BARING THE IRON HAND

BARING THE IRON HAND

DISCIPLINE IN THE UNION ARMY

STEVEN J. RAMOLD

Northern Illinois University Press

DeKalb

© 2010 by Northern Illinois University Press
Published by the Northern Illinois University Press, DeKalb, Illinois   60115
Manufactured in the United States using postconsumer-recycled, acid-free paper.
All Rights Reserved

Library of Congress Cataloging-in-Publication Data
Design by Shaun Allshouse

Ramold, Steven J.
Baring the iron hand: discipline in the Union Army / Steven J. Ramold.
    p.   cm.
Includes bibliographical references and index.
ISBN 978-0-87580-408-8 (clothbound : alk. paper)
1. United States. Army—History—Civil War, 1861–1865. 2. Military discipline—
United States—History—19th century. 3. United States—History—Civil War,
1861–1865—Social aspects. 4. United States. Army—Military life—History—19th
century. 5. Military offenses—United States—History—19th century. I. Title.
E491.R36 2010
973.7'1—dc22
2009028416

Beware the People weeping,

When they bare the iron hand

—*"The Martyr," Herman Melville (1866)*

For my parents,

George and Elaine Ramold

CONTENTS

ACKNOWLEDGMENTS

The debts of gratitude that I owe for this project can never be repaid, so I hope that those who contributed their time, talent, and advice for this project will simply accept my humble thanks and gratitude. I began this project while teaching at Virginia State University, where I had the pleasure of working with some outstanding colleagues and enjoyed the support of two excellent department chairs, Joseph Goldenberg and Arthur Abraham. Both were very generous with research funds, and I am grateful for their help in getting this project off the ground. I have also received generous financial support from the department, college, and university administrators at Eastern Michigan University. Department heads Phil Schmitz and Kate Mehuron provided research funds when I needed them, as did the Office of the Provost in the form of a Faculty Research Fellowship and a Support, Services, & Materials Grant. I must also mention with gratitude the financial support of the United States Army Military History Institute in Carlisle, Pennsylvania. This is not only a world-class research facility, but their financial support in the form of a General and Mrs. Matthew G. Ridgway Research Grant also was greatly appreciated. There are also a large number, too many to mention, of archivists, librarians, and researchers who helped out in dozens of research sites. My research took me from Virginia to Wisconsin and Oregon to Massachusetts, but regardless of where my travels took me I always found dedicated professionals who made my research much easier.

A number of colleagues and friends also deserve mention for their research assistance and general encouragement. Jeff Flannery, who runs the Reading Room at the Library of Congress, not only aided my personal research but also has my eternal gratitude for the "beyond the call of duty" assistance he provides to my student groups. Bob Kirby at the Petersburg National Battlefield guided me to a number of wonderful research sites and also runs a great operation at Petersburg. Don Pfanz, the staff historian at the Fredericksburg and Spotsylvania National Military Park, oversees a veritable treasure trove of information at his facility, and a Civil War historian could write several books just on the materials in the Park Service library there. Other colleagues provided valuable criticism on various chapters of the book, so I also thank Richard Nation, Robert Citino, and John McCurdy at Eastern

Michigan University for taking the time to look over my ideas. Professor McCurdy's own research into gender and manhood in colonial America was especially useful in shaping my own thesis on the role of masculinity and manhood in relation to Civil War discipline.

Finally, I would like to thank my wife, Paula. She is always a great inspiration to me and always has a word of encouragement, a bit of advice, and infinite patience with her oft-distracted husband. So, I reserve my final and biggest thanks for her.

BARING THE IRON HAND

INTRODUCTION

Soldiers in the Civil War committed crimes. In many Civil War histories, that reality is often overlooked in the broad operational depictions of the war. Historians concentrate on the course of battles and the personalities of leaders and generals, and consider things like logistics and strategy to determine why winners win and losers lose. The motivation of the respective armies, however, often escapes study. Discipline also goes a long way in explaining why armies were successful, serving as a measuring stick of determination and will to persevere. But which definition of "discipline" is more important? "Discipline" in one definition is the traditional measurement of combat efficiency: the willingness to enter battle, risk one's life, and kill the enemy. In the other definition, "discipline" represented the willingness to obey orders, subordinate oneself to military practice and custom, and accommodate the needs of the group over the wishes of the individual. In theory, if soldiers embraced the demands of the latter definition, they would take on the characteristics of the former definition. As far as the army was concerned, a disciplined soldier who did what he was told in camp became a disciplined soldier on the battlefield. It is a plausible theory but one that failed in the mass armies of the American Civil War. The ultimately victorious Union army was certainly possessed the former definition of discipline, but it certainly lacked the latter.

Three concepts came into conflict when the Union created a mass civilian army to fight the Confederacy. First was the clash between the mentality of the Regular Army and the new volunteer regiments. These volunteers are the soldiers that Alexis de Tocqueville meant when he described "the soldiers of a democratic army . . . do not consider themselves as seriously engaged in the military profession and are always thinking of quitting it. . . . Among democratic nations the private soldiers remain most like civilians."[1] In antebellum conflicts, American volunteers rallied to the defense of the flag, but the presence of the Regular Army provided a regulating factor. The culture, traditions, and attitudes of the Regular Army rubbed off on the volunteers or, at the very least, provided a standard to which the army hoped the volunteer regiments might emulate.[2] In the Civil War, however, the mass of volunteers overwhelmed the relatively small Regular Army, and amateurism became the norm instead of the exception. The sheer volume of soldiers, and their subsequent poor behavior, simply overwhelmed the ability of the existing military justice system to function.[3] As a result, the previously harsh and rigid forms of military justice had to relax its standards and practices to ensure a minimal amount of discipline and manpower. The army struggled throughout the war to reach a point where they could accommodate the populist inclinations of its volunteers with the more stringent traditions of military law. The result was a flexible legal system that entirely satisfied neither the volunteers nor the professional soldiers.

The next conflict pitted the political and social concept of the citizen-soldiery against the establishment represented by traditional military controls. The Regular Army governed itself through codified standards, such as the Army Regulations and the Articles of War. To the Regulars, standards and regulations meant order, and order meant discipline. Such a belief was a longstanding precedent, and the army had history and tradition on its side when positioning itself as the model for the Union army. The standing army, however, represented everything that the citizen-soldier resented: elitism, regimentalization, and deprivation of free will. The army seemed a monolithic structure, governed by an excessive number of rules, and designed to deprive the common soldier of the individuality that symbolized the American character. Whereas soldiers in the Regular Army were accustomed to such behavior, the untrained and ill-disciplined citizen-soldiers possessed an entirely different ethos. In their belief system, individuality, the freedoms associated with citizenship, and general permissiveness did not, by definition, defy the definition of a good soldier.[4] Quite the opposite, a free citizen, fighting in the defense of the nation that guaranteed these rights, was the superior soldier. Blessed with the guiding motivation to protect the Constitution, nation, and Union, the citizen-soldier believed that they were the true guardians of the American legacy. Davy Crockett, who perhaps only to Andrew Jackson personified the citizen-soldier ethos, professed, "I love a good gun, for it makes a man feel independent, and prepared either for peace or war."[5] Claiming the heritage of the Revolutionary War, the citizen-soldier defied the enemy, but also defied an army that tried to tell them what to do, when to do it, and how to do it. Faced with obeying well-defined codes of behavior, a clash was inevitable.

The final conflict in the Union army was an extension of social behavioral norms, with the freedoms associated with bachelor manhood challenging the rigid expectations of Victorian morality. Mid-nineteenth-century America was a nation in transition. The rugged, rural America symbolized by the frontier was giving way to a growing urban industrialism marked by a different brand of social expectation. The individuality of American manhood, the rural view of America, emphasized independence in thought, aggressive pursuit of self-interests, and a reluctance to accept conformity. Central to this behavior were demonstrations of manly behavior, where young men vied for status and recognition in the community though acts of bravery and physical ability. Whether demonstrating their ability to work hard or consume the most liquor, bachelor manhood emphasized the absence of restraint, with the individual defining their own recognized limits. The self-made man of the antebellum United States, as defined by Michael Kimmel, stood for self-promotion, democratic politics, and producerist economics. Andrew Jackson, who lent his name to a period of American development marked by unrestrained growth and expansion of individual personal liberty, emerged as the symbol of American rural manhood.[6] Although America was changing by the time of the Civil War, Jackson's cultural and political influence remained, and Western states and territories, rural areas of Eastern states, and newly arrived immigrants still embraced Jacksonian political philosophy. Abraham Lincoln himself was as symbol and beneficiary of the characteristics of rural masculinity. Springfield, Illinois, was the capital city of a settled state, yet even by the 1860s it still had the feel of a frontier town, with shifting and uncertain economic conditions and a violent streak that reflected an unsettled dynamic in the population.[7] As a Western candidate, Lincoln received favorable support from his native region because of his rustic independence compared to his effete Eastern predecessor, James Buchanan.[8] Victorian morality, the emerging urban/industrialized behavior model, prized the exact opposite elements. Victorians prized restraint, group cohesion, and suppression of the individual as a means to gain status within the group. Victorian morality abhorred wild behavior, the very essence of nonrestraint, and excluded non-Victorians from their social circles while at the same time trying to persuade non-Victorians to emulate their actions.[9] To those who espoused Victorian morality, Lincoln represented everything they feared: a crude, semieducated, ambitious upstart who married outside of his class.[10]

In the context of military discipline, the two behavioral models had clear proxies. Military discipline, represented by the Articles of War, embodied the elements of Victorianism: clear behavioral expectations, emphasis on restrained conduct, and suppression of the self for the well-being of the broader institution. The army expected officers to behave as gentlemen as well as leaders and imposed upon them the burden of representing to their men the code of behavior the army wanted. In turn, many officers, whether gentlemen or not, embraced the army view as the benchmark for evaluating themselves against other officers, using conduct from a Victorian perspective to assess competency. Furthermore, forcing soldiers to behave in a Victorian manner made the officer's life much easier, as soldiers modified and controlled their own behavior, reducing the need for the officers to discipline them.

Issues developed, though, when recruits that embodied the masculine ethic joined an army shaped by Victorian philosophy, causing a reevaluation of the definition of battlefield discipline. Masculinity required its adherents to practice their own code of behavior that included elements that clashed with Victorian military discipline. Privileges taken for granted in civilian life, such as physical mobility, freedom of expression, and economic opportunism, came into direct conflict with an army that wanted its soldiers to stay in camp, shut their mouths, and not steal everything in sight. Masculinity's demand that soldiers uphold their honor though force if necessary clashed with army restrictions against internal violence, fighting, and other disruptions of general order. Worst of all, the army tried to stop men from getting drunk, one of the fundamental rights of manhood, not to mention a favorite recreational activity. Yet those same soldiers who drank, fought, reviled their officers, and found themselves court-martialed repeatedly stood their ground, fought hard through both victory and defeat, and ultimately won the war.

Caught between these divergent forces, the soldiers and officers of the Union army engaged in a constant reassessment and reevaluation of the need, procedures, and outcomes of military justice. Far from the perception that military justice was hidebound and immovable, the various forms of Civil War discipline (camp punishment, regimental courts-martial, and general courts-martial) regularly shifted and changed based upon a variety of factors. Officers, many of them themselves temporary citizen-soldiers, often identified more with their men than with the traditional officer corps and their view of traditional discipline. The sheer number of cases, generated by a rebellious need to demonstrate individuality and masculinity among the enlisted men, forced the army to adjust its judicial system to accommodate the caseload. The morality of Union soldiers proved flexible throughout the conflict, but so did the morality of the army leadership. Offenses—particularly property crimes—that earned an offender a quick punishment early in the war went largely unpunished by the end. The outcome of this philosophical struggle was both positive and negative. On the positive side, the evolving nature of military justice allowed the Union army to accommodate change and create a system that emphasized justice over a restrictive definition of law.

Despite the complaints of many soldiers, discipline in the Union army was usually not abusive, although there were exceptions to every rule. On the negative side, such a flexible system meant that soldiers often did not know to what disciplinary standard the army held them, creating confusion and uncertainty as to proper conduct. Civilians also paid the price for a shifting code of justice. More often than not, changes in the army's disciplinary system was to the benefit of the soldier/offender, leaving Confederate civilians more vulnerable to offenses because Union soldiers felt less deterred from committing certain crimes.

Altogether, there was no easy way to characterize discipline in the Union army. It was an army that seldom obeyed the rules yet performed well on the battlefield. It was an army of individuals that often seemed a faceless blue mass. It was an army that justified its actions in the name of the Constitution and the need for law and order but often descended into near chaos. It was an army that identified with high ideals of nation, personal rights, and liberty that also committed violent crimes, devastated property, and menaced unarmed civilians. The Union army violated both criminal and military law, committing traditional criminal violations, such as murder, theft, and assault, and far too often defied military regulations by desertion, straggling, and defiance of orders. Someone who observed a typical Union army camp might characterize the assembled body of men as little more than a mass of hooligans, with a thin line of officers as all that kept the entire mob from unrestrained lawlessness. What the observer might miss, however, was the social, cultural, and legal battle going on between soldiers who considered themselves men first and obedient soldiers second, officers who demanded respect for their position but who often failed to live up to their own standards, and an army struggling to redefine the concept of military justice while in the midst of the gravest war in American history.

"ANCIENT UN-AMERICAN ARTICLES"

American Military Justice to 1861

The United States went to war with itself in 1861 with little idea of the carnage that lay ahead, an army with little preparation for a major war, and a volunteer spirit that generated thousands of volunteers eager to fight for their respective causes. It also went to war with a military justice system that was unclear, untested, and unready to deal with the legal challenges of a civil conflict. Before the Civil War, American military justice comprised a series of limited and makeshift legislation designed to cope with the problem of the moment more than establish any permanent system of military jurisprudence. Many in the army complained about the makeshift nature of the system, but no officer or politician could come up with something better. So, for eighty-six years, the United States fought foes, both foreign and domestic, and administered an army in peacetime, with a legal code essentially copied from America's English antecedents. These "ancient un-American articles, thus adopted to meet the emergency"[1] sufficed for the small antebellum army but were not entirely satisfactory.

Instead of a comprehensive military legal system based upon tradition, custom, and experience, America—created in the midst of rebellion and expanding rapidly into an open continent—relied upon experience to shape its system of military justice. Three factors shaped American military justice before the Civil War. The first was history, or, more specifically, the body of historical knowledge passed down among the community of nations that enabled the armies of various countries to create essentially common codes of military behavior. The British code of military justice inherited by the American Army traced its own history back to previous rules created by its rivals and neighbors. Next, the legal and Constitutional debates of the new nation fashioned a unique American military justice tradition. The codified Constitution, distinctive at the time of its ratification, provided a broad spectrum of personal liberties that military justice had to accommodate. Reflecting the separate nature of military discipline, however, the Constitution also granted wide latitude to the military to design its own structure and process. The legal system also played a part in arbitrating disputes between the Constitution and the separate military justice establishment. Finally, military experience delineated military law. Without a distinctive philosophy of military justice and acting in a legal realm not entirely defined by the Constitution, the army found itself creating impromptu policy on military law intended to fit the particular situation. In doing so, however, the ad hoc solution became precedent for later action as well. Although failed short-term solutions soon disappeared, successful quick fixes for immediate problems tended to stay. The successful experiments proved how adaptive American military law could be, but it also prevented a more permanent and comprehensive system that America could rely upon in future wars.

MILITARY JUSTICE EMERGED out of a long history, a process that paralleled the professional development of armies themselves. Hammurabi's Code contained restraints on military forces, and the Roman legions faced severe discipline for infractions of a formalized code of behavior. Structured military justice evolved during the Middle Ages, where medieval knights regulated themselves through Courts of Chivalry, proceedings to settle disputes by combat. Codified military justice systems returned slowly during the Renaissance, only fully reemerging under the guidance of Gustavus Adolphus of Sweden in 1621. Several factors drove Adolphus' adoption of a structured military justice system during the Thirty Years War (1618–1648). First, Adolphus' army used the innovative technology of the age, and Adolphus needed tight discipline to integrate his force of pikemen, musketmen, and artillery. Second, the Swedish army fought most of its battle on foreign soil, and tight discipline kept the army intact. Last, shocked by the atrocity and counter-atrocity nature of a religious war, Adolphus sought to restrain the baser nature of his men through rigid discipline. Adolphus' system of military justice provided for general courts-martial staffed by senior officers to try significant violations and regimental courts-martial to handle lesser offenses. Adolphus detailed trusted soldiers to serve as an early form of military police, charged with arresting and imprisoning soldiers accused of crimes. Punishments ranged from fines and extra duty for small infractions to the death penalty for major offenses such as cowardice, plunder, and theft. Adolphus, however, banned flogging, a rare exception to a widely practiced form of punishment.[2]

England soon adopted Adolphus' system. With the decline of the medieval system and the rise of a standing British army similar to the Swedish model, the responsibility for maintaining criminal justice passed from aristocratic knights to professional soldiers. Instead of ad hoc regulations established in the field that governments and armies later formalized, the British system emerged out of a series of legal ordinances (or "articles" of British law) that the British army collectively labeled the Articles of War. As the British system of justice evolved over several centuries, the Articles of War reflected British attitudes of military justice versus the rights of citizens, embracing many elements of not only the future American Articles of War but also elements of American constitutional rights. The English medieval Courts of Chivalry gave way, by 1644, to a more formal arrangement during the English Civil War, when both the royalist and parliamentary armies implemented a military justice system to restrain the passion of their troops. The articles passed by the royalist army were particularly important, as they created a two-tier system similar to Adolphus' system. The Councils of War, as the royalist articles were known, provided for a court of war to hear evidence on significant criminal offenses, balanced by a lower marshal court authorized to hear lesser charges at the regimental level.[3] The courts-martial were especially important in imposing order upon the new standing British army, created upon the restoration of Charles II in 1660.

Later revisions of the Articles of War provided increased rights and protections to soldiers accused of offenses, guarantees and privileges later copied by the American army. The 1685 articles required the presence of a sworn clerk to record the court proceedings, as well as a review of all punishments by a representative of the crown. This royal review served as the soldier's only form of appeal, because the crown's agent had the authority to suspend or reduce the severity of any punishment. The 1753 Mutiny Act obliged the clerk to provide a copy of the court transcript to every courts-martial defendant within three months of the end of the trial. After 1718, all witnesses in British courts-martial had to swear to tell the truth, and the administration of an oath became part of military justice. In the same year, Parliament added an article that required the British army to read aloud the Articles of War be read aloud to British soldiers at least every two months, lest soldiers claim ignorance of the law as a defense. Articles passed in 1753 required that a court try an accused soldier within eight days of his arrest, an early example of habeas corpus.[4]

The creation of the British Articles of War reflected the monarchical nature of Britain at the time. Establishing, defining, and implementing the Articles of War remained a privilege of the monarch, recognizing that the king was both the military and political leader of the nation. English monarchs retained this power until Parliament assumed the responsibility for the Articles of War in 1803. Recognizing the unique nature of military offense and the military's close ties to the throne, English kings established the tradition of military courts separate from civilian authority. This separate system, later adopted by the United States, was unique in Europe at the time. The separate system was not absolute, however. The 1765 Articles of War obligated the army to turn soldiers wanted for civil offenses over to civilian authority. In addition, the army could not "protect any Person from his Creditors on the Pretence of his being a solider," in recognition that soldiers still bore responsibility to the civilians they protected.[5] There were still restraints on the king's military authority, however, lest the king use the army to usurp the Parliament. The main restraint was the prohibiting of issuing the Articles of War in peacetime, an attempt to prevent the imposing of martial law and to restrict military law to only those English citizens subject to its punishments. This element is particularly important, because the monarch not only commanded the army, but governed it as well. Moreover, officers and soldiers alike swore their allegiance to an individual monarch, not the institution of government or the state. Another restraint was the requirement of the monarch to submit the Mutiny Act to Parliament for annual renewal. The Mutiny Act, passed in 1689 in response to a revolt of a sizeable portion of the British army, reinforced the monarch's authority to issue Articles of War in wartime. But the requirement of an annual renewal ensured that the monarch could not institute them at the monarch's discretion in peacetime.[6]

While British military courts became more formal, the application of discipline also evolved. From the sixteenth to the eighteenth centuries, British military discipline became relatively more humane and limited. The widespread use of torture and maiming to impose order gave way to more restrained punishment starting with the 1689 Bill of Rights, which banned cruel and unusual punishments a century before the American Constitution. Permanent punishments, such as branding or mutilation, died out quickly, but flogging remained a popular punishment well into the nineteenth century. Reflecting the opinion that a disciplinary offense was an affront to regimental honor and reputation, some British officers opted to flog soldiers by having them run the gauntlet between lines of their fellow soldiers, allowing the soldiers themselves to administer the flogging instead of a designated punisher. There was no practical limit on how many lashes a convicted soldier might receive, and some British courts-martial ordered as many as three thousand lashes. Changes to the Articles of War in the 1740s, however, mitigated the scale of floggings while permitting the practice to continue. A thousand lashes became the maximum number permitted under a general court-martial, and three hundred was the limit for a regimental court-martial. Instead of administering them all at once, a soldier received them over a period of weeks. A regimental surgeon supervised the floggings, with the surgeon held responsible by the army if the convicted soldier died. Opponents of flogging managed to persuade the British army to ban flogging in 1881, twenty years after a similar ban took place in the American army.[7]

The use of codified Articles of War came to America as part of the English military tradition, and, like the British military model, underwent significant alteration. Even before the American Revolution various colonies established codes of military behavior that reflected the circumstances of colonial warfare. The most significant difference between colonial American and British military law was the absence of standing professional armies in America and the reliance upon local militias. All of the colonies established militia laws, creating universal militia service, schedules for militia drills, and the equipment with which each colonist had to equip himself. Colonial legislatures passed these laws early in their history to deal with the threat posed by Native Americans. The exception was Pennsylvania, which maintained more harmonious relations with Native Americans than other colonies and did not pass a militia law until 1755. Whereas most colonies limited their militia laws to matters of equipment and schedules, others addressed broader issues of soldierly comportment. The Virginia colony, seeking a greater level of discipline, passed a revised militia law in 1755 that provided for fines for a variety of lesser offenses (swearing, drinking, or insubordination), corporal punishment for more serious offenses (desertion or mutiny), and the death penalty for treason.[8]

Most colonies, however, did not follow Virginia's example and found themselves without any true Articles of War to regulate their troops when the American Revolution broke out. The confrontation between the British army and the Massachusetts militia after the passage of the Coercive/Intolerable Acts triggered the need for further regulation of the colonial militia as war with Great Britain seemed inevitable. Lacking a clear set of directives, the Massachusetts colonial legislature adopted a modified version of the British Articles of War as their own in April 1775. The wording was almost verbatim, but Massachusetts did include some significant revisions to suit colonial needs. A dual system of courts-martial existed, but general courts-martial also served as an appeal for their regimental counterparts. The commanding general of the militia acted as a last appeal for dissatisfied soldiers and officers convicted of offenses. The commanding general also served the function of the royal review in the British articles, confirming and approving all punishments handed down by the military courts. Finally, the Massachusetts Articles of War instructed all officers sitting on courts-martial to "behave with calmness, decency, and impartiality."[9]

Two months later, the Continental Congress, also lacking any formalized mechanism to control its new Continental Army, adopted a modified version of the Massachusetts Articles of War. The army needed its own central code of law to override restrictions present in the individual colonial militia laws. The 1755 Virginia militia law, for instance, demanded that all reviews of sentence take place within the borders of Virginia. Members of Virginia militia units serving with the Continental Army had to return to Virginia for their appeals if their officers court-martialed them. This requirement caused considerable delay in the administration of justice, cost a great expense, and took men away from the army.[10] The new national Articles of War superseded all of the colonial articles, creating a centralized military justice system for the first time. Reflecting the populist nature of the former militiamen that comprised the Continental Army, the new American Articles of War had no appeals mechanism and made abandoning an assigned post a capital offense. The Articles mandated that those who abandoned their post, or induced others to do so, "shall suffer death immediately."[11] To restrain the penalties inflicted upon America's citizen-soldiers, the Articles limited courts-martial punishments to "degrading, cashiering, drumming out of the army, whipping not exceeding thirty-nine lashes, fine not exceeding two months pay . . ., [and] imprisonment not exceeding two months." The primary intent seemed to be public humiliation instead of punitive discipline. If a court ordered a flogging as punishment, for instance, the lashings were "to be laid on publicly with vigor."[12] A public punishment might induce others to obey the regulations, a hope the U.S. military retained when the Civil War began.

Both of the 1775 versions of the Articles of War included two articles that remained a part of the military's legal system until the adoption of the Uniform Code of Military Justice in 1951, causing a great amount of debate the entire time the articles were in force. Article 46 of the Massachusetts Articles required the dismissal of a commissioned officer for conduct "unbecoming an Officer and a Gentleman." Article 49 permitted courts-martial to prosecute common soldiers for actions that threatened "good order and military discipline," even if the purported offense was not officially punishable by the Articles of War. Together, these clauses gave courts-martial the authority to punish anyone for any action the military deemed inappropriate though not strictly illegal. The articles caused considerable debate from the moment of their enactment to the Civil War and into the twentieth century.[13]

George Washington, commanding the Continental Army encamped outside of Boston, was not satisfied with the Articles as passed by Congress.

Accustomed to inflicting the harsher punishments permitted under the Virginia militia law, Washington believed that thirty-nine lashes was not a significant deterrent to many of his tougher soldiers. Washington claimed that some men, punished for drunkenness, offered to take an additional thirty-nine strokes for a bottle of rum.[14] Washington himself had sat on the five-person committee that recommended the 1775 Articles, but the other members of the committee overturned his frequent requests for harsher punishments.[15] Acting upon Washington's recommendations, the Continental Congress appointed John Adams and Thomas Jefferson to consider revisions to the 1775 Articles. Adams approached the project with all the relish for which he became famous. With the British occupying his native Boston, Adams was keenly interested in formulating an army that could liberate his home city. Moreover, as Jonathan Lurie has written, Adams and the other revolutionaries had a vested interest in success. The failure to prosecute a successful rebellion would fall hard on Adams and the others that the British perceived as traitors.[16] Although he lacked military experience, Adams embraced the idea of military law separate from civilian law. Military success demanded discipline, and though control might seem an anathema to liberty, Adams saw the threat to liberty posed by an ill-disciplined army. "There can be no liberty . . . where the laws are not revered and most sacredly observed," Adams wrote his wife, "nor can there be happiness or safety in an army for a single hour when discipline is not observed."[17] To this end, Adams at one point proposed to adopt the British Articles of War verbatim. Considering that the Romans and British each dominated the world in their respective time periods, Adams concluded "it would be in vain for us to seek in our own invention . . . a more complete system of military discipline."[18]

Thomas Jefferson and the other members of the committee, by contrast, favored a more American set of Articles.[19] The 1776 Articles of War contained 102 separate articles divided into eighteen sections. The new Articles retained large portions of the 1775 version but expanded the range of punishments and the options available for punishment. Instead of corporal punishment, the 1776 Articles included a range of fines for lesser offenses, such as "two-thirds of a dollar" for profanity. Flogging was still permitted, but the committee increased the number of maximum lashes from thirty-nine to a hundred. The committee expanded the death penalty for additional offenses and identified new offenses based upon the experience of the army since the adoption of the 1775 Articles. The new offenses included sleeping at guard post, plundering, desertion to the enemy, and assault on quartermaster personnel. The appeals process from the earlier Articles was also retained, with regimental courts-martial obliged to obtain confirmation from a commanding officer or garrison commander. General courts-martial required the confirmation of Congress or the general-in-chief of all sentences.[20] Finally, in a move that reflected Adams' recognition of a separate system of military law, the 1776 Articles provided for a position of Judge Advocate General (JAG). Instead of pursuing legal proceedings through Congress, the JAG, a military officer appointed by the General-in-chief, conducted investigations, prosecuted offenders, and oversaw punishments within the army itself. Washington selected William Tudor, a prominent Boston lawyer and colonel in the Continental Army, to serve as the first JAG.[21]

CREATING A CODE OF MILITARY JUSTICE was not just an academic exercise; the Continental Army was in serious need of real discipline. The framers of the 1776 Articles included specific articles to counter specific and reoccurring offenses, as reported by the army. Articles existed to prevent the forcing of safeguards, drinking on duty, and abandoning posts because these offenses, and others, occurred with alarming regularity. Fighting, profanity, and slovenliness became the hallmark of many units in the Continental Army, and throughout the war Washington despaired of the behavior of the army. Soldiers claimed a number of justifications for their actions. Dangerous duty, alternating with months of boredom, depressed martial spirit. The quality of army rations left much to be desired, but soldiers also commonly went hungry when even these meager rations were not available. Often their monthly pay was months in arrears, leaving them and their families destitute. When pay did arrive, the collapsing value of the American currency meant that the soldiers' purchasing power was less than before. The length of the conflict, much longer than anyone could have anticipated, also caused a decline in dedication to the nationalist cause.

Hungry, disillusioned, and poorly paid, the Continental Army often lacked even the basic discipline of a standing army. Alcohol was widely available from a variety of sources, including the army itself, and drunkenness was a common plague among the enlisted men. The standard ration included a daily dose of rum, whiskey, or hard cider. The portion itself was not enough to cause inebriation, but soldiers often hoarded their ration until they had enough to trigger a case of "barrel fever."[22] If soldiers did not want to wait to get drunk, there were other sources of alcohol besides the army. The army permitted each regiment to have a sutler, an itinerant merchant that traveled with the regiment, to provide items and services that the army did not. Alcohol was always a popular sutler commodity, especially because most sutlers were willing to sell whiskey on credit, pending the next payday.[23] Wherever soldiers encamped for any length of time, taverns invariably sprung up beyond the periphery of the camp, enticing the soldiers into another common offense, being absent without leave (AWOL). Taverns also attracted prostitutes, which further eroded the discipline and control of the army. The army could have contained the alcohol problem with relatively minor changes in procedure. First, the army could have made drunkenness itself an offense, but this was not the case under the Articles of War. Drunkenness while on duty was an offense, but simply being drunk was not, and soldiers took advantage of that distinction.[24] Second, the army could have made some effort to provide recreation, amusement, or some activity to pass the time instead of forcing soldiers to turn to alcohol for relief from the boredom. But there was no organized effort to amuse or entertain the soldiers of the Continental Army, so the pursuit of alcohol took up much official time and effort.[25]

In addition to the alcohol problem, Washington's army combated other offenses, big and small. In an attempt to maintain moral purity in addition to military discipline, the Articles of War forbade profanity in the ranks, something that proved impossible to achieve. Louis Beebe, a physician in the Continental Army, complained of the soldier's propensity to "ridicule the Bible, mock Hell and damnation, & even challenge the Deity to remove them out of this world by Thunder and Lightening."[26] Gambling also challenged the moral fiber of the army, and Washington opposed any form of gaming that might detract his soldiers from their duty. In 1777, Washington issued a missive threatening to punish any soldier who wasted their time engaging in idle recreation. The same message also chastened officers to better use their time to "devote . . . vacant moments . . . to the study of Military authors."[27] Malingering, the faking or overrepresentation of an injury or illness to avoid duty, was another relatively minor offense that caused more irritation than injury to the army. One physician in 1777 complained of his hospital overflowing with more than five hundred men, many of whom had complaints the doctor described as "trifling." Often doctors had to have their malingerers escorted from the hospital and back to their units, but at least the soldiers remained in the army.[28]

The intent of these measures was to prevent small problems from developing into bigger issues. Another good example was Washington's demand that soldiers maintain their weapons. A spot of rust might not seem much one day, but failure of that weapon in combat might have severe consequences. Early in the war, the Continental Army relied upon written reminders to junior officers to inspect their soldiers' weapons frequently and to punish those who did not maintain their muskets. By 1780, however, the absence of polished firearms led to more severe repercussions. The commander of the New York Brigade made his sergeants responsible for the maintenance of their squads' weapons. If an officer spotted a rusty musket during an inspection, the soldier immediately received thirty lashes and the sergeant was demoted to the ranks.[29]

Unfortunately for the Continental Army, disciplinary offenses much more serious than a rusty musket occurred with alarming frequency. Suffering from a lack of food or tired of the monotony of their fare, soldiers began to forage from local farmers without permission. Attempts to halt the foraging were largely unsuccessful, as would be the case in the Civil War, despite the application of the death penalty. When not stealing from civilians, soldiers stole from each other or from the army. Soldiers pilfered the money and personal goods of their fellow soldiers and, when the opportunity presented itself, from the stores of the army itself. Food was an obvious target when supplies ran low, but alcohol was the favorite. Soldiers found out the hard way that the army did not take kindly to the thievery of its rum, with flogging the usual punishment for the offense.[30]

The most damaging offense to the army, and one that occurred most frequently, was desertion. Desertion ran the spectrum of motivations and justifications. Some soldiers deserted temporarily, returning to the army after a short stay at home, but others abandoned hope for the cause and attempted to leave the army permanently. Even worse, other soldiers deserted to the enemy, betraying those with whom they previously served. Because of the severity of the offense, desertion earned the harshest punishments that the Articles of War could levy, but because of the diverse nature of the offense, punishments also varied. The army was most lenient with those whose desertion took the form of refusing to serve. Several states, including Virginia, imposed mandatory militia service during the American Revolution that included the possibility of service with the Continental Army. Failure to appear for militia service constituted desertion, even if the soldier-to-be had never left home.[31] The Continental Army also suffered this problem. Soldiers, who went home to clear up their affairs after filling out their enlistment papers, sometimes had a change of heart and decided not to report for duty. This obliged the army to compel them by force to serve their term, but punishments were usually light as the reluctant soldier was at least at his duty.[32]

Soldiers who deserted after joining their units, however, faced mixed discipline. The 1776 Articles granted the army license to inflict the death penalty for desertion, but did not mandate the punishment. Washington himself, while certain of the benefits of tight discipline, was not quick to inflict capital punishment when he did not think it appropriate to do so. Private Adam Wolf, for example, deserted from his command, but instead of a death sentence he received the relatively light sentence of ten lashes and was returned to his unit. Another example of Washington's magnanimity came on July 4, 1778, when the commanding general issued a general order commemorating America's second birthday. Besides ordering a thirteen-gun salute, "the Commander-in-Chief thinks it proper to grant a GENERAL PARDON to all prisoners in the army, now under the sentence of death."[33]

The death penalty was no real threat, of course, unless exercised, and not all convicted soldiers got off as easily. Allen Bowman's research on Revolutionary War discipline found 225 cases of desertions ending with a court-martial sentence of death. The army carried out at least forty of these sentences.[34] The 1776 Articles did not prescribe the means of death, and the condemned soldiers died by either hanging or firing squad. Some officers, however, added punishments of their own. In one case, Washington denied General Henry Lee's request to decapitate a soldier convicted of desertion, while Captain Philip Reed, later a Congressman from Maryland and veteran of the War of 1812, decapitated a condemned deserter after he was shot by firing squad and then displayed the head as a deterrent.[35]

More often than not, however, soldiers who deserted escaped harsh punishment during the American Revolution. Out of more than a thousand documented courts-martial for desertion, 70 percent resulted in a flogging as the most significant punishment. Other deserters received generous pardons for their actions from an army simply glad to have soldiers available in camp. Still others simply waited for one of numerous desertion amnesty calls issued throughout the war. Moreover, the penalty for assisting soldiers to desert was very lenient. In the 1775 Articles of War, abetting desertion earned the offender (whether civilian or military) a 5 pound fine and ten lashes. The 1776 Articles, though, dispensed with the lashes and retained only the modest fine.[36] In the end, most deserters simply got away with their offense. So successful were deserters at escaping punishment that the amnesty calls usually netted only a handful of returning offenders.[37]

The major exception to this trend was the punishment meted out to soldiers who deserted to the enemy. Soldiers who simply went home might no longer aid in the quest for independence, but soldiers who went over to the enemy betrayed the cause and might even cause the death of American soldiers. Such treachery usually ended in death for any soldier unlucky enough to desert to the enemy and then find himself back in American hands. After the Battle of Hobkirk's Hill in 1781, for instance, five captured deserters to the enemy were hanged without benefit of court-martial.[38] Also in 1781, a soldier caught in mid-afternoon attempting to desert to the British was shot by firing squad before the evening roll call.[39] Washington at various times issued orders to execute captured deserters to enemy as soon as possible. The first was outside Boston in 1776, and the last was during the siege of Yorktown, where he ordered the death of any deserter found within enemy lines.[40] Evidence of this policy appeared in a case near Germantown, Pennsylvania, in 1777, when an artilleryman named Thomas Mattross failed in his attempt to desert to the British. Found guilty in the afternoon, the court ordered Mattross' death at noon the following day.[41] Quick discipline was considered necessary because of British success at enticing men to desert. One of the most effective British methods was to pay Continentals to switch sides. After capturing New York in 1776, British General William Howe offered to pay 3 pounds and a parole to any American soldier who turned himself in, 4 pounds if he brought his musket with him. Other British officers offered generous amnesty terms at various times during the war, offers that many American soldiers accepted.[42] The success of these offers, however, varied with the relative success of the British. Following the British defeat at Yorktown, Americans soldiers seized two envoys from British General Henry Clinton soliciting desertions and hanged them.[43]

Espionage also brought a quick death sentence. Captured enemy spies, especially native-born Americans, fell under the same category of treachery as deserters to the enemy, and the execution of spies was also standard practice under the accepted laws of war. In 1776, Congress sanctioned the death of "all persons not members of nor owning allegiance to, any of the United States of America . . . found lurking as spies in or about the fortifications or encampments of the armies of the United States." The Continental Army executed several civilians for such spying, including Daniel Taylor, who was caught smuggling a message to the British in a hollow silver bullet that he swallowed but was forced to vomit up.[44] Later in the war, Captain Robert Kirkwood dispatched another accused spy. "This Day was Executed by hanging," Kirkwood wrote, "a Certain Solomon Slocum being a Spy from the Enemy Likewise a Deserter from the 2nd M. Regt."[45]

Death was also the primary penalty for acts of mutiny. Minor acts of mutiny occurred throughout the war, and Washington was content to let his subordinate commanders handle such matters as they saw fit. Large mutinies at the end of the war, however, forced Washington to crack down by using the death penalty. When Pennsylvania troops mutinied at the Morristown, New Jersey, winter encampment in January 1781, Washington restrained the impulse to simply execute the ringleaders because he understood that poor conditions motivated the uprising, and the Pennsylvania men did not engage in any other criminal acts, such as theft or pillaging. A mutiny by New Jersey troops three weeks later, however, resulted in the execution of two mutineers and an end to the mutiny.[46]

Although the 1776 Articles of War proved sufficient to hold the army together enough to win the war, they were clearly inadequate as a permanent solution to discipline problems. The most pressing issue, from Washington's viewpoint, was the inflexibility of the disciplinary system. Fining a soldier for a minor offense was suitable, as was a hundred lashes for a more serious offense and the death penalty for capital offenses. The problem was the lack of a suitable punishment for offenders in the middle range, when a hundred lashes were not enough of a punishment but death was too harsh. The limitation often led to predictable outcomes of courts-martial, as the maximum number of lashes became almost the standard punishment regardless of the offense or its severity. Near Princeton, New Jersey, in 1777, for instance, a court-martial tried three soldiers; one soldier stole a horse, one stole a horse and a wagon, and one stole a shirt. In all three cases, the court handed down the same hundred-lash punishment to all of them.[47] To rectify the shortcomings of the 1776 Articles, Washington proposed some sweeping changes in 1781. Washington asked that his Provost Marshals possess the authority to impose more flexible punishments to fit the severity of the crime. Among the new proposals were sentences at hard labor, sea duty for captured deserters, raising the maximum number of lashes to five hundred, or to allow the court-martial to determine the number of lashes themselves. With peace negotiations with the British underway and the war seemingly winding down, the Continental Congress declined to accept Washington's changes, and the Continental Army spent the remaining months of the war with the 1776 Articles in place.[48]

Unable to inflict the punishments he believed appropriate, Washington instead had to concentrate upon efforts to deter crime from occurring in the first place. Washington used appeals to patriotism, exhorting his men to not behave like the hated British enemy. He also singled out the soldiers who behaved in an exemplary manner for special praise, rewarding them with extra pay and specially established medals.[49] Washington also placed more of the burden of maintaining discipline upon his officers. He required his subordinates to regularly search the camps to prevent looting and foraging and also demanded frequent roll calls to thwart soldiers from deserting and going AWOL.[50] Washington also made every effort to get his men paid and fed regularly as a means of alleviating the primary sources of discontent. Receiving regular pay and food was the obvious answer to forestall the offense of foraging civilian property. Washington was especially sensitive to the offense of foraging, as the despoiling of civilian property caused a decline in public support for the war. Foraging was especially bad when the army went into winter camp and soldiers stayed in one place for a long time and hand plenty of time on their hands. Only the most stringent efforts, including the threat of and use of the death penalty, managed to keep foraging under a modicum of control.[51]

LEARNING HOW TO FORGE a system of criminal justice and discipline was not the only lesson the Continental Army learned in the American Revolution. From the British, Washington gleaned knowledge of how to discipline an army firmly, knowledge used to justify the failed proposed changes to the 1776 Articles of War. The Americans also got a close tutorial on how to administer occupied territories. Like the Union army later in the Civil War, the British army occupied various American cities, some for extended periods of time. The British occupied New York from 1777 to 1783, and Boston, Philadelphia, Savannah, and Charleston for shorter periods. Obliged to control sizeable portions of the American landscape, the British established policies to regulate the occupied areas and the potentially rebellious population within their control. Some of these policies reflected the accepted laws of war, but others mirrored the unique nature of the colonial conflict. In regulating the hostile population, the British established precedents that the American army would integrate into future conflicts, emulating the British in how to control and administer occupied areas. Last, the Americans observed from the British how the legal sanctity of civilian property became vague and flexible when fighting an enemy that was nominally fellow citizens.

The British army suffered many of the same disciplinary problems as the Continental Army, despite Britain's well-established Articles of War. Desertion was an issue, although much less than in the Continental Army because British soldiers were far from their homes and had nowhere to go.[52] Nevertheless, about 3,700 British soldiers deserted during the war for reasons ranging from harsh discipline, youthful indiscretion, or intolerable service conditions. Like the British, the Americans also appealed for British troops to desert, although with less effect.[53] Many British deserters became deserters through no fault of their own, as hundreds of British soldiers taken as prisoners of war found themselves accused of desertion as defined by the British Articles of War.[54]

The benefit that the British enjoyed when it came to military discipline over the Continental Army was the ability to inflict a broader range of punishments relative to the offense. British courts-martial were free to impose punishments ranging from minor fines to substantial floggings. A soldier suffering a sentence of a thousand lashes or more was relatively common, though courts applied the death penalty only with great restraint. Courts also had the liberty to set the punishment as they saw fit, but a commanding officer had to approve the sentence. This flexible system allowed the British to maintain discipline far from centers of control and was exactly why Washington wished to implement a similar system for his own army.

Washington could not persuade Congress to adopt the British court-martial system, but Washington did emulate one feature of British discipline. Both the American and British Articles of War created a dual court system of general courts-martial for serious offenses and regimental courts-martial for lesser offenses. Lesser offenses warranted lesser punishments, and regimental officers, left to their own devices, created a variety of punishments intended to use humiliation and physical discomfort to correct aberrant behavior. To address basic problems, for instance, British noncommissioned officers (NCOs) could inflict corporal punishment to induce preferred behavior, such as dressing a line or obeying orders in a prompt manner. For more serious offenses, soldiers might face additional duties or requirements to do unsavory duty, such as digging latrines. If an offense was yet more serious but did not warrant a full court-martial, a regimental court-martial could sentence a soldier to a variety of camp punishments. These punishments, intended to humiliate or cause nonpermanent pain, included tying an offender up by their thumbs, standing on a barrel, or "riding the horse"— sitting on a wooden structure shaped like a horse with weights strapped to the limbs—for extended periods of time. Humiliated by the public spectacle of their punishment and with the pain as a reminder, soldiers knew the price of stepping out of line. Some of punishments, however, could exceed the objective of pain and cause permanent injury, just as the case with excessive floggings. The opportunity to abuse these types of punishments was very high, as regimental punishments did not require confirmation from a higher authority.[55] At a loss to contain breaches of discipline within his own army, George Washington also imposed corporal punishment in the Continental Army. American punishments included all of the British afflictions, but the Continentals showed a special affection for forcing offenders to "run the gauntlet." [56]

The British also demonstrated to the Americans how to control a potentially hostile civilian population after occupying enemy territory. The occupation of enemy territory for the British was different from previous conflicts where Britain had seized foreign territory. Against foreign adversaries, only the rules of war regulated the behavior of British soldiers. In the American Revolution, however, the British goal was to reunite the colonies with a minimum of violence and damage to avoid lingering hostility that might inflame another rebellion in the future. This difference forced the British constantly to consider the impact of any policy, especially any brutal or violent policies, that might affect the outcome of the conflict.

Unlike the formal codified Articles of War applied to soldiers, the occupation of enemy territory had no hard and fast rules, although some precedents did exist to provide guidance. The 1765 Mutiny Act for North America, for instance, granted the British military the right to try "Persons, not being Soldiers . . . which are not within the Limits of Jurisdiction of any Civil Government there hitherto established.[57] Theoretically, under this law the British could court-martial any accused rebel in any occupied area on the grounds that the "Civil Government" was no longer operating, even if the occupation of American cities was, from the British perspective, the reestablishment of civil government under British law. The British could also apply the law of belligerent occupation, a broad set of concepts first developed during the Seven Years' War (1756–1763). The law of belligerent occupation held that nations at war were entitled to exercise military control over conquered regions to further their war aims and to protect occupied citizens. This included the right to create new courts and legal systems, regulate trade, and appropriate private property for military purposes as long as the army properly compensated the owners of the seized property.[58]

On the basis of these justifications, the severity of British occupation and treatment of American civilians depended upon various factors: the size of the occupied population, level of civilian opposition, and proximity of an American military threat. Frederick Wiener's research into the British occupation of American cities during the American Revolution reveals that the British application of martial law in occupied areas came in a broad spectrum of policies and attitudes. Boston, the cradle of the rebellion, suffered a brief but harsh occupation marked by the suspension of civil rights and popular government. Charleston, South Carolina, also suffered a full military occupation. The city was the only reliable bastion of British control in the South late in the war, and the British also tightly regulated the citizenry there. The British, however, administered New York and Philadelphia less harshly. The British held the city for such a long time that it could permit the creation of civil administration under military control to run the city. The same situation occurred in Philadelphia, but for the opposite reason. The British held the city so briefly that they did not have the time to dismantle the civil administration.[59] The occupations of Savannah, Georgia, and Newport, Rhode Island, were the least oppressive, again for different reasons. The British needed Newport as a naval base and were not generally concerned about the surrounding countryside, so their presence there was relatively brief and mild. In Savannah, the British could rely upon a sizeable loyalist population to obey the law and assist in restraining rebel influence, so harsh military measures were not necessary.[60]

The British, under pressure to suppress the rebellion in a manner intended to prevent future outbreaks of resistance, had constant troubles finding the appropriate level of military pressure to apply to locals sympathetic to the rebel cause. The Union would find itself in a similar circumstance during the Civil War, precipitating a debate on the merits of what became known as "soft war versus hard war." On one hand, the British could appeal to American reason by acting in a respectful and law-abiding manner, in the hopes of convincing the rebels of the benefits of remaining British citizens (soft war).

On the other, the British could inflict punishing blows by depriving rebels and their supports of their rights and property in an effort to undermine the revolutionary military effort (hard war).

British troops, and their accompanying camp followers, had plenty of justifications for foraging. Pay was low, logistical failures led to short supplies, and prorebel civilians were often hesitant to provide sustenance. The general wealth of the country also provided tempting opportunities to plunder for personal gain.[61] The British army also claimed a legal justification for seizing property in the form of the 1775 Prohibitory Act. Intended by Parliament to stifle the colonial economy into submission in the early months of the rebellion, the Prohibitory Act authorized British officials to seize colonial merchant vessels in the same manner as enemy vessels in time of war. The British army extended this practice to property on land, especially when it came to contraband, property that aided the enemy's war effort.[62] In these circumstances, foraging and pillaging by the British became commonplace, though the level of foraging and the tolerance of it varied. Hessian mercenaries, with no loyalty or identity with the rebel population, became some of the worst pillagers, as did camp followers. Trailing behind the army where control was lax, camp followers took every advantage to pillage and plunder in the wake of British offensives.

A prime example of British efforts to curry favor with the local population in New York was efforts to protect their property from the army and pro-British civilians under their jurisdiction. British officers attempted, at least at first, to restrain the impulse to pillage, with varying degrees of success. Like Washington, the British imposed tight controls on troops leaving camp, used camp punishments to compel compliance with established regulations, and even executed the occasional egregious offender.[63] In 1777, for instance, General William Howe ordered the execution of a private found "Guilty of the Crime of Marauding & Detect'd with plunder upon him." Moreover, Howe announced in the private's death warrant that in "the future [Howe intended] to show no mercy to any man guilty of that Crime."[64] Of the camp followers court-martialed in New York, the sample found that the typical punishment, regardless of gender, was five hundred lashes. Other camp followers and pro-British citizens faced harsh punishment, including death, for other property crimes including robbery, embezzlement, and receiving stolen goods.[65]

But very quickly the British attitude turned from cultivating good relations with local civilians to retaliating against the civilian population for real or perceived support of the rebellion. Instead of using their courts-martial to restrain and punish those accused of property and violent crimes, the British military courts increasingly exonerated soldiers and pro-British civilians and, by extension, endorsed their offenses. This turn to hard war took several forms. The British increasingly supplied themselves at the expense of colonial property holders. As in the later Civil War, the pillaging was justified in the name of striking an enemy that proved difficult to defeat on the battlefield. In a foreshadowing of Union actions, the British engaged in the destruction of property that they themselves could not use to prevent its use by the Continental Army, an act justified on military grounds. Also similar to Union efforts during the Civil War, the British established a legal justification for their property appropriations. British soldiers on campaign extended the definitions of the Prohibitory Act to seize property beyond the supervision of the king's agents.[66] This led to further property damage and seizures, mostly by individuals seeking plunder and profit.

The hard war waged by the British also took on more assertive forms. British occupation provided some employment for occupied colonials, but the British also demanded involuntary labor when also needed. In New York, Philadelphia, and Charleston, British officials used colonial forced labor on fortifications and public works.[67] Violent crimes against colonials by the British army and pro-British civilians also increased during the war and also generally went unpunished. An analysis of Wiener's New York court-martial data finds that more than half of the courts-martial for pro-British citizens were for the violent offenses of murder, plunder, and robbery. There was also a significant percentage of attempted murder, assault, and robbery cases. The courts found the defendants not guilty in nearly 60 percent of the cases, including fourteen of the twenty-five charges of murder.[68]

A prime example of British leniency was the case of Richard Lippincott, a captain in the New Jersey loyalist militia, who summarily executed Joshua Huddy, an officer in the New Jersey militia, in retaliation for the execution of the murder of loyalist Philip White. Washington demanded that General Clinton turn Lippincott over to the Continentals for trial. If the British failed to do so, Washington threatened to select by lot from the British officers held as prisoners of war by the Continentals and put him to death. Clinton instead court-martialed Lippincott, and the court subsequently acquitted him of all charges on the grounds that he was following the orders of his superior officers. Washington never followed through on his threat to execute a British officer, and Lippincott fled to Canada after the end of the war.[69] For British soldiers, their courts-martial were equally lenient. In one sample of British criminal justice during the American Revolution, military courts issued findings of not guilty for ten of the fifteen murder cases tried before it. Of the five found guilty, only two faced the death penalty, with the others receiving pardons or their charges reduced to manslaughter. Rape was also rarely prosecuted, and punishments for the few found guilty was generally light.[70]

The end of the American Revolution left American military justice in a nascent state. The fledgling American army received practice in the application of military justice in a time of war. The experience was not always smooth, perfect, or universally popular, but it was experience upon which the American army could build. The army and the Congress resolved many issues, but others remained undetermined and ill defined. The army had a JAG to organize its methods of military justice, but the officers in the position could never overcome the daunting number of cases and systemic resistance to military law by common soldiers. Moreover, the lessons the British taught the Americans about occupying enemy territory provided only marginal assistance for the future. The British had successfully contained anti-British fervor within their occupation zones, but they could neither compel pro-British behavior nor restrain the impulse for national independence. Frustrated in their efforts, the British adopted a hard war approach to dealing with obdurate rebels. The hard war method demonstrated that relatively harsher policies could feed an army, cow the civilians into compliance, and relieve the hostility that soldiers had toward the rebels, but hard war could not create loyalty or guarantee victory. The Revolution had created the concept of American military discipline, but it was not yet fully defined.

IN THE DECADES AFTER the American Revolution, the image and role of American military justice changed very little. The time period from 1783 to 1846 was marked by long periods of relative peace and a small American army that did not require much in terms of supervision and administration. With but a few changes, the Articles of War adopted in 1776 remained a sufficient instrument to regulate and maintain the army. The ratification of the Constitution in 1789 did not significantly alter the system of military justice already in place. Quite the opposite, the Constitution served to cement the system adopted during the Revolution into semipermanence. The military maintained its two-tier system of regimental and general courts-martial and remained more or less an independent legal body, unregulated by the Congress or the civilian legal system. Instead of a trial by fire, as during the Revolution, American military justice settled into a period of evolution defined by political and legal action.

While the role of military justice is not one of the great issues that come to mind regarding the 1787 debate over the Constitution, the creation of an effective military was an outgrowth of the debate in Philadelphia. The delegates created the framework in which the American army was expected to operate, and in the process solidified the criminal justice system pioneered during the American Revolution. This should not be a surprise; at least thirty signers of the document were veterans of the Revolution. With the recent conflict in mind, the delegates perceived several broad security issues that the new Constitution, and the army that it would create, needed to address. The framers wanted the Constitution that would cement the new union of former colonies. "A Union is necessary for the purpose of national defense." wrote Oliver Ellsworth during the ratification of the Constitution in his native Connecticut, "United, we are strong; divided we are weak."[71] The Constitution also envisioned a force sufficient to be a bulwark against foreign aggression and intimidation, to guard the long, extended American frontier, to contain the Indian threat (both real and perceived), and to preserve internal order and rule of law.[72] The latter responsibility was fresh in the delegates' minds considering the recent Shays' Rebellion, and it would have greater meaning later on when the Civil War broke out.

An early debate was what kind of army should protect America's newly won liberties. The framers of the Constitution generated many quotable opinions on the dangers of a standing army in peacetime, but the real question concerned whether there was a real alternative to a standing army. Proponents of a militia-based defense espoused the view that militias were the greatest safeguard against political tyranny. James Madison, writing in *Federalist* number 46, felt confident that any attempt to usurp the national authority "would be opposed [by] a militia amounting to near half a million citizens with arms in their hands . . . fighting for their common liberties."[73] Other framers, however, preferred that the defense of the nation rest in the hands of a standing army akin to the Continental Army of General Washington. Supporters of a standing army cited the unequal performance of the colonial militia during the Revolution, the potential for disaster if militia confronted a professional European army, and the disunity of command that would result from thirteen different militias instead of a single national army.[74]

In the end, like many issues in the Constitution, the solution was compromise. The state militias would persist, but only as an adjunct to the standing army. Moreover, as the framers defined the Constitution relative to the new army, the militia became subordinate to certain controls of the standing army, losing many of the militia's distinctive elements. The end result was a Constitution that contained many broad conceptual powers related to military justice of both the standing army and the militia. The Constitution obligated the government to provide for the "common Defense," to "punish Piracies . . . and Offences against the Law of Nations," and to "raise and support Armies," though the budgetary function of this power was limited to two years. The Constitution empowered the government to "erect Forts, Magazines, Arsenals, Dock-Yards, and other needful Buildings." The Constitution provided for a mechanism to organize the militia to not only fight as a supplement to the standing army but also to "execute the Laws of the Union, [and] suppress Insurrections." If called into federal service, any militia accused of military violations would face the same discipline as the standing army. The Constitution granted the power to establish "Regulation for the land and naval Forces," which included the Articles of War and process of court-martial, and placed the militia under the same standard by "provid[ing] for . . . disciplining, the Militia . . . and Authority of the Militia according to the discipline prescribed by Congress."[75]

The Constitution also reinforced other issues relating to military justice and issues in the impending Civil War. The document continued the practice of a military justice system separate from the civil system, recognizing the distinctive nature of military offenses and the unique offenses that military courts adjudicated. The document designated the President as the Commander in Chief of the armed forces, including the federalized militia, but granted the right to declare war to the Congress. This division of war-making powers worked well in conventional conflicts but would cause political strain when Americans began to fight Americans. In cases of civil insurrection, the Constitution provided for the suspension of writs of habeas corpus, but the question of who had the authority to suspend the writ was ill defined. The Constitution permitted the suspension of the writ but did not say what individual or which institution wielded the power to do so. The language providing for the suspension of the writ existed in Article I, which listed the powers of the Constitution, so the implication was that the power rested with the Congress. That implication, however, would not be so clear when the Civil War began.[76]

In the presence of a stable Constitutional government and the absence of major conflict, the Articles of War remained relatively unchanged between the Revolution and the Civil War. Instead of abrupt changes caused by the pressures of conflict, the Articles evolved to reflect a garrison force dominated more by political concerns than military ones. The first notable revision came in 1786, when Congress added several items intended to assure a fair trial for the accused. The new additions included a more formal appeals process, obligations to the JAGs to ensure fairness, and provided for a Court of Inquiry process for officers only. A Court of Inquiry was broadly the equivalent of a grand jury and provided the opportunity for an officer to resolve an accusation of misconduct before a charge went to a full court-martial where his reputation and career might suffer. These changes were in place when the nation adopted the Constitution, but the change in government did not alter the existing Articles.[77]

In 1806, President Thomas Jefferson and Congress made several major revisions under the direction of an ad hoc committee, resulting in what

Congress considered a new set of Articles. The 1806 Articles contained several changes designed to reflect the language and intent of the Constitution, as well as to reflect other political considerations.[78] The 1806 Articles reduced the severity of corporal punishment available to courts-martial, limiting floggings to fifty lashes instead of the previous hundred. It also more precisely defined the process for seating regimental and general courts-martial. The changes also provided for a new type of hearing in the form of a garrison court-martial. Regimental courts-martial, which the army presumed would take place in the field, were given a wider amount of latitude in the behavior of the court panel. Garrison courts-martial, however, required tighter adherence to formal policy, as the army unit administering the court-martial was close to a center of authority and appeal. The addition of the garrison court-martial reflected the nature of the army in the early nineteenth century as a relatively immobile frontier defense force and not a mobile offensive army. Article 5 of the new regulations included punishment for any officer or soldier who "shall use contemptuous or disrespectful words against the President of the United States," the government, or other federal official. The 1776 Articles forbade members of the armed forces to use "traitorous or disrespectful words against the authority of the United States," but the word "traitorous" resonated too much like the hated Sedition Act passed by Jefferson's rival, President John Adams. When Jefferson became president, he approved the different wording, despite the obvious issue of the limitation of First Amendment rights. Jefferson required the change to silence his military critics who opposed his reduction of the army and navy.[79]

After 1806, Congress changed the Articles of War only slightly, and generally to the favor of potential defendants, until the outbreak of the Civil War. In 1830, for instance, Congress removed the death penalty as a potential punishment during peacetime, reserving the harshest retribution for wartime offenses.[80] The only significant procedural change was the introduction, in 1821, of the first General Regulations. General Regulations were policies on behavior, dress, protocol, and other military matters that required less legal expertise and more administrative flexibility. An example of General Regulations might include descriptions of mandatory uniform appearance, disbursement of payroll forms by a certain date, or changes in the army's standard diet. These policies were flexible, and the War Department changed the General Regulations to suit the shifting needs of the army. In adopting the General Regulations, the army gave the policies contained within all of the weight of military law but without the need to gain the approval of Congress to alter minor matters.[81] After 1835, changes to military justice took the form of alternations to the General Regulations, provided that they did not conflict with the Constitution or the 1806 Articles.

As the nineteenth century continued, the only other defining influence upon the administration of military justice was the court system. In a variety of cases before 1860, the Supreme Court and lower federal courts issued rulings that strengthened the separate nature of military law and clarified possible conflicts between the jurisdictions of military and civil law. Although many of these cases did not attract much notice at the time of the Courts' rulings, they had huge importance later as they provided precedence in providing discipline to Civil War armies. A prime example was the 1858 decision in the case of *Dynes v. Hoover*. In 1854, Frank Dynes, a seaman in the U.S. Navy, deserted from the service, but was subsequently arrested. Instead of convicting Dynes for desertion, the court-martial hearing his case opted for leniency and instead convicted him merely "attempting" to desert. Dynes' attorney appealed the verdict on two grounds. First, the navy did not charge Dynes with attempted desertion, and his attorney argued that the court-martial panel could not convict him of a charge for which he was not accused. Second, at the time of the trial the navy's Articles of War did not contain "attempting to desert" as an offense, and Dynes' lawyer argued that the court-martial could not convict his client of an offense that the navy did not recognize until that moment. The navy's representative, Attorney General Caleb Cushing, conceded that the offense of "attempting to desert" did not exist until Dynes' case but countered the appeal on two grounds. First, denying the court-martial's attempts at leniency could only result in a conviction of desertion, which would cause a harsher penalty for Dynes. By denying the court-martial's ability to render an appropriate penalty, the Supreme Court would actually cause more harm not only to Dynes, but also to defendants in future possible cases. Second, the Constitution provided for separate civil and military legal systems, and, because Dynes' case was exclusively a military matter, his appeal to the Supreme Court was inappropriate. The Supreme Court concurred, and, by and 8 to 1 vote, supported the navy's finding against Dynes.[82]

The Court's action had far-reaching consequences. In denying Dynes relief from punishment, the Court justices reinforced the separation between civil law and military law by strengthening the authority of the military to regulate itself, as the *Dynes* case seemed entirely at odds with the Court's 1812 ruling in *United States v. Hudson*. In *Hudson*, a civil case, the Supreme Court ruled that lower courts, including the one that convicted Barzillai Hudson of libel against President James Madison, were the product of Congress and that Congress alone had the authority to set their jurisdiction and scope. In Hudson's case, that meant that the lower court ruling exceeded its authority by convicting Hudson of a crime that did not exist within their jurisdiction. In short, the lower court erred in its opinion because it convicted Hudson of a crime that

Congress had not yet created. But when the same circumstances came up forty-six years later in a military court, the Supreme Court chose not to cross the civil/military court boundary.[83] The ruling in *Dynes* also established an important precedent for the later Civil War by giving courts-martial the ability to mitigate the punishments imposed upon the large number of wartime deserters. Desertion in wartime mandated a death sentence, but by creating a loophole the Supreme Court gave later courts-martial the ability to sentence offenders to lesser punishments than to the original charge and thus prevent unnecessary deaths in an already bloody conflict.

The Massachusetts Supreme Court also chose not to stray across the military/civil court divide in the issue of *Walker v. Morris* in 1830, a case regarding the power of the navy to court-martial an offender even after he had left the service. In 1829, William Walker enlisted in the navy for a term of one year. During his service, Walker committed several offenses, and his commanding officer, Captain Robert Morris, preferred charges against him and seated a court-martial. Before the proceedings began, however, Walker's term of enlistment ended, and his lawyer argued that he was no longer under military jurisdiction. The Massachusetts high court rejected that argument, stating that there was "sufficient commencement of the prosecution to authorize a court-martial to proceed to trial . . . notwithstanding the time of service had expired before the court-martial had been convened."[84]

The final major antebellum court decision regarding the authority of military vs. civil law and future Civil War issues was in 1827, when the court issued a ruling in the case of *Martin v. Mott*. Jacob Mott was a member of the New York militia during the War of 1812. When President Madison federalized the state militias for military service, Mott refused to report, on the claim that he enlisted in the militia to protect his home state and his home state only. A court-martial tried Mott for disobeying orders and fined him $96. When Mott refused to pay, the army authorized William Martin, a federal marshal, to seize Mott's property as compensation. Mott sued in local court and won. Martin then appealed to the Supreme Court, and the Court unanimously overturned the state opinion. "We are all of opinion, that the authority to decide whether the exigency has arisen," Justice Joseph Story argued, "belongs exclusively to the president, and that his decision is conclusive upon all other persons."[85] The ruling not only bolstered the strong case for a separate military justice system; it also reinforced the ability of the standing army to regulate the militia in time of crisis. It also had a lingering influence upon the future Civil War by asserting the President's authority to define a crisis and the methods necessary to contain the crisis.

Despite these clarifications of military authority, their impact was minimal in the post-Revolution to pre-Mexican War time period. The relative peace of the era led to a diminished role for the military, marked by small budgets, minimal personnel, and scattered garrisons. With only a small force to regulate, military justice was often an ad hoc affair that relied heavily upon harsh discipline to maintain any semblance of order. Several factors combined to create poor discipline. The pay the soldiers received always lagged behind civilian wages, so military service tended to attract the financially desperate. Service in isolated posts in remote areas of the frontier also did not attract many recruits, nor did the risk of death in combat with Indians. As a consequence, a high percentage of the army consisted of immigrants and the unemployed. The status of the state militias was not any better.[86] In the absence of a direct foreign or domestic threat, regular militia drills became scarcer and scarcer as militia numbers declined in the antebellum period. The relatively few drills that did occur became more of a social event than a military exercise, providing the opportunity for rural communities to congregate for entertainment and social interaction.[87]

Not surprisingly, discipline in the antebellum army was poor, with several factors that mitigated any effort to improve discipline. The Congress proved unwilling to allow the army to tighten discipline through the threat of harsher punishments. The 1806 Articles actually reduced the maximum number of lashes a court-martial could impose, and, from 1812 to 1833, Congress temporarily suspended floggings altogether.[88] Believing that Congress was leaving them to their own devices, some officers took discipline into their own hands and meted out unregulated justice. Beating and capital punishment were common, painful forms of camp punishment (such as continued use of the "horse") proliferated, and officers even conducted illegal executions.[89] In an attempt to halt desertion at his isolated post in Pennsylvania, Major John Wyllys summarily executed three men for desertion in 1786. An internal investigation by Secretary of War Henry Knox exonerated Wyllys, but Knox suspended him from duty pending further investigation by Congress.[90] Left to decide discipline issues for themselves, officers relied very heavily upon local regimental courts-martial to control their troops instead of relying upon general courts-martial involving the War Department. Between 1823 and 1828, for instance, 7,058 soldiers faced a regimental court-martial, almost 23 percent of army personnel, but only about 3 percent faced a general court-martial.[91]

Discipline in the antebellum army might have been better if the army were able to impose some judicial and administrative changes. The first was the preventive measure of containing the use of alcohol. Alcohol use and abuse was prevalent throughout the antebellum army. Alcohol caused a variety of disciplinary problems, the greatest of which was desertion. In the 1820s and 1830s, nearly 20 percent of the army deserted every year. To make matters worse, alcohol was widely available to antebellum soldiers, including a daily whiskey ration issued by the army itself. The daily measure of corn whiskey (the army substituted other spirits when available) amounted to one gill, about four ounces, issued before breakfast. That amounted to 11.4 gallons of whiskey per soldier per year, or about a quart a week. To provide this ration in 1830, the army issued 72,537 gallons of whiskey at a cost of $22,132.[92] In addition, soldiers could buy liquor, despite regulations against the practice, from regimental sutlers. Alcohol was their biggest seller. The inventory of one sutler in 1855, for instance, amounted to eighty-four bottles and twenty-nine casks of various liquors.[93]

Isolated in remote garrisons, underpaid by the army, and ostracized as the least desirable members of society, soldiers turned to drink and the disciplinary infractions occurred as a natural outcome of dissolute behavior. General courts-martial were not common during the antebellum period, but when they did occur it was often for alcohol-related offenses, about 20 percent of the cases. The army tended to correct alcohol-related offenses at the regimental level; 80 percent of regimental courts-martial involved the use of alcohol.[94] Nothing the army tried—camp punishments, floggings, temperance advocacy—had any effect. In the end, the army simply tried prohibition. In 1832, the army ceased issuing the whiskey ration, except for men conducting arduous labor or for medicinal purposes. It had little effect, because alcohol was still available from sutlers or the ubiquitous saloon on the edge of camp. Soldiers would also obtain whiskey from their families through the mail, by foraging for it, or by simply stealing it. It was not until well after the Civil War that the army got a handle on its drinking problem.[95]

The army also suffered from a lack of organizational control to regulate breaches of discipline. The Judge Advocate General Corps, established by the 1776 Articles of War, remained in existence, although its impact was minimal. William Tudor, the first JAG, served less than two years before, overwhelmed by the number of cases and amount of travel, he resigned and returned to civilian life. Washington appointed Colonel John Laurance to replace Tudor. Laurance served for five years, and his tenure included the in absentia prosecution of Benedict Arnold. He left the post in June 1782 when the Revolution was winding down, to return to the New York legislature, and Washington had difficulty finding a replacement. Congress offered the job to two candidates, both of whom declined to serve. Finally, Congress granted the position to Laurance's deputy, Lieutenant Thomas Edwards, who held the post until the end of the war. The Treaty of Paris, however, signaled the end of the Continental Army and the post of JAG.[96] In addition to the JAG, the army employed fifteen assistant JAGs, who were distributed among the army formations and regional districts. Among the fifteen was Captain John Marshall of the Fifteenth Virginia, later a distinguished Chief Justice of the Supreme Court.[97]

The army did not employ a JAG from 1783 until 1794, when the diminutive standing army of the era did not need such a specialized officer. In the latter year, however, military affairs created the need for a revived JAG. The army faced severe difficulties in removing the Indian threat in the Ohio River valley, and Major General Anthony Wayne appointed Lieutenant Campbell Smith to the post of "Judge Marshal and Advocate General" for the army he was recruiting for operations in the Ohio country. The growing possibility of war with France, soon to bloom into the Quasi-War, also necessitated the appointment of a legal advisor for the army. Smith remained at the post until his position again disappeared, this time as part of a March 16, 1802, act of Congress. The act specifically created the Army Corps of Engineers, established the U.S. Military Academy at West Point, New York, limited the size of the army to three regiments, and dispensed with the JAG office. In its place, the Act of March 16 authorized that the "President of the United States may appoint some fit person to act as judge advocate." In the absence of a presidential appointment, the ranking officer of the court could appoint a judge advocate for the proceedings.[98] The 1806 Articles of War further defined the powers of these temporary and ad hoc advocates, a system that remain in place for the next forty years.[99]

During the War of 1812, Congress permitted the army to appoint a number of advocates, similar in function and responsibility as the assistant judge advocates appointed during the Revolution, to each military formation to administer justice to the expanded armed forces. The posts were temporary only, and the post of JAG remained closed by act of Congress. Subsequent congressional acts (March 3, 1815, April 14, 1818, and March 2, 1821) reduced the size of the army to pre–War of 1812 levels, and the temporary advocates disappeared. The office of JAG did not return until after the Mexican War. The absence of a JAG during this period hampered American military law during the conflict, and aggravated several tense legal issues introduced by the war.[100]

ALL OF THE ISSUES RELATING to military justice in the period from 1783 to 1846—the obsolescent Articles of War, the ill-defined constitutional issues, the diminished JAG office, the entrenched peacetime attitudes regarding discipline, and the inability to impose regular discipline—came to a head during the Mexican-American War. For the first time, America fought a war deep in foreign territory, far from centers of political authority and surrounded by hostile civilians. The army conducted the war with a Regular Army hastily expanded by the recruitment of large number of immigrants and a mass of enthusiastic, if poorly trained and ill disciplined, volunteer state regiments. All of these elements combined to create a disciplinary nightmare that taxed the army's ability to wage the war effectively.

Soldiers enlisted in the Regular Army for a variety of reasons. Economic necessity, youthful adventure, chronic unemployment, and professional advancement all attracted men into the service.[101] The war was very popular in the South, but less so in the North where antiwar attitudes intensified during the conflict, and attracting recruits was more difficult there. As a result, army recruiters relied on coercion and compulsion to meet its goals, along with a considerable number of recent immigrants seeking some form of employment.[102] Nativism was very strong in America at the time, however, and perhaps strongest of all among the officers of the U.S. Army. In addition to their foreign birth, most early nineteenth-century immigrants came from Catholic regions of Europe, such as Ireland and southern Germany, causing more nativist friction in a Protestant-dominated America. Officers were often dismissive of the abilities of their new soldiers, labeling them as "Dutch" or complaining about the pack of "unsophisticated, untutored, and intractable sons of Erin" assigned to their commands.[103] Predisposed to finding fault with their men, officers in the Mexican War allowed this prejudice to create major disciplinary problems once they reached the combat zone.

The army's reaction to the new volunteer regiments was not much better. An influx of volunteer regiments made up of existing militia formations and new recruits outnumbered the standing army.[104] Problems started almost immediately. Many units formed and reported for duty without a clear understanding of their obligation and rights. The Fourth Indiana Regiment, for instance, organized in 1847 without predetermining how long their military obligation lasted or even how much the government intended to pay them.[105] Many regiments volunteered only for fixed terms of service, and not for the length of the conflict. This meant that volunteer units were constantly coming and going from the battle zone, usually at the point when their experience finally made them effective combat units. In 1848, for instance, the end of twelve-month enlistments among volunteers threatened General Winfield Scott's campaign into central Mexico, when a sizeable portion of his army left when their terms of service expired. Scott was deep in Mexican territory in the midst of a potentially decisive campaign, but the volunteers left anyway, reducing Scott's army to barely seven thousand men.[106] The volunteers also balked at obeying the rules of army discipline. Despite the constitutional definitions, and subsequent Congressional legislation, that placed the militia under the authority of the army and President in wartime, many volunteers were either ignorant of the mandate or chose to ignore it. Volunteers expected to serve only in their state-oriented units, demanded to select and dismiss their officers at their own discretion, and rejected the leadership of officers who seemed to demand too much discipline and protocol. "They [volunteers] are composed of a different material from the regulars," wrote one Pennsylvania soldier, "and should be differently managed."[107] Disciplinary problems specifically escalated after many volunteers became disillusioned when the mundane and often boring nature of army life clashed with their romantic image of war.[108] As a whole, many officers did not have much confidence in making true soldiers of their volunteers, but some held out hope. "The American volunteer is a thinking, feeling, and often capricious being." wrote Major Luther Giddings, "He is not and never intends to be become a mere moving and musket-holding machine." Giddings opined that if the army could blend the volunteers' "native courage and intelligence and a proper degree of discipline, [it would] make him the most formidable soldier in the world."[109]

The disciplinary divide between officers and men grew wider when officers attempted to impose prewar methods of discipline upon their new soldiers. Men in the prewar Regular Army were accustomed to military discipline, but new soldiers and volunteers were not. When officers refused to recognize that fact, problems almost invariably developed. Discipline was perhaps the worst among General Zachary Taylor's forces, operating along the Texas-Mexico frontier. Taylor was far from any sort of judicial support, so discipline was his matter and his matter only. Moreover, he had to rely more heavily upon volunteer units after the War Department reassigned most of his Regular troops to operations elsewhere. That left Taylor with new and untrained volunteer regiments, along with the Texas "Rangers," an irregular frontier force that supported the army to defend the border. The Rangers were simultaneously one of Taylor's biggest assets and biggest headaches. The Rangers were invaluable for scouting and reconnaissance, but their primary motivation was plunder, and the activities quickly alienated any support Taylor might expect from the local Mexicans. Compounding the problem, Taylor and his officers were not certain they had the authority to impose discipline, as the Rangers were neither Regular Army nor formal state militia.[110] A prime example of the army's powerlessness to contain the Rangers came after the American capture of Monterrey in October 1846. While most of Taylor's army remained encamped outside of the city, Rangers went on a killing and plunder spree that left more than a hundred civilians dead. No record exists of any court-martial or punishment for the crimes.[111] Taylor proved generally unwilling to restrain his men, and his occupation of northern Mexico soon devolved into a cycle of violence and counter-violence. The American pillaging of the village of Agua Nueva, for instance, led to the murder of a lone cavalryman, Archibald Colquitt. In retaliation, American troops killed a number of Mexican civilians after claiming they found some of Colquitt's personal effects. Taylor attempted to punish the offenders, but threats by the volunteers to refuse further service led Taylor to suspend the investigation.[112]

On their own and left to their own devices deep in enemy territory, Taylor's officers resorted to brutal and often inequitable punishments to keep their troops in some semblance of order. Caleb Cushing, a diplomat before the war and future Attorney General of the United States, served as the colonel of a Massachusetts regiment. Catching a volunteer and a sutler selling liquor without permission, Cushing "took the law into his own hands, and had the fellow soundly horse-whipped."[113] Another soldier suffered the penalty of being "gagged with a bayonet, his teeth broken and loosened, and his mouth cut severely," while others "rode the horse" or worked at hard labor while encumbered by a ball and chain. When these measures proved incapable of stemming disorder, officers escalated the punishment to include branding. Officers intended the imposition of a permanent mark constantly to remind the soldier of past offenses in the hopes that they would not repeat them. The brand represented the offense; habitual drunkards received a "HD," deserters a "D," and soldiers deemed worthless received a "W."[114]

Nativist prejudice further exacerbated Taylor's disciplinary problems. Although harsh punishment was the rule, observers noted that officers tended to single out immigrant soldiers and take special delight in the punishments imposed upon them. When tried at regimental courts-martial with native Americans, almost invariably the immigrant soldiers received harsher treatments for identical offenses. Instead of the traditional forms of camp discipline, immigrant soldiers suffered from a wider range of punishments than native soldiers did. Hanging Irish and German soldiers by their thumbs with their feet barely touching the ground, unable to support their weight, was a common punishment. "Bucking and gagging" were other commonly inflicted punishments, where a soldier sat on the ground, his knees drawn to his chest, and his hands tied in front of his knees. The supervising officer placed a stick under the knees so the soldier could not move, and left them there for several hours; this bucking was also accompanied by gagging, in which the soldier was forced to clench a rag, or sometimes his bayonet, in his teeth. Nativism was not only the prejudice of officers. American troops also held contempt for immigrant soldiers, which escalated into mass violence, as when a riot broke out between Irish and Georgia troops near the town of Camargo that left one man dead.[115]

The response of soldiers, both native and immigrant, to the discipline in Taylor's army varied widely. Some wrote bitter letters home to their families, asking them to forward their complaints to their congressmen. Some soldiers, overcome by the experience, committed suicide.[116] Others retaliated with violence of own, only to face force in return and a charge of insubordination. When Irish members of the First Ohio Regiment resisted the abuse dealt to them, their "officers were obliged to use force and blows to put down the disturbances, and a number of blackened eyes and broken heads were the result."[117] Even General Taylor himself got a taste of violent retribution. After barking orders at a German soldier who understood little English, Taylor roughly grabbed the man by his ear. The soldier, in pain, turned and floored Taylor with a single punch. Officers with swords drawn rushed to arrest the soldier, but Taylor ordered his release, telling them to let the man go as he would "make a good soldier."[118] Other resistance organized itself into open mutiny. Most mutinies occurred in the volunteers' home states, resulting from last-minute disputes over pay and personnel matters. But several small mutinies occurred in Mexico, for reasons ranging from anger over harsh camp punishment to which officer should lead the regiment.[119] Resistance to authority even escalated into attempts to murder unpopular superior officers—"fragging," in the terminology of the Vietnam War. Private John Meginness, for instance, explained the high number of officer casualties at the Battle of Molino del Rey as the product of disgruntled soldiers shooting their officers under the cover of battle.[120] Captain Braxton Bragg, a future Confederate general, survived one fragging attempt when soldiers lit an artillery round and rolled it into his tent. Miraculously, Bragg survived the resulting explosion with only slight burns.[121]

The primary means of resisting military discipline, however, was to desert, and desertion became a critical problem by the middle of the war. By one estimate, 13 percent of the soldiers in Taylor's Regular Army regiments deserted by the time his campaigns ended. Desertion rates were equally high among the volunteer regiments. The Second Pennsylvania Regiment, for instance, lost 6 percent of its strength alone while passing through New Orleans on it way to the frontlines.[122] Soldiers deserted because of low pay, poor living conditions, and the disillusionment with soldier life, but harsh discipline was the single greatest cause of desertion, a problem that the army failed to address. The nativist bias against immigrant troops, and the malicious discipline that came with it, drove many immigrant troops to leave the army and even to side with the enemy. Almost as soon as Taylor's army arrived on the banks of the Rio Grande, soldiers took the risk of swimming across the river to desert. On April 1, 1846, alone thirty-six soldiers successfully escaped into Mexico. Taylor responded by posting additional pickets and threatening to shoot any man seen in the river who did not respond to warnings to return. Between April 1 and April 11, at least forty-three of Taylor's men reached the south bank of the Rio Grande, according to the local Mexican newspaper, but the number was probably higher. At least nine men died or were shot by pickets while attempting to desert.[123] The desertion problem only became worse after Taylor crossed the Rio Grande on his campaign against Monterrey, as soldiers found it easier to disappear into the vast countryside.

The Mexican government, playing upon the nativist backlash in the American forces and appealing to the common Roman Catholic religious tie between Mexico and many Irish/German immigrants, made a concerted effort to induce disgruntled soldiers to leave. The Mexicans used propaganda leaflets to compel desertion, followed by promises of safe conduct through Mexican territory, land grants, and even officer commissions if the deserters enlisted in the Mexican Army.[124] In occupied towns, priests attempted to compel soldiers to desert, despite warnings to stay out of army affairs. "The reverend gentleman was placed in confinement and shipped to Camargo." wrote the officer who arrested him, "If he gets his just deserts [sic], he should be hung, in spite of his sanctity."[125]

Most deserters preferred to avoid further military service, but some opted to enlist in the Mexican Army. This group, the San Patricio (St. Patrick) Battalion, numbered between two hundred and five hundred men at various times during the war. The term "San Patricio" gives the impression that most were Irish immigrants, but, though Irish were the plurality, they were not the majority. The San Patricios contained significant numbers of British and German immigrants and a number of native-born Americans.[126] By enlisting in the service of the enemy, the San Patricios faced treason as well as desertion charges, so they tended to fight ferociously and to the death when in combat with American forces. Those whom the U.S. Army did capture faced severe punishment. By the end of the war, the United States had recaptured seventy-two San Patricios, and their fate lay in the hands of General Winfield Scott. Courts-martial found seventy of the seventy-two guilty of deserting to the enemy and sentenced them to death. The facts of the case were not in dispute; all of them were captured while wearing Mexican Army uniforms. But Scott faced a considerable amount of pressure to apply leniency. When many of the San Patricios described the harsh conditions that led to their desertion and foreign diplomats asked Scott to show mercy, the general had to consider the impact among his remaining immigrant troops if he ordered a mass execution. The Mexican government, with whom Scott was attempting to negotiate a peace treaty, also asked for leniency, and he did not want to sour relations if a political end to the war was near.

In the end, Scott exercised as much leniency as he could, and, after reviewing each individual case, revised a portion of the courts-martial findings. Scott eventually pardoned five men (including two underage soldiers) and sustained the death sentence against fifty of them. The remaining fifteen men received sentences less than death because of mitigating factors. The most common mitigating factor applied to San Patricios who deserted from Taylor's army. They deserted before Congress issued a formal declaration of war, and the 1830 revisions to the Articles of War forbade the use of the death penalty in time of peace.[127] Their punishments, however, were still harsh. Scott mandated that each man "receive fifty lashes each upon their naked backs, and to be branded with the letter D high upon the check-bone, near the eye, without jeopardizing it sight."[128] One San Patricio, John Riley, suffered doubly. General David Twiggs, supervising the punishments, noted that Riley's brand was upside down. To obey the letter of Scott's order, Twiggs had Riley branded again, this time properly, on the other cheek.[129]

Besides adjudicating desertion cases, Scott had to deal with discipline issues of his own. In the spring of 1847, Scott led an expedition into central Mexico with the goal of capturing Mexico City and bringing the Mexicans to the negotiating table. After capturing Veracruz in March, Scott defeated a Mexican force at the Battle of Cerro Gordo on April 18. Soon after this victory, however, Scott's volunteers left for home at the end of their terms of service. Instead of retreating to Veracruz, Scott elected to press forward toward Mexico City without a logistic line back to the coast. Scott intended to live off the land by foraging and appropriating food from the local population. Isolated and vulnerable deep in enemy territory, Scott had to adopt a different approach to his relations with his army and with the vast civilian population around him. In doing so, Scott established some Soft War precedents for later Civil War officers in occupied territories of the Confederacy.

Scott had to manage the delicate task of managing his army, successfully waging a military campaign, and keeping the local population from destroying his army in the same manner as Spanish guerillas undermined Napoleon in Spain. Scott tightened discipline within his own army, a process made easier by the limited opportunity to desert. Whereas deserters from Taylor's army sought to flee back to Texas, deserters from Scott's army had nowhere to go deep in the Mexican countryside. Scott still had to worry about property crimes and other depredations upon civilians, so he moved to limit such temptations. The army cracked down on liquor consumption, gambling, and contact with civilians. All of these moves proved unpopular, especially the latter. Soldiers had come to enjoy the local fandangos, or local dances, because it provided contact with women and the opportunity to drink.[130] Scott required the army to pay for supplies requisitioned from the civilian population, either in script or in notes of credit.[131] Officers had wide latitude to monitor and control their soldiers to avoid the pillaging of towns and homes. Scott also curried favor with Mexican civilians by avoiding any clash with the cultural dominance of the Catholic Church. Scott maintained the church's property and status as a demonstration that the Americans were not there to change Mexico or even necessarily to stay very long. Scott went so far as to attend Catholic Mass and to order his men to extend respect to Catholic clergy, a move that did not sit well with the Protestant and nativist segments of his army.[132]

After capturing Mexico City, Scott also had to establish a bureaucracy to run a major city and prevent outbreaks of violence with the city's inhabitants for an occupation that lasted nine months. The immediate problem was the issue of legal mechanisms. The Mexican legal system had broken down, and the Articles of War contained no provision for punishing soldiers for crimes against foreign citizens. In the absence of a legal mechanism, Scott created one. On his march to Mexico City, Scott had permitted Mexican courts to try Americans accused of killing Mexican civilians. Local authorities misused the courtesy, so Scott did not repeat it. Instead, in his General Order 20, Scott established a court system that included representatives of the army and civilian government to try cases stemming from alleged illegal acts by Americans and vice versa. The intent of the courts was to try those who committed "grave offenses not provided for in the act of Congress . . . by, or upon, individuals of those armies, in Mexico, pending the existing war between the two republics."[133] Scott's court system soon proved it was serious; in January 1848, a soldier from a regiment of Regulars hanged for the "killing of an inoffensive Mexican."[134]

Scott always balanced his use of leniency, however, by the tacit threat of violence. He managed to suppress dissent after capturing Mexico City by threatening the *ayuntamiento,* or civic leadership, with unregulated looting if local resistance did not cease. With their assistance, Scott was able to quell civil dissent, but only after several days.[135] Scott also imposed an assessment of $3 million per year on the Mexican population. Scott intended this assessment to pay for the administration of the Mexican government if and when a peace treaty came into effect, but the implied purpose was more in line with the assessment that Taylor imposed in northern Mexico for the sole purpose of compensating the United States for their wartime expenses.[136] Scott was not entirely successful in containing breakdowns of discipline, as boredom caused by a long occupation still created disciplinary problems. The lure of female companionship continued to entice soldiers to fandangos, despite a $1.50 tax imposed by the army to stop them.[137] Soldiers still committed acts of violence and murder against civilians and each other, and drinking continued to cause such problems that the army established a 6 P.M. closing time to combat their corrosive influence.[138] While not perfect, Scott did maintain sufficient discipline to keep his army intact, maintain reasonably good order in Mexico City, and preserve enough good will with the Mexican people and government to permit an eventual negotiated end to the war and subsequent American withdrawal.

BETWEEN THE MEXICAN WAR and the outbreak of the Civil War, the army reverted to its pre–Mexican War status. By 1850, the dissolution of the volunteer regiments had reduced the army to its congressionally mandated size of 12,937 officers and men.[139] The army dispersed its manpower to frontier posts and coastal forts, and life reverted to its prewar routine. With but one exception, the Mexican War did not significantly alter the course of American military justice. That single exception was the recreation of the office of Judge Advocate General. After the war, Generals Winfield Scott and Gideon Pillow engaged in an unseemly public spat over who deserved the most recognition for the victory over Mexico. Scott attempted to silence his subordinate using policies in the General Regulations that prevented officers from issuing reports directly to newspapers. Pillow had a strong ally in President James K. Polk, however, and the so-called "Leonidas incident" dragged on until it became a public embarrassment for the army. Recognizing the need to regulate army discipline in the field, and to provide an impartial judge for quarrels between officers, Congress reestablished the post of JAG on March 2, 1849, and named Captain (Brevet Major) John F. Lee to the post. Lee held the position until 1862, overseeing general courts-martial, but leaving field officers to oversee their own regimental courts-martial.[140]

Lacking any substantive change, military justice was in the same unprepared condition when the Civil War broke out as it was when the Mexican War occurred. This time, however, the war created issues and contentions far beyond the comparatively limited scope of the Mexican War. Instead of an enemy defined by a congressional declaration of war, the Regular Army and its adjunct volunteer regiments would face fellow Americans in murky political conflict turned violent. Instead of a few thousand volunteers, the Regular Army had to contend with hundreds of thousands of volunteers, each cognizant of their rights as citizens and as citizen-soldiers. Even more potentially dangerous, the Mexican War had created a perception of a mode of behavior in both the army and the new soldiers. Memories of the Mexican War involved pillaging and retribution as seldom-punished offenses, if not outright encouraged practice. Officers, both veteran and newly commissioned, retained a memory of strict discipline that maintained the combat power of the army in hostile territory. When accented by the combat of the Civil War, these memories clashed, creating a situation that made military justice even more difficult to maintain.

2

"DAMN FOOL!"

The Uneasy Relationship between Officers and Enlisted Men

Union soldiers had many motivations for fighting in the Civil War. Some fought for Union, some fought to define their manhood, and still others fought to end slavery, but all fought the establishment. America was a country where the citizen-soldier defined its military history. Whether Massachusetts Minutemen or Tennessee Volunteers, Americans associated military service as an honorable, responsible, and most important, temporary expedient for the defense of the country. As citizens with rights codified in the Constitution, Americans knew the history of their nation and recognized that their ancestors fought and won previous wars only through pain and sacrifice. To many soldiers in 1861 and after, the call for sacrifice was just as clear. The veterans of previous wars, because they were not professional soldiers, knew that their service to their country was only a brief interruption of their lives. Once the enemy threat disappeared, citizen-soldiers became merely citizens again. As a result, the standing professional Regular Army remained small, and the nation continued to place its defense in the hands of its latent force of amateur soldiers.

When wars did occur, the professionalism of the Regular Army clashed with the desire of citizen-soldiers to exist more as "citizens" and less as "soldiers." Maintaining this desire, however, caused a fundamental problem with the relationship of organized armies. The problem was convincing an army of citizen-soldiers, who were accustomed to speaking their minds and exercising their rights, that someone was not only going to tell them what to do, but that they had to obey without question. A clash between the two definitions of discipline was inevitable, as citizen-soldiers found themselves in the position of knowing what had to be done to win the war but hesitant to surrender their freedoms to accomplish it. On one hand, the soldiers of the Union army were disciplined enough to organize into a potent force, stand their ground in the midst of deadliest battle, and ultimately win the war. On the other hand, the soldiers of the Union army constantly fought against the institutional controls of the army and those who represented the institution, the officers. In the end, no one won this battle. Instead, the struggle between citizen-soldier and institution-army settled into a general, if uneasy, stalemate, punctuated by occasional skirmishes that threatened to cause outright war.

   DURING THE MEXICAN WAR, the mentality of the Regular Army dominated. The volunteer, however, dominated the Civil War. Vastly outnumbering the Regulars, the volunteers formed a collective mindset shaped by the perception of their rights and privileges as citizen-soldiers. Using the imagery of the minuteman from the American Revolution as their guide, the Civil War citizen-soldier accepted the burden of fighting for their country and their Union, but that same imagery caused them to reject the harshest elements of military discipline as an anathema to their natural rights. They accepted the hazards of military life but would not permit military discipline to change their fundamental rights or privileges of citizenship. The result was an army that only grudgingly obeyed the rules, followed their officers, and tested the limits of permissiveness at every turn.

   Some soldiers accepted the dangers of military service as patriots, personally identifying with their revolutionary ancestors. "It really seems as if our time of revolution and great change has come," James Ames wrote to his mother, "The future historians will write about the dates of '60 and '61 and the great 'American revolution.'"[1] These men embraced the mantle of commitment thrust toward them, shaped as a three-part argument for duty. The duty took the form of an argument that citizen-soldiers had the obligation to defend the Constitution and the citizens who enjoyed its benefits, soldiers had to defend the high ideals that America and its government promoted, and that the needs of the community of American citizens prevailed over the interests of the individual. Through their lens of perception, the American Revolution was a legitimate and moral crusade for freedom, and their cause was right because their country was right.[2] Other patriotic soldiers, especially those who were recent immigrants, felt a responsibility to defend the country that had embraced them and provided the opportunity for social and economic advancement. "[I]t is right and the duty of citizens and those who have lived long enough in this country to become citizens to fight for the maintenance of law, order, and nationality," wrote Private Peter Welsh to his brother, "but the country has no claim on you and never bring upon yourself the dangers and hardships of a soldier's life where the county nor cause has no claim on your service."[3] In theory, a soldier who embraced this patriotic challenge fought because of principle, and coercion and material gain played no part in their decision to risk their lives for their nation. With such determination, military discipline was unnecessary because soldiers were self-motivated to discipline themselves.[4] In the course of time, however, this idea disappeared in the face of reality and modern war.

Associated with this idea of patriotism was war as the test of manhood. Combat represented, to many a naïve soldier, the ultimate test of maturity and masculinity, and the social pressure to succeed in the test of combat motivated many soldiers to embrace the patriotic cause to bolster their own individual confidence. In the mode of the political crusade for the nation, citizen-soldiers were to view desertion and cowardice in the face of the enemy as a great personal failure. Cowards deserved scorn as failures to their country and to their fellow citizens.[5] "i [*sic*] often think of home but home has no charams [*sic*] for me when there is work to do," David Lilley wrote to his sister, ". . . Be what it will i will never fill a Cowards grave."[6] In response to his cousin's hints that his place was at home helping his father, John Lynch could only respond that "I could not remain at home . . . while others would be performing my duty in fighting the battles of our country."[7] Manhood in the defense of the Union was not the exclusive impulse of the young. "I am 65 years old [but] am able to do a fair days work," Daniel Edwards wrote to President Abraham Lincoln in 1864, "[I] am willing to go to the army . . . Avery Coon is a stout man of about my age—[he] will go too."[8] Although often fearful of the experience, soldiers braced themselves for their first taste of combat, hoping they measured up to their own expectations of manhood. Private James Dunn wrote to his wife in 1861 that he expected to "smell powder" soon, while Joseph Baer reported that his regiment was about to "gad [go] to se [*sic*] the allafent [elephant]." "Going to see the elephant" was common Civil War slang for a soldier's first combat experience, a verbal allegory for undergoing a new experience.[9]

Associated with this idea, self-discipline was again important. To patriotic citizen-soldiers no amount of punishment, or threat of punishment, could instill the moral character necessary to stand and fight, so military justice was superfluous. Soldiers were to accept their duty, no matter how dangerous or unfulfilling their duty was.[10] When military discipline was necessary, soldiers expected the punished to take it like men. "Tell the boys if they want to be free & not be obliged to come & go at the beck of an over to stay at home & leave sogering [*sic*] to those that like it," Private Henry Matrau wrote his parents, "A person in the army must mind his own business & let other people's alone or it will be apt to go pretty hard with him."[11] James Wiggins grew weary of soldiers who, after considerable time in the army, still complained about tough discipline. "Some men will always growl," Wiggins wrote his parents, "It makes no difference how well they are treated. We all know that military laws are severe."[12] This public pressure was often enough to persuade men to join the army who were personally not convinced they should go. "Nine-tenths of them enlisted just because somebody else was going," wrote Captain Samuel Merrill to his wife, "and the other tenth were ashamed to stay at home."[13] The demands of manhood and public masculinity, however, did not mean that soldiers forgot for whom they were fighting. "The men, too, are thinking of absent and loved ones. The roughest soldiers among us has a quiet corner of his heart that he keeps hidden from his comrades' eyes," Private Samuel Partridge wrote to his wife, "There he keeps green the memory of those who are all and all to him. Occasionally a tear starts in the eye but is hastily wiped away."[14]

The acceptance of this patriotic mission helped to create a determination among Union soldiers to see the war through despite the challenges, deprivations, and hardships of war. "I know not how I will feel in battle," Elijah Cavins wrote before leaving Indiana in June 1861, "but it seems to me that I would a thousand times prefer that I should be wrapped in a winding sheet, than falter or pause in the coming conflict."[15] Such sentiments regarding the importance of manhood were common among other soldiers as well. Major Claudius Grant, writing in his diary of an officer accused of cowardice, confessed that "For myself I prefer 6 ft of sod to lie under with my soul" than accept the premise that "a live coward is worth more than a dead hero." "Life at the expense of honor," Grant believed, "is worse than death."[16] The "cowards have been sifted by the thousands out of the ranks," wrote one Wisconsin soldier, "and the huge talking men, the braggarts and boasters have gone home. The men who are left are real warriors."[17] Expressions of manhood also manifested not only in protecting the reputation of the individual, but the family as well. "I know my grandfather was a soldier in the War of 1812 . . . and I heard father say that my great-grandfather was a Revolutionary soldier, and that he enlisted for the Blackhawk War . . .," Private Billy Davis wrote in his memoirs, "I feel that if I do not go that I will be disgraced, and by staying home will bring reproach upon the family name."[18] The need to protect one's reputation loomed over even the threat of death. "Should it be my lot to fall during the present struggle," James Woodworth wrote to his wife, "let the shout that I die in the defense of my country console you. And when peace with its happy train of attendants shall once more visit the land, may it be your greatest job to teach my child that I was one who loved my country better than life. This is the only legacy I can bequeath to him, but is one that a Prince might well be proud of."[19] Even when faced with difficulty, the need to protect one's reputation and manhood often defeated the temptation to quit. Writing to his father, Lieutenant James Carman resisted the urge to resign his commission because "I have taken an oath to Support the Constitution of the U. States and obey the President."[20]

Soldiers also stated their willingness to defend the broad concepts of "home," "nation," and "Union," or rather the specific liberties and freedoms identified with these broad concepts. "What is home with all of its endearments," Private George Beidelman wrote to his father, "if we have not a country freed from every vestige of anarchy, and the tyrannical and bloodthirsty despotism which threatens on every side to overwhelm us?" Beidelman also saw the war as a challenge to the nation from God. "This war has been, and is, a terrible thing . . .," he wrote, "but I firmly believe it is the judgment begun in the house of the Lord—the refining fire that will purify our nation."[21] Surgeon William Philips also saw the conflict as preserving and improving the nation by removing slavery as an obstruction to democracy, and providing an opportunity to expand the Northern model of yeoman agriculture to the "backward" South.[22] George Cadman was also willing to die for the Union. "And [if] I do get hurt I want you to remember that it will be not only for my country and children," he wrote his wife, "but for liberty all over the world that I risked my life; for if liberty should be crushed here, what hope would there be for the cause of human progress anywhere else?" Cadman did die for his country, from wounds suffered during General William T. Sherman's campaign to take Atlanta.[23] "As long as the war lasts I expect to be a soldier. . . ," William Bentley wrote his family, "I never appreciated the blessings of a free country till I came into the Army."[24]

Converse to the preservation of the Union, soldiers were determined to see the war through to destroy the perceived treason of the Confederacy and its "monstrous and unholy rebellion."[25] In the effort to preserve the Union, George Avery emphasized that he was fighting "not for wealth—tis not for honor, but for the benefit of mankind."[26] In an exuberant letter to his local newspaper, William Barnitz looked forward to when "these hell hounds who have been plotting the destruction of our temple of liberty, cemented by the blood of our fathers and reared at so great a cost of life and agony, would be hanging on every tree, objects for the execration and loathing of patriots all over the civilized world."[27] Private George Remley echoed the sentiment.

"Much as I would like to be at home and see all of you once again, I would not, were it offered me, take a discharge," Remley wrote his family, "I want to see the boasted strength of the Confederacy complete broken, every hand that is raised against our Government struck down peace once more restored to the whole country."[28] Even when the war dragged on and victory seemed distant, the determination to finish the task and win the war remained. "Shall I abandon the ship that has so long carried us in safety," Captain George Avery wrote his wife, describing the Union as a ship of state, "one which has rode majestically & triumphantly over so many troubled seas, & for so many years & one too which as cost the life blood of so many noble patriots[?] No! [M]y patriotism says, No!—my manhood says, No! Then, I must finish my task."[29] Private Jacob Bartmess, writing to his wife in the aftermath of the Battle of Stone's River, grieved over the "spot where lies the boddies [sic] of hundreds of our brave men . . . the many little orphans calling and crying for pappy . . . and the widowed, and heartbroken wife," but determined to fight on.[30] Private Charlie Mosher fought on because he believed "this Southern confederacy ought to be sunk to the lowest hell, and lower," while Private John Brobst dreamed of the day he could get his hands on "old Jeff Davis, wanting him tied up to a fence post and let the grasshoppers to kick him to death."[31] Private James Abraham mourned for the "desolate homes, widowd [sic] wives and orphaned children" but pledged never to quit "while Hell-born[e] treason stalks the land of the free and the home of the brave. Better for humanity that this and the next generation should be draped in mourning than our glorious institutions perish and freedom and Democracy bow to Slavery and despotism. Better that our land should be drenched in blood now, before we're bound hand and foot, than that posterity should do it rending the shackles."[32]

The resolve to win the war generated a grim determination to persevere despite great risk, great horrors, and great risk of personal injury and death. "I've been where death was thick and close around me," Charles Brewster wrote his parents, but he was determined to fight out the war, chastising his wife to "don't take it for granted that I am dead and stop writing until you know the facts."[33] Surgeon Robert Mitchell, who knew the human cost of the war, wrote in the aftermath of the Fredericksburg debacle that "the only way to close this war is to fight it to the bitter end . . . we have nothing to gain and everything to lose by truces and attempt to patch up a peace."[34] Mashies Lord, another surgeon, saw the horrors of war up close. "[A] vast hospital . . . was filled with wounded soldiers, lying on the floor, many of whom had just had an arm or a leg amputated . . .," Lord wrote in his diary, "human beings were being cut and sawed and subjected to the weapons of the surgeon . . . And all of his for what? For the salvation of our country. The cause justifies the cost."[35] Under the pressure of combat, unlikely soldiers emerged and men did incredibly courageous acts. The Twenty-third New York included a "belligerent member of Co. H., aged 15 years and 18 days—a precocious warrior who . . . can keep his arms in order, endure fatigue, use expletives, and chew tobacco as well as "any other man.'"[36] Another motivated soldier, George Remley, died in action bear Berryville, Virginia, in October 1864. Ordered into position against the enemy, Remley joined his unit even though a friend "told him it was useless for him to go into the fight without any weapon. . . . I will never forget his reply to me. 'I came into the Army to fight and I am going to get me a gun.'" Remley took a rifle away from a soldier frozen by fear but was killed in the ensuing Union charge.[37]

Soldiers that demonstrated such dedication to their cause tended to favor the promotion of discipline in the ranks, and officers who tried to motivate their soldiers to behave to the highest possible standards received the appreciation instead of the scorn of their determined men. Although soldiers embraced the idea of the citizen-soldier temporarily suspending their personal liberty toward a greater cause, they recognized that, while in the army, they must passively accept discipline that they would not accept in civilian life. To do so was to create a better army that might win the war sooner and return them to civilian life quicker. Sergeant Peter Welsh appreciated the high level of discipline that his regimental officers maintained. He conceded that "their [sic] is a good many of our regiment who have out Colnel [sic] because he is a man of discipline" but also favored the colonel because "he will alow [sic] neither Officers nor men to shirk their duty. . . if there is any cause of complaint he makes it his buisnss [sic] to look after it immediately." Welsh even favored the wider use of capital punishment by the officers. "A commission gulentine [guillotine] is much needed," he wrote to his wife, "by which all inefecient [sic] commissions should be beheaded and men from the ranks put in their [sic] place."[38] Private Rufus Robbins also spoke well of his strict commander. "He [the regimental colonel] is a very smart man and I think will make better soldiers of us than we could ever have been . . . Every order has to be obeyed to the letter and the slightest offense subjects us to some kind of punishment."[39] Injured in battle, the colonel commanding the Eighth Maine had to take medical leave. Upon his return, some privates were glad to see that discipline came with him. "I am glad for some reasons that he is back," Private Daniel Sawtelle wrote. "One of them is that he will have disaplin [sic] and this we have not had since he left. The regt had been little better than a mob."[40] Colonel Lysander Cutler won the admiration of the men of the Iron Brigade because "he imposed upon us severe duties— but only for our good as he told us, and we came to know this in time and thank him for it."[41] Officers, in turn, appreciated soldiers who recognized that discipline was necessary to win the war. "His whole thoughts seemed to be the suppression of the rebellion," Captain Alfred Duncan wrote to the family of William Abraham after he was killed in battle, "and most earnestly and willingly was his time and attention devoted to it[.] As a subordinate[,] he was always obedient and respectful and every ready to perform any duty assigned him which was always done cheerfully and highly commendable both to his own credit and that of his officers."[42]

Willing to accept discipline and recognizing the value of it, soldiers came to appreciate good officers. Officers who did their duty, who did not consider themselves better than their men or who protected the lives of their soldiers earned the special regard, or even love, of their men. The best officers knew what their soldiers could do, knew what they could expect from them, and knew when not to push too hard. Unfortunately, the attitudes of many officers made this insight all too rare. West Point–educated officers were a minority of the Union officer corps, but they tried to instill their Regular Army attitudes on the citizen-soldiers under their command, often with unsuccessful results. Soldiers accustomed to the rights and belief systems of the citizen-soldier mystique refused to accept such cut-and-dried forms of authority, resulting in the friction so common in the army. But many of the former civilians who found themselves wearing an officer's uniform, with no other form of guidance, looked to the West Pointers as an example to follow, with equally unsuccessful results. Their failure to lead their men was particularly harmful because the soldiers, besides rejecting their symbolic authority, labeled them as violators of the citizen-soldier ethos, making them even worse than the West Pointers. For the fortunate few with the ability to lead their men, however, the reward for flexibility and concern for the general welfare of their commands was a respect and admiration from their soldiers that most other officers could only envy.

Officers who empathized and shared their soldiers' hardships often received the respect of their men. "O! wife, I do hate to drive tired men," General Alvin Voris confessed to his wife, "I can order, perhaps like to command. [But] [t]he exercise of authority is pleasing to me when not allayed with the quality of pain, fatigue, & ill temper of those I rule." By demonstrating his concern for his regiment, Voris could rightly claim that "I believe that my Regiment have an affection for me. All treat me kindly and with confidence. Both officers and men get out of patience with the exercise of authority, but . . . concede that I only do what I think is necessary.[43] The men of the Seventh Illinois Cavalry respected Colonel Henry Forbes because he lived up to his promises to "administer military discipline without fear or favor to good and bad alike."[44] Major John H. Grider of the Ninth Kentucky earned the respect of his men by sharing a particularly unpleasant task: standing picket during a cold October night. "Maj. Grider . . . shouldered a rifle, accoutrements, and a roll of blankets, fell into line on the left of our company and went with us on picket," one of his soldiers remembered. "[He] insisted on being allowed to take his turn at standing—this was granted. . . . I then offered to let him act as corporal of the relief for he would thereby get to remain by the fire all the time, but he refused the offer and stood on outpost four hours that night."[45] Sharing hardships also meant sharing food. "We had in the company and regiment a splendid and kindly set of officers," Private Robert Strong fondly remembered, "Scott was the kindest of all. He would divide his last cracker or last water in his canteen with the boys."[46] Lieutenant Colonel Robert Cameron earned the respect of his men for his willingness to fight with them. When a drummer boy mistakenly rolled an alarm instead of tattoo, soldiers were pleased to see Cameron "ready for fight, with nothing on but shirt and pants." Another soldier believed that "our leutendant [*sic*] Col [Cameron] is the best man i ever seen. We all just love him. i [*sic*] would rather hear him talk than eat any time."[47] Battle brought out the best in some officers, just as it sometimes brought out the worst. "I remember a certain colonel whom because of his nervous peevishness, the boys all dubbed 'granny.'" Private James Abraham wrote in his memoirs, ". . . We all expected to see him run away at first signal of danger . . . But we were disappointed. Singing bullets and bursting shells was the very music needed to quiet his nerves and enlarge his soul. There was no cooler head at South Mountain or at Antietam than this same colonel, and no one handled his troops with greater skill or better judgment, nor courted death with sublimer courage."[48] Major Henry Abbott earned the respect of his men by leading his men under fire "with the same indifferent air that he has when drilling [his men]."[49]

Soldiers recognized good officers when they had them, so the loss of a good officer, for whatever reason, triggered a reaction from the men they left behind. When Colonel Henry S. Briggs of the Thirty-seventh Massachusetts received a promotion, his appreciative men wrote to their hometown newspaper praising the "prudent man, and a brave man. . . . while he relaxes nothing in discipline, [he] will permit preterit no effort to secure their health and comfort."[50] Soldiers also felt the loss of Lieutenant Colonel Walton Dwight. He took temporary command of the One Hundred Forty-ninth Pennsylvania while their colonel convalesced from a wound. The men did not initially appreciate the discipline he brought with him, but they all stood sharply at attention in bad weather when he gave his farewell speech.[51] When General Don Carlos Buell relieved Colonel John Turchin of command, some respectful soldiers walked more than seven miles to see off their commander.[52] Soldiers felt the loss of good officers even more when good officers died. General Edward Lander, despite severe wounds, continued to lead his men during the disastrous Union defeat at Balls Bluff, earning the respect of his men. When he died of pneumonia in 1862, one letter described "In General L[ander], a brave, magnanimous, heroic man has died. He was of reckless daring, of rough manners, but a kind & generous heart, perhaps not a great General but was a noble soldier."[53] Even former enemies could gain the respect of their men. "Captain [Charles A.] Bell, of the 20th Indiana, was hit today by a fragment of shell and died within a few minutes," Private Charles Haley wrote, "He was formerly a Rebel, and deserted to our side. Captain Bell was highly respected by his own men, and his loss deplored. He was a brave fellow."[54] The command relationship between white officers and their African American soldiers in the segregated regiments of the United States Colored Troops (USCT) was often contentious, so the soldiers felt the loss of a good officer even more. Lieutenant Charles Oren, of the Fifth USCT, was one such officer, and his death hurt his company badly. "If my Brother Had of Bin [sic] shot it would Not of Hurt me any worse then it Did when He was shot," Sergeant Dillon Chavers wrote to Oren's widow, "He Was a good officer not only That But He Had His men At Heart. . . . Our Company Has Bin of no use Since His Deth."[55]

An outgrowth of the dedication of the citizen-soldier and the determination to win was a large degree of self-discipline within the army, even in the absence of officers. Soldiers took it upon themselves to police their own behavior, maintain their own discipline, and perform well on the battlefield in the absence of any other external leadership figure. Two privates of the Third Minnesota, for instance, chose to leave a prisoner exchange compound, where they were awaiting a formal end to their parole granted by the Confederates after their capture in battle, to go back into the fight. Instead of awaiting a parole, the two privates, Frederick Schilplin and John Pope, joined the Eighty-second Illinois on their way to fight in Virginia. This was a violation of the Twenty-second Article of War , unfortunately, and the Third Minnesota considered the two men deserters. When the officers of the Eighty-second Illinois decided to send the men back to clear their names, they considered the two privates so trustworthy that they returned to their old unit without a military escort.[56] When the Nineteenth Indiana, a regiment of the famed Iron Brigade, lacked a number of officers, including a colonel, because of disease, a local journalist reported that "the boys are not disposed to take advantage of his absence" and instead maintained discipline in the camp by themselves.[57] The self-discipline even extended onto the battlefield. At the 1862 Battle of Mill Springs, soldiers of the Tenth Indiana became separated from the rest of the regiment in the confusion of the fighting. Instead of retreating in panic, however, the men returned to their regimental camp, assembled into position, and awaited orders to return to the battle. General George Thomas, finding them "in front of their encampment, apparently awaiting orders," sent them back into battle, ensuring the Union victory.[58] Even with their duty completed, some volunteers felt compelled to stay. A "change which has come over our men . . . is very curious," described Captain John W. DeForest, "Not so very long since they [the men] were like the nine-months' fellow; they nearly all wanted to go home. Now it is difficult to get even a broken-down man to accept his discharge."[59] Private James Hughlett demonstrated perhaps the clearest example of self-discipline. In a November 1864 letter to Abraham Lincoln, Hughlett confessed to his Commander in Chief that he had accidentally received his monthly pay twice and was ready to accept the consequences. Lincoln forwarded the note to the War Department with the instructions that "mercy should be extended" to the honest private.[60]

THE SAME WAR THAT PRODUCED such dedication and determination also produced an equal, if not greater, amount of pessimism and defeatism. As the war wore on, many soldiers lost their patriotic zeal and determination to fight for abstract concepts like "Union" or "nation." Supply problems caused hunger, late pay created financial difficulties, and ghastly casualties eroded the sense of glory or glamour of war. "Half starved, bare footed, marched to death, and slaughtered by the enemy," Lemuel Jeffries wrote in his diary in 1862, "our patriotism in on the decline."[61] Soldiers consequently saw themselves less as instruments of a great crusade, and more as expendable assets that others exploited for their own agendas. The same officer who was so proud of his tough tobacco-chewing fifteen-year-old soldier expressed a different belief only a short time later. "There is no mistake in the matter that we are here only to pander to the political aspirations of some men or set of men," Lieutenant Colonel William Colby wrote his father a month after the Battle of Antietam, "and that the war with its immense cost of blood and money is a mere political machine to be continued long or made short as shall most conduce to the interest of the managers. . . . I believe that most men in the army now think as I do."[62] Other soldiers saw themselves as the victims of profiteers. "I see by your note that there is considerable patriotism in you," Samuel Budd wrote to his brother, "but if you should serve one year in the ranks of the country's defenders, your patriotism would be at low ebb. We no longer look on it as a war for country, but as a great speculation."[63] That same uncertainty of purpose sapped the offensive spirit of many soldiers, leaving them only willing to participate in combat as much as they felt obligated to. "The phrensy [*sic*] of soldier rushing during an engagement to glory or death has, as our boys amusingly affirm, been played out," wrote a chaplain, "Our battle-worn veterans go into danger, when ordered, remain as a stern duty [only] so long as directed."[64] Other soldiers shared the chaplain's view. "I don't believe there are any cowards in the 95th [Illinois] Regt., . . . but I believe that there are very few men who would rush into a fight alone on account of their patriotism."[65]

Adding to the lack of dedication, the long stretches of mind-numbing tedium also sapped the soldiers' will to fight as the glamour of combat and army life disappeared. "War is an organized bore" Oliver Wendell Holmes, Civil War soldier and later Supreme Court Justice, once said, and few soldiers would have disagreed.[66] "I have no news to write . . . ," a soldier wrote his sister. "I am as bad as in a Jale [sic] [as there is] nothing going on."[67] Private Wilbur Fisk bemoaned the constant boredom in the spring of 1863. His diary entry for April 23 reported that there was "No drill. Nothing to read; dull times; ho hum. Well this camp life." Later, on May 16, Fisk is even more bored, reporting that the men "did nothing but lay around and kill time—murder it."[68] Even the officers had to admit that life in camp, especially the long stretches of inactivity during the winter lull in the fighting, could be dreadfully boring. Inactive in winter camp during the Siege of Petersburg in 1865, Alvin Voris reported to his wife, "Yesterday we celebrated the anniversary of Washington's birthday by doing noting in particular and many things in general."[69] Garrison duty in occupied areas of the Confederacy also produced boredom, as the war had seemed to pass the soldiers by. Garrisoning a fort in Tennessee, the men of the Seventy-first Ohio whiled away their time by "lying their tents. Some of them were playing cards . . . reading in their Testament . . . reading novels, and some were writing." Other soldiers at the fort "were quarreling, and some of them were talking about their homes . . . and some of them were damning the war. This is the way it goes all the day when it is raining and the troops have no other amusement."[70] Thomas Bennett, writing from remote Fort Barrancas near Pensacola, Florida, confessed to his sister that "I had much rather see good hard fighting than be cooped upon a fort like this."[71] Boredom bred the associated side effect of laziness. "Soldiering is certainly not beneficial to the mind . . . ," a Michigan surgeon wrote. "It certainly engenders laziness . . . [caused by] the alternation of very hard work, which is compulsory, and nothing at all to do, with very few resource for amusement."[72] "The health of the Regiment is excellent," George Wagner wrote his friend, "with the exception that everybody is inflicted with that spring epidemic—laziness."[73]

Pessimism, in turn, led to diminished discipline, as individual soldiers no longer felt obligations to the nation, army, or each other. Enlisting because of dreams of glory or a sense of obligation to a higher cause, soldiers quickly discovered the disenchanting nature of army life. "Too many such lies had slid down our necks like sweet syrup," wrote a Maine volunteer in dismissing rumors of a great victory in 1864, "Fewer lies and more bread would suit much better! Patriotism, like religion, is closely allied to a full belly and comfortable quarters."[74] Other soldiers also felt betrayed by an army that was supposed to be in the fight together. "I am sick of the army, for there is no fair play in it," wrote Private Daniel Sawtelle, "The officers have everything their own way. An honest man stands no sight here. He gets used worse than the meanest drunkard."[75] Some soldiers held on to their faith deep into the war before finally relinquishing it. "I am tired of such a life," Herman White wrote to his parents from outside Richmond in May 1864, "We are fighting or marching all the time . . . I am nearly played out. We are now on the peninsula again, where we were 2 years ago. I never was sicker of war, would like peace on any turms [sic]."[76] Francis Elliott perhaps put it the most succinctly: "Shits what poor soalgers [sic] Sees."[77]

The drudgery of army life was a significant cause of declining dedication, but the horrors of the battlefield sapped the determination of soldiers even more. Nothing dashed the naïve illusions of military glory like the masses of dead after every engagement. "I cannot write of the horrors I saw," Private John L. Smith wrote, beginning his letter with the same words that started hundreds of other similar letters, "men with a leg or arm shot off, being carried back every way, with no conveniences, and dead lying just where they fell. . . . It was simply murder."[78] Samuel Partridge lost his illusions in the first major battle at Bull Run. "When a bullet goes into a man's head," he wrote his family, "it makes a crash among the bones that can be heard for some feet . . . and a torrent of blood from his mouth gush[es] all over your face."[79] The sights of the battlefield also horrified Daniel Pulis of the Eighth New York Cavalry. "I passed over the field where they fought the day before," he wrote his wife, "There were men with one leg, one arm, bodies without heads or with only part of a head. I saw one man who was hit with a piece of shell with the back part of his head cut entirely off, he was still alive. At one of the hospitals, I saw a stack of arms and legs 4 feet high."[80] Alden Murch also went into detail about the effect of nineteenth-century weaponry. "I saw 4 men struck down by a single [artillery] shot," he described to his wife, "The first man's head was taken off, the next one's face was blown off against my head, the next lost his underjaw, and fourth had his throat tourn [sic] entirely out. . . . I saw a man's brains spattered all of the next man's head and other sights as bad."[81] Disgusted at the endless violence he witnessed in Georgia and Tennessee in 1864, Marshall Miller reported, "Nothing but butchery from Spring till Fall. It commenced with chickens and has ended in butchering men."[82] Soldiers never seemed able to inure themselves to the sight of severed limbs. "I found 8 dead bodies, members of the first Brigade," Private Henry Gangewer wrote. "A few Rods further, I wound 5 more bodies besides a pair of legs the owner of which was in the hospital and at nearly every step I found sad evidences of yesterdays work. I however soon sickened of the horrid scene and turned back to the Battery to think of the stern realities of war."[83] Even seemingly innocent actions produced horror. James Abraham remembered a soldier who, in the dark of night, thought he saw his tentmate sleeping under a blanket and slid in next to him, only to discover the next morning that his blanketmate was "minus a head and wore the gray."[84]

It is not surprising that many soldiers began to doubt that the death they saw around them was for any great purpose, as high casualties led to a growing defeatism. Soldiers took note of their feelings of futility, especially after disastrous defeats. There is a verry [sic] strong & rapidly increasing feeling in the army in favor of peace," wrote Private Emory Sweetland after the Union debacle at Fredericksburg. "I hear many curses about this war every day by Officers & men."[85] Defeatism even lurked on the eve of great victory. "There is no use in disguising the truth," Sergeant Charles Bowen confessed to his wife on the eve of the Battle of Gettysburg. "[T]he south has better Generals than we have & . . . tis easy for blind man to see, that will all our superior numbers & strength, we shall be the whipped party."[86] No amount of material or logistic support could alter the sense that the rebels were unbeatable. As one soldier observed, referring to some shoddily dressed Confederate prisoners, "We have learned that clothes do not make the soldiers."[87] The defeatism was not limited to the enlisted ranks. Brigadier General Marsena Patrick was not particularly confident of the Army of the Potomac's chances of success in October 1863. "They [the rebels] are either making a feint, preparatory to an evacuation of our front," he gloomily wrote in his diary, "or they are preparing to give us our annual Bull Run flogging."[88] In a similar vein, Colonel Elijah Cavins had little confidence in the appointment of Major General Ambrose Burnside to high command. "I tremble for Burnside," he lamented to his father. ". . . [T]oo much is expected of him, and the same causes that brought about his promotion [the shortcomings of General George B. McClellan] may possibly consign him to private life. The press and people seem to expect him to take Richmond this winter. It can't be done from this point."[89] Often, soldiers placed their blame for their failures on their commanding officers. In the aftermath of the Fredericksburg debacle, Private Charles Chase wrote his family, asking the rhetorical questions: "And who is at fault [for the army's failures]? Are not our soldiers as brave as those of the South? . . . Have we no generals? I think we have some good ones but too many cooks spoil the broth"[90]

In its most extreme form, pessimism became fatalism, as soldiers became convinced that their deaths were inevitable, with seeing home and family again a virtual impossibility. "Many a brave flower of our country has been sacrificed for our government," Sergeant Franklin Boyts mourned, ". . . but this is our lot."[91] Private Beidelman, initially convinced that the war would purify America, believed that he would not survive the Battle of Gettysburg. Tucked into his coat pocket was a note asking "To all whom it may concern" to write a note to his father if "I, in the providence of god, be killed or seriously wounded" in combat.[92] "I have made up my mind that my chances of coming out of he war alive are less than even," wrote Lieutenant Charles B. Haydon in his journal, a perception that he accepted very early in the war. This was not a brief moment of pessimism. A month later, Haydon vented his wish that "May the curse of God light on the men who brought me here. . . . As often as I escape a danger, I consider it as so much net gain of duration of life & as an unexpected gain where death or wounds would be the natural course of events." Haydon was not the only one in his unit, the Second Michigan, to feel that way. Haydon reported two years later on the widespread drunkenness that engulfed the unit because "A soldier never know one day where he may be the next & and his hold on the future being so uncertain he crowds the present to the utmost. 'Eat drink & be merry for to morrow [*sic*] you die.'"[93] As deadly as past battles had been, soldiers resigned themselves to the idea that future battles would be worse. "Thousands of fellows who, a year ago, were full of life and promise, are today among the dead," Private John Follmer despaired on New Year's Eve 1863. "How many more thousands are still to be sacrificed ere the end comes to this rebellion? God only knows and He wisely with-holds the knowledge from us."[94] Even officers felt the same way. Captain Thomas Livermore, all of nineteen years old, saw no purpose in planning for the future. "The thought of what I should do after I left the army never stayed in my head long enough to fix a plan there," he wrote in his postwar memoirs, "for I presumed it very likely that I should be killed before the war was over."[95]

The belief system that led the citizen-soldier into the army, also, ironically, helped to undermine the army. That same determination to fight for rights, privileges of citizenship, and future of the nation that drove people into the ranks also made them determined to defend their sense of citizenship and liberty to the extent necessary to maintain rigid discipline. Frank Dickerson, a lieutenant in the Fifth U.S. Cavalry of the Regular Army, disparaged the lack of discipline among the volunteers, noting the corrosive effects that the presence of volunteers had on the rigor of the Regular soldiers. "Their carelessness, uncleanliness, familiarity with the lack of respect to officers and superiors, and lack of discipline generally," Dickerson wrote, "had had a tendency to impair somewhat the fine state of discipline we possessed before we were [forced to] associate with them."[96] Unlike in the Mexican War, the influence of the Regulars was not enough to create a culture of Regular-level discipline. Quite the opposite, volunteer soldiers seemed to revel in the opposite viewpoint. They, at the minimum, refused to accept the Regulars' level of discipline and, at the maximum, pointedly rebelled against it. The result was an army that learned the hard way that discipline was necessary for survival, much less victory.

The volunteers' opposition to army discipline fell into general complaints about the restrictiveness of army discipline, the inability to select their own officers, and the undemocratic nature of the officers that the system placed above them without their permission. True Americans, from the volunteer perspective, went where they wanted, said what they wanted, and did what they wanted without having to ask permission or explain why they needed to do what they did. To have to explain their motivations to officers and NCOs, strangers at that, was a foreign concept. Moreover, citizen-soldiers resented the notion that the army had to control them. As good patriots who knew their duty to their nation, most volunteers believed that rules and regulations was a sign that the army did not trust them to do the right thing, did not think they knew their duty, or did not think the were capable of the task at hand. Offended by the perceived accusation of inability, and defiant of army regulations, soldiers bent and broke the rules as a demonstration of their personal independence.

Instead of viewing discipline as a necessary practice that would win the war and perhaps save their lives, many soldiers chose to view discipline as an infringement upon their civilian liberties, as "Each day brought some restraint upon our freedom," in the words of one soldier.[97] "Many of the men seem to think they should never be spoken to unless the remarks are preface[d] by some words of defferential [sic] politeness," Charles Haydon wrote in 1861, as he tried to get his platoon into shape. "Will the gentlemen who compose [sic] the first platoon have the kindness to march forward . . . is about what some of them seem to expect."[98] Haydon was not far off, as new soldiers expected the liberties, or at least the courtesies, of civilian life. "I would not advise anyone to enlist," a Wisconsin soldier complained. "It is irksome to be so closely confined and to have to implicitly obey all orders."[99] The inability to come and go as one pleased was a common complaint. "Many soldiers are in the Capitol, who move about as if they were on their own farm," a Vermont private wrote home. "I hear arguing in this wise: 'We've as much right here any anybody; Abe Lincoln has no more. We are freeborn Americans, and have come here to defend our own property.'" The mundane tasks of maintaining an army camp—digging latrines, policing the area for trash, or finding firewood—tasks collectively known as "fatigue duty," was also seen as beneath the dignity of many free-minded citizens. Troops later in the war were little different in their attitudes from early volunteers. "A West-point officer and a strict disciplinarian may make good machine soldiers," artilleryman Silas Stevens, who enlisted in

1862, opined, "but to us free born citizens of a free republic, we could not present him the affection that men give toward a real commander."[100]

Stevens was one of many soldiers who thought themselves well suited to select "real commanders." Raised in a democratic society, where voting was the most public manifestation of the rights of a free individual, soldiers believed the right to vote extended into the army and the selection of officers. The choosing of officers by their own soldiers was a time-honored, if not always effective, means of designating army leaders throughout the militia history of America. The army tried to prevent the election of officers in the War of 1812, but with only limited success.[101] Soldiers rejected alternative means of picking officers as a means of defending their right of association and maintaining their community and state identity. When the army did not see the wisdom of that logic during the Civil War, the vehement reaction of common soldiers reflected their outrage at the suspension of their presumed rights, leading to challenges to army authority. It is not surprising that soldiers felt the right to select their officers. By an act of Congress dated July 22, 1861, all appointments to rank of captain and above required the approval, by vote, of the other commissioned officers in the regiment.[102] If officers had the right to confirm their fellows, the soldiers reasoned, why could they not have a vote? Unfortunately, this led to the selection of officers based upon popularity rather than ability. Popular officer candidates sought votes by treating men as "clients" instead of soldiers, creating a gap between electability and combat ability, a shortcoming discovered only under the steep learning curve of battle.[103] The failure to get the officers they wanted caused hard feelings among the men. "The appointment of [Robert A.] McKee [to the rank of lieutenant] was unexpected by the whole company," Private John Campbell ranted in his diary. "The appointment caused much ill-feeling in the company. The company desired to choose their own officers."[104] Charlie Mosher felt the same way. When his regiment received an appointed colonel, instead of elected, to replace their previous commander, the move did not please the Eighty-fifth New York. The regiment crafted a resolution accusing their departing colonel, Uriah L. Davis, of "despicable political trickery, and the grossest fraud . . . to force upon us a colonel who is an entire stranger to us."[105] The army leadership, of course, saw the need for discipline and competence as more important than the extension of citizen-soldier rights into the army hierarchy, but the clash with the mass of enlisted men was an ongoing battle, especially early in the war. "We have been weeding out some of the worst [elected] officers," then Brigadier General George Gordon Meade wrote his wife, "but owing to the vicious system of electing successors, which prevails, those who take their places are no better."[106]

That did not mean that soldiers could not do anything about officers selected rather than elected. When the 154th New York received a new major, Jacob Ten Eyck, without soliciting the opinion of the soldiers in 1862, the new officer did not get a warm welcome. Within a matter of days, under pressure from the soldiers and fellow officers alike, Ten Eyck submitted his resignation, knowing where he was not wanted. "[F]or the reason that it is not agreeable . . . that I remain with the regiment," Ten Eyck found another assignment.[107] Even late in the war, when voting for officers had all but disappeared, soldiers still felt they knew better than the political leadership about which officers deserved promotion and which ones did not. Believing that Ohio Governor John Brough was operating under political influence when he made unpopular promotions in 1864, Corporal Josiah Hill complained that the decisions "makes us feel like poor dogs rather than men . . . [Brough] has done more to injure the service by his mode of appointing officers than he can ever do good as governor."[108] Although the army ended the election of officers relatively early, the practice still existed on a small scale throughout the war. In May 1864, Private Virgil Andruss noted to his mother that his "100-Day" regiment "elected officers this morning" in preparation for duty.[109] In June 1864, the men of the Fifth Iowa held a vote on candidates to replace a captain who had resigned his commission. The men elected a sergeant, W.C. Pennywitt, to the post. Colonel Ezekiel Sampson, however, overruled the vote in favor of two 2nd lieutenants, Robert McKee and John Campbell. Sampson reasoned that McKee and Campbell, both "tried on the field of battle and never found wanting," deserved the promotion more. Instead, McKee became captain, Campbell became lieutenant, and Pennywitt had to settle for the rank of 2nd lieutenant.[110] Only a few months before the end of the war, in January 1865, Corporal Aurelius Voorhis of the Forty-sixth Indiana noted that "A sergeant was elected. . . . Corpl. Ingham was elected Sergeant and so ended the campaign [for the position]."[111]

Soldiers wanted to elect their officers partly to remind them that, as officers, they were still a member of the masses. The nature of American democracy and the philosophy of the citizen-soldier perceived leaders as temporary authority figures only, with an obligation to restrain any imperial impulse in relation to their momentary control over their fellow citizens. Officers who seemed too imperious, demanding, or prone to tight discipline seemed haughty to their enlisted men, and therefore more deserving of scorn and resistance than obedience and loyalty. Some soldiers disparaged their officers, attempting to puncture their exaggerated status. "With them all argument and justice ends by a significant tap on either Shoulder," Corporal Royal Bensell complained about the indignity of obeying officers, "indicating that in those 'tinsel appendages' is a 'Might that makes Right.'"[112] Stripes, epaultes, and other symbols of authority became, not honored symbols of authority, but gaudy apparel on a man who needed decoration to overcome personal flaws and general inability to lead. "Our officers, by reason of their shoulder straps," cursed a Maine private, "are (in their minds, at least) the embodiment of human wisdom. They look down in lofty scorn upon men who are their superiors in everything but rank."[113] Sergeant James Abraham, unwilling to denigrate himself by rising in rank, proudly notified his sister that "I was offered a Capt. Commission in this Regt. which I contemptuously declined . . . having no aspirations in that direction."[114] This attitude was not only for enlisted men. Junior officers also felt the right to dismiss the abilities and attack the pomposity of their superiors. "It takes every bit of force I have to keep cool and turn away without a word from men that because superior in rank attempt to lord it," Lieutenant William Ferry complained to his wife, "Men that at home I would not wipe my dirty shoes on."[115]

Other soldiers saw officers themselves as symbols and instruments of the army discipline that diminished their personal liberties, and therefore became the target of general scorn and displeasure at army discipline. As a means of separating themselves from the Regular officers they despised, soldiers denigrated the bearing with which Regular officers carried themselves, identifying the behavior as a sign of elitism. "They had jaunty and effeminate ways about them," Private Eugene Ware observed, "for instance, one led around by a string a dwarf terrier; one wore a monocle. I had never seen a monocle before, except in comic pictures."[116] Sergeant Onley Andrus could only wait until "My time will run out in course of time & then I'll be just as good a man as he [Colonel Lawrence S. Church] is or any other Officers either."[117] Often only the recognition of a higher mission kept soldiers from rebellion against what they considered intrusive and oppressive rule by their officers. "We had enlisted to put down the rebellion," an Indiana private ranted, "and had no patience with the red-tape tomfoolery of the regular service. Furthermore, the boys recognized no superiors, except in the line of legitimate duty."[118] The tension between appointed officers and liberty-minded enlisted men continued for the duration of the war. Although the tension was highest in the early months before declining, soldiers never entirely lost the will to exert personal freedoms by deflating the egos of their officers.

A byproduct of the friction between citizen-soldiers and their officers was a rejection of commanders who tried to make their soldiers more than the soldiers wished to be. Officers who tried to instill order through tight discipline faced opposition and outright resistance. "We hold these truths to be self-evident that all men are created equal," wrote Private Marcus Woodcock, citing the Declaration of Independence, "but this is a great principle of Republicanism usually departed from by the petty officers of the U.S. Volunteer Army."[119] John P. Wood, the adjutant of the Iron Brigade, was such a petty officer. The men despised him for his close attention to detail during regimental inspections. "Adjutant Wood is a good officer, but rather tyrannical," one soldier wrote. "He takes delight in 'putting a man through,' especially when he can do it before the whole Regiment."[120] Wood was simply upholding the standard of dress and appearance that the army required, but soldiers still hated submitting to the practice, even if it instilled the discipline that might keep them alive on the battlefield. The colonel of the Twenty-first Wisconsin was "a brave, well meaning man," an officer wrote, "whose only fault was that he stook [sic] to[o] pertinaciously to the West Point regulation which could not be applied to the Volunteer soldier."[121] Private Charles Wills recognized this dichotomy between popularity and discipline. "We love and respect all our officers, but one," he wrote in his diary, "and he is the best officer we have, but [he has] a little too much regular army about him."[122]

With dedication to cause flagging and without a predisposition to obey symbols of authority, some soldiers engaged in little self-discipline and were prone to disciplinary violations at the first opportunity. Released from the parole camp following their exchange, the aforementioned Third Minnesota went from a unit known for tight discipline to an almost absence of discipline. The reason was the absence of their officers. While the Confederates paroled the enlisted men, the commissioned officers stayed in captivity in Georgia. Deprived of their regular and trusted commanders, the unit's cohesion and discipline vanished.[123] Winter encampments were a particular problem, when soldiers had too much time on their hands and officers could not be everywhere. In the absence of drill or other activities to fill the day, bored and pessimistic soldiers occupied themselves by defying their officers and creating disciplinary chaos, as when Vermont troops occupied a "neutral" plantation for the winter, much to the chagrin of the owner.[124] The Fifth USCT also suffered from little self-discipline in winter camp, forcing their colonel to levy fines, impose extra duties, and demote NCOs to hold the unit together.[125]

Soldiers often lacked self-discipline because officers often failed to provide a good example. Just as good officers inspired their men and created a bond with them, bad officers damaged the perception of army discipline and the need for common soldiers to obey it. As the visible symbol of military authority, officers had to measure up to the expectations of the authority above them. In a letter to Northern governors, the War Department provided some insight on what the army believed were the qualities of a good officer: "None should be appointed except such as were of undoubted moral character and patriotism, and who were of sound health."[126] Even if officers convinced their state governors of their qualifications, they also had to meet the personal standards of the citizen-soldiers beneath them on the rank scale. Officers who failed in their duty lost credibility with their men, and provided justification for those soldiers who violated the legal and military definitions of discipline. When officers behaved or performed badly, soldiers reasoned that if officers did not have to maintain a standard of discipline, why should they. An officer who demonstrated incompetence on the battlefield and got his men killed obviously lost the respect of their men, but other actions had the same result. If an officer was lazy, lacked common sense, or did not take care of his men in camp, that officer often failed to maintain discipline and the soldiers made their feelings toward him plainly known.

The adjutant of the Twenty-first Wisconsin found this out the hard way. In the midst of a thirty-mile march, the Wisconsin men stopped at the only water source available, a pond filled with "a muddy, filthy warm mixture, with a slimy cover on the surface." The soldiers had no sooner skimmed off the muck and began filling their canteens, when the adjutant rode his horse into the pond so the animal could drink. The horse muddied the water the men were trying to drink, and the soldiers responded with a barrage of stones, "not willing to be treated in such a hoggish manner."[127] Officers who ignored such negative feedback from their soldiers did so at the peril of losing the confidence of their men. "He was one a class of men who labor under the astronomical error thinking the earth cannot move in its orbit not revolve on its axis without their consent," Charles Davis wrote his colonel, ". . . becoming very wroth when anything happens to mar their beautiful conceit."[128] Conceit also drove some officers to disregard their men in the pursuit of promotion and glory, or at least give the impression of such ambition. A sergeant in the Ninety-five Illinois believed his colonel was "looking for Stars [a general rank]" and is willing to sacrifice every man in his Regt to accomplish His aims."[129] Other officers abused the labor of their men. After troops of the Thirteenth Vermont constructed a theater for amateur shows and other amusement, they soon lost control of the structure. A few days after completion, soldiers noticed a nighttime meeting taking place inside. When they inquired what was going on, an officer opened the door with a drawn sword and order the men back to their tents. The soldiers found out the next day that officers who were members of the Masons had appropriated the building for their own use. "It was a clear case of bunco," as one soldier put it.[130] Exercising their rights as citizen-soldiers, some regiments tried to use political pressure to get rid of bad officers by appealing directly to their state governors. Charles Haydon wrote in his diary that "there is a petition in circulation to have Colonel [Israel B.] R[ichardson] resign. The governor has been telegraphed [regarding the petition]," while officers of the Twenty-seventh Indiana petitioned for the removal of Colonel Silas Colgrove on the grounds that they "have patiently submitted to insults until forbearance is beyond endurance."[131]

Even more than a stupid or incompetent officer, Union soldiers despised commanders who acted in an imperious or autocratic manner. Officers whose conduct was remote or arbitrary alienated their soldiers by appearing to be above them, both in rank and social standing. To the equality-minded citizen-soldier, an officer who put on airs or abused their rank at the expense of his subordinates did not deserve their position or the respect usually conferred by an officer's uniform. Whereas Regular Army troops accepted that officers would flaunt and abuse his rank, volunteer soldiers seldom accepted such pomposity. In their minds, an officer in a volunteer regiment was not a true officer in the same sense that they were not true soldiers. Citizen-soldiers temporary accepted the obligation of soldiery to defend their cause and just as temporarily accepted the rule of officers above them. But the arrangement was a tenuous one, justified only by the political crisis, grudgingly allowed for the duration of the crisis, but not a moment longer. Volunteer officers, the soldiers believed, should not become accustomed to the privileges of their rank, as it was to exist only as long the citizen-soldiers permitted it to exist. Officers who embraced their new status, regardless of their competence on the battlefield, often found themselves on the end of a soldierly snubbing and overt criticism.

Whether actually abusive or not, some officers garnered a reputation for abject tyranny in the eyes of their subordinates. "You must understand," Robert Strong explained to his parents, "that a private has not rights that an officer is bound to respect, and the officer if he sees fit can be a regular tyrant." Colonel Colgrove, whom the Twenty-seventh Indiana petitioned for removal from office, was one such officer. "Colgrove . . . has an abuseful disposition," a soldier complained, ". . . He would be a good officer to lead an attack but that is all. He is very tyrannical."[132] Other soldiers shared this opinion of Colgrove. "The colonel is getting more tyrannical," Simpson Hamrick wrote. ". . . The colonel has marched the regiment several times unmerciful and then cursed the officers and men because they could go no further. He is very unreasonable sometimes."[133] Tyrannical behavior was not the preserve of senior officers, and even the greenest lieutenant sometimes exceeded their authority. "Lieutenant [Silas] Wagoner was the officer in charge of the detail . . . ," William Wiley of the Seventy-seventh Illinois recounted. "He was a very small man in a very large body. He was very over bearing [sic] and abusive. His little authority seemed to hurt him. He cursed and abused the men at a terrible rate."[134] John Westervelt, an engineer with the First New York Engineers, had no use for officers who looked down on him as an enlisted man. "He [Lieutenant Peter Michie] is a miserable little upstart," Westervelt wrote in his diary, "and because he happens to belong to the Engs [Engineers] of the regular service he pretends to look down on us Vols [volunteers] as so many slaves."[135]

Even officers had complaints about fellow officers. Patrick Guiney, who rose to the rank of colonel during the war, had little good to say about the leadership ability of Colonel Thomas Cass, who blamed anyone but himself for any faults. "The officers receive abundance of oaths and curses for not performing," Guiney wrote his wife. ". . . Censuring rudely the officers if anything is wrong with the men, and then telling the men, if they make complaints about anything, that the fault is with their own officers . . . his habitual manner is anything but that of a gentleman."[136] Colonel (later Brevet General) Voris believed that West Point–trained officers discriminated against volunteers such as himself. "I ought to be with my regiment," Voris complained to his wife, "but Col. [George B.] Dandy of the 100th N.Y. is in command . . . who is my junior, [but] being a Regular Army officer . . . cannot be relieved by a volunteer." Voris was not happy with the arrangement, and resented the treatment because he was a volunteer officer, or a "political officer," as he called himself. "I grant that there is an advantage in favor of the man who has made the art of war his study," Voris continued, "but that is only the advantage of theory. . . . I must say that the advantage is not verry [*sic*] great over a thorough, intelligent, practical business man. . . . I know we "political" colonels (as we are called by the West Pointers) are despised, but I would remind these gentlemen of the fate of Gen [Edward] Braddock when advised by a militia Col, derided it, and ran into ruin."[137]

Officers who acted in a haughty manner earned the enmity of their men by denying them privileges that they enjoyed as citizens, but which the army now deemed detrimental to common discipline. A captain in the Fourth California, for instance, publicly berated a corporal who had the temerity to smoke in his presence, while another officer in a different regiment, incensed at a soldier smoking, "knocked, the pipe out of the man's mouth."[138] Other officers were sticklers for saluting, a sign of diminished status that particularly rankled citizen-soldiers accustomed to widespread social equality in civilian life. Corporal Bensell mocked a petty lieutenant named James Davison who, while commanding a temporary encampment away from the main post, insisted that sentries "salute all Officers according to rank." But when the lieutenant left camp in civilian dress, he was not entitled to a salute, eliciting an assessment of "Damn fool!" from Bensell.[139] At least Lieutenant Davison maintained some restraint. A lieutenant colonel in another regiment, when confronted by soldiers who refused to salute, became violent. "One of them [that would not salute] said 'he would be God Damned if he would salute him' and jumped and struck both feet in the lieutenant colonel's face," Private Mark Rogers wrote his parents, "The lieutenant colonel caught him by the throat and threw him down under his feet and drawed [*sic*] his revolver and placed it to his [the soldier's] breast, but couldn't get it off. So, he took the butt of it and cut his head and face pretty bad."[140]

Confronted by disrespect to their rank or some other perceived slight, imperious officers frequently used force or weaponry to punish the offender. "The picket guard yesterday interrupted Capt. [Reuben A.] Beach very unceremoniously," Charles Haydon wrote, implying that the soldiers disturbed the officer while he was relieving himself, "He sprang to his feet, asked what in hell they wanted, drew his pistol & ordered them to retire on pain of death."[141] When Sergeant George Stotsenberg hesitated when ordered to lead his men across an icy stream, Lieutenant Alexander Wilson "pulled out his pistol" and forced the men forward at gunpoint.[142] Lemuel Jeffries of the Fourth Ohio described how an unidentified brigadier general who, "knocked off his horse by the mules" of a wagon master, "picked up a club, knocked the wagon master senseless from his horse, then galloped away, all done so quick and he was gone before the few boys near by had time to see the cowardly outrage and shoot the fellow."[143] To get through a tangle of wagon trains and other traffic, Brigadier General Marsena Patrick admitted he "[h]ad a very hard time [getting through] & had to use my riding whip more than I wished" to persuade soldiers to move out of the way. Later in the war, Patrick complained that "My shoulder is a little Sore tonight, probably owing to my having knocked a man down, this evening, who was insolent to [Lieutenant James] Winfield."[144] In the Arizona Territory, a captain of the First California had a teamster staked out in the hot sun because he did not like where the teamster had parked his wagon.[145] The Eighteenth Illinois had a reputation for officers with harsh, even perverse, discipline. One lieutenant, pistol in hand, forced a soldier to dance about on threat of death if he stopped, while the regiment's colonel, Michael Lawler, punished soldiers held in the regimental guardhouse for drunkenness by sending them a bottle of whiskey tainted with ipecac.[146]

Often the only means that soldiers had to complain about their officers was in their letters and diaries. Because open and verbal challenges and complaints invited the possibility of punishment or criminal prosecution for insubordination, soldiers had to rely upon the written word. Letters and diaries are filled with criticisms and comments about the shortcomings of certain officers specifically and the leadership of the army and the war generally. It also reinforced the conception of their rights as a citizen-soldier. The army, at least for the duration of the war, may control certain portions of their life, but enlisting in the army did not strip them of their democratic right to criticize those who they felt deserved it, who overstepped their authority as officers, and who squandered lives through incompetent decisions. Luckily for the common soldier, the army did not censor personal mail to the extent it did during later wars, because many of the comments, if known to the target of the criticism, justified prosecution for insubordination or even mutiny.

Many written comments sought to place blame for military defeats, and the criticism started early in the war. Private Samuel Partridge, describing the Union defeat at the Battle of Bull Run in 1861, criticized the plan of General Irvin McDowell as "a military blunder as I ever heard of. A boy would have or ought to have known better [than to attack the Confederates there]."[147] James Dunn was even more blunt; he considered McDowell to be a "traitor and a jackass."[148] Henry Abbott, although an officer himself in the Twentieth Massachusetts, had little good to say about the leadership of the army after the debacle at Fredericksburg. "What an awful greenhorn [Major General Ambrose] Burnside is, don't you think so too?" he wrote his mother, "His letter [explaining his actions at Fredericksburg] is the letter of a high-minded donkey, if it is high-minded at all. . . . All the generals lie like dogs, except old bull-headed [Major General Edwin] Sumner, . . . He was shamefully served, however, by that useless piece of furniture, [Major General Henry] Halleck, who seems to be good at nothing but equivocating. Pity us sacrificed by a dishonest government and an honest general."[149] After the Battle of Perryville, where casualties reduced his regiment until "not 100 men left," Sergeant Elmore Day placed the blame upon "our Traitor Gen. D.C. [Don Carlos] Buell [who] kept our Reinforcements back."[150] Soldiers also blamed poor leadership for the loss at Chancellorsville. "Do not entertain for a moment that thought that we were whipped," Jershua Jenkins wrote to the New York *Sunday Mercury*, "We were only 'out-generaled.'"[151]

Even when not in battle, soldiers offered their less than reverential opinion of those put in charge over them. Unimpressed with Major General William H. "Baldy" French, a soldier opined that he "looks precisely like of those plethoric French Colonels, who are so stout, and who look so red in the face that one would suppose someone had tied a cord tightly round their neck."[152] Lieutenant Edmund Haley pondered the competency of Lieutenant General Ulysses Grant. "Nor is Grant the best strategist in the world," Haley wrote his wife, questioning Grant's decision to disband two of his corps formations to reinforce his remaining units.[153] Many soldiers, aware of Grant's prewar reputation, referred to him in writing as "the Old Drunk."[154] Even Abraham Lincoln, on the occasions when he reviewed troops in person, received his share of hidden insubordination. "Ugly as sin" is how one soldier assessed his first image of the President. "Mr. Lincoln on horseback is not a model of beauty . . . a more awkward specimen of humanity I cannot well imagine" is how one soldiers recounted his impression of seeing Lincoln in person, while an officer described Lincoln passing the army "with his long legs doubled up so that his knees almost struck his chin, and grinning . . . like a baboon."[155]

While soldiers penned a significant amount of criticism aimed at the senior command of the army, their regimental, brigade, and divisional officers had more direct control over their lives. Consequently, these officers received the brunt of the written questioning of their ability and authority. Visiting a relative in another regiment, John Holahan described the officers in less than flattering terms. "Capt. Patterson is a scholar, but nothing else," Holahan opined. "He is a snorting, blowing boy, if not [a] simpleton. His 1st Lieut. . . . is of the same pattern, minus the knowledge, and the 2nd Lt. is a boy in years and knowledge."[156] William Moore was relieved to report that "Colonel [James H.] Trimble had discovered he was not preeminently adopted to the military life and resigned and gone back into mental oblivion."[157] Lieutenant George Bliss believed his regiment had "good men and good . . . officers" but "Col. [Robert B.] Lawson is a God damned fussy old pisspot utterly incompetent for the position he holds . . . [a] lunk headed old fool." Worried that his opinions might become known, Bliss requested the recipient of the letter to "burn this letter" when done reading it.[158] Private William Wiley had no confidence in Major Memoir V. Hotchkiss, claiming the "major could not handle the regiment on drill without getting us all doubled up and we did not care to be doubled up in the face of the enemy." Soldiers may fairly criticize the shortcomings of an officer, but in Wiley's case his assessment of Hotchkiss may have been premature. Only a few weeks before, during the capture of a rebel position during the siege of Vicksburg, Brigade Commander William J. Landram cited Hotchkiss and two other officers who "waved their swords and rallied their men who opened upon the enemy and by a brilliant charge drove them again from the fort."[159]

Soldiers were quick to find reasons why their officers did not meet their expectations. A common belief among soldiers was that alcohol was to blame for the failure of officers to lead effectively, and incompetent officers soon earned the label of drunkard whether they deserved it or not. John Follmer conceded that "We have a greater degree of confidence in our officers than we had starting out," but "some of ours seem never to have learned the trade and are more at home in saloon brawl."[160] William Martin blamed the combination of "whiskey and incompitent [sic] officers" for the Union defeat at Chancellorsville, while Alfred Holcomb described seeing officers "drunk and carousing about the streets every day. some times half a dozen at a time."[161] Soldiers of the Second Massachusetts Cavalry were so incensed by Captain Zebdial Adams' "tyrannically conduct [through which] he has lost the esteem and incurred the hatred of his men; [and] by his habitual intemperance he has lost their respect and forfeited every claim to decency" that Adams soon transferred to another cavalry regiment.[162] After the alert that got his regiment out of bed in the middle of the night turned out to be a false alarm, Private Henry Kaufman attributed the disruption of his sleep as "I supose [sic] some of the generals had one snort of Whiskey to [sic] much and felt like fighting but as they sobered up their mind changed and so we did not move."[163] The association between military failure and alcohol abuse became so strong that it seemed a perquisite for high command. "Another brigade drill today," Corporal John C. Williams complained after a lengthy drill on a cold January morning, "and if our brigadier possesses the necessary qualifications for General, then drinking and swearing are the chief requisites."[164]

Soldiers were also quick to discern other personality faults in their officers. A soldier of the Eighty-seventh Indiana characterized Colonel Kline Shryock as "too confounded lazy to get out of his tent," while William Ray believed his "Col. is good enough, but the line Officers are lazy, verry [sic]."[165] Soldiers also longed to puncture the air of pomposity they believed surrounded too many officers. "The [volunteer] officers are as stiff and distant as those of the regular army," Edward Wightman complained. "They scarcely ever speak to the privates even to give orders."[166] Tired of the constant wait for medical treatment, Private Aaron Kepler considered his regimental surgeon as little more than "a conceited, pompous little fellow, full of airs and red tape."[167] Pomposity also included the trappings of officery and the claims of success before the army claimed victory. Colonel Voris noted, with scarcely hidden sarcasm, "We had a Grand Review last week. . . . [for] Gen. [John A.] Dix and his cortege of mounted ossifers. . . . These Grand Reviews will soon crush out the wicked rebellion. . . . They cost but few lives, and as a consequence one can show off without much danger," Emory Sweetland also had no use for large entourages, claiming "Generals are as plenty here as wood churches at home."[168] Officers did not impress many soldiers because in far too many cases officers had failed to achieve the victory the soldiers sought. "It is strange, but nevertheless true, that this war has not yet developed a real military genious [sic]," Elijah Cavins perceptively wrote. "There are quite a number of good generals—but no Napoleon or Alexander or Ceaser [sic] has made his appearance." Pontification on grand strategy also did not impress the common soldier. "We think we have performed one of the greatest strategic movements of the war," Henry Bear confided in his diary, "but darn the strategic movements. Talk is talk."[169] In the absence of superior leadership, soldiers believed themselves the equals of generals in terms of military acumen. "There is one thing certain that i [sic] know," Sergeant Peter Welsh confided to this wife. "[I] am more competent to fill an officers position then more then [sic] one half of the officers that are in the regiment."[170]

AS SOLDIERS INCREASINGLY HELD officers in lower and lower regard, more and more soldiers refused to obey even some basic tenets of military discipline. In these cases, the soldiers were not overtly challenging the authority of the army but rather pushed the boundaries of basic rules to test what they could get away with. The minor infractions also were a means to assert the rights of citizen-soldiers by acting in a way that was acceptable in civilian life but not the army. In civilian life, a man was free to speak what he wanted and when he wanted, to come and go from his residence, to set his own standards, and to earn his own living. But in wartime, the army expected citizen-soldiers to leave these ideas of personal choice at home. The army was a place of tight discipline, stringent behavior, and regulated existence where the group mentality dominated. A problem arose, however, when soldiers refused to accept the army's limitations on their personal choices, and instead brought their peacetime expectations to war with them. What resulted was a constant battle between the army and its citizen-soldiers to define a mutually acceptable coexistence.

One basic challenge to authority was soldiers who refused to be quiet when officers ordered them to. As antebellum civilians, soldiers were free to speak not only what they wanted, but when they wanted. Military discipline did not permit such latitude, silencing soldiers not only on certain topics but also at certain times. Officers expected soldiers, for instance, to be quiet and go to sleep when the bugler played Taps and the call of "lights out" circulated through the camp. Soldiers, however, resented the treatment on the grounds that it treated them like children instead of grown men, and also denied them their citizen's right to speak at their leisure. They also resented that officers escaped such restrictions, another privilege that soldiers felt their officers did not deserve. Many soldiers complained about attempts to abridge their rights to talk amongst themselves. "The Whole Compy [sic] were most justly indignant by two Sergts and one Corpl endeavoring to force obedience to certain seemingly uncalled for restrictions," Private Bensell complained, "such prohibiting talking after 'Taps' or even walking out [of their tents] after retiring, and actually arrested certain innocent Men who were released for want of evidence."[171] Private Moses Harris perhaps stated the soldiers' position in its most basic, if somewhat crude, form. "Commissioned officers can make as much noise as they choose [especially] when they get drunk," Harris complained when an officer ordered him to stop talking, "but privates are not allowed to fart."[172] Harris' complaint notwithstanding, soldiers making noise after Taps did cause a disruption, and not just to the officers. "They beat a big bass drum furiously in the middle of the night," Edward Wightman complained. "They worked the most hideous noises out of a trombone . . . They got on the roof and . . . yelled through the knotholes till everyone was worn out and disgusted. They mounted guard at the door where they . . . prevented egress and ingress. Their dog, Jack, tore the seat square out of the trousers of a Massachusetts man who incautiously walked near their sleeping place."[173] The requirement for silence included singing in addition to talking. Private Joseph Heffelfinger complained that, although soldiers were "very noisy singing Star

Spangled Banner, John Brown, etc.," their captain did not appreciate their display of patriotism and "has just now forbidden us to sing."[174] Likewise, officers forbade soldiers stationed in Beaufort, North Carolina, from "the habit of singing and dancing" after hours because they were "making a great deal of unnecessary noise" after the sounding of Taps.[175]

Nativist soldiers, prejudiced against foreign-born troops, often characterized soldiers of Irish ancestry as lacking the ability to observe the "lights out" order. "In the tent [next door] they are having an Irish wake," Private Charles Chase complained, "[E]ach one trying to make the most noise and shake the floor the worst."[176] Compounding the problem, only one or two disruptive soldiers could ruin the good night's sleep of a whole regiment. "I . . . shut my eyes and tried to make myself comfortable, as a philosopher should," Edward Wightman wrote to his brother, "But two noisy Irishmen got quarrling about some ridiculous trifle and kept up yelling until we rose as a body and expelled them."[177] To achieve peace in camp, officers cracked down on the noise. "We can talk and tear around as much as we want to until after 8 P.M. or 'taps.'" William Henry Clayton wrote his parents in Iowa, "After that time there must be silence in camp. A night or two ago a corporal in the tent joining ours got to talking in Irish style with an Irishman in another tent. They made quite a noise and the colonel sent the officer of the guard and some men after him."[178]

Besides complaining about regulations that tried to silence them, soldiers, especially those from rural areas, resented attempts by officers to improve their personal hygiene. Bathing, from a viewpoint of a typical American, was an unnecessary, effete, and potentially hazardous activity. Regular bathing did not become commonplace until the widespread application of indoor plumbing in the late nineteenth century, so most Americans simply did not bath with any consistency. A quick bath in a river or stream, or a washtub every few weeks, passed for acceptable hygiene. Even the White House did not boast a bathtub until 1851. Middle- and upper-class Easterners in urban areas were the few Americans who did bathe regularly, something that clashed with the personas of rough and tumble Westerners who were proud of their sparse but self-established existences. Many Americans also perceived bathing as potentially unhealthy. Hydropathy, better known as the "water cure," was a medical fad of the 1840s and '50s, and established the connection between bathing and general health. But a consequence of hydropathy was a perception that bathing was only needed to cure an existing disease, not prevent a potential one. Americans sensed a general connection between hygiene and health, but until the germ theory gained acceptance most Americans did not tie clean bodies to good health.[179] Soldiers, therefore, resented attempts by their officers to make them bathe and improve their living conditions. Many recruits saw only efforts to impose upon them a military mentality that, as citizen-soldiers, they did not accept, an effete practice that insulted their manhood, or treatment reminiscent more of how parents dealt with children than officers dealing with grown men. "Our officers are very busy trying to make Sunday soldiers of us here," George Cadman complained, "and there are more brushes being worn out in polishing shoes & clothing for inspection than would pave the road from the toll gate to Cincinnati."[180] Instead, most soldiers probably preferred to "lay around loose, with sleeves up, collar open, hair unkempt, face unwashed, and everything un-everything."[181]

Conversely, officers felt it their duty to keep their men clean. The military context of discipline included the concept that soldiers had to accept the army's way of doing things, in direct conflict with the attitudes of citizen-soldiers. The army's way included maintaining a soldierly appearance, with body, equipment, and uniform in good order.[182] If a soldier obeyed the regulations regarding cleanliness, their commanders could count on them to obey other more critical orders, to charge an enemy on the battlefield for instance, without inquiring why. The same theory applied to drill. It had a practical purpose of massing firepower against the enemy, but it also inculcated soldiers to the practice of obeying orders without question. Regulations regarding hygiene created better, and healthier, soldiers. Officers attempted a variety of methods to improve hygiene, usually in the face of opposition from the soldiers. John DeForest described the disgust of a general when a filthy soldier requested a day pass to leave camp. The general refused the pass and proceeded to dress the man down in front of the entire camp. "All of this with the air of intense disgust and entire desperation," DeForest recounted with disapproval, "as if the spectacle of an unclean soldier were more than humanity could bear."[183] To ensure military bearing and appearance, some officers set a high personal standard for soldiers on guard duty. It "takes a person almost all day to get ready to go on guard duty the next day," Private James Newton complained to his parents. "No one is allowed to come out on guard or dress parade without having his boots blacked, his clothes well brushed, and his gun so bright that you can see your face in it, and it is no fool of a job to do it either."[184] Such standards were not just for early-war recruits; commanders later in the war tried to instill the same discipline. When Major Ira Brown took temporary command of the Thirty-ninth New York in 1864, he instructed his officers to prepare their men for visual inspection before they went on guard duty, including all equipment in good order and their shoes blackened.[185] Other Union soldiers underwent white glove inspections, with officers examining even the bores of their rifles.[186] The most common time for inspection, however, was on payday, when all of the enlisted men eagerly lined up for their monthly wages. To receive their pay, however, soldiers had to pass inspection, and often soldiers did not pass. "We were mustered for pay," John Holahan remembered. "The inspection was very strict, and a number of the boys were sent to quarters in disgrace, for their untidy appearance."[187] The cleanliness standard not only applied to individuals. Larger formations faced criticism if its members did not meet an officer's expectations because of only one or two unkempt soldiers. Company F of Fifth New Hampshire, for instance, failed inspection in 1863, with the inspector noting that the company contained three especially filthy men. Chagrined by the failure, the company commander, Captain Albert Cummings, reinforced the demand for hygiene. A few days later, the company passed inspection, with the inspector taking special note of the unit's cleanliness.[188] Lieutenant Colonel John T. Lockman, commander of the One Hundred Nineteenth New York, was another stickler for hygiene. "He is up and about at reveille," Captain Theodore Dodge wrote in admiration, "and he has his eye everywhere. At guard mountings he is present, inspects himself each man; dirt ones are put down on the black list and doomed to fatigue duty."[189] Soldiers sometimes found ways around such stringent requirements. "The general had many of the men unbutton their coats to see how clean their shirts were," Captain George Hugunin observed. Word spread like wildfire through the camp, and soldiers, now aware of the spot inspection, donned their cleanest shirt, causing Hugunin to comment that "needless to say that the last company inspected were much cleaner than the first, as each man had on a clean shirt."[190]

Persuading soldiers to stay clean was not easy, especially as it was far easier to get dirty in the field than it was to get clean. Despite this obvious problem, however, some soldiers became noticeable for their personal filth as much as any other attribute. The One Hundred Fifty-fourth New York, for instance, had two particularly filthy soldiers, nicknamed "Ash-Cat" and "Beauregard," the latter described as looking like a bum, "with holes burnt in his pants and overcoat from sleeping too close to campfires."[191] Soldiers in the Fifty-seventh Massachusetts had the untidy habit of relieving themselves whenever convenient instead of using the latrines. In response, the regimental colonel had to issue a directive warning "men will use the sink [latrine] intended for their use, and anyone committing any nuisance in or around the barracks or campground will be dealt with accordingly."[192] Soldiers in a Michigan regiment were similarly disposed, with the result that "Some dozen men were arrested for pissing on forbidden ground."[193] To ensure cleanliness, sometimes officers resorted to the practice of ordering the forced bathing of chronic or especially dirty soldiers. The act of forcibly bathing a resistant soldier not only reinforced the authority of the officers to dictate conditions in the camp, it used the threat of humiliation to impress a lesson upon the other soldiers. Soldiers who had to bathe against their will were reminiscent of unruly children, and the implicit lesson was that if soldiers intended to act like children their officers would treat them as children. By turning their sense of manhood against them, officers maintained a minimal level of hygiene. "There are two brothers who are especially dirty," George Cadman wrote, "and if they are left alone for a few days they get such a coat of dirt upon their faces it is impossible to tell one from another. They would be eaten alive by vermin if it were not their messmates cursing them. The other day they were both send down to the creek under the charge of a corporal and two men were detailed to wash them."[194] In the absence of a vigorous scrubbing, officers could always camouflage the worst smelling offender. In addition to "several cases of fine liquors, brandy claret, and porter" discovered aboard a wrecked blockade runner, officers of the Fifteenth Maine found "large quantities of fancy toilet articles, such as nice perfumes, soaps and pomades" that the officers forced the more malodorous of the regiment to use until "the whole camp is redolent with perfumes, and reminds me very much of the Methodist Church at home on a warm summer afternoon."[195]

In the end, soldiers had their personal level of hygiene imposed upon them by officers, usually in the form of informal regulations and policies that varied from officer to officer and regiment to regiment. Officers ordered their men to bathe when the opportunity presented itself, despite the grumbling the orders produced. Marcus Woodcock partially obeyed the order to bathe when "a general order came for all . . . to fall into line and be marched to the creek . . . and plunge into the stream." Woodcock was not enthusiastic about a bath, stating "this did not suit me very well" and wound up only "washing the upper part of my body" instead of whole thing.[196] John Gibbon, when commanding the Iron Brigade, required the unit to bathe at least once a week, the same frequency arranged by Colonel Thomas Roberts of the Seventeenth Maine in his order that "Each man must wash his legs and feet at least once a week" if not their entire body.[197] Officers created other regulations to ensure general cleanliness and health. The colonel of one regiment banned eating in the barracks due to the common garbage lying about, while the colonel of another issued orders to ensure "that quarters are kept clean and all offal and filth promptly removed and the sinks [latrines] daily kept in repair" to ensure "health, convenience, and comfort."[198]

Soldiers also groused about the army's attempts to limit their ability to make money during the war. Soldiers earned a monthly wage, plus a clothing allowance, but some soldiers sought to expand their income by engaging in private enterprise. Most of the financial hustling conducted by soldiers was not illegal by civil law nor banned by the Articles of War, but it did represent the diversion of a soldier's focus away from his soldierly duties and onto his side ventures. Officers also feared that soldiers who engaged in pseudo-business in camp or barracks might create a tension within the regiment or company that might decrease unit cohesion. Soldiers competing for business or holding a debt over the head of a fellow trooper might cause disruptions of discipline that officers did not desire. Consequently, soldiers had to keep their business activities low-key and relatively inoffensive, lest it attract unwanted attention.

Soldiers were very creative in establishing and maintaining their financial enterprises. Some soldiers provided a service. Fairfield Goodwin of the First Illinois Light Artillery made a few dollars from his musical talent. "I made an effort at composing another song," he wrote in his diary in January 1862. "Got a man to help sing it. We went to all the companies in our regiment and sung it to them. The boys passed around the hat each time we sung. Raised $14.32." Goodwin continued to write and sell his songs, and within a week had collected enough money to cover for his printing costs, pay off his singing partner, treat his friends to an oyster supper, and still "I had about ten dollars clear."[199] Private Henry Bear found a soldier to cut his hair for him because the last barber charged him "Nothing more nor less than Half a dollar, the son of a bitch. I toled [*sic*] him it was the last he would get of me."[200] During the Peninsula Campaign in 1862, Henry Charles bolstered his income and whiled away the time by "making bone rings and selling them to the cavalrymen." Charles did not mention whether the bones were animal or human.[201] Other soldiers made money by selling goods and services. While at Camp Carrington near Indianapolis, for instance, Private Jacob Bartmess parlayed his good behavior into a quick two bits. "I got a pass to go out of camp yesterday," Bartmess wrote to his wife, "and Sold it for 25 cents."[202] John H. Ferguson of the Tenth Illinois, describing the hardship of standing watch all night, reported that "Some are paying other $1.50 cts. to stand two hours for them."[203] A soldier ordered to the picket line offered Private Wilbur Fisk "a dollar if I would take his place which I willingly decided to do."[204] John Smith "saw a fellow with a lot of tobacco," purchased as much as he could, and immediately resold it to men in his regiment, making "about $4.00 on the same."[205] Corporal Leander E. Davis also supplemented his income by buying "fourteen dollars of tobacco and sold it for $18.60" and selling "paper and invelops [envelopes], one bunch of each. I sold the paper for 35 cents and the invelops the same. You will make 27 cents on a pack of the invelops and 18 cents on a quire of paper."[206] Wilbur Fisk was also in the stationary business. He reported in his diary that he "Received a dozen pens from A. Morton last night. Sold all but four of them," followed by "Sent for another lot of pens. $32 is considerable to risk in such a speculation but the die is thrown."[207]

Wilbur Fisk did not sell pens, but he still made money by using one. "Wrote a letter today to a lady in Poughkepsie for another fellow," Fisk told his wife. "Rather of an ungentlemanly way of doing business but I was paid for it and if the lady ain't shrewd enough to "see it" she deserves to be taken in."[208]

The one thing that most soldiers wanted was whiskey, and if soldiers could obtain in and restrain themselves from imbibing their product, they had the opportunity to earn a great rate of return. Some soldiers sold their whiskey rations, a relatively rare reward provided by the army. Sergeant John Hartwell sold his Christmas bonus, informing his wife that "This morning each had a gill of Ale. I sold mine for a dime."[209] William More observed soldiers selling their Christmas whiskey rations "from one to another for from 20 [cents] to 50 [cents]."[210] Leander Davis paused from his stationary business to let his wife know that "I have done something the last two days that I have never done before. We was served out with whisky, and I drew my rations and gave them to another man," presumably at the right price.[211] John Holahan engaged in the questionable practice of selling whiskey to soldiers jailed in the regimental guard house, but justified his actions due to the "fabulous prices for it."[212] One audacious soldier "under the guise of a waiter" crashed an officer's-only party featuring a spread of "wine, ham, beer, lemonade, beer, horseradish, whiskey punch, claret, ale, and shad." The soldier helped himself ("I drank as much lemonade as some of the officers drank beer and whiskey."), and then made sure to take some whiskey with him because "when I do get whiskey I always sell it or trade it for something else."[213] If soldiers could obtain a large volume of whiskey, they had the opportunity to set up shop, of a sort. "It is a heavy fine if caught at it [selling whiskey]." William Jones wrote to his brother, "but these old regulars are to [sic] smart for them. They buy there [sic] whiskey by the gallon & then hide it in the woods. . . . They then ask you how much you want, and . . . they ask you for your money. They won't go to get it until you pay for it. Then they start back, . . . In about 5 minutes they comeback with it, give it to you & walk right off."[214]

Soldiers even sold the food off their plates. Men who could cook often "confiscated hogs, butchered and cooked them, then sold the hind quarter," but not all such enterprises were successful. A sergeant in the Fiftieth New York Engineers had purchased a "huge cheese" for thirty cents per pound and was selling it out of his tent at eighty cents a pound, "making quite a nice little speculation." When discovered by his colonel, however, the sergeant "was required to cut it up and dividing it among the companies free of charge."[215] One particularly adventurous entrepreneur, "with more cupidity than conscience," capitalized on the hunger for fresh beef by collecting the discarded lungs from the army butchers and selling them for twenty cents per pound.[216] William Morse and his comrades cooked up and sold a product that only the most desperate of soldiers could eat. "The boys are mixing up their flour and water and frying it in tanned hogs" oil and selling the "doughnuts . . . for 25 [cents]," he proudly testified. "Cliff Jones is hard at work making up our batch which we calculate will be a little extra as we have nutmeg and sugar. . . . I have [also] been busy cleaning and boiling tripe."[217]

Other soldiers raised money the old-fashioned way: they got a job. Private John Brobst worked in a livery stable on the side, Henry Kaufmann found work by cooking for his captain and serving as an ad hoc mail carrier for his company, and John Haley worked as clerk for the regiment's sutler.[218] John Smith also worked for a sutler, at least until officers forced the sutler out of camp.[219] General Charles Heckman had to crack down on the large number of men in the Eighty-first New York finding outside employment with various sutlers, ordering Colonel J.J. DeForest to put an end to the practice.[220] Confined in a prisoner exchange camp, Sergeant Hamlin Coe found employment by "an old Dutchman [who] came after me to go and build him a hayrack." Coe not only earned $1.25 for his day's work, but he enjoyed "plenty of good victuals and the ladies [of the house] to talk with. . . . I would work until I became weary and then go into the parlor and talk with the fair ones."[221]

Officers also engaged in a bit of moonlighting, and took advantage of situations where they could add to their paychecks. Besides earning a wage as a regimental surgeon, James Dunn also invested in sutlery, and even worked behind the counter on the odd day.[222] Major Henry Forbes operated his own sutler shop as well, but found himself on the wrong side of the law. Accused of improperly selling liquor to soldiers, Forbes found himself under arrest by the order of his brigade commander, Colonel Edward Prince. After languishing under arrest for a few days, Prince let Forbes go with only a warning.[223] Private Bensell, already disgusted at Lieutenant James Davison's insistence on saluting too much, noted that Davison had purchased three tons of potatoes for the regiment at 75 cents per bushel. Other regiments, however, purchased theirs for 37 cents per bushel, and Bensell opined that Davison was engaging in a bit of speculation ("one of his 'savings schemes'"), if not outright fraud.[224] Lieutenant Welcome Crafts of the Fifth New Hampshire earned the wrath of Colonel Edward Cross by loaning money to short-handed privates at high interest rates. Cross ordered Crafts to cease his usury business, return any collected interest, and to collect only the principle on his current loans under threat of much harsher penalties.[225] One officer, Captain John Morris, profited from financial dealings with enlisted men, even as a prisoner of war. The Confederates captured Morris and about two thousand other Union soldiers after recapturing Plymouth, North Carolina, on April 20, 1864. Just before their capture, most Union soldiers had received their pay, in the form of a check from the regimental paymaster, checks they still had with them when they arrived at the Andersonville prisoner of war encampment. Morris, who had "a quantity of Philadelphia stocks and bonds" with him, swapped the bonds with Confederate officers for their value in Confederate money, and then used the Confederate money to purchase the soldiers' paychecks for "one-third the face of the checks, which are as good as the gold." The soldiers sold their paychecks to Morris to purchase extra food from their Confederate guards, who accepted only Confederate currency. Private Charlie Mosher resisted selling for as long as he could, but, weak from hunger, he sold his paycheck after seven months of imprisonment.[226]

THE CLASH BETWEEN CIVILIAN LIFE and military duty was one campaign that the army establishment could not win. Citizen-soldiers had a clear expectation of the rights they possessed and a strong memory of the privileges they enjoyed before enlistment. No amount of discipline, tradition, or protocol could change that. When confronted with limitations on their perceived liberties, soldier ignored, adapted, or changed the nature of the disciplinary boundaries that the army sought to erect. The result was a Northern army that embraced the expectations of combat discipline. Despite pessimism and defeatism, the Union army and its soldiers kept coming back for more. Soldiers might have decried the abilities of their officers, but they did not back calls for surrender, negotiation, or mass disobedience. Instead, soldiers realized that they themselves had to be the saviors of the Union, an ideology that fit in well with their self-perception as citizen-soldiers.

That left the army in the position of enforcing discipline when it could and in the manner it could. Martinets and sticklers for detail and protocol found themselves ignored or disobeyed, while officers who adopted a flexible attitude toward discipline and the rights of citizen-soldiers found soldiers willing to fight and die for the preservation of the Union. Smart officers recognized what level of discipline they could enforce, while bad officers did not. The uneasy relationship between officers and men evolved over the course of the war. Neither body of soldiers nor officer corps dominated the other, but an uneasy and flexible level of discipline remained for the duration of the war. This tenuous relationship was never more clearly demonstrated than in the army's reaction to soldier activity that existed in the gray areas of the Articles of War.

"FIELDS OF SATAN"

The Impulse of Indiscipline

The inability of the officer corps to compel direct obedience to the military definition of discipline had long-lasting influence. The army maintained discipline during the Mexican War through the presence of the Regular Army and its ability to convey its code of behavior upon the mass of wartime volunteers. The Civil War was a volunteer war, however, and the well-developed attitudes regarding the rights of citizen-soldiers were to invariably clash with the army's desire to establish, monitor, and maintain military as well as legal discipline. The citizen-soldiers, however, brought their ideas with them into the army. To maintain their connection to civilian life, soldiers attempted to live as much like civilians as they could. Moreover, the definitions and perceptions of manhood from the antebellum period defined how soldiers selected the elements of army life they would accept and which ones they would reject. Soldiers resented the officers' privileges and control over their lives. They identified with soldiers who bent and broke the rules, and denigrated officers who did not allow them the latitude they desired. They wanted to demonstrate their achievement of manhood, but would do so under their own terms, with fewer and fewer demonstrations of earlier naivety.

Not the innocents who went off to war, soldiers shaped their own parameters of existence. By mass demand and populist insistence, soldiers forced the army to accept, if not embrace, a more flexible view of legal discipline, especially for behaviors that existed on the fringes of military discipline. No codified legal system, such as the Articles of War, could cover every exigency, and the citizen-soldiers of the Union army proved adept at finding the gray areas of the Articles of War. This adeptness generated a massive amount of behavior that straddled the line between the military definition of discipline and the legal definition of discipline, between acceptable and unacceptable behavior, and between illegal and inappropriate action. When this questionable behavior occurred, the army was at a loss to deal with it. The behavior in question did not clearly violate the Articles of War, so the army could not impose punishment or conduct a court-martial. On the other hand, the behavior was not conducive to collective discipline, and the army believed its soldiers should avoid such behavior, even if they could not punish the offender. From this loose conundrum came a mass of conduct that was improper but not illegal, usually conducted on such a scale that the army proved hesitant to tackle the problem. Furthermore, many of the issues involved included topics that the army believed were none of its concern or best left to local authorities. At its worst, the army chose simply to ignore disruptive behavior or left the disciplinary question up to regimental officers to tackle instead of instituting an army-wide policy. This neglect further played into the hands of citizen-soldiers, who exploited this vacuum of authority to challenge further the limits placed around them.

WITH THE DECLINE IN DEDICATION and Regular Army influence, and rise in pessimism and defeatism, soldiers saw less and less reason to behave in the manner proscribed by the dreams of glory and valor in war. The average soldier developed a more practical mode of behavior, and one result was a decline in morality relative to prewar behavior. Victorian morality, marked by family-based values and the gospel of self-denial, was the norm for upper and middle classes and the goal of the lower classes. The Victorian ideal of masculinity was self-restraint and public virtue, and the ideal setting was the family home. Home represented the reward of Victorian social achievement, the place where women (the ideal Victorians) provided a secure hearth and home against the temptations and pitfalls of the outside world. Even if lower-class Americans and immigrants did not have the trappings of Victorian middle-class life, American culture and society emphasized that morality and self-restraint led to success, which opened the door to social mobility. Hence, if the lower-classes were not Victorians, the lesson was that they should strive to be Victorians.

Self-restraint was the badge of Victorianism—restraint against sin, carnality, greed, and ambition. Indulging in sinful or earthly delights diverted effort away from this remanifestation of the Puritan work ethic, and threatened to tarnish one's social reputation, if not the immortal soul itself. Drinking, gambling, and other forms of vice were wastes of one's time and talents, and reflected a flawed personality by the inability to control one's desires. Not surprisingly, alcoholism in the antebellum period was seen as weakness instead of as a curable disease.[1] The sexual impulse was for the purpose of procreation only, with Victorian men expected to restrain their urges because fragile women could not. "The young bride is more or less capable of over-exciting the sexual appetites. . . ." wrote Dr. Augustus K. Gardner, one of the most respected antebellum physicians. "Unfortunate is the imprudent man who dares to drink without care from this cup of delight."[2] In a similar vein, the antebellum temperance movement became an instrument of Victorian morality. Curbing the impulse to drink bolstered the individual's self-restraint, improved the financial circumstance of the family, removed a source of crime from the neighborhood, improved the reputation of the community, and cleansed the moral health of the nation. Liquor went from the convivial shared beverage of the rural community to the cause of all society's ills, and a definite negative to any aspiring Victorian.[3] While a non-Victorian streak existed among single men, the lower class, and frontier settlers, Victorian morality cemented middle-class influence in America and provided a model of behavior for which other Americans were to strive.[4]

Removed from the control mechanism of middle-class society, and unrestrained by the Regular Army's tradition of military self-discipline, the mass of Civil War volunteers created their own definition of morality in a military environment of long boredom, hard living, and easy death. Simply being in the army was justification enough to convert many antebellum Victorians into the very examples of nonrestraint they feared. The rough nature of army life, ready availability of temptation, and disillusion from the war created plenty of opportunities for some very un-Victorian behavior. "War is pretty sure to relax the morals of everyone it comes in contact with," was the justification of Charles Haydon, and few soldiers would have disagreed.[5] "War is a horrible thing." perceived John Follmer. "It makes men heartless, brutal, and in many instances sinks out of sight all of higher and nobler manhood" that Victorian men aspired to represent.[6] "War is hell broke loose," Cyrus Boyd believed, "and benumbs all the tender feelings of men and makes them brutes."[7] Boyd's statement was both an explanation and a justification. To many soldiers the nature of army life made Victorian morality impossible, so instead of trying to change it, army life became the excuse to indulge in it. James I. Robertson, writing about the lives of Civil War soldiers commented that "In the military, sin competed with salvation on an equal footing for quite human reasons. . . . [Soldiers] found excitement in the usual attractions and novel experiences that soldiering offered."[8] A quarter century earlier, Frederick Shannon also explained lapses in discipline by soldiers who were finally "Freed from the restraint of home, or never having known moderation" as the product of the army life in which they found themselves.⁹

Once morality weakened, its increasing absence became noticeable to soldiers perceptive enough to perceive the difference that army life had on their compatriots. The tendency to participate in immoral activity is best summed by a soldier on Sherman's March to the Sea. "Both officers & men appear to have cast off all the restraints of home," Emory Sweetland wrote from the hospital, "& indulge their passions to the fullest extent."¹⁰ Morality in general suffered, and soldiers made note of the change in moralistic tones. "Those in the midst of it can tell what a terrible thing war is." Charles Musser wrote from Arkansas, "It makes demons of men. It corrupts the pure and innocent." Later, even more depressed by the sinfulness around him, Musser dreaded that "a few short years and we will all be gone and forgotten and nothing to show that we ever existed except the evil acts we do, for who does any good acts these times? Alas, a very few, and the evil predominate."¹¹ Observing the misbehavior of the men in his own regiment, Lyman Ames lamented "O! what a school war is. It is the field of Satan."¹² Religion became less and less important, to the point of seeming irrelevant in a mass organization dedicated to killing. "Preaching all over Camp to day [*sic*]," Private Daniel Chisholm write in his diary soon after enlisting, "but I am afraid not much good done, for Cards and Sermons don't mix well, and we have both." Chisholm noted that the lack of religious devotion was attributable to the absence of restraint that many men felt. "The boys are very wild as a general thing," he described. "[T]hey feel like young Colts or at least they act so."¹³ Hallock Armstrong, chaplain for the Fiftieth Pennsylvania, echoed the opinion that symbols of restraint no longer had an effect upon the soldiers. "Some one has said that three things are out of place in the army." Armstrong wrote to his wife, "Bibles, Ministers, and Women!"¹⁴

The decline in morality translated into a wide range of misbehaviors that, while not technical violations of the Articles of War, represented a lack of discipline. Instead of violating the definition of discipline as courage under fire and ability to achieve military objectives, these breaches of societal and personal morality represented an inability or unwillingness to obey the moral code that the country and the army wished the soldiers to uphold. Despite the generally religious nature of antebellum America, adherence to institutional faith in particular and organized religion in general eroded as the war progressed. From the general belief that the war was a moral and Christian crusade early in the war, soldiers turned away from religion. To many, organized religion represented two of their worst experiences during the war: authoritarian organization and blind belief in cause and country. Early-war volunteers widely held the conviction that God led the army into battle for a higher purpose. "Every day my conviction becomes firmer that the hand of God is in this," confessed John Campbell, "and that in spite of victories and advantages he will deny us Peace unless we grant to others the liberties we ask for ourselves."[15] Responding to his wife's letters stating that the local priests and bishop are split on the moral nature of the war, Sergeant Peter Welsh retorted "The clergy being devided [sic] upon the war question does not therefore go to prove that God has nothing to do with it. God in his justice allows [sic] evil men to ferment discord and precipitate . . . people of the same nation against each other as a chastisement for their ofences [sic] against his devine [sic] laws."[16] Officers attempted to reinforce these types of beliefs by encouraging religious devotion. As the Seventy-seventh Illinois left home to go to war, for instance, the ladies of Peoria donated a library of religious books to each of the regiment's ten companies, and the men received a send off from a local minister who reassured them that "they need not fear to go into battle that any one who was killed in such a holy cause was sure to go strait [sic] to heaven."[17] Religion also enjoyed a considerable amount of revivalism later in the war. Instead of being tinged with early-war optimism, the later revivalism was a sign of pessimism, as soldiers dedicated themselves to moral behavior on the belief that their lives were soon to end. A chaplain in a Kansas regiment reported in 1864 that "Quite a religious influence in Camp. At our prayer meeting 7 arose for payer, with tears in their eyes told me that they were resolved to lead new & Christian lives. . . . The Col. appears willing to aid me in any thing I desin [design]." The men were apparently serious in their efforts at reform, as a fellow soldier reported that there was "scarecely [sic] no drinking at all" in camp, and even an "anti-tobacco pledge . . . and several old tobacco users have sined [signed] it."[18]

Intense religious devotion by some soldiers, however, was often surpassed by derision of organized faith, as religious devotion and symbols of religious devotion became targets of rejection, disbelief, and scorn. Soldiers were quick to recognize the dichotomy between the government's orders to kill and the Bible's dictates against killing. "The Minister opened the pages of Holy Writ on an Arm Chest." Corporal Bensell wrote, "Around him were polished and improved instruments of Death, and his audience, Men drilled each day to perfect the Art of Warfare, to distroy [sic] one another. Yet the text was, 'Love ye one another,' Such is human consistency."[19] The reality of death and war often overcame the abstract of religion, and soldiers rejected the moral message offered by many chaplains. "If a [religious] meeting was called and the men were ordered out to listen to the preaching," Daniel Sawtelle remembered, "there was so much grumbling that it was no doubt discouraging to the chaplain."[20] Not content with just grumbling about having to attend services, soldiers sometimes did their best to disrupt the religious pursuits of others. Chaplain Henry Lowing of the One Hundred Fifty-fourth New York suffered the indignity of having mule urine sprayed on his flock of the faithful and gunpowder cartridges dropped down the chimney of his tent heater. The exploding power panicked the occupants and nearly burned down the chaplain's tent.[21] At the Judiciary Square Hospital in Washington, DC, a group known as the Evangelical Brethren disturbed the wounded and ill soldiers with their "yelling of prayers" so much that Private Benneville Leno fired a warning shot with his pistol to shut them up.[22] Chaplain Louis Beaudry, attempting to distribute testaments in his regiment, found himself rudely rebuffed. "A young man," Beaudry later recounted, "took a huge quid of tobacco from his mouth, placed it in the center of the book, contemptuously closed it with force, that as much of the book might be destroyed as possible by the saturation of the filthy spittle in the weed."[23] It is not surprising then that chaplains became exasperated with their spiritual flocks, and religious soldiers found army life not conducive to pious faith. "This world is full of iniquity, and especially here," Private Francis Strickland wrote, "that I sometimes become almost discouraged and feel like giving up and was it not for the confidence that I have . . . [in] God . . . I should completely despair."[24]

The vast majority of chaplains toiled in obscurity, but soldiers did recognize the efforts of the best of them and showed their appreciation for their efforts. Sergeant Major Stephen Fleharty, for instance, was sorry to hear that his chaplain had tendered his resignation. The chaplain was "not particularly noted for his spiritual qualities" but was known as a good card-player, and the men would miss his common approach to their spiritual salvation.[25] "There are some grand old men in the army who are preaching the gospel who are like fathers to the boys." Private Follmer related, "These men have the respect of all their men" because they took a broad view beyond religion and became true authority figures.[26] Chaplain John Stuckenberg may have held some of his flock in low regard, but his men certainly thought highly of him. When Stuckenberg contemplated resigning because of poor health, the regiment, reduced to barely two hundred men, donated $115 toward a horse for his use.

One of Stuckenberg's colleagues was also highly valued by his men. Unarmed and riding alone, the chaplain came upon two Confederate soldiers watering their horses from a spring. The chaplain "secured their carbines, ordered them to surrender and brought them and their horses and mules to camp."[27] Because many father/son relationships existed within Civil War regiments, there was the occasional father/chaplain administering to son/soldier, but sometimes with mixed results. Private Silas Wesson of the Eighth

Illinois Cavalry described the relationship between his regiment and their chaplain as "Chaplain [Philo] Judson preaches and prays to us and his son [Sergeant Philo P. Judson, Jr.] swears at us, and one does as much good as the other." Judson did not have much influence as a man of God, but he did have the respect of the men. Wesson assessed Judson as someone who "can't preach for sour apples but he seems to be a good man."[28]

But just as good chaplains distinguished themselves from the mass of ministers, the bad ones also stood out in sharp relief. For soldiers seeking religious comfort, an incompetent or lazy chaplain was worse than having none at all. John Follmer thought highly of some of the chaplains he encountered, but admitted that "some have missed their calling, greatly." Instead, Follmer observed, "They might make fair shoemakers or auctioneers, but it is plain that they will never make preachers."[29] Aurelius Voorhis was also not impressed with his regimental chaplain. "Heard a preacher try to preach but to my mind it was a perfect failure," he complained, "He done nothing but chew tobacco and tell fool stories and they were poorly told at that."[30] As many men had rejected organized faiths, they had no use for chaplains, who seemed only to consume resources and generate nothing in return. We "have a fine chaplain" a Maine soldier wrote, ". . . never gives us any trouble, we see him but once in two months and then it is on pay-day."[31] "Our chaplain is good for nothing," one officer complained, "except to relieve the government of money. He is too lazy to do anything and has preached only twice since he is with us. He never visits a sick man, but is always on hand when pay day comes."[32] Joseph Johnson derisively described his regimental chaplain as "aloof and a tent peeper" but did show the chaplain the courtesy of removing a mocking note from the back of his coat placed there by a mischievous soldier, the nineteenth-century equivalent of the "kick me" gag.[33] On other occasions, however, chaplains lost their jobs for earthly violations of their own teachings. Stopping a man engaged in plundering a Southern home, General William T. Sherman demanded to know the offender's name. "Oh, hell, General," the man responded, "I am Abner F. Dean, Chaplain of the 112th Massachusetts."[34] Other chaplains faced accusations of establishing their "quarters in the rear . . . they show the white feather [symbol of cowardice]; hence the men dispise [*sic*] them," and for drunkenness, theft, or other moral weakness.[35]

PARALLELING THE DECLINE OF RELIGION, the rise of questionable behavior shocked and alarmed chaplains as soldiers shaped their own collective view of proper morality. The bending of societal norms became with basic moralistic offenses, often seen more as the sign of bad breeding and less the sign of moral turpitude. From basic offenses, however, soldiers escalated to much more serious breaches of moral behavior. Cursing and profanity was one of the most common basic violations of Victorian morality that most, if not all, Civil War soldiers engaged in at one time. Profanity represented the language of masculinity, expressed frustration and anger, and allowed soldiers to assert a voice of independence in a military culture that sought to control such independent thoughts. As evidence that soldiers were aware that profanity was socially unacceptable behavior, written accounts mention the widespread nature of profanity in the company of other soldiers, but profanity is virtually absent in soldiers' letters themselves. Only the rare letter home contains profanity, and those that do are addressed to other masculine figures—a father, brother, or male friend. In a letter to his brother, for instance, Private David Myers complained about the "god Damn sons of B——" in the army that failed to forward his mail to him, while Henry Thompson penned a letter from a location simply identified as "Camp Shit."[36] Amongst soldiers themselves, however, profanity became the common language. "It is wonderful how profane the army is," observed Captain DeForest, "Officers who are members of the church, officers who once would not even play a game of cards, have learned to rip out oaths when the drill goes badly, or when the discipline 'gets out of kilter.'"[37] DeForest was not alone in his bemused attitude about casual cussing. "Our boys are, like most privates in the army," Edward Wightman wrote his brother, "disgustingly unprincipled and profane. . . . They swear perpetually for the sake of swearing."[38] The range of one's profane vocabulary became a means of defining an individual, as when William Moore lamented the death of a fellow soldier. "Poor fellow," Moore bemoaned, "he was a gallant soldier if he was a bad swearer."[39]

The prevalence of profanity dismayed religiously devout soldiers and discipline-inclined officers alike. "I have never heard more obscene, profane, low and vulgar words, remarks, and innuendoes than ever fell on my ears in all my past life," Captain Joseph Blackburn wrote in astonishment to his wife. "A camp is the world in miniature for all extremes meet—intellectual and animal, moral and immoral."[40] The prevalence of swearing could be particular bad if a soldier had to share space with someone prone to profanity. "My tentmates are too profane," Private Edwin Emery complained to his sister, "too vile to suit my tastes. They cannot prevent my having prayer. I hope, though it is not too pleasant sometimes to kneel and pray before these profane fellows."[41] Even the most pious soldiers felt eroded by the constant profanity around them. "After having served in the army almost 17 months," Colonel Elijah Cavins commented about his soldiers, "where men are constantly swearing, I cannot become so used to it."[42] Despite Cavins' complains, officers often swore just as much as their men, or even caused swearing. "Up to this time our Regiment was free from this foolish sin and an oath was rarely heard," Wesley Brainerd recounted, "but on one evil day all our morality in this respect vanished." An officer, angry at the sloppy drill of his company, "popped a hideous oath." Hearing an officer swear, "the ice once broken . . . that night oaths rolled from the right to left with wonderful volubility. The charm was broken."[43] Colonel Edward Cross of the Fifth New Hampshire tried to stem the use of profanity among his officers, pleading with them to set a good example. In a circular to the regiment, Cross believed that "Nothing so weakens the authority of officers over their men as rough vulgar language to one another. The men "reason" if the officers do not respect each other why should be respect them? . . . Let us remember that we have a character to preserve and that honor and chivalry are the true gems of a soldiers' life."[44] But soldiers found it difficult to cultivate these gems of their existence when even generals cut loose with profanity when the opportunity struck. "Profanity may be classed second on the list of degrading camp vices." Captain Thomas Orwig of the First Pennsylvania Light Artillery complained, "Even Generals may be heard trying to emphasize their command by the utterance of loaded oaths."[45] Lafayette Church, who rose to the rank of captain in the Twenty-sixth Michigan before becoming a chaplain, held General Judson Kilpatrick in high regard. "Gen. Killpatrick [*sic*] . . . is brave and dashing, and can swear more than any other officer in the service except perhaps Gen. [Winfield Scott] Hancock, our commander— they say he can beat every other man."[46]

Chaplains complained to their commanding officers to do something about the sinful practice. Chaplain Stuckenberg, dismayed by an incident of public profanity by the aforementioned Major General Winfield Hancock, penned a note to the general chastising him for his breach of morality, and implored him to set an example and curtail swearing in his division. "Finding that profanity prevails to an alarming extent in our midst, I have, as my duty required, attempted to banish it from our regiment." Stuckenberg wrote, ". . . It is, therefore, with the deepest regret, that I find so many [incidents of swearing] pointing to our Division General as an Example of the grossest profanity. What can my feeble labors accomplish, when in conflict with an example of so high authority?"[47] Despite the pervasiveness of vulgarity, officers did attempt to curtail the uttering of public oaths. Officers did not have to rely entirely upon their own sense of moral outrage to curb profanity; the Articles of War made profanity a punishable offense. Section I of the original 1775 Articles of War contained six articles related to "Divine Worship" that governed moral behavior, the expectations of chaplains, and the penalties for not attending church services. The 1806 revisions removed some of the Articles regarding the duties of chaplains, but still retained articles regarding church attendance and profanity. Soldiers in 1861 went off to war governed by Article 2, that "earnestly recommended" that all soldiers and officers attend divine service, and punished only those who "behave indecently or irreverently at any place of divine worship." The punishment was a dollar for officers and one-sixth of a dollar for enlisted men on the first offense, and the fine and twenty-four hours of imprisonment for every subsequent offense. Article 3 provided the same punishments for "any non-commissioned officer or soldier who shall use any profane oath or execration."[48] Armed with these powers, officers attempted to use legal force to silence the swearing. Colonel Thomas Gallagher, commanding the Eleventh Pennsylvania Reserves, tried to impose the mandated punishment to stop the cussing, but reported that the effort had no impact.[49] Officers in Wesley Brainerd's regiment tried to fine soldiers for swearing, but after the officer swore in public there was "No more punishment for swearing, for with what propriety could the men be punished for an offense when even the Lieutenant Colonel indulged in it unrebuked."[50]

Other officers tried to use common sense and good leadership to curb swearing instead of formal military procedure. One officer tried to increase their sense of refinement by entertaining his men with high literature. "In the evening I related to them one of Shakespeare's plays (The Two Gentlemen of Verona)," George Cram wrote to his mother. "It had an excellent effect—they listed attentively and I noticed that there was much less swearing for a long time afterward."[51] Officers pledged to give up swearing in the hopes that their men would follow their example. These public pledges, however, soon became very difficult to maintain. Chaplain Armstrong was proud of the religious nature of the major in his regiment, although he broke his promise not to swear by cussing as a function of "military necessity." Relating the paradox to his wife, Armstrong reported hearing the major order his men to "stop that their d——d swearing, without a smile and in all sincerity."[52] Colonel Charles Lowell of the Second Massachusetts Cavalry also tried to end the swearing by setting an example and enforcing the Articles of War if necessary. The example did not last long. In battle soon after his pledge, Colonel Lowell ordered a subordinate to "god damn you get out of the road," ending his abstinence from cussing.[53]

With the army unwilling and unable to contain something as simple as profanity, other forms of vice proliferated as soldiers continued to define their own sense of morality. In the absence of collective restraint, swearing combined with other forms of vice to create a camp climate that surprised or appalled many observers and participants. The most popular, but certainly not only, vices were drinking, card playing, gambling, and the use of tobacco. Stricter faiths considered playing cards or other games of chance, even if the participants did not wager money, a form of sin. Victorians associated card playing with professional gamblers, prostitutes, and other possessors of low morals, and hence a practice that virtuous souls should avoid. Unfortunately for the pious, gambling and profanity seemed a matched pair. "You may want to know how I like Soldiering by this time!" George W. Squier wrote his wife, "Very well, was not the society so awful. Gambling is the common practice of nearly all and swearing is the common dialect of the Soldier."[54] Sergeant John Hartwell wrote his wife of his disillusion at seeing so "many young men that left home determined to resist all temptations of a demoralizing influence," only to take up the liberal use of drink and profanity. "Gambling like swearing," he continued, "is carried on to great extent by a large majority of the men, first they commence for playing for pies, apples, cigars or any other small innocent stakes, by & by they are captivated by the play & venture large sums of money."[55] Chaplains expressed the loudest disapproval of gambling. "Oh! The curse of gambling!" Chaplain Beaudry lamented, "It is ruining thousands [of men] in the army. In some tents, they gamble all the time from early morning till late at night. . . . This universal gambling in the army breeds pilfering, and gambling soon educates a man to wholesale swindling. Should the war continue long, we shall become a nation of swindlers."[56] As the war progressed, chaplains complained that the gambling problem seemed to only get worse. "They [the men] have plenty of money, and many seem to place little value on it," described Chaplain Stuckenberg, "Some staked 100 dollars a time on their way down here. One said he had lost over $10,000 in his life by gambling, another that he had lost more than he ever expected to be worth again."[57] As with religious principle, some soldiers rejected the sin of gambling from the start, while other developed a conscience relating to the practice. Virgil Andruss reassured his mother that since he entered the army "I know no more about cards than I did when I left and have no desire to."[58] Other soldiers, facing the possibility of death in a looming battle, developed a sudden aversion to gambling. Commenting on the men of the One Hundred Eighteenth Pennsylvania just before entering battle, John Smith noted, "I never saw so many packs of cards thrown away by so many men in my life as I did this particular afternoon. A soldier who is not so very particular all his life has an utter dread of being found dead with a pack of cards in his pocket and the result is that they are scattered all around. There is no accounting for taste."[59]

Gambling and other forms of vice, of course, seemed perfectly acceptable to many soldiers. Vice offered not only entertainment, but camaraderie. "Card playing and gambling was quite a pastime with some of the officers, as well as the men." James Avery wrote after the war in defense of gambling, "but I believe . . . from my own observations, that the soldiers that today are left from the ranks of that mighty army are more united, and have a more friendly and better feeling for one another, than any other class of men."[60] Other soldiers downplayed the popularity of gambling. "Our Regt. is pretty temperate as a whole," Edward Bassett wrote, "and playing [cards] for money is forbidden to soldiers."[61] While card playing and gambling became associated with those of low morals in the opinions of some men, many young soldiers associated gambling and vice with the masculine world of soldiering. In their belief system, a good soldier embraced the masculine elements of the existence, including "cursing, drinking, gambling, and wenching."[62] A veteran informed the newly enlisted Cyrus Boyd that "unless a man can drink, lie, steal, and swear he is not fit for a soldier," with the absence of gambling on the list probably just an oversight on the part of the veteran.[63] Reinforcing this view, veterans engaged in gambling most frequently, setting an example (for good or ill) on the newer recruits. "The men are not so good as they were once," John DeForest wrote, "they drink harder and swear more and gamble deeper."[64]

To combat gambling, officers used a variety of methods to persuade their soldiers to hang on to their hard-earned pay. In his plea to his officers to stop swearing, Colonel Cross also urged them to cease gambling as a standard of behavior. "To a game of cards, now and then at proper hours, there is no objection." he reasoned, "But the practice of assembling evening after evening and day after day is pernicious—especially when it becomes know to the enlisted men." This is remarkable forbearance for Colonel Cross, who only days before had stormed into a late-night poker game "with a pair of handcuffs in one hand and a saber in the other."[65] Some officers tried a total ban on gambling, essentially forcing their men to go "cold turkey" off gambling. Other officers tried threats. Colonel Daniel Woodall took command of the Thirty-ninth New York (the "Garibaldi Guard") in 1863, and issued warnings that "men of the Garibaldi Guard who were found at and reported for playing cards were to be punished most severely." The orders obviously did not stand, because when Colonel Augustus Funk took command in 1864, he had to issue similar orders: "All parties who are caught gambling will be punished, and those winning money or articles will be compelled to return them to the original owners."[66] On the frontier, in the New Mexico territory, Sergeant George Hand commented on an attempt to ban gambling that backfired. The "Officer of the day was ordered to stop a gambling game and arrest all soldiers engaged after Taps." Hand wrote, "He went there and found an officer betting and disobeying his orders. That is what I call neglect."[67] At least one officer tried public humiliation to stop gambling. Brigadier General Patrick wrote in his diary of seeing "A couple of men caught in a sweat cloth, gambling, were set to work in the rain, in a public place, near my Office, playing with beans instead of dice & having a placard on their backs 'Gamblers'—They were at it from early morning until dark with nothing to eat."[68]

Despite all efforts to halt gambling, however, the practice went on without constraint. Soldiers gambled to ease the boredom, to take their minds off the war around them, and for the opportunity for quick wealth. Thomas Bell found life so boring while encamped near Nashville that "it is not to be wondered at that men allow themselves to get excited over cards and gambling is the consequence."[69] Games came in a bewildering variety, with the troops of a Delaware regiment playing "Euchre, Old Sledge, poker and mante, and a sort of betting game with dice called the *sweat box.*"[70] Because gambling provided so many diversions and was such a portable form of recreation, soldiers took their chances and bucked the odds whenever and wherever they could. "Night before last I found some men gambling and made them stop it." Chaplain Stuckenberg wrote, "But scarcely had I turned around when they were at it again and continued at it till 3 o'clock the next morning."[71] Sometimes only extreme weather could halt the gambling. "The Guard tent here was struck by lightening yesterday evening, seriously injuring several," wrote James Abraham, "besides breaking up a Game of Cards that was in progress at the time."[72] Even when close to combat, the lure of gambling brought men together. In the midst of the Peninsular Campaign in 1862, an officer noted the widespread popularity of a dice game known as Chuck-Luck. Soldiers used the game to supplement their meager wages, and "Almost every soldier in turn becomes Banker and Better. When he is flush, he opens a game and plays until his adversaries break him, when he goes off to break someone else, or to raise a new pile." Between skirmishes, the games went on. "Today I saw a twenty-acre field black with Chuck-Luck parties squatting on the grass," the officer described, "The rattle of dice in the tin boxes . . . was almost ear-splitting."[73] Gambling only increased on payday, as soldiers, flushed with cash, took the risk of expanding their personal gains. "There is a good deal of gambling among the men since they were paid," wrote Charles Haydon, "There is one fine thing about, that is that they money will soon be gone."[74] When money was not available, soldiers gambled with what they had. Corporal Bensell reported that "Small pieces of tobacco, valued at 10 cents each, are used in lieu of money," while Private Sawtelle observed soldiers using the percussion caps for their rifles as chips, noting that the soldiers were careful to "give them back after they got through playing" in case they needed to use their rifles the next day."[75]

Although not considered as corrosive as gambling, officers also tried to curb tobacco use by associating use of the product with personal weakness or failure. One Massachusetts colonel associated tobacco use with such eroders of discipline as alcohol, profanity, and other practices that "had no place in an army of moral virtue and discipline."[76] Efforts to halt tobacco use were doomed to failure, however. Tobacco use was common before the war, many new soldiers saw tobacco use as a sign of manhood, and tobacco, like gambling, was an easily-portable form of comfort and recreation. "The way I comensed [sic] using it, I use to get lonesom [sic] that I did not know what to do with myself." Orlando Poe wrote his wife, "I took up chewing [tobacco]."[77] Altogether, these factors ensured that tobacco use remained a common vice in the army. To make matters worse for those who wanted to stamp out the use of the plant, charitable organizations frequently offered tobacco as a sign of the comforts of home. One chaplain was proud of the Christian Commission's efforts with the army, particularly the issuing of "large number of beautiful medals" for men who signed a pledge to stop drinking, smoking, or swearing. His hope for improvement was dashed, however, when he "went directly to the Sanitary Commission, and found them issuing large quantities of tobacco free to the boys!"[78]

Some officers, realizing that boredom was the most corrosive detriment to good discipline, attempted to provide entertainment for their men. Sports were an easy option. Young soldiers had energy to burn and time on their hands, so sports filled the free hours and provided beneficial exercise as a bonus. Baseball, already growing in popularity before the war, became the national pastime thanks to the Civil War, as soldiers spread the game wherever they went, providing a welcome change of pace. Depressed in recent days because of the dreariness of his existence, Joseph Johnston happily reported in his diary that "I have been brightening up by base ball play."[79] Regimental teams played intramural games within their camps, but also played other teams to defend the pride of the regiment or their state. The level of competition, however, was often uneven. The Fourteenth New York, a regiment that included many men who played in well-organized baseball clubs in the New York City area, dominated any other team they played. The team "whitewashed the nines of all the country regiments" that dared face them.[80] Although a popular pastime, the army required that officers maintain a respectful distance from the activities of their men, so baseball was often off limits to them. "At first the line officers used to take a hand with us," wrote Private Sawtelle, "but some of the higher officers decided it was not military enough. An order was read to the regiment forbidding their [the officers'] playing ball with the privates."[81]

Football, however, seemed a different matter. Although closer to rugby than contemporary American football, the rough and tumble sport still attracted soldiers eager to prove their manhood, officers included. Taking a break from his baseball games, Joseph Johnston appreciated his regimental colonel's effort to keep his troops busy, including reminders to company officers that "they had not forgot to play foot ball" with their men.[82] Charles Mattocks, a young officer from Maine, noted in his diary that "We have been having a game of football every evening for more than a week. Capt. Golderman [Augustus Goldermann] obtained it [the football] while a home. Quite a number of sore shins have already appeared."[83] George W. Benedict, an officer in a Vermont regiment, also mentioned officers playing football. "The colonel had procured a foot ball," he wrote in November 1863, "Sides were arranged by the lieutenant colonel, and two or three royal games of foot ball—most manly of sports and closest in its mimicry to actual warfare—were played. The lieutenant colonel, chaplain, and other officers, mingled in the crowd; captain took rough-and-tumble overthrows from privates; shins were barked and ankles sprained; but all was given and taken in good parts."[84]

When winter weather prevented baseball or football, snowball fights helped to pass the long and boring hours of winter camp. Private David Lilley described a brief snowball skirmish between his unit and a nearby artillery battery that lasted about twenty minutes, ending when "we quit with Cold hands."[85] Starting with these impromptu skirmishes between small groups of men, some snowball fights escalated into miniature wars themselves. In March 1864, for instance, the Second and Sixth Vermont regiments fought a full-scale snowball war, led by their officers, with the goal of capturing the other regiment's makeshift flag. "It was lively sport," an observer reported to the local newspaper, "charging and snowballing, capturing and recapturing officers, though it was ruinous for army coats, and the wear and tear of clothing in some encounters was immense. . . . As our surgeon was on the ground, I am confident that all the wounded were well cared for."[86] In early 1863, the colonel of the Twenty-second Iowa, encamped near Rolla, Missouri, also organized a snowball fight to relieve the boredom. He "divided the Regiment into two battalions," wrote Private Jacob Switzer, "set them in line of battle fronting each other on the parade ground, and . . . directed a battle with snow balls to ascertain which side could capture the banner. I do not know which side was victorious . . . but I do know that the banner suffered more in the contest than any of the contestants themselves."[87] Snowball fights could get out of hand, however, with physical injuries as a result. In March 1863, a Vermont and a New Jersey regiment fought an epic snowball fight featuring fortified positions, flanking movements, and hand to hand fighting. "The snow was crimsoned with the blood issuing from the olfactory organs of the Vermonters," a New Jersey soldier wrote, "and the appearance of the battle field indicated the fierce nature of the contest." After a two-day melee, the battle finally came to an end, with casualties reported as "Bloody noses, 53. bunged peepers, 81. extraordinary phrenological developments, 29. shot in the neck after the engagement, unknown."[88]

Despite the innocent and beneficial attributes that sports offered, soldiers often turned sporting activities to their own purposes, which often meant the opportunity to gamble on the sporting events in question. Baseball provided wholesome recreation, but it also provided the opportunity to place a wager. In April 1863, Private Hayward Emmill noted that "This afternoon the 9 best base ball players of the 2nd New York Troy regiment played the best 9 Jerseymen in our brigade for $300. The Jersey boys beat [in] 20 innings & a inning not played."[89] A few days later, the "19th Mass[achusetts] regt and the 7th Michigan have had a great game of ball to day." Private James Decker wrote his sister, "The stakes were one hundred & ten dollars a side. the [sic] Mass boys beat & won the money."[90] If baseball was not in the offing, then soldiers found their own sports upon which to wager. Isolated in distant Oregon, Corporal Bensell related the bets that soldiers placed on the catfights at their post. Soldiers pitted their cats against each other, and, when catfights got boring, against a weasel captured from under a wood pile. Bensell reported that the weasel won every time until "Skookum," the champion cat, "mimeloused" the weasel.[91] Boxing matches were another common sporting event that involved wagering, but not always as planned. Private John Bowman of the Iron Brigade was a noted country brawler that openly challenged any man to face him. A New York regiment included a professional prize fighter in its ranks, and bet heavily on their man to defeat Bowman. Bowman, however, thrashed his opponent, and the New Yorkers took a beating of their own through their lost bets.[92]

With so much horseflesh around the army, horse racing soon became the preferred animal sport upon which to place a bet. Officers vied with each other to prove their horsemanship and to show off their prized animals, providing the soldiers a spectator sport and an opportunity to wager. In a race between horses posted by the II and V Corps, only a broken stirrup permitted the II Corps horse to win "by three feet," and, with entire corps betting on the outcome, "about $25,000 changed hands," including the money of General Joseph J. Bartlett, who alone lost $1000.[93] To ensure the security of their wagers, soldiers were not above a bit of cheating. Soldiers in the Eleventh Indiana not only possessed a fast horse, but a "little fellow in our regiment that had been a professional jockey." The soldiers arranged a race against an officer and his horse from a New York regiment, but the New Yorker would only race against other commissioned officers. The Indiana troops simply dressed their rider in a captain's uniform, arranged the race, and cleaned up on the bet.[94] Horse racing between officers occurred regularly throughout the war, but it was not without danger. Deaths and serious injuries occurred with alarming regularity, and because the races were public spectacles, the deaths occurred in front of hundreds of witnesses. General Joseph Hooker even banned horse racing after one particularly horrendous accident. In March 1863, two horsemen participating in a steeple chase collided, and "the sound of the horses [*sic*] heads as they struck each other could have been heard far across the field. Both riders were thrown together with such force as to mortally injure one, who died the following day, and cripple the other for life."[95] Samuel Cormany of the Sixteenth Pennsylvania Cavalry witnessed the accident, but reported that it was not the only one. He recorded in his diary "3 men killed and 4 horses."[96]

Officers who did not provide some form of diversion for their troops usually regretted it, because soldiers with time on their hands and no enemy to fight often turned upon themselves. Fights broke out over unit pride, the oddest of possessions, or simply because there was nothing better to do. "There were five up us in Company C that were wounded fighting among themselves." Henry F. Charles remembered in his postwar memoirs, ". . . our company always held the record for the most wounded before we got to the front. But, if we had no Johnnies to fight, we would fight among ourselves."[97] Private Alfred Bellard barely avoided involvement in a fight among the members of his regiment as soldiers fought because of "a dislike between the city boys and country ones" from different companies.[98] Other soldiers fought over pilfered firewood, to defend the honor of their officers when insulted by other companies, or over simple things like pet dogs. Private Bensell's diary contains the description of a fight triggered when the dogs of another company killed the pet fawn of his company, "a fight in the mess room was the result."[99] Although deaths were rare, soldiers suffered for their violent clashes. On their way from Indiana to Tennessee, some Indiana soldiers engaged in a bout of drinking. Fighting resulted when "at least half were drunk. They had several fights, and quite a number came away with bruised faces and black eyes."[100] Officers tried to punish soldiers for fighting, but soldiers still had to exist within the same unit, and short of discharging one or the other, the army could do little to deter soldiers who wanted to beat up each other. "Private Mark Whitebread and [Orderly] Charles Russell had a fight." Lieutenant Lewis Luckenbill jotted in his diary, "Whitebread was ordered to the guard house and orderly Russell to his tent under arrest. At dress parade, it was read that Whitebread was to carry a log weighing 20 pounds for five days and Russell reduced to the ranks."[101] Soldiers did occasionally die as a result from these brawls, sometimes in the oddest of ways. Private Charlie Mosher noted the death of a fellow soldier, Nathan Wright, in his diary. "The night before he died," Mosher reported, "he got into a fight with a fellow prisoner, and bit off his finger." Mosher did not provide evidence if the chewed digit caused Wright's death or if that was simply a coincidence.[102] Although fighting rarely accomplished anything constructive, on some occasions it did produce positive results. "John Richardson gave [George] Tumblin rather a severe thrashing, wich [*sic*] gave the boys, generaly [*sic*], great satisfaction, as Tumblin has been the bully heretofore."[103]

Fighting was often the by-product of rivalries that developed between groups of young men who focused their attention on other adversaries when their Confederate foes were not present. Some Union soldiers created enemies more than they created friends among their fellow soldiers, and challenges to honor or unit pride soon escalated out of control. Soldiers even quarreled within the ranks of their own regiment. A significant example of this is the rivalry between the men of the Second Massachusetts Cavalry. Massachusetts men made up most of the regiment, but the unit included one company, Company A, made up of California volunteers. Although nominally a unit, an internal rivalry developed because of the attention lavished on the Californians. "The other companies are red-hot with jealousy," wrote Californian Charles Briggs. "[W]e are so much better dressed; more uniform in size; more particular in our dress [when] on duty." According to at least one source, the Californians also deserted from the unit in smaller percentages than did the Massachusetts men. Rivalries between the two groups also included complaints by the California officers that they were too low on the seniority list compared to Massachusetts officers, and the senior California officer, Major DeWitt Thompson, also complained about the practice of excluding him from command decisions. The tensions continued until the regiment permitted Thompson to return to California, ostensibly to recruit replacement soldiers but really to relieve themselves of a quarrelsome officer.[104]

Rivalries developed between regiments in close quarters with each other, especially if the regiments were from different service branches. Charles Wills of the Ninth Illinois jotted down such a clash in his diary after "an artillery man stabbed one the 9th and got knocked, kicked, and bayoneted for it. The artillery [men] have sworn to have revenge and every hickory man [member of the Ninth Illinois] . . . they see they pounce onto." Two years later, the rivalry with the artillery still simmered. "Cogswell's battery attempted to pass us on the march," Wills wrote in September 1863, "but our two advanced companies fixed bayonets, and by a few motions stopped the proceedings. Cogswell got very wrathy, but when Colonel Wright proposed to shoot him . . . he became calmer." The Ninth soon developed a reputation as "the meanest set of men, that was every thrown together," prone to fight any perceived challenge. If any soldier was "foolish enough to ask a question [that the Ninth did not like] . . . he'll wish himself a mile under ground before he hears all the answers, and ten to one not a whit of the information he asked for will be in any one of them."[105] Regimental rivalries even encompassed soldiers from the same state. Rivalries between the Second and Fifth Michigan regiments became so strained that one officer believed that the men of the Second "would today rather shoot or bayonet one of the 5th Mich. than a Secesh."[106] Basic issues like food could also trigger regimental clashes. Two Pennsylvania cavalry regiments clashed over limited food supplies, which "started a row, and a small engagement ensued" before officers could get their men under control.[107] Rivalries were not only between the enlisted men; officers got into the act as well. "The col. of the 25th N.Y. challenged the 118th Penn. Vols. To fight his regiment," Herman White informed his parents, "and gave order to his sentinels to shoot any of the 118th that crossed his lines."[108]

Moving up the organizational chart, rivalries also developed between different army corps. "This 19th Corps is a portion of [General Philip] Sheridan's command and helped him win those glorious victories in the [Shenandoah] valley," an Illinois soldier wrote, "They . . . have already had some difficulty with our troops. . . . I saw the wind up of a snug little fight between a portion of the 20th and 19th Corps. Noticed about 40 bloody faces. All this kind of work grows out of corps pride."[109] If a corps performed poorly in battle, or if it consisted of particular troops that other corps found easy to discriminate against, rivalry was also a result. The best example of this was the scorn heaped upon the XI Corps after the disastrous defeat at Chancellorsville. Commanded by Major General Oliver O. Howard, the XI absorbed the brunt of Confederate General Thomas "Stonewall" Jackson's flank attack that nearly collapsed the entire Union position. As the first unit to collapse under Jackson's onslaught, the XI Corps took the blame for the subsequent Union defeat, regardless of whether the accusation was correct or not. Because nearly half of the soldiers in the corps were of German descent (thirteen of the twenty-seven regiments in the corps), the foreign troops became an easy excuse for the general failure of the Army of the Potomac. "We found many panic-stricken Dutchmen, whom we endeavored to rally, by pounding them vigorously with our sabers and leveling the bayonets of our men at them," James Ames wrote, squarely placing the blame for the failure on the German members of the XI Corps.[110] The stigma of failure went with men of the corps wherever they went. "The new men [assigned to the regiment] are most[ly] all dutch and two or three of them were in the eleventh Corps at the time of thier [sic] big skadadle at Chancelorsville," Private James Miller of the One Hundred-eleventh Pennsylvania wrote his parents, "but is my opinion that is they try that trick with us . . . the old men of our regt will shoot them like dogs as they will deserve."[111] Miller was not the only one with that attitude. "We know the 11th Corps is not far from here," David Nichol wrote his sister, "but this is poor consolation for it there is a fight, we expect to see the country overrun with "Flying Dutchmen," as before."[112] The men of the Second Massachusetts Cavalry paused from their internal rivalry to criticize the XI Corps. "The 11th Corps disgraced themselves," a soldier wrote, "but what can you expect from Germans."[113] Soldiers of the XI Corps' themselves felt ashamed of their unit, and only the successful participation of the unit in the defense of Chattanooga in late 1863 restored some of the unit's pride. The damage to the corps' reputation was too great to recover, however, and the army soon merged the depleted XI and XII Corps to form the new XX Corps.

The troops of the XI Corps were not the only ones to face nationalistic prejudice, and ethnic rivalries strained relations within the army throughout the war as Irish, German, and other foreign-born troops became the targets of nativist discrimination. Compounding this problem, units often drew components from the diverse American melting pot, so discrimination and stereotyping became difficult for troops to overcome. One soldier described the makeup of his unit as "the Yankee with supposed knowledge of every thing, the German whom you must not cross, the keen Frenchman, and the fiery Irishman, all strangers to one another like a lot of new horses together, if one got cross and kicked, other would kick."[114] Irish troops, already subject to antebellum social discrimination, were the most frequent target of bias because they more than any other immigrant group reveled in their non-American identity. Irish units took time out to celebrate St. Patrick's Day, highlighting their separate ethnicity. "As St. Patrick's Day approaches," Thomas Galwey recollected, "great preparations for its observance are made by the Irish Brigade," and Colonel Patrick Guiney permitted his Irish troops to decorate their camps, take time out for special games, and issue three extra whiskey rations.[115] The maintenance of Irish heritage did not sit well with nativist Americans, and trouble was the result. "Three or four men got into a row the Irish Saturday night." Private William Lamson wrote to his sweetheart back home, "Bill knocked down two or three and got a Brickbat on his ankle which makes him lame and another one was hit on head with a club."[116] Major General Alvin Voris believed that "The intelligent colored man is much more respectable and safe as a voter than the Irish."[117] Even Chaplain Stuckenberg allowed his nativist bias to overcome his Christian charity. "The very fact of being placed in an Irish brigade was very disappointing to us," he wrote his wife. ". . . Irishmen in this brigade are rough, a week ago yesterday many were drunk, they were fighting et cet, and that after attending mass in the morning."[118] At Newport, Virginia, in March 1863, a clash between Irish soldiers and a Rhode Island regiment almost became tragic. After Rhode Island men picked on a lone Irish soldier from the Forty-eighth Pennsylvania, the incident escalated into a general brawl between the two regiments, with the Pennsylvanians getting the upper hand in each clash. In response, the Rhode Islanders "brought out their Pistols and began firing and the bullets whistled past my tent. . . . There were none of our boys wounded but the Rhode Island Regt carried two to the Hospital next morning[;] they were wounded by their own men. . . . There were eleven shots fired by the Rhode Islanders but none of our boys [were] wounded."[119]

The imagery of Irish constantly drinking and fighting, regardless of the reality of the representation, certainly fit the stereotypical view most antebellum Americans had of the Irish, perceptions that found a home in the army as well. Anything "Irish" became an insult, as when John Haley described the redundant effort of the Christian Commission to give Bibles to the men in his regiment who were already so pious that "Bibles are plentiful as dogs in an Irish neighborhood." Haley also played upon the stereotype of the drunken Irishman, claiming that an Irishman in his Maine regiment believed that there was no sense in paying for meat "since half of it is bone." The Irishman preferred to "buy whiskey with no bones."[120] Describing his fellow soldiers in his unit, John Westervelt of the First New York Engineers played upon traditional stereotypes of drinking to describe an Irish colleague. "John McKee, an Irishman," Westervelt described, ". . . is sloven in his dress and manners, using his fingers in preference to knife, fork, or spoon. Is immoderately fond of whiskey . . . He enlisted as a carpenter but knows more about distilling liquors."[121] Even when Irish soldiers performed well, stereotyping allowed nativists to diminish their accomplishments. An oft repeated Civil War tale involved the brave and heroic actions of an Irish soldier on the battlefield, who repeatedly exposed himself to the enemy, only to admit later that he was simply recovering his whiskey flask, his most important possession.[122] This particular stereotype even appeared in the 1993 move *Gettysburg*, where Captain Ellis Spear (Donal Louge) capped the triumphant defense of Little Round Top by offering Colonel Joshua Chamberlain (Jeff Daniels) a swig from his flask.

The antagonisms caused by nativist bias were matched by another open rivalry, the contentious relationship between veteran soldiers who had enlisted in the first months of the war and newer recruits who entered the army much later. The early volunteers considered themselves true patriots, citizens who enlisted to save their country in its time of need. They did it for the sake of the nation, to ensure that the government would not, as Lincoln put it, "perish from the earth." To the early enlistees, the later recruits were little more than mercenaries, joining the army simply to collect the lucrative enlistment bounties offered by the federal, state, and local governments. Even worse, as far as the early soldiers were concerned, were the draftees. The passage of the Enrollment Act in March 1863 created the first true conscription in U.S. Army history (the Confederacy committed itself to conscription in 1862), creating soldiers whom the old veterans despised as unpatriotic and unworthy soldiers whom the government had to compel to defend the nation. Whether true or not on an individual basis, the veteran soldiers singled out newer recruits for special mistreatment and abuse, such as the accusation of cowardice. "Thoes [sic] *money* soldiers," as Private William Dunn described the later recruits, "are not worth as much as they *cost* for when you heer [sic] firing ahead you may see them hid in the woods."[123] Despite their bias against new recruits, veteran soldiers found themselves surrounded by new men, whether they wanted them or not. The presence of new and untried soldiers threatened unit cohesion, broke long standing chains of command, and undermined the proud reputations that units had earned through long months of fighting. The Iron Brigade, for instance, was outraged when the army broke its purely Western identity by reinforcing the brigade with the One Hundred Sixty-seventh Pennsylvania after the Black Hats suffered huge casualties at Gettysburg. The replacements could not have been more unsuited to join the brigade. They were Easterners, they were mostly draftees, and, worst of all, they had enlisted for only nine months of service.[124] While the Iron Brigade was nearly destroyed at Gettysburg, the Pennsylvanians had yet to see major combat. The men of the Iron Brigade were glad to see the Pennsylvanians gone when the unit disbanded at the end of its term of service, losing only two fatalities in combat, a far cry from the blood shed by their Iron Brigade compatriots.[125] But every unit that received replacement soldiers had to deal with an awkward new arrangement. "Our corps is filling up with drafted men." Private Charles Barber wrote, "We expect 700 in our regt in a few days. There is only 40 men on duty in our regt now but seven hundred will make quite a regt but the old troops do not like to be put in with conscripts. They [the conscripts] look down hearted and of course are awkward in the ranks."[126] A common means of demeaning and degrading the new recruits was to insult not only their motivation, but their social standing and moral proclivities as well. This permitted the veterans to accentuate the differences between their higher moral decision to enlist with the deeply flawed draftees who came after them. "Thieves, cutthroats, robbers, [and] police criminals now make up a large proportion of the men who are sent to fill the ranks," an officer of the Tenth Connecticut complained to his hometown newspaper, "They rob the few honest men who are with them on their way here, rob or steal as soon as they get here . . . do you call it 'supporting' us to send us such material?"[127]

The reaction of other units to the arrival of new recruits and replacements was more or less the same, although some units took the opportunity to vent their frustrations and animosity upon the unsuspecting arrivals. "We have got a lot of new recruits." John Brobst wrote his wife, "They are as green as were when we first came out. They make real nice play-things for us. We have our own fun with them and call them four hundred dollar men [the amount of their enlistment bonuses]. They do not like it very much, but it can't be helped. We do not want them."[128] Wilbur Fisk described the reception the Twenty-sixth New Jersey, a nine-month regiment, received when brigaded with the Second Vermont. The New Jersey troops did not make a good first impression. "A regiment of nine months men," Fisk mocked, "came out here with big bounties, and, of course, has seen more hardships, endured more privations, and suffered more generally than any of the old soldiers ever dream of." The "two hundred dollar men," as Fisk called them (apparently the New Jersey bounty was not as lucrative as Pennsylvania's), became the victim of every prank and trick the Vermonters could think of. After bearing the brunt of this abuse, officers of the brigade "advised the Jerseys to let the Second boys along or they would find more than they could handle, and the Jerseys are beginning to think it best to accept this advice."[129] Harassing newly arrived recruits helped the veterans to establish a form of social separation and pecking order that they expected the replacements to observe, thereby justifying their actions, as Private Henry Abbott indicates when he proudly proclaimed that "We have put the screws to them [the new recruits] like the Devil."[130] Private Edward Wightman, as a new recruit, saw firsthand the mistreatment and hazing that late enlistees had to endure. Wightman, however, did not take the abuse sitting down. Set upon by several veterans, Wightman "let fly right and left with such effect that after a short and violent contest, the 'boys' were dumbfounded" and left Wightman alone after that.[131] But recruits rarely got the upper hand on veteran troops. When a "great feud" developed between veterans in one regiment and volunteers in a nearby regiment led to assaults on some of the veterans, "a party of chosen fighters, generally under the leadership of Sergeant Broadus, a strapping fellow, of the kind who professes to be able to "whip his weight in wildcats," started in to avenge these attacks."[132]

Veteran soldiers were so dedicated to their claim of moral superiority over the new recruits that they even spurned other veteran soldiers who left the army when their terms of enlistment ended. The Union faced a manpower crisis in 1864. The vast majority of the early enlistees signed up for three-year terms of service, terms set to expire in 1864. If the early volunteers, the most seasoned veterans of the army, went home, the Union lost not only a significant portion of its armies, but the most experienced troops as well. To entice soldiers to reenlist, the army offered incentives. Regiments that reenlisted at least three-quarters of its remaining men earned the designation of a "Veteran Regiment" to distinguish themselves from the new drafted or bounty recruits, as well as a chevron on their sleeves to distinguish their status. They also received a thirty-five day furlough to go home, ostensibly to recruit replacements for their depleted formations, but in reality a thinly disguised reward for renewing their service. The decision of some veterans to not reenlist caused some hard feelings among their fellow soldiers who chose to stay. By leaving the army in its time of need, veterans considered the nonreenlistees as little better than the despised bounty men. "Several more have re-enlisted, men who up to the last hour condemned the Officers as designing Knaves," wrote Private Bensell, who himself chose not to reenlist. "These 'Veterans' have created a dangerous feeling in abusing those who choose not to serve longer. It would be impossible for "D" Co[mpany] to live on amicable terms again."[133] The lure of additional funds from other regiments led even Regulars to abandon their old units. "Inducements have been offered to the men to reenlist but as yet none have accepted them." George Merryweather wrote, "No man will bind himself for five years & $400 Bounty [in the Regulars] when he can get $1300 bounty in the Volunteer Service."[134]

The most intense and violent rivalries emerged when troops originating from, or fighting in, the Eastern Theater of the war came in contact with troops fighting or born in the Western Theater. Each side saw each other through the prism of stereotypes. Easterners perceived Westerners as crude, ill-bred, and unpolished by discipline. Westerners saw Easterners as effete, over-educated, and cowed by the prowess of Robert E. Lee. When the soldiers of the two regions came into contact, or when men from one region found themselves attached to armies in the other region, these stereotypes created friction that led to nasty rivalries. Westerners liked to mock the Easterners as less than manly, based upon the belief that factory work and shop clerking did not create a manly physique like the rough work in the rural West. "Eastern troops don't look like our Western men," George Cadman opined. "[T]hey have not the weight or the muscle that the Western men have. [T]he 17th N.Y. was the rattiest rowdiest looking regiment I have seen yet, small ill-shaped fellows looking as if they were the rakings of a pile after Old Nick had done with it."[135] Conversely, Captain Daniel Oakley of the Second Massachusetts considered the Westerners lacking in basic military discipline when he wrote "We observed in the Western troops an air of independence hardly consistent with the nicest discipline."[136] General John Gibbon agreed. Assigned to the Iron Brigade, Gibbon found Western men to be "active, intelligent young men" but also discovered they "would not take any nonsense from anybody, with or without shoulder straps" and insubordination was a common problem.[137] For their part, the Westerners accepted as a matter of pride that they did not accept discipline blindly, a shortcoming they perceived in their Eastern counterparts. Discipline and tight drill looked impressive, the Westerners conceded, but it did not translate into military success. What Westerners lacked in spit and polish, they made up for in victories, and their triumphs led to a scornful attitude toward the Army of the Potomac. "The Army of the Potomac has never done anything and never will," was the simple analysis of Wisconsin soldier John Brobst, "If they had done half as much as the western army, this war would have been rubbed out before this time. This army [Brobst was a member of the Twenty-fifth Wisconsin of the VII Corps, part of the army of Arkansas at the time of this letter] will have to go down there and take Richmond for them, poor fellows."[138] Lack of regard led to stereotyping of Eastern troops, and Western soldiers cast broad aspersions on their abilities without gaining any firsthand knowledge. "The rest of the troops here are all "Eastern men," with whom we have little Sympathy, or they with us." William Abraham wrote his brother, "The fact is there is no men I like so well as those from West Va. and Ohio, the real 'Black Eastern Yankees' and 'Marylanders' I don't like nohow."[139]

Proud of their accomplishments in conquering the West while Eastern troops seemed unable to capture Richmond, Western troops sought reasons to explain their claimed military superiority over their Eastern compatriots. Brevet Major General Alvin Voris, an Ohio native, believed that Western troops, while frequent violators of the legal sense of discipline, were more apt to obey the military definition of discipline. "This brigade has had hardly a case of desertion," Voris wrote his wife, ". . . while several of the Eastern Regiments here have had more desertions from a single Regt this winter. . . . I know Regiments that cannot be trusted on the picket line . . . to keep from desertion. I need not say to you these are not Western troops." Voris also believed that Westerners had a stronger constitution, and were healthier than Easterners, describing "some of the Yankee Regts have more than half of their men sick. They do not stand the grief as well as the Western men do."[140] Supporting the theory that Eastern troops were more prone to desertion, Private Robert H. Strong also believed the Westerners adhered to military discipline to a greater degree, pointing out that Eastern troops usually had a camp guard to keep them from leaving. "We troops of the West seldom set a camp guard when we had a strong picket out." Strong remembered in his memoirs, "As long as the boys were in camp at drill and rollcall, they were allowed at other times to go where they pleased."[141]

When forced to serve together, troops from different regions usually perceived a favoritism of one type of soldier over another. Such was the case during Sherman's March to the Sea in 1864. The XX Corps was the only formation that contained a majority of Eastern troops amidst Sherman's predominantly Western army. Among the members of the XX Corps, in turn, was a minority of Western regiments in its ranks. Although fighting in the Western Theater, the western-born troops of the XX Corps believed themselves the victims of Eastern bias, claiming that Western troops received fewer promotions and benefits relative to their Eastern compatriots.[142] Robert H. Strong, a Westerner in the XX Corps, held a grudge against his Eastern officers even years afterwards when he wrote his memoirs. "Part of the trouble between the general and us was the difference between Western and Eastern troops." Strong wrote, "They, the Easterners, would stand for more than we [Westerners] would. . . . General [John W.] Geary was a martinet, much stiffer with his boys than we of the West could stand."[143] Soldiers of the Twenty-seventh Indiana, attached to the XII Corps in the Army of the Potomac, also claimed regional bias. "What a detestable brigade we are in," complained Simpson Hamrick wrote to his brother, "We had an inspection of all the regiments owing to the prejudice Eastern officers have for us Western soldiers. They reported us in a bad condition and poor discipline. We and some other of the best regiments in the army was condemned."[144]

Rivalry between the two regions soon begat open competition that escalated beyond simple matters of pride, often with dire results. In New Orleans, the Eleventh Indiana troops mocked the Easterners in their "white starched linen shirts . . . profusion of plumes and cockades . . . [and] white paper collars and white cotton gloves." To manifest their disdain for the troops from the East, the Eleventh "began introducing ourselves by giving them lessons in the fine art of pugilism," by picking fights with any Easterner who crossed their path.[145] Private Jacob Switzer was a soldier of the Twenty-Second Iowa, a Western unit in the same brigade with two New York regiments. In 1863, enmity between Easterners and Westerners translated into a marching challenge. Breaking camp on a hot day, the rival regiments set a blistering pace as they marched to a new campsite. By the end of the day, the New York regiments had fallen out of formation by the side of road, while the Iowans arrived at the new site intact "without a dozen stragglers except our sick." Switzer gloated that the "clodhoppers of the prairie" had subdued the New Yorkers, seemingly unconcerned about reports that sixteen New Yorkers had died from heatstroke.[146] The rivalry within Sherman's army became so intense that a brawl broke out between the XX Corps and the XIV Corps in Fayetteville, North Carolina, resulting in numerous injuries and the death of a soldier. The most pointless violence occurred after Lee's surrender at Appomattox, when the fighting and killing should have ended. The most public attempt at regional upstaging occurred at the end of the war during the Grand Review of the Armies, the massive public parade of Union forces in May 1865 that signaled the end of the war. Sherman's army, despite its rustic appearance and reputation, was determined to outshine its rivals. Daniel Chisholm wrote in his diary that his unit was getting "ready for the grand review in Washington. We drew new clothing, and are busy as nailers getting ready, and it takes no little work to get ourselves in shape. . . . The Army of the Potomac, Sherman's

Boys, and Phil Sheridan's Troopers are all bent on the same point."[147] On May 24, 1865, after Sherman's army paraded up Pennsylvania Avenue, a clash between Sherman's army and soldiers from the Army of the Potomac turned deadly. Sherman's Westerners, returning to their camp, taunted the Easterners by calling them, among other things, "bread and butter men," a comment on their "soft" abilities. "Hot words were followed by blows and then by a resort to firearms," wrote a witness, "Two were killed and several wounded" in a futile waste of life when the war was essentially over.[148]

The unleashing of firearms was not surprising, considering that Union soldiers had a propensity to discharge their weapons whenever they wanted. The concept of army discipline included the idea of restraint of behavior; soldiers were not to do what they wanted whenever they wanted. When it came to their weapons, however, soldiers frequently ignored concepts of discipline. Citizen-soldiers rationalized that they were soldiers, and their weapons were an extension of themselves. Soldiers seemed to squeeze off shots whenever, and at whatever, the fancy struck them, despite the efforts of officers to control them. The level of proficiency with firearms varied as widely as the backgrounds of the soldiers themselves. Soldiers from the western states and rural areas had more experience with weaponry, and the frontier ethos of associating proficiency with firearms as a badge of manhood was very strong. Soldiers in the more established eastern states and urban areas had generally less experience with firearms, although some former members of immigrant urban gangs knew how to use a weapon. A systemic effort at introductory firearms training could have produced soldiers that at least respected the power of the weapon in their hands, but the concept of army Basic Training was decades away, and soldiers received little in the way of weapons training. Private Jacob Switzer remembered the extent of his training at Camp Pope, Iowa: using "wooden bayonets we challenged the salute of the wooden sword of the officer of the guard . . . while the private had a private 'confab' with his best girl who had just called to see him a few minutes."[149] The firearms training of the One Hundred-tenth Ohio amounted to two sessions, two weeks apart, where soldiers fired only one round apiece.[150] Weapons training was so infrequent that when the Third Minnesota finally got to fire live rounds, soldiers in a nearby camp presumed that they were under enemy attack.[151] The men of the Ninth Maine only got to fire their weapons as part of Christmas celebrations in 1862, when offered a "Jeff David effigy to shoot at" and their colonel offered a $20 gold piece for the sharpest marksman.[152] These examples were the rule rather than the exception, and formal training remained a rare thing. Consequently, the mixture of youthful exuberance, inadequate knowledge, and live ammunition made life dangerous in the vicinity of army camps.

Soldiers were particularly keen on trying out rifles as soon as the army issued them. The soldiers of the Twenty-ninth USCT exuberantly tested their rifles until their colonel issued a general order threatening to arrest anyone firing their weapon without orders.[153] Lieutenant John Campbell found himself under arrest because "one of the boys in the company fired a charge of damp powder out of his gun, for which he was arrested by the Colonel and I was arrested by the same power because I did not arrest the man who fired the gun. Not being in command of the company, I didn't consider it my business."[154] Returning to camp from picket duty, soldiers of the Thirty-ninth New York would "gamble on who could hit designated targets, branches, posts, etc. . . . When stray bullets whizzed over the heads of officers they believed to be under attack."[155] Not realizing the deadly power of modern weapons and ammunition, soldiers had a frightening tendency to shoot any anything that caught their eye. "Sometimes a Shark Shows [sic] itself along shore," Private Charles Musser wrote his father from Clarksville, Texas, "and then you ought to see the scatterment among the boys. He invariably gets cropped by a Minnie ball or two before he gets out of reach of our rifles."[156] Instead of the laborious process of extracting a loaded round, soldiers of the One Hundred Forty-ninth Pennsylvania fired out the round, usually at a distant building occasionally occupied by civilians.[157] On their way to defend Washington, DC, early in the war, witnesses claimed that men of the Second Massachusetts "fired their muskets out of the windows of their [train] cars, killed hogs, and endangered life."[158]

Because random firing was not expressly forbidden by the Articles of War, the worst action a soldier could face was a court-martial for disobeying orders. "Many stray shots are fired on picket." Captain Theodore Dodge wrote, "In camp it is different: there we are strict, and I am sorry to say that two of my men are now at Head Quarters awaiting a court-martial for 'willful discharging of fire arms.'"[159] The loose discipline with firearms was so prevalent, however, that prosecuting offenders threatened to tie up the military legal system indefinitely. Instead, the army left the problem of finding solutions to regimental and company officers. More often than not, soldiers refused to confess to random shootings and, unless an officer actually observed a soldier pulling the trigger, finding an offender was difficult. A good example of this is found in a memoir by a soldier of the Sixth Michigan. "A hog came along, and our boys . . . could not resist temptation . . . [a soldier] leveled his musket and brought Mister Hog to a halt." Private Ben Johnson remembered, "No sooner did he do so, then bang, bang, bang, went the picket line, all along, and the whole force was turned out under arms to resist the incoming foe." Officers tried to find out who was responsible for the false alarm, but Johnson proudly reported that "it was useless to try to find out from Michigan men, because they stood in together."[160] Despite the soldiers' code of silence, officers tried their best to curb the practice, if for no other reason than to protect life and limb. Colonel John Taggert of the Twelfth Pennsylvania Reserves cracked down hard on his men, beating and striking some of them after they haphazardly fired their weapons out the window of a moving train.[161]

The discharge of weapons was a serious problem in the Union army, made even worse because, of course, some of the shots hit things and people that the shooters did not intend to hit. A stray shot wounded Colonel Thomas F. Gallagher's horse, although the "wound is not fatal" and the horse recovered.[162] The attempts by officers to control the random firing by pickets were to avoid accidental deaths, such as the unfortunate soldier of the Twenty-first Massachusetts. "It appears that the guard of the Eighth Heavy Artillery (colored troops) are in the habit of going down to the bank on the railroad, each morning as soon as relieved, to discharge their muskets," a soldier wrote in May 1865, "On the opposite bank of the road a detachment of the Twenty-first Massachusetts are encamped. Yesterday the darkeys poured their volley into the soldiers' camp opposite, mortally wounding one and slightly wounding another."[163] But USCT troops were not the only ones guilty of such reckless behavior. Second Lieutenant Samuel Rikker described the accidental shooting of a First Lieutenant while searching a home. Fortunately, the wound proved nonlethal, but Rikker darkly ribbed the man who pulled the trigger that if he "did not shoot well enough for my 2nd lieutenancy" to get the wounded man's rank and to "take better aim next time" to ensure his promotion.[164] Other soldiers also had close calls. "A careless man this moment let off his piece." Edward Wightman noted while in the midst of writing his brother, "The ball pierced the tent next to this one in which I am living and passed through the thigh of a man not 12 feet distant."[165] A Pennsylvania soldier "had his arm dreadfully shattered by the accidental discharge of a musket," forcing a surgeon to act, and he "under the shade of a tree amputated the limb."[166]

Careless soldiers occasionally managed to shoot themselves, causing a great deal of concern to the soldiers around them. The discharge of weaponry was serious enough, but soldiers oddly seemed more shaken by the accidental maiming or death of a comrade by their own hand than by enemy bullets. "A sad accident happened in my tent this morning, resulting in the death of Frank Johnson," a shocked John Campbell wrote in his diary, "He was placing a loaded revolver away when it accidentally went off and the ball entered his head at the corner of the right eye. . . . Nothing, not even the horrors of the battlefield—ever game me such a shock as this."[167] A Wisconsin private, attempting to extract a round from his musket, caused the weapon to discharge and "ramrod and all went through his right hand, tearing it to peaces [sic]. The Dr's [sic] have concluded to cut off the hand."[168] Searching for a suspected spy, another soldier "stuck the stock of his gun into it [a bush] and when he pulled it out the hammer caught and discharged the gun killing him instantly."[169] Others who shot themselves were fortunate enough to survive. A major in the Second Massachusetts Cavalry carelessly allowed a pistol to discharge as he inspected it, narrowly missing him as the ball passed through the visor of his cap.[170] Thomas Walton, in a brief diary entry, noted that "Andrew Elles shot himself in the leg" but "was taken to Hospital" and expected to recover.[171] Elisha Peterson, who prided himself on the care with which he handled his weapon, mentioned to his parents that his company sergeant accidentally shot himself while "playing with a pistol."[172]

Far too often, however, the tragic result of careless gunplay was the needless death of another Union soldier. A careless discharge took the life of John Bell of the One Hundred Fourteenth Pennsylvania. "The bullet penetrated [his] left eye and took away the left side his head," a comrade wrote. "It was a ghastly sight."[173] Another soldier lost his life to a tragic oversight. "One gun had been left loaded after the battle . . ." Frank Shiras wrote, "it went off killing one of our best Men Named Charles Bright."[174] Harlan Bailey noted to his sister of the "terrible accident in this regiment yesterday. Two fellows were scuffling when one fiered [sic] a gun in fun not knowing it was loaded and shot the other dead on the spot. The ball went in back of his ear and came out the top of his head," killing him instantly.[175] The hazardous gunfire frequently came from new recruits for whom army life was still filled with novelty. "Some recruts [sic] got to fooling with the muskets and bursting caps at each other." John Ferguson observed, "One gun being loaded, went off, blowing the whole pate from one of there [sic] fool heads and scattering his brains all over the place. He was killed imediently [sic]. Green recruts, like regts, has got to learn by sad experience."[176]

Like most accidents, shooting deaths were avoidable, as in the accidental death of one officer. "Notwithstanding orders to remove the [percussion] caps from our guns," Billy Davis wrote, "one soldier failed to do so, and slipping fell and accidentally discharged the piece, the bullet struck and killed an Ohio lieutenant."[177] A similar accident caused another death in the Twentieth Maine. "The man [who fired the fatal shot] supposed he had his own gun that he had discharged [to unload it]," William Lamson described, "but [instead] got a loaded one that was standing beside it. He was careless or he would have seen that it was capped." Careless handling of firearms seemed tragically common in the Twentieth. On another occasion, Lamson related that "A sad accident happened while I was eating dinner. A man of Co. G took a gun by the muzzle to pull it out of a tent . . . when it went off wounding one man severely in the bowels and 2 others in the arms. . . . Night before last a man in Co. F on guard was fooling around with his gun when it went off wounding his leg so that he had to have it amputated."[178] Accidents also occurred with much larger guns, as Henry Bear noted in his diary. "There was a sad accident occurred today." Bear jotted, "While the Artillery was practicing today with blank cartrige [cartridge] there was a canon [sic] went off while the gunner drawing out the ramrod, and tore his right arm off close to the elbow, and tore the whole side of his face off and burnt the hair off his head. . . . The Captain was not noticing, he gave the word to fire."[179]

A by-product of poor weapons discipline was the propensity to fire at potential threats before determining their true nature. Approaching a picket line, especially at night, manned by soldiers with a propensity to shoot first and ask questions later was a dangerous practice. Private Henry McCaslin of the Twenty-seventh Indiana lost his life when accidentally shot by the picket of his regiment, who thought him a rebel scout.[180] Charles Haydon gruesomely described another victim of a picket with an itchy trigger finger. "One of the Mass. 14th was shot last night by a sentinel of his own Co. whom he insisted on attempting to pass." Haydon mentioned, "Half his lower jaw, all his left cheek & left eye were blow entirely away. He is still alive."[181] Hunting for food to supplement their diet, "two privates of the 9th Ind[iana] went foraging, and when after some chickens one shot the other."[182] Larger groups of men also fired upon each other in confusion. "The 18th and 22nd Indiana regiments . . . had a battle among themselves last night through mistake." John Campbell noted, "[T]he pickets mistook each other for enemies and the scouting companies fired on each other, killing several and wounding quite a number. . . . The sad affair was caused by criminal dereliction of duty among the head officers."[183] Poor weapons discipline was also to blame for the death of two soldiers of the Sixty-third USCT when, on a raid in Arkansas, two members of the regiment were wounded due to "careless shooting."[184] Near New Bern, North Carolina, in 1862, Union soldiers fired upon each other because the state quartermaster had issued one of the regiments gray overcoats, causing the other regiment to mistake them for Confederates, and "as soon as our men saw them they fired three volleys into them before they found out their mistake."[185]

A final subject that vexed the army's sense of discipline, but which it did little to curb, was prostitution. While not a socially acceptable practice, the public did not shun prostitution to the point of extinction either. Brothels, streetwalkers, and other elements of the sex trade were common features of every significant American city in the nineteenth century, and were permitted to exist for a variety of reasons. Although Victorian-era morality demanded restraint and moral piety, middle- and upper-class Victorian men justified the patronage of brothels on the grounds that prostitutes provided sexual release in a manner that Victorian men could not achieve with their morally idealized wives. The same attitude justified the taking of mistresses among the affluent classes, an outlook that did not apply to women seeking sexual pleasure. Lower classes also tolerated prostitution as "working girls" provided sexual release for young men and bachelors who either lacked, or could not afford to support, a wife and household. Consequently, the status of brothels corresponded to the class of their clientele, with "Parlor Houses" servicing the upper class and "Panel Houses" providing for the lower classes. There was also a "boys will be boys" attitude regarding masculine behavior, with sexual conquest demonstrations of sexual virility as a measure of manhood and adulthood. As a general rule, the army tolerated prostitution as long as the local community tolerated it, and arrests only occurred when brothels became disruptive and forced either the army or the community to act. Civic and law enforcement leaders also tolerated prostitution. Pragmatic municipal politicians reasoned that prostitution was an evil not likely to disappear any time soon, and regulated and restricted prostitution was the best for which a city could hope. Police also shared this attitude. Brothels could not operate openly without a minimal level of police consent, and prostitution existed within the bounds permitted by police turning a blind eye. In the 1860s, for instance, police in New York City recorded more than six hundred operating brothels in the city, although reformer Dr. William Sanger considered that estimate as considerably below the real number.[186] New York was not the only place where prostitution enjoyed a thriving business. By 1865, more than six thousand prostitutes worked in Chicago, about 3 percent of the total city population.[187]

There were some attempts at reform, but the demand for sex workers and the scope of the business defied attempts to eliminate it. There were individual reformers, like Dr. Sanger, who tried to shed light on the evils of prostitution and the moral damage it inflicted. Some civic leaders, like Boston mayor Josiah Quincy, tried to purge their cities of the sex trade, but their efforts were either insufficient to the task or lasted only as long as the crusader stayed in office.[188] Private organizations engaged in the great reform movements of the antebellum period also targeted prostitution. The Female Moral Reform Society (FMRS), founded in Oberlin, Ohio, in 1835, was the largest reform group, with chapters in most northern states by the early 1840s. Unlike earlier benevolent societies, which catered to the prostitutes as the victims of society, the FMRS also targeted the solicitors of the sex business. Instead of simply blaming the prostitute for her moral failings, the FMRS sought to illuminate the social failings of men who perpetuated prostitution. Among the FMRS agenda were efforts to criminalize adultery, thus punishing those who victimized the victims. Their efforts were unsuccessful, however, and the FMRS died out by the time of the Civil War.[189] Small groups of reformers continued the crusade against urban prostitution, however, throughout the course of the war.

Faced with this type of mixed pubic message, the army was ambivalent about curtailing the solicitation of prostitution, or even shaping the general behavior regarding sex, among its soldiers. Sex was a sensitive issue, and when it came to sex the army took a very different approach from its normal position of controlling a soldier's life. The army considered prostitution a civilian issue, despite the proliferation of prostitution in several areas simply because soldiers were there. Moreover, when it came to other forms of solider/civilian interaction, military justice was quick to assert its authority, but the army was content to turn a blind eye to problems that soldier-supported prostitution tended to create. The army also insisted upon molding recruits into the behavioral model of discipline that the army wanted, but refused to shape attitudes regarding prostitution. The army declined to impose itself on the economic aspect of prostitution, refusing to fine soldiers soliciting sex or even to suggest what a soldier could or could not do with their well-earned pay. This was especially the case at antebellum frontier posts, where prostitution represented one of the few diversions available to soldiers in remote locations. The army also reinforced the antebellum definition of masculinity, supporting (by not condemning) the precept that men were entitled to sex and prostitution was a victimless crime and therefore not a moral offense. Instead of shaping a formal policy regarding prostitution, the army took the position that since soliciting was not banned by the Articles of War, what a soldier did was his own business. Like so many other forms of discipline in this gray area of the Articles, the army left policy-making and its enforcement to regimental and company officers.[190]

Officers certainly had their hands full dealing with prostitution, especially when stationed near urban areas where vice loomed just beyond the boundaries of the camp. Soldiers adopted a casual response to the availability of sex workers, as the war and its horrors blurred the prewar line between the moral and the immoral. What behaviors seemed so easy to codify before enlistment became difficult to defend during the war. Soldiers who casually killed each other one day found it difficult to be critical and judgmental of prostitution the next. Morality became looser, just as religious devotion lost its appeal to many soldiers. Writing to a friend at home in regards to prostitutes, Private Charles Tallman of the Sixth New York Heavy Artillery, agreed with his friend when "you say that there is no harm in it [soliciting prostitution]. . . . for my part, I dont [sic] think that there is, and I would not care if there was. If I could come acrost some gall down here that sold tail to the boys, but we are so far from any city or village that they are some thing that we dont see very often."[191] In this vacuum of principles, soldiers could justify many actions that would have appalled them only months earlier.[192] Instead of shunning the sex trade, the redefined morality of the war (coupled with traditional views of masculinity) meant that a soldier was not a real man if he did not solicit prostitutes. "There was an old saying that no man could be a soldier unless he had gone through Smokey Row," a soldier wrote of his experiences in Nashville's "red light" district. "The street was about three fourths of a mile long and every house and shanty on both sides was a house of ill fame. Women had no thought of dress or decency."[193] Some soldiers also had little decency. Sergeant Major Charles Nickerson, stationed in the New Mexico territory, scandalized his regiment by openly living with a prostitute. A soldier described that Nickerson "has just gone to the river with a Spanish lady, soap & towels."[194] If soldiers missed roll call, officers often had a good idea where to find their men. "At 5 ock Roll Call a number [of] men were absent," wrote Samuel Cormany while encamped near Harrisburg, Pennsylvania, "[a] squad was sent to [the] City, a Doz[en] of us. We visited some 6 or 7 whorehouses, [and] found [Privates] Brough, Bradley, Arnold, White, Earich & May. On way [back] to camp, [we] met some coming, we took them back."[195]

If soldiers were not close to urban areas, prostitutes still managed to find them. In Falmouth, Virginia, a soldier resisted the offer of a women "to marry me last Sunday," even if the marriage was a temporary and financially motivated arrangement. The soldier declined, not because of any moral scruples but because the woman "was homely enough to turn a pail of hot water into ice, forty rods off, by looking at it."[196] Prostitutes made similar officers in Philadelphia by "offering to accompany us to the front," as Charles Haley recounted, but "Their invitations were respectfully but firmly declined."[197] Other "ladies" managed to make it to the camps, however. "To keep prostitutes off the ground . . . [officers] roam about in squads wherever there is a probability of their services being needed." Charles Haydon described, "They took about 25 bbls. of liquor & beer to day which had in some way been smuggled across the river & also 3 women."[198] Sergeant Hartwell wrote to his wife about recent regimental orders restricting the presence of women in camp to assure her that it did not preclude her from visiting him. Instead, he noted, the order was "only to stop a general rush of *bad women* here. If it were not for this order the camp would be over run with prostitutes."[199] The pursuit of the army was so great that Provost Marshal Patrick had to send out "a Cavalry force to examine the Trains for Women" trying to reach the camp.[200] Stationed in Kentucky, Aurelius Voorhis noted the presence of "Two or three women of ill fame [who] had located themselves in a cave not far from town and . . . two of our Regt. [Fourteenth Kentucky] were in the habit of making their quarters there," at least until authorities rooted them out. "The boys were sent to camp," Voorhis related, "and the women shipped across the river."[201] Prostitutes even found their way into hospitals. In a Washington, DC, hospital, John Vautier and "some of the

Stewards caught 2 women of bad repute in some of the wards, where they had been smuggled in by the Ward Masters & had remained over night."[202]

There were dangers associated with prostitution, however. Colonel Newton Colby, responsible for order in Indianapolis, wrote his father about "investigating into the facts connected with the murder of one of the men last night in a house of ill fame. He was shot and instantly killed by a person connected with the house, and the city authorities here are not remarkable for sound loyalty and care not much for the death of a soldier. . . . It is the second or third instance since I have been here of soldiers meeting their death in these houses of prostitution."[203] In Robertson County, Tennessee, an argument over a prostitute led Private Commodore Workman to shoot and kill Private Joshua Wilson "at a house of ill-fame, kept by one Mary Williams." Workman wound up serving three years at hard labor, while Wilson wound up dead.[204] At isolated posts in the New Mexico Territory, the local fandangos were the place to find trouble. If a soldier "becomes disgusted with life" and wished to die, Ovader Hollister wrote, "let him to go a fandango, raise a row, and be killed decently."[205] Eastern cities were equally dangerous. John Holahan, assigned to military police duty, was often busy in Annapolis, Maryland because "Many soldiers and others [are] shot . . . in bawdy houses with which the city abounds. Prostitutes are flocking here from every large city in the Union, and they are reaping a harvest."[206] Even if no one was killed, brothels were still dangerous places. "A great many of the boys . . . went to the houses were common weman [*sic*] were harbered." John Ferguson wrote of the brothels in Terre Haute, Indiana, "Then they got into truble and had there not been so many of them, some would a been killed. . . . But as it was they came out tollereable well. One or two got there nozed cracked a little and some a black eyes."[207]

Although prostitution flourished in every major city, cities close to the war zone experienced the greatest effect of mass prostitution. Nashville's "Smokey Row" was not the only notorious red light district. Soldiers also spent their free time in "Hooker's Division," an area filled with bawdy houses near the Potomac River in Washington, DC. Different brothels identified themselves by colorful business names, such as the Ironclad, Fort Sumter, the Wolf's Den, Unconditional Surrender, or the Bake Oven. By the height of the war, Washington boasted more than 450 brothels (compared to only forty before the war), employing more than seven thousand prostitutes.[208] The situation became so bad that some brothels became too dangerous even for soldiers in large groups. One particularly bad spot, nicknamed Castle Thunder, "was evidently too dangerous for a soldier, as we never found one there," noted a private attached to a military police detail in the area.[209] The prostitutes swarmed into DC almost as fast as did the soldiers. "Soldiers still continue to pour into the city from all quarters," George Bliss wrote in 1862, "and I am told an army of 8000 whores is quartered in the city to supply them with all the pleasures of home. In the city yesterday two passed us in a splendid barouche and threw kisses at Capt. [John B.] Wood and myself."[210] In Louisville, Kentucky, Marshall Miller marveled at the unabashed attitude of prostitutes who, in plain view at the train station, "threw kisses and some wanted to throw something else."[211] Prostitutes were just as brazen in New York City, where Colonel Cavins complained, "An officer can scarcely walk any considerable distance on Broadway . . . without having some pretty miss to smile sweetly at him and slip her card in his hand."[212]

Even communities with relatively small populations gained a reputation for raunchy entertainment when soldiers arrived in large numbers. Pine Bluff, Arkansas, was a prime example. A peaceful town before Union soldiers occupied the area, the community suffered an influx of prostitutes when the Twenty-eighth Wisconsin arrived. Soon officers and men alike were "gambling . . . drinking . . . running after and around, publicly, with fast women, women whose characters are not in the least questionable, for no on suspects them of possessing a spark of virtue or decency."[213] Soon after its capture in 1862, Corinth, Mississippi, became "full of 'fast womin [*sic*]' who have come in a few days and are demoralizing many of the men and with the help of bad whiskey will lay many of them out."[214] Northern cities had similar experiences. Portland, Maine, a city so virtuous that it banned alcohol before the war, still saw an invasion of "ladies of easy virtue," although local newspaper editors were quick to observe that the prostitutes were not locals, as "There has been a great influx of these characters from abroad lately."[215] The Seventy-ninth New York found plenty of diversions in Louisville, Kentucky, especially when payday came around, engaging in conduct described as "deplorable in the extreme."[216] In Alexandria, Virginia, across the river from Washington, DC, the overflow from Hooker's Division also plied their wares. "It is said that one house out of every ten in the city is a bawdy house— it is a perfect Sodom," described Colonel Cavins, ". . . An officer cannot walk the streets without having indecent advances made towards him by a woman." The frank expression of female sexuality seemed to unnerve Cavins, especially when "Women pass along the bank of the Potomac and look at men while they are bathing. I believe I have never seen more loathsome and disgusting sights here than I ever saw before."[217] Other soldiers were also not impressed with the morals of Alexandria. "We read in the Bible of Citys [*sic*] being destroyed on account of wickedness in them,'" George Bates wrote, "If they were destroyed now Alexandria wouldent Stand one day longer."[218] In other smaller cities, however, the army tried to do something about the prostitution problem. "We are making quite a reform in the morals," Daniel

O'Leary wrote from Tennessee, ". . . by sending all the frail ones who infest Chattanooga, and increasing daily in numbers, to Nashville . . . much to the relief of well disposed persons who had too great a regard for their own good name to associate or come in contact with such degraded beings." O'Leary characterized most of the prostitutes removed from Chattanooga as wives of Confederate soldiers, preferring to disparage them instead of pondering the economic condition that led them to their profession, claiming, "If they [their husbands] were aware of their conduct I have no doubt they would pray for a friendly bullet to put an end to their existence."[219]

As with other forms of indiscipline, officers were some of the worst offenders. Charles Haydon noted with disapproval that his tentmate, "Benson came home [from leave] last night. A little child of love in Washington took all the strength out of him. He is nearly used up."[220] Warren Isham, a reporter for the Chicago *Times*, published a story about an unnamed colonel who, in "an advanced state of undress," narrowly avoided capture at a brothel by Confederate soldiers.[221] Colonel Ebenezer Peirce faced a court-martial in 1862 for, amongst other charges, leaving camp to visit prostitutes. Among the witnesses were the picket guards who reported that "Colonel Peirce made no attempt to disguise himself." Colonel Lafayette Riker also faced a court-martial. Among Riker's infractions was arranging the enlistment of "Private Walter Harold," who was actually a prostitute named Helen Lambert who dressed as a man, lived in Riker's quarters, and collected a private's salary. When questioned about "Private Harold's" duties, a captain testified that her duties were "Nothing in particular—just looking out the window." In an attempt to defend himself, Riker called upon his fourteen-year-old daughter to testify that Lambert was not a prostitute, was madly but secretly in love with Riker, and joined the regiment without Riker's knowledge to be near him in hopes of future marriage. Perhaps entranced by the soap opera–like plot, the court-martial found Riker not guilty of all charges.[222] Sometimes, however, the officers were caught, not by other officers, but by their own wives in the uncomfortable situation of supporting an in-camp prostitute. "Quite a number of officers' wives are out here." Colonel Elijah Cavins observed in 1862, "The most singular thing about that is that in several instances the second wife has very unexpectedly appeared in the presence of the astounded husband."[223] The arrival of important dignitaries also caused disruptions, as when Abraham Lincoln visited the Army of the Potomac and its commander, Major General Joseph Hooker. Hooker, a man of low reputation, hastened to tidy up his command, including the removal of several "Hooker's girls" from camp.[224]

But just as some soldiers retained their religious fervor, other soldiers reflected the antebellum reformer's opinion that prostitution was a moral wound on the army and the nation. Determined to remain loyal to his (appropriately named) wife Fidelia, Private James Greenalch was disgusted by the behavior of the men in his regiment, the First Michigan Engineers. "I am I supose [*sic*] as great a lover of the fair sex as most men," he explained, "and as I trust I left a virtuous wife at home, I have tride [*sic*] to respect that virtue: If I had of asked myself to disregaurd the wish of a virtuous companion as some married man that is going home, I should not want to look my wife in the face." Others in Greenalch's unit, however, did not share his virtue: "I am satisfide [*sic*] from what I have seen that some of the women [of the South] . . . have been convinced that the Yankees have horns, but not horns on the top of the head." Greenalch complained of the pursuit of local prostitutes, "I should have hesitated to of believed that men or those that pretend to be men would become so demoralized and void of all decency or respect. I would expect if I had been guilty of what I have seen to have some plague or sin come upon me for it."[225] While sympathetic to the plight of Confederate soldiers, Captain Daniel O'Leary was shocked by the behavior of Southern women. "And what is worse . . . ," O'Leary wrote his wife, "the Mothers, Wives & daughters of these men have becomes strangers to virtue and female modesty—which is the greatest ornament of the sex—worse than the most degraded creatures which abound in the cities of the north. I do not Know what standard of morality was in this country before the rebellion but if it has been the means of bringing about the present state of depravity and vice its authors deserve the execrations of all honest people."[226]

However, as the saying goes, "it takes two to tango," and prostitutes could not exist without clients. At least some critics of prostitution placed the blame on those who solicited, also in general moral terms. Stationed in Little Rock, Captain George Avery despaired at the "moral desolation which seems every where to pervade the Army," particularly the "Men & women-married and unmarried-black & white [who] seek only to gratify their sensual desires, & it matters little whether or not there is a commingling of the races." Avery placed a large part of the blame on the soldiers, who had the attitude of "we have only one short life to live & we cannot afford to loose [*sic*] these three years [in army service]. We will make the most of the opportunities presented to us, but . . . expect our wives at home to maintain a character which is beyond suspicion" as society and their husbands required.[227] "[This] evening two Ladies (?) call on Capt., whereupon I left the tent," Sergeant Cormany wrote his wife, "But Cap and Lieut put their arms around them before I got out. O, where are their marriage vows?"[228] Some soldiers, however, could resist the temptation by placing the manly obligation of saving the county over the masculine impulse for sex, especially if it marred their patriotic zeal to save the nation. After conveying the body of a soldier to Washington, DC, "the lieutenant led us to a hotel to rest," James Avery recorded in his memoir, "and we were no sooner seated than a number of, I may say, devils in women's garb, came into the rooms to rob the soldier and ruin the man." Avery was proud to report, however, "I passed through the furnace without a burn" by remembering the virtuous slogan "When rum and temptation are thrown in our sight, we'll think of our nation and fight for the right."[229] Edwin Brown was also tempted by the easy sex available in Washington, but reassured his wife that "I determined when I came into the army to steer clear of those vices which cast a shade on the character of so many military men."[230]

The army did conduct some limited efforts to control prostitution, but only when it became obvious, inappropriate, and disruptive. Colonel Selden Conner, for instance, "Arrested a cavalry soldier for having connection with a negro wench in a horse stable" only because their activity disturbed the horses. Conner earlier arrested and removed four prostitutes from his regimental camp near Martinsburg, Virginia after blaming them for an outbreak of venereal disease. Conner reported to his brigade commander that he had the women "arrested for whoring. They were dirty things."[231] Even high-ranking officers were not immune from either the lures of available women or the punishment that such behavior attracted when taken too far. Any number of officers consorted with prostitutes, both in and out of camp, but when Colonel William Grosvenor became too public in his dalliances with "a woman, not his wife, by the name of 'Belle Fisher,'" the army had to court-martial and remove him from command. Oddly, while Grosvenor pled guilty to the charge of keeping a woman in his quarters, he appealed his sentence to President Lincoln, who overturned the guilty verdict because "the sentence appears not to be sustained by the evidence."[232]

While the army did not have much interest in curbing the sex trade as a social ill or disruptive influence on discipline, it did have a medical interest. Prostitutes spread venereal disease, and every soldier in the hospital with syphilis, gonorrhea, or any other "social disease" was a soldier not doing his duty. Venereal disease removed a considerable number of Union soldiers from the ranks. The Army Medical Corps treated more than 73,000 cases of syphilis and about 96,000 cases of gonorrhea during the war.[233] These numbers included only the reported cases. It does not include unreported cases or soldiers who treated themselves with a variety of over-the-counter remedies. What is particularly shocking about these numbers is that the army should have known that venereal disease on this scale was going to occur, based upon prewar experiences. In the twenty years before the Civil War, an average of 7 percent of the soldier in the U.S. Army suffered from syphilis and/or gonorrhea in any particular year.[234] Based upon that experience, and the knowledge from the Mexican War that volunteers were less disciplined than Regulars, the army could have predicted the scope of the venereal disease problem.

There were more successful efforts to stem prostitution once the war ended. The army tolerated a looser form of wartime behavior and morality during the time of crisis, but once the war ended the army dismantled its attitude regarding prostitution as quickly as it dismantled its army of citizen-soldiers. Less than a week after Lee's surrender at Appomattox, army authorities in Washington, DC, issued an order requiring "All brothels and bawdy-houses will be visited as frequently as possible during the evening." If found in a disorderly state, "the inmates will be ordered to report to the Central Guard House on the following morning" to face judgment and possible fines. But this was a far as the army, even in the nation's capitol, was willing to go; prostitution was still a local issue, and if local politicians wanted the brothels closed they had to close them.[235]

The army lacked, however, a clear policy on prostitution, and consequently different attitudes and strategies to deal with the problem emerged in different locations. The antebellum existence of prostitution was one of the primary determinants of what policies the army put in place. Cities where prostitution was accepted and existed before the war typically had looser policies in place, while cities facing prostitution for the first time or had a sudden expansion of the profession tended to impose stricter controls. Other considerations helped to shape Union decision-making, such as the length of time a city remained under Union control. The character of the Union officers in charge of establishing and maintaining policy also had a direct impact upon the procedures put in place, as did the distance of the location from higher authority. The latter consideration was particularly important, as most of the large Confederate cities occupied by the Union for a lengthy period of time were all in the West, far from the War Department in Washington.

Communities under a long Union occupation, like Alexandria and New Orleans, where the locality accepted prostitution saw minimal Union interference with local practice, although General Nathaniel Banks cancelled Mardi Gras in 1863 because he feared the results of too much drunken revelry in the city's red light district.[236] The first military supervisor of New Orleans, General Benjamin Butler, earned the eternal hatred of the city when he threatened to treat disrespectful ladies as "women of the town plying her avocation" but did little to control the brothels of the community. Other communities, however, saw a more direct approach by Union occupying authorities. Both Memphis and Nashville had well-established brothels, and Smokey Row's reputation had nothing on Memphis' red light district centered on Beale Street, featuring such noted establishments as Shirt Tail Bend, Happy Valley, and Hell's Half Acre.[237] In both cities, the Union army permitted prostitution to continue, although the officers in charge of both locations initially took a different approach. In Memphis, General William

Tecumseh Sherman acted as military supervisor from July to December 1862, replacing the ad hoc occupation of the city after it fell in the aftermath of the Battle of Shiloh. Reflecting the general attitudes of the army, Sherman chose not to meddle in the sex trade, letting local government handle matters "which the military authority has neither time not inclination to interfere with." Recognizing that his soldiers needed entertainment, or would seek it despite efforts to stop them, Sherman ensured that the soldiers' amusements remained open. When the city leaders sought to impose a series of taxes, including one on "a bawdy house or house of ill fame," Sherman permitted all the taxes except the duty on brothels.[238] The local prostitutes, if not the general population of Memphis, welcomed the arrival of the Union army. "Women and whiskey are plentiful here," George Cadman wrote, "and our men had been so long debarred fro both that it did not take long for them to raise hell generally."[239] If prostitutes became a disruptive influence, however, Sherman did not hesitate to evict them from the city. When an argument erupted into gunplay at one brothel, soldiers assisted local authorities in "emptying the contents of the doggery into the bayou."[240]

After Sherman left to resume combat operations in 1863, however, Union attitudes changed, but only because rates of venereal disease rose sharply. Subsequent commanders began an aggressive crackdown on prostitution, issuing orders to steamboat captains banning them from bringing additional whores into the city. Under the terms of a May 1, 1863, proclamation, brothels within city limits had ten days to shut down or face arrest and property confiscation. When this failed to curb the sex industry, authorities began a system of mandatory registration in September 1864. All "sporting women" had to register their occupation with the city, pay a $10 registration fee, and submit to a medical examination that cost an additional $2.50. The funds, $6,429 raised by April 1865, paid for a medical ward to treat venereal disease at a local hospital.[241] Not everyone was pleased. Local clergy raised the obvious moral question of legitimizing crime by licensing it, but the city plan finally brought the prostitution and venereal disease problem under control.[242]

Authorities in Nashville attempted a more direct approach, but wound up settling for a similar policy. Under the auspices of Brigadier General Robert S. Granger, the military governor of Nashville, the army attempted to exile of all prostitutes from the city starting in July 1863. Assisted by city police, soldiers rounded up a number of prostitutes, herded them aboard the steamer *Idahoe*, and planned to deposit them further upriver where they could do no harm to soldiers in the war zone. Two problems undermined Granger's plan, however. First, other cities did not want Nashville's surplus whores. When the *Idahoe* arrived in Louisville, civic leaders refused permission for the ship to dock, forcing it further down the Ohio River. Cincinnati, as well as river cities in Indiana, refused to accept the sordid cargo, and *Idahoe* eventually returned to Nashville a month later with its unwelcome passengers still aboard. The second problem was that black prostitutes filled the void created by the absence of white prostitutes, and behaved "So barefaced . . . that they parade the streets, and even the public square, by day and night."[243] The solution to the problem was the registration system eventually copied by Memphis. Begun in August 1863, the registration system required prostitutes to register their names with city authorities and to submit to regular health inspections. If any prostitute failed the checkup, they had to submit to treatment at a designated hospital, funded by a 50 cent per week tax imposed upon every registered prostitute. Anyone found in "plying their avocation" without a license faced a penalty of thirty days in a work house. In the first year of the law's tenure, more than five hundred prostitutes registered in Nashville, collected taxes amounted to nearly $2900, and the venereal disease hospital was full, but the venereal disease rate among soldiers was down and a modicum of respectability returned to the city.[244] The system of licensing and regulation proved so successful it became unofficial army policy duplicated elsewhere. When Charleston fell to the Union in 1865, a licensing policy was in effect in a matter of weeks.[245]

Associated with prostitution was the issue of pornography. The army did little to curtail prostitution until it became a medical issue, but actively tried to suppress the possession of pornography by soldiers. There is no clear answer why the army behaved differently to the impersonal sex trade than it did to the live sex trade. One possible explanation is that pornography was in camp while prostitution was not. The army could tolerate a soldier's absence for a brief period of time while consorting with prostitutes, but would not tolerate a soldier's mind on sex if pornographic material was readily available. Prostitution and sex were a personal matter that the army did not believe it had a right in which to intervene, but pornography was a public matter, often arriving in the public mail, that permitted an open view of sex, something that properly belonged behind closed doors. Another possibility is linked to the medical issue of venereal disease. Questionable medical theories of the antebellum period associated masturbation with "self-abuse" and even mental deficiency. If the army regulated prostitution in the name of medial purity, than curtailing pornography was an equally valid endeavor.

Soldiers had access to pornography at "peep shows" in urban theaters and in mobile shows offered by regimental sutlers. There was also a thriving business in photographic and printed pornography, often imported from Great Britain.[246] Because it was easy to ship and easy to carry around, pornography was a common item in army camps. Attempts to rid the army of it included searching the mail. Marsena Patrick, Provost Marshal of the Army of the Potomac, noted "Amongst other thing I have seized upon & now hold, [are] large amounts of Bogus jewelry, Watches, etc. all from the same houses that furnish the vilest of Obscene Books, of which I have made a great haul lately." Two days later, Patrick reported, "There has been a bonfire in rear of my Tent, burning up a large quantity of Obscene books, taken from the Mails."[247] Patrick had help from regimental chaplains, who tried to use moral suasion to curb the sin of pornography. "I discovered a young man looking over very unbecoming and indecent engravings in a book." Chaplain Beaudry recounted, "I succeeded in borrowing the book with intention of purchasing it for destruction." Beaudry purchased the book from its owner the next day, and burned it the day after that (after giving it a good look?), but his efforts were in vain as "He had told me he had seen other quite similar books among his fellows."[248] Despite their best efforts, however, Patrick and other officers could not stop the arrival of pornography as long as men wanted it. "My stock of reading material is very limited," Charlie Musser complained to his father, "unless I take up the "yellowback literature" that almost deluges every Camp, but I don't much fancy such 'pass times.'"[249] An orderly for the colonel of the Twenty-ninth Massachusetts lost his job and was returned to the ranks when discovered in possession of two "vulgar books" titled *Frances Hall*, which included pictures of nude women, and *Memoirs of a Lady of Pleasure*.[250] To elude potential censors, pornographers in New York produced collections of graphic images that outwardly resembled pocket Bibles.[251] Only in 1865, in response to the massive amount of commercial pornography available, did the federal government pass a statute granting the postal service the power to restrict the mailing of pornographic materials across state lines. Pornography itself did not become a crime until the passage of the 1872 Comstock Act (named for Anthony Comstock, the founder of the New York Society for the Suppression of Vice) made the mailing of pornography itself illegal.[252]

THE ARMY'S ATTITUDE, if not policy, regarding these fringe behaviors set the pattern for the rest of the war. By demonstrating both the unwillingness and inability to curb even marginal offenses of military discipline, the army set a precedent of failure when it came to curbing more serious offenses, including those that required clear enforcement under the Articles of War. Instead of setting the disciplinary tone by forcing soldiers to toe the line on relatively marginal undisciplined behavior, the army emboldened soldiers to test the boundaries of both military law and the army's willingness to enforce it. From the soldiers' perspective, the ability to shape their wartime experience in the face of codified discipline was not perceived as a military failure, but rather as a successful demonstration of their rights as citizen-soldiers. The men of the Union army demonstrated a clear appreciation for the military definition of discipline, while demonstrating that the legal definition of discipline was flexible and even irrelevant to their existence. Soldiers embraced the idea that they could, and should, create their own form of morality. In shaping their own morality, soldiers redefined their relationship to army discipline, in the process creating a more flexible and populist form of discipline than that illustrated in the Articles of War.

The rights of citizen-soldiers to define their wartime existence did not demonstrate a clear challenge to army authority in regards to the issues raised here. Fighting amongst themselves, gambling on any occasion, or ignoring the advice of a chaplain were things about which the army could do nothing. The army's failure to regulate the soldiers' behavior, luckily, did not affect the efficiency of the army. But when soldiers applied this reinforced sense of citizen-entitlement to other areas of army discipline, the army was less flexible. Contesting, but ultimately allowing, soldiers to earn money on the side or to solicit a prostitute was one thing; permitting a flaunting of more established, codified, and serious rules was another. When soldiers breached the disciplinary code on more significant offenses, officers could not look the other way. The army expected discipline, but the citizen-soldiers expected freedom. The two rival ideas clashed over one of the most basic of symbols of adult freedom and the item that most threatened the army's control over its soldiers. The army had to contend with the moment when a soldier decided he wanted to have a drink.

4

"BRAWLS, RIOTS, AND MIDNIGHT ORGIES"

Alcohol and the Union Army

The Union army liked to drink. Everyone drank, from the highest-ranking general (see Ulysses S. Grant's reputation) down to the lowliest recruit. They were not picky about what they drank, as long as it provided the necessary level of intoxication. The army drank on a scale both epidemically and endemically, creating disciplinary problems from the top ranks to the lowest and from the first days of the war to its very end. As the bulk of the Union army, privates drank more than did officers, but they also demanded access to alcohol much more than officers. Enlisted men wanted alcohol, in as large a volume and as frequently as possible, because of their perceived right to drink and what alcohol and alcohol consumption symbolized. From a corporeal standpoint, it alleviated the hardships of battle, weather, and both physical and mental weariness. For citizen-soldiers raised in a culture where drinking was prevalent and accepted, drinking became a connection to their past and, hopefully future, status as citizens. In an army that emphasized distinct levels of status between officers and enlisted men, alcohol consumption became a means to break down rank differentials and celebrate the status of the enlisted man. As symbols of masculinity, making war and drinking alcohol went hand in hand as outward demonstrations of manhood, with soldiers gauging each other's ability to consume alcohol as a measure of manhood within their peer groups.

Such pervasive use of alcohol, however, came with a disciplinary burden. Alcohol use bred violence, upheaval, and crime. Alcoholism became an obvious by-product, with the subsequent loss of public esteem. Officers in particular faced a heavy penalty for drinking, in terms of blows to their reputations if not to their freedom. Drunken soldiers damaged the reputation of their units and their states, and also damaged their bodies, brains, and their lives. Worst of all, from the army's standpoint, alcohol eroded discipline, making soldiers unmanageable and unresponsive to orders. Attempts to halt the use of alcohol proved futile, and the army's leadership dealt with alcohol as a problem they had to manage and not as a behavior that they could command. Despite the obvious fact that alcohol was the source of much of the army's disciplinary problems, the army could not, despite its best efforts, regulate, moderate, or restrain the use of alcohol by men determined to have it.

ASIDE FROM THEIR ADHERENCE to the ethos of the citizen-soldier, Union troops took no stronger perception of themselves into the army than their right to drink. Americans liked to drink in the nineteenth century, and, while they accepted the obligations of fighting for their country, soldiers still expected the right to consume alcohol in a manner that connected them to the idea of home and civilian life. Alcohol flowed through the collective veins of most Americans for both practical and philosophical reasons. Alcohol was the common drink of the masses before the Civil War, despite the temperance activities of the antebellum moralists. It was safer than most sources of water, and provided a cheap form of recreation for agrarian and working classes. Philosophically, drinking was one of the universal symbols of masculinity. Besides associating drinking with the attainment of male adulthood, the volume of alcohol that one could consume, along with how one behaved while consuming it (how you 'held your liquor'), was a measuring stick of virility and manliness. Alcohol was also associated as a reward for manly behavior. Workers at the end of a long day, winners of athletic events, or the successful conclusion of a hunt were all causes not only for drinking but establishing bonds of male contact, events that almost always excluded respectable women. When men engaged in war, the most masculine of activities, the idea of separating drinking from warfare seemed out of the question. As a reflection of this attitude, Civil War soldiers emulated the manner of antebellum drinking in that social drinking was almost unknown. Relatively rare does one find instances of restrained or modest drinking during the Civil War, and those that do exist are almost always written by officers demonstrating their level of refinement. Instead, virtually all accounts of drinking by enlisted men (and many by officers) describe unrestrained alcohol consumption—drinking simply to get drunk. A possibility for this conduct is the soldiers' pessimistic assessment of a long life and the decision to live in the now instead of the tomorrow, but a larger measure is also due to a general consensus of what equated to masculine behavior. A visiting British naval officer provided a good description of the antebellum masculine attitude regarding whiskey. "American can fix nothing without a drink," Captain Fredrick Marryat opined. "If you meet, you drink; if you part, you drink; if you make acquaintance, you drink; if you close a bargain, you drink; they quarrel in their drink, and they make it up with a drink." Marryat found little use for water among Americans, who considered it only "good for navigation."[1]

As citizen-soldiers, Union troops believed they possessed the right to speak their minds on any issue and occasion, and alcohol certainly fit into this perception. A sign of how desperately soldiers desired whiskey appears in their complaints. Soldiers either complained that they did not have any whiskey, complained about the quality of the whiskey they had, or complained that the decent whiskey they had was nowhere near enough. "With deepest melancholy and disgust I am compelled to announce that there is nary whisky nary a drink within these barracks," George Bliss grumbled to a friend at home, "and that I have been beastly sober for many a day."[2] Massachusetts soldiers, unsatisfied about the quality of the local hooch in Virginia, proposed to use it as a weapon against the Confederates. By squirting the stuff "through a force pump," the men claimed the vile concoction could "kill at forty rods."[3] Officers also complained about the lack of quality liquor. In January 1863, officers of a New York regiment toasted the New Year "with some hot punch brewed out of such wretched whiskey that I got a severe headache from it. . . . [It] was my habit of using *good* liquor when I use any that made it disagreeable to me."[4] Even when quality product was available, soldiers still preferred quantity over quality. A shot of good whiskey lasted but a moment, but a bottle or keg could dull the senses for a considerably longer length of time.

One also finds evidence of the association between soldiers drinking and masculine behavior in the social setting where soldiers drank. If drinking for the pleasure of drinking was the sole objective, than soldiers would drink alone, but that was usually not the case. Instead, soldiers generally drank in groups, providing an opportunity to demonstrate their masculine control of alcohol to their peers. Despite fifteen straight days of rain that made roads nearly impassable, for instance, James Holmes wrote to his wife that a large group of soldiers still planned to "go to town & get drunk."[5] After a hard campaign, one group of artillerymen decided it was time to relax. After a night when the camp was "full of Wine, Brandies, and whiskies," the company captain found his sergeant of the guard passed out between two bales of hay and "only about ten men fit for duty."[6] At one point in 1862, the Iron Brigade had to contend with "A thousand drunken men the brigade" at the same time.[7] In Frederick, Maryland, James Gillette estimated "about three thousand drunk soldiers [were] lying in the gutters and streets or staggering about town."[8] A newspaper correspondent described the Army of the Potomac's camps as "more like . . . bacchanals than enlisted soldiery. Brawls, riots, and midnight orgies proclaim the supremacy of a drunken god."[9] The use of alcohol as a group activity extended beyond lines of rank to include officers. At a commemoration of the Battle of Gettysburg, the drinking of the Iron Brigade became so widespread that "the officers of this brigade and the Generals within any convenient distance of us were almost unanimously drunk."[10] In Arizona, a soldier recorded that nearly the entire regiment was "in a whiskeyficated state," and their officers could do nothing with them and the soldiers did not care.[11] Soldiers were determined to drink because war and drinking were what men did, and, moreover, that is what soldiers in the past had done.[12]

Whiskey, the pursuit of whiskey, and the effects of whiskey were issues that confounded the antebellum army well before 1861. In the antebellum period, the army recognized the threat to unit cohesion and general discipline that liquor posed, and the army made a wide-ranging, if uncoordinated, effort to control the drinking of soldiers. In 1832, for instance, the army banned the issuing of a daily liquor ration. The army instituted the liquor ration in 1782, during the American Revolution, with a gill of whiskey issued daily, and additional gills served for arduous duty or duty during inclement weather. In an average year, the army provided, free of charge, 11.4 gallons of whiskey to each soldier as part of their standard rations. The dispensing of alcohol, however, came with considerable disciplinary problems. The army blamed alcohol use for its 20 percent desertion rate in the prewar years, along with a slew of other offenses. Officers complained, for instance, about the "hell of gamblers and liquor venders where they [soldiers] can easily get drunk" that sprang up near any body of soldiers.[13] Finally, the army banned the liquor ration in 1832 (the U.S. Navy retained it for another thirty years), hoping that the financial burden of providing their own drink would persuade soldiers not to imbibe.[14] Soldiers continued to drink, however, and the army never found an effective way of curbing the influence of alcohol. Instead of searching for alternative forms of amusement or improving the quality of barracks life, the army brushed the issue under the rug, addressing alcohol use only when it became a noticeable problem, as when liquor destroyed the antebellum military career of Ulysses Grant.[15] Unfortunately, the problem was never far away. The inventory of one regimental sutler in 1855, for instance, included "seventy-two bottles of schnapps, twelve bottles of bitters, eight kegs of whiskey, seven barrels of gin, six casks of assorted brandies, six casks of sherry, and two casks of ale."[16]

THE EXECUTION OF THE DESERTER WILLIAM JOHNSON IN GENERAL FRANKLIN'S DIVISION, ARMY OF THE POTOMAC.—[See Page 827.]

Harper's Weekly December 28, 1861—The execution of a deserter by firing squad. A typical execution, the condemned soldier sits upon his coffin, and the execution is witnessed by a large number of his fellow soldiers. Courtesy of HarpWeek, LLC

Harper's Weekly **July 15, 1865—** Soldiers playing "chuck-a-luck," a dice-based form of gambling. The impulse to gamble was so intense that soldiers took the opportunity to wager whenever and wherever they could. Courtesy of HarpWeek, LLC

Harper's Weekly **September 26, 1863—** Execution of bounty jumpers. Five bounty jumpers meet their fate in an execution viewed by the entire V Corps. Like many executions, this one seemed to not go off as planned. Despite a massive firing squad, one of the condemned men appears to have survived the initial volley. Courtesy of HarpWeek, LLC

Harper's Weekly **June 28, 1862**—Wearing the barrel. Caught drunk on duty, a soldier endures his punishment (and the mockery of his compatriots) while wearing a heavy barrel. Referring to his heavy shell, the other soldiers compare him to *USS Monitor,* the Union Navy's first ironclad warship. Courtesy of HarpWeek, LLC

Harper's Weekly **June 28, 1862**—Drummed out of camp. Head shaven, uniform stripped of all army insignia, and surrounded by disapproving onlookers, a soldier accused of cowardice is drummed out of camp. Courtesy of HarpWeek, LLC

THE ARMY OF THE POTOMAC—GAMBLERS AT THE PROVOST MARSHAL'S HEAD-QUARTERS.—[Sketched by A. R. Waud.]

Harper's Weekly **November 7, 1863**—Humiliation as punishment. Caught in violation of camp rules against gambling, an officer forces two soldiers to wager for beans and wear placards announcing their offense while under the observation of a sentry. Courtesy of HarpWeek, LLC

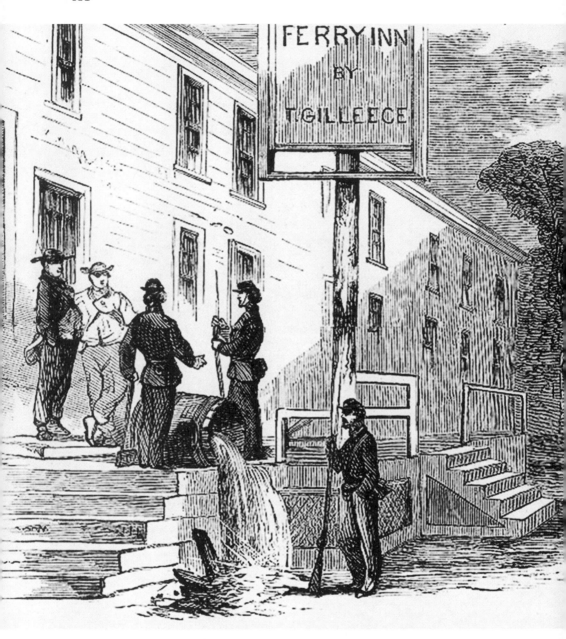

Harper's Weekly **November 8, 1862**—Destroying illegal whiskey. In an attempt to prevent their men from drinking, officers often cracked down on civilians who sold liquor to soldiers. Those caught selling liquor usually had their stocks dumped on the ground, but the lure of money ensured active liquor smuggling. Courtesy of HarpWeek, LLC

Harper's Weekly **January 3, 1863**—A court-martial in session. Although a special circumstance (the court-martial of General FitzJohn Porter), the setting and arrangement is typical of court-martial cases. The panel of officers, serving as both judge and jury, sits around the table to hear the evidence. Courtesy of HarpWeek, LLC

James B. Fry—Provost Marshal General of the Union Army. Colonel Fry supervised the soldiers of the Provost Guard, pursued and arrested deserters, operated and enforced wartime conscription, and suppressed political dissent in the North. Although an effective administrator, his unpopular activities cost him his post after the war. Courtesy of the Library of Congress, Prints and Photographs Division

Joseph Holt—Judge Advocate General of the Union Army. A civilian, Holt oversaw the administration of courts-martial and other formal military judicial proceedings, established policies relating to legal issues and the war, and provided advice to the Lincoln administration on legal matters. Courtesy of the Library of Congress, Prints and Photographs Division

Sutler's Tent—A sutler offers his wares. Although sutlers were popular when soldiers had money to spend, soldiers criticized their high prices and cutthroat approach to business. Officers despised sutlers who smuggled whiskey into their camps. Often unpopular, sutlers became the targets of thieves, swindlers, and robbers. Courtesy of the Library of Congress, Prints and Photographs Division

Execution of William Johnson—Execution by hanging. Private William Johnson, convicted of desertion, hangs from the gallows near Petersburg, Virginia. Courtesy of the Library of Congress, Prints and Photographs Division

Pillaging of Fredericksburg—Union soldiers pillage Fredericksburg. Looted civilian property lies scattered in the streets as Union troops destroy the city in pursuit of loot. Devastated by both the nearby battle and Union foraging, Fredericksburg was the worst example of Union property crimes on a vast scale. Courtesy of the Library of Congress, Prints and Photographs Division

Morning Salute Whiskey Flask—Liquor as recreation. The use of alcohol pervaded the Union Army, and many a soldier would have welcomed a "morning salute" from this highly decorative whiskey flask. Soldiers found plenty of ways to transport their whiskey but often had to go to great lengths to obtain it. Courtesy of the North Carolina Museum of History

Camp Punishments—A variety of camp punishments. This vignette from the *Illustrated London News* shows the typical camp punishments imposed upon soldiers who committed minor violations of army discipline. Soldiers carry logs; wear a ball and chain, stand on a barrel, stand tied to a tree, or sit "bucked and gagged" under the watchful eye of the Provost Guard. Author's collection

Soldiers continued to drink through the Mexican War, the development of the sectional crisis, and right into the start of the Civil War. More often than not, whiskey was the preferred beverage of the Union army. Whiskey was the common drink of antebellum America, thanks to the surplus wheat and corn crops produced by American farmers. Crops that had only a limited shelf-life in grain form could last indefinitely once distilled into liquor. It was relatively cheap, easy to make, and widely available. In rural areas where hard currency was in short supply, whiskey served as ersatz currency in local transactions. From the soldiers' perspective, however, the great asset of whiskey was its portability. For a soldier who wanted to alter his consciousness but who also faced a twenty-mile road march, whiskey provided the proverbial "more bang for the buck." A soldier could get drunker on a single bottle of whiskey than he could with a similar volume of beer, so soldiers largely turned to sour mash instead of barley wine. A good reflection of America's affinity with whiskey is the colorful names associated with various whiskey recipes. Private James Horrocks, an English citizen who enlisted in the 5th New Jersey Artillery, wrote to his parents in England about the diversity of America's alcohol spectrum. "Yankees are ingenious and in the mixture of spices and Liquor they have exercised their ingenuity," Horrocks wrote, "These are a few names of said mixtures: Gin Sling, Milk Punch, Brandy Smash, Egg Nogg, Mint Julip . . . I have tasted a few of these but the best of all is the Sherry Cobbler."[17] Names reflected the appearance or content of a drink, but names also indicated the feeling the whiskey produced or its quality. Soldiers euphemized their quality liquor as "Oil of Gladness" or "O, Be Joyful.[18] Low quality whiskey, which produced nasty hangovers, became known as "Spider Juice," "Bust Skull," "Kill at the Counter," "Death Bed Confession," or "Tanglefoot."[19] Even if soldiers did not relate an interesting name, they softened the record of their drinking behind other euphemisms, such as "drinking something harder than water" or "partaking in a variety of tonics."[20]

In the absence of whiskey, however, soldiers were not above turning to wine or beer. Getting drunk was the intent of most soldiers, and when granted the opportunity, most men were not too picky about the beverage. Wine was a rare delicacy, especially for those who appreciated a good vintage. Cornelius Courtright, a sergeant in the One Hundred Fourth Illinois was pleased to see that the regimental foragers "brought in Tobaco [sic] and Wine," but "some of the boys had too much wine for their own good."[21] In Cheraw, South Carolina, soldiers from the XVII Corps discovered eight wagonloads of fine wines hidden there for safekeeping by the well-heeled citizens of Charleston. The corps commander, Francis P. Blair, appropriated some of the finer bottles, but he shared the rest of the lode with his men, whose palates were perhaps not as appreciative of the vintner's skill.[22] Wine was good in a pinch, but beer was more appropriate to the citizen-soldiers of the Union army, and a serving of beer was just as welcome as a good whiskey. George Bliss was not happy about the constant rain in Washington, DC, in March 1862, but he could not complain as "my bowels are lined with ale."[23] Isolated without booze on the remote Oregon coast, California soldiers celebrated when a "wagon load of Lager arrived," causing the men to "hy-you zigzag."[24] A passing peddler did not have any whiskey, but a group of Michigan officers in the Army of the Potomac were glad to "purchase a 10 gal. keg of beer for $3" instead.[25] Some New Jersey men enjoyed an evening of recreation including "two kegs of Lager bier provided by the Captain" to maintain unit cohesion.[26] The German soldiers in General Louis Blenker's brigade were always well-supplied with beer, much to the delight of non-German troops encamped nearby. "Andy Knapp and I went over to Blenkards [division]," John Hawk of the Nineteenth Indiana wrote, ". . . and we [soon] felt as independent as a hog on ice."[27]

Acquiring alcohol from Blenker's brigade was possible because of German and Irish soldiers who demanded and received alcohol as a component of their cultural identity. The Irish troops who celebrated St. Patrick's Day as a component of their Irish character used alcohol to commemorate the day, and resisted efforts to separate them from the whiskey that was so much of their ethnic consciousness.[28] Germans also requested alcohol in the form of the beer that formed part of their traditional civilian diet. When General Sherman attempted to ban alcohol in his army during the Vicksburg Campaign, Colonel Augustus Willich, commanding the Thirty-second Indiana, persuaded Sherman to allow his regiment to keep their daily ration of six kegs of beer per day to maintain the unit's high morale.[29] The main difference between the two nationalities, however, was that the Germans seemed more willing to share, whereas Irish troops tended to isolate themselves because of native persecution of the Irish in the antebellum period. When alcohol was in the offering, it tended to produce more conflict among Irish and nativist than national unity. "During the night we were disturbed by John Madigan, an Irishman, who had got some Apple Jack [fermented cider] and was drunk," James Avery complained. "He was all for fight with everyone and was very noisy . . . until he got knocked down."[30] On the other hand, the German soldiers were more likely to establish friendly relations with non-German soldiers. Considering the willingness to blame German soldiers for military failures, such as the XI Corps at Chancellorsville, one suspects that the nativist contact with the German troops was more to gain access to their beer and less to establish nationalistic ties. The Ninth New York, made up of nativist troops, for instance, developed a friendship with the largely German One Hundred Third New York. When the two regiments met up again in Virginia, "the Dutchmen danced around like lunatics. . . . Dutch canteens were sent around until many a brave fellow of the 9th found it easier to lie down than to stand up."[31] Soldiers of the Iron Brigade also liked encamping near German soldiers, who were more than willing to offer the chance to "come and take some lager."[32]

With alcohol such an embedded feature of American life, soldiers drank when they could and when they could afford it. Money was an important issue, as alcohol was a commercial product and soldiers could only legally obtain liquor if they had the currency to pay. Money came only on irregular paydays, and the arrival of the paymaster made mass drunkenness a fair prediction. "Today we were called out to receive pay," Sergeant Hamlin Coe wrote. "It is now sundown, and a more drunken set [of men] I never saw then Company K."[33] Payday coincided with a torrential downpour in the camp of Captain John DeForest. The combination of money, mud, and whiskey soon produced a cacophony of action, as "men splashed through the sludge and halted on the little company parade, jabbering reeling, and scuffling . . . payday had worked its usual mischief: one third of them were as drunk as pipers."[34] Order soon returned, however, when the soldiers exhausted their funds. "The town is getting quiet again," Sergeant George Hand gladly reported. "The money is gone and the whiskey will not come."[35] Soldiers were now penniless, but most considered it worthwhile fun. "We had a jolly time here for a couple of days after we got paid," Sergeant Welsh innocently wrote to his wife, ". . . it is all over ecept [sic] that a few of the boys are in the guardhouse yet for getting drunk."[36]

THE ARMY DID NOT WANT SOLDIERS to drink, but, similar to the issue of prostitution, could not or would not interfere with a soldier's activities when he was on leave from duty. The simplest way to acquire alcohol was to buy it at a commercial outlet. If soldiers chose to purchase their alcohol, they expected to pay a high price. Like any other wartime commodity, liquor was in high demand and it was a seller's market. With such a large body of men searching for alcohol, sellers could also inflate their prices to what the market would bear, knowing that even if most soldiers could not afford their prices there were still enough that could. Encamped in Virginia in preparation for the attack at Fredericksburg, the Army of the Potomac consumed all of the alcohol in the area, leaving a soldier to complain that the "last whiskey he saw sold was not two weeks ago and brought $10 per gallon."[37] To a private in the Union army, who made only $13 per month, ten-dollar whiskey was an expensive luxury. Soldiers found similar prices in North Carolina, where "three dollars a bottle for whiskey [was] no bar to indulgence."[38] Presuming the bottles were quart bottles, that whiskey was even pricier at $12 per gallon.

One can infer from the prices that perhaps it was quality whiskey instead of the inferior commissary whiskey, because another soldier in North Carolina reported that his regimental sutler sold food at outrageous prices, but sold "Whiskey common [for] 2.00 per qt," or only $8 per gallon.[39] That was still more than half a soldier's monthly pay in 1862, making whiskey a very profitable commodity during the war. But when soldiers wanted their drink, most proved willing to pay the price. To celebrate New Years 1863, "one company used up 9 canteens of whiskey at $6 per canteen."[40] At nearly $16 per gallon, it was an expensive celebration. Franklin Boyts listed the highest whiskey prices. In winter camp after the Battle of Fredericksburg, Boyts mentioned "whiskey $3.00 a pint bottle from sutler," a lavish $24 a gallon.[41]

With a tavern featured in nearly every city, town, and village in America, soldiers did not have to go far to find someone willing to accept their hard-earned money. "Saloons are open on every hand and whiskey and beer was abundant to the boys," Private Sawtelle happily remembered. ". . . It was a great treat to be able to get all they could pay for at an open bar."[42] A popular place for soldiers at Camp Douglas in Chicago was a spot known as the Cottage Grove, described as "a poor excuse for a grove, being a series of beer gardens and bowling alleys scattered among some scrub oaks."[43] Corresponding from the field, a reporter from the *Cincinnati Enquirer* observed the "disgraceful conduct of a portion of the Ninth Ohio Regiment . . . They fill the saloons and coffee-houses, and . . . their revellings and riot have greatly disturbed the quiet."[44] Access to taverns deeply dismayed the regimental chaplains. After receiving liberal passes to go into town, many soldiers of the Fifth New York Cavalry returned to camp drunk, much to the disgust of their chaplain, who commented "There are more drunkards, drunk men, in camp tonight, than I have ever seen in a long time."[45]

If soldiers could not purchase alcohol openly, they would use alternative methods to acquire a drink. This usually involved considerable subterfuge to elude the sharp eye of their officers, but soldiers occasionally did not have to take the risk themselves. Selling alcohol to soldiers was a profitable business, so civilians took the risk to smuggle alcohol to soldiers despite the possibility of punishment. The opportunity for smuggling was certainly present. The military could place entire cities under military control when in an urban setting, but in the field army authority extended only to the edge of the camp. Just beyond the reach of regimental control, liquor dealers, just like prostitutes, hovered nearby in anticipation of entering the camp to sell their wares. With liquor so close, soldiers were tempted to obtain it, but getting alcohol past the guards and pickets involved something more subtle than stuffing a bottle in a coat pocket or boot. One observer noted that in one camp that one soldier "fills a stone jar [with whiskey], covers the top with butter, and passes in[to camp]," while another smuggled alcohol in a bag of potatoes. A creative soldier "discovered that his musket barrel would hold just one pint" and marched into camp with his shouldered musket full of whiskey.[46] He was not the only soldier to use such a ruse. "The Officer of the Guard noticed that all who returned to camp were very particular to carry their pieces at Support Arms," Colonel Wesley Brainerd wrote. "An inspection of arms discovered the fact that the barrel of each musket was filled with whiskey, the muzzle & nipple being carefully plugged."[47]

Soldiers would have no whiskey to smuggle, however, if liquor dealers did not exist on the fringes of their camps, and army officers struggled to control their presence. Like many circumstances regarding vice in the Civil War, the Union army had no formal guidelines on the presence of such entrepreneurs, leaving regimental officers to set their own policies. Officers could not reach beyond their own camps to proactively deal with the problem, and could act only when dealers attempted to bring alcohol across the lines of authority. One particular whiskey dealer, for instance, followed the Eleventh Pennsylvania Reserves for weeks. He set up camp a safe distance away from the control of angry officers, that is until local authorities forced him to leave.[48] Another liquor dealer established a site "where two casks of 'Red Eye' were buried in the ground, and the man who sold it had it so arranged that when he pumped the rum out, one would suppose that it came from the bowels of the earth."[49]

Making the problem even more difficult, some suppliers of legitimate goods smuggled whiskey as a side business, and the army had to sort the illicit from the legal. In the Army of the Potomac, soldiers smuggled banned objects into camp by hiding them in the turkeys procured for Christmas dinner. Private John Follmer wrote, "some of the fowls were stuffed with queer filling, packs of cards, flasks of brandy, pocket Bibles and Testaments."[50] One supplier of vegetables brought whiskey into camp by placing smaller kegs in the middle of larger barrels of produce, forcing officers to roll the barrels and listen for the whiskey sloshing within.[51] Other liquor dealers stretched their ingenuity, and "every scheme was used to avoid detection . . . Tin cans were made with false bottoms, or double sides, with whiskey between and jellies, preserves, etc., on the top or inside."[52] Another vendor provided alcohol by opening an establishment that sold "lemonade," at least until authorities shut her down.[53] Women, thanks to their voluminous clothing and feminine charm, also proved an effective way to smuggle alcohol. Two caught in the act, Mary Welsh and Katherine Hartnett, gave themselves away when a guard took notice of the "unusual size of Mary's lacteal fountains," while another woman was captured smuggling four gallons of whiskey under an "extensive and unseemly bustle."[54] John Holahan discovered "the 'loose' women of

Baltimore giving a grand 'treat' to the boys" of the Forty-fifth Pennsylvania in an effort to persuade them stay behind and sample their wares. Holahan managed to get his men back to the train by carrying those "too far gone to walk, and drive like sheep those who could."[55]

Without any official policy or oversight, regimental officers sometimes took the law into their own hands, using threats, intimidation, and physical punishment to impose control when the army and the law were silent. In New York, an officer threatened to tear down the shanty of a liquor dealer selling whiskey to troops during a train stop, and nearly precipitated a gunfight with the armed owner.[56] Another officer forced a dealer on the outskirts of his camp to "take a hatchet, go into your doggery, burst in the head of every whiskey barrel you have, and pour the infernal stuff on the ground." If he did not, the officer threatened to "make a bonfire of your business house, and I will tie you up by thumbs. . . . I will dry up this infernal traffic even if I am compelled to resort to fire-brands and hempen ropes."[57] Other officers did not stop at mere threats. Fed up with the constant stream of drunken men returning to camp, "Capt. [John] Raines took a squad and went down to the city and broke up a grog shop."[58] Sergeant Charles Scribner described his most important duty as "to prevent the selling of liquor to Soldiers," and when the officers in his unit, the Fifth Vermont, captured alcohol smugglers, "most of them are sentenced to be chained to a tree . . . with a large placard pinned to their backs . . . painted in letters large enough to be read ten rods away—Whiskey Venders, this to those who tried to destroy both *body* and *Soul* by selling Liquor to Soldiers."[59] When two civilians ignored Colonel Samuel H. Starr's order that forbade the selling of alcohol to soldiers under his command, Starr convened, with War Department approval, a regimental court-martial, found the men guilty, and "sentenced [them] to receive 20 lashes on their bare backs and to be set adrift in the Potomac [River] in an open boat with no oars." Despite their protests, the two men were flogged, one with a "coach whip and the other a long waggon [sic] whip" until "their backs looked like raw beef."[60] The punishment was particularly harsh, as the officer could not levy it upon soldiers after the army banned flogging as a punishment in August 1861.[61] Another smuggler, "a woman who cooked for Colonel [Patrick] Kelly . . . managed in some way to get licquor .[sic] and used to put in about half water and then sell it for five dollars a canteen," paid the penalty for engaging in the liquor trade: "she was sent to prison at Washington."[62]

Smuggling by outside sources was bad enough, but the most common smuggling came from a semi-official source. Each regiment had a sutler, an outside merchant who sold items not provided by the army, attached to it. Sutlers sold personal items (like stationary), basic sundries (like tobacco), and luxury items (like pies) not available through the normal channels.

The armies required sutlers to apply for and possess a license to operate in a regimental area, with a single sutler permitted to each regiment. Following the pattern of shifting decision-making powers downward, the army permitted the regimental officers to select their own sutler.[63] Through this mechanism, sutlers played an official role within the army. On the other hand, sutlers operated with very few restrictions. They could set their own prices, choose what goods to sell, and decided for themselves when to open and close shop. One of the few limits placed upon them by the army was the restriction on selling whiskey to enlisted men. Officers faced no such restraint, but the army wanted to control the soldiers' alcohol intake and forbade sutlers to sell to enlisted men.[64] The demand for alcohol and the tidy profit it generated, however, prompted many sutlers to set up a legitimate looking operation in the front and sell whiskey to the soldiers out the back. To officers who tried very hard to fend off alcohol smuggling from the outside, having a quasi-official smuggler in their midst was frustrating.

Sutlers could thinly claim that any alcohol in their inventories was intended for officers, and sutlers claimed ignorance or theft if soldiers wound up with their products. Only relatively late in the war, in March 1863, did the Army of the Potomac decree that sutlers could not sell alcohol at all or even keep in on inventory. The decree came down from Major General Joseph Hooker, himself a noted imbiber, who generated the order as part of the general reorganization of the army after the debacle at Fredericksburg four months earlier. Deprived of their plausible deniability, sutlers could no longer justify hiding alcohol, and the level of overt smuggling, at least in the Army of the Potomac, declined. The smuggling continued, however, in other armies, and sutlers became craftier in the Army of the Potomac. One sutler "pretended to be loaded with apples but a good share of her apple barrels proved to be whiskey barrels, the liquor being put up in bottles and then packed with sawdust in the rough."[65] Another sutler, claiming to offer a wagonload of pickles, did a brisk business until the large crowd of soldiers around his wagon prompted an officer to order a search, revealing "liquor bottles outnumbered pickle jars by five to one."[66] Another sutler offered "sausages" to the soldiers—sausage casings filled with whiskey.[67] The most elaborate ruse was "The Bosom Companion," a flask of whiskey shaped to look like a pocket hymn book.[68]

A major factor in limiting the smuggling of sutlers, however, was that sutlers were so important to the operations of the regiment. Sutlers provided creature comforts that the army could not, or would not, provide, little touches of home to which citizen-soldiers felt entitled. The regiments simply could not dispense with their sutlers. Hence, the punishments extended to sutlers engaged in liquor smuggling usually amounted to nothing more than dumping their stock on the ground. "The guard emptied 10 barrels of beer & whiskey which were brought up by peddlers on to the ground," Charles Haydon wrote approvingly. "The men have entirely emptied two or three peddler's wagons of their contents in a tenth part of the time it took to load them."[69] A sutler who came into came ostensibly to sell pies instead began to sell whiskey until discovered, and "seventy-three bottles of whiskey were . . . unloaded and a corporal broke the bottles and spilled the Irishman's spirits upon the earth."[70] Dumping the liquor did not always dissuade soldiers from taking a sample. "Eight barrels of whiskey were emptied upon the street," Corporal Daniel Mowen recorded. "Some of the . . . lovers of the ardent liquid dipped it out of the gutter with tin cups or tried to run it into their canteens."[71] Sutlers also came under scrutiny when their products caused health problems, as in the case of a sutler attached to the Seventy-seventh Illinois who was in the habit of "making bad whiskey . . . to the demoralization of some of the weaker comrades."[72] Authorities shut down another sutler, who hid his whiskey in vats labeled "Wigwam Tonic," after a soldier/customer drank his product and lapsed into "a fit of insanity."[73] Even if not causing actual illness, a sutler's whiskey caused otherwise normal soldiers to go wild. "Our suttlers [sic] bring rot gut whiskey into camp," Sergeant Darius Starr complained, "and the soldiers get it. The result is that they get, not merely drunk—they will do that on good liquor—but they get perfectly crazy and in that condition are ready for anything."[74] Occasionally the army made an example out of a sutler by imposing a harsher punishment. The sutler for the Thirty-fourth New York "was drummed out of camp . . . for selling whiskey," Edward Bassett wrote. "The whole Brigade was drawn up in line. He was marched the whole length of it, with seven or eight big bottles around his neck . . . They took him outside the lines and warned him not to appear among us again."[75] Shutting down a sutler, however, was potentially disruptive, especially if soldiers had become accustomed to their liquor. "Col. [Ernest W.] Holstedt to-day confiscated $3,000 worth of liquors, brought in by the sutler," Rufus Kingsley of the Eighth Vermont noted in his diary. "The best was turned over to the hospital. The most was turned out on the sand. No wonder the officers don't like the new Colonel."[76] When a lieutenant from the Eighty-third Pennsylvania tried to shut down his regimental sutler, "a large number of intoxicated soldiers had congregated around the Guard undoubtedly for the purpose of assaulting them . . . yelling and brandishing clubs in a threatening manner."[77]

When the usual methods of obtaining a drink failed, soldiers relied upon their families at home to provide them with alcohol through the mail. This was not the preferred way of acquiring liquor. Soldiers asking for booze through the mail were openly admitting their intemperance and sinful behavior when out of sight of the idealized Victorian home. Therefore, only soldiers from lower social strata, especially those whose chances of moving into the Victorian middle-class were slim, defied social norms and openly placed their orders with family members. "Every day some of the boys secure . . . some kind of box with something nice to eat," James Holmes informed his wife. "[S]ome get several oyster cans filled & sealed with Pittsburgh Whiskey."[78] Noticing the contents of a mail delivery, Henry Heisler observed that "Nearly every box had a bottle of whiskey in which soon created a lively time in camp and filled the Guard House in a short time by drunken men."[79] Soldiers may have received their intended packages, but the cost of mailing alcohol and the risk of breakage meant that it was only a stopgap measure to slacken the army's thirst. Although not a very useful means of acquiring alcohol, receiving it through the mail was at least a reliable method. The army tried to curb the postal delivery of alcohol by requiring packages to list their internal contents and randomly searching parcels, but the sheer volume of mail, not to mention army wagons and civilian commercial vehicles, meant that the likelihood of receiving whiskey was very high.[80]

Another reliable way to obtain alcohol was to request it for medical purposes. Even some temperance advocates believed that alcohol had therapeutic advantages, and the army permitted surgeons to stock liquor as a panacea for many medical ills. Soldiers generally wanted alcohol as a preventative measure, believing that whiskey fortified the constitution, warded off the cold, or sharpened the senses. The army tended to agree to the extent that whiskey became a vehicle to get soldiers to, literally, take their medicine. Alfred Bellard partook of a "ration of whiskey and quinine" to ward off malaria, as did the men of a New York regiment based upon the belief that "The ration of whiskey with quinine in it does our men much good these cold mornings."[81] Captain John DeForest was not a believer in the theories, however. "Beware, too, of trying to march on the strength of whiskey," he advised in his memoirs, "you go better for a few minutes, and then you are worse off than ever." DeForest instead believed that "Opium is a far superior as a temporary tonic . . . I started out sick, took four grains of opium . . . and at the end of twenty-two miles came in as fresh as a lark."[82] Most soldiers, however, decided not to become drug addicts and stuck to their more familiar beer and whiskey. Discovering the soldiers of the Sixth Michigan to be "bilious and complaining," the regimental surgeon, Charles V. Mottram, "managed by some device to smuggle a barrel [of beer] into camp, and told the boys to help themselves" for health reasons.[83] The army also permitted whiskey as a remedy. Soldiers from Nantucket, for instance, were glad to receive packages from their local Soldiers' Relief Society that included personal items, bandages, and some "medicinal wine and brandy."[84] By 1863, however, the army began to forbid the shipping of alcohol directly to soldiers themselves, but the "medical" option remained tacitly open. "We have been able to smuggle in 2 boxes of whiskey," Captain Dodge was proud to report, ". . . a few days ago Major Baldwin informed us of a chance to get some thro' as 'Medical Stores.' Of course we immediately confided the money to his care to secure the desired 'drugs.'"[85] Private Albert Allen also used the mail to acquire "medicine," requesting and receiving a bottle of "Pain Killer" from his sister at home. Private Allen was apparently in a lot of pain; within a month he informed her, "I have used about half of it."[86] William Jones was less subtle. "Harry, I tell you what I would like you to do for me," Jones wrote his brother, "That is, send me down a bottle of Chestnut Grove whiskey for medicinal purposes. I tell [you] it would do me a good deal of good. I have a belly ache once in awhile, and [on a] rainy night it would do one good to take about a tablespoonful before he goes on guard."[87] Medical sources of whiskey also included those driven by a profit motive. Sergeant Wyman White was shocked to find that local agents for the Christian Commission "sold whiskey to anybody at five dollars per bottle. . . . Charity and Christianity, what crimes are committed in your names."[88]

Soldiers often did not have to pay for whiskey, however, as the army itself often provided the soldiers with liquor. The Regular Army banned the liquor ration in 1832, but drinking remained a significant feature of the national militias. To many of the militias, their annual training sessions were little more than an excuse to socialize and drink.[89] When the mass of volunteers arrived in 1861, bringing with them their citizen-soldier's defense of their right to drink, the liquor ration enjoyed a renaissance among the new state regiments. An easy way legally to dispense whiskey was to justify it as compensation for harsh conditions and poor accommodations. According to official army policy, "one gill of whiskey is allowed daily, in case of excessive fatigue and exposure," and officers liberally dispensed alcohol when weather conditions caused hardship or when soldiers had to endure arduous labor.[90] When the army did issue a whiskey ration, it dispensed its own whiskey instead of purchasing it locally. Army regulations permitted officers the privilege of drinking as they wished, and officers could purchase their own liquor or draw it as supplies from the Commissary Department. This caused no end of hard feelings among the soldiers. Officers who wanted alcohol "had only to send to the commissary to obtain as much as they pleased, whenever they pleased, by paying for it," John Billings complained in his memoirs, "but the private soldier could only obtain it of this official on an order signed by a commissioned officer."[91] Officers obviously drank a lot. The relatively small District of West Florida alone requisitioned 2,345 gallons of whiskey per month, a rate of almost two gallons for each officer.[92]

Commissary whiskey was not always of the best quality, but it was available when officers decided when conditions warranted a ration. The Fortieth New York received a ration after a snowstorm dumped eight inches of snow on their camp, and one soldier reported that the "guard house was [soon] full of drunken soldiers before sundown."[93] Commanding troops during the grueling siege of Petersburg, General Edward Ferraro ordered that a "half gill of whiskey be issued to each of the men of this command each day until further notice."[94] Private Rufus Robbins reported the same policy. "We never draw rations of whiskey," he wrote to his brother, "except when it is very strong weather or on fatigue duty."[95] To alleviate their discomfort because "many of the boys could not lay down on account of their tents being flooded with water," the commanding officer of the Tenth Illinois issued "3 canteens of whisky" for each company.[96] When illness related to poor weather became particularly widespread, senior officers were also inclined to use whiskey to improve the health of their men. On May 19, 1862, the Army of the Potomac doubled the whiskey ration to two gills per day "upon the recommendation of the Medical Director." The army revoked the extra whiskey a month later.[97] The army permitted a liquor ration, but left it to the regimental officers to ensure that the privilege was not abused. Taking this duty seriously, Charles Haydon "distribute[d] the whiskey which I made out to do in such a manner that no one got drunk. This is quite unusual & cost much swearing on the part of the men & a little on mine."[98]

Another way the army violated its own rules was to distribute alcohol as a reward for special or outstanding duty. The soldiers wanted alcohol, the officers needed something done and had access to alcohol, so the obvious commercial relationship existed. Many soldiers, as discussed before, engaged in private commercial ventures while in the army, so volunteering for extra duty for alcohol, on one hand, seems like an obvious thing to do. Moreover, soldiers resented the implication that officers were their social betters, so alcohol was a lure to persuade soldiers to perform extra duties that they might otherwise refuse to perform. Captain Dodge persuaded a soldier, "a mason by trade," to construct a fireplace for his winter quarters, but instead of cash the soldier "takes his pay in tobacco and whiskey, which the men prefer to money."[99] Private Wilbur Fisk was one of a group of soldiers detailed to construct a fence around the officer's quarters in the regimental camp. Upon completing their task, Fisk reported, "they treated us to some whiskey and let us go."[100] Colonel Voris, concerned about the hard labor conducted by his men, told his wife that "I got my boys a few gills of whiskey Sunday & have been giving it out to them by 1/2 Gill doses when they get verry [*sic*] tired. . . . Of course, they do not get enough to make any one tight [drunk]. I wish I could get it for them oftener."[101] Veteran troops in particular required some form of compensation for hard work. Members of the Iron Brigade, for instance, grumbled about their assignment to a railroad construction project, work they considered beneath them. To keep them motivated, officers permitted them a whiskey ration.[102] Proof that whiskey kept the complaining down is also found in an account by an officer during the Peninsular Campaign. Large numbers of men labored to construct field fortifications in blistering hot July weather, but complaining was minimal because "as they got 'the whiskey ration' for extra work they were all happy and worked with a will."[103]

Sometimes an officer did not need a reason to reward his men. Captain Thomas Donnelly of the One Hundred Fifty-fourth New York issued extra whiskey on top of his men's usual ration simply because he felt they deserved it.[104] When his officers seized some illegal whiskey, Colonel William Stone give it to his men in a supervised fashion, having the "companies march, one at a time, to the front of his Quarters, and every man was treated to a glass of whiskey."[105] On other occasions, alcohol became the reward for jobs that soldiers actually anticipated and enjoyed. John Bates, participating in the Carolina Campaign in early 1865, was happy to report his company "Serenaded Gen. [William T.] Sherman in the Evening and got a good Drink of Licker [sic]" as compensation.[106] Regimental bands took turns serenading the officers of General Philip Kearny's III Corps in the summer of 1862. The First New York's band performed admirably, and received a whiskey ration as a reward, but another regiment was so awful that "General Kearny gave this band a gallon of whiskey to go away."[107] For a canteen of whiskey, Corporal William Coxhall constructed the gallows on which the army hanged the assassins of Abraham Lincoln. Coxhall complained that he never got his whiskey, but there were many soldiers that would have constructed that particular gallows free of charge.[108]

The army also bent its own rules by permitting, or even providing, alcohol for special occasions and events. As already mentioned, St. Patrick's Day was a special occasion for Irish troops, with extra whiskey rations to mark the day.[109] National holidays, such as Christmas and the Fourth of July, shared by all soldiers also generated alcohol-fueled good cheer. John Mottram certainly enjoyed the celebration of Washington's Birthday in 1865, marking the day with "little fatigue [duty] and a good glass of Whiskey."[110] The men of the Ninety-fifth Illinois were very joyful on Christmas when "Col. Tom [Thomas Humphrey] turned out 15 gall of Rotgut & several of the boys got happy."[111] The men in William Jones' regiment "have been drinking and 'when the rum is in, wits are out,'" as Jones put it, further noting that they were "making a pretty good deal of noise, but [the officers] let them be merry as it is Christmas."[112] New Years became the most common holiday for officers to treat their soldiers to a celebratory beverage. "A ration of whiskey and an extra ration of sugar has been served out today," Captain Dodge noted disapprovingly, "of which to make the New Year grog. The men have most of them already partaken of the luxury and are now making manifest by songs and cheers."[113] Sylvester Hadley appreciated the gift when "The Officers bought a barrell [*sic*] of whiskey and gave [it] out to the men and if there wasn't a Circus that night than I miss my guess."[114] To celebrate the New Year in 1865, Corporal John L. Smith attended a party where General Gouverneur Warren invited all of the V Corps' NCOs to "share a whiskey punch."[115] Providing liquor on New Years was a risky venture, as men could get out of control, but some officers took the necessary precautions. John Chester White, a lieutenant in the 130th Pennsylvania, described the Christmas festivities prepared for the regiment as, "camp-kettles of Commissary whiskey, mixed with canned milk and styled milk-punch, and others [kettles] full of beer, had been sent by the officers to their respective companies, and a number of the former, as well of the men proceeded to get beastly drunk, after a double cordon of sentries had been thrown around the camp."[116] Not receiving alcohol for special occasions, on the other hand, produced only grumbling soldiers. "General [Thomas] Meagher promised us last sunday [*sic*] that we would have our whiskey today," Peter Welsh complained on Christmas 1862, "but we have not seen it yet."[117]

When soldiers could not pay for alcohol and the army would not give it to them, they could usually forage for it. Acquiring alcohol from civilians, with the additional advantage of not paying for it, combined two disciplinary issues in a single event. The fact that alcohol was available in rural areas close to army camps was a sign of the antebellum drinking culture. As most battles occurred in rural areas where home distilling remained a common practice, soldiers knew quite well that alcohol was probably available if they made only minimal efforts to acquire it. In this sense, the common Union soldier had to revert to civilian modes of thinking to locate his favorite beverage. The other issue was the practice of foraging. The Union army widely conducted economic warfare, the process of weakening enemy armies by consuming the economic assets that kept the enemy in the field. That necessitated foraging, even when the army possessed adequate supplies, to deny food and other essentials to enemy forces. As discussed later in greater detail, there was a thin line between legitimate foraging and illegitimate pillaging. Alcohol certainly existed in that gray area between the two concepts. On one hand, alcohol was a product of the fertile Confederate countryside, and therefore a legitimate target for seizure. Considering the corrosive effects alcohol had on the Union army, however, and the zeal with which Union soldiers pursued liquor, the Union army might have done better to leave the Confederates as much alcohol as they could drink.

Union soldiers were determined to consume their fill when the opportunity presented itself, and foraging operations often degraded into simple whiskey hunts. "I suppose over half of the detail as drunk," Henry Charles wrote of a foraging expedition near Petersburg, Virginia. ". . . Most of us filled our canteens and there was a keg of brandy there . . . [but] then a Provost Marshal rode up and dismounted and with his little George Washington hatchet he gave a heavy rap and soon the brandy. . . was on the ground."[118] Another soldier, caught red-handed while being "very irregular in getting a jug of whiskey . . . smashed the jug on a stone wall" instead of turning it over to the officer who caught him.[119] Faced with authorities intruding with their pursuit of alcohol while on formal foraging expeditions, the occasional soldier decided to embark upon a personal foraging expedition. "William Jones had a natural longing for something stimulating," Sergeant Austin Stearns recalled, "and he was up to all manner of tricks to get past the guard." Jones' favorite trick was to either "swim down the canal" with his clothes tied to the top of his head to keep them dry or to "creep through the brush with cat-like stillness" to avoid the picket guard. Another private who was "often thirsty" did not have to go to such great lengths. Assigned as a messenger, "he would take a large yellow envelope and . . . he would walk as though he carried an order . . . and so pass unquestioned."[120] An Indiana artillery unit foraged so much alcohol they could not drink it all, and their officers gathered up the remainder for return to its rightful owner, but soldiers still stashed some away and "every hollow log and stump was full of it."[121] Sometimes soldiers found it easier to let Southern civilians bring the whiskey to them. "I like to stand picket around Nashville," Patrick Brennan wrote, ". . . we serch [sic] the wagons and if they have whiskey we make them fork it over till he have all we wont and it takes a prity good lot to do us."[122]

As much as the army tried to restrain their soldiers from foraging, their own officers undermined their efforts. "Lieutenant John Barry of the First Cavalry who was a wonderful forager, especially when it came to foraging for anything that was . . . stronger than water" led his brigade to a demijohn of "homemade blackberry brandy." The soldiers, having imbibed a considerable amount soon "noticed the fence that we halted by commenced to zigzag," Charles Veil recalled. "I wanted to take a nap and did so right there . . . when I woke up I saw all the rest of the staff, the general included, taking a nap too."[123] The occasional cache of alcohol was a welcome sight, but most soldiers preferred to hit the main lode and find the distillery itself. "Sometimes we were so fortunate as to find a still," Thomas Livermore of the Eighteenth New Hampshire wrote, "and could replenish our canteens with the warm beverage" found in the vats.[124] "Soldiers from the Twelfth Maine, part of the force occupying New Orleans in 1863, discovered a distillery "and were enjoying themselves drinking sugar-cane rum. There were all jolly in less than half an hour; one gill makes a man drunk."[125] Captain John Otto wrote how glad his men were when they "struck Oil" by finding a still, returning to camp with "an 8 gallon Keg of bourbon."[126]

Alcohol was such an important part of the soldier's life that if he could not buy it, smuggle it, or forage it, he would simply steal it. The process of stealing whiskey itself reflected several general attitudes held by Union troops. Soldiers stole from civilians because they could justify it as part of a foraging campaign. They stole liquor from officers because they resented their status and privilege. They stole alcohol from taverns and sutlers because these merchants cheated them, charged too much, or sold substandard whiskey. Some thefts were by individuals, but most thefts occurred when soldiers acted as mobs exercising a form of group democracy to redress a perceived wrong. Sometimes theft was simply an individual rebelling against army authority, demonstrating their status as a citizen-soldier.

Taverns and sutlers paid the price for insulting or overcharging soldiers prone to acting out in a violent manner. "A fight occurred at Hulton station," wrote a soldier of the Eleventh Pennsylvania. ". . . [S]ome of the Erie boys made a charge on a lager beer saloon, tearing down the sign and handling the proprietors in a very promiscuous manner . . . The guard had to be called out . . . several of the men received a bayonet gouge apiece before they could be quieted."[127] In Indianapolis, soldiers became angry when a tavern owner refused to serve them and "made a rush" at the establishment, resulting in the wounding of a soldier, "the ball striking him in the breast and glancing downward."[128] When tavern owners clashed with men of the First Michigan Sharpshooters, the owners "lost the shape of their faces and the contents of their grand saloon" in the ensuing fracas.[129] The Tenth Illinois plundered a store in Indianapolis when the owner locked the door instead of accepting their business. "Something to drink they were bound to have," John Ferguson wrote, "so they quickely [*sic*] brock [broke] open the doar." In the ensuing flurry of activity, soldiers "carried off bottles from the bar," then "took hold of watter buckets . . . broke in the heads of whiskey bbls. and dipped in and carryed off." Others "could be seen carrying kegs on there [*sic*] shoulders . . . The whole thing was cleened out in less time than one could reed the circumstance." This was the second such performance by the Tenth Illinois; a week before they cleaned out the liquor in a grocery in Terre Haute, Indiana.[130]

When soldiers could not steal liquor from civilians they stole the army's whiskey, but such an acquisition required a certain level of bravado. Sometimes stealing was a case of misplaced trust by the army. Assigned to guard several barrels of whiskey included among the general supplies of the Commissary Corps, several soldiers of the Iron Brigade instead plundered the whiskey themselves.[131] Officers had to keep an eye on their privileged liquor, lest it disappear. Soldiers crashed a reception for officers of the Second Wisconsin, managing to acquire what "they could swipe, which was no small amount."[132] Even an officer's personal stash of whiskey was at risk. A lieutenant in the

New Mexico territory found out when "He went to get his "bitters" from the ten gal. keg in the corner when to his great surprise it was gone, keg and all. . . . Everyone wonders who has the keg. And while all are wondering, some soldiers are drinking it."[133] The soldiers of the Fourteenth Vermont were proud of their ability to filch alcohol, considering the theft of a quart of whiskey from General Edwin Stoughton's saddlebag as their greatest achievement.[134] Stealing an officer's whiskey sometimes took some subterfuge. Captain George Hugunin of the One Hundred Forty-seventh New York thought he misplaced his coat. He was next perplexed when he tried to draw whiskey from the Commissary, but was denied because his monthly allotment was already filled. Hugunin found out later that "my bugler had taken my coat, got a mule . . . & went off to another Brigade, putting on as much style as a Brigadier [general] & got 5 or 6 canteens full [of whiskey]."[135] When their whiskey was not at risk, an officer's horse was still fair game. A soldier in the Tenth Massachusetts, detailed to hold Major General Don Carlos Buell's horse, instead leapt upon the animal and headed down the road looking for a drink until Buell's staff caught up to him.[136] There were risks when stealing alcohol, not all of them obvious. "Anson Keene found a small red keg full of something at Brigade Hd. Qrs," Silas Wesson of the Eighth Illinois Cavalry remembered. "He thought it was beer so he stole it . . . [he] called the boys to come and take a drink. . . . It was vinegar and the boys got mad. They took a cup, put in some vinegar and salt and made Anson drink it. We call Anse Keene 'Red Keg' now."[137]

WHEN THE ARMY COULD not control drinking, soldiers behaved in a manner that most officers found objectionable. Faced with improper conduct, officers had a choice of trying to control the situation themselves or letting the drunks sober up before inflicting punishment. Either choice was problematic. Controlling a large number of drunks, or even sober soldiers looking for alcohol was usually impossible, considering the citizen-soldiers' penchant for dismissing authority figures when their perceived rights were at risk. On the other hand, permitting soldiers to engage in improper behavior and then try to correct them the next morning only fed the soldiers' sense of alcohol entitlement. They had bent or broken the rules, and the army was now (unfairly in their view) trying to punish them for something ex post facto, especially bad for soldiers who were so drunk they could not remember what offense they had committed. Regardless of how officers tried to curb their men's behavior, the one certain fact was that alcohol had an effect on how men behaved and none of it had a positive outcome for the army.

An inevitable behavior problem was noise, especially after Taps. Soldiers believed they possessed the right to speak as they wished, and none more so than soldiers who were drunk. Peace and quiet, and not to mention sleep, were impossible when "a good many of them feels there [*sic*] whisky a little too well."[138] Private William Wiley had to endure the ruckus caused by soldiers who got drunk and "yelled and howeled [*sic*] all night and some of us felt like getting up and shooting them."[139] James Avery was less forbearing. Weary of a drunk soldier who "began to yell and holler," Avery recalled. "I took him by the collar and seat of the pants . . . I threw him on the bed . . . bump[ing] his head severely on the iron head piece. . . . I think I knocked the whiskey out of his thick head."[140] Captain DeForest, tired of the noise in his company camp, decided to use the physical approach after growing weary of the "bacchanals, which I quieted by sending one man to the guardhouse, pushing others into their tents, and ordering lights out."[141] DeForest was gentle compared to the officers in a Vermont regiment forced to deal with a soldier who was "drunk and in for fighting." Five men struggled to control him, and in the process the soldier "bites one of them quite badly," before "his hands are tied behind him, he gives up in despair, and the poor fellow cries like a child."[142] Trying to subdue noisy drunks, however, was a risky venture. Soldiers of the Fourth Rhode Island resisted efforts to quiet their carousing with a barrage of "jeers, groans, hisses, sticks of wood, stone, [and] old shoes."[143]

Drinking also led to fighting, and drunken brawls between soldiers inevitably broke out when drinking bouts turned into physical bouts. Despite the escalation of misbehavior from simple noise to physical conflict, the punishments' consequences were still the same. The army left the decision of punishment to regimental officers, who tended to ignore the problem because it was relatively infrequent and punishing soldiers might damage unit cohesion. A good example are the exploits of Sergeant Al Sanborn of the Thirteenth Massachusetts. A chronic drinker who bounced between the NCOs and enlisted ranks because of his alcoholic tendencies, Sanborn also had a habit of picking fights for the fun of it. "Not being satisfied with the sport he was having in his regiment," a fellow sergeant wrote, "he thought to have some with the 39th Mass." The "sport" was not as much fun as Sanborn thought; "they got the best of him," and his company captain reduced him back to the ranks.[144] Soldiers had to bear the bumps and bruises of fighting. On Christmas Day 1863, Private Frederick Pell reported that "The boys had a big drunk today with considerable fighting." The next day, Pell reported, "The boys are all sober this morning some with sore heads and faces."[145] Fighting or conflict happened seemingly at any time. "There is a fuss on [my] hands just now," Henry Bear wrote in a letter as it happened. "John Fields is half tight. He wants the Cracker box I am writing on but he wont [*sic*] get it by a damn sight till I get done with it. He is now fussing with Bill Hickman. I wish Bill would knock hell out of him the son of a bitch."[146]

For every source of alcohol, there seemed to be a fight as a by-product. The custom of supplying soldiers with drink also caused unintended violence. A generous treating of whiskey by one regimental colonel resulted in the men becoming "pugilistic, and as a consequence some had Eyes Red & some Black" the next morning.[147] In a similar case on the West Coast, a captain "issued 2 Gallons of Whiskey" to his men as a treat, which "made a number of the Boys drunk and pugilistic. Several bloodless fights occurred."[148] After issuing a whiskey ration to soldier working on fortifications, "two of them conclude that each of them 'is monarch of all he surveys,'" Marcus Woodcock noticed, "and fall out . . . to decide it by a pugilistic contest, this action seeming to disagree with the peaceful inclinations of their company commander; he orders them to be separated."[149] Even NCOs behaved like common soldiers. "Yesterday the Sergeants of Company H spent their money on not a few bottles of so-called champagne," Captain Dodge wrote, ". . . jolly drunk they both got; after which they set to fighting and gave each other a mutual merciless beating." Dodge never determined the cause of their disagreement.[150]

The most frightening instances of fighting, however, was when large groups engaged in massive brawls, ignoring the efforts of their officers to stop them. Private Bellard remembered a spat between two officers "who were jealous of each other." Each drew his sword on the other, but they calmed down "without any whiskey being spilt." But the clash got the officers' respective companies riled up, and soon "a regular old fashioned free fight was the consequences for about half an hour, during which bloody noses and black eyes were freely given and received" until extra guards quelled the fight.[151] Company-sized fights swelled into regiment-sized fights. "Some of the boys of our Regiment," John Ferguson described, "became intoxicated and got into a difficulty with a Ky [Kentucky] Regiment" that took nearly an hour to break up.[152] Even worse still were the instances when alcohol so degraded the sense of subordination that officers found themselves fighting enlisted men in an absence of all military control. "While we were gone one day we got a ration of whiskey," Herman White wrote to his parents, "Our officers all got drunk and they had a h——l of a row, privates and all fighting with the officers . . . swords & pistols was swinging in evry [sic] direction. No respect was shown officers. Our LieutCol got knocked upside down with the rest of them."[153] Sometimes fights exceeded mere fisticuffs. "All of the men who are in the habit of it, as many of them are, got liquor enough to get drunk," Charles Haydon wrote in exasperation, ". . . the Big Sailor & another quarreled in our tent. One suddenly drew a sword & the other a dirk & were parted with difficulty. We are in as much danger from our own men as from the enemy."[154] Two soldiers drunkenly squabbling in the Arizona Territory stopped fighting when one "seized a gun and struck him on the side of his neck," knocking his adversary unconscious. Later in the same unit, a series of commotions occurred, including a report that "Pat Connelly & Tom Lloyd had a fight—both cut with knives and bruised badly" but still alive.[155]

Officers also had to respond to soldiers who appeared publicly drunk or whose antics threatened to disrupt the efficient running of the camp. Also, officers reined in drunks whose public behavior threatened to undermine the officer's position as an authority figure. Camps with drunken soldiers staggering around did not send the message of an efficient and competent officer. In June 1862, officers patrolling the perimeter of the Army of the Potomac rounded up a number of offenders, including a drunk Pennsylvania soldier "dressed in female dress and very disorderly."[156] Another drunk soldier took the opportunity of a small crowd to leap atop a log to give an exposition on the polices of Abraham Lincoln. At least he would have, had he not "lost his balance and plunged to the ground," leaving an observer to postulate that "the rest of this extraordinary harangue would have been was left to our conjecture."[157] Napoleon Bartlett described to his brother his amusement at seeing a drunken soldier named "James Bass come tumbling out of a tent and rolled over about half a dozen times clear in the middle of the street."[158] Another soldier awoke in the guardhouse wondering where he was after officers found him "dead drunk in the road [along] with his canteen full of whiskey."[159] Mocking an officer who inquired about his state of sobriety, one soldier responded by admitting, "I am drunk. I report myself unfit for duty, too much intoxicated to be on dress parade, and sink or swim, live or die, survive or perish."[160] After the Battle of Shiloh, officers of the Eighteenth Regiment of the Regular Army thought they found a live soldier accidentally placed with dead soldiers in preparation for burial. Instead of a fatality, however, they discovered a live drunk who, in searching for a place to sleep, thought the dead were his comrades and laid down to join them.[161]

When sending drunks to their tents or the guardhouse to sleep it off was not enough, officers had to impose harsher discipline, including arresting and punishing drunk soldiers to curb their behavior. This tactic, by itself, was an uncertain proposition because officers had to have an associated offense to justify an arrest. The Articles of War did not list intoxication as a punishable act, so simply being drunk was not an offense for enlisted men. Soldiers could drink as much as they wanted, and their state of inebriation was not in itself a crime. Only if soldiers committed another offense, or failed to perform some assigned duty, could a drunk trooper face disciplinary action. This presented both good and bad circumstances for an officer. Invariably, a drunk soldier would commit some sort of offense, so tolerating a drunk was usually not a lengthy process. On the other hand, an officer had to accept whatever disruption a soldier caused until they could justify arresting him, causing breaches of discipline that need not have occurred.

The severity of the offenses that led to arrests varied widely, with some arrests for trivial violations of the regulation and others creating major violations of safety and sanity. General Marsena Patrick reported the arrest of two Scouts, cavalrymen deployed to screen the movements of the army, "two of whom have been drunk."[162] Authorities in Washington, DC, arrested Private John Scherer of the Fortieth New York for "strolling around the city without a pass hunting for whiskey."[163] Officers were content to quiet drunks who made noise after dark, but when they were insubordinate to officers trying to shut them up, arrests occurred, as in the case of a sergeant and a corporal in the Thirty-ninth New York.[164] Instead of sleeping it off in the guardhouse, two soldiers of the Fifth Iowa found themselves under arrest for missing roll call. "They resisted," an observer noted, causing "a scene . . . disgraceful to them, and through them to the [entire] company."[165] Arresting drunks, just like trying to quiet them, carried its own risks. Private Marshall Miller was of the opinion that being a soldier was risky enough, but "he runs more risks in arresting drunken soldiers."[166] A captain of the One Hundred Seventy-eighth New York found that out the hard way in August 1863 after a drunken soldier nearly shot him.[167] A soldier of the Fifty-first Indiana struggled with the officer trying to arrest him for public intoxication in Indianapolis. Unable to overcome him, the officer shot him, but luckily the "ball struck his head and glanced [off]; another inflicted a slight wound in one of his hands."[168] That was not the only time that gunplay was necessary to subdue a drunken soldier. Weary of a chronically drunk soldier named Charley Counsel, his captain placed him in the guardhouse. Counsel promised to escape, prompting the officer to order the sentry to shoot the miscreant if he attempt to do so. Counsel managed to get hold of the sentry's bayonet, at which point the sentry shot him, leaving "a hole through his thigh an inch or so in diameter." For obeying his orders, the captain gave the sentry $5, and his lieutenant colonel promoted him to sergeant.[169]

Because intoxication itself was not an offense, officers had to decide for themselves what the appropriate punishment a drunken soldier deserved. An officer could take the soldier's inebriation into account when judging their actions, or they could take a more serious approach. Either way, the punishment of alcohol-related offenses varied widely. Early in the war, when disciplinary offenses were a new experience and the likelihood of long war seemed remote, regiments opted to remove drunkards from their midst and sent them home. The Californians attached to the Second Massachusetts Cavalry did just that before leaving their home state, stripping a chronic drunk of his uniform and dismissing him from the unit.[170] As the war progressed, however, sparing manpower so quickly was no longer an option, and officers had to deal with disruptive imbibers. John Haley, describing how "the requisite amount of tanglefoot" could change a man's disposition, recalled an aggressive soldier who, after threatening the officer who took his whiskey away, wound up in leg irons, becoming "as meek as a lamb."[171] Time in the guardhouse, a temporary jail established at the regimental level, was the standard punishment, although the time period varied depending upon the severity of the offense. Edward Marshall, otherwise described as a "clean and good soldier," spent seven days in the guardhouse for his drunken offense.[172] One Union soldier, however, who "was saucy to the captain," spent only a few hours locked up and "was let out the same day."[173] Other officers tried alternative punishments. Combining the humiliation of a public bathing with the old belief that a cold shower sobered up the inebriated, some officers tried the "cold water" method to punish drunkards, usually with no effect. "The Captain devised a new means of punishment" for a chronic drunk, James Harrocks recalled, "He made a spread eagle of him, that is tied him with his hands and feet as far from each other as possible, and then poured buckets of water on his head." Instead of inflicting a memorable punishment, Harrocks remembered the soldier piously repeating, "This is nothing to what the Saviour suffered," portraying himself as a "Christian but unhappily drunken martyr."[174] The method also did not work in the Western Theater. "Our Capt. [Thomas Wellman] says that putting men in the guardhouse for getting drunk is played out," Sergeant Hand recorded from New Mexico, "and the next one who missed a roll call . . . he would give him a cold bath." Private Pete Susee was the first test; Wellman "ordered him tied in the corral and detailed three or four men to perform the hydropathic operation." Hand did not think it would work, stating, "He stood it like a man but . . . He is still in a whiskey state." Sure enough, a few hours later, Hand recorded that "Pete was brought to the guardhouse . . . very drunk. The bath is not good."[175]

Besides disciplinary punishment, soldiers had to pay a physical price for consuming alcohol, and the inevitable hangover and physical purging provided enormous embarrassment to those who suffered and considerable glee to those who witnessed it. Marcus Woodcock amused himself by watching inexperienced tipplers attempting to drink as much as the other soldiers, "but [they] were finally left weltering in their gore, completely subdued." Later in the war, the same soldier witnessed another massive imbibing near Knoxville, Tennessee, that left "many helpless forms . . . stretched over the *spewy* field."[176] After a drinking binge in an officer's tent, Corporal William T. Mack "spewed all over the ever unfortunate [Corporal William] Hadlock who ran to the Sergts." tent for redress."[177] The embarrassment of vomiting was not limited to enlisted men. When officers of the One Hundred Twenty-sixth Ohio held a function to see off departing Lieutenant Colonel William Harlan, "a bucket each of egg nog and whiskey were the centers of attention," leading to a "weaving, spewing sick set of men" that included "One Capt. who was a Presbyterian elder at home."[178] When officers in another regiment also failed to control their stomachs, their soldiers "would forget their own troubles at the fun of seeing the officers heaving."[179]

One of the most tragic by-products of alcohol use was alcoholism. Unfortunately, at the time of the Civil War physicians had not yet embraced the perception of alcoholism as a treatable disease. Instead, the public and the medical community tended to view the alcoholic as a flawed individual that possessed weak self-control.[180] Consequently, the Union army's medical statistics regarding alcoholism reflect only extreme cases that required medical attention. According to post-war compilations of wartime medical cases, the army treated only 4.6 alcoholism-related medical cases per 1000 soldiers. The incredibly low number of medical cases compared to the massive consumption of alcohol reflects more the misunderstanding of alcohol's influence than the general morality of the Union soldier.[181]

Hallucinating is one of the symptoms of advanced alcoholism, and such bizarre behavior invariably caught the attention of soldiers who witnessed a hallucinatory episode. A drinking binge by one soldier resulted in visions of "snakes and devils" and howls of terror until officers could medicate him into submission.[182] Charles Haley described a new recruit who "was seeing a menagerie of snakes in his shoes."[183] A Maine soldier also had to contend with a drunk in their tent who "go the delirium tremens and the snakes were all over and around him and in his shoes."[184] Alfred Bellard was almost the victim of one soldier who "was taken by the Jim Jams (Dilirum Tremens) [sic] and seizing a knife was soon running amuck through the camp looking for his enemy." Only a few days later, Bellard experienced another similar episode. "One of our men having imbibed too much corn juice was taken with an affliction of the brain," Bellard marveled. "While my squad was forming on the street. . . this mad man made a rush and jumping from the window landed in the middle of us. Had not some of them seen him as he made the jump and got out of the way, he would have been impaled on our bayonettes [sic]."[185]

There were other side affects associated with alcoholism, including loss of status and rank. Private Augustus Curtis had great potential according to his company captain "when not under the influence of liquor" but failed to reach his potential because "his love for the beverage seems to be a passion" that he could not shake.[186] "The color sergeant and his right hand corporal were as drunk as could be . . . ," Captain Theodore Dodge observed at dress parade. "I had the two first reduced to the ranks for their behavior . . . They can't be moderate."[187] Henry Martin enlisted as a private in the One Hundred Fifty-fourth New York before rising rapidly to the rank of captain. Martin lost his rank and the respect of his men, however, for his inability to control his drinking, including embarrassing himself by appearing drunk before General Oliver O. Howard, a noted temperance advocate.[188] Lacking any mechanism to deal with alcoholism, soldiers committed drunken disciplinary offenses, sometimes chronically, without any means of preventing it. A chaplain described one alcoholic acquaintance who would "come to my tent, he would cry, and promise to be a good man, but whiskey was too strong for him."[189]

There were other victims of alcoholism as well. Captain John DeForest received a letter from the wife of one of his soldiers inquiring if her husband was dead as she had not heard anything from him nor received any of his pay to support the family. Consequently, she and her children were both penniless and homeless. DeForest knew the soldier was alive but "I fear she will get little aid from her husband. He is a mild, weak young fellow, easily led away by comrades . . . and given also to seeking courage in whiskey." DeForest could only sympathize that a "quite worthy girl has married a good-looking youth of inferior nature and breeding."[190] Besides alcoholism, whiskey fueled other psychological problems. Depression often prompted alcohol consumption, as soldiers turned to the bottle to ward off the blues. "Sid Prentice's old lady love is just married," wrote a Michigan soldier, "& he swears that he will either go into a battle or get drunk within 3 days."[191] Another Michigan soldier turned to the bottle after receiving the news that his wife had died.[192]

The harshest consequence of drinking, however, was death, and alcohol claimed a number of Union soldiers through destruction of their health, alcohol poisoning, or by placing the soldiers in such an intoxicated state that they could not respond to a dangerous situation. Encamped near Annapolis, Maryland, on the campus of St. John's College, a soldier of the Eleventh Pennsylvania, described as "full of whiskey" by a fellow Pennsylvanian, "fell out of the third story window of the College buildings and fractured his skull. He died next day."[193] An accidental fall also killed a soldier in the Eighty-ninth Illinois when he "found some whiskey and abused it and . . . fell in the opening of the bridge . . . We buried him at midnight."[194] Whiskey also caused deaths by associated accidents. "Last night, a wagon pertaining to the commissary caught fire," a Colorado volunteer recorded. "[I]t is supposed from a candle inside, by which the sergeant was reading, and he, being stupid with liquor, was consumed with the wagon."[195] Onboard a transport heading down the Potomac River, Sergeant Hartwell wrote in his diary that "Some of our men got drunk during the night & one got so rich he walked overboard & was lost."[196] A similar accident claimed the life of a soldier in the Eighteenth Illinois. When the regiment embarked on a transport, the regimental colonel asked the sutler traveling with them if he had any alcohol in his inventory, and the sutler promised he did not. During the night, however, soldiers broke into "boxes marked soda, candles, and soap, and it proved to be bottled liquors." In the ensuing riotous drinking, a "man of Company D, Hugh Carr, fell overboard and was drowned. He was one of the principle [principal] men of the riot and was drunk when he fell over." This was the second member of the Eighteenth to drink and drown. Eight months earlier the regiment received word that "One of our men was found on a sand bar [in the Mississippi River] drowned . . . when he fell he was Drunk and he sunk and was never seen until today."[197]

Alcohol and trains also did not mix. A soldier of the First New York Engineers "became intoxicated . . . and fell asleep on the track of the horse rail road while in this position . . . a passing car crushed both his legs."[198] A private named Sash-ko-bon-quot, a soldier from the Pinconning nation in the First Michigan Sharpshooters, died when a railroad car crushed him as he lay intoxicated on the back of another car.[199] A New Jersey artilleryman described in graphic detail the death of another alcohol-train collision. "He had got enough liquor to make himself dull and stupid," James Harrocks wrote, "and sat down on the railway which runs alongside the camp. . . . The man seemed asleep although the engine driver did his best to stop the train . . . it was too late; in a few moments his head lay by the side of the rails and his body entangled in the wheels was carried about 30 yards further and there left the most shocking mangled body one can imagine."[200] Drunken soldiers were also unable to protect themselves from the enemy. On patrol in rural Virginia, some members of a Maine regiment became drunk, "and fell by the wayside, stupefied." Unwilling to linger in enemy-held country, the patrol had to leave them behind, and "while in they in this state of stupor, a party of Southrons [local partisans] came upon them and nearly severed their heads."[201] Similar circumstances led to the death of a Pennsylvania soldier "found lying outside the camp this morning with his throat cut from ear to ear." The soldier passed out in a state of "intoxication and some rebel here took the opportunity to give vent to his hellish spleen."[202] Others simply drank themselves to death. Captain Blackburn informed his wife that one of his men "died last night from the effects of bad whisky and took [so] much of it" that he died.[203] "On Christmas night [1862] a man by the name of Samuel Rodgers of Co. D., 26th Reg., Pa. Vol., died from intemperance," George Stephens wrote to a newspaper. "Just think of it, a man to die from excessive drinking in the U.S. Army, under the eye of military authority."[204]

UNABLE TO PERSUADE SOLDIERS to behave as they wanted, the army tried various means of regulating alcohol consumption among the enlisted men. Invariably, however, every method fell afoul of the citizen-soldier's desire to behave as an individual in an army dedicated to a group mentality. One means adopted by the army was the most basic and most likely to fail: the army tried to simply order soldiers to not drink. At various locations and at various levels of authority, the army tried to ban presence of alcohol in an attempt to force soldiers to stop drinking. But even if soldiers were inclined to obey the bans (which their sense of citizen-soldier privilege would not permit them to do), the irregularity of antialcohol regulations and the disparity in the level of enforcement ensured that the prohibitions were doomed to failure. Officers banned alcohol for good reasons, but soldiers often failed to see the justification, especially if alcohol was the primary, or only, form of recreation. At Plum Creek in the Nebraska Territory, Captain George Bailey declared that "under no circumstances will Ranchmen, Storekeepers, or Sutlers be allowed to sell Spirituous, Ale or Malt Liquors to any troops this command" despite the absence of any other form of entertainment at the remote location.[205] The decision to ban alcohol was often at the discretion of the local commander, whose tenure in that position might change along with the policy in that locality. When General Benjamin Butler, a political appointee, assumed command of Fort Monroe, Virginia, in 1861, he imposed his own personal ban on alcohol, with the sole exception of officers who produced a letter from a physician prescribing alcohol for medicinal purposes. But when Butler left a few months later to participate in the capture of New Orleans, his replacement rescinded the restriction.[206] To deny alcohol to the Iron Brigade, their commander posted "argus-eyed guards" at chokepoints like bridges to search soldier and cargo alike "so that the old subterfuge of putting a keg into a barrel of vinegar or cider, or bottles into sugar and molasses, does no good."[207]

This technique worked well with the Iron Brigade, but its colonel could not extend his authority beyond his own formation, so ultimate success proved impossible. Colonel Francis Lee of the Forty-fourth Massachusetts had the same problem of limited authority to control alcohol in areas beyond his command. Within his command, however, he was very active. "Colonel Lee has military jurisdiction over a territorial radius of one mile," Zenas Haines wrote, "and has no bowels of compassion for those fellows who open rum and refreshment booths along the highways and in the bushes about the camp." Lee zealously pursued liquor within his area of authority, but could do nothing about the regiments around him.[208] Particularly stringent officers even tried to control their soldiers' drinking when on liberty. When the men of the Seventy-sixth Ohio returned home on their veteran furlough, Colonel William B. Wood sent word ahead to the scheduled stops for their train to prevent the sale of alcohol. Even the regiment's officers were included in the ban, much to their chagrin.[209] Colonel (later General) Alvin Voris also restrained his soldiers while on a train trip, requiring them to remain in their cars when the train was in station, and exhorting his officers to set an example by engaging in "wholesome prohibition."[210]

Wholesale banning of whiskey only worked if an officer had absolute control over a wider region than their own camp. On Ship Island, off the coast of Louisiana, officers had authority over the entire island, and could, therefore, successfully ban alcohol, and under the auspices of General Order number 7, General Benjamin Butler successfully banned "All intoxicating liquors" on the island.[211] Officers in occupied regions of the South also enjoyed more autonomy to establish rules and policy. General Charles Heckman, commanding a pocket of Union occupation around New Bern, North Carolina, ordered all local taverns to close for violating his rules against selling liquor to soldiers.[212] As post commander for the entire city of Indianapolis, Colonel Newton Colby could control the activities of soldiers and citizens alike, but with less success. On March 19, 1864, Colby issued General Order number 2, prohibiting "the sale, or giving away, of intoxicating liquors, of any kind, to soldiers, or any soldier, with the limits of this command." A month later, however, Colby reported "some of the saloon keepers are violating the order, and they may soon get themselves into trouble for so doing." At the same time, however, Colby had to admit "the liquor saloons are very numerous and it is next to impossible to entirely stop their selling . . . and to exercise a wholesome restraint over them."[213] Earlier in the war, Washington, DC, had the same problem. On September 7, 1861, military authorities "made a descent upon 25 saloons which had been selling liquor to soldiers," earning each a $25 fine. But there were too many saloons to police, illicit profits were too high, and army attention was too inconsistent to curb the alcohol problem in the District.[214]

Weary of its failures to stem the flow of illegal alcohol, the entire Army of the Potomac tried to go cold turkey. On September 15, 1864, General George G. Meade issued General Order number 36 that banned both the importation of any alcohol to the army and the commercial sale of alcohol in the vicinity of army camps.[215] With the army in the midst of the siege of Petersburg, however, officers had better things to do than constantly search for a hidden bottle or improper package. The ban, moreover, did not include hard cider, which was plentiful in rural Virginia, until Meade added the spirit to the banned list, despite efforts by Provost Marshal Marsena Patrick to keep it available lest it force "men to drink Commissary Whiskey" instead.[216] Patrick had good reason for wanting Union soldiers to avoid the whiskey sold by the Commissary Department. A soldier from the Fourteenth Indiana opined that commissary whiskey was little more than "bark juice, tar-water, turpentine, brown sugar, lamp oil, and alcohol" with perhaps only a small amount of sarcasm.[217]

Not all soldiers drank to the point of insensibility. A minority opposed the use of alcohol for both practical and religious reasons. In the clash between Victorian morality and the rights of citizen-soldiers, a number of men decided that public virtue was more important to them than the recreational use of liquor. In some regiments, this attitude was the majority, and temperance was the rule instead of the exception. In other regiments, single soldiers were the only voice of restraint, as they described the debauchery around them. The movement toward temperance received support from a well-organized campaign before the war. Reformers, such as Benjamin Rush and Lyman Beecher, along with well-organized temperance societies, such as the American Temperance Society and the Washington Temperance Society, promoted sobriety as a Victorian virtue long before the section rivalry flamed into open war. Membership in these societies not only indicated a dedication to the promotion of temperate living, but also an adhesion to the Victorian code of restraint and moral living. Bound up in the religious exuberance of the Second Great Awakening, temperance was a strong moral force in antebellum civilian life.[218] Judging others through this righteous lens was an indicator of someone opposed to drinking for moral reasons. "[Sergeant William] Sawyer has proved himself a very small potato," Captain Joseph Blackburn judged. "He came into camp with hymnbook in hand, was first in speaking and praying, but alas he has been drunk a number of times."[219]

Some soldiers refused to imbibe for practical reasons, recognizing the destructive effects that alcohol had on discipline and good order, none more so than Major General George B. McClellan, first commander of the Army of the Potomac. As one of the first generals to lead the new army of citizen-soldiers into battle, he was also one of the first to recognize his soldiers' penchant for drink. Instead of accepting and managing the proclivity, however, McClellan railed at alcohol's evil influence and tried to ban it from the army. "It is impossible to estimate the benefits that would accrue to the service," McClellan wrote, ". . . [If the army practiced] total abstinence from intoxicating liquors. It would be worth 50,000 men to the armies of the United States."[220] To the minds of many soldiers, such as Private Charles Chase, "Whiskey is one of the greatest scourges to the army," and one that commanders could not purge.[221] One chaplain believed that "It is a well established fact in the minds of all who are acquainted with army men and movements, that were it not for *whiskey*, our war would have been terminated before this time."[222]

A few soldiers targeted the liquor ration specifically, noting the inconsistency between the army issuing alcohol while at the same time complaining about alcohol. "The government furnished whiskey and when the men got drunk punished them for drunkenness," Private Sawtelle complained. "I was so tired of it all that I wanted to go home where I should not have to come into contact with it."[223] Major Henry C. Forbes also opposed the whiskey ration, to the point of filing an official complaint against the officers in his regiment because of the "loss of efficiency" caused by whiskey.[224] Other soldiers could not comprehend the wastefulness of drinking. "There is men here that has got wives at home that is needy," Joshua Jones of the Nineteenth Indiana wrote incredulously, "and they are Spending their money for whiskey and getting drunk and buying all other foolery that does not profit them one cent."[225] George Cram complained that, while his company did not have enough to eat, the army devoted wagons to deliver "the meanest of whiskey to steal away their brains and injure their systems." When issued a whiskey ration, Cram was pleased to note that "a large number of Company F refused theirs."[226] The effects of alcohol scared some soldiers straight. "One of my Tent Mates died the other night of Gastroenteritis from the effects of drinking that execrable stuff called Whiskey," George Merryweather wrote, but a positive outcome of his death was that several men "who were his companions in his sprees . . . have sworn off drinking."[227] John Westervelt had a slightly different complaint, one that resonated with the attitudes of citizen-soldiers and antielites. Offended because the officers observed his unit while they drank their whiskey ration to prevent them from saving it up to get drunk, Westervelt refused his ration, stating, "if I cannot drink it when and where I please I will not drink it at all." He further equated the presence of "an officer standing over me is too much like contrabands [escaped slaves] and entirely repugnant to my feelings."[228] Captain DeForest despaired at controlling his men, recalling the reaction of one of his junior officers. "If I was the angel Gabriel," DeForest's second lieutenant stated, while observing a drunken revelry, "I should take my trumpet out of my mouth to swear."[229]

Other soldiers and officers opposed alcohol because it offended their moral or religious principles, and wondered why their fellow soldiers did not hold themselves to the same standard. John Campbell could only shake his head while "some of our 'boys' disgraced themselves today by getting beastly drunk. Oh, that men should barter their manhood for the gratification of their appetites."[230] Appalled by the drinking and misbehavior around him, John Pardington promised his wife "so much for Whiskey. Coming here has cured me. I think if I ever get home that no one will ever see me raise whiskey to my mouth only in case of necessity." In another letter, Pardington reiterates his temperance promise to his wife, along with a pledge to give up swearing as well.[231] Sergeant Hartwell rejected the idea that whiskey had positive medicinal value. "I have stood it as well as the best of them on long marches," Hartwell bragged to his wife, "sleeping hundreds of night with nearly everything I had on wet . . . yet I got along without liquor & took no more colds than others."[232] Sergeant Peter Welsh, himself a hard-drinking Irish soldier, still recognized the effect it had upon him and tried to dissuade his younger brother from drinking. "Shun the wine cup and company keeping," he advised, "shun the use of intoxicating drink as you would a foul and venemous [sic] serpent. It is the destroyer of happiness and prosperity of three fourths of the human race."[233] Some soldiers did more than just talk temperance; they acted upon it. Incensed by the presence of a sutler/liquor dealer in their regiment, soldiers of the Seventy-seventh Illinois resolved to remove this "eye-sore to the members of regiment." After warning the sutler to desist from selling liquor and observing the sutler ignore their warning, soldiers of the regiment "many of them . . . religious and many of those who made no pretensions to a religious character [but] were temperate in their habits" dismantled the sutler's tent and ejected him from their camp.[234]

Steeped in the antebellum reform movement, soldiers organized temperance societies in several regiments. Unable to watch the dissolute behavior around him, Chaplain Louis Beaudry tried to do something, at least in his regiment. Emulating the antebellum societies, Beaudry established a temperance society, with the design to "strengthen each other against the evil of Intemperance and to save therefrom our comrades in arms," with each man signing a public oath that "I hereby solemnly pledge myself, on honor as a gentlemen and soldier, to abstain entirely form the use of intoxicating liquors" for the duration of the war. Chaplain Beaudry was such an effective temperance speaker that he persuaded at least two hundred men of his regiment to sign a pledge not to drink while in the army. He also influenced a certain Mr. Doggett, who owned the property on which the regiment encamped, to also sign a pledge, leading Doggett to change the "name of the area from 'the Devil's Leap' to 'Temperance Hill.'"[235] In a similar society in a Maine regiment, more than 70 percent of one company signed a temperance pledge, including all of the officers.[236] Western soldiers also created societies. In the One Hundred Twenty-ninth Illinois, the men formed a society because "there is a great many that never drank a drop at home [who might] return tipplers, if they stay long" in the army.[237] The concern of the Illinois troops reflects the citizen-soldier mentality. Drinking whiskey may be acceptable to soldiers, but a citizen was not a long-term military man, and soldiers had to protect their virtue for the time when they returned to civilian life. Chaplains also became the source of strength for individual soldiers who wanted to change their habits. Chaplain Stuckenberg counseled a man who pleaded, "I am not yet 25 . . . yet my hair is gray. . . . Drink, drink has done it."[238] While many temperance societies failed, others persisted and persevered. "At noon, I issued whiskey to men on the works,"

Lieutenant Owen Hopkins noted in his diary. "Over one-third of the Seventh Kentucky detail refused to drink, as they . . . were nearly one half of them Sons of Temperance, having taken the pledge at Baton Rouge."[239] The Sons of Temperance were also active in the Twenty-third New York, concentrating their efforts on reducing drinking on paydays and persuading soldiers to send their wages home to their families.[240]

TEMPERANCE MIGHT HAVE ENJOYED more success if officers had not consistently set such a poor example for their men, but officers enjoyed more unrestrained access to alcohol and their behavior was often worse then their charges. The relationship between officers and drinking is clear evidence of the separation between the dominance of the Regular Army in earlier wars and the new breed of citizen-soldier. The mass of elected and appointed officers in the volunteer regiments swamped the pro-Victorian morality of the Regular Army's officer corps, molded at West Point. In its place, the army found itself led by many officers whose social attitudes more closely mirrored their men than their fellow officers in the Regulars. While Regulars and West Pointers prided themselves on their personal restraint and adherence to rigid discipline, volunteer officers refused to accept the same standard of personal behavior. As citizen-soldiers themselves, the volunteer officers were prepared to accept the military definition of discipline, in that they were prepared to lead their men into battle and defeat the enemy. But they were not, as a group, prepared to accept legal discipline, preferring to retain their identity as a citizen in the midst of the army. The antebellum culture of drinking remained strong, and officers maintained many peacetime attitudes toward alcohol. When William Sherman served as military governor of Memphis, for instance, he responded to a Confederate general's pledge to retake the city within sixty days by gentlemanly betting him a bottle of whiskey he could not.[241]

The problem with this belief system, however, is that enlisted men looked to their officers as examples of leadership, and were very quick to dismiss those who failed to measure up. From the perception of Union soldiers, officers who drank violated both the precepts of masculinity and Victorian morality, leaving officers in a social quandary. Masculinity included accepting burdens (including responsibility), courage, and good-natured comradeship. Victorian morality demanded restraint, propriety, and class identity. When officers drank, they blurred the lines of both social models, and tended to alienate the proponents of each social model. From the perception of a citizen-soldier, a drunken officer was a leader who failed in his responsibility, a coward that required liquor to provide "liquid bravery," and an elitist who drank freely while denying the privilege to their enlisted men. Supporters of Victorian morality viewed a drunken officer as an intemperate tippler, an unprincipled pretender to the ranks of gentlemen, and an embarrassment to his rank and his service. Officers who appeared drunk or who failed to control liquor in their camp faced a variety of criticisms from both sides of the social divide, making decision-making an unpopular task. The lack of discipline in camp denoted an officer who ran a lawless camp, earning him the scorn of his fellow officers and pro-discipline subordinates. Officers who abused alcohol (especially in battle) earned the perception that they were incompetent in the military arts, bunglers who got their men killed. Major General George McClellan certainly believed this. "Nothing can be more erroneous than to suppose that as long as an officer is not drunk to insensibility," he wrote in a General Order. ". . . [H]e is not drunk at all. The fullest possession of his faculties, by every officer, is necessary to fit him to discharge his duties properly."[242] Officers who drank whiskey too freely garnered the outlook that they could not lead by presence or example and had to lead by persuasion and permissiveness. Leaders who relied upon alcohol sometimes believed it made them popular with their men, or they convinced themselves that by issuing whiskey they were somehow controlling the unit's imbibing by deciding what they drank and when. Conversely, if an officer did crack down on alcohol use, he received a different set of censure. Disciplinarians earned the scorn of their men as someone exceeding their place or trying to make themselves better than their men, defying the code of the citizen-soldier. Teetotaling officers seemed to lack manliness, and risked the loss of masculinity in the eyes of their soldiers. Restricting booze might make the chaplain happy, but it tempted soldiers to leave camp to find recreation, creating different disciplinary problems. With soldiers split on the issue of alcohol in the ranks, officers found themselves unable to make everyone happy. As citizen-soldiers themselves, more officers drank than not, and officers under the influence of alcohol played an unfortunate role in the story of army discipline.

Officers who drank, however, found themselves in a different set of legal circumstances than enlisted men. Article 45 of the Articles of War stated, "Any commissioned officer who shall be found drunk on his guard, party, or other duty, shall be cashiered" from the army. Cashiering meant the army immediately dismissed the officer from the service with all pay due to him. In some cases, the army dishonorably discharged an officer and retained his accumulated pay as a further punishment. The army further barred a cashiered officer from service in the army in the future, as opposed to dishonorably discharged officers who could attempt to redeem their reputation by joining another regiment. Article 45 presented an enigmatic trap for officers who chose to drink, especially the phrase "or other duty."

When was an officer ever not on duty? If an officer attended a social function, chose to imbibe, became intoxicated, but then had to rush to his post when an alarm sounded, the army considered the officer drunk on duty. This situation placed officers in a precarious position if they chose to drink because the army essentially decided that officers were always on duty. Moreover, the army defined drunkenness on duty to include any activity begun by an officer but incomplete when the officer became drunk. This definition encompassed such potential snares as construction projects that took several days, marches to a distant location, or a lengthy siege or other military operation.[243] Officers had to be wary when opening a bottle, never knowing when the army would deem their personal time as time on duty.

The other side of side of this legal tangle was that officers faced only limited punishments if found drunk on duty. Article 45 stated that enlisted men found drunk on duty automatically faced a court-martial and whatever punishment the sitting officers chose to inflict. Officers, on the other hand, faced nothing worse than a cashiering from the service. Whereas enlisted men faced the possibility of a major fine or incarceration at hard labor, an officer faced a fine, a public reprimand, or a discharge from the service. Officers might find cashiering a humiliating experience, with the army declaring that they were a deficient officer, but enlisted men certainly considered that a lesser punishment than a fine (when they only earned $13 a month) or back-breaking labor wearing a ball and chain. To protect their reputations, officers often covered for each other, and if a regiment's officers decided to tolerate drinking amongst themselves, there was little the soldiers could do. Soldiers were quick to point out the hypocrisy in the differing situations. A Pennsylvania soldier claimed that "the men needed whiskey just much as the officers did. The private, who did the shooting, needed something to steady his nerves just as much as did the officer, who did no shooting," making a clear statement on the usefulness of officers.[244] "There are Capts. and Lieuts. who get fairly drunk," Charles Chase complained. "Of course they are not punished but the poor private is thrust into a cell and fed on bread and water."[245] When New York soldiers found one of their officers drunk near the enemy's lines, they dragged him back to camp, but one of them bitterly remarked "a like offense on the part of a private is death by firing squad" for attempted desertion.[246] Complaining that his company captain was "too drunk to stand and far too drunk to walk straight," Wilber Fisk bitterly protested that "He is a captain so it is all right. If he were a private he would have lodging in the guard house and perhaps worse penalties."[247] John Campbell resented the "officers [who] became intoxicated and behaved with all the simpleness, foolishness, and disgust that drunk men generally do," noting, "some of these same officers have had their men punished for getting drunk and making a disturbance in camp. Oh! consistency, thou art a jewel!"[248]

The army could not cashier every officer found drinking, however, and the army had to tolerate behavior among their officers in the same manner that they endured the antics of the enlisted men. This meant, of course, a shift of responsibility down to the regimental commanders, whom the army held responsible for the behavior of their own officers. This system created a patchwork of policies that varied widely from regiment to regiment, with the commanding colonel setting the tone for each unit. The most common tone was to let officers drink as they liked as long as their overall conduct did not affect the operations of their companies and the regiment as a whole. In the end, the citizen-soldiers' perspective on drinking won out over the Regular Army mentality of holding officers accountable for virtually every second of their day. Freed from most of the stringent restrictions on their behavior, officers tended to drink in patterns reminiscent of the citizen-soldiers they commanded, only with more access to alcohol and less accountability.

Enlisted men, as a rule, looked disapprovingly upon drinking by officers, judging them with by a standard to which most soldiers failed to hold themselves. Strangely, while most enlisted men viewed alcohol consumption as a masculine trait, drinking was not considered a measurement of a good officer. The occasional soldier defined masculinity in their officers through their drinking abilities. "Old Jack was very strict with the rest of the battery," Private John Cook wrote describing Lieutenant James Stewart, "but would at the same time drink more than any one else."[249] Cook was the exception rather than the rule, however, and wise officers recognized that their standing with their men was only as good as their reputations. Consequently, officers were more reticent to brag about their drinking exploits than were enlisted men, so most accounts of officer drinking come from the observations of their soldiers.

Some officers kept their drinking to a minimum. Charles Haydon related discussing "items of business" with a fellow officer over "glasses of iced brandy," although for a second round Haydon "took the ice minus the brandy."[250] While visiting his corps headquarters for an afternoon meeting, Captain Dodge, "in company with some other officers," convened and "dispatched several bottles of Rhine wine and some doughnuts."[251] Although not drunk, a soldier observed officers on General Alpheus Williams' staff "in high feather drinking punch" in the middle of the afternoon.[252] Much like their men, officers associated drinking with manliness and camaraderie, and officers felt pressured to partake "because it will not do at all to reproach other officers by refusing to drink with them."[253] Captain Thomas Orwig was of the same opinion. "There is much to be seen in the army that is disgusting and degrading," Orwig wrote critically to a friend, "But the greatest vice is *intemperance* and this is also among the officers. Many . . . entertain the idea that they cannot be hospitable or gentlemanly without offering something to drink."[254]

While officers comfortably enjoyed their whiskey, they had to be careful about their liquor intake because their soldiers were watching. Soldiers barely tolerated the authority of officers above them, and when officers abused their privileges they destroyed their legitimacy as leaders and it became nearly impossible to restore their lost standing. Wesley Gould had little regard for any officer appointed over him because of their intemperance. "There is a great maney [sic] of our Office that have not seen one sober day for the last month," he complained to his brother. "Even our Division Commander General [Robert B.] Potter is a cussed drunkard. All he ever was before the war was a dancing master and a whore house bully . . . [Lieutenant Colonel Theodore Gregg] is so drunk that he don't know what he is about half of the time."[255] One soldier complained about going to Sunday church services, only to find his regimental "adjutant also there, intoxicated." The soldier was appalled to see "while the minister is engaged in prayer," several officers "pass the bottle and take a drink" during services.[256] When not drinking in church, officers also drank while on duty, in direct violation of Article 45. Lieutenant John Sheldon, responsible for prisoners in a Washington jail, attended his duties "conspicuously flourishing a brandy bottle," much to the embarrassment of his men.[257] Another officer humiliated himself in front of his soldiers when, "having gone into a jollification time," he fell headlong into one of the latrines.[258] "The officers are haveing [sic] a gay and festive time, the majority of them being pritty well corned before night," Private Ferguson observed with some humor, "So much so that the ground would fly up and hit them in the face ocationly [occasionally]."[259] The appearance of officers under the influence particularly disappointed relatively small number of soldiers who opposed the use of alcohol. "Officers all drunk as fools tonight," a teetotaling Sergeant Hartwell told his wife. "Oh, misery."[260]

Soldiers lost respect for officers who appeared drunk, but suffered under those who became abusive while under the influence of alcohol. Captain Robert Erwin of the Seventy-seventh Illinois, for instance, discredited himself when he "got on a big drunk that night and abused his men shamfully [sic] and had them out in line at all hours of the night."[261] Soldiers of the One Hundred Twenty-second Ohio rushed to their posts in the middle of the night, only to find the alert was a false alarm caused by an officer who "attempted to cross the picket line without giving the countersign and they fired on him. He was drunk."[262] In the Sixth Wisconsin, an unusual turn of events occurred when soldiers had to complain about the "noise in their tents" caused by drunken officers. The noise "made some of the boys mad . . . there was a fuss . . . and one of the boys was wounded" by an irate officer.[263] Colonel William Weer, assigned to command the military prison in Alton, Illinois, had the dual problem of a short temper and advanced alcoholism. Weer terrorized enlisted men and junior officers alike, and allowed conditions at the facility to deteriorate badly. After several months of incompetence, Weer faced a court-martial for his failures, resulting in his expulsion from the army.[264] Drunken officers not only destroyed their reputations and standing with the enlisted men, as inebriation diminished their abilities to perform their duties. Major William Cook humiliated himself while trying to drill his regiment drunk, ordering improper maneuvers until "he was got away" by some embarrassed lieutenants.[265] Likewise, Second Lieutenant Thurston Owens of the Fifth USCT also created a drunken disturbance during a morning roll call, causing his dismissal from the army.[266] He was not the only USCT officer with a drinking problem. When assigned to the Second Louisiana Native Guard, Nathan Daniels reported the regiment in "good condition though somewhat dissatisfied with the conduct of Col. [Alfred G.] Hall," who had the habit of "being drunk—beastly so—for three days" or more.[267]

Drinking by officers was also potentially lethal to their men, especially when impaired officers tried to lead their men in battle. During the Battle of Bull Run, Colonel Dixon Miles appeared on the battlefield drunk, with observers noting, "He spoke with a mouth full of tongue. He rolled on his horse and could not keep his balance."[268] Observing General Blenker during the Fredericksburg campaign, John Haley noticed one morning, "Although it was barely daylight, Old Blinkey was 'fuller 'n a goat,'. . . It is not uncommon for this general to be muddled any hour of the day."[269] While on the Red River Campaign, a soldier noticed "Col. [Lysander] Webb having filled up with whiskey to keep the water out got pretty drunk and made us marched right in the center of road," causing a massive traffic jam.[270] One of the highest-ranking officers to lose their command due to whiskey was Colonel William Tilton, a brigade commander in the V Corps, who the army sent home because of conspicuous drunkenness during the Battle of Globe Tavern in 1864.[271] Even if generals and other high-ranking officers were not drinking or drunk during combat, soldiers on the losing side often blamed drunkenness as the reason their generals performed so badly. General Irvin McDowell, the loser at Bull Run, became the first, but certainly not the last, general to face charges of incompetence due to drunkenness.[272] A soldier who witnessed the Ambrose Burnside's disastrous Union attack at the Crater during the Siege of Petersburg characterized "The attack a perfect humbug. Caused by whiskey."[273] Because of his reputation and proclivity for alcohol, critics inevitably attributed Joseph Hooker's great defeat at Chancellorsville to alcohol, a charge Hooker vehemently denied.[274] Although he found Hooker's drinking habits unsavory, Captain George Barnard decided that he preferred a drunken Hooker to a sober Ambrose Burnside.[275]

With the exception of the insignia of their rank and the high expectations that came with them, officers were still common everyday individuals, and the product of their American upbringing. They, just like their men, faced the pressures of living up to Victorian standards while at the same time tempted to challenge authority by the citizen-soldier ethos. Caught between two conflicting standards of behavior, some officers became the paragons of responsibility and virtue. A minority, however, embraced the masculine attitudes of their soldiers, and the same experiences, pitfalls, and consequences of drinking that affected their men landed upon their shoulders as well. Officers celebrated special events and holidays just as did the enlisted men, providing further opportunities to imbibe, such events carried disciplinary risks. To prevent consorting with their men, officers celebrated amongst themselves, which seemed elitist to soldiers who scorned elitism. Officers celebrated when they deemed it proper, causing soldiers to complain that they celebrated only and to the extent to which officers permitted them. Officers commemorated the passing of colleagues in past battles, events that seemed ghoulish remembrances to past bloodlettings to their men. At one event, a sword presentation to Major General George Meade, a young captain described that "After the speeches came the feasting in which about Three hundred officers . . . took an active part. . . . Champagne and about a dozen different etcs were disposed of."[276] In celebrating the anniversary of a battle, John Ferguson disapprovingly noted that "Some of the officers of our regiment disgraced themselves & dishonored the dead of Iuka by celebrating the anniversary of the battle of Iuka by getting drunk last night." On an earlier occasion, Ferguson judged an officer gathering to celebrate George Washington's birthday by believing "Satan was more honored than Washington by it."[277]

When officers did drink to excess, they ran the risk of losing their standing with their men by engaging in conduct that lacked the decorum associated with an officer's rank. The army demanded peace and quiet after Taps, but drunken officers themselves violated this rule with their behavior. Colonel Charles Knobelsdorff, for instance, disrupted the quiet of his own camp for an entire month with his inappropriate antics.[278] Fighting, like that among the enlisted men, was also a by-product of drinking, and officers often came out the worse for wear because of it. Lieutenant Haydon described one brawl that occurred in his tent when a group of officers and NCOs met to play cards. After consuming twenty bottles of ale and six bottles of champagne "together with some liquor," an argument broke out over a card play. Soon, "Mason & Prentice came out with black eyes, Butler & Mack with noses skinned & bloody & Benson with some hard knocks in the bowels." The fight did not end there. "Mason then insisted on whipping the officer of the guard for ordering them to make less noise . . . Benson & North at once seized him [to keep him quiet] & rolled him all ends uppermost outdoors into a ditch."[279] In the Iron Brigade, Lieutenant Benjamin Hancock, filled with liquid courage, tried to pick a fight with Private Abraham Oliver, who had a reputation as someone good with his fists. Twice Oliver refused Hancock's baiting, even when Hancock removed his coat with his officer's insignia, indicating that they were then equals and Oliver could fight him without fear of repercussions. Finally, on his third foray against Oliver, the enlisted man slugged Hancock, knocking him senseless. The army court-martialed Hancock and exonerated Oliver.[280] Officers were also susceptible to alcohol-related deaths. "Col. [William] Dewey of the 23rd Iowa is dead," Sergeant Cyrus Boyd reported. "Old Whiskey at last laid him out as it is laying out many a thousand other men in this Army. It is killing more than the Confederates are killing."[281] Colonel Thomas A. Zeigle of the One Hundred Seventh Pennsylvania enjoyed the respect of his men with the exception of "that one vice which men in the army get into that is drinking too much *Whiskey*. He died with delyrium Tremens."[282]

In an effort to curtail the abuses and offenses that alcohol generated among their officers, the army tried various means to force their compliance with the army's standard of behavior. Some commanders tried to ban their officers from drinking, despite the officers' protests that the restrictions equated them with common soldiers and denied them their privileges as officers. When Colonel James T. McIvor assumed command of the One Hundred Seventieth New York, he found most of the regiment's officers unfit for service because of alcohol. McIvor responded by requesting that the Commissary Bureau "not sell any more Whiskey to the officers" of the regiment for fear that "before four weeks expire there will not be a Line officers for duty."[283] McIvor faced a storm of protest from his officers, but he stuck to his position. Other officers followed suit. During the Siege of Petersburg, General Napoleon Bonaparte McLaughlen, rejecting the excuses that the siege left officers with too much idle time, banned alcohol in his brigade by forcing the sutlers in his regiments to cease selling whiskey.[284]

Alcohol had a corrosive effect on personal standards of everyone in the army, and officers were no different. Crimes, both serious and petty offenses, inevitably occurred where alcohol was present, and officers were frequently as guilty as the enlisted men of criminal behavior. Colonel Alfred Hall's replacement in the Second Louisiana Native Guard accused him of chronic drunkenness and "selling passes to his soldiers."[285] Another officer faced disciplinary action for selling whiskey to soldiers after an inventory of the camp's supply came up "40 Gallons [of] Superior Whiskey short."[286] A similar offense occurred in the Seventh Kansas regiment, where the Commissary officers had converted the supply hut into a "grog shop," selling liquor freely to the officers and occasionally to the enlisted men.[287] In a major lapse of judgment, Lieutenant John Acker of the Twenty-fourth Ohio faced a court-martial for failing to retain control of a group of Confederate prisoners of war, "permitting soldiers and prisoners to enter drinking saloons" in Sandusky, Ohio.[288] Colonel Newton B. Lord, commander of the Thirty-fifth New York, set the standard for drunken behavior. When finally court-martialed for his antics, the army charged Lord with, among other things, appearing drunk at a brigade review, indecently exposing himself to a lady while intoxicated, and riding his horse into a tavern and ordering a brandy for each of them, not once but twice.[289]

When denying access to liquor did not work, the only solution was to levy punishment. Officers found solely of drunkenness on duty faced dismissal from the service, but only as a maximum punishment. To avoid wholesale turnover of officers, the army often eased its punishments for alcohol offenses. For drinking after hours in violation of regimental rules, the officers of a Wisconsin regiment found themselves in the guardhouse for a change. "They are very nice birds playing checkers with their noses through the iron gates," John Brobst wrote in great amusement.[290] Sometimes a public chastisement was sufficient punishment. Charles Cox wrote to his mother that "Capt. M is released from arrest having made a public confession to the Regt . . . his sacred word and honor that he would not touch another drop during his connection with the service."[291] Other commanders were not so lenient. Private James Sneden was pleased to hear that Colonel James Kerrigan of the Twenty-fifth New York was also cashiered because of "Too much rye" and believed "There are lots of other officers who would benefit the service" by receiving the same punishment."[292] When his adjutant became "gloriously drunk, and fell off his horse in the presence of the whole Regt," Colonel Charles Mattocks, declaring "I am death on a man who well get drunk on duty," placed the adjutant under arrest and "assigned him [to stay within] the limits of the Regimental Camp." At the subsequent court-martial, the "Adjutant tried to make an opium defense," but the court ruled against him and sentenced him to be cashiered.[293] Falling off one's horse was embarrassing, but nothing compared to the humiliation of Lieutenant Effingham Hyatt when he sobered up. According to his court-martial proceedings, Hyatt "did in a state of intoxication, sing bawdy songs and did propose to strip himself naked and dance to such songs in the presence of officers and enlisted men," behavior that earned him a cashiering.[294]

ALCOHOL WAS MANY THINGS to Union soldiers. It was a form of comfort, a recreational outlet, a source of bravery, and a demonstration of individuality. Whiskey turned boys into men, and men into idiots. It made officers popular when they served it and unpopular when they drank it. Booze made army life easier and it made army life harder. Officers despised it, but soldiers would not tolerate life without it. Alcohol, by its very nature, loosed restrictions and relaxed morals, both attributes of the masculine existence espoused by most enlisted men. Alcohol became a means to, and an excuse for, temporary suspensions of reality that most Union soldiers embraced as part of their privilege as citizen-soldiers. The right to drink alcohol, so prevalent in the antebellum period, was part of the rite of passage for young men, and if that resulted in disciplinary problems for the army, it was an issue that the army had to accept. If soldiers stepped beyond the bounds of disciplinary expectations only when they were drunk, however, the army might have more readily accommodated such behavior. But other behaviors demonstrated that soldiers frequently refused to subordinate themselves to army discipline, creating problems that made many officers think about taking up drinking themselves.

"THERE WERE THREATS TO SHOOT THE OFFICERS"

Insubordination in Various Forms

The soldiers of the Union army learned very quickly from the start of their enlistments that military duty meant obeying orders, and discipline and regulations governed their lives. For better or worse, military law as symbolized by the officers appointed to lead them was the last word on what was right and what was wrong. Soldiers might periodically have the Articles of War read aloud to them, as required by army regulations, but few probably spent much time contemplating the philosophy that created the system of military justice that regulated their lives, at least until they broke one of the army's rules and faced the consequences of their actions. Then the dual nature of military law became evident. Civilian law, as characterized by Edward Byrne, was a negative procedure in that it only punished those who committed offenses only after the offenses occurred. Furthermore, the application of the legal system could only deter future criminal acts because the law lacked the authority to correct the behavior of potential criminals. Civilian law attempted only to "regulate behavior so that people can live together in peace and tranquility." Military law, Byrne believed, was a positive legal procedure because it not only punished those guilty of criminal offenses, it also imposed discipline upon soldiers to forestall offenses from occurring in the first place. Hence, military law included offenses that had no corresponding crime in civilian law, such as desertion, cowardice, or insubordination. The purpose of this additional control was to create "self-discipline," a mode of behavior amongst soldiers that would "promote good order, high morale, and discipline" so that the individual soldier "will instantly obey a lawful order, no matter how unpleasant or dangerous the task may be."[1] A fine aspiration, but an aspiration that soldiers did not share.

As citizen-soldiers, the new recruits had a fresh memory of the civilian legal system that controlled their pre-war lives. They recalled, in their civilian existence, that no one punished them for saying what they wanted, being late for work, or for quitting their jobs. Factory workers or clerks had to obey the orders of an employer while on the job, but were the masters of their own homes when not working. Soldiers from an agricultural setting were particularly unaccustomed to the level of personal restraint they were expected to accept. Not surprisingly, soldiers often did not embrace the "positive" existence that the army created for them. In their desire to assert their independence, soldiers often had to reject the army's demand to subordinate themselves for the benefit of the whole. Whether for personal liberty or self-preservation, soldiers had to make the decision whether subordinating themselves for the greater good was more important than their own perceptions of honor, manhood, and group identity. The consequence of that choice varied as widely as the soldiers themselves. Soldiers ran the risk of being court-martialed, punished, or ostracized by their peers for failing to obey the rules, share the burden, or accept the same risks as their comrades. Sometimes a soldier's behavior received the blessing of their fellows because they approved of the expression of individuality, and sometimes the actions earned scorn, derision, and hatred because the decisions reflected cowardice, a lack of masculinity, and a fragmentation of unit cohesion.

A FREQUENT BEHAVIOR that, literally in this sense, split units was straggling. For all of the railroad's impact upon the Civil War, soldiers still walked more than they rode. Marching was the most time-efficient means of moving large numbers of soldiers, with marches of twenty miles or more occurring with regularity throughout the conflict. An army marching in tight formation to a steady cadence made for good imagery, but the reality was usually quite different. Soldiers had any number of reasons to fall out of a march, some legitimate and some not. Soldiers suffered from physical weariness, hot weather, or lack of water. Others failed to keep up with their units because they wandered off to forage or were simply too lazy to continue. Officers, of course, tried their best to limit straggling from the column. Straggling soldiers were no longer under the eye, and hence control, of their officers and liable to commit some infraction of the rules. Stragglers made an officer look bad to his superiors, implying that he could not control his men or that their straggling was indicative of other poor discipline. More dutiful soldiers also looked down upon stragglers as shirkers from duty and weaklings who lacked the masculine traits to bear up to a long march. An undercurrent to all of the criticism of straggling was an unspoken accusation of cowardice, with loyal soldiers measuring their comrades who straggled as weak souls who were also likely to falter in battle as well. "I have spoken to stragglers upon the march," Corporal Zenas Haines noted. "There are two or three distinct kinds of straggling. One is involuntary—the result of sickness or exhaustion. Another comes from laziness or the want of spirited determination to bear up, and another comes from cowardice."[2]

Long marches that lasted several days taxed the physical ability of soldiers to keep marching on aching and blistered feet. Captain DeForest described one such tortuous march. "In the morning the whole regiment starts limping, and by noon the best soldiers become nearly mutinous" from the exertion, leading them to "curse the general for order such marching, [and] they curse the enemy for running away instead of fighting." As bad as the soldiers felt, the officers had it worse because "the company officers, as sore-footed as anyone, must run about from straggler to straggler" to keep them moving. Finally reaching their destination, DeForest's men were "ready to fight the bloodiest of combats rather than march a mile further."[3] Other regiments had it just as bad. "Straggling became almost a mania," one soldier wrote before the Battle of Chancellorsville. "[S]ome regiments not being able to account for half their men."[4] If distance did not cause soldiers to lag behind, the frequently harsh Southern weather did. "The load of 150 rounds of cartridges, which the men had to carry, broke many of them down," Theodore Dodge wrote, "and the intense heat melted them."[5] Sergeant Benjamin Hirst described one particularly lethal march. At mid-morning "the Suffering of the men commenced," Hirst remembered, ". . . we seemed to be suffocated eat each step. The Ambulances were soon filled with sick and utterly used up men. Several were Sun Struck and Died in a few moments. I saw one man fall down; in 3 minuets [*sic*] he was Dead and in 30 Burried."[6]

Such marches damaged the health and enthusiasm of the most ardent volunteer, but most observers tended to portray stragglers as morally rather than physically weak. As if determination alone could sustain the body on a physically debilitating march, ideal soldiers pressed on while those who lacked in spirit or fortitude lagged behind. While recognizing "some of these stragglers are good soldiers, who are sick and footsore," Captain Thomas Galway characterized most stragglers as "systematic shirkers who are anything and everything but the soldiers they enlisted to be. . . . driven ahead like sheep."[7] Another witness described the devolution of a passing regiment, with the "strong soldiers, with their eyes on the road ahead" leading the "squads that lounged forward lazily and unevenly," followed by "a shambling rabble of laggards—old skulkers, convalescents, limping recruits . . . [who] scrambled over the ditches and into the fields or prowled off towards the farmhouses."[8]

The only thing the army could do on a march was to manage the stragglers the best they could. If a soldier needed to fall out during a march, an officer, if he trusted the soldier, might issue a pass. This written document informed army authorities that the soldier had permission to leave his unit to rest with the understanding that the soldier would rejoin his unit at the earliest possible moment. A good example of this occurred to Corporal Thomas Mann while his unit moved to the Battle of Antietam. After Mann marched all day while suffering from a bout of jaundice, "the captain gave me a pass to fall out of the ranks, and the first thing I did was to lie down in the corner of a fence . . . and immediately fall asleep" before rejoining his regiment the next day.[9] Soldiers quickly took advantage of the pass system, leaving some regiments with more soldiers lagging behind than keeping pace. Marching through Mississippi in July 1863, William Wiley found "a great deal larger of the regiment" was straggling like him, while only "the officers and about one third of the men" arrived at their destination as scheduled.[10] Commanding generals detailed other soldiers to bring up the rear of the column to scoop up the stragglers and keep them moving. Describing such a task, Private Bellard described his orders as "to drive before us all stragglers who were resting in the woods . . . all men found laying in the woods or straggling along the road were picked up and taken along with us."[11] Even when tasked with this duty, officers still extended some leniency. Wilbur Fisk had just begun to prepare his breakfast when officers ordered his regiment to fall in and move out. "I love my breakfast better than I did the order," Fisk decided, "and concluded to remain and eat it." When discovered by a passing officer, "We told him how it was and he waited several minutes for us" to finish the repast.[12]

This permissive attitude with stragglers reflected the realities of human endurance, but some officers tried to compel their stragglers to keep up with their formations, efforts that usually ended in failure of its designed intent and with generating resentment among the enlisted men. Regimental leaders, not their men, faced the consequences if they failed to obey a commanding general's orders to move their regiments to a specific place by a specific time, so junior officers felt the pressure to perform up to expectations. Officers also had to be wary of granting too much leeway to their men, lest they earn a reputation in the eyes of their superiors as someone who lacked leadership skills or the respect of their men. At least one officer, Colonel George Hays of the Eighth Pennsylvania, faced a court-martial for allowing his regimental formation to disintegrate on a march. One witness testified the "regiment was scattered over four miles," with many men "sitting by the side of the road playing cards."[13] Officers who tried to use physical force to punish stragglers and keep them in line found themselves frustrated by the sheer numbers of exhausted men or, even worse for them, marked as a brute that cared more about discipline than the care of his men. Captain Francis Barlow, in addition to using guards to round up stragglers, himself beat and kicked soldiers who could not keep up, earning him the eternal hatred of his regiment.[14] Private Timothy Bateman of the Twelfth New Jersey believed officers in his regiment overreacted when they arrested three soldiers for "falling out [of the march] to cool Coffee."[15] One officer pursued the arrest of three stragglers all the way to a regimental court-martial that found three stragglers guilty and fined them each $10.[16] Fines became the most common means of compelling men to stay with their regiments, although the practice was not popular. "Every man that fell out in out company had deducted from his pay $13.00," John L. Smith complained, "and I regret to say that nearly half of the men of the regiment were victims of this robbery."[17]

Another behavior that damaged collective cohesion was malingering: the willful falsehood of a physical or mental impairment to avoid combat or undesirable duty. Soldiers who faked such an ailment to avoid unpopular or dangerous tasks represent a curious blend of masculine expectations and self-preservation. Unlike those who actively mutinied, malingerers did not challenge the totality of army discipline, but instead only temporarily stepped outside of the army command structure for their own perceived self-interests. Unlike those who deserted, malingerers would not or could not openly face a charge of cowardice by their peers or reject their duties as a soldier, but their desire to protect their own selves meant that they took the chance to remain physically a soldier while at the same time avoiding the obligations of a soldier at a critical time. Malingerers found themselves in a moral quandary that found them struggling to act out the requirements of manhood, while submitting to the fear and desire to preserve oneself. Soldiers who malingered, however, found little sympathy from the army and their peers, who considered the conduct as, at best, laziness, or, at worst, craven cowardice. In its least disruptive form, soldiers malingered to avoid unpopular duty around camp. To avoid picket duty on a rainy night, for instance, Private Louis Leonhardt, according to his commanding officer, "dodged off & hid himself so that I could not find him."[18] Other soldiers found ways to avoid the everyday tasks of maintaining the camp and functioning in the army. Such behavior angered their comrades, who had to work extra hard to cover for their less-useful colleagues. "A few brave men do all the fighting and a few industrious ones all the work," Thomas Galway complained, "whilst the rest go off behind clumps of bushiness or into deep ravines and grow fat and save their bodies."[19]

Malingerers from duty caused minimal problems because they at least stayed with their units and officers had the chance to modify their behavior. Soldiers who malingered to avoid combat, however, caused much more problems. The purpose and duty of a soldier in wartime was to engage and defeat the enemy, a purpose negated when soldiers avoided their duty and refused to fight. Combat was also a test of manhood, which malingering also complicated. A soldier could avoid the threat of combat by malingering, yet still claim to have upheld his masculinity by remaining within the army institution. A malingering soldier may have missed the opportunity to share the risks of combat with his fellows, but a medical excuse permitted him to avoid the charge of cowardice. "It is not that men are wanting either in courage or patriotism," one soldier reasoned when trying to explain malingering, "but each man has some private reasons of his own why he would escape danger or death or maiming if an honorable chance" presented itself.[20]

To soldiers who stayed in the army, accepted the hardship, and faced the enemy in battle, malingerers were poor excuses for men. Instead of facing their fears, they hid behind perceived weaknesses and failed to stand with their comrades. Edward Wightman had little good to say about the "beats" in his regiment who "while in the army, by living off their wits, feed from the fat of the land and in the event of a battle are either on the sick list or drop out of the ranks at the first favorable opportunity."[21] Officers with reduced commands because of an excessive number of malingerers believed the "prodigious sick list might be reduced by half by taking out the lazy & shirks" and returning them to duty.[22] Soldiers felt the same scorn for those who managed to acquire a medical discharge. "Tell me what the brave boys that have got home have to say about the war," a New York soldier wrote his wife. "The most of us think they were [only] home sick."[23] Others were less subtle in their accusations of cowardice. Writing to his parents of two deserters from his company, James Newton characterized one of them as "as great a coward as ever lived" because at the Battle of Corinth "he pretended to be sick but did not get any sympathy from any of the boys."[24] Charges of cowardice followed many soldiers, imposing a penalty upon them even if they achieved their aim of leaving the army. Private Samuel Cobb, who fled in panic in his first battle, tried to afterwards return to his unit with a bandaged hand, claiming a wound. A medical examination found but a "neat little puncture," and his comrades branded Cobb a coward, a charge that followed him when he returned home in 1865.[25]

Soldiers had a variety of methods and reasons to malinger, depending upon their goal. For those who wanted a break from the labors of army life, the answer was Sick Call. Immediately after reveille every morning, soldiers with medical ailments made a sick call to the regimental physician for medical treatment. If their ailment was sufficiently dire, the doctor kept them from their daily duties to recuperate. "If the doctor thinks any of them to [*sic*] sick for duty he can excuse them from duty and they will not have anything to do on that day," Sergeant Welsh observed. "A great many go and make a long face and play sick when there is scarcely anything the matter with them."[26] In some regiments with malingering soldiers and compliant physicians, the number of men on Sick Call reached unrealistic numbers. In July 1864, for instance, 20 percent of the Sixty-seventh Ohio were routinely on sick call.[27] For soldiers who wanted out of the army entirely, a medical discharge was the goal. One man emptied his medicine supply looking for something that would earn him a trip home. "I have been taking Pulsotil, Bryvina, Beladonna, Acoute, Nuy Pom," and anything else he could get his hands on to make himself "look pale and sickly."[28] One Pennsylvania solider, described as "a first class coward," managed to obtain a discharge after eating soap to make himself ill.[29] A Minnesota soldier arranged a discharge by soaking his feet in lye, creating painful but temporary blisters.[30] An army doctor discovered one soldier, who "complained of passing enormous quantities of urine," was padding his urine sample by partially filling the sample vessel with water before he started.[31] A Maine volunteer, described by his recruiting officer as "bristled all over with fight and spoiling for a scrimmage," became disenchanted with the army after only five days and wanted to go home. Informed that the army only granted discharges for disability, the soldier "drawing down the corners of his mouth and planting both hands over his bowels . . . fetched a fearful groan and fled to the surgeon."[32] When Private Joseph Hotz was informed by his wife that his child had died, he resolved to get out of the army. Promising his wife "when we go into battle again I'll hold back as well as I can," Hotz planned to "report sick as so many others do," and pressed his wife to find a doctor at home that could arrange a discharge. When finding such a corrupt doctor proved difficult, Hotz instructed his wife to "tell him that I broke my shoulder and also a rib," and if "he can get me discharged, I'll pay him well for it" when Hotz got home. "It would be fine with me," Hotz determined, "if I wouldn't have to fight again."[33]

Often the goal of malingering was simply to avoid the harshness of army life, and for those seeking an easier military existence for a few days a hospital seemed a good place. Hospitalized soldiers did not stand guard, did not engage in practice drill, received good food and attention, and rested in comfortable beds. As a consequence, hospitals became collecting grounds for malingerers. After the Battle of Chancellorsville, a soldier "threw a stack of guns down on his head and posed as wounded man" to seek temporary refuge at his division hospital.[34] Sergeant Welsh looked forward to punishing a man in his company who "never got wounded but went to [the] hospital sick" when he finally came back.[35] Some soldiers, however, understood the impulse to escape, if only temporarily. "Dan Reagan went to the Hospital . . . unable to do duty." Private Herman White wrote, "I think he was more afraid than sick."[36] Hospitals seemed a particularly good place to be if a battle loomed, and the threat of combat always seemed to increase the need for medical care. Lieutenant Thomas Durham recalled a soldier who "could smell a battle from afar and would take the 'dry-grypes' before the battle."[37] Sometimes a soldier did not need to go to the hospital to find temporary relief. Knowing that whiskey was a handy medical remedy and needing a drink on a hot day, one soldier "threw himself down on the side of the road pretending to be sun-struck . . . they poured ab[out]t a pint of whiskey down him, when he slowly recovered & went on."[38]

Soldiers who malingered had to accept the consequences of their actions, and the consequences were often not what they anticipated. They lost the respect of their comrades, and they also faced the possibility of alienating their families and communities. A malingerer who managed to procure his release from the army bragged about how he fooled his commanding officers, earning him the label of coward at home and making it impossible to find work.[39] When a family friend suggested that he mutilate himself to get out of the army, David Ashley of the Third New York Cavalry refused, knowing the reception his home town was likely to give him. "In regard to having one of my fingers shot off so as to get me out of danger," Ashley wrote his parents, "I would say, I do not desire any such 'glory.'" Besides, he added, "I don't wish to come home until I see Richmond in our hands."[40] It was not only a community that could turn on malingering soldiers; sometimes the families of the malingerers themselves turned in a faker rather than receive a coward in their midst. When army authorities checked on Private Elihu Parker to make sure his medical discharge was legitimate, Parker himself, according to the reporting officer, "claims to be sick, but his parents, wife, and brother say he feigns it all."[41]

The most drastic form of malingering came in the form of self-injury, as soldiers inflicted wounds upon themselves to escape army life. Like feigned illnesses, army doctors had a difficult time discerning accidental injuries from intentional ones. Given the army's loose discipline when it came to firearms, accidental shootings were not unusual. Suspicious shootings that occurred without witnesses and in nonlethal areas of the body, however, always raised an eyebrow. "There have been several accidents last week here," Amos Downing of the Sixth Maine suspiciously told his brother, "Some got shot through the hand, others lost two fingers."[42] James Wiggins' company had some similar "accidents." "There are two of our boys that were wounded since we came here," Wiggins wrote his parents. "Corporal Alton . . . had his

Carbine resting on his foot and [his] bridle rein caught the hammer and it went off and took his toe off," while another soldier "shot himself with his revolver in the toe."[43] Accidents inevitably happened, but when convinced that a soldier inflicted the wound himself, his comrades quickly applied the label of coward. When a private of the Twenty-ninth USCT, a soldier long disenchanted with army life, claimed a fellow sentry accidentally shot him in the hand, the other sentry vouched for him, although the rest of his company remained skeptical.[44] Private Frederick Clark, writing from a hospital after the Second Battle of Bull Run, claimed a bullet wound in the hand. "Nobody doubts that he shot himself," a fellow soldier noted, ". . . he was a trembling little coward."[45] Other self-mutilations, however, were more overt. Reporting on casualties among the One Hundred Seventh New York after the Battle of Antietam, Bushrod James noted that "some of the cowardly men would shoot off the ends of their right forefingers, hoping it would be considered accidental . . . [and] they could be protected from the dangers of an engagement."[46] A newly arrived recruit in the One Hundred Forty-fifth Pennsylvania "shot off his little toe last night no doubt hoping thus to be discharged."[47]

Soldiers shooting their own fingers under the duress of combat are certainly shocking, but self-injury is understandable only in the context of masculine behavior. If a soldier no longer wanted to be in the army and shooting off a toe was sufficient to remove him from the obligation, why did he not do it before he left home? A possible answer is that he wanted to demonstrate his willingness to fight, and hence masculinity, by donning a uniform and going to the front lines. Once there, however, he could injure himself while in uniform and return home to claim the masculine status of a wounded veteran. Similar to the practice of self-mutilation was the hope of receiving what later soldiers in World War II called a "million-dollar wound," a wound serious enough to receive a discharge but not enough to debilitate them for life.[48] Lieutenant Tully McCrea, writing to his fiancée, confessed that he on occasion "wished I could be wounded in the battle . . . just enough to give me a sick leave." McCrea recalled, however, that the Major in his regiment "wished the morning before the battle that he could get a slight wound so that he could go home," but wound up "inflicted with a mortal wound."[49] Daniel Mowen of the Seventh Maryland complained that a mule kicked him, but complained more that the kick did not injure him enough to get a medical furlough.[50] Elisha Stockwell, struck in the arm by a spent artillery round at Shiloh, was "as tickled as a boy let out of school" when the injury got him out of the army.[51] Officers also malingered and used self-injury to escape the army. Due to the higher responsibility placed upon them, however, the punishment for shirking their duty was usually a humiliating court-martial for cowardice or conduct unbecoming an officer. John Holahan had nothing but contempt for an officer who "kept sick" when a battle was imminent, but returned in great health after the battle "put[ting] on more airs than a country stud horse."[52] Lieutenant Albert Thomas of the First Michigan Sharpshooters faced disciplinary action for languishing in a rear-area job while claiming to suffer from wounds received at the Battle of Spotsylvania. His senior officer charged him with cowardice, denying that Thomas had fought at Spotsylvania and that he was further "guilty of self-mutilation."[53] The army court-martialed and cashiered Captain Alfred Brooks of the Twenty-ninth Massachusetts for constantly claiming illnesses that kept him from his command in the field while at the same time enjoying a "course of riotous living, attending balls, parties, picnics, dinner parties, etc."[54] Captain Edward Bowen of the One Hundred Fourteenth Pennsylvania went home to recover from a slight wound, what one private described less as life threatening and more as "a wound in the shoulder strap."[55]

As the only authorities with the training to discern the actors from those truly ill, army doctors played a key role in detecting malingerers. Army authorities warned physicians to be "absolutely incredulous . . . sharp, shrewd, cunning, and quick" lest they be deceived by "every unfit recruit, sound drafted man, and rascally substitute."[56] Under the crush of wartime necessity the army had to hire the services of many newly trained physicians, so William Fuller, a surgeon of the First Michigan, formulated a set of eight principles to guide new surgeons in their treatment of soldiers and to detect malingering. The principles stressed, above all else, patience and observation, and while most surgeons operated under compressed circumstances, Fuller's principles were sound nonetheless.[57] Using a bit of patience, reasoning, and observation, surgeons could locate at least some malingerers and return them to their units. One surgeon, suspicious that a soldier was faking his claim of a bad back, ordered an unusual treatment instead of letting the soldier lay about in bed. The surgeon ordered his nurses to lacerate the soldier's back in several places as if they were drawing blood and then cover the lacerations with a "blister," a poultice to protect the incision. Finding hospital treatment much worse than he thought, the soldier pronounced his back much better and asked to return to his regiment.[58] Another soldier, pleading weakness in one of his legs, miraculously recovered when a suspicious surgeon announced that the only remedy was to amputate the leg. As proof of his recovery, the soldier returned to his regiment by escaping the hospital ward in the middle of the night, "and the only means of escape was over a fence twelve feet high."[59] William Stewart, a surgeon in the One Hundred Twenty-third Pennsylvania, found a soldier "rubbing a copper coin over a slight irritation of the skin, thus producing an aggravated ulcer which kept him safe in the hospital." When Stewart informed the soldier that "if there was no marked signs of improvement . . . within twenty-four hours, I should be obliged to amputate his leg." That prognosis "had the effect of putting him into fighting condition again very soon."[60]

Punishing soldiers who malingered, however, was a difficult proposition. Only trained physicians knew for sure if a soldier was actually ill or just faking it, so the army could only levy punishment after allowing time to determine a soldier's true status. The army considered malingering a formal offense, and not an impulsive act, because the offender had to consciously plan and carry out his charade. Consequently, the army held malingerers liable for their actions.[61] The colonel of a Maine regiment, for instance, ordered a chronic malingerer drummed out of camp in disgrace, despite his protests of innocence.[62] Granting a soldier a discharge, even one as humiliating and painful as a drumming out, essentially granted the soldier what he wanted, so instead of discharging offenders, the army usually fined them and imposed additional duties to try to make soliders out of them. Private James Griffith of the Fifth Infantry Regiment of the Regular Army was one such case. Convicted of seven counts of malingering, the army merely fined him and put him to hard labor for three months.[63]

A way to avoid a malingering charge and still preserve one's masculinity was to find work behind the lines as a clerk, quartermaster, blacksmith, or any of a number of other service jobs. These tasks permitted a soldier to stay in uniform but avoid the hazards of combat. James Avery felt no shame that his position as aide-de-camp to a colonel kept him out of the front-line fighting, justifying his position by stating "I think I have done my portion of hard labor in the field—now I am willing that others may occupy my place."[64] James Horrocks, writing to his parents in England, wrote of his desire to attain the position of quartermaster sergeant recently vacated when its occupant was promoted to lieutenant. Horrocks liked his current position of company clerk, "but whenever there is fighting I shall have to take part, as either cannoneer or driver." Instead, as quartermaster "there is then a chance of a commission and a good prospect of returning safe and sound." The average soldier tended to scorn medical malingerers, but soldiers serving in noncombat roles did not earn the same disregard. Horrocks believed that other soldiers would try for the quartermaster position just as he might because such an act of self-preservation "is here regarded universally as a *Smart thing* and the person who does it is a *dem'd smart fellow.*"[65]

Union soldiers might debate the cowardice of a malingerer when a possibility of danger arose, but there was no question about the cowardice of men who fled when battle was clearly imminent or actually commenced. Those with the weakest nerve left before the battle even began. Officers of the Fourth Maryland, for instance, issued orders to arrest Private Charles

Williams, who fled "from his company when it was drawn up in like of battle, expecting to meet the enemy."[66] Austin Stearns wrote derisively of men who lost their courage when the first "minie would come singing over," causing them to "lie down till the main part of the army had passed, and they would go double-quick to the rear."[67] Disgusted at the actions of his comrades during the Union army's defeats in the Shenandoah Valley, Sergeant Welsh opined that soldiers running just as combat loomed "believe a living coward is better than a dead heroe [*sic*]."[68] At least one fleeing soldier attempted to justify his personal retreat by claiming that he had a family to support at home, preferring to "let the young men who have no families fight."[69]

One indicator of the potential for flight was an excess of bravado. Many soldiers noted that those who spoke the loudest about coming to grips with the enemy were often the first to run in a fight. "The bruiser who goes around at big musters with a chip on his shoulder," James Abraham observed, ". . . seldom ever carries it into battle," while "the little, quiet, modest fellow whom everyone expects to see faint at the first sniff of gunpowder will perhaps forge to the front every time" a battle occurs.[70] "I find that men who talk the most are not always the bravest," Chauncey Cooke wrote his parents, "Maybe they are more anxious to die for their country than I am but . . . I am doubtful."[71] Private Sawtelle had little good to say about a soldier in his company who seemed proud of his early-war photograph, depicting him sitting aggressively holding a "revolver [in one hand] and in the other a big dirk knife," but thereafter he "was always hanging around the officers after a soft job . . . that would keep him out of the fighting."[72] Instead of being impressed by loud pronouncements and physical prowess, one officer opined "that the fisticuffs and bully bluffers were as rule the worst cowards in battle."[73] The obvious implication is that a coward was masking his fear by excessive aggression, but it is also likely that many soldiers, in youthful masculine exuberance before their first fight, expressed such bluster. They remembered the ones who ran away, while silently regretting their own bravado.

It was easy to charge someone who fled before a battle with cowardice, as the outcome of the fight was still in question. It was much harder to label a coward, however, once a battle commenced. In the confusion of combat, soldiers and officers often had to decide for themselves, through their own small prism of experience, if staying on the battlefield was a good idea or not. While a battle might unfold favorably in a large scale, an individual soldier did not have the big picture and had to make personal decisions based upon what he was experiencing and what was going on around him. Unit cohesion and instilled discipline constantly battled with the chaos of battle and the urge for self-preservation to decide if a soldier opted to stay in a fight or if he chose to leave. In the midst of the great Union victory at Gettysburg, for instance, Marsena Patrick "had my hands full . . . to keep the Troops from breaking. It was hot work & I had several lines formed [to catch retreaters] so that very few succeeded in getting entirely through."[74] Instead of retreating in good order when flanked at the Battle of Stones River, the Forty-fourth Indiana fled as a group despite the "officers vainly endeavoring to rally at the fence where lay the 13th O[hio] as our reserve."[75]

As the soldiers of Union army shed their idealistic aspirations for the war, became more pessimistic, and challenged the authority of their officers as the war progressed, the definition of cowardice became harder to find.[76] Instead of a general definition of bravery accepted by all, with all exceptions labeled as cowards, bravery and cowardice became a personal choice. Those who chose to leave the battlefield believed they did so for the correct reasons (impending defeat or lack of support from other units), and thus felt no shame for their actions. Those who remained on the battlefield while others left could claim the mantle of bravery and accuse others of cowardice, often knowing full well that in similar circumstances they would behave in the same way. This duality when it came to cowardice became a convenient means of judging personal behavior on the battlefield, with the cowardice of others becoming a ready excuse for battlefield failures. By identifying the few cowards amongst the larger group of brave and loyal patriots, entire units could pin the blame for failure on the few and preserve the honor and masculinity of the group. Private David Lilley, for example, was not sorry to see a former soldier in his regiment cowering at home because "he never was much of a Soldier" and he was "not fit to be where good men are wanted."[77] Consequently, cowardice became the cause for the failure of the Union's efforts and an inevitable outcome of every defeat. At the same time, charges of cowardice appeared most often as an outcome of defeat. When the Union was victorious in battle, there was plenty of credit to go around, but when defeats occurred someone had to bear the blame.

The extent of cowardice had to be measured against what soldiers considered bravery. Gerald Linderman charted this shift in the concept of bravery in his *Embattled Courage*, documenting how soldiers blamed cowardice for defeat, especially early in the war. Later in the war, personal bravery became less overt and demonstrated as the war forged a new definition of bravery. Soldiers branded a soldier who hid himself from enemy fire early in the war as a coward, but very soon such cowardly behavior became the key to survival. Instead of standing bravely in the open during the Battle of Yorktown, Private Herman White made no apologies for concealing himself during an artillery barrage. "You better believe I lay pretty flat," he told his parents without a hint of shame. "I stuck my head down behind a stump and if ever I lay flat twas then."[78] Even more telling was the willingness of soldier to admit their cowardice, something unthinkable in the early months of the war. Although relatively rare, the occasional honest soldier admitted their fear in their writings. Private John Cuzner heaped praise on the bravery of his comrades in the Sixteenth Connecticut at the Battle of Antietam, but "As for myself, I am a big coward."[79] As self-preservation became the primary goal of Union soldiers, cowards became something less to be pitied and more something to be hated. Soldiers who fled the battlefield risked the lives of the comrades left behind, threatening the chances for self-preservation. The evolving disregard for authority also clouded the definition of cowardice, as soldiers could justify their retreat off the battlefield due to incompetent or cowardly officers, another example of self-preservation as soldiers refused to remain in situations that threatened their lives.

Because cowardice became such a personalized event, and therefore difficult to define, soldiers viewed the unwillingness to fight through a spectrum of opinions. The anticipation of battle affected each soldier differently. "Our Colonel told us to keep our guns dry for we would have a chance to try them," Thomas Douglass of the Twenty-seventh Iowa wrote his parents. "Some of he boys felt brave and some looked sick."[80] Some soldiers found it easy to label anyone who fled or refused to fight as a coward and unworthy of consideration. Lieutenant Charles Brewster spent the better part of one day looking for a soldier who fled from a battle during the Peninsular Campaign. Angry at the "miserable coward," Brewster promised that "if we have another battle and I get him started for it he won't run from it alive. I can tell him that if he is afraid to face the enemy and take his chances for life and death, I'll make it a certain thing for him if he undertakes to run away."[81] In an effort to preserve a soldier's honor and manhood, his comrades might try to compel bravery and prevent cowardice. At the Battle of Chattanooga, Private Howard Whitford began to run until a corporal stopped him, steadied his nerves, and persuaded him to return to his post.[82] All of these examples of cowardice, however, reflect the expectations of bravery that one soldier or officer had for others, and expecting a soldier to meet someone else's standard of behavior was difficult when bravery became so individually identified. Instead, most Civil War soldiers would have agreed with James Abraham's assessment of bravery. "'To die for one's country is glorious and honorable" is a beautiful sentence," Abraham recollected, ". . . but quite a different phrase when analyzed amid screeching shells, plunging shot and singing, zipping, thugging bullets, with charging, yelling masses all around, mingled with the cries of wounded comrades and the agony of dying friends. . . . I conclude much of the battlefield poetry is written on a distant hill and the scenes gathered through a long range field glass."[83] A soldier who fled from battle was not ashamed to admit that "he did not stop to attend to the duties of nature [while running away] and so when he returned home he had to have a new seat put in his pants."[84]

Inept leadership in battle further softened the perception of cowardice as something more justifiable. Soldiers believed they had the right to preserve themselves when incompetent officers launched foolhardy attacks or even when well-conceived plans simply failed against staunch Confederate defenses. General Patrick noted in his diary that during the fighting in the Shenandoah Valley in 1862 an entire regiment in his brigade "had fled & I could get their whereabouts for more than 2 hours."[85] At the height of the Battle of Spotsylvania, with the outcome of the battle still in doubt, a veteran Maine regiment refused to move into the battle in a mass act of self-preservation. Viewing the carnage going on about them and recognizing the likelihood of their own deaths, the soldiers "firmly refused to sign our death warrants or be driven or bullied further," entirely unrepentant and clearly not considering themselves as cowards.[86] A similar event occurred in June 1864 during the Siege of Petersburg. Ordered to make an assault upon an enemy position "which was in plain view across an open field probably 4 or 500 yards in our front," the soldiers of the Twelfth New Jersey "positively refused to attempt it and no urging to get them to make even a show of going."[87] Another soldier justified his departure from the battlefield by claiming that he needed to tend to a wounded comrade, not just removing him to a collection point but also going in the ambulance with the wounded man to ensure the ambulance took the best road. He then returned to his regiment without any retribution.[88] So many uninjured soldiers joined the stream of wounded heading to the rear that by the time of the Battle of the Wilderness in 1864 anyone leaving the battlefield had to "show blood," provide evidence of a wound to proceed further.[89]

The perception of cowardice fell especially hard on those who bore a higher expectation than common soldiers did. Color bearers, soldiers who carried the national, state, and regimental flags during battle, earned the honor because they distinguished themselves to the regimental officers as the best soldiers. Carrying the flags, however, was a risky venture. The flags attracted enemy fire, and the unarmed color bearers had to maintain their position while unable to fire back. They also had the responsibility of ensuring that the colors did not fall into enemy hands, as captured enemy colors were the most-sought prize of any regiment. Those who failed in their duties earned a particularly harsh rebuke. Sergeant William Law of the Sixth USCT, for instance, served as regimental color bearer until he dropped the colors and fled to the rear during the opening assault on Petersburg in June 1864. His regimental colonel demoted him to private, and Law never regained the esteem of his regiment.[90] The colonel of one Wisconsin regiment imposed an additional dishonor upon a color sergeant who fled by publicly stripping him of his stripes in front of the entire regiment.[91] NCOs also had to uphold a higher standard of conduct due to their higher rank, and cowardice was a quick way back into the ranks. Corporal Thomas Stewart lost his rank after he deserted his company while in battle near Tupelo, Mississippi. A soldier in Stewart's company stated he would "rather have been *under ground*, than to have been branded a coward before the whole Reg't."[92]

When it came to cowardice among officers, however, the soldiers had no problem identifying the cowards amongst them. Soldiers had high expectations of themselves, but had even higher ones for their leaders. Soldiers risked their lives by following the judgment, planning, and example of their officers. A cowardly officer, therefore, not only humiliated himself; he also placed the lives of his men in jeopardy. Once identified as a coward, soldiers quickly tried to discredit and disassociate the officer in an effort to find a better replacement. In the Iron Brigade, Captain Alexander Hooe lost the respect of his men, who described his performance in battle as someone who "will not run but he is so terrified that he can't give a command," and at Bull Run he crouched so low to avoid enemy fire "you would have thought he was trying to sneak up to a wild turkey."[93] Instead of receiving orders from one of their captains during the Battle of Stones River, an Indiana regiment last "heard from him *three miles to the rear*. He was making a straight line for Nashville."[94] The army cashiered Captain Calvin Spear of the Fifth USCT for cowardice on the battlefield and behavior that characterized him as "an adventurer, a dishonest speculator, unworthy to associate with gentlemen and wholly unfit for the responsible position he occupied."[95] Captain Joseph Lawton abandoned his regiment during the Battle of Shiloh, "making for the river about as fast as his legs would carry him," with the excuse that "he was going down to the river to draw rations so that the boys could have something to eat as soon as they were done fighting."[96] Officers were equally prone to empty bravado when the enemy was not in sight, including Lieutenant Silas Wagoner of the Seventy-seventh Illinois. William Wiley described him as "over bearing and abusive," and someone "from his talk and actions . . . would tear the confederacy all to pieces in a little while," but Wagoner "was the first to resign [his commission] when we got where rebel bullets begun to sing around in a careless manner."[97] An officer himself, Charles Haydon had no use for boasting and bravado among his high-ranking colleagues. "I look upon an officer's bravery very much as I should on a woman's virtue," he confided to his diary. "When much is said of either I look upon it with suspicion."[98]

The highest ranking regimental officers became the target of cowardice accusations by their men as a means of explaining away a defeat or poor performance by the soldiers themselves. Instead of leading from the front, standard procedure had the regimental colonel, lieutenant colonel, and major coordinating the fight from the rear, causing soldiers to accuse them of hiding from combat and not sharing the dangers with their men. In the First Minnesota, for instance, Colonel Willis Gorman lost the leadership of his regiment after the inexperienced regiment could not account for his absence at the First Battle of Bull Run. Gorman did not absent himself from his command, but instead was directing the regiment from the rear, as was appropriate. Gorman was already unpopular in the regiment because of his staunch discipline, so a charge of cowardice became a convenient means to remove him.[99] Other officers, however, fulfilled their soldiers' accusations of cowardice. When his regiment came under fire near the Rapidan River in Virginia, Lieutenant Colonel John Rodgers ran "behind a barn and called to the men to 'rally on the barn,'" while "Captain Robinson of F Co. formed his squadron and charged down to the water's edge, opened fire, and . . . drove the enemy away."[100] At the Battle of Perryville, soldiers observed Colonel J.R. Taylor of the Fiftieth Ohio "lying on his face, crouching behind a stump, and . . . far to the rear of his regiment, while his men were in line of battle."[101] General J.H. Hobart Ward, a brigade commander in the III Corps earned the eternal hatred of his men after Chancellorsville because "he was in such haste to reach the rear that he ran over two men, one of whom died a few days later."[102]

Sometimes it was not individual officers, but an entire regimental staff that fell apart. The Ninth New York, after the Virginia Campaign in 1864, had a total breakdown in command according to Edward Wightman. Its commander "disgraced himself by remaining out of the battle at Palmer's Creek . . . he has offered his resignation," while Captain John Fay "was so badly frightened during our raid against Petersburg that he pretended to be sunstruck while walking through a shade pine forest." Wightman characterized the next senior officer, Captain Alexander Mann, as a "notorious coward" who "mysteriously disappeared from the men of his company and . . . could not be found," while Lieutenant John Hoes, while "enscouncing [sic] himself behind a stump or tree" urged his men forward. The worst officer, however, was Captain James H. Wicks, who "was fired on by his men for running away from Proctor's Creek."[103] A similar collapse of leadership occurred among the officers of the Forty-sixth Indiana at the Battle of Champion's Hill in 1863. During the battle, Thomas Durham "rushed back to the right of the regiment and found Colonel [Thomas] Bringhurst and his regiment apparently bewildered. They reminded me of a flock of ducks in a hail storm," while nearby "a half dozen of his officers huddled behind a big tree."[104]

Hiding behind trees was a smart thing to do during the Civil War, except if you were an officer. Held to a much higher standard of personal bravery, soldiers expected officers to not only share their hazards but provide an example from the front. Hiding behind their men and concealed from the enemy was a quick means of shifting a soldier's perception of an officer from an effective leader to blatant coward. "The man despised most by our Regt," wrote Charles Chase was a "Lieut. who . . . was found behind a large tree," one of several officers who "showed the white feather," the symbol of cowardice.[105] During the fighting in the Wilderness, an officer tried to "induce a fellow to vacate a position behind a stump" so the officer could hide there, but the soldier merely "put his fingers to his nose and made a motion of contempt."[106] A fellow officer found Lieutenant Isaac Witemyre of the Iron Brigade "skulking behind a tree some four hundred yards in the rear of the regiment," while Colonel David Williams of the Eighty-second Pennsylvania earned the nickname "Stumpy" for his proclivity to seek cover.[107] Later in the war, however, when deliberate exposure to the enemy brought only quick death, soldiers saw overt exposure to the enemy less as brave and more as suicidal, and hiding oneself behind trees, breastworks, or other defenses lost much of its stigma.[108] Marsena Patrick noted by 1864 that "the men are refusing to assault any more, and the Officers cannot or will not expose themselves as heretofore."[109]

The Union army used a variety of means to prevent and punish cowardice. The army quickly cashiered officers found guilty of cowardice, occasionally drumming out the worst offenders as an additional humiliation. Captain Hooker DeLand and Lieutenant Moses Powell of the First Michigan Sharpshooters faced such shame when, before the assembled regiment, their fellow officers stripped off their uniform buttons and broke their swords before drumming them out of camp.[110] Enlisted men, however, faced more serious penalties. At the point of occurrence, the most common preventive measure was lines of cavalry to intercept fleeing soldiers. The horsemen were much faster than the running soldiers, "so that if a man attempted to run, they would stop him or take his head off."[111] If arrested for cowardice, soldiers faced the possibility of a court-martial as a violation of Article 42 of the Articles of War, but if found guilty at a military tribunal the punishment was relatively light. The army and its soldiers might have despised cowards, but they pitied them more. Viewing cowardice as a personal weakness, the army tended to impose harsh punishments, but punishments short of the death penalty. Common court-martial punishments included stretches at hard labor, public forms of humiliation, and drumming out of the service coupled with a dishonorable discharge. Unlike other military offenses, cowardice often earned the unique punishment of public announcement. Playing upon the soldiers' fears of loss of face and denigration of manhood, the army forwarded the news of a soldier's cowardice to hometown newspapers for publication. The news wrecked the soldier's reputation amongst his family and friends, who usually did not know the circumstances that led to the charge of cowardice in the first place. Captain Luther Brown of the One

Hundred Tenth Ohio, for instance, notified a local newspaper that Private Edwin Lamme had fled from the Battle of the Wilderness. Lamme and his father attempted to protect the family name by accusing Brown and other regimental officers of incompetence, creating a flurry of charges and counter-charges over the next several issues of the paper.[112]

One remedy for cowardice that seemed very dramatic but was seldom, if ever, actually applied was the threat to shoot anyone retreating from a battle. Commanding officers, as a battle neared, often issued a general warning to kill on the spot anyone caught retreating, an act that accentuated the seriousness of the coming fight. There are also specific instances of officers threatening individual retreating soldiers with death if they did not return to the fight. Despite the patriotism and enthusiasm of early-war recruits, officers found it necessary to threaten death for deserters from the very start of the war, with the earliest occurrences at the First Battle of Bull Run.[113] A year later, after several regiments broke and ran during the Battle of Shiloh, Brigadier General William Sherman assured one Ohio regiment that in the next battle they would have "a battery of artillery behind them and if they attempted to run they would open on them with grape and canister."[114] Following the orders of General George McClellan, officers tried to stem the flow of retreating troops at the Battle of Gaines Mill by threatening to shoot anyone who tried to cross the Chickahominy River.[115] Individual officers also threatened the lives of soldiers leaving ongoing battles. At the Battle of Dallas in 1864, General John Logan encountered an artilleryman fleeing the field. Logan persuaded him to return by drawing his pistol and proclaiming "if you move even a foot further to the rear . . . I'll blow your brains out."[116] On occasion, officers delegated the threat to an enlisted man. When a Zouave regiment broke and ran during the Battle of Chancellorsville, a sergeant in an adjacent regiment received orders "to fire into them. We did not obey the order."[117] Also at Chancellorsville, Colonel Silas Colgrove selected Private Henry Daniel to stand behind his company and shoot anyone who tried to retreat, a burden that Daniel opted not to exercise.[118] There is no evidence that threats prevented soldiers from retreating if they determined on doing so. Quite the opposite, the potential application of such an arbitrary punishment raised the possibility of retaliation. When an officer threatened soldiers with death if they retreated from the Second Battle of Bull Run, "One of our men . . . told the officer, that if he shot any one [sic] he would be shot himself."[119]

Mutiny was another serious offense that threatened military discipline and the ability of officers to lead. The army from its start in the American Revolution recognized the menace of mutiny to unit cohesion, military discipline, and the chain of command. George Washington had to deal with the threat of mutiny on several occasions, and grievances by soldiers occasionally triggered outbursts by soldiers throughout the antebellum era. Due to the dangers of large numbers of armed men refusing to obey the orders of their outnumbered officers, the Articles of War provided a harsh penalty for those convicted of mutiny. Not only did Article 7 dictate that "any officer or soldier who shall begin, excite, cause or join in any mutiny . . . shall suffer death or such other punishment as by a court-martial shall be inflicted," but Article 8 imposed the same penalty upon "any officer, non-commissioned officer, or soldier who, bring present at any mutiny or sedition, does not use his utmost endeavor to suppress the same." The Articles also addressed mutiny committed by an individual by potentially imposing the death sentence upon "any officer or soldier who shall strike his superior office, or draw or lift up any weapon, or offer any violence against him, being in the execution of his office" or who "shall disobey any lawful command off his superior officer." Through these articles the army made it clear that challenging its established authority had dangerous consequences, and that the army interpreted mutiny in a broad fashion in an attempt to deter potential malcontents from acting upon their anger. Recognizing the seriousness of its statutes, however, the army imposed rigid definitions on all of the charges to determine actual offenses of the relevant articles. A court-martial had to prove, for instance, that a soldier accused of striking a superior officer was aware the man he struck was a superior officer, but did it anyway. Charges of sedition came with the burden of proof that the language spoken by an officer or soldier actually caused a mutiny, as mere complaining about army authority did not constitute mutiny.

The Articles of War also made a distinction between mutiny and mutinous conduct. Mutiny was a retroactive charge; the army could only charge a soldier with mutiny after the mutiny had occurred, with all of the potential punishments. Soldiers who acted in a way that threatened to become mutiny or to disrupt collective discipline faced a charge of mutinous conduct, with less harsh penalties because a breakdown of authority nearly occurred, but did not actually happen.[120] An example of such a distinction occurred in the Western Theater of the war. In a drunken stupor aboard the transport *Isabella* in 1864, three soldiers of the Seventh Kansas Cavalry who had complaints against Lieutenant Colonel Thomas Herrick threatened to throw him overboard. Recognizing their state of inebriation and their lack of success in rousing action against Herrick, at their subsequent court-martial the three soldiers faced charges of resisting the lawful authority of their commanding officer instead of mutiny, although all received long sentences at hard labor.[121] Volunteer officers, unaware of the precise definitions enunciated in the Articles of War, usually labeled any incident that involved a sizeable number of men a mutiny, causing much confusion on the matter later. Records and personal accounts from the Civil War frequently cite examples of mutiny, events that encompass everything from true mutiny to mutinous conduct to spontaneous rioting. Incidents best characterized as insubordination also incorrectly earned the label of a mutiny.

The army did not approve of the practice of mutiny, but citizen-soldiers certainly claimed the right to do. What the army considered mutiny, common soldiers considered a legitimate protest in response to a perceived grievance. Just as any other American citizen, soldiers wanted their voices heard. If the army did not listen, citizen-soldiers had only limited means to make the army listen. Unable to vote for a change of leadership or policy and powerless to leave the army if they were unsatisfied with their condition, the only option was to refuse to act and serve as soldiers, essentially going on strike. By pointedly refusing to obey orders, however, such an action struck at the heart of military discipline and the army could not abide such an action and had to react. Caught between their citizens' sense of justice and personal rights and the army's demand for obedience, soldiers did not lightly engage in mutiny. They were aware of the consequences of their actions, but in most cases believed that either the army was abusing them or their rights were threatened. Mutinies tended to occur spontaneously, demonstrating that soldiers had no plans to overthrow army discipline, but only wanted redress of specific issues. Consequently, most soldiers participated in riots as part of a large group, demonstrating that their complaints were not the simple gripes of one man but the concerns of many. "Although I am not in favor of mob law," John Haley reasoned after observing an example of mutinous conduct, "still there are cases where justice can be accomplished no other way. A private might complain till doomsday and it would be only so much the worse for the private, as the officer always escapes persecution [for complaining] and subjects the private to the most vigorous prosecution."[122]

There are numerous examples of what offended officers called mutiny that seemed simple exercises of democratic rights to those participating in them. The Thirty-ninth New York, encamped in Alexandria, Virginia, marched out of camp en masse with the intent of marching to nearby Washington, DC, to enunciate their complaints directly to the War Department. The Ordnance Bureau had issued rusty antiquated firearms to the regiment, and they refused to risk their lives in battle with such weapons. The mutinous mass nearly reached the Long Bridge across the Potomac River before surrounded by other regiments and forced to yield.[123] Mutiny was also a means by which enlisted men demonstrated their resentment against imperious behavior by superior officers. Moving through Mississippi on a horrendously hot day, the Seventh Kansas Cavalry halted in a shady spot to fill their canteens. An officer approached them representing Major General John Logan and ordered them to keep moving. A few minutes later the officer returned, stating that if the regiment did not move immediately General Logan "will order out a battery [of artillery] and drive it out." The Kansans responded by threatening to take any battery sent against them, and "the men sat silent and grim and would not stir," until finally cajoled into leaving.[124] The charge of mutiny itself became a form of punishment, especially when applied to officers who acted too much like citizen-soldiers. When Colonel Henry Eustis of the Tenth Massachusetts brought in an officer of another regiment to serve as major instead of promoting one of the officers within the regiment, eleven of the officers resigned their commissions in protest. Instead of caving in to this form of dissent, Eustis arrested and charged all of them with mutiny against his authority. Despite protests that Eustis was abusing his position and that protest did not equate to mutiny, the army cashiered all of the arrested officers.[125]

Mutiny became a means to demand change and protect their identity as individuals in an army that demanded mass obedience. One means that soldiers possessed to assert their rights and identity was through their regimental formation. Regiments, recruited in the towns and counties of the soldiers' own state, became an ad hoc home. Surrounded by fellow residents of their locality, soldiers often fought alongside relatives, neighbors, friends, and coworkers, and the regiment came to represent a comfort zone for many soldiers. When the army proposed to change or disband that erstwhile home, soldiers became indignant, especially in regiments depleted by hard fighting and great sacrifice. In 1864, the army amalgamated regiments who failed to attain veteran status, but the army also periodically merged regiments before 1864 that lacked enough manpower to remain viable fighting units. The mergers, however, did not go unchallenged. When the army proposed to merge decimated regiments in 1863, for instance, Edward Wightman predicted "the proposal . . . likely is to be productive of much trouble." And he was right, as the consolidation of two New York regiments "was only accomplished by force and then at the cost of many men who deserted at the first opportunity" because of their dissatisfaction with the process.[126] Alfred Bellard described an open mutiny caused by consolidation of two small companies in his regiment. "The men refusing to obey were placed under arrest" when they refused to join the new company, "The mutineers were ordered to walk up and down the rifle works with a log of wood on their shoulder as punishment. . . orders were orders and had to be obeyed or take the consequence."[127] When troops from a disbanded New York regiment arrived to join another regiment, the surrendering of their old colors was too much to bear, so "they took them back" and refused to join, submitting only when "the Brigade surrounded them, with a battery in front."[128] A more peaceful resolution took place in the Second Maine. Most of the regiment enlisted for two years of service, and the survivors of these men went home in June 1863. One hundred twenty soldiers, however, signed on for three years and had to remain. When they resisted amalgamation into the Twentieth Maine, the army cracked down hard by holding them under close armed guard and denying them meals. Colonel Joshua Chamberlain, when he received the disgruntled men from the Second, removed the guards and treated the offenders as soldiers again. His more measured approach convinced all but six of the Maine men to join the new regiment, providing much needed reinforcements to the Twentieth on the eve of Gettysburg.[129]

Similar mutinies occurred when the army forced regiments to change their branch of service. The army, for instance, randomly selected one hundred fifty men from the Second Ohio Cavalry to form the Twenty-fifth Ohio Light Artillery because artillery pieces were available but recruits were not. None of the men obeyed the order to report for artillery training, and "Squad after squad having refused, were under arrest and on their way to the guard quarters" despite their officers "remonstrating and earnestly entreating a return to obedience" and reminding them of "the pains and penalties attached to mutiny and disobedience of orders." The soldiers agreed only after the officers promised the reassignment was only temporary, a promise that proved a lie. After four months, the artillerymen held a very democratic meeting to collectively vote on their next course of action, and decided to refuse orders for duty or even to confirm their presence at the morning roll call. Officers again promised to look into their complaints and again the men returned to duty, but the unit remained disgruntled for the rest of their term of service.[130] When soldiers of the Mechanic Fusiliers, trained technicians who enlisted on the promise that the army would utilize their skills, mutinied on a cold January morning when they found out that the army intended to use them as common infantry. To persuade them to fall into line, "those that would not were turned out of camp after being stripped of their overcoats and blankets." Exposed to the elements, the soldiers soon mustered for drill.[131]

Mutiny and mutinous conduct also arose over the issue of terms of service. In some cases, especially early in the war, soldiers became disruptive over exactly how long their term was to last. In the weeks after Abraham Lincoln's inauguration, the President issued several calls for volunteers to suppress the rebellion with the volunteers committed to various short terms of service. When the war promised to last longer than expected, soldiers expecting short military commitments suddenly found themselves facing a much longer obligation. Feeling the government had manipulated their patriotism, some soldiers reacted angrily. In August 1861, the Seventy-ninth New York mutinied when the soldiers believed the army cheated them into longer terms. When the war began, volunteers had the option of enlisting for three years of service or for the duration of the war. Believing as many did in 1861 that the war would be brief, most of the soldiers in the Seventy-ninth signed up for the duration. After the humiliating defeat at Bull Run and the realization that the war would last at least into the next Spring, the New Yorkers claimed the army deceived them and they demanded their immediately release. Emulating Washington's strong stance against mutineers during the Revolution, Major General George McClellan, commander of the Army of the Potomac, confronted them with force. In the face of armed soldiers prepared to fire, the mutineers stood down and accepted their obligations. McClellan further punished the regiment by stripping them of their regimental colors, but restored them a month later after the regiment demonstrated improved discipline.[132] McClellan was not the only one to take a hard line. Confronted by a captain who promised to leave as soon as his three-month enlistment ended, Brigadier General William Sherman promised him, "If you attempt to leave without orders, it will be mutiny, and I will shoot you like a dog!"[133]

Other mutinies occurred over disagreements of when terms of service ended. The Eleventh Pennsylvania mutinied and refused to perform duty on April 20, 1864, the third anniversary of their "entry into the service of the State" of Pennsylvania. The army, however, calculated their term as ending three years after "the date of their being mustered into the service of the United States." There was a gap of one month because the regiment formed in April 1861, but did not join the Union army until May, and the army claimed the latter date. In the end, the army released the Eleventh rather than cause undue problems with other Pennsylvania recruits.[134] A similar revolt by the Sixty-ninth New York ended the same way, but only after the mutiny turned lethal. The men of the Sixty-ninth represented volunteers who answered Abraham Lincoln's initial call for men to serve for three months. When the army tried to coerce the Sixty-ninth to stay in the army, the men "revolted a day or two ago and killed two of their officers" before the governor of New York intervened and brought them home.[135] Another New York regiment, the Twenty-fourth, made up of "two-year" men also mutinied when they refused to participate in the Chancellorsville campaign because "the men felt that their term was too close to expiring to risk possible death or injury in the upcoming campaign."[136] The Twentieth New York, however, stuck to their mutiny and paid the price for it. They also refused to cross the Rappahannock River on April 28, 1863, because their terms of enlistment ended in three weeks. Instead of fighting in the upcoming battle, nearly two hundred men of the regiment refused to cross the river. Their subsequent courts-martial sentenced all of them to hard labor for the duration of the war, followed by a dishonorable discharge.[137]

Food, either the lack of it or the poor quality of it, also provided a justification for mutiny. Mutinous conduct over food was a by-product of the expectations that soldiers had of their leadership. Soldiers knew the army expected them to face danger, follow orders, and be good soldiers. In return, however, the soldiers expected the army to not abuse them, not squander their lives, and provide the tools necessary to win the war. The soldiers had certain tasks to perform, and in exchange they anticipated that the army would provide for them. Food was certainly part of this arrangement. Soldiers could not fight the enemy and fend for themselves at the same time, so the army had the burden to feed its soldiers. Moreover, the army, if it wanted peak performance from its soldiers, had to feed them well. If the army did not fulfill its end of the bargain, the soldier did not feel obligated to hold up his end. The attitude was analogous to a worker holding his employer to the terms of a labor contract, except the soldier could not quit his job. "We had all we could do to prevent a mutiny," Samuel Partridge wrote his family, "They gave us bad hash the other night, it tasted just like kerosene oil and smelt oily." The smell and taste was not surprising, as the mess hall was, before the war, "an unfinished machine shop." When the "next day at dinner the beef stunk a little," the soldiers demolished the mess hall and assaulted the cook, accusing him of being a "God damned black hearted white livered son of a bitch."[138] California soldiers bound for the war aboard the steamer *Ocean Queen* rioted because "before you eat the hard bread you must rattle the vermin out of it" and the beef "was rotten, rice wormy."[139] Less often, housing also caused discontent and mutinous conduct. Officers of the Seventh Kansas Cavalry court-martialed one sergeant in December 1861 for "mutinous and disorderly conversations with his men" when he encouraged the enlisted men to burn down the officers' quarters. While the soldiers encamped in the open, the regiment's officers resided comfortably in a nearby hotel, prompting the sergeant to agree with the enlisted men that the officers should share their hardship and burning down the hotel would serve them right.[140]

Another expectation that soldiers held firm was that the army would pay them on time. Antebellum army regulations mandated that soldiers receive their pay at least every two months, but that time frame proved impossible to meet during the war. The army often owed soldiers pay that was months in arrears, leaving soldiers to justify their mutinous conduct on the grounds that that the army failed to live up to its end of their enlistment bargain. "Boys are awfully out of humor," one soldier noticed, "[they] almost mutinied" when the paymaster failed to appear.[141] Some soldiers preferred to sit in the guardhouse rather than soldier without pay. "[S]eventeen men this afternoon refuse to drill," Corporal Bensell noted, ". . . mutinied on account of not having received any Pay since Enlistment, over nine months."[142] Money was also the reason a number of soldiers refused to leave Philadelphia for their frontline units, men "who refused to go for various reasons, principally the non-payment of their [enlistment] bounty."[143] Lieutenant George Bliss faced a near mutiny when his "men swore they would not leave camp until they received their pay. . . Capt. [Lycurgus] Sayles and myself had to speechify considerably before they came around." Bliss was sympathetic: "I can not blame them much under the circumstances. Six months in the service and no pay, many of them with families suffering for want of money."[144] Alvin Voris was also sympathetic to his soldiers' plight. When his regiment refused to move without their pay, their colonel threatened to bring in reinforcements and arrest them. Voris stepped in and promised that he could get them to move. After gathering the men around him, Voris "got off a few jokes" to lighten the mood, "had the boys sing 'The Star Spangled Banner'" to boost their patriotism, and ended with a speech about how their comrades were fighting and they needed to join them. Soon "they were wildly cheering the train" as it carried them forward to their destination.[145]

The most dangerous circumstances when soldiers resorted to mutiny came over the issue of punishment. An officer's right and authority to mete out discipline and punishment to those soldiers under his command was one of the clearest delineations between officers and enlisted men. Under ideal circumstances, officers imposed appropriate punishments to those who deserved them, but ideal circumstances depended upon the eye of the beholder. If an officer abused his authority and punished a soldier too severely, his comrades might mutiny to demonstrate their resistance to what they considered to be inappropriate leadership. Soldiers particularly targeted punishments they deemed too harsh or that lasted too long. Unfortunately, this came into conflict with a particular punishment that officers favored. After Congress banned flogging as a punishment in 1861, officers often imposed another painful punishment by tying an offender up by his thumbs. Officers ordered the wrongdoer's thumbs tied to a crossbeam with his arms above his head so that his toes barely touched the ground, to remain there for a designated period of time. The soldier's weight did not entirely rest on his thumbs, but enough did to cause excruciating pain, especially as the penalty might last for hours. Viewing the penalty as little more than torture, soldiers resented the imposition of thumb tying upon their comrades and often acted to end the practice.

Private Bellard observed a near riot when a tyrannical colonel tied up two men by their thumbs and their company mates intended to cut them down. Confronted by a near mutiny, the colonel "never tied up a man after that and shortly after resigned" his commission.[146] In other cases, however, full-blown mutinies broke out over the use of the punishment. In 1862, a major riot broke out between the officers of the Eighteenth Regiment of the Regular

Army and the citizen-soldiers of the Ninth Ohio. The volunteers, resenting the harsh discipline the Regulars inflicted upon their own soldiers, decided to enter the Eighteenth's camp and cut down two Regular soldiers tied up for drunkenness and negligence. When the Eighteenth's officers tried to restore order, the Ohio troops resisted with violence and injured a number of officers. The Regulars had to call for reinforcements and threaten to shoot into the crowd if they did not leave.[147] In another episode, John Haley observed "how hard it would be to stop this army if it ever did become mutinous." An officer in Haley's brigade ordered a guard to shoot a soldier from the Thirty-seventh New York found pillaging a house near his camp. The "seriously but not fatally wounded" soldier crawled back to his camp and told his friends what happened. In retaliation, soldiers from the regiment massed together and assaulted the officer, and he was "cudgeled over the head and ears . . . the mob took rails from the fire and smashed him over the head . . . It is nothing short of a miracle that he didn't immediately require the services of an undertaker."[148]

Because mutinies often involved large numbers of angry soldiers, officers placed themselves at great risk to control the mutineers. In their efforts to reassert discipline, officers had limited options. When large groups of soldiers refused to perform duty, the army usually countered with a show of force or some other form of counter—escalating the conflict. This demonstration of resolve could take various forms, from subtle pressure to lethal force. Angry at not receiving a promised enlistment furlough, the soldiers of a Kentucky regiment seized control of the steamer *Texas* to prevent the army from moving them to another location. Colonel Henry Carrington, leading the Eighteenth Regiment of the Regular Army suppressed the mutiny by firing several volleys across the steamer's bow, prompting the mutineers to surrender.[149] Another officer used soldiers of the Eighty-fifth New York to help subdue resisters in the Fifty-third New York, "an ugly looking lot of men, nearly all of them had a bowie knife or revolver in sight and they would have given us a hard fight" but they chose to acquiesce instead.[150] In another demonstration of force, soldiers of a Michigan regiment nearly had to "charge bayonet on the N.Y. 12th" when they refused to drill. After the Twelfth twice refused General Israel Richardson's orders to fall out for drill, "he then ordered us to load & cap our guns, then to fix bayonets," and backed his threat to use force with "two brass 12-pounders loaded with grape[shot])." The Twelfth complied thereafter, but other regiments did not. In Richardson's own brigade courts-martial ordered sixty-three members of the Second Maine and thirty soldiers of the Thirteenth New York to imprisonment at Fort Jefferson, Florida, until they decided to fulfill their enlistment obligations.[151] If to be used to curb a mutiny, deadly force was also an option. When Colonel Charles Lowell of the Second Massachusetts Cavalry threatened to shoot anyone who resisted his efforts to arrest some mutineers, he meant it. Lowell personally shot one mutineer who resisted arrest, killing him instantly, and placed five others in custody pending a court-martial. The subsequent proceedings cleared two of those of mutiny charges, but sentenced the other three to death. One died while awaiting punishment, President Lincoln commuted the sentence of a second, but the army hanged the third, Private William Lynch, on June 16, 1863.[152] Soldiers of the Twentieth Ohio mutinied to affect the release of one of their members tied up by his thumbs for stealing. In response, officers fired into the mob, killing one soldier outright, mortally wounding another, and placing twenty-two soldiers under arrest.[153]

A consistent trend that emerged out of these demonstrations of force is that violence occurred because the officers initiated it, not the soldiers. The soldiers wanted the army to rectify a grievance, not to disband the army or to surrender to the rebels. They usually were very specific about the person or thing that was the cause of the grievance, not engaging in general chaos. When violence, bloodshed, or deaths occurred, the vast majority of the blame must fall on officers who resented challenges to their authority, panicked in the face of opposition, or had reasons of their own to emphasize their status. An armed and uncontrolled mob of soldiers was undoubtedly an intimidating sight, but many officers seemed too ready to use violence when negotiating might have produced better results. Officers of the Thirtieth USCT, for instance, imposed disproportionate punishments on soldiers who looked too slovenly for the officers' liking. In response, the soldiers "kicked up a big row and there were threats to shoot the officers and for a while it looked bad," but cooler heads prevailed in a situation that need not have happened if the officers had acted appropriately.[154]

Instead of force, some officers took an empathetic position regarding their men, often a useful means of defusing a tense situation. Faced with an internal rebellion against drill exercise, Colonel James Carleton took a less confrontational approach. After letting the ringleaders spend the night in the guardhouse, Carleton addressed the regiment by appealing to their patriotism, urging them to live up to their manly obligations, reminding them that drill was necessary to save their lives on the battlefield, and promising that if they followed orders he would forget the whole incident. Carleton's patience paid off, as most of the miscreants returned to duty with nary a complaint.[155] Another officer challenged his regiment's manhood to get them to comply with his orders. When a Pennsylvania regiment refused to cross the state line into Maryland because they claimed they enlisted only to protect their home state, their colonel ordered them into formation, commanded every coward to step forward, and informed them that he was heading South with the remaining troops. "There was not a man had the courage to step out" of formation, and the mutiny ended right there.[156] In other occasions, officers thought it best to simply let the matter drop. Acting upon their morals, the soldiers of the Twenty-first Wisconsin roughly handled two slavecatchers looking for escaped slaves in their camp in 1862. As the 1850 Fugitive Slave Act was still in effect, the slavecatchers not only had a legal right to search the camp but the officers and soldiers of the army were obliged to assist them. General Lovel Rousseau tried to arrest those who opposed the slavecatchers, but their comrades refused to give them up. Despite threats to punish the entire regiment, Rousseau decided to forget the whole affairs as the brigade prepared to march. Under the Articles of War the collective resistance to Rousseau's authority constituted a mutiny (not to mention that the soldiers torched the houses of the slavecatchers that evening), but the general decided in this case to let the matter rest.[157]

However difficult the army found mutiny to delineate, the attempt to define insubordination was even thornier. At its simplest, insubordination was as clear cut as a soldier refusing to obey a direct order. In more specific terms, however, that was only part of the issue. The Articles of War listed refusing to obey an order as a specific offense within the broader issue of insubordinate behavior, delineated separately because it was the clearest challenge to military authority. If soldiers did not obey officers when told to do so, then there was no discipline. A soldier defying the power of a superior to dictate his actions struck at the heart of military discipline, and those who dared to do so faced the possibility of death or other appropriate punishment under the same Article 9 that defined mutiny. Insubordination, however, encompassed broader behavior than just disobeying orders. Insubordination included other behaviors and infractions such as insulting or denigrating a superior officer, criticizing the army or the conduct of the army, and such actions that impaired efforts to maintain discipline. With such a wide range of potential offenses, insubordination became difficult to define and impossible to eradicate. Insubordination was, at its essence, free speech. To citizen-soldiers who embraced their status as free Americans who sacrificed their liberty, and possibly their lives, the right to speak one's mind was essential to maintaining one's individuality and personal rights. Consequently, insubordination came in a variety of forms, some more subtle than others. In addition to active insubordination, challenging an officer's authority directly, there was passive insubordination. The latter type took the form of actions committed behind an officer's back, written criticism, or spiteful behavior intended to demonstrate displeasure or anger. This type of insubordination proved difficult to control because it occurred without an officer's knowledge or was committed in such a way that the transgressor remained hidden in the ranks of his regiment. Regardless of the source, the army had little success in compelling soldiers to accept a subordinate position or behavior just because the army wanted them to do so.

The basis of subordinate behavior was the belief that soldiers should respect their officers. The army expected officers to maintain a respectful social distance from their men because casual or informal interaction "would encourage contempt of authority. Nothing is so true as familiarity breeds contempt."[158] That expectation clashed, however, with the citizen-soldiers' sense of general equality, and officers who remained remote faced the possibility of losing the deference of their men because they remained aloof from their charges. Officers who interacted too much with their men in a personal manner risked accusation of consorting with enlisted men, an act that diminished the status of their rank. On two separate occasions, for instance, the commander of the Fourth California had to issue orders prohibiting NCOs from gambling with their men, believing his NCOs "speak or act familiarly with privates" far too much.[159] Captain Otto Van Borries, a German-born officer in a New York regiment, resigned his commission after a fellow officer accused him of "gambling with some of the privates of his Company." Borries did not resign because of the charges, but rather was offended that anyone interfered in his private affairs.[160] West Pointers used the frequency with which officers consorted with enlisted men as an example of the lack of professionalism in many volunteer units, decrying the lack of deference where "a colonel felt free to ride companionably . . . with a private, both smoking cigars."[161] Finding a perfect balance between accessibility and respect was hard to find.

An officer rank, however, carried the burden of acting in a way that deserved respect. Soldiers, as mentioned previously, could respect officers that behaved appropriately and who treated them properly, but were quick to dismiss officers who abused or insulted them. One of the most hated forms of abusive and imperious behavior by officers was the use of their swords as tools of discipline. Soldiers mocked the trappings of an officer's rank, from their shoulder straps to their shiny boots, but the sword carried by an officer was the most obvious symbol of his authority. Consequently, when officers used their swords in an inappropriate manner, soldiers perceived it as literally beating them over the head with a sign of their authority. Even worse, officers tended to use their swords to move soldiers out of the way, again using the sword to control a soldier's behavior or as a sign of an officer's privilege. In a defensible manner, Colonel Silas Colgrove subdued three drunken and insubordinate soldiers by "slapping, hacking, and prodding" with his sword. Luckily for the soldiers, it was Colgrove's dull dress sword and the injuries were not serious.[162] Colonel Edward Cross also used his sword to quell an unruly mob around a sutler's wagon, not bothering to "distinguish the back and edge" while swinging.[163] Use of the sword in such a manner could quell insubordination, or it could escalate it, with the officer facing the backlash. When General John Geary struck a soldier with the flat of his sword because he did not move a mule out of the road fast enough for his liking, the soldier threw Geary off his horse and "pounded and kicked him" before escaping into the anonymous mass of blue uniforms around the incident.[164] Colonel Henry Carrington's rash use of his sword resulting in the amputation of one of his soldiers' arms and a court-martial for Carrington.[165] Some officers were under the impression that soldiers did not mind the use of the sword as a corrective tool, or at least found it preferable to other forms of discipline. "They prefer any time a smart rap over the head with the back of the sword," one officer believed, "to having their pay stopped by a Court Martial or dragging a ball & chain."[166]

Soldiers usually committed insubordination because they believed themselves insulted or snubbed by officers who exulted a bit too much in their position. As citizen-soldiers, Union troops merely tolerated the chain of command, and would not suffer anyone who created a sense of superiority by diminishing their status as free men. Writing home while on the Vicksburg Campaign, one soldier dismissed the status of his officers "when these Shoulder Straps put on so many airs and try to show their Authority" by wishing he could "hasten that day when we shall once more stand on equal footing with them and tell them what we think of them."[167] In one Wisconsin regiment, a captain faced constant insubordination because "whatever he did say was said in such a bluff, repulsive manner that the boys seldom cared to heed it unless compelled to."[168] Captain John Marsh of the Sixth Wisconsin was so despised that his men "would like to see him sunk o the lowest pits of hell," and, when Marsh was under house arrest for insubordination of his own, they openly spoke of their hopes that "May he die under arrest" within easy earshot of his tent.[169] Incompetent officers especially earned their share of insubordination, as their ineffective leadership made them targets for derision. Often the harshest criticism came from their fellow officers. "The Colonel[']s lack of military knowledge was perfectly wonderful," Wesley Brainerd recalled. "He did not know the simplest movements and it seemed impossible for him to learn."[170] At the court-martial of Colonel Ebenezer Pierce, a witness described Pierce's inability to lead the regiment on the parade ground. "Our drill is full of errors and the colonel does not correct them," Lieutenant Ezra Ripley testified. "I have seen him holding his sword in his left hand."[171] When a specific officer did not earn a soldier's wrath, the officer corps as a whole became a target of abuse and insubordination. Angry at the inability to produce winning generals, one soldier blamed his woes on a war that "has been prolonged by the influence of them *miserable, low flung Villains wearing the Uniforms of American Army Officers.*"[172]

While keen themselves to drink at any opportunity, soldiers used drunkenness as an easy excuse to violate the orders of their officers. Drunken officers were unworthy officers, and citizen-soldiers felt no obligation to follow any officer who threatened their well-being. Edward Wightman held little regard for Lieutenant Colonel E.A. Kimball: "our acting Colonel, is . . . an [*sic*] habitual drunkard and so testy, ignorant, and muddle headed that he is no more fit to command a regiment than an untaught schoolboy."[173] A Maine soldier feared going into battle under the command of his regimental major, who "cannot go into battle without his whiskey. I once saw him so drunk that he could hardly sit on his horse."[174] Major George West of the Seventeenth Maine was so prone to imbibing that a private believed he spent most of his time looking at the world through "the bottom of a tumbler" of whiskey.[175]

Mocking officers was another demonstration of insubordination, with soldiers taking the liberty of demeaning their officers through personal attacks. Marching with their unit past elements of General Daniel Sickles' III Corps who were hopelessly drunk and uncontrollable, soldiers of the Fifth New Jersey struck up an ad-libbed song "Johnny stole a Ham, and Sickles killed a Man," ribbing Sickles' infamous past.[176] Soldiers of the Iron Brigade called General John Gibbon the "Southern Renegade" because of his North Carolina heritage and his brothers fighting in the Confederate army.[177] Besides mocking their appearance, soldiers relished moments when officers lost their superior bearing and embarrassed themselves in front of their men. Embarked on the steamship *De Molay*, William Wiley enjoyed watching the seasick officers run to the rail "to heave Joner."[178] A captain in the Seventy-ninth New York also humiliated himself, much to his men's amusement: many soldiers of the unit were Scottish immigrants or were of Scot descent, so the unit unofficially labeled themselves the "Cameron Highlanders" and many wore kilts to reflect their ancestry. Pursuing a pig for dinner, one kilt-wearing captain got his garb caught on a fence rail, making an "exhibition of his attenuated anatomy as to call forth a roar of laughter."[179]

If soldiers did not dare tell an officer what they really thought of him or if their displeasure was more general than specific, soldiers denigrated their officers through insults, name-calling, and other generally juvenile behavior. Private Haley was a good example of someone whose ability for insulting officers often surpassed his ability to obey orders. Haley considered General Eugene Carr "a fine specimen of conceited flatulency," and thought General Amiel Whipple so filthy that he was "perfectly safe form any missile weighing less than a ton, having a casing of dirt of unknown thickness supposed to be invulnerable."[180] Soldiers employed other forms of verbal harassment to demonstrate their displeasure with their superiors. When Union troops captured a Confederate fort near Shreveport, Brigadier General Andrew Jackson Smith opted to destroy the position. When the demolition accidentally detonated an ammunition magazine and killed two soldiers, Smith's men took to hissing at him when he passed.[181] Soldiers also heaped group verbal abuse upon officers if they were hungry or undersupplied. After an eighteen-mile march on empty stomachs, for instance, soldiers of the One Hundredth Illinois "hollowed [hollered] for hard tax [tack]" when General Andrew Humphries rode past, as did hungry soldiers in the Army of the Potomac, who chanted "hard tack, hard tack" at a passing General George Meade.[182] Such disrespect had its consequences, however. When men of the One Hundred Twenty-first New York embarrassed their colonel, Egbert Olcott, by "cheering derisively" at a passing general, he punished the regiment with extra drill and tying some of them up by their thumbs.[183] General Ambrose Burnside, known more for his military gaffes than his successes, seemed a particular target for soldier abuse, especially after he orchestrated the debacle at Fredericksburg. A month after the disastrous battle, "Burnside visited the 2nd Army Corps," assistant surgeon Albert Sprague observed, "and many of the men groaned and hissed [at] him."[184] Private John Smith observed different, yet both insubordinate, responses to Burnside. One group of soldiers' response to Burnside was to chant "to h—l with Burnside," while another unit insulted Burnside by giving him the silent treatment when he visited their camp.[185] Pranks also allowed soldiers to tweak the status of a superior officer. Angry at orders requiring them to remain quiet after Taps, soldiers of the Fortieth Illinois filled their canteens half-full of water, loosely placed the stopper in the canteen, and placed them in the campfire. Periodically, a canteen blew its stopper out with a loud pop, forcing the officers to stay up all night trying to discover who was making all the noise.[186] Band members of the Fiftieth New York Engineers drove all of their officers out of bed by staging an impromptu concert in the middle of the night, but escaped punishment by claiming they were serenading the commanding colonel.[187]

If relations between officers and soldiers became especially dire, then a situation quickly escalated into a potentially dangerous argument. Soldiers who refused to cede their position to an officer equally determined to assert army authority created situations where the possibility for physical confrontation was likely. In situations such as these, insubordination took the form of threats to commit physical violence against an officer. After a soldier in the Second Kansas Cavalry wound up "in chains and Confined [to] the Military Prison" for calling an officer a coward, the soldier's comrades "Swore that if he was not released they would burn the town and the have hearts blood of the Gen'l."[188] Private Frank Kelly was a frequent imbiber who usually took out his drunken energy on the nearest officer, claiming that he could "whip any captain, sergeant, or man in the camp." When confronted during one drunken spree, Kelly pushed a captain too far, found himself in irons, and soon faced a court-martial. Found guilty of threatening a superior officer, Kelly received a death sentence, although Lincoln commuted the sentence to three months hard labor.[189] Most cases where a soldier threatened an officer, however, resulted in a less dire punishment. Angry when an officer proposed to punish a soldier who dropped out of a march to wrap his aching feet, the soldier "placed his fist under the captain's nose and with fixed teeth and stern eye informed the captain of his displeasure." The soldier found himself under arrest, but was released the next morning.[190] When a soldier refused to attend morning roll call, his company captain arrested despite the soldier's warning "that if I came near his shack he would kill me" and had him tied up by his thumbs for an hour.[191]

Verbal insubordination, prankish behavior, or dire threats usually sufficed to get a soldier's point across or release anger and frustration. In some instances, however, insubordination not only turned threatening but also violent, especially if soldiers felt aggrieved. Angry at the constant badgering of an officer, Corporal George Erwin "drew a bayonet on [Lieutenant] Jordan" and tried to kill him.[192] Similarly, when soldiers in a Michigan regiment grew tired of the tight discipline issued by their company officers, the soldiers waylaid the officers in a darkened tent, with the officers "landing abt. 10 ft. in front of the tent . . . [and] their posteriors well booted."[193] When an officer haughtily dismissed soldiers on picket duty when they challenged him for the password, the pickets taught him a lesson by knocking him off his horse, beating him badly, and spooking the horse so that the officer had to humiliatingly walk back to camp.[194] A horse also failed to protect an officer on General Joseph Hooker's staff who, after trying to rouse his men into giving three cheers for Hooker, instead "was pummeled almost into jelly . . . [and] torn from his horse."[195] Outraged when a colonel threatened to strike them with his sword if they did not move faster, Private Robert Strong and another soldier "pulled him off his horse, rolled him in the dirt, kicked and cuffed him, and . . . [threatened to] shoot him." Strong also threatened to shoot officers on another occasion. Sent to the rear to make contact with the rest of the One Hundred Fifth Illinois, Strong encountered two officers who accused him of cowardice and tried to arrest him. "I cocked my gun and told him to put up his sword," Strong responded, "or I would shoot him on the spot."[196]

When faced by physical intimidation and insubordination, some officers did not seek assistance and instead confronted the threat with force of their own. When a private "sauced" Colonel James Gavin, the officer "knocked him down" and personally hauled the soldier to the guardhouse. Earlier in the same regiment, Private Edward Meyers "got drunk enough to be foolish and accused the Capt. to his face of being a coward." In response, "the Captain . . . slapped Meyers over."[197] When confronted by a soldier aiming his rifle at him during the Battle of Fredericksburg, General George Meade struck the man over the head with his sword, breaking the blade in the process.[198] In the Seventh Indiana, Captain Jesse Armstrong felt it necessary to put his adjutant in his place by "striking him in the face and kicking him in the stomach."[199] Transiting through Baltimore with half his regiment drunk, the colonel commanding the First Massachusetts dealt with one disorderly subordinate when "took the musket out of his hands & struck him over the head 2 times with it."[200]

Officers were often hesitant to impose punishment in cases of mutiny because of the potentially large number of soldiers involved, but individuals engaging in insubordination did not have the protection of numbers. Backed by military law, officers used the military legal system to single out and punish offenders. Sitting on a regimental court-martial, Lieutenant Haydon fined a soldier and placed him on twenty days hard labor for "telling a Sergt. to 'kiss his ---.'"[201] More serious, three soldiers of the Eleventh Pennsylvania faced court-martial for insubordination and threatening the life of an officer, resulting in the drumming out of one soldier and ten days hard labor for the other two.[202] Private Michael Keefe threatened an officer who intervened in a fight between Keefe and his sergeant. As the officer testified in the subsequent court-martial, Keefe said "that it was none of my business and that if I meddled with him he would shoot me." Keefe spent the rest of his term of service at hard labor.[203] Other soldiers charged with mutiny, however, received mere slaps on the wrist considering the severity of their crimes. Sergeant Charles Amelin found himself convicted of mutiny but served only a month at hard labor as a penalty, while eleven members of the Excelsior Brigade who mutinied received only a fine.[204]

Officers themselves often questioned the orders of their superiors, and by extension engaged in insubordination. After an exhausting march that left the men of Tenth Indiana exhausted, at nightfall their officers permitted them to sleep alongside the road instead of making camp. Brigadier Charles Gilbert passed down the road and demanded that the tired men rise and render a proper salute. In response, Colonel William Kise informed Gilbert he would not "hold dress parade at midnight for any d——d fool" and suggested to Gilbert that he should keep moving.[205] In January 1863, in the aftermath of the Fredericksburg disaster, Ambrose Burnside ordered the arrest of Brigadier General William T.H. Brooks for his insubordinate comments about Burnside's plan for the battle. Although accused of "complaining of the policy of the Government" and "using language tending to demoralize his command," Brooks escaped a court-martial but suffered nevertheless. Brooks lost his division command, and Congress refused to promote him to Major General later in the year. By the time of the Gettysburg Campaign six months later, Brooks was in charge of the defenses of Pittsburgh.[206] When pushed too far, officers used violence against their superiors just as did the enlisted men. Ovando Hollister of the First Colorado noted in his journal that "Lieutenant McDonald is here, under arrest for whipping Capt. Lord." McDonald beat Lord badly during their brawl, as Hollister noted that the lieutenant "has a pocket full of Lord's whiskers torn out in the scuffle."[207]

Officers used their ability to resign their commissions as a form of protest, especially when officers threatened to reign en masse, leaving a regiment without leadership. The army resented this form of blackmail, and tended to view such actions as insubordination. When Colonel Richard Byrnes of the Twenty-eighth Massachusetts filled officer openings in his regiment with officers from other units instead of promoting from within, "the officers of regiment protested against it . . . and he put two captains under arrest." A court-martial, however, refused to punish the officers for such minor infractions.[208] At Ship Island, Louisiana, all of the African American officers of the Second Louisiana Native Guards resigned in protest of army policies that offended their sense of propriety, particularly the impressments of slaves into the Union army.[209] The officers of the Sixth Wisconsin resigned their commissions to protest the removal of George McClellan from command of the Army of the Potomac in 1862, although the officers later withdrew their resignations under pressure and threat of punishment.[210] Insubordination was also a means to an end, albeit a drastic one. Captain August Steffens of the Twenty-fourth Wisconsin used insubordination as a way out of the army. Steffens survived a leg wound at the Battle of Perryville and received another wound at Chickamauga, and he determined that two wounds were enough. Steffens purposely provoked his colonel into court-martialing him by calling the colonel a horse thief. Knowing that a dishonorable discharge was the worst punishment that could befall him, Steffens gladly took the punishment and went home.[211] Officers had some leverage when it came to insubordination against their superiors, but they still ran the risk of punishment. Captain Dodge, for instance, was quick to deal with an "important" lieutenant who refused to go on picket duty. "He will either have to resign or be dismissed," Dodge predicted, ". . . and I rejoice at the prospect of getting rid of him."[212] Captain John Davis of the Ninetieth Pennsylvania, unhappy with the location of the regimental camp, faced a court-martial after he purchased a large amount of fireworks, distributed them to the enlisted men, and instructed them to discharge them after Taps "with the apparent intention of offering insult to his commanding officers."[213]

The most serious direct challenge to army authority involved instances where soldiers murdered their officers, not for any overt reason but simply to remove them as an authority figure. During the Vietnam War, such murders became known as "fragging" an officer, named for the use of fragmentation grenades as the preferred weapon.[214] The fragging of officers was an inevitable by-product of the clash between citizen-soldiers and the army authority that sought to control them. The army gave soldiers weapons and permitted them to kill, yet expected soldiers not to turn the weapons upon officers who, from the soldiers' perspective, abused and misled them. Given the pervasive death around them, it is not surprising that soldiers pondered killing the officers they most disliked. Mostly, soldiers satisfied themselves with threats to kill their officers in the hopes that intimidation would persuade them to change their behavior. Sergeant John Avery, angry at Captain Joseph Lawton because Lawton received a promotion that he rightfully thought his, threatened Lawton so often that the captain was afraid to go into battle because "he was in danger of his life from one of his own men," implying that Avery intended to kill him and place the blame on Confederate bullets.[215] The threat of murder in the midst of battle was not a new one. Soldiers under the command of Lieutenant Robert Beaumont became so angry at his rough handling of drunken soldiers that "Many openly swear that they will shoot him the first time they have a battle with the enemy."[216] Often threats to frag an officer were simply that. As one soldier wrote in his memoir, "Many a wearer of shoulder-straps was to be shot by his own men in their first engagement. But . . . there seemed to be Rebels enough to shoot without throwing away ammunition on Union men."[217]

There was a big gap between wanting to kill an officer and actually attempting it, but soldiers did attempt to frag officers in cases where they deemed it justified. When the aforementioned Private James Orr could not obtain a medical discharge for faking insanity, he attempted to shoot Captain John Otto by claiming that Otto had fired at him first. Only the timely intervention of another soldier, who pushed Orr's musket away, saved Otto's life.[218] In 1863, Lieutenant Virginius Van Gieson shot Sergeant Andrew Ekens dead for mutinous conduct. In retaliation, seven of Ekens' comrades attempted to kill Van Gieson, who managed to escape by wounding two of his assailants.[219] General Thomas Williams apparently lived a charmed life. Considered "a tyrant in every sense of the word," his men openly tried to kill him. "They would shoot at him as he rode through the bushes, and when he was in his tent," but without success.[220] General John Geary's men so disliked him, Robert Strong recalled, that "One of them told me that he had shot at General Geary more than once. Another told me that he put a bullet through the carriage that Geary and his adjutant were riding in."[221] When the colonel of a Michigan regiment ordered the removal of a sutler for illegally selling beer, three soldiers "charged on him with their bayonets" but the officer eluded their attack.[222]

Because the punishment for murder was the death penalty, soldiers did not blatantly admit to their crimes, so examples of fragging are more likely than proven. In Missouri, for example, Colonel William Worthington, described by his discontented troops as "a military martinet from some soldier school in Kentucky," died when a sentinel shot him. Although the sentinel claimed it was an accident, most of the regiment's officers considered it premeditated murder as "More than once his life had been threatened by soldiers who regarded themselves as having been badly treated by him."[223] Another possible fragging occurred at Shiloh with the death of Lieutenant P.T. Keyes. The day before the battle began, several soldiers, who Keyes had struck for not marching fast enough, threatened to kill him the first chance they had. In the aftermath of Keyes' death, a soldier in the regiment confessed he was not entirely sure if the rebels killed Keyes or one of his comrades did, "but the co[mpany] were glad to be rid of him."[224] A similar event occurred at the Wilderness, where Lieutenant James M. Brown died of wounds. "I do believe he was so hated that he was shot by some of his own men," John Haley opined. ". . . Whoever sped the bullet did this regiment an inestimable service."[225] Remembering one of the few overt fraggings, Sergeant Hartwell recorded in his diary that in the adjacent Twentieth Massachusetts "a conscript shot his Captain dead . . . The Capt was standing at a camp fire after dark when it was done." The unknown assassin escaped into the night, and "as yet no clue is found."[226]

THE ARMY FOUND CONTROLLING their enlisted men in the "positive" way as outlined in the Articles of War much easier said than done. The army clearly demonstrated that, at best, it had no idea how doggedly the common soldier would cling to his individual sense of identity and well-being or, at worst, stubbornly refused to believe that its will to assert authority was more powerful than the soldiers' will to resist it. When volunteer officers themselves, steeped in the belief systems of the citizen-soldier, challenged authority by disobeying orders, hiding instead of leading, and assaulting their superior officers instead of showing deference, the army's way of viewing military justice suffered a serious blow to its credibility. Instead, unpredictable elements such as unit cohesion, personal loyalty, and demonstrations of masculinity kept soldiers fighting much longer than simple adhesion to some written rules. These were powerful incentives to keep soldiers in the army and risking death, but they were not enough to keep everyone in place. Soldiers demonstrated their decisions to flaunt authority, mock their superiors, or even leave the battlefield based upon their own interpretations of discipline, and no officer or regulation would make them stay, obey, or respect just because an officer told them to the contrary. Officers may not have liked insubordination, but it was a fact of life that the wisest of them came to manage more than control. At least those soldiers who committed various forms of insubordination stayed within the army, and there were hopes the army could modify their behavior. Much worse were those soldiers who chose to leave the army altogether.

"THE PERNICIOUS PRACTICE OF TREASONABLE PERSONS"

Desertion in the Union Army

In every army, commanders cannot account for their soldiers at all times. As seen in the previous chapter, soldiers straggled, malingered, hid, and ran away. All of these acts were serious breaches of discipline that had a common causation. Soldiers became insubordinate most often when a battle loomed or began, providing at least a minimal justification for their deeds. Soldiers usually characterized such insubordinate behavior as cowardice, but some soldiers rationalized insubordination as the realities of war, the product of poor leadership, or the desire for self-preservation. Under the pressure of combat, some soldiers could place themselves in the shoes of those who committed insubordinate acts, and see themselves doing the exact same thing. When it came to desertion, however, the offense did not have the presence of combat to justify it. Instead, soldiers deserted when they became angry, disillusioned, or pessimistic of their chances of surviving the war. Like many other wartime transgressions, desertion reached epidemic proportions, and the army found itself swamped by too many offenses to handle by traditional means. The Articles of War, specifically Articles 20 and 52, permitted courts-martial to issue death sentences for desertion and misbehavior before the enemy, but absences from duty involved so many soldiers that capital punishment was simply not an option.

Instead, the army tried to contain disgruntled soldiers, hunted down those who left, rewarded those who stayed, spent huge sums of money for rewards and compensation, and enticed absent soldiers to come back into the ranks. When caught deserting, the army applied a mixed approach. If soldiers returned on their own, the army proved lenient. If arrested for their absence, soldiers faced the harshest possible punishments, including death. As will become evident in a later chapter, the army certainly proved willing to execute soldiers for desertion, but preferred to rehabilitate instead of shoot a deserter. The different approaches to desertion, however, created a dichotomy, as the army tried to stress the dire consequences of desertion while at the same time refusing to carry through on its threats of harsh punishment. This, in turn, promoted more than hampered desertion, as soldiers believed they had a real possibility of escaping serious retribution for one of the most serious of military offenses.

DESERTION WAS MORE than just a disciplinary offense. Unlike other forms of disruptive behavior, desertion critically weakened the army, often at the most inopportune times. James Connolly explained away the Union defeat at Chickamauga by admitting to Confederate numerical strength, bolstered because "they didn't have enough desertions" unlike Union armies.[1] Desertion also damaged recruiting efforts. While the Union army tried to build up its forces for offensive actions, desertion undermined these efforts by reducing strength at a time when the army needed to build its strength. Desertions amongst recruits reached such a scale that Ulysses Grant in 1864 believed that only about one in every five recruited soldiers actually reached their units.[2] Desertion created poor morale, or exacerbated periods when morale was already low. Deserters demonstrated a lack of confidence in the Union war effort, often spreading that pessimism to the home front and causing even more damage to the Union cause. A few deserters could not cause significant damage, but desertion occurred on a massive scale, especially in the Army of the Potomac. Whereas the Western armies fought hundreds of miles from home in hostile territory, soldiers who deserted in central Virginia only had to find their way to a major railway to reach their comparatively close homes. From April 1863 to April 1865, nearly 279,000 desertions occurred in the Union army.[3] That number included both enlisted deserters and those who refused to report for service when drafted. For the entire war, the Union army suffered 421,627 desertions (260,339 enlisted deserters and 161,286 absent draftees). About one in every eleven Union soldiers deserted at some point during the war.[4] These numbers are not atypical when compared to the antebellum army. In 1830, the army lost

21 percent of its strength to desertion, and roughly the same percentage in 1856. These were particularly bad years for desertion, as the average desertion rate between 1820 and 1860 was just under 15 percent of the army.[5] Finding, arresting, and returning deserters to the ranks became a major task for the army, but it was often a futile one. The Provost Marshal Corps (or PMC) arrested 75,526 deserters according to its final report to Congress in 1866, or about only one in every six deserters.[6]

Desertion, however, was difficult to characterize across the Union army. Some regiments suffered a high rate, while others knew virtually no desertions. In cases of polar opposites, desertion reduced the One Hundred Twenty-eighth Illinois down to only thirty-five men in the ranks by March 1863, while the Forty-forth Massachusetts lost only four men to desertion for its entire, albeit brief, existence. Discipline in the One Hundred Twenty-eighth Illinois was so bad that more than seven hundred of its soldiers deserted in a five-month period, forcing General Lorenzo Thomas, the Adjutant General of the Army, to disband the regiment and cashier the officers.[7] Within regiments, wide discrepancies existed, depending upon such variables as unit motivation or the quality of their officers. The Second Massachusetts Cavalry, which included some companies from California, suffered a 42 percent desertion rate in its Massachusetts companies, but only 12 percent in the California companies.[8] Different types of units had different experiences with desertion. The desertion rate across the Union army was 62.5 desertions per 1000 men. For USCT soldiers the rate was slightly higher. Despite many instances of mistreatment and racism from their own army, USCT soldiers deserted at a rate of only 67 per 1000.[9] Complaining about the poor treatment he received in the Fifth USCT, a contraband recruit justified his desertion by making the unfavorable comparison "that he was no better treated in the army than he was by his former master."[10] Specific events, such as major defeats, also affected the desertion rate. While an otherwise steadfast regiment, nineteen men of the Nineteenth Indiana deserted within only a few days of the loss at Fredericksburg.[11] Desertion continued even when the nation sensed that Union victory was within their grasp. In February 1865, army muster rolls showed 630,924 men present for duty, compared to 338,536 absent from their commands. The latter number included deserters, but also encompassed men on furlough, in hospitals, or other authorized leave.[12] Statistics became difficult to compile because officers often simply did not know the disposition of some of their men. The army continued to search for a soldier "who was missing sometime since & supposed to have deserted" from Charles Haydon's regiment until he was "now reported killed."[13] Private Oliver Gosler did desert from his regiment, but found himself a prisoner of the Confederates. He died in a POW camp in

North Carolina some months later, but his regiment listed him as a deserter for the rest of the war, unaware of his death.[14] John Westervelt likewise did not know the disposition of one of the young drummers in his regiment. "He left camp one night when the rebs were shelling," Westervelt wrote. "It is not known whether he has deserted, been shot in the woods, or gone home."[15]

Among the enlisted men, opinions about deserters by those who chose to stay ranged from understanding to pity to anger. Like many other disciplinary infractions, desertion was a personal choice that reflected a soldier's state of mind and level of commitment. Unable to discern the thought process that led a comrade to desert, the remaining soldiers practiced a form of transference, projecting their own fears and worries as the reasons that soldiers left. Departed soldiers also became an easy target of denigration, with remaining soldiers bolstering their own sense of patriotism and valor by comparing it to the lesser men who failed the test of soldiering. Unable to devise a single perception of desertion, soldier attitudes ranged from justifying the departure of their comrades to palpable rage, with the majority of opinion on the angry end of the spectrum. Soldiers also frequently associated desertion with a lack of manhood. Writing to his father-in-law to inquire about a deserter who perhaps returned to his hometown, John Pardington expressed no surprise that he deserted, expecting "his Patriotism would soon die out. It dont [sic] last long in the army." Pardington, on the other hand, determined to stick it out and prove his worth, writing, "as bad as I want to see my Wife and child I do not think I shall ever desgrace [sic] them or you as a son in law." Emory Sweetland echoed the sentiment, promising, "Your husband will never disgrace his wife and child that way."[16] In response to his mother's fears that he might desert and dishonor the family name, Eason Bull replied, "Tell her as long as my name is Eason Bull I will fight before I desert."[17]

Viewing themselves as examples of masculine idealism, soldiers who stayed in the army viewed those who left as something less then men, worthy of pity and punishment for their personal failures. While recovering at a hospital, Sergeant Francis Bowen spotted a deserter from his company on the street. Describing the encounter, Bowen's anger spilled over: "I pitty [sic] him; his just desserts is death. He is cowardly & tretcherous [sic] but I hope justice may fall with a downy hand for his is a weakness impossible for him to overcome."[18] After five soldiers deserted his regiment, Ovando Hollister could only fathom their actions by determining "Cowardice is their only ground. They ought never to call themselves men again. After proving insensible to all the dictates of pride, honor, or interest that usually influence men, they should sneak off to some region where manhood forms no necessary ingredient of character."[19] When caught, deserters garnered no sympathy from their compatriots. "I am glad to see deserters brought to their regiments," Anson Shuey wrote to his wife, "if they have been willing to enlist they ought to be willing to serve their time."[20] Other soldiers marked deserters as less than men, but favored no punishment for them because, as poor examples of masculinity, the army was better off without them. Viewing the army as a masculine testing ground, soldiers expected the process to weed out the unfit, and finding the unfit proved valuable because the soldiers who remained staked the claim of being masculine survivors and superior men to those who left. Former comrades, for instance, characterized deserter Cyrus Hadley as "worthless," while an officer diminished another deserter as "a worthless hound and is no loss" to the army.[21] Various members of his regiment recalled Private Shelley Martin after he deserted as a "worthless drunkard from youth. . . He was as likely to lie as to tell the truth. He has a reputation of running with lewd women."[22] Silas Wesson was glad that "Forrester Graham deserted and gone. He was no good anyway, he was a thief and a coward."[23] Soldiers also liked to believe that patriotism bolstered their determination to fight, an attribute that foreign-born soldiers lacked. A postwar compilation of statistics made the unsubstantiated claim that "desertion is a crime of foreign, rather than native birth, and that but a small proportion of the men who forsook their colors were Americans."[24] In the fall of 1863, Henry Abbott reported a high rate of desertion among foreign-born soldiers, "particularly the Dutch and French" and claimed, "Desertion in the field . . . was almost unknown before this jumble of French, Italians, Germans, & in some cases, *Chinese* came to us."[25]

Soldiers also associated desertion with a general lack of will, patriotism, or duty. As citizen-soldiers with obligations to defend the nation, soldiers who took up the burden of soldiering had a duty to see the task through. Although dissatisfied with the leadership of the army and progress of the war, some soldiers could not bring themselves to desert, even if they felt justified to do so. "The soldiers as a general thing are very much discouraged about ending the war," Augustus Hall wrote to his cousin. "Lots of them are deserting every day and a good share of those left [in the army] though, I think they enlisted from patriotic motives, remain only from principle."[26] Those who deserted were not just failed men, they were also failed patriots who let down their country, their army, and their comrades in arms. Subsequently, captured deserters deserved no pity and had to accept the consequences of their actions. When guards brought in a deserter from his regiment, George Cram expressed disgust at the deserter's lack of determination and expressed "no doubt but what he will suffer for it now."[27] Cruel punishment was preferable, some soldiers opined, to the failure of their cause, as harsh times caused for harsh measures. Leniency, they believed, only bred more indiscipline. "Stern punishments would have prevented many offenses," a soldier recalled in his memoirs, "but, at that time, the highest echelons [of the army] seemingly neither could nor would learn . . . the administration of justice must be prompt, fast, and strict" to be effective.[28] "Desertion has increased at a most alarming extent," one officer believed. "It must *at once* be punished with *Death* speedy & certain or the army is ruined.[29] Benjamin Baker certainly grasped the necessity of such treatment. "I understand that the law is to be executed to the limit on deserters & that means death," he wrote his mother, "for my part I would as soon die any other way as to be set up against a stump & shot at."[30]

Who, then, was the typical deserter? Simple identifiers are difficult to establish, but some statistical models suggest some answers.[31] Age was not a factor, with deserters representing the entire age range of eligible soldiers, nor were casualty figures at the company level, signifying that soldiers determined to desert regardless of their optimism regarding the war. Companies with common demographic makeup (i.e., same home, occupation, or age) contained soldiers more likely to desert, reflecting a belief that men of a similar background and lifestyle would understand why a soldier deserted more than a colleague with a different background. Not surprisingly, married men and fathers deserted more than single men. Community cohesion was a major factor in desertion, with soldiers less likely to desert back to communities that actively supported the war than to communities hostile to the Lincoln administration. The presence of experienced officers and NCOs tended to suppress desertion, while regiments with new officers tended to suffer higher rates of desertion. Education level also factored into desertion rates, as educated soldiers created an army that, as General Henry Halleck put it, "reads and thinks."[32] Able to evaluate and criticize the war effort, many educated soldiers opted to desert instead of stay.[33]

FOR MANY A SOLDIER, their first flirtation with desertion came when they temporarily distanced themselves from their units. On many occasions soldiers were AWOL, physically separating themselves from the army for a brief time. Unlike straggling, AWOL was a premeditated offense, with the soldier fully intending to leave army control. As a sign of insubordination, the army found AWOL far more damaging than malingering, straggling, or disrespecting an officer. Soldiers who committed one of the insubordinate offenses was a disciplinary problem for certain, but they committed those offenses within the reach of military discipline. They were still in a position where the army could hopefully apply some corrective measure or punishment that might prevent such behavior in the future. A soldier who went AWOL, on the other hand, physically separated himself from the army structure, even if for only a brief period of time, and existed beyond the control and discipline of the army or the soldiers' peers. A soldier who was AWOL was not susceptible to orders, did not have any regulations to obey, and no officers to lead him. This type of independence was the very thing that military discipline sought to purge, and the army consequently took a very dim view of soldiers who decided for themselves when a little vacation from the army was necessary. The army did not like soldiers going AWOL, but their own regulations tended to promote the practice. An officer who noted a soldier missing from duty immediately recorded him as AWOL. If the soldier remained missing for more than ten days, the army declared him a deserter, a much more drastic and heavily punished offense. AWOL soldiers, therefore, kept an eye on the calendar, and made certain to return to duty before they moved from the AWOL to deserter category.[34] The only other difference between desertion and AWOL was intent. The AWOL soldier expected to return, while the deserter did not.

Going AWOL, however, was entirely within the expected behavior of citizen-soldiers who wanted to assert their rights and individuality. Committing the offense of going AWOL undermined the very elements of control that the army sought to impose (stay where the army wants you to stay, do what the army wants you to do), and demonstrated the perceived rights that citizen-soldiers embraced (leave when you want to leave, do what you want as long as you still do your duty). Absenting one's self from camp and command permitted citizen-soldiers to demonstrate that they still had some sense of decision-making in their lives, even if the decision to go AWOL was for such base reasons as getting drunk or finding a prostitute. Often, simply the lure of something different than the bland and boring existence in camp was enough to entice men beyond the borders of their regiments. Lieutenant Colonel John Cook, commanding the Fifth USCT, found it impossible to keep his soldiers in camp for this reason. After garrison duty in remote areas, the Fifth was pleased to encamp close to New Berne, North Carolina, and with all of the recreational opportunities that such cities provided.[35] Therefore, unlike most of the other insubordinate behaviors, going AWOL was usually a premeditated act and therefore less likely to be tolerated or rationalized. If a soldier was willing to leave the army for a few hours, a soldier might opt to leave the army altogether. Consequently, the army took a dimmer view of AWOL, tried harder to stop it, and punished the offense much more harshly.

According to the War Department, only three reasons existed why soldiers might legitimately absent themselves from their units: official leave, disability from wounds that required hospitalization, and disability caused by disease. If a soldier wanted temporarily to leave his unit, it was at the discretion of his commanding officer, with any unauthorized absence without leave constituting desertion.[36] Horrified by the idea of soldiers wandering around without supervision, commanders quickly imposed tight boundaries around their camps, and permitted soldiers to leave only under the most limited of circumstances. In the Twenty-third New York, Private Seymour Dexter noted the tightened restrictions. "The training grounds now have a complete guard staff of soldiers. . . . Nobody in and nobody out without a pass," he observed. "No more than three men can leave the grounds at one time and no more than six per day."[37] In an effort to maintain order in Indianapolis, the local garrison commander imposed tight controls over all regiments within his jurisdiction, including three roll calls per day supervised by at least one commissioned officer, and company captains could issue only one pass per day that permitted a single soldier to leave their encampment.[38] Such basic restrictions were not enough in some regiments, and their officers took even more drastic measures. In the Fifty-seventh Massachusetts, Colonel Edward B. Hollister ordered a roll call every three hours, while in the Third New York a soldier needed "the signature of his Colonel, Brigade Commander, and of the Provost Marshall [*sic*] to pass him ten feet out of the lines."[39]

Ordering soldiers to stay in camp was one thing, while keeping them there was another. In some regiments, efforts to halt the transit of soldiers seemed to cease entirely, with the officers having little concern what their men did so long as they answered the morning roll call. Edward Wightman witnessed the same loose discipline in his regiment. "The camp guard was instructed to permit no one to go out . . . [but] the orders might not have been given," he wrote his brother. "The whole regiment could not keep our boys out of the city, and the camp guard gave so little heed to the instructions that the camp was habitually empty."[40] Sergeant Charles Ramsey of the One Hundred Forty-eighth Pennsylvania observed that it was difficult to keep soldiers in camp when the under-equipped pickets had only clubs to stop them. Without arms to back up their orders, soldiers simply walked past the guards and ignored their orders to halt.[41] Not even brick walls could stop soldiers determined to leave their encampments. When officers of the Sixth Michigan housed their men in a sturdy building constructed "with solid masonry brick walls eighteen or twenty inches thick" and required a "written pass, signed and countersigned" to leave, they thought they had contained their men for the night. Their determined soldiers, however, "removed some of those sacks from over against the wall and commenced drilling for liberty" and soon carved "an opening . . . large enough to admit a man's body to pass through on his hands and knees." The tunnel worked well until "some of the boys became indiscreet and the officers "put masons to repair the break . . . and several other attempts to burrow out were discovered and frustrated."[42] Frequent roll calls did not always work, especially if the person who called the roll was himself AWOL or showed up only for roll call. In the Sixteenth

Pennsylvania one morning, "Orderly [Sergeant John] Barnes [attended] an all night dance. . . . He came in time to call the Roll and escaped [out of camp again]."[43] To avoid the roll calls altogether, one soldier recommended becoming friendly with the orderly sergeant tasked with the roll, or "if the orderly was not sharp" a soldier present for the roll call might call the name for someone who was absent.[44]

Sometimes stealth or force was not necessary to leave camp. If soldiers could not legitimately obtain a pass from their company officers, they could always try to forge one. "This afternoon H.C. & C.J. Simmons and myself made a pass of our own," Charlie Mosher noted in his diary. ". . . We have had a good trip [to Washington, DC], and no one the worse for our forged pass and running the guards."[45] On May 27, 1865, John Ferguson obtained an expired pass dated the 26th. Ferguson, however, "scratched out the 6 by means of a sharp pointed knife and placed a figer [figure] 7 instead . . . So we started out for the City of Washington."[46] William Lamson devised a clever way to leave camp in plain view of the pickets. "An officer and eight men can pass the guard any time to drill," he wrote to his sister, "so one takes command and marches eight or more out and then we go back when we please."[47]

As with some forms of insubordination, the occasional officer tried the soft approach, hoping that leniency might produce results where inflexible treatment did not. Some officers tried the strategy of giving passes freely when they could in the hopes that soldiers would conversely stay in camp when officers could not let them leave. Such was the case with the Tenth Illinois as it prepared for Sherman's Carolina Campaign. "Our whole regt. has been in town today," John Ferguson wrote. "No passes been required and no orders given to remain in camp. The boys feels at liberty to go and come at pleasure."[48] During the Siege of Vicksburg, a group of soldiers slipped out of camp to find some relief from the boredom. After engaging in an "aligator [sic] hunt," the soldiers returned to camp expecting "to get into trouble . . . but got off with a lecture" not to leave camp without permission again.[49] And, of course, the infractions of officers themselves undermined efforts to control the problem. Colonel Patrick Guiney arrested two of his own captains for overstaying a pass, lamenting, "Will I ever get through with these men?"[50] Because officers themselves violated the rules and went AWOL, some of them punished absence without leave only lightly. "One of our Corporals run the guard the other day and he has been put back in the ranks for doing it," James Newton informed his parents. ". . . [H]e was put on guard today as a private."[51] A demotion is a significant penalty, but considering he received nowhere near the maximum penalty, the corporal got off lightly. John Cook of the Sixth Wisconsin spent "three days on short rations" for leaving camp to visit Washington, DC, but gladly accepted the punishment because "I got what I deserved . . . [and] we had a bully time."[52] Soldiers who failed to return in time for roll call had their names "pricked" on the roll sheet, marked by pressing a pin into the paper next to their names, singling them out for punishment or extra duty. James Avery, for instance, hurried to complete a letter to his family because, he explained, "I fear my name will get pricked for being tardy" to roll call.[53]

Other officers, however, did punish AWOL severely and in line with the Articles of War, so soldiers who brazenly left camp without permission found out that getting back and escaping punishment was not an easy matter. Soldiers had to be aware, as Private Edward Bassett was, that "If we go into the country we might run into the Patrol and turned over" for punishment.[54] Guards and officers on the prowl for absent soldiers considered everyone they met outside of the camps as a potential violator, and suspicion was a normal part of the search process. John Brobst stayed in Helena, Illinois, for a few days after the transport carrying his regiment to Cairo, Illinois, moved on. He had to "dodge around" to keep authorities from "taking me as a deserter," but eventually returned to his unit.[55] Soldiers in the Forty-fourth Massachusetts dodged their way into camp by, at one point, boldly posing as guards themselves and brazenly checking the papers of anyone they suspected were guards looking for those absent, and, at another point, crawling "crab-like" past the pickets and into camp unseen.[56] Daniel Sawtelle tried to slip past the pickets by telling the guard that he and his comrades had gone to town to attend church. Although they actually did go to attend services, the guard thought it an unlikely excuse and arrested them.[57] The army also imposed fines. "For the most trivial thing a man is punished severely," James Simpson complained in a letter. "A man absenting himself for a week or so—$8 to be forfeited [from his pay every month] for the balance of his enlistment."[58]

A soldier faced only the risk of punishment if a guard caught him, but soldiers who tried to sneak out of, or back into, camp under the cover of darkness took a deadly risk. In enemy country with danger close, pickets had to keep a sharp eye out for potential danger. A shadowy figure lurking in the darkness presented a difficult situation for a jittery and trigger-happy picket. Was the figure a comrade sneaking back into camp after a night on the town or was it an enemy soldier bent on more lethal goals? Sentinels also, in some cases, received specific orders to shoot absent soldiers who tried to sneak back into camp instead of permitting themselves to be arrested and accepting their punishments. For an offense as serious as AWOL, the army certainly considered such an order perfectly legitimate, and soldiers died in the darkness at the hands of their own comrades. "The guards shot at another man" trying to sneak through the picket line, one officer recorded, "I think they will soon learn that it wont do to fool with guards with loaded muskets."[59] Private James Miller certainly knew the consequences of fooling with a loaded musket. "No privates go out of the Camp and the boys do not run the guard here," Miller wrote his father, "for the [pickets'] rifles are loaded . . . and they have the order to shoot any one who does not stop when hailed three times." Miller himself nearly fired upon a captain, having "brought my gun to my face to fire when he stoped [stopped] and the Corporal of the guard" let them through.[60] Other guards, however, pulled the trigger. "2 men of Company B tried to run out pas the gards [*sic*]," David Lilley wrote to his sister, "and the gard Run the Bayonet through his hand and . . . Captain Ricketts shot at a man with his revolver as the men tried to escape" from camp.[61] When confronted by an officer bent on arresting him for being AWOL, Private Joseph Updegraff "was shot and instantly killed . . . for refusing to halt when ordered to." It is uncertain if Updegraff intended to shoot his way out of an arrest, but the officer in question testified that "Updegraff paid not the slightest attention to the order" to halt and instead "began to cap his gun," forcing the officer to fire to protect his own life.[62]

While most shootings were singular affairs, in other cases the death toll mounted. "The Twelfth is winning a terrible name for discipline," Captain DeForest complained. "Within a few weeks past its sentries have shot three men dead for trying to run guard." Instead of being angry, "with this punctilious execution of orders our general is much pleased."[63] Even worse, because soldiers guarded their own camps, the men they were shooting were soldiers from their own units. "A sentinel of the 63rd Penn. Regt. shot two of his own Co. last night at one shot," Charles Haydon wrote, approving of the soldier's accuracy, "They had been outside & were trying to creep in unobserved."[64] Private James Greenalch had little pity for soldiers killed while AWOL. "Last night two men were shot by the guard," he wrote to his family at home. "They were told to stop and did not and they [the guard] fired. They were drunk I suppose. One was shot dead, the other was brought in to the hospital this morning and another was shot the night before. They were our men and shot by our men, that was their orders."[65]

Blazing away at any possible AWOL, however, was potentially dangerous and carried the risk of a deadly confrontation that need not have happened. In one instance, two soldiers of the Eighth New York Heavy Artillery who "ran the guard and went down to the city" returned to camp only to find a guard confronting them. One of them "drew a revolver and threatened to blow out the sentinel[']s brains unless he allowed them to pass," whereby the picket aimed his weapon and ordered the soldier to drop the pistol. Authorities immediately arrested the soldier and forwarded him to the corps headquarters to face a court-martial.[66] A lieutenant in a Maryland regiment "in some way got beyond his outpost" by accident. "He failed to hear the challenge of the picket," one of his soldiers reported, "and he was severely wounded by being shot in his arm and side."[67] When an officer observed a number of unknown men entering a barn outside of their lines one night, Wesley Brainerd participated in an armed reconnaissance to determine who they were. After debating whether to storm the barn or open fire on it from a distance, the detachment decided to wait and evaluate the situation in daylight. It was a fortunate decision, as the suspected intruders were "15 or 20 of our own men . . . having . . . a comfortable nights lodging in the hay."[68]

FOR OTHER SOLDIERS, however, a brief hiatus from the army was not enough. For a variety of reasons, soldier decided that their association with the army had to end, and a permanent desertion was the only solution. There is no shortage of causes for desertion during the Civil War. Ella Lonn, for instance, identified no fewer than nine causes for desertion ranging from poor officers and late pay to low-quality recruits and war weariness.[69] In determining the "cause" of desertion, however, the idea of causality is itself misapplied. Lonn and other historians promoted the externalization of causality, placing the blame for desertion upon conditions the soldier found intolerable. By presuming that the deserters had "cause" for their actions, their actions were defendable, as no one could blame a soldier for leaving if he thought the war was unwinnable, if his commander was incompetent, or if the government did not pay him. Such a description of "causes" for desertion placed the blame for desertion on the army, not the soldier who committed the offense. What this view lacks, however, is the perspective of the citizen-soldier and the expectations of manhood in that it does not explain why only some men deserted while most decided to stay. The very same ethos of the citizen-soldier that prompted one soldier to leave because the army appointed an inept officer to command him was the same ethos that kept another soldier in the field who had the same complaint. The same sense of masculinity that convinced a soldier to go home and take care of his impoverished family was the same sense of masculinity that kept other soldiers fighting even after disastrous defeats. It also ignored the obligations of military service. They were soldiers, and military law and the army regulations dictated where they would go, what they would do, and how they would do it. To desert was to shed not only one's uniform but the status of a soldier altogether. Soldiers obviously knew that deserting was wrong; that is why they snuck away when no one was looking and hid when someone came to find them. When soldiers believed the army abused their manhood and citizenship, soldiers obviously reacted to defend their status as citizens and men, but they did so because they felt they had the right to do so and their reaction was warranted. If soldiers were going to openly flaunt military law they needed something more than just a "cause." They needed a justification.

Unfortunately for the Union army, their soldiers had plenty of justifications. The army's failure to provide pay on a regular basis proved damaging to morale. Dozens of soldiers in one regiment grumbled "that if they cannot get their pay they will desert and go where they can support their families."[70] The horrors of the battlefield evaporated any misplaced dreams of the glamour of war. Following Ambrose Burnside's ill-advised assault at Fredericksburg, desertions from his army skyrocketed, with estimates as high as a quarter of the army absent from their units.[71] Claiming that their "regiment meant nothing to us," several soldiers pondering the course of the war decided that "desertion was the only cure we could see" to save their lives.[72] Defeatism particularly festered in winter encampments, where soldiers spent months doing very little but thinking about their condition. A large number of men deserted during one such winter encampment, failing to "see the propriety of laying inactive a whole winter at an unimportant point."[73] The failure of officers to effectively lead also convinced many a soldier to depart. Several soldiers from Company H of the Fifth USCT deserted instead of entering battle under the command of their captain, a notorious coward.[74] Edwin Stark justified his desertion from the Eleventh Michigan Cavalry by describing an altercation where an officer "drew his saber and struck me a hard blow on the face and cut open my lower jaw. . . . I took him from his horse and gave him a severe whipping."[75] The turnover of unpopular and ineffective officers also affected the morale of the Twenty-seventh Indiana, where "the privates are beginning to talk of deserting."[76] Private Miles Kellogg chose to leave, according to the officer who arrested him, because he was "changed from Co. I to Co. M which he did not like and for that reason he deserted."[77] John Klotzbucher of the One Hundredth Pennsylvania simply deserted because he was "tired of the service and concluded to go into the Boot and Shoe Business."[78]

Politics also provided a justification for desertion, especially the controversial enacting of the Emancipation Proclamation. By making the war an abolitionist crusade, the Lincoln administration alienated those who preferred to characterize the war as a struggle for Union without any consideration of the status of slaves. The Proclamation proved a polarizing event, with numerous soldiers deserting rather than fight to free the slaves. Within days of the enacting of the Proclamation, for instance, nine soldiers of the Sixty-sixth Indiana deserted because of the document.[79] "If the nigger is the object [of the war]," George Sinclair wrote his wife, ". . . I am out of it forever and shall act conscientiously in leaving the army."[80] James Decker wrote to his sister of numerous desertions in his brigade because "the soldiers say they won't fight by the side of the nigger."[81]

Timing was the key to a successful escape, but often the timing involved the arrival of a soldier's pay. "I shall go [out of the army] very soon," James Horrocks wrote his parents, ". . . but if there is a likelihood of getting two months pay, I will wait a little longer."[82] The issue of pay, or rather the absence of it, played a clear role in desertion. Soldiers justified their desertions because they were not paid, and the army was afraid to pay its soldiers because they knew that many were only waiting until payday to desert. "Should our Troops be paid off before the next action," Marsena Patrick postulated, "I predict very large desertions & no possibility of staying them." He was correct. Less than a week later, Patrick had a full scale spate of insubordination and desertion on his hands, where "the Excelsiors [an all New York brigade] are determined to run if they can get a chance, having been paid off today" and "15 men from the New York Regt. of [General Joseph J.] Bartlett's Brigade deserted."[83] Albert Sprague, a surgeon in the Seventh Rhode Island, observed the same phenomenon, telling his wife that "we expect our Regt. to be paid off soon, and then look out for desertions. Men are deserting every day."[84] James Harrocks complained that his regimental paymaster had enough cash on hand to pay the regiment, but his colonel wanted to wait until the army left the environs of Washington, DC, and into a field encampment before paying them "as he knows it will be more difficult to desert there."[85] The colonel of the Sixteenth Connecticut had the same idea, causing a soldier to accusingly state that "i [sic] think the reason they don't pay us off is they kno [sic] that half of the soldiers will run away."[86] The tactic was useful, but it caused undue hardship that made desertion more likely. Due several months pay, a soldier of the Sixth USCT lamented his financial hardships that reduced his wife and children to abject poverty, and prompted him to ponder desertion as her letters "have brought my patriotism down to the freezing point."[87] When arrested after deserting from their respective Vermont regiments, Private Louis Bee justified his desertion because the army had not paid him in six months, while Private George Badger left because his pay was eight months in arrears.[88] Soldiers who deserted before the army paid them, however, lost their accumulated income, making desertion a costly business. When Sergeant Charles Watson deserted from the Seventeenth Vermont, for instance, he left behind $340 in unpaid wages and bounty money.[89] Thirty soldiers of the Sixth New York Artillery deserted over several days in September 1864, leaving behind more than $60 per man.[90]

Because desertion was such a momentous choice, soldiers did not act rashly and suddenly when they concluded to desert. Soldiers planned or threatened to desert as a means of expressing their displeasure with army life. Sometimes the threat was only a means of venting frustration or expressing disapproval. Sergeant Welsh often noted that "it is no uncommon thing to hear men swear they will never fire another shot if they can help it" when unhappy with their lot in the army.[91] George Squier confessed, "I am sick of soldiering . . . I certainly do not feel like exposing my life, ruining my health and enduring all the hardships of military life." Squier knew his duty, but at the same time, "in case of another fight, if there is a chance of 'playing out,' I do not know what I may do."[92] Corporal John Rhoades worked out a precise plan for his desertion, informing his wife to expect him in "about twenty days."[93] James Horrocks worked out an elaborate scheme for his desertion, detailing his plot in a letter to his parents. Horrocks planned to desert in Washington, DC. Presuming that he could convince army authorities that he was simply AWOL if arrested within a few days of his departure, Horrocks' goal was to reach Philadelphia, a city with "not the most remote chance of meeting anyone I know," within ten days. Horrocks planned to stay in Philadelphia instead of returning to New York, confident the he would be "able to get employment in some shape very soon," safe in a city where there was "as much chance of my being arrested as there would be finding a needle in a bottle of hay."[94] Some soldiers were brazen in their planning. Austin Stearns noted that a soldier named Joseph Martin told him, "I'll pitch my poncho just three more days" and, true to his word, successfully deserted three days later.[95]

Soldiers needed careful planning because not every desertion was successful, as the army was quick to impose measures to stem the problem. Many soldiers attempted to desert, but not all were successful. Private James Carl attempted to desert on six separate occasions, but the army caught him every time, while Private Chester Blake failed three times before finally deserting successfully in December 1863.[96] Trying to mingle with a detachment leaving camp to forage, some potential deserters tried to escape by "lay[ing] down in the wagons . . . while others went on the horses and tried to play wagonmasters."[97] Geography stymied some desertions. Chaplain Stuckenberg noted several men querying him about the distance to the Rappahannock River, especially one he described as a "prissy, sharp looking fellow, in the corner of whose eye desertion lurks."[98] Despite recent bad weather that meant "the Rappahannock was swollen by the rain," several men attempted to desert from Wilbur Fisk's regiment. Unfortunately for them, a nearby detachment of cavalry soon ran down most of them; "six were retaken and one escaped."[99] Trying to manage his "drunk & . . . very noisy" men aboard a transport, Theodore Dodge had to fish out of the water "four [men who] tried to desert by jumping overboard."[100] Detailed as an orderly sergeant to a captain in the Seventy-eighth New York, Lorenzo Stewart managed to get out of camp by "donning the [captain's] shoulder straps . . . and walking out past the guards" before a patrol captured him down the road.[101]

Usually, soldiers caught trying to desert received a relatively light punishment, such as extra duty or a fine, but the army cracked down on some offenders. "George Perry got his sentence for attempting to desert," John Bates noted in his diary. "It is to lose all pay and allowance and confined at hard labor during his term of service three years at Dry Tortugas, Florida."[102] When captured, soldiers who attempted to desert received little sympathy from their colleagues. "Last night 100 men deserters were brought into headquarters . . . They were caught while attempting to make a raft to cross the river Potomac," John Dunbar wrote his sister. "They have to stand up all night and have had nothing to eat. It seems hard to treat men so but they know better than to desert."[103] Some attempted desertions ended tragically. Trying to cross a creek with "a large number of canteens . . . fastened around his body under his arms" as a makeshift lifebelt, James O'Brien of the Third New Hampshire drowned instead.[104] Another soldier, in the Western Theater, "was drowned . . . trying to get across the river to desert."[105] Observing a soldier trying to desert in a rowboat, a sergeant verbally warned him to return. When the soldier ignored both the verbal warning and a "shot fired over his head," the sergeant "fired again, hit the deserter in a vital spot, and he died shortly afterward." The army considered charges against the sergeant, but General Hooker "ordered the sergeant's release and personally wrote to him a very complimentary letter and promised him speedy promotion."[106] When "an entire company . . . attempted to desert *en masse*," the New York *Herald* reported, ". . . They were stopped . . . and ordered to return to the camp, and on refusing they were fired on by the patrol. Two men were killed on the spot and five were severely wounded."[107]

MAKING THE PROBLEM of desertion even more difficult for the army was the abundant opportunities that existed for soldiers to desert. Long marches provided both a reason and an opportunity to desert. Grueling marches were the type of activity likely to convince a soldier pondering desertion to act upon his plans. Marches also provided cover, as an officer might presume that a missing soldier was simply temporarily straggling instead of permanently leaving. Considering the large numbers of stragglers in an army's wake, an officer might not realize for several days that a soldier had deserted. More than a dozen men from the Eighteenth Regulars deserted on the march during Sherman's Atlanta Campaign in 1864.[108] Even if the "march" meant travel by train, desertion still occurred. Knowing that the conductors had to keep to tight schedules, soldiers slipped off the train and managed to desert by hiding only long enough for the train to pull away.[109] The only way to contain the deserters was to use the same tactics to limit straggling: extra guards and vigilant officers.[110]

The majority of deserters, however, left the army from an encampment. Soldiers spent most of their service in various encampments as the war dictated the movement of their units. Soldiers might encamp for only day or two, or might stay for months. Regardless of the duration of their stay, the camp was their army home, and the place they left to return to their civilian home. The positioning of camps in remote locations and the general comings and goings of a large army provided the opportunity for deserters to leave camp and disappear. Just as in preventing AWOL, the officers relied upon vigilant sentinels to keep an eye out for deserters, but sentinels were only effective when they did their duty. The officers of the Second Massachusetts Cavalry found containing desertion difficult when, in Baltimore, the pickets left camp to go get drunk.[111] While the hardships endured in sparse frontline encampments provided plenty of justification for desertion, soldiers chose to desert even from relatively comfortable camps. Stationed at Camp Douglas to guard the Confederate prisoners housed there, the First Michigan Sharpshooters had the advantages of an established camp located only a few miles from the recreational opportunities of Chicago. Despite this relatively comfortable assignment, forty-nine men deserted the regiment during their six-month stay at Camp Douglas.[112] Soldiers opted to desert even in places where getting home proved difficult. Serving on the frontier, four soldiers deserted by jumping from the *Jesse H. Lacy* as it steamed up the Missouri River at "the mouth of the Niobrara [River]" in a remote section of the Nebraska Territory.[113]

Desertion from camp became particularly popular after demoralizing defeats or frustrating activity. After the loss at Fredericksburg, the One Hundred Twenty-first New York immediately "lost by desertion about 70 men," with an officer fearing "that there will be more deserters tonight."[114] After their luckless attack at the Crater in 1864, soldiers deserted the Twenty-ninth USCT at steady rate for the next month.[115] A good example of desertion bred from frustration was the reaction to Ambrose Burnside's "Mud March" that commenced on January 20, 1863. Eager to redeem his reputation after the debacle at Fredericksburg a month before, Burnside tried to take advantage of unseasonably warm weather to seize an advantageous position on the Army of Northern Virginia. The warm weather, however, thawed the ground, turned the roads into muddy streams, and bogged down the army. After two days of struggling in the mud, the Army of the Potomac slogged back to camp, utterly undone by the conditions. Frustrated by the inept movement and taunted by jeering Confederates on the south bank of the Rappahannock, many soldiers chose to leave. "A great many men . . . took advantage of this mud march to desert," Private Bellard noted. ". . . The woods were full of them. The mud I suppose sickened them."[116] In two days, the Second Wisconsin alone intercepted sixty soldiers attempting to desert, including sixteen men crammed on a makeshift raft trying to cross the Potomac.[117] Disgusted with the effort, five men from the Seventeenth Maine left together in hopes of a successful desertion.[118] "I saw where lots of soldiers had gone, having left everything," Wyman White reported, "their tents, their equipment, and in many cases their rifles and ammunition, everything lying on the wet ground. It struck me that they must have deserted, and I afterwards found that to be the case. Hundreds of men, being entirely discouraged, broke to the rear and started toward the north and home. Not because they were not patriotic, but because they were discouraged beyond endurance."[119]

Frustration also drove many soldiers to desert from the various exchange camps set up as part of the prisoner of war exchange cartel. Paroling prisoners was still a part of warfare in the nineteenth century, with armies sometimes sending captured soldiers home instead of tending them in prisoner of war camps. The largest parole came after Ulysses Grant captured Vicksburg in July 1863, and paroled nearly the entire 30,000 man garrison.[120] The conditions imposed by a parole prevented soldiers from engaging in belligerent action until exchanged by a like number of prisoners held by the other side. Instead of allowing men paroled by the Confederates to go home, because they might not ever see them again, the army held paroled Union troops in special camps, where they sat until released from their obligations. The parole camps, designed as temporary quarters and surrounded by armed guards to keep the parolees from wandering away, were very unpopular places. The parolees had no freedom of movement, there was nothing to do, and parolees resented their incarceration when they thought they were going home.[121] Weary of life at the largest parole camp near Annapolis, Maryland, a number of men deserted. Private Henry Kaufmann was one of the few deserters caught leaving the Annapolis camp, getting only as far as Manchester, Maryland. As punishment for attempting to leave, the army charged Kaufmann $13.67, the cost of finding and returning him.[122] So many soldiers deserted the senior officer at the camp believed that "If the men in my camp were a sample of our army, we would have nothing but a mob of stragglers and cowards."[123]

One of the great aids to soldiers who wanted to leave the army was the circumstance that deserters left the army in large groups, by either design or coincidence. A handful of deserters had little chance eluding the huge army around them, but when desertion became a flood there was a high likelihood that a deserter could escape. In some cases deserters conspired to leave the army as a group, doing so for various reasons. Some group desertions occurred because the deserters had the same complaint, they were friends or relatives, or because a large number of deserters made it more likely that at least some of them might successfully escape. Demoralized by the "perpetual rain and piercing cold" of their winter camp, forty men deserted together from their company, leaving an observer believing "the remainder [of the company] wished last night that they had followed suit."[124] Also weary of the winter weather, William Howe and nineteen other members of the One Hundred Sixteenth Pennsylvania all deserted together in December 1862.[125] In other cases, deserters decided for themselves to leave, but happened to do so at roughly the same time that others decided to desert. Typical of these cases are desertions after demoralizing events or when soldiers received unpleasant news or information. Unhappy about heading to the front lines in Virginia, twenty-five men of one regiment deserted in a single night by leaping off their transport ship in the middle of the Potomac River, preferring to risk death by drowning to death in combat.[126] In the week between the Battle of the Wilderness and the Battle of Spotsylvania in 1864, the Fourteenth Connecticut lost forty-six men, while earlier in the war Battery M of the First Connecticut Artillery lost seventy men in a single day.[127] Regardless of how or why they left in large groups, desertions took a sudden toll on any Union army formation. In six weeks, General Louis Blenker's division lost 731 of his 8616 men to desertion in early 1862, 8 percent of his force before they ever encountered the enemy.[128] Marching his regiment to Fort Monroe, Virginia, Edward Wightman warned his men against deserting, assuring them "that they would be entrapped at half a dozen places on the route." His warnings proved hollow, however, as he arrived with only sixty-eight men out of the more than four hundred that started the march.[129]

With the army determined to stop as many deserters as it could, deserters needed to look less like soldiers. The best way to do that was to shed their blue uniforms and dress like the civilians that they hoped to once again become, and civilian clothing became a means for a soldier to escape his obligation to the army. Without the distinctive blue uniform, a soldier in civilian dress looked just like any other local, making detection almost impossible. One soldier recalled how easy it was to desert in civilian clothing from his regimental camp. "If a man wanted to leave," Henry Charles recalled, "all he had to do was to put on his uniform over his civilian clothes. When he would get outside [of camp] he would go behind a stretch of fence that was handy, strip off his blues, throw them away, and be on his way in his citizen outfit. Some times you could pick up 20 to 60 blue suits along back of a fence."[130] Robert Sneden agreed. In a "suit of civilian clothes," anyone could elude capture as the "lynx eyed officer of the guard" fell only on soldiers wearing army blue.[131] Even in confined spaces, like a steamboat, civilian clothing provided the means of escape. Leaving Philadelphia with his regiment, Private George Jones reported that the next morning "there were 15 empty uniforms stowed on the deck" and the officers did not know "how they managed to desert but they were gone."[132]

Aware that soldiers were using civilian clothes to desert, the army began to seize and destroy all civilian clothing that a soldier might have. Upon his enlistment in the army in 1864, Daniel Chisholm underwent an inspection where "They made us unsling our knapsacks and examined them to see that we hadn't any civilian clothes stowed away in them."[133] If soldiers did not bring civilian garments with them, there were other ways to obtain a change of clothes. A soldier might request that his family mail him a package of clothing, either with the knowledge of the soldier's intent to desert or unaware of what the soldier planned.[134] In regions of Pennsylvania where the war was decidedly unpopular, families aided the desertion of Union soldiers by mailing them civilian clothes in boxes marked as food or medicine.[135] Tipped off by a patriotic citizen, officers of the One Hundred Thirty-second Pennsylvania began systematically to search the regiment's mail, uncovering two packages of civilian clothing intended to assist desertion attempts.[136] Convinced that more such parcels existed, General Seth Williams, the Assistant Adjutant General of the Army, tried to stop the flow of civilian clothes at the source. Most civilian packages sent to the army came by way of the Adams Express Company, the largest private shipping company in America at the time. Williams forced the Adams Company, if they wanted to continue doing business with the army, to require external invoices on all packages and to refuse any boxes containing any clothing other than overcoats, which soldiers might need during the winter. The intent of the new restrictions, as Williams put it, was to halt "the pernicious practice of treasonable persons sending citizens' clothing to soldiers here to encourage and facilitate desertion."[137] When mailing civilian clothes no longer worked, direct delivery sometimes did. "The wife of a man in my own company brought him a suit of citizen's clothing to desert in," John Billings wrote, "which he availed himself of later."[138]

Soldiers could also purchase a new civilian outfit, either from an unaware but enterprising merchant or from unscrupulous providers who profited from the desire to desert. Having no intention to desert, a Union cavalryman found himself solicited by one such dealer who thought he had a sale. "A rough looking chap came along and asked me if I did not wish to buy some clothing," James Avery mentioned in his memoirs, "saying he could show me where I could get clothing very cheap."[139] Other soldiers attempted a bit more subterfuge with their selection of civilian garb. One Ohio soldier, who deserted his unit while in Tennessee, made it half way home before a railroad conductor noticed that his dress and petticoats did not quite fit.[140] Civilian clothing, however, did not necessarily make a soldier a civilian, and military mannerisms sometimes gave deserters away. Captain Henry Schlutz arrested a deserter in civilian clothes named Henry Coffman from the One Hundred Fifty-seventh Pennsylvania in Washington, DC, because he reflexively saluted an officer who passed.[141] Other soldiers deserted using military uniforms, just not their own. In January 1863, a New York cavalry regiment preparing to go home at the end of their enlistment offered to sell their uniforms to other soldiers who could use them to disguise their desertion attempts.[142]

Providing civilian clothing was only one of several means of abetting, encouraging, or facilitating a soldier to desert. Families and other sympathetic parties pressured, cajoled, and enticed soldiers to desert, and then did everything in their power to assist the subsequent offense. Sarah Sleeper wrote her mother that she intended to encourage her husband to "skedaddle to Canada" were his name selected for the draft.[143] Abetting desertion itself, however, carried a risk. Under the terms of the March 1863 Enforcement Act, anyone who abetted desertion by enticing a deserter, harboring them as a fugitive, providing monetary assistance, or obstructing the recovery of a deserter faced a trial by military court-martial, a penalty of at least six but not more than twenty-four months in prison, and a maximum $500 fine.[144] Tried in Washington, DC, under the terms of the new law, two women and one man received six-month prison sentences, in Massachusetts and New York, respectively, for providing clothing to deserters.[145] Sometimes the abettors were right under the army's nose. In January 1865, General Patrick noted he spent the day "ferreting out some leaks" in the Army of the Potomac, including clerks who sold "Genl. Grant's Passes" for as much as $125 each (a pass from such a senior officer permitted the bearer to go practically anywhere) to Quartermasters employees hiding deserters in their wagons when they headed to the rear.[146]

There were other means of eluding army service that required a bit of assistance and luck. A soldier could separate himself from the army by appealing for political relief. Volunteer regiments were state formations engaged in federal service, and the regiments retained political connections in their state capitals. With politicians vulnerable to lobbying and pressure, a soldier with the right connections could find a way around any army attempts to hold him. Colonel Edward Cross of the Fifth New Hampshire, for instance, constantly struggled with his state adjutant general. The adjutant freely discharged soldiers over Cross' protests, soldiers that Cross considered deserters and shirkers of duty.[147] Soldiers also found it easy to desert while on legitimate leave from the army. Soldiers who had furloughs and passes to go home on legitimate business found it tempting not to return. Private Frank Huff of the Nineteenth Indian, for example, overstayed his furlough by five weeks, and might have stayed longer had his regiment not listed him as a deserter.[148] Many other furloughed soldiers, however, did not return even after accused of desertion. In an effort to stem the abuse of furloughs, the army tightened its policies governing the issuing of passes. In the One Hundred Seventh New York, recognizing "the absence of non-commissioned officers and privates . . . have grown into an evil," officers permitted only three passes per company at any one time.[149] In 1862, the War Department announced that any soldier who remained away from the army past their allotted furlough time was subject to desertion charges, and the soldier could not use the furlough itself as evidence of permission to leave the army.[150]

Because of this behavior, most officers made it difficult, if not impossible, to obtain a legitimate furlough. One soldier complained to a reporter that a soldier requesting a furlough had to pass a uniform inspection four times (company, regiment, brigade, and division levels) to qualify for a furlough, and even then the division commander granted only one furlough amongst the small group of soldiers who survived the process.[151] Other regiments set up a system that defined eligibility for furlough and prioritized who was first to apply. In the First New York Engineers, anyone who had joined the regiment within the last year, had been home for any reason recently, or was about to receive a discharge was ineligible, as was anyone who had committed a serious breach of discipline.[152] The rigid requirements to obtain a furlough created considerable acrimony between enlisted men and their officers, especially when serious home issues arose that required a soldier's presence. A soldier in the One Hundred Fourth Ohio, who enlisted in the army at the age of sixty-four, needed more than a month to obtain a furlough home when his wife died, "leaving a family of small children with no one to care for them."[153] At least he received one, unlike a soldier in the One Hundred Fourth New York who received the news in a "letter his wife was dead leaving three small children without any means of support. He tried to get a furlow [sic] but could not and he wept like a child."[154] In hopes of improving his chances for furlough to see his dying father, one soldier provided a note from his mom. "You need have no fear but that he will return," Augustus Shippy's mother wrote, ". . . I have three sons in the army, and I would much rather they fall on the battle field than to desert thier [sic] Country in this her hour of trial. . . . They are true patriots Grandsons of one of the noble heroes of the revolution inhaling patriotism with their first breath."[155]

Oddly, the most effective means of stopping desertion by way of furlough became to grant more furloughs. With desertion rampant in the ranks after Fredericksburg, the new commander of the Army of the Potomac, Joseph Hooker, issued a liberal furlough policy in early 1863. The new policy permitted company captains to grant ten-day furloughs, but only to obedient soldiers with "the most excellent record for attention to all duties." Captains could issue only two furloughs per company, and, to ensure that soldiers came back from their furloughs, other soldiers received furlough only when a soldier on leave returned. This created peer pressure on soldiers to not desert, lest they ruin the furlough system for their comrades.[156] Charles Brewster was pleased to tell his wife that the system seemed to work in his regiment, as "one lot of nine men and two Officers have just gone [on furlough] to take the place of the same number who have just returned."[157] By giving soldiers a more likely chance of legitimate leave, Hooker's policy took away a soldier's temptation to desert while on furlough because he might not ever get another opportunity. The move, along with other reforms, greatly boosted the soldiers' confidence in their new commander.[158] The desire to desert, however, was too strong for some dissatisfied men, who abused the policy and deserted anyway. Such decisions cost their units their leaves, as when men on furlough from the Twenty-third and One Hundred Seventh failed to return on time and the entire regiments lost their furlough privileges.[159] Hooker also created a furlough system for officers, who also unfortunately abused it on occasion. "Lieut. Orleman came back last night and Capt. Lockman this morning," Theodore Dodge complained. ". . . [T]hey had so far outstayed their leave . . . selfishly keeping others from getting leave until they reported."[160] Overstaying a furlough could be expensive, as in the case of one soldier who returned late, costing him a $40 fine and "the respect of the whole company."[161]

Another relatively easy means of desertion was from an army hospital. Filled mostly with bedridden soldiers, hospitals did not maintain the high level of perimeter security and internal discipline of field encampments. The army located its field hospitals close to the main encampments, so there was still a minimal level of monitoring and discipline, but nothing compared to the containment around the field units. In the absence of the unusual restraints, wounded soldiers with sufficient mobility simply walked out of the hospital in large numbers with no one to stop them. The chief physician of the Army of the Potomac reported to the War Department that his hospitals discharged approximately 7000 of the nearly 52,000 hospitalized men to their units in the first two months of 1862. Of the 7000 discharged soldiers, nearly 600 (9 percent) deserted instead of going back to their regiments, and that number does not include soldiers who deserted from the hospitals before the surgeons could discharge them.[162] Western soldiers also had little trouble. Sergeant Major James Bruce of the Fifteenth Regulars recovered from his wounds at a Chattanooga hospital, and then simply walked away.[163] Not all soldiers entered the hospital with intent to desert, as at least some, bored with hospital life, decided that recuperating at home was just as beneficial. Three soldiers from the First Michigan Sharpshooters, for instance, decided to recover at home without telling their doctors or the army.[164] Soldiers under threat of military justice found the hospital a convenient conduit to escape both punishment and the army. Private George Morgan stole a horse, but instead of facing a court-martial he faked an illness, went to a field hospital, and then was never seen again.[165]

While soldiers had little problem deserting from field hospitals, state hospitals were even easier. If soldiers required a lengthy recovery time, the army transported them to a hospital in their home state, freeing up a bed in a field hospital, until the soldier recovered. Far removed from the army and supervised only by civilian physicians (who were often sympathetic to their plight), deserters simply left through the front door. Aware of the ease of desertion, wounded soldiers tried their hardest to arrange a transfer to a state hospital. John Baum, a private in the Ninetieth Pennsylvania, wrote to Pennsylvania Governor Andrew Curtin asking for his intervention in gaining such a transfer. Claiming that his officers cared little for his health and the regimental surgeons were incompetent, Baum asked that Curtin arrange a transfer so Baum might escape medial care where "Patients . . . are treated more like dogs than men."[166] Governors had reason to intervene, especially the ones facing reelection. Hoping that finding a soldier a hospital bed in his home state would translate into a vote (not all states allowed soldiers to vote in the field), Northern governors by 1863 had secured the transfer of almost 200,000 men. The vast majority of them never returned to their units.[167] Other soldiers simply went into the hospital system and their regiments never knew their disposition. Corporal Peter Welsh wanted a promotion to sergeant but could not obtain it because his company technically already had five sergeants, although "one has been absent in hospital over a year and we do not know where he is."[168]

Eventually, the army tried to tighten security at hospitals, but the measures were perfunctory at best. The army needed every soldier it could get, and guarding wounded men was not the best use of limited manpower. The Sanitary Commission, the organization that ran most of the larger hospitals, had no authority as a civilian organization to prevent soldiers from leaving and instead requested the army provide some form of military guards. The best hospital security had dedicated guards housed in the hospital, working regular shifts with supporting facilities. In other hospitals, however, ambulatory patients received guns to serve as makeshift guards, providing a cursory barrier against desertion but little more.[169] The army also tried to do a better job of screening which wounded men required significant medical care and who needed only basic care at the attached field hospitals. Fearful of losing large numbers of soldiers, for instance, General Ulysses Grant ordered his medical staff to send only the men requiring the most urgent care to the large hospitals in Memphis and St. Louis.[170]

There was a final means a Union soldier could use to desert, but it came with extra dangers and a greater chance of retribution if caught. While Union soldiers did not always agree in their considerations of deserters who went home, they were universal in their hatred of deserters to the enemy. A deserter who went home abandoned his duty and his manhood, but a deserter to the enemy became the enemy, another soldier tying to kill the defenders of the Union. Instead of a minimal attempt at understanding and empathy, deserters to the enemy earned only the desire for retribution. In addition to the discomforts of his prisoner of war camp, Lieutenant George Lodge found it "more insulting than necessary" that a Union deserter was one of his guards, and hoped that "if he ever falls into our hands, 'God have mercy on his soul.'"[171] Angry that deserters to the enemy told the Confederates that morale in the army was cracking, William Winters hoped to recapture them to prove them wrong, as "the determination [*sic*] is to take Vicksburgh [*sic*] at all hazards."[172] Sometimes the soldiers' wish for retribution came true. William Ormsby deserted from the Second Massachusetts Cavalry while in Virginia and became a scout for John Mosby's band of partisans, responsible for the harassment of the Union army's supply lines and death of dozens of Union soldiers. Two weeks after he deserted, members of his old company recaptured Ormsby, who received a death sentence for his treachery.[173]

Not all deserters to the enemy did so for philosophical reasons or for self-preservation, but rather to take the offer of a quick journey home. A particularly easy way to desert was to merely walk away from picket duty and desert to the enemy only a short distance away. Exposing oneself in the no-man's land between the armies was hazardous, but both armies welcomed deserters from the enemy. Both sides in the war actively encouraged enemy soldiers to desert with promises of less dangerous duty. On the Union side, the Lincoln administration formally offered amnesty to any Confederate soldier who switched sides, promising the Confederate deserters duty either as service troops or on the Western frontier so that they did not have to fight against their former comrades. If Confederate deserters did not wish to fight, the army provided transport to their homes if their homes were in Union-held areas. To counter this effort, the Confederate War Department issued General Order number 65, promising to parole all Union deserters and send them home.[174] Lured by the possibility of an easy trip home, a considerable number of Union soldiers took the risk to cross over to the enemy. George Cram wrote disapprovingly of a number of men in his regiment who successfully "went over to some guerillas to get paroled."[175] Of a group of 625 New Hampshire recruits, eighty-two of them deserted to the enemy within days of arriving at the front lines, compared to only thirty-six who deserted by infiltrating north through Union lines.[176] So many men from the Fifth

New Hampshire deserted across the lines during the long siege at Petersburg that the Confederates mockingly erected a sign within their lines indicating the "Headquarters, 5th New Hampshire."[177] After the Battle of Perryville, Sergeant John Dey of the Twenty-first Wisconsin opted to use the same method to get out of the army. Encountering a rebel patrol, Dey, according to witnesses, walked over to strike up a conversation, whispered something to the Confederates, removed his sword and handed it to them, and became their prisoner. "Perhaps Sergeant Day lost his share of patriotism there in the cornfield," one soldier postulated, "or . . . concluded to let the other boys do the fighting."[178] But taking the Confederates up on their offer came with risks of its own, as the Union army scoured the no-man's-land between the armies for soldiers attempting to cross the lines and tricked those searching for the Confederates into incriminating themselves. "Seven of these worthies who were suspected [of wanting to desert] have been cunningly trapped," John Westervelt wrote approvingly. "They were put on picket and told it was the outpost when in realty we had a fort a mile farther out." When the deserters left their picket posts and approached the "rebel" fort and "called out not to fire as they were deserters from the Union army," officers quickly arrested them and returned them to camp for quick punishment, with Westervelt noting, "one was shot to day and buried without a coffin. The rest will no doubt suffer the same penalty."[179]

SOMEWHERE BETWEEN ABSENCE without leave and full desertion an unusual form of desertion existed where soldiers deserted only temporarily. Soldiers who took "French leave (or French furlough)" left the army for an extended period of time, but fully intended to come back. Because the length of time these soldiers remained away from the army could stretch to months, these are not cases of absence without leave, where soldiers left camp for only brief respites from military life. Soldiers decided to leave the army for lengthy periods of time to avoid tedium and long stretches of inactivity. The most common reason to take French leave was to prevent the boredom of winter camp, although lesser numbers of cases occurred throughout the year. Civil War armies rarely fought major battles during the winter, and instead used the cold season to build up their strength for the coming spring campaigns. For soldiers, the mind-numbing boredom of winter camp was too much to bear, especially when spending a few weeks or months at home seemed much more desirable. Soldiers who "face instant and almost certain death," one soldier wrote in justifying his French leave, "becomes the most restless mortal in existence" after long stretches of inactivity, resulting in "laziness, sulkiness, and desertion."[180]

Opportunities for French leave presented themselves at almost every turn. In February 1865, an Ohio regiment marching through the state while deploying from the Eastern Theater to the Western Theater lost almost all cohesion when "nearly all of our officers and a great many of the men went home on French Furlough when we came thro [*sic*] Ohio."[181] Another Ohio regiment also liberally partook in French leave. A member of the Ninth Ohio, noting, "many men were absent for long periods," explained that those who were absent "decided to rest from recent dangers and hardships," although the burden of their absence "markedly reduced our strength" to less than five hundred men available for duty.[182] The chance to take French leave was so prevalent that some soldiers did it repeatedly. Henry Charles admitted that "I went home 3 times myself without leave to see my folks and my sweetness."[183] Bored and frustrated at a prisoner exchange camp, Jacob Bartmess informed his wife that he planned to come home soon "furlough or no furlough."[184] Even officers and NCOs took extended unauthorized leave. "[Sergeant Joseph] Bachman went him on a French furlow," Private Thomas Walton noted, and Sergeant Thomas Smith, denied an official furlough to go home because his father was ill, decided that if he could not get a pass, "I shall take French."[185] Weary of the war and pessimistic of its outcome, Lieutenant Edward Williams pondered taking French leave as his brothers intended, telling his parents to look for them soon as they were only waiting until the next payday before heading home.[186]

An important element of French leave, however, is that the soldier deserted with every intention of returning to the army at the appropriate time. These were not cases of full desertion, where the soldier had no intention of ever returning to the unit from which they fled. Instead, after spending their time in a more comfortable place, the soldier returned to their unit prepared to accept whatever punishment the army intended to administer. Because they returned to their units of their own volition, both the army and the soldiers' comrades treated them differently than true deserters. In the vast majority of cases, the army did not administer the harshest penalties upon a soldier returning from French leave, and their fellow soldiers did not characterize them as cowards. They might harbor some resentment for pulling extra duty while their colleague was away, but partakers of French leave more often than not found their reception a reasonably warm one. Instead of harboring resentment at the men who left, a surgeon in a New York regiment jokingly reported that "over fifty had taken French leave without waiting say 'goodbye' to the colonel, or even to call upon their surgeon to ascertain whether he though it would be healthy to leave this cold weather without purse or script."[187]

Timing, however, was of the utmost importance. The main difference between desertion and French leave, as a far as the army was concerned, was if a soldier returned on their own or if the army arrested him at home. A soldier who showed up and took the punishment waiting for him usually found a regiment glad to have a soldier ready to carry a weapon and, therefore, less likely to inflict a harsh punishment. If soldiers timed their return right, courts-martial were usually content to impose a fine, a stretch at hard labor, or to add time to the soldier's enlistment period to compensate for the time missed. At a court-martial in the Department of Texas in February 1864, four soldiers were accused of desertion, but were found guilty of absence without leave, and fines were imposed on all of the offenders. In addition, the each of the four had to make up the ten months they were away "after his term of enlistment would otherwise expire."[188] The cases of French leave were so numerous that soldiers got plenty of opportunities to see its consequences. Describing the activities around his camp, Private William Anderson included "there were some been kept busy diging [sic] stumps all day for taking French furlows."[189] If the soldier overstayed his French leave, however, and the army arrested him before his return, then the soldier could not claim the good will of showing up on his own. Unable to demonstrate his best intentions, an arrested soldier received no special mercy from the army, who treated him as any other deserter. Because of the threat of very real punishment, some soldiers resisted the urge to temporarily leave. Marshall Miller fended off his wife's demands that he take French leave because "I do not believe you would like your neighbors to say, 'There goes a man who deserted and got a dishonorable discharge.'"[190] Other soldiers feared more than just a dishonorable discharge. "Though I should like to see you very much," Joseph Baer wrote his wife, "you must understand once in a while a fellow gets sent to the Rip Raps for three years for his playing off."[191]

WITH DESERTION SPIRALING out of control, the army had to make serious efforts to curb the problem. An obvious means of dealing with desertion was to prevent it from occurring in the first place. The army might address some of the reasons that soldiers deserted, like late pay or lousy food, but the army also recognized that some soldiers would attempt to desert regardless of changes to their conditions, and to at least some extent the army had to force men to stay. One means to stem the flow of desertions was to reinforce the first line of defense by bolstering discipline at the regimental level. To ensure that company and regimental officers supervised their soldiers more closely the army tried to make the officers more accountable if their men deserted. High ranking officers believed that officers who practiced lax discipline or who failed to perform their duties as officers created too many opportunities for desertion by not policing their camps or maintaining order on the march. One critic chastised an officer who tried to supervise a marching column of eight hundred men by himself, especially when the officer allowed 132 men to desert along the way.[192] Commanding officers of various regiments, brigades, and divisions all imposed regulations mandating periodic roll calls, closely monitored hospital rosters, and limits on furloughs, but no formal policy existed that detailed the obligations of officers, nor the applicable penalties, if they failed to keep their men from deserting. Instead of instituting and enforcing a specific policy, the army relied upon the vague expectation, as expressed by one colonel, that officers should do something about the "loose company discipline which is prevalent and the worse than careless manner in which the general duty of the camp is performed."[193] The army also placed additional pressure on officers who themselves deserted. Officers usually enjoyed a certain level of protection when it came to courts-martial as the usual punishment was only a dishonorable discharge. That changed in March 1863 when, by executive order, President Lincoln permitted courts-martial trying officers for desertion to reduce the officer to the ranks as part of the punishment, making them eligible for whatever sentence the court-martial opted to impose.[194] The law had its intended effect, as desertions by officers declined, but the occasional court-martial still took place. Colonel John Rust refused to take command of the Eighth Maine just before the Battle of the Crater in 1864, and the army, unaware of his whereabouts, charged him with desertion.[195] The army also tried to shift some of the burden onto NCOs. The commander of the One Hundred Twenty-first New York issued a general order in 1863 that required an NCO to accompany any group of soldiers going outside of the lines. If the NCO returned with fewer men than he left with, the colonel would demote him to the ranks.[196]

The larger problem was how to stop enlisted men from leaving in the first place. One prevention method was to punish more harshly to demonstrate resolve in regards to the desertion problem and to deter possible attempts. For relatively minor AWOL offenses, for instance, one regiment exercised the full range of punishments that the army granted regimental colonels, including hard labor with a ball and chain, solitary confinement, and reducing rations to bread and water. Regimental courts-martial could not impose the death penalty, but regimental officers could instruct their pickets and guards to shoot any attempted deserters on sight.[197] One divisional commander offered twenty-day furloughs "to those who will arrest or shoot deserters," while another promised "a furlough and a recommendation for promotion."[198] Such punishments tended to backfire, however, as they generated only more discontent or solidified a soldier's determination to leave. Despite frequent roll calls, extra guards, and more vigilant officers, the army could not watch all of its soldiers all of the time. If a soldier decided to leave, there were always opportunities at least to attempt a desertion. The choice to leave or stay always came down to the balance between risk and reward. Disgruntled or demoralized soldiers knew more than anyone the rewards of leaving and returning to their homes. The risks, however, were the great unknown. There were hazards in the attempt, of failure and discovery, and the subsequent and inevitable punishment that came with an unsuccessful desertion. Even if successful, a deserter remained a fugitive, always looking over his shoulder for the hand that might arrest him. There was also the risk of rejection, as soldiers measured the reaction of their comrades, families, and communities to their abandonment of their military obligation.

Desertion could decimate a regiment and render it ineffective almost as quickly as battle casualties. In the fall of 1862, for instance, desertion cut the available manpower of the One Hundred Fourteenth Pennsylvania in half in a matter of days when more than four hundred men deserted.[199] To avoid such a loss, regimental officers determined to keep their men together, and, if soldiers deserted, to tirelessly hunt them down and recover them. In a concerted effort to reclaim his deserters, Colonel Victor DeLand dispatched his officers and NCOs to various locations throughout the Detroit area to effect arrests, including two deserters "upon the steamboat for Saginaw" and fugitives who crossed into Canada.[200] Other units had less success. When five men deserted together from a Kansas regiment because they disliked their commanding officer, they disappeared into the countryside despite the efforts of search parties to locate them.[201]

Despite efforts to elude capture, the army did enjoy some success in finding deserters and returning them to their units. Marsena Patrick, as Provost Marshal General of the Army of the Potomac, received captured deserters in large groups for redistribution back to their regiments, 344 in one particular parcel and 400 in another.[202] An officer in New York had to organize transport for a single batch of 509 deserters captured in his jurisdiction.[203] In individual regiments, soldiers noted the return of their escaped comrades and their subsequent punishment. Charles Cox of the Seventieth Indiana informed his sister that "Those men who deserted this Regt. have mostly been caught, a number are here undergoing a court-martial. . . . We are looking for Capt. Scott this evening, he will bring 8 or ten more deserters back."[204] Often the best tactic was simply to wait until a deserter returned to his home and arrest him there, but sometimes it took longer. The One Hundred Thirteenth Massachusetts knew the whereabouts of one of their deserters, but had to wait until he finished an eight-month prison sentence for larceny before they could pick him up.[205] Arresting deserters was an unpleasant task for some officers, especially those who had to arrest soldiers at their homes and in front of their families. Major Abner Small, unhappy about the "bitter task" of arresting a deserter despite the pleas of his wife, decided that "I never performed a more disagreeable duty. I shouldn't have cared to repeat it for a ninety days' leave or a brigadier-general's commission."[206]

Arresting deserters proved a difficult and hazardous task, with deserters melting into the general population and doing their utmost to avoid detection. Instead of going home, some deserters tried to start new lives elsewhere, including on the Western frontier. Captain Oscar F. Davis, responsible for hunting deserters in Omaha City, Nebraska Territory, arrested one Anton Shoaf, a private who deserted from the Army of the Potomac four months earlier and fifteen hundred miles away.[207] Conversely, Musician Herman Helbing of the Second Regulars deserted from his unit's post in the Nebraska Territory and remained at large until arrested in Virginia four months and an equal distance away.[208] Privates Eugene Sampson and William Simmons avoided arrest for desertion because they "went to sea" before authorities could apprehend them, as had Private John Donald, who had "gone whaling on a 3 years voyage." Officers failed to arrest Private Frederick Fries after he "moved away with his furniture at night to parts unknown."[209] Because deserters proved so difficult to detect, some officers opted for more subtlety. Detailed to New Orleans to find deserters from his regiment, Captain Rufus Kinsley donned "planter's dress" instead of his uniform to blend better into the crowds.[210]

If the army did find them, deserters desperate enough to leave were certainly capable of anything to avoid going back. Some deserters pulled off multiple escapes before authorities finally cornered them. An officer searching for deserters in Illinois described Private William McMullen as a "slippery customer" who had eluded him before, and warned anyone dealing with Private Thomas Wood to keep an eye on him as he had escaped from custody six times already and seemed capable of "slip[ping] off any irons that can be put on him."[211] After the capture of Private Wilber Williams, the arresting officer noted in his report that Williams was a "desperate character" who had already escaped from a previous arrest. Deserter Walden Dutchen had also eluded arrest twice before, causing his arresting officer to describe him as "of the worst character possible and should be shot." Thomas Atkinson elicited a similar attitude from his arresting officer, who "recommends that this man be shot at the earliest convenience."[212] When sent to arrest two soldiers named Stewart and Dustin, "deserters and smugglers," Captain Benjamin Thomas found Dustin under the floor of a house "with his Henry rifle." Failing to extract him peacefully, Thomas "ordered the men to fire under the house and set the house on fire in three places" before Dustin finally surrendered.[213]

Among the most ardent hunters of deserters were the men of the Veteran Reserve Corps (VRC). In an effort to maximize available manpower, the army created the Invalid Corps on April 28, 1863. The name soon changed because of its unfortunate acronym. Damaged government property slated for disposal received the stamp "I.C.," meaning "Inspected and Condemned," and the soldiers of the Invalid Corps did not consider themselves useless. The VRC comprised wounded and injured soldiers who, though incapable of full physical duty, performed less demanding tasks, freeing fit soldiers for combat duty. VRC soldiers performed "orderly duty at hd qrs, clerks at the offices of the many administrative departments and frequently garrison & light duty at the posts to the rear of the armies."[214] The first VRC troops came from hospitals at the time the army created the organization, and wounded soldiers could request a transfer to the VRC thereafter. In the six months after its creation, the VRC had sixteen regiments manned by 18,000 troops, led by nearly 500 officers. By the end of the war, about 70,000 men served in the VRC.[215] While themselves guilty of desertion (2538 soldiers deserted from the organization), the VRC became one of the most effective tools for hunting deserters.[216] Driven by the citizen-soldier ethos to serve their country's cause even if not fully physically able, the VRC held deserters in even lower regard than most frontline soldiers. One of their main jobs was to guard arrested deserters on their way back to their units, and the VRC rarely allowed an escape. Just one VRC regiment alone arrested 1,355 deserters and rounded up 3,062 stragglers in two years of service.[217] The Sixteenth VRC, stationed in southern Pennsylvania, arrested 2,793 deserters during the winter of 1863–1864 alone.[218] The army posted VRC units that proved particularly adept at hunting deserters in key locations to exercise their talents. Colonel Adoniram Warner's Seventeenth VRC, for instance, relocated to Indianapolis to quell problems there. Warner persuaded state officials to let him establish a temporary prison ground where he could hold his captures until he could parade them, publicly and in shackles, to the train station for their trip back to the front.[219] The VRC proved especially valuable by providing military muscle in regions of the country where the war, conscription, and/or Abraham Lincoln were unpopular. VRC troops played a prominent part in suppressing dissent in several parts of the North, allowing the draft to occur relatively smoothly, and arresting deserters in regions that abetted their presence.[220]

Getting soldiers back to the army, however, was a dangerous task. Instead of surrendering meekly, some deserters resisted with force, like Sergeant George McDonald of the Third Maryland. He tried to shoot the sergeant sent to arrest him, adding additional charges to his subsequent court-martial.[221] Only the use of armed guards prevented deserters from escaping army custody, and transfers were always tense missions. After escorting one group of arrested deserters to a holding station, the guards informed their prisoners that their "guns were not loaded and not a cartridge in the crowd," angering the deserters because they remained docile only because they feared "some of us would have given them a dose of cold lead."[222] Once back in the ranks, officers had to convince soldiers to stay and not attempt another desertion. Colonel Augustus Gibson tried shame to impress a lesson upon deserters returned to the One Hundred Fourteenth Pennsylvania by ordering the returned deserters to parade at the front of the regiment during afternoon drill, hoping to "render a public exposure of the disgraceful conduct" of the deserters.[223] An officer in New York wanted to parade his captured deserters down Broadway in irons to make an impression upon any deserters still at large, but the army refused to grant permission for the demonstration.[224]

The army also tried to reclaim its deserters by offering rewards to anyone who found, apprehended, and delivered a deserter to lawful authority. In the antebellum period, regulations authorized the payment of $30 for each deserter returned to the army. With the onset of war, however in September 1861, the government reduced the reward to a maximum of $5, plus compensation for housing, feeding, and transporting a deserter. The reward was less because the government believed that a combination of dutiful citizens, law enforcement, and army officers could control the desertion problem themselves without any outside assistance. Any law enforcement or federal employee was obligated to look for and report the location of any deserters within their jurisdictions. Those under this obligation included postal workers, county sheriffs, and federal marshals. These officials, and other civilian agents affected by the policy, did not produce many results. With their own duties to perform, looking for deserters was a decidedly secondary task.[225] In addition to relying upon existing federal authorities, the government simply could not afford a higher reward amount, and tried to recover deserters on the cheap.[226] Neither strategy proved superior, as the government found that private enterprise was an effective means of finding deserters, but bounty hunters had no incentive to hunt deserters for only small reward. One bounty hunter, for instance, received only 10 cents for arresting Private Edward Garrison, while another received only 75 cents for capturing Private John Thomas.[227] Considering the monthly wage of an officer, it was also not cost-effective to detail officers to hunt deserters, especially deserters who managed to find their way back to their hometowns. Eventually, the army recognized the utility of a sufficient reward, and returned the reward to $30 in September 1863.[228] This, in turn, helped to create more interest in hunting deserters. Between June 1863 and June 1865, for instance, the army recovered 310 deserters from New Hampshire regiments. Bounty hunters arrested 206 of them, thirty-six soldiers returned on their own, army officers arrested thirty-five, and local police arrested thirty-three.[229]

Offering rewards, however, was an expensive way to find and return deserters, but, then again, desertion itself was a costly enterprise. Besides losing the deserting soldier, the Union had to dispatch personnel away from the army to hunt and arrest them. To justify their actions, deserters often concocted exaggerated stories of their experiences in the army, stories that undoubtedly deterred other potential recruits from volunteering. There was also a financial cost. The Quartermaster Bureau reported that it spent more than $157,000 in the 1863–1864 fiscal year to recover deserters, money expended on reward payments and travel costs. Soldiers who deserted also took their uniforms and accoutrements with them, costing the army even more to replace lost material. In one area of Pennsylvania with a high number of deserters, a government agent noted, "Almost every man in the State, he declared, had a rifle, saddle, or some piece of government property."[230] General William Rosecrans observed a similar situation in the region north of Nashville, the main Union railroad hub in the area and a path frequented by absent troops, where he believed "some 30,000 men belonging to this army" hid in the countryside.[231]

Due to the army's efforts to hunt down and arrest deserters, some absent soldiers only felt safe in the sanctuary of Canada, a region characterized by one army officer as "the Traitor's Refuge."[232] Recognizing the long reach of the U.S. government, deserter Private Henry Sayers tried to cross the border near Detroit. A barking dog, however, alerted the owner of the boat he tried to steal, and Sayers found himself under arrest.[233] Sayers was the exception, though, as Canada became an easy refuge. "There is but little doubt but that Ben Morgan & Dick Lewis have gone to Canada," William Charles opined. "I hope that shame if nothing else will for ever keep them from coming" back again.[234] The government tried to prevent desertions to Canada by requiring internal passports in August 1863, but the plan proved unworkable when protesting states refused to comply.[235] In at least one case, the matter of Private Alpheus Cross, the army tried to hold the deserter's family liable for his departure to Canada. Colonel Victor DeLand, commanding the First Michigan Sharpshooters, pressured his father to "return the deserter inside of thirty days . . . [or] I will lay the matter before the U.S. attorney and move for your speedy prosecution," but to no avail.[236] Canadian soil soon harbored vast numbers of deserters. Officers in the Sixth District in Michigan maintained lists of local deserters and tried to determine which ones were in Canada. By the end of the war that district alone recorded 3,177 desertions, of which 267 (8 percent) were in Canada.[237] Some deserters to Canada soon regretted their decision, and made inquiries about returning to their units. In July 1863, the editor of the Detroit *Daily Advertiser* wrote a letter to Secretary of War Edwin Stanton to inform him that many deserters in Canada "are anxiously waiting the opportunity to return . . . [if] they shall be pardoned the offence" of desertion. A year later another request for amnesty came from deserters in Canada, but the War Department rejected both inquiries.[238]

After arresting deserters, the army had to decide how to punish them. Article 20 permitted the army to execute soldiers convicted of desertion, but the circumstances and authority changed due to wartime conditions. The army could only apply the death penalty in wartime, so commanders had to consider the penalty once the war began. The Articles also required the President to confirm all death sentences before the application of the penalty. The rapid expansion of wartime courts-martial, however, led Congress in March 1863 to alter the law so that only the general commanding the army or district where the court-martial took place needed to approve the sentence.[239] The intent was to speed up the approval process on court-martial cases and give the impression that the army intended to impose the death penalty more frequently in the hopes of using the impression as a deterrent. Colonel Patrick Guiney, for instance, tried to impress upon his men the likelihood of lethal punishment, arguing "it is safer for them to fight well than to run fast."[240] As desertion became epidemic, however, the army simply could not shoot every deserter lest the firing squads kill more soldiers than did the Confederates. The army did put nearly three hundred men to death during the war, the vast majority of them for desertion, but compared to the scope of the offense, the execution rate was very low.[241]

Although, as will be seen later, a large number of deserters did receive the death penalty, courts-martial usually took a more lenient approach, and a range of punishments for desertion took the place of the firing squad. If a soldier escaped the firing squad, the most common penalty was a prison sentence. The army operated its own prisons by 1862, most notably the Old Capitol Prison in Washington and Fort Jefferson in the Dry Tortugas, but also used state prisons if necessary. The New York state prison in Ossining (better known as Sing Sing) often housed Union soldiers with long-term sentences. On the West Coast, the army incarcerated soldiers on the fortified island of Alcatraz. In addition to the prison sentence, early in the war regiments often drummed deserters out of camp. The philosophy behind this penalty reflected the idealistic nature of citizen-soldiers new to combat. Viewing themselves as patriots to a great cause, drumming out those who failed the cause reinforced their own sacrifice and valor for staying. Also, by ejecting those who failed, the drumming out ceremony came to symbolize a form of Darwinistic adaptation, with the larger entity getting better by shedding its weaker elements. When Private Oliver Gorham deserted from his artillery battery, a court-martial sentenced him to imprisonment at a military prison for the duration of his army obligation, but his unit also drummed him out of camp to demonstrate their separation from this weak element in their midst.[242] Private John Mallory received the same treatment, but he performed his six-month prison sentence first before his unit drummed him out.[243]

The penalty of drumming out became less common as the war continued, as disillusioned soldiers who wanted out of the army gladly accepted a drumming out if it meant leaving the army.

In addition to a prison sentence, the army imposed other particular penalties depending upon the nature of the desertion, the character of the deserter, their length of service, and any recommendations for clemency the soldier might produce. Although soldiers usually received one or two of the special penalties, brothers Hiram and Spencer Kelly received all of them. Convicted of deserting together just after the Battle of Gettysburg, the brothers escaped a firing squad but faced imprisonment at hard labor wearing a ball and chain for the duration of their term of service. The army extended the date when their service ended by five months, which was the amount of time they were away from their unit, and also forfeit all pay and allowances due to them in addition to compensating the army for the costs associated with their arrest.[244] In addition to these extra penalties, the army also sentenced deserters to imprisonment in solitary confinement or a diet of bread and water. Such punishments, however, were not always appropriate. Prison sentences took soldiers away from their regiments, so officers sometimes preferred to punish soldiers within their own camps instead of sending them to a general court-martial. "Two of these were caught [deserting] in St. Louis and returned to the authorities here last Sunday," George Remley wrote. "Since that time they have had the pleasure of carrying what in camp parlance is called 'wooden knapsacks,' that is a piece of wood, weighting about 50 pounds . . . to be worn all the time."[245] In other cases, particular elements of the soldiers' service played a part in their punishment. Private Alphonso Cherry deserted from the Sixth USCT in 1864, only to appear a few months later serving as a sergeant in a USCT cavalry unit. When arrested, Cherry argued that he did not desert, but simply changed units because he preferred to fight while riding instead of walking. As Cherry remained in the army, his only punishment was a brief stint in the guardhouse and a return to his original unit.[246] Punishment also did not just occur in the army, as the label of "deserter," "coward," and "failure" dogged soldiers even after they completed their court-martial sentences. When Corporal Miles Card deserted from his regiment, his company officers made sure his family knew of his crimes because "All his letters are sent back with 'Deserted' written under his name."[247] William McCutcheon promised to let the hometown folks back home know "what they are doing and who had deserted" by notifying the local newspapers.[248]

But for all of the harsh rhetoric in official dispatches, regimental orders, and the Articles of War, the army did not necessarily take a hard line when prosecuting deserters. One reason was the concern that harsh discipline would adversely affect morale and recruiting. Soldiers frequently reacted angrily to excessive discipline, and if courts-martial followed the letter of the Articles too stringently, an excessive number of executions might cause wholesale mutiny in the ranks. In addition, the army had concerns about the effect that harsh discipline might have on recruiting. The army might reasonably expect soldiers to enlist to defend the Union despite the risk of death on the battlefield, but if potential recruits perceived the army as a brutally repressive institution that commonly executed its own soldiers, the enlistment numbers were bound to go down. The biggest reason for leniency, however, was the simple impracticality of imposing harsh punishments on everyone. Desertion was so prevalent that courts-martial simply could not order the execution of every soldier accused of the offense lest the number of execution deaths equal the number of a major battle. As Abraham Lincoln put it, "you cannot order men shot by dozens and twenties. People won't stand it."[249]

The primary means of leniency was to reduce the findings of a court-martial, and many soldiers charged with desertion instead found themselves convicted only of absence without leave. The prewar case of *Dynes v. Hoover* set the precedent for courts-martial to charge a defendant with one offense, but convict him of another, and many Civil War deserters found themselves the beneficiaries of *Dynes*. Private Patrick Sullivan, for instance, defended himself against a charge of desertion by claiming he was still sick when his medical furlough expired. Unwilling to convict a sick man, the panel instead found him guilty of AWOL and fined him $20. Charles McRoberts also pled illness during his court-marital for desertion, telling the court he had been "sorely afflicted with diarrhea for the last four or five months," resulting in a lesser finding and a $50 fine. Even multiple deserters received this leniency, such as Private John Addelman who deserted twice but received not only the lesser charge but a dishonorable discharge and a trip home.[250] For some soldiers, however, the leniency seemed excessive and misplaced. Private John Lepper deserted four times during the war, never receiving any punishment higher than forfeiture of his accumulated pay.[251]

There were also other forms of leniency. Courts-martial considered good past behavior as a mitigating factor. Henry Stone, accused of deserting his regiment in early 1863, received only a $10 fine and a reprimand when his company captain informed the court of Stone's heroism at the Battle of South Mountain, where Stone carried the regimental colors after bullets cut down the previous five color bearers.[252] Patrick Leonard received only a minor punishment for deserting from the Fourth New York Cavalry in 1862 because he had reenlisted in another cavalry regiment, where he had served honorably enough to earn promotion to corporal.[253] Marsena Patrick had in his custody a deserter named Daniel Stiles, but opted to send him home instead of court-martial him because he was the "husband of the woman who was victimized here last summer, and Patrick did not want to further traumatize her.[254]

In other instances, however, leniency itself was a punishment, especially when it insinuated a lack of manhood. On the belief that sending cowards home to face the scorn of their family and friends was itself a harsh punishment, the colonel of the Fourteenth Indiana sent three attempted deserters home in disgrace. Such punishment worked only in the early months of the war, before the disillusionment made soldiers perceive pubic bravery in a different light. But at the time of these discharges, the Fourteenth Indiana still retained its early-war perceptions of personal bravery as a sign of masculinity. Private David Beem rejected pleas to come home by explaining, "If I was to turn back now, many would say I was a coward. I would rather be shot at once than to have such a stigma rest on me."[255]

Another form of general leniency was to offer amnesty to any soldier who returned to duty, hoping that the promise of no punishment might shame, cajole, or placate soldiers at home to return to their units. At first, the War Department dug in its heels on offering amnesty, believing that relaxing regulations sent the wrong message. "The crime is too serious in its consequences," Secretary of War Edwin Stanton stated, "to be made light of even for the sake of securing the return to the ranks of a few effective men."[256] When desertion reached epidemic proportions by 1863, the army had to rethink its position. In need of veteran soldiers when the spring campaigning season commenced, the Lincoln administration issued an amnesty proclamation on March 10, 1863. "All deserters and absentees from the Army," the offer stated, ". . . may deliver themselves up agreeably . . . [by] the 1st of April, subject to no other punishment than the forfeiture of their pay and allowances during the time they may have been absent." The amnesty deal did not apply to soldiers already punished for desertion, but the army chose to construe the law broadly, to include "all persons now undergoing punishment for desertion, those awaiting sentence, and those awaiting trial for that offense."[257] The amnesty offer had its desired effect as the ranks swelled with returning deserters who knew that "If they don't go to their Regts they will be shot or work out the balance of their time in disgrace sure as the sun shines."[258]

The majority of soldiers who stayed thought of those who left as cowards. The soldiers who took advantage of the amnesty program or who returned to their units of their own accord, however, faced very little retribution from their comrades. While one might expect some resentment and hostility to their presence, most soldiers welcomed the returnees back into the ranks as someone who was once again taking up the burdens of manhood and performing the obligations of the citizen-soldier. In a mix of fact and a bit of resentment, a Pennsylvania soldier noted that "Washington Gailbreath has got back [under the amnesty] and they didn't do anything with him."[259] In his memoir of military service in the Ninth Ohio, Constantin Grebner likened the amnesty returnees as chastised schoolboys, returning after "having reconsidered their truancy."[260] Private John Lepper returned to his regiment "after an absence of nearly 6 months" because he found the local pressure to return "too hot for him."[261] Wilbur Fisk returned to his regiment because of the "wear and tear on my nervouse [*sic*] system in consequence of my dangerous position as a deserter," and he feared his fiancée would not marry him, worrying, "Should Angie accept me as her husband she will be surprised to find what a weak affair I am."[262] When Private Benjamin Duke returned under the provisions of Lincoln's amnesty proclamation, he slipped back into the routine of army life without any acrimony from his company, while only three months earlier the same company shaved the head of a soldier and drummed him out of the army in disgrace for the same offense.[263] Private Charles Balke not only faced no punishment when he returned from his brief stint as a deserter; he soon received a promotion to corporal.[264]

Not every regiment however, received its deserters back with open arms. "Henry Hutchinson, who deserted at Cumberland, arived [*sic*] here last night from Baltimore," Henry Kaufmann reported. "He was put under arest [*sic*] immediately" and drummed out of the regiment the next morning.[265] When Sergeant John Gansz returned to his regiment, he faced a court-martial before a letter from Pennsylvania Governor Andrew Curtin convinced his superiors to demote him and place him back in the ranks.[266] Private William Wood returned to his regiment presuming to receive a warm welcome, which he hoped to promote by bringing his company captain a bottle of brandy. Instead, the "next morning the customary charges and specifications [for court-martial] were forwarded to Corps Headquarters."[267] Private Nasby Mills of the Seventh Kentucky faced a delayed court-martial. He was absent from his regiment due to illness for nine days, and upon his return his company captain ordered him to report to a hospital for treatment. After six months of recuperation, he rejoined his regiment in January 1864. Six months later, the same captain who ordered him to the hospital arrested him for deserting the previous year, although he was present for duty for the previous six months. Despite his protests, Mills found himself convicted of desertion and spent the rest of the war in the Dry Tortugas.[268]

MANY RECRUITS DID NOT HAVE TO desert from army camps because they never reached them, instead deserting almost from the moment they enlisted. These early deserters left the army for a variety of reasons ranging from an unappetizing first taste of army life to a sudden waning of their peacetime bravado. The First Michigan Sharpshooters lost at least forty-five men to desertion almost immediately as their camp was "cold and dreary

[and] the barracks utterly unfit for winter quarters."[269] Charles Haydon derided the men who immediately wanted out of the regiment, scorning them because they "enlisted hastily & . . . desertions have become frequent."[270] As his regiment prepared to move South, J.C. Switzer noted that "a number of our weak-kneed patriots learning that we were about to get near to the rebels deserted while we were in this camp, thinking it was easier I suppose to get to the north from there than further south."[271] The army gave new recruits a few days to go home to settle their affairs before heading to the front, and soldiers who had a change of heart often deserted during this time. If the army tried to force an enlistee to report for service, state courts often intervened. Claiming that military service was a form of imprisonment, reluctant recruits applied for writs of habeas corpus from their county courts, jurisdictions very likely to take the side of a local citizen over the army. Recruiting officers had to spend considerable amounts of time in local courtrooms simply to get a recruit to fulfill his army obligations.[272]

Many of the recruits did not want to go anywhere near the front line because they had been there already. Bounty-jumping, the practice of enlisting in the army to collect bounty money and then deserting to do it all over again, plagued the recruiting process in the second half of the war, and many of the new recruits arriving never had any intentions of picking up a rifle. Bounty-jumping was certainly a lucrative business by 1863, with local, state, and federal bounty money available to entice soldiers to enlist instead of face the draft. Unscrupulous men collected large sums of money, only to leave at the first opportunity and swell the numbers of deserting soldiers. If soldiers remaining in the ranks had no love for deserters, they absolutely despised bounty-jumpers. Soldiers characterized jumpers as unmanly for failing to remain at their posts, corrupt for accepting money to do what good soldiers were doing for no extra pay, and unpatriotic for enlisting only for financial incentive when true citizen-soldiers, like the first 1861 volunteers, signed up without the lure of financial incentive. To bounty-jumpers, a soldier's uniform was simply a means of collecting money by illegal means, and oaths and pledges of fidelity meant nothing. Soldiers also delineated the difference between bounty-jumpers and deserters by measuring their length of service. A soldier who deserted after a period in the army at least sacrificed something, be it time or blood, before they decided to leave, but bounty-jumpers had no intention of serving any time at all. Consequently, soldiers despised the bounty-jumper as someone who diminished the role of a soldier, mocked its value, and was therefore not worthy of mercy or consideration. Because of their propensity to desert, bounty-jumpers tainted the veterans' impression of new recruits, damaging efforts to integrate them into their new units. Veterans immediately suspected any new recruit was a bounty-jumper, characterizing them as "Most if not all of them were bounty-jumpers and about as tough and reckless a gang of daredevils as was ever gotten together in one organization."[273] Made up of the "worst characters in the universe," the Twenty-seventh Michigan needed three thousand recruits to fill up the one thousand man regiment because of "2,000 deserting before they could get away from Detroit."[274] The officers shared more or less the same attitude. Bounty-jumpers were not just deserters; they were also thieves who stole their bounty money on the pretext of answering the nation's call to duty. If the officer's job was to make soldiers out of reluctant citizens, then bounty-jumpers proved the greatest challenge of all. Searching for reasons why bounty-jumping occurred, the army leadership arrived at a number of possible explanations ranging from cowardice and a lack of patriotism to simple greed and the intellectual weakness of foreign-born soldiers.[275]

Bounty-jumping soon attracted the efforts of professional criminals, who used their previous criminal experience to gain money illicitly. Hardened criminals clustered in urban areas, with the added benefit that large cities contained both places for bounty-jumpers to hide and new recruiting depots for perpetrating their crimes again. The army estimated that nearly six thousand bounty-jumpers were operating in New York City alone in November 1863, and one raid by military police netted 590 bounty-jumpers in a single day.[276] Consequently, New York recruits had the highest rate of desertion in the Union army, leaving at a rate of eighty-nine per thousand recruits compared to the rate of 62.5 per thousand across the entire Union army.[277] Among the bounty-jumpers arrested in New York, the rogues gallery included deserters with previous convictions for counterfeiting, assault, horse theft, and attempted murder.[278] When army authorities arrested one deserter in Connecticut they found burglar tools and stolen property in his pockets, having just returned from a heist.[279] The professionalization of bounty-jumping included means to alter the appearance of multiple jumpers. A newspaper investigator found that experienced jumpers "have disguises of civilian clothes, false beards, and all varieties of wigs, paints, and eyebrows" to alter their appearance.[280] Enlisting under an alias also created confusion as to a deserter's true identity. The disguising of names began immediately after enlistment, where bounty-jumpers "disowned their names under which they enlisted, exchanged names with one another, mixed as much as possible with the recruits . . . and employed every possible means to remain incognito."[281] To disguise his identity in case he opted to desert, James Horrocks "enlisted under the name of Andrew Ross," but he jokingly worried that "if I remain the full three years here I shall have forgot who I am."[282] It was a joke to Horrocks, but some bounty-jumpers did forget their aliases, and when addressed at roll call, "Many had forgotten the name they gave then they enlisted and others would try to make them believe that was their name when one was called and there was no answer."[283] Despite some barriers to overcome, bounty-jumpers inflicted considerable harm upon the Union army's recruiting system, and some brazen jumpers became so proficient that nothing but bad luck seemed to stop them. Thomas Ryan, alias John Reagan, confessed to jumping at least thirty bounties before his arrest and execution at Camp Morton, Indiana.[284] Some bounty-jumpers committed their crimes in different parts of the country, but Private Smith Turner deserted from six different Indiana regiments before finally falling into army hands.[285] Private Thomas Mansfield found a way to steal even more money. Draftees could avoid service by hiring a substitute, and Mansfield not only collected his bounty money; he also pocketed $150 by enlisting as a substitute for a Mr. David Perkins.[286]

Men with medical disabilities also used their physical limitations to bounty-jump. These jumpers disguised or did not reveal their medical conditions until they passed the entrance examination, received their bounty money, and reported for duty with their new units. Once in the field, they revealed their handicap, received a medical discharge, and started the process all over again. Wary of the practice, Major Abner Small refused to enlist a soldier after, "stripped of his clothing and the mysteries of hair dye," he discovered his advanced age and sent him home after his "visions of large bounties and an early discharge on a comfortable pension had vanished."[287] Other soldiers managed to get through the examination process, like the soldier who managed to jump twelve bounties by faking his way through the physical examination portion of his enlistment process despite his glass eye.[288] Colonel Elisha Rhodes uncovered another medical bounty-jumper who feigned insanity in the First Rhode Island and determined to try it again in Rhodes' Second Rhode Island. When the soldier attacked him, Rhodes described "picking up a club I used it upon him until he begged for mercy and owned up that he was not crazy. . . . [T]he men are pleased to have him exposed."[289]

Like any other deserter, the army wished to arrest and punish bounty-jumping, but catching them proved a difficult proposition. Stopping the average soldier from deserting was difficult enough, but stopping an experienced and determined bounty-jumper was even harder. The average deserter usually went home, providing a starting point for the army to locate them and bring them back. Bounty-jumpers, on the other hand, were looking for the next army recruiting station, and their constant movements made detecting them difficult. Aware that "Their favorite time for leaving was during their first tour of picket duty," General Martin McMahon "found it necessary to throw a cordon of cavalry outside of our picket lines." McMahon also tried to intimidate potential bounty-jumpers by ensuring a "gallows and a shooting ground were provided," but the threat did not deter the jumpers.[290]

The army caught some bounty-jumpers in the act. When two soldiers "were caught on their way to the rebel lines," Louis Beaudry observed it usually did not cause much excitement, but these two men "were both recruits and had been here but two days. . . [and one] is said to be here under a fictitious name" and the other "boasted that he had jumped two bounties before by desertion and he would jump another."[291] Other arrests were from pure luck. One unfortunate bounty-jumper happened to meet his former captain on the streets of Elmira, New York, resulting in his prompt arrest.[292] Seven bounty-jumpers from the One Hundred Eighteenth Pennsylvania, who each had "about $300 apiece and thought they would just take the bounty and run away," instead ran right into the arms of waiting camp guards who had anticipated their attempt.[293] Sometimes soldiers recognized deserters in the ranks of other units and pointed out the miscreant. When records-keeping improved, the army detected increasing numbers of bounty-jumpers at the point of enlistment, but far more succeeded than failed.

Once the army arrested deserters and bounty-jumpers, the next step was returning them to their units. The army accumulated arrested soldiers until either their units came to retrieve them, or armed guards could escort them back. The supervising officers received a receipt from the jailer for each deserter, and the officer in charge of the escort was responsible for safely conveying the deserters back to their units. Confident that he was up to the task, Lieutenant Cyrenius Knight promised his regimental colonel that he would either "bring back a receipt for each man returned to his regiment or a receipt for his death."[294] To ensure that bounty-jumpers did not escape, officers took extra precautions. When escorting six confirmed bounty-jumpers and a number of potential bounty-jumpers to their regiments, Captain Charles Mattocks took no chances. He ordered the six confirmed bounty-jumpers chained together, and harshly punished any potential bounty-jumpers who stepped out of line by either pistol whipping them or tying them spread-eagle on the deck of their transport ship.[295] Colonel Joel Baker tried a different approach. Baker arranged for his group of deserters to receive "a good breakfast and comfortable cars to ride in" attempting to convey the idea that "if they behaved they would be treated well and if they did not some of them would get shot."[296]

Getting bounty-jumpers back to their units proved extremely difficult and hazardous. Desperate to avoid the harsh punishment awaiting them at the end of their journey, bounty-jumpers took great risks to escape army authorities and disappear back into the civilian population. Some bounty-jumpers attempted, and occasionally succeeded, in escaping from jails and barracks before the army shipped them back for trial. Jumpers tried to escape from moving trains, although such a foolhardy idea often resulted in unintended consequences. Some managed to escape, but many injured or killed themselves in their desperate efforts. One unfortunate jumper leapt from a car directly into the path of an oncoming express train, killing him instantly, while others died from injuries sustained by unwise departures.[297] Jumpers also took their chances by jumping from steamboats, preferring to take their chances in the water instead of facing military justice. New York was the central receiving point for arrested deserters, and New York Harbor witnessed several dramatic escape attempts, some successful, some failed, and some fatal. In addition to the risks of escaping, bounty-jumpers risked death at the hands of their armed guards, who possessed the authority to shoot fleeing deserters without warning. Escorting five bounty-jumpers back to the Ninetieth Pennsylvania, Major Alfred Sellers shot and killed one of them as they jumped from the boat. A subsequent investigation cleared Sellers of any wrongdoing.[298] A new recruit observed the fatal consequences of the attempted escape of four bounty-jumpers in New York. As the first ran, "the guard near me turned on his heels quickly, threw his heavy rifle to his shoulder, covered the running man, and shot him dead," a fate soon visited on two other escapees. A "tall, lithe officer, pistol in hand," ran down the other escapee, but "he made no attempt to arrest the deserter, but placed the pistol to the back of the runaway's head and blew his brains out as he ran."[299] At a collection point in Baltimore, John Holahan noted, "One bounty-jumper was shot whilst trying to escape last night," and two others "killed themselves by falling whilst trying to slide down the [rain] spout" from a fourth floor window.[300] Fraught with danger, soldiers rarely enjoyed the task of returning deserters to the army, preferring to stay with their units instead of engaging in such nerve-wracking duty.

THE ARMY NEVER MANAGED to solve its desertion problems. The best description is perhaps that they contained the desertion epidemic to a manageable level. In a broader view, however, it is apparent that the army could never resolve the desire to desert. Soldiers deserted because they lost their naïve perception of war, honor, and glory. Soldiers deserted because of Confederate military successes, an element somewhat beyond the control of the Union army. The plight of families of at home convinced others to desert, a condition that the army had no control over. Instead of justifying or supporting those that went absent, soldiers viewed them as cowards that weakened the army and shamed themselves by failing to act like men. If they returned to face danger with their comrades, however, they redeemed their lost manhood and their companies accepted them back. Because the soldiers themselves did not have a consensus on the behavior of deserters, it is not surprising that they army lacked one as well.

The army tried harsh discipline, and when that proved impractical it tried leniency, and that proved just as unsuccessful. Like many other disciplinary offenses, the sheer scale of desertion proved more than the army could handle. Also just like other offenses, the only real solution was to manage the problem to a controllable degree. Hence, the army largely tolerated AWOL and French leave, and granted deserters as much leeway as the military justice system allowed. For an offense that the army considered one of the most serious a soldier could commit, the best result was to ameliorate the problem in the hopes it would not get worse. This also became the policy for a number of other serious offenses, including crimes that civilian society would not tolerate.

"DESCEND TO THE LEVEL OF THE BARBARIANS"

Theft, Property, and Violent Crimes

Throughout the Civil War, the soldiers of the Union army demonstrated a flexible morality. As death and destruction mounted around them, the naïve soldiers who went to war to save the Union turned into hardened veterans with a pessimistic outlook on the goals of the war and the likelihood of their own survival. New definitions of bravery and manly deportment replaced the early-war expectations of bravery and dedication to cause, country, and army. Instead, soldiers accepted mere survival as a small form of victory, living in fortifications as preferable to dying in the open, and viewing desertion as an acceptable alternative to upholding the obligations of the citizen-soldier (as long as they had a good justification). This evolution of outlook created a malleable morality, whereby soldiers redefined what passed for acceptable conduct and created a new standard of what constituted moral behavior. Plain morality, cast in black and white, found itself replaced by multiple shades of gray, with each soldier relying more upon their own intuition and needs rather than a group morality to endorse their conduct. Chief among them were the acts that, in their civilian antebellum lives, would have stained a man's reputation, created public outcry, and led to lengthy prison terms, or even the death penalty. In the chaos of war, traditional modes of behavior changed, and actions that would have shocked and stunned them in civilian life became acceptable or even expected.

Instead of receiving a blanket condemnation as they might in civilian life, Union soldiers who behaved as thieves, thugs, and murderers found a mixed response in military life. There were some offenses committed by Union soldiers that received a strong reaction similar to crimes in the civilian sector. Those who killed for no reason or who killed for financial gain received nothing but scorn from their fellow soldiers, while soldiers considered any punishment inflicted upon a convicted rapist as nowhere severe enough. Other offenses, however, received a neutral or even positive reaction. A soldier who assaulted another soldier in defense of their honor received no great derision from their comrades, nor did soldiers who stole army or civilian goods to feed or equip himself. Under these conditions, soldiers perceived the offender as simply doing what he had to do to maintain his standing or perform his duty as a soldier. The theft of civilian property, especially when done behind the veneer of legitimate army policy, was approved or even praised if a soldier proved especially adept at it. Consequently, the army committed massive property crimes against Confederate civilian lands and goods, with only a tiny minority of protesting voices.

While conducting such crimes, additional nuances appeared besides the new flexible morality. A darker element to human behavior began to appear, as not only did antebellum social expectations begin to erode, but taboo behaviors gained a modicum of acceptability. It became broadly accepted to pillage corpses on the battlefield, and the deep-seated fear and respect for the dead began to disappear. Sexual assault, especially upon African American women, increased in frequency, although the army's swift repercussion kept the offense from becoming common or chronic. The defiling of the home, the Victorian symbol of all that was good and holy in life, received little negative repercussions, and soldiers began to desecrate private homes and insult the security of Confederate families in ways that were unthinkable before the war. Instead of acting as breaks on this behavior as officers and gentlemen, commanders in the Union army largely tolerated, promoted, or, in some cases, actually led the process of property violation and pillage that so damaged the Confederate economy. Lacking clear examples of restraint from their officers, and often even following their own officers' examples, soldiers felt little reason to not steal, pillage, and engage in violence, safe in the thought that they could blame the war for their change of attitude and aware that the army was prepared to do little to stop them.

THE THEFT OF PROPERTY, belonging to civilians or to the military, plagued the Union army throughout the war. Soldiers stole items at every turn, and there was little the army could do to stop it. The opportunity to steal was everywhere, and the anonymity of army life promoted the notion that once could easily escape retribution for engaging in thievery. Also, no one knew who or where theft might occur, and while hardened criminals stole items, so did otherwise upstanding and law-abiding citizen-soldiers who saw the opportunity and took it. Because theft came in so many forms and had so many different victims, the soldiers' response to the problem was just as varied. A soldier who stole from his comrades suffered the most serious penalties his comrades could inflict, ranging from a formal court-martial to public ostracism to a physical beating. As citizen-soldiers, Union troops expected soldiers to maintain good faith with their fellow citizens and not engage in criminal behavior, such as stealing, that seemed more akin to the lowly behavior of the traitorous enemy than a defender of the Union. Likewise, the masculine belief system entitled any man to defend the property he had gained from his own labor, and to resist and deride anyone who tried to profit without effort. But soldiers who stole from the army, from merchants, or from southern civilians received little rebuke or scorn. Stealing from the army was simply acquiring what the soldier needed to do his job, while merchants profited from the sacrifice of citizen-soldiers without risking their own lives. Stealing from the enemy became almost expected by the end of the war, as theft escalated into open pillaging of the Confederate countryside.

The things that soldiers stole most often were food and money. Money was an obvious asset, and any common thief in the army had opportunities to enrich himself at the expense of the army establishment or his fellow soldiers. Food, however, was a different matter. Soldiers could minimally justify their theft as an act of necessity because, whereas soldiers did not necessarily need money to fight, they had to eat. On occasion during the war, the Union army outstripped their supply resources, leaving soldiers to go hungry, but overall the Union army's Subsistence and Quartermaster Departments did a credible job of making sure the army remained fed. While quantity of food was seldom an issue, quality and variety presented problems. Army regulations established the standard diet of the U.S. soldier, a diet that seldom varied.[1] The cornerstones of the soldiers' diet were hardtack and raw meat, which the soldiers had to cook by whatever means they could obtain. The monotony of their diet compelled soldiers to find alternatives on their own, as did the quality of the standard diet. Hardtack was tough and difficult to chew, and greasy meat, while filling, was often poorly cooked and of indifferent quality. Moreover, few soldiers knew how to prepare food, as one soldier noted when he observed that "if they ate a cooked meal they must cook it themselves, something they had not counted on."[2] Theft was also a by-product of the army's habit of paying its soldiers so irregularly. Without funds to purchase goods, soldiers made the leap in reasoning that theft was the only way to get what they desired. Instead of receiving regular pay on a regular basis, soldiers went months without pay, only to receive large sums at once. Corporal Cornelius Courtright, after not seeing a paymaster for more than four months, received all of his back pay, $139.05, in one lump sum, while a year later Lieutenant James Sinclair finally got his back pay, $422.86, for which he waited five months.[3] Corporal Frederick Pell of the Seventy-sixth Illinois was glad to report that "We mustered today for two months pay," but tempered his enthusiasm by remembering, "We have six months pay due."[4] Exacerbating the absence of pay was the common inflation of prices for soldiers who did have money to pay. The wartime economy caused a degree of inflation by itself, but the huge demand for civilian goods near army camps created a high demand that merchants satisfied at even inflated prices.

Driven by simple criminality, economic need, or sense of deprivation, theft took on many forms. Due to the variety of theft, however, soldier reaction to the offense was mixed, with soldiers approving or justifying some forms while condemning others. Soldiers were not above stealing from stores, but in the field, merchants were few and far between. The exception was the regimental sutler. Soldiers enjoyed a love/hate relationship with their sutler. The merchant smuggled in the whiskey they desired, but also charged them what the market would bear for the goods. Demand was high, and prices were consequently inflated. One sutler sold rancid butter at $1 per pound, spoiled tobacco, and pies so foul-tasting the soldiers called them "condensed cholera."[5] Another soldiers accused the sutlers of "gathering up the scraps and refuse from the camps and bringing it back the next day in the shape of mince pies."[6] Sutlers also sold products on credit to soldiers who had no money to pay, often charging interest and demanding immediate payment when soldiers did receive back wages. "We have in camp what we call a Sutler," Private James Holmes wrote to his sister, "one who has everything you want but you have to pay three or four prices for them. You get them on credit, but when pay day comes he gets your money before you get yours."[7] Offended by sutlers amassing small fortunes while they sacrificed and suffered for the survival of the nation, soldiers had few qualms about taking advantage of a sutler and relieving him of his goods. "As far as I am conserned [*sic*]," Henry Bear wrote, "I would not care if they would take all he [the sutler] had. He would skin a louse for its hide and tallow." Private Charles Bardeen had even less regard for sutlers. "The only place where a sutler could find sympathy," he quipped, "was in the dictionary."[8]

Justified by the exorbitant prices charged by their only sources of civilian goods, soldiers often took out their frustrations on the sutler's wagon by helping themselves to his products. "The soldiers looked upon them as thieves," Wyman White opined about sutlers, "and were not slow in taking advantage of them as often as the opportunity afforded." Cleaning out a sutler was not a long process. Lieutenant Lewis Luckenbill of the Ninety-sixth Pennsylvania noted that "In the afternoon our Sutler . . . came in with a load of goods" and by "8 o'clock he was robbed of nearly all his goods and all his money."[9] Another soldier described the practice of rushing the sutler's tent, with the yell of "rally" as the signal, and "the tent would come down and the goods would be going in all directions; the crowd of excited soldiers striving to get all they could and not be caught by the guard or the officers."[10] A sutler's stock of illegal booze also fueled robbery attempts. "Our Brigade cleaned out the sutler in the 10th Illinois today," John Bates recorded, "The way they made the beer kegs and cigarettes[,] etc. fly was a scene."[11] Robbing the sutler came with a risk, however, as they were not going to give up their products without a fight. Franklin Horner reported that "Our boys were rather noisy last night. They tried to rally on a sutler, but were repulsed."[12] In the fracas of a sutler raid, deaths were an occasional unplanned result. Franklin Boyts recorded one such raid upon a sutler that resulted in "One man killed and another wounded by the guard as they try to rob [the] sutler."[13] Describing an assault in his regiment, Private George Hitchcock of the Twenty-first Massachusetts observed, "They made a grand charge on the sutler's tent, but were checked for a few moments by the occupants who showed resistance . . . Two of the roughs were shot during the melee."[14] Trying to halt "a raid on a sutler's shop tearing it to pieces and taking out everything," a colonel "discharged his pistol among the crowd, wounding one man in the arm and making amputation a necessity."[15] In an attempt to make an assault upon their regimental sutler easier, Private Charles Curtiss admitted "the boys got the sutler drunk" so he could not oppose them.[16]

Such raids were far from rare, and some sutlers endured unrelenting theft. Sergeant Evan Gery of the Ninety-sixth Pennsylvania recorded a barrage of attacks upon his regimental sutler, starting on January 7, 1863, when "The boys of the regiment robbed the sutler of his cakes" up to May 20, when the sutler left camp after he "was robbed of $500."[17] Once soldiers stole from the sutler, the army found it difficult to get the items back or even to identify and prosecute soldiers in the mass of blue-clad suspects. Few ever faced prosecution for their thievery. "Private Thomas Green was arrested for stealing feed boxes belonging to the sutler and sent to the Guard House for ten days," John Mottram noted, but Green was the exception rather than the rule.[18] One of the few offenders caught red-handed was a brazen soldier who stole cash out of the sutler's cash box with a "stick to end of which he had attached a bulb of tar from a wagon-wheel."[19] Not surprisingly, when faced with the loss of their property, sutlers became wary of engaging in trade with some regiments. "A sutler takes great risk because the soldiers often upset their wagons and steal everything they have got," John Smith observed, "so there are not many sutlers who want to come here and take those risks."[20]

Getting what they needed when no other option was available was also the justification for a considerable amount of counterfeiting during the war. The war saw the introduction of millions of dollars worth of paper money by both sides, and the ability to duplicate legitimate currency became a possible, although highly technical, means of obtaining goods illegally. General Patrick ordered the arrest of an entire company of the First Pennsylvania Cavalry "up for Counterfeiting," culminating with the imprisonment of the three ringleaders in the Old Capitol Prison in Washington, DC, and lesser punishments for the rest of them.[21] When soldiers of the Eighty-seventh Indiana defrauded a local woman by giving her counterfeited Confederate money for her produce, she complained to their commanding officer. General James Steedman gave the Indianans thirty minutes to come up with the money to compensate the woman, or he threatened to imprison all of them.[22] Members of the Seventy-ninth New York were also good at copying Confederate currency, and some "sharpies had crudely counterfeited Confederate money and passed it on a loyal but ignorant southerner" for a quantity of whiskey.[23] Some Union soldiers did not have Confederate or Union currency to counterfeit, so they made their own. "The boys could not get the proper vignette" to make the imagery on the money look realistic, a sergeant found out, so "they used advertising cuts of cabinet warehouses and restaurants. Many of our men have passed Mustang Liniment advertisements on the people."[24] In some cases, the inequitable exchange of monies was more a case of exploiting ignorance than purposeful deception. "The boys passed of 15 or 20 dollar of Allegan & Berrien County money," Charles Haydon wrote, referring to the money issued by local banks in his native Michigan, "to peddlers to day for 95 cnts on 100 & in some cases got silver" in exchange for paper dollars of dubious value outside of Michigan.[25]

The acquisition of some items from the battlefield was also broadly acceptable, even if the army and local civilians might object. Such theft had to occur under very sensitive conditions. If removing items off the battlefield did not injure or insult anyone, or if it was unclaimed property, soldiers had no problem with such activity, but abusive or insensitive theft risked a harsh backlash. Some soldiers took the opportunity to improve their firepower. Unhappy with the "common musket" that the government issued his regiment, Colonel Cavins "took the responsibility of ordering each company to supply themselves with superior guns" from the weapons left by Confederates on the Antietam battlefield.[26] Colonel Newton Colby acquired from Antietam "a fine Remington Rifle, with sabre [sic] bayonet complete" to improve his own personal arsenal.[27] Also, no one objected if soldiers acquired a few souvenirs or momentos from their campaigns. Many a soldier, in search of a souvenir of their wartime experience, emulated Private Henry Gangewer and "went over the Battle field in search of relics."[28] Corporal John Smith sent his mother two buttons off an abandoned Confederate coat, Private James Holmes took a "piece of wood off the Pew" of the church where George and Martha Washington wed, Amos Abbott visited the tomb of George Washington's mother and "got a piece of the monument to send home," while Henry Kauffman preserved "some cherry blossoms of the tree that General Lee surrendered his army under."[29] William Bentley told his family of the "$1 Confed[erate] bill in my jacket," which he obviously obtained only as a memento as "I could have got hundreds of dollars out of the trash if I had wanted it."[30] Souvenirs from dead Confederates were also generally accepted, but barely. Private Sawtelle wrote of comrades who searched through dead Confederates and "had brought [back] a lot of letters they had found in their pockets. . . . It seemed very sad to me."[31] Even the most grotesque items became souvenirs. After coughing up a spent bullet lodged in his throat, a soldier dropped the projectile in his picket, deciding "I'll keep that as a souvenir."[32] On other occasions, families at home wanted relics, and soldiers tried to satisfy their curiosity. "You ask me to send mementos," Sergeant Charles Woolhizer wrote his family, "what shall it be [—] gun, knife, pistol, cannon ball, or what?"[33]

Soldiers also justified and overlooked battlefield theft to supply themselves of desired items. Captain Jeheil Wintrode of the Seventy-sixth Ohio discovered a dead Confederate officer with a pair of boots lying next to him. Finding those boots superior to his own, Wintrode appropriated them. He later found out that a Union private had discovered the body first, had removed the rebel's shoes, and left his own used boots for Wintrode to find later.[34] After the Battle of South Mountain, Edward Wightman discovered soldiers "so famished with hunger that they fed from the well-filled knapsacks of the dead rebels."[35] Private John Smith retrieved a small sewing kit from a dead Confederate soldier, but searching the knapsack of another he found only "two ears of green corn and one Johnnie cake the size of a saucer."[36] Smith obviously had no problem searching the bodies of dead soldiers, as he told his mother he did not need her to knit him any more socks as "I can get plenty of stockings from dead soldiers' knapsacks."[37] Some soldiers got more than socks. William Landon, having returned to the site of Battle of the Wilderness a year later to bury newly discovered remains, pried the gold teeth from the skulls of dead Confederates. He made no attempt to hide his activity, even relating it in a letter to his hometown newspaper.[38]

Officers, of course, objected to indiscreet behavior, but there were other forms of theft that earned the offender only scorn and abuse from his comrades. These were cases when soldiers took advantage of those who did not deserve to have depredation visited upon them or circumstances where the theft reflected a lack of honor. Often it was simple as a soldier stealing or robbing another soldier. Authorities in Washington, DC, arrested Private John Martin of the Twelfth Ohio Artillery for not only deserting, but also stealing $100 from his tent mate to finance his escape.[39] Wilbur Fisk complained "I lost my wallet as I was taking a nap in my tent," but another soldier saw who took it, leaving Fisk to "think I have enough evidence to make it a sorry job for him."[40] A soldier and his comrades awoke one night to the cries of their tent-mate, who thought he felt a snake crawling under his bunk. After finding no snake, the men went back to sleep only to find that a haversack was missing in the morning. The "snake" was "the thief pulling at his haversack and he felt the strap move in his bunk."[41] John Holahan complained that "Someone has stolen my flannel shirt and drawers from my haversack" and presumed the thief "has pawned them for whiskey."[42] Private Jonathan Stowe wrote in his diary of the "worst possible practice of robbery and land piracy [that] has been practice daily" by two sergeants in the medical service who stole the personal possessions of wounded soldiers under their care at a hospital in Falls Church, Virginia.[43] In an attempt to shame a potential thief into not taking his diary, Private John Mottram poetically wrote "Steal not this Book for fear of shame for here you see the owner's name," inside the front cover.[44]

Theft of the mail was also not tolerated. The soldiers relied upon the mail to receive their highly desired letters from home, to receive boxes of civilian luxuries, and to forward their pay to their families at home. Anyone who undertook to disrupt or threaten the mail made himself an enemy of the soldiers in the Union army. A "considerable excitement" arose in Private Joseph Taylor's regiment when officers arrested "Jerome E. King of our company on the charge of robbing the regimental mail box." King confessed to the robbery, admitting that he had stolen a total of $225, although only "Forty-one dollars were found on him" at the time of his arrest. "He is a miserable fellow," Taylor declared, "and has never had a good name in the co."[45] King was lucky; the army docked his pay to compensate those he robbed, but he avoided any real severe sentence. Others were not so fortunate. "The mail was broken open . . . and 400 letters thrown into the Potomac," William Lamson wrote his sister. ". . . The man that robbed it has been sent to prison for ten years."[46] Worst of all was the violation of the mail by those trusted to disperse it. "Our mail was robed [sic] the other day by a soldier that carried the mail," Private John Withrow wrote his sister. "They cot [sic] him at it or found some of the letters that he had tore open. . . . The way he robed it, he would take and look at the letter and any he thought had money he would open them . . . I shouldn't wonder if there is a good deal of such work that is going on."[47] Withrow was not the only one to believe that mass postal theft occurred. Sergeant Elmore Day of Thirty-sixth Illinois wrote to his parents that he was delaying the postage of his pay to them because he "can't send money now because of mail thievery."[48] Even boxes were not safe. James Ames came across a "whole lot of musty packages that have been unearthed from the express office" that had sat undelivered for months. Although most of the boxes contained only "rotten papers of loaves, blue mould [sic] masses of putrescence & filth," Ames noted that "I have broken into one . . .thrown away some decayed matter and appropriated some chocolates, olives, preserves, and crackers."[49] Sergeant Welsh was pleased that "the bottle of whiskey and the bottle of bitters" sent by his wife arrived safely, but was angry that "some scoundrell [sic] opened the bottom of the box and took the bottle of brandy" while the box was en route.[50]

Soldiers tolerated some scavenging on the battlefield, but other forms of battlefield theft were off limits and soldiers risked retaliation for practicing such activity. For instance, it was alright for soldiers to acquire mementos off a battlefield, but citizens could not. Characterizing the population of Gettysburg as "nearly all Copperheads," Marsena Patrick noted with disgust the number of civilians who "came in Swarms to Sweep & plunder the battle grounds."[51] While soldiers accepted the necessity to acquire useful items off the battlefield, the plundering of personal items was not. "The Fourteenth Kentucky . . . disgraced the name of soldier," Private Owen Hopkins wrote after a clash near Paintsville, Kentucky. The Kentuckians engaged in "indiscriminate plundering of the dead and wounded, in some instances stripping boots and shoes from dying men." Hopkins blamed the behavior on "influences created by the Medusa head of their cherished institution: Slavery."[52] When an officer discovered the body of Captain William T. Bryan of the Ninth Kentucky on the battlefield at Stone's River, he raged that "some of these villains had robbed his body of a valuable watch and his pocket-book." Infuriated, the officer wished to see the pillagers "tied to a cannons mouth and blown in pieces" for their "unexcelled depravity of heart."[53] In a sorrowful letter to his parents, Private Herman White broke the news of his brother's death to his parents. Unable to retrieve his brother's personal effects as he had "to advance again soon after and leave him," White returned to find "His pockets were rifled before I could get the chance" to collect any items.[54] When Captain Nathan Messick of the First Minnesota died on the battlefield, "His sword and pocket book were taken from him within fifteen minutes after he fell" according to the soldier tending his body, "Who took them, I don't know."[55] Just before the Battle of Gettysburg, John L. Smith left his cash with a family friend in case he was killed in the battle "I knew [what] would take place. I did not want my soldier friends to take my wealth."[56] Disgusted at the "camp cormorants and stragglers" who "clean out the pockets and knapsacks" of the dead, Private

Ames was pleased that the thieves could not rob a Union corpse that "had a ring glittering on its cold hand" as "it was on tight."[57]

Union soldiers approved of removing items from dead Confederates, but became indignant when Confederates practiced the same behavior. It was an article of faith among Union soldiers that Confederates, especially in the early months of the war, routinely scavenged uniform parts and weaponry from Union dead, but rumors also flew about Confederates fashioning trophies from Union corpses. "Skulls were frequent tent ornaments, and were also used for soap dishes," and, according to one newspaper rumor, ". . . Soldiers of the Brooklyn 14th . . . on the field of Bull Run . . . [lie] unburied and headless."[58] Private Davis Ashley wrote to his parents of his recent assignment to hunt locals and Confederates "who were caught in the act of disfiguring our dead who had been killed." Angry at the desecration of the dead, Ashley hoped for a lethal end to his assignment: "I wish they were all hung."[59] That was also the desire of Union troops who found alive, three days after the Battle of Cedar Mountain in August 1862, a wounded soldier "stripped of his clothing and left for dead" by Confederates who held the field after the battle.[60]

Because theft was such a diverse offense, and because soldiers held such a spectrum of attitudes regarding the crime, punishment also fell across a wide range of practices in the relatively few cases when the army decided to inflict a punishment. Sharp contrasts occurred in the administration of justice, with a wide range of mercy and hostility. In the Thirty-ninth New York, the regiment handled thieves internally, inflicting additional duties on two soldiers who stole a shirt and a small amount of cash.[61] A former slave hired as a servant in the Eighth Illinois who "stole our canned fruit, jellies, and oysters" and "the colonel's liquor" lost his job, although as a civilian employee he was liable to face military justice.[62] In contrast, when a soldier detected a thief in a Pennsylvania regiment, he soon had "a whole host of Irishman after him throwing stones, bottles, et.cet., and threatening to kill him."[63] Arrested for stealing a box of goods mailed to a comrade, a young Massachusetts soldier was let off easy with only repaying the $20 value of the stolen goods, but in an Illinois regiment a soldier who "stole a blouse from the quartermasters was cortmarsheled [sic]" and sentenced to a year in a military prison.[64]

Another form of intolerance when it came to theft occurred when officers committed the crime. While soldiers had a flexible morality about stealing things, both soldiers and the army establishment maintained absolutely no tolerance for officers who abused their rank, defrauded the army, or took advantage of their men to line their own pockets. Officers, due to their responsibilities, had a wide range of opportunities to steal. The army entrusted them with great amounts of equipment, provided them access to the logistic network, placed them in charge of disbursing pay, and managing the records that kept all of it straight. If an officer wanted to make money by illicit means, the opportunity certainly presented itself. Unfortunately, enough officers did avail themselves of illegal wealth to become a noticeable problem. When caught, officers faced a loss of status, reputation, and rank. As an officer and gentleman, the army establishment and its soldiers demanded a higher standard from its leadership, and had little sympathy for any officer who denigrated his uniform and rank by abusing the position, trust, and responsibility thrust upon him.

Embezzlement was a common crime, with officers diverting army funds or supplies to their own purposes. An audit of a regimental ration fund (the army allowed company commanders to return unconsumed rations in exchange for cash) found that Captain Hiram Edwards had embezzled the funds instead of buying supplies as intended. His company pressed to have him court-martialed and cashiered, but Edwards "begged so doggedly and promised to refund the money" that he kept his rank, although his regiment held him in low regard for the rest of the war.[65] Under the right circumstances, an officer could embezzle a considerable amount of money. Quartermaster John W. Howland of the Tenth Massachusetts deserted his regiment and fled to Canada with more than $16,000 in cash.[66] Captain John F. Andrews of the Sixth Michigan Cavalry faced a military trial for embezzling for the "intent . . . to convert to his own use, one cask, containing, to wit; about twenty gallons of alcohol," leading to his dismissal from the service.[67] Major Henry A. Gallup and Lieutenant William C. Davidson of the Third Missouri Cavalry conspired to add fake names to Davidson's company, with payrolls confirmed by Gallup, and the two officers splitting the money. A senior officer discovered their caper, leading to the prosecution of both of them. George Avery, a lieutenant in the unit, approved of the prosecution of those who committed monetary crimes, "Some by appropriate public property to their own private use—others by receiving money and giving no account of it," although he believed that the crimes of Gallup and Davidson were just the tip of the iceberg. "I will venture to say," Avery opined, "that there are not ten officers in the Regt. who have not to a greater or less degree swindled the government."[68] Captain Barnabas T. Hayden of the Seventh Kentucky Cavalry was a prime example of another common form of embezzlement when he purposely added names to his muster rolls to collect pay for soldiers who did not exist. Barnabas faced charges in 1865 that he "knowing at the time" that William Boyd was "not a soldier of the United States Army," knowingly had him "entered upon the pay rolls of his Company."[69] Embezzling funds and supplies was only one way that officers abused their authority. General Judson Kilpatrick spent three months in jail in Washington, DC, for accepting bribes from sutlers in his division.[70] Colonel Silas Colgrove of the Twenty-seventh Indiana did not have to receive bribes from his regimental sutler; the sutler was his son and Colgrove profited from this nepotism. Officers complained that instead of using army wagons "to haul clothing for our . . . regiment," he used them "to haul goods for the sutler." Colgrove also managed to appoint one of his sons his adjutant, another the regimental mail carrier "at $80 per month," and entered into a partnership in another sutlery, leading critics to complain that Colgrove "looks like all he cared for is to advance his own pecuniary interests."[71] Extortion was also a profitable venture in areas where officers had direct control over the lives of civilians. In Kentucky, Brigadier General Eleazer A. Paine forced civilians to labor on military construction projects, unless they were willing to pay to be excused from their obligations.[72] In the same state, Major General Stephen G. Burbridge, who led the District of Kentucky in 1864–1865, turned his command into a massive extortion scheme. Burbridge levied fines upon towns in retaliation for guerilla raids, banned the shipment of goods within the state unless the dealer had signed a loyalty oath (and purchased a license), and perpetrated the "Great Hog Swindle." Burbridge issued an order in October 1864 that required all farmers to sell their surplus hogs to the army at a set market price, a price several cents less than the market value in northern cities. Critics charged that Burbridge pocketed the difference on the subsequent sale, with some estimates claiming a profit of $300,000.[73]

No officer, however, could surpass Colonel George Frederick D'Utassy for sheer volume of crime, variety of offenses, and brazen openness about his activities. As colonel of the Thirty-ninth New York, the Hungarian-born D'Utassy ran his regiment as his personal fiefdom and used it to generate as much personal wealth as possible. When the army finally arrested him in 1863, D'Utassy had to answer for a wide variety of offenses. Among the charges were stealing horses (reporting the loss of horses actually still alive, receiving replacements from the army, and then selling the supposedly dead animals), opening private mail, extorting money from sutlers to gain an operating license (and then revoking the license to give it to someone willing to pay more), accepting bribes to appoint applicants to officer positions, and forging payrolls and pocketing the money. To hide his offenses, D'Utassy forced officers to resign their commissions when they threatened to expose him, and persuaded a number of enlisted men to desert so they could not testify as witnesses. Although military trials usually only punished convicted officers with a dishonorable discharge, D'Utassy's court-martial ended in an unusual sentence of a year imprisonment at hard labor in a civilian prison. Also, to further shame the errant officer, the court-martial ordered the "crime, name, and punishment of the delinquent to be published in at least three of the public [news]papers of the state of New York."[74] In May 1863, D'Utassy arrived at Sing Sing prison in New York to serve his term. D'Utassy reacted indignantly when, like any other prisoner, the guards issued him a striped uniform and shaved his head. Instead of hard labor, he demanded office work, and even a salary for his labors.[75]

THIEVERY DID NOT ONLY OCCUR amongst soldiers and the army. The army also acquired civilian property by force, although the level of criminality depended upon which months of the war the incident occurred. Most early acquisition of civilian property fell under the legitimate practice of foraging, or seizing property for the use of the army. Foraging was a traditional practice in wartime, with the expectation that soldiers had the right to seize items that might aid their enemy (contraband) and use it for their own purposes. The laws of war expected the seizure of contraband to be limited and restrained, with minimal imposition upon the health and life of civilians in the army's path.[76] In reality, a very thin line separated legitimate foraging from improper pillaging, and during the war Union soldiers made no distinction between the two and blurred the difference between justifiable seizures of military goods and wanton acts of pillage and destruction. To make matters worse, both formal and informal military polices made the distinctions vaguer instead of more defined.

Early in the war, the seizure of civilian property was limited and moderate. Attempting to wage war in a manner that did not inflame Southern public opinion, senior officers in the first months of the war practiced what later historians characterized as "soft war." By protecting civilian property, especially slaves, generals like Irvin McDowell, George McClellan, and Don Carlos Buell tried to demonstrate that Southerners still enjoyed the protection of federal forces and the nation's laws.[77] Despite their secession, the Lincoln administration still considered Southern residents to be citizens, and therefore entitled to the protection of the government. Moreover, as Winfield Scott demonstrated during the Mexican War, a "soft" approach to a hostile civilian population could contain hostile attitudes and permit military victory.[78] In early-war campaigns, officers enforced strict orders forbidding foraging, especially on McClellan's 1862 Peninsular Campaign, with mixed levels of success. After members of his staff observed soldiers foraging "fowl, vegetables, and a small pig" from a farm, McClellan had the men arrested, fined, and placed in the guardhouse.[79] McClellan's subordinates tried to enforce his orders to their utmost, but his own officers joined members of Congress to question if such a lenient policy did not treat Confederate traitors too lightly. When McClellan failed on the Peninsula, his soft war strategy suffered as much as his military reputation. When Lincoln announced his Emancipation Proclamation in September 1862, the era of "soft war" was over and McClellan's approach to the war became as unpopular as McClellan himself.[80]

The army's policies regarding civilian property changed, as attitudes about the Confederates evolved. Officers began to reject the idea that "soft war" might entice loyal Southerners back into the Union fold. Rather, loyalty and confidence in the Confederate cause seemed stronger than ever, bolstered by Union military failures. Instead of "soft war," in the absence of military victories against the Confederate army, generals such as Ulysses Grant, Benjamin Butler, and John Pope advocated a "hard war" to damage the Confederate economy and infrastructure as a replacement for battlefield success.[81] On July 18, 1862, for instance, General Pope issued orders permitting the Army of the Potomac to "subsist upon the country" to deny agricultural products to the Confederate army.[82] Although Pope intended for Union soldiers to issue vouchers so that the government could compensate civilians for lost property at a later date, soldiers saw the announcement very differently. Describing the previous policy of protecting civilian property as "the greatest Curse to us in this army," Private James Miller welcomed the perceived permission to escalate the war from foraging to pillaging as part of a campaign to "to have war in earnest," and the soldiers could pillage as part of that campaign and "we are to be suported [sic] by the Government."[83] Policy changes also occurred as a recognition that soldiers were likely to forage whether permitted or not. Sargeant Austin Stearns noted Colonel Samuel Leonard's pointed disobedience of General John Abercrombie's order against pillaging when he openly permitted his men to steal hay for bedding and fence rails for firewood.[84] Because of these reasons, the army's collective attitude toward foraging relaxed after the first year of the war. Colonel Elijah Cavins noticed the shift in policy. "Horse stealing, negro stealing, and all other sorts of stealing are common occurrences," he wrote in May 1862, ". . . [during] last summers campaign, stealing was not allowed, but now a man may be punished if he steals a chicken, but if he only steals a fine horse or negro, it is all right."[85]

Regardless of policy, there was no shortage of justifications for pillaging amongst the soldiers. The men of the Union army saw little difference between the government ordering them to seize or destroy Confederate property as a military tactic and their own decision to take what they wanted as an individual. If the government was inclined to destroy or acquire Confederate property, they reasoned, they could do the same. If other circumstances also occurred, soldiers had en even easier time in justifying their behavior. When poorly supplied by their own army, Union soldiers supplemented their meager rations by taking what they needed, regardless of their officers' promises of resupply. "Discipline counts for nothing," John Haley wrote, "once a certain state of hunger is reached."[86] Edward Wightman wrote his brother that his company engaged in foraging after eating the only food available—twenty huge rats. Wightman reported the rodents tasted, "like chicken, only a good deal better."[87] When foraging something to eat, however, soldiers had to be careful. Presuming he had stolen "a quart cup full of flour," John Smith and a friend sat down to "bake flapjacks," only to find "to my utter disgust . . . it was plaster [of] paris."[88] Some soldiers claimed poverty, and unable to obtain extra rations or lacking the funds to purchase goods because their pay was in arrears, soldiers felt the right to take what they needed. Soldiers justified pillaging when civilians did not act like civilians and actively resisted the Union military presence. Colonel John Turchin, for instance, permitted his regiment to pillage Athens, Alabama, after soldiers claimed that the town's citizens had fired upon Union troops retreating from the town in previous days.[89] The most convenient excuse for pillaging, however, was simply the fact that Southerners were the enemies of the Union, and any property of the enemy was susceptible to plunder. Kansas troops, for instance, pillaged a town in Arkansas because "every family in and around [the town] . . . [has] male members in the rebel army or among the licensed banditti of the CSA."[90] Likewise, soldiers helped themselves to the bee hives of a Mississippi farmer with the justification that "If it had been a Union man it would have been too bad to use up his property so, but as it was it was all right, for the owner was away from home with the Guirillas [sic]."[91] Wilbur Fisk felt no different. "Virginia is a guilty state," he reported to his local newspaper in describing the pillaging of the landscape, "and day of her retribution seems to be at hand."[92] Associated with this idea, soldiers pillaged on the thin justification that they were part of the army's wider strategy of destruction and were only doing what they thought the army wanted them to do. "We felt more at liberty to ransack," Charles Williston reasoned, ". . . as we were [there] . . . for the main purpose of crippling the enemy's resources . . . [so] we felt justified in helping ourselves and conscience did not rebuke us."[93] Furthermore, at least in the mind of William Bentley, "it may prove a warning for the future, that Rebellions against our Government won't pay."[94] The destruction of civilian property troubled Private Julius Murray of the Sixth Wisconsin, but in the end he reconciled himself to the devastation around him by deciding "they have brought it on themselves."[95]

The products of Southern farms were the most common targets of pillaging, as the destruction of these items served the dual purpose of feeding the Union army and depriving support to the Confederate army. Legitimate foraging crossed into illegitimate pillaging, however, when the destruction of food stores became an end unto itself, with no purpose other than senseless destruction. Ordered to acquire a boatload of "Secesh Corn" along the banks of the Yazoo River, soldiers from the Twenty-third

Wisconsin could not load the corn and return to their post as ordered, so instead of leaving it "we set fire to the Corn" and left before Confederate forces could respond.[96] Soldiers of the Ninth Ohio not only appropriated a farmer's apples, they set fire to a haystack to roast them, "by spontaneous combustion of course" according to an eyewitness.[97] In retaliation for the loss of a number of horses to a Confederate raid, Colonel Francis V. Randall of the Thirteenth Vermont ordered his men into the countryside to seize an equal number of replacement animals from Confederate civilians. The soldiers responded with alacrity, seizing, among other animals, two old plow horses from a farmer in the process of working his land, leaving him to curse the soldiers as they rode away with his livelihood.[98] Nor did cotton escape the eye of Union soldiers. Unable to confiscate a crop, "we set fire to a large barn filled with cotton and a cotton gine [*sic*]," John Ferguson wrote with satisfaction, "In a few minutes it was all in flames. The old lady came out to the doar . . . When she saw what was dun, she . . . went to praying with both hands extended upewards. I did not hear the words she uttered but I do not think she prayed for the Yankees."[99]

The targeting of items that supported the Confederate war effort soon expanded into the pillaging of private property, leading to destruction that was entirely wasteful and pointless. "At nearly every halt" of General Sherman's march through the Carolinas in 1865, William Bentley observed, "some mischievous Yank would set fire to the pitch on the tree and in a short time the woods would be on fire as far as you could see. Of course this will kill the trees and help to remind the natives of the march of the Yankee Hoards through their state."[100] In Tennessee, soldiers also senselessly destroyed forests, as an anonymous soldier reported that "the boys are just slaying the timber; they cut the trees down, I guess, just to see them fall."[101] The most pointless pillaging was the theft of items that soldiers could not or would not use in their military lives. "A soldiers is a very funny animal," John Smith noticed. "He will take things that are of no more use to him than geography would be to a cow and will carry it for two or three miles and then throw it away."[102] Private George Remley recorded a soldier who stole a pair of ice skates who explained his acquisition by saying, "I couldn't find any thing else to steal so I thought I would take these."[103] Soldiers also stole questionable items from a farm in Arkansas. Besides taking every bit of stored grain and livestock, Union soldiers also cleaned out the house of all personal luxuries, including, the lady of the house testified, "my wedding slippers."[104] Another soldier, also apparently at a loss to find something worth taking, "passed us dressed as a lady, only his toilet was rather crudely made."[105]

As the war progressed and pillaging became a more common activity, some soldiers dropped all pretense of foraging and engaged in pillaging simply for the fun or profit of it. Campaigning against Vicksburg in 1863, Union soldiers joked they could mark their passage by the "Mississippi headstones," the smoking chimney that was all that remained of a torched house.[106] Edward Wightman wrote proudly of his friend Private James H. Folan's, aka "Cockroach," ability to pillage and plunder. Folan had a sixth sense for locating hidden goods and a penchant for stealing anything he thought he needed.[107] John Brobst was also proud of his loot-detecting abilities. "The woods are full of trunks and boxes filled up with dresses, bed clothes, and all manner of stuff that they thought they had hid from us," Brobst wrote to a friend, "but hide from a Yankee soldier if you can."[108] The pillaging, in defiance of the government's claim of reuniting the Union, included the homes of Unionists as well. "There are a good many man in this army that will steal from the Union people," Corporal Thomas Wasson complained, "so we have to have a guard around our camps."[109] Unable to determine true loyalty, soldiers simply treated all Southerners as enemies. Despite claims that the occupants were "loyal Union people," the soldiers of the Sixth Michigan pillaged a farm in Louisiana anyway and "felt no remorse of conscience in the least."[110] "Every man and woman down here is loyal as soon as a soldier comes around the house," a Wisconsin soldier observed, ". . . But we have no respect of persons down here. They must all suffer alike."[111]

Much of the pillaging had a class component to it, with soldiers taking particular pleasure in destroying the comforts and trappings of the Southern upper class. As the leaders of Southern culture and possessors of most of the slaves, the upper class embodied the enemies of the Union and the cause of the war. Destroying plantations, cotton gins, and other physical representations of slave-based wealth became a way for Union soldiers to manifest their displeasure at slavery and the war it caused. "On our line of march back down the bayou were several fine mansions," Private Benjamin Johnson of the Sixth Michigan wrote. "We were eager for some chance to satisfy our desire for revenge in having been . . . very needlessly put to this exposure and fatigue. We were told that we would be . . . reducing these same mansions to ashes, and we were not slow in so doing, leaving no vestige of habitation on those accursed plantations."[112] John Ferguson was proud of the work of his regiment, who demolished a plantation house by "scattering and upsetting everything" before setting the house afire. "The whole cost of the wealthie [sic] mansion includeing the funitur," Ferguson calculated, "could not fall short of one hundered thousand dollars."[113] Particular items that indicated upper-class status earned special attention, such as expensive furniture or personal libraries. "The soldiers pillaged the houses," an Iowa soldier recounted, "carrying off almost every thing moveable, looking glasses, chairs, carpets, Dishes & every thing, books included. . . . I have a volume of

Plutarch's Lives with which I spend my leisure moments."[114] Pianos became a particular target as a symbol of wealth and sophistication. During the Battle of Chancellorsville, General Oliver O. Howard approved the burning of a plantation house near his lines "full of furniture and valuable things . . . especially their piano."[115] In Arkansas, among the troops pillaging a house was an "Irishman caught dancing on top of the grand piano in one woman's home."[116] Robert Sneden was proud of his regiment's new theater, constructed by the men themselves and featuring padded seats and "a piano from some Rebel house."[117] Sergeant John Hartwell, supervising the pillaging of a home, noted, "Thare [sic] was a splendid piano in the parler but spoiled by a bullet," which disappointed Hartwell because "I wanted to a play a little."[118]

The most organized pillaging was for cotton. The North had an insatiable demand for cotton, and seizing it provided the most convenient and immediate source of the product. The North needed cotton to not only supply its own textile mills, but also keep European textile mills operating. The British and French reliance upon Southern cotton, which they could not obtain in sufficient amounts due to the Union naval blockade, raised the specter of European intervention into the war in support of the Confederacy. If the North could obtain enough cotton to keep the European textile mills operating, however, then the Union had some means of maintaining European neutrality. One means of obtaining cotton was through open commerce with Southern citizens who claimed, at least in terms of business, either pro-Union or neutral sentiments.[119] This method did not provide sufficient amounts of cotton, so other methods of obtaining the product emerged. The Union government instituted policies to grow cotton in occupied areas of the Confederacy, generally employing former slaves working the lands of their erstwhile owners in exchange for wages.[120] The government also permitted the confiscation and resale of captured Confederate cotton. Driven by the possibility of personal financial gain, the military services set about confiscating cotton with a vengeance. The navy in particular, with its own means of transport, became adept at confiscating and moving cotton before the army could get it. When the navy seized cotton purchased already purchased by the Confederate government, bearing the C.S.A. stamp, they stamped the bales with U.S.N. on the other end, leaving peeved army soldiers to claim that the initials stood for "Cotton Stealing Association-United States Navy."[121] After a cotton barn near an army camp burned before the army could confiscate its contents, "Gen. [Nathaniel] Banks got in a terable [sic] rage about it and said he would have it [the cost of the cotton] assessed against our brigade," William Wiley wrote with some amusement, "but we got our poor little $16 all the same."[122] Soldiers took the opportunity to enrich themselves, although not with the army's blessing. Sergeant William Rogers and five other men of the Fourth

Illinois Cavalry, for example, faced a court-martial when they conspired with a cotton smuggler to provide him with fifty bales of cotton in exchange for $2,500 in cash.[123] A captain in the Forty-sixth Indiana found himself under arrest when he "thought to make some money" by smuggling thirteen bales of cotton aboard the transport carrying his men.[124]

Perhaps the worst and most concentrated pillaging occurred during General Ambrose Burnside's assault at Fredericksburg, Virginia. Most of the fighting took place west and south of Fredericksburg, but to get to the battlefield Union soldiers had to cross the Rappahannock River on pontoon bridges that led directly into town. Both soldiers newly arrived on the battlefield and those from units shattered in the fighting thoroughly plundered the town from December 11–13, 1862. "In plain english," Bruce Catton wrote of the plundering, "the town had been sacked [by] unrestrained rowdyism," and soldiers despoiled nearly every house in the community.[125] Many an observer described scenes of utter chaos and absence of discipline. "The streets were filled with the confusion of all things," Private Oliver Norton described, "splendid furniture and carpets, provisions, bottles, knapsacks, dead men and horses, blankets, muskets, the pomp of war and paraphernalia of peace mingled together."[126] Private John L. Smith "could see the men carrying chairs, sofas, beds and doors and they would throw them right in the mud in the streets so they could lie on them," and later "stood at the river looking at soldiers diving for tobacco which was thrown over before the town was evacuated."[127] Lieutenant Curtis C. Pollock of the Forty-eighth Pennsylvania offered another chaotic scene. "The men wandered all over town bringing in tobacco," he observed, ". . . they also brought a number of books, some very handsomely bound and works by the best authors. Co. G got a complete set of Waverly novels." Pollack wandered into another area where "Everything was apparently left in great haste and the men could be seen walking around with every imaginable article of household good. One man brought into camp a large doll . . . others had lace, shawls silk dresses . . . I was told that a man belonging to one of the batteries found a whole set of silver and carried it off."[128] Chaplain Stuckenberg observed most men securing foodstuffs, but tobacco was also a preferred commodity for pillage. Soldiers also helped themselves to "the very finest china ware and silver knives and forks and spoons . . . [and] some very excellent libraries." Stuckenberg himself was the beneficiary of the plunder. "A soldier gave me two books," he noted, "'Life of Washington,' which I afterwards gave to Col. Brown and 'Life of Lafayette' still in my possession."[129] "One man . . . packed up a sewing machine which he found . . . to send home," Thomas Galwey described. He also noted that some soldiers blew open the safe at a nearby bank only to find it contained "nothing but worthless paper."[130]

A key indicator of just how widely the army accepted pillaging is the number of cases where soldiers pillaged openly, with neither any apparent shame nor any concern with punishment or retribution. Soldiers took what they wanted when they wanted, and destroyed what remained, seldom concerning themselves with who saw them engaging in such conduct. Quite the opposite, pillaging was often a group activity, with whole units engaging in the practice. Sometimes the thievery occurred outside the view of a superior officer, but on other occasions it happened with the full knowledge and tacit blessing of officers. The plundering of towns was the best example. "Men were at work all last night with dark lanterns and candles in shops and stores all over town," wrote Robert McMahan of his regiment's plundering of Van Buren, Arkansas. "Guards were of little consequence and the officers seemed to care not" until "[General James] Blunt made his appearance revolver in hand and drove us all out."[131] Upon the rumor that a local town had murdered some soldiers, the Seventy-seventh Illinois "thought it was their duty to retaliate by raiding the town which they did in good shape by raiding the stores and firing a good many buildings." Dressed up in the "dry goods whey they had taken from the stores," the Illinois men "came marching back to the boats looking like a lot of Indians."[132] The pillaging of one town in northern Georgia was so bad that General Alexander McCook could only impose order by posting "2 regiments on provo duty and aresting [*sic*] every soldier they finde doing anything rong."[133] Senior officers became uneasy about the broader effect of pillaging, but soldiers had much less concern. Chaplain Armstrong, observing "most of the boys have some confiscated article," feared that "It will take a generation to repair the loss" to the South from Union pillaging, but Captain William Lusk estimated that only $200 "would probably cover any damage" done to Germantown, Virginia, after his men looted the place.[134] Such behavior occurred in sharp contrast to every moral and legal ethic of antebellum life, but the war challenged traditional notions of masculine conduct and bravery, and many a soldier saw no contradiction between stealing while in the army and returning to antebellum modes of behavior after the war ended.

While soldiers had no qualms about engaging in open and unrepentant pillaging, they still had to worry about their reputations at home. Many soldiers bragged openly about their thievery, but others, concerned about how their family members perceived their behavior, chose either to not mention what they were doing or disguise their conduct through a justification or euphemism. Encamped on the farm of Confederate General Marcus Wright, Sergeant Hartwell noted that the general "had a very Splendid barn which it is supposed took fire by accident last evening."[135] Theodore Dodge, with tongue firmly in cheek, denied that his men were pillaging livestock, but "The fact is that the animal creation about here are very pugnacious, and insist on attacking our picket line so often that our boys are fain to bayonet them out of pure self defense."[136] An equally aggressive pig "bit one our boys. He was sentenced to die without trial," wrote one soldier, while another soldier received permission from a lieutenant to shoot some wild turkeys so the beasts "did not bite any of the boys."[137] In the Sixth Wisconsin, stealing a sheep became known as "killing a rabbit," as "'rabbits' are covered with wool in this country" according to an exasperated officer.[138] Even officers used misleading language. Brigadier General Stephen Burbridge instructed his men "not to get bit" if encountering any chickens or geese, implying that they were to defend themselves against hostile Confederate poultry.[139]

Many soldiers found a way to reconcile the conflict between their upbringing and their desire to pillage, but other soldiers could not. Some men found the practice anathema to their status as experienced soldiers, and were aghast at the depredations of new recruits. "The men . . . were allowed to do as they please, and many acts were committed that a veteran would be ashamed of," criticized William Westervelt. "Houses were pillaged and burned, women and children were insulted, barns were fired, and immense amounts of property unnecessarily destroyed."[140] Soldiers with families at home found it difficult to pillage the property of another family without considering the effect such pillaging might have on their own family. Other soldiers with a strong sense of Victorian morality objected to the violation of a house and home, even if it was the enemy's. Citizen-soldiers, possessing a strong sense of the honor and obligation of soldiery, opposed the destruction of property as simple lawlessness, deeming pillagers little more than common criminals. "Now what is the need of this lawlessness?" James Avery asked, ". . . [I]t is a shameful fact there were men, calling themselves soldiers, who would not stop at robbery, but even insult defenseless ladies. I say such men were not soldiers, but the worst kind of sneaking dogs."[141] Edward Wightman agreed. After observing Union soldiers pillage a house while its frightened female occupants "locked themselves in the upper chambers," Wightman asked his brother in a letter, "What do you think of such a scene? Most of our common soldiers are scarcely above brutes by nature."[142] William Chittenden expressed disgust at his comrades' propensity to steal all "eatables [intended] for the sustenance of old men women & helpless children."[143] The "entreaties of a tender little girl" also failed to stop the thieving of Ninth Kentucky, who engaged in plundering that disgusted soldiers believed 'would disgrace the humblest convict in 'Sing Sing.'"[144] When a fellow officer threatened to burn a civilian's home for failing to provide information on the location of nearby rebels, Lieutenant Colonel David Strother rebuked the officer and told him the army was there to defeat the rebels and not burn out civilians. Instead of complaining, soldiers in his command "cried out 'That's the way I like to hear a man talk'" in support of Strother's decision.[145]

With pillaging so popular amongst the enlisted men, officers tried appeals to their moral Victorian values to protect vulnerable citizens, values that had degraded because of the death and destruction around them. In an effort to stave off pillaging, Colonel Warren W. Packer implored the Fifth Connecticut to refrain from pillaging. "The path of the regiment," he desired, "shall not be cursed by the tears of women and children, weeping over raved homesteads." An army of pillagers, Packer declared, "will, sooner or later, prove an army of cowards."[146] Colonel Elijah Cavins counted himself among the "decent or honest men [who] has been disgusted with the management of this division of the army. The army has become a marauding party, plundering everyone- Union men, women & children as well as rebels. Not leaving anything for them to live on."[147] Henry S. Sherman, colonel commanding the One Hundred Twentieth Ohio and nephew of General William Sherman, was aghast at the behavior of his men. "I did not think that those who were battling for the Sacred Cause of the Union," Sherman wrote in his diary, "could be so forgetful of all that makes them civilized and descend to the level of the barbarians."[148] James Garfield, colonel of the Forty-second Ohio and future President of the United States, chastised his men for foraging, urging them to "Show these Kentuckians, who are your comrades under one flag, that you did not come to rob and to steal." The Forty-second temporarily moderated their conduct, but one soldier who listened to Garfield's plea recorded, "we then thought it wrong to confiscate rebel property, but as time moved on and our faces became bronzed, so also did our conscientious scruples, and we totally forgot the moral teachings of Colonel Garfield."[149]

Some soldiers, however, did not become barbarians, and while they could not stop the pillaging of their comrades, they preserved their own sense of honor. Private Thomas Bennett of the Twenty-eighth Connecticut could not bring himself to steal. "Every valuable was stolen by the soldiers," Bennett wrote his sister, describing the sacking of a house, "I could have got you a handsome set of china here if I had thought it right to take it."[150] James Dunn recognized the need to feed the army but objected to taking everything for fear of leaving "women and children to starve."[151] Also objecting to leaving civilians with nothing to eat, Laurinan Russell, a bugler in the Thirteenth Massachusetts, considered the actions of his comrades as "nothing but robbery, and that of the worst kind."[152] Private John W. Bates objected to the desecration of churches, and when his regiment "tore a church down for wood," he decided, "I don't like the idea; the pulpit should be respected."[153] Recognizing the backlash that pillaging was certain to generate, John Follmer derided the too-common practice where a "house was entered and ladies insulted. . . . These men claim to come from an enlightened country, but are a disgrace to the army. . . . This cannot help us conquer the enemy."[154]

Opposition to pillaging generated no small amount of hypocrisy on the subject. John Haley was certainly not above his fair share of pillaging, but still felt the right to denigrate fellow soldiers who stole a family's meal, food, plates and all, by wrapping it up in the tablecloth and hauling it away, considering the action "a nasty, contemptible trick, deserving prompt punishment." Haley, often unaware of his own hypocrisy, was quick to point it out in others. Haley and his comrades plundered an apothecary because its owner had removed the bucket from his well so the Union men could not use it. When Lieutenant Colonel Charles Merrill chastised the men for stealing medicines, Haley reminded the colonel of some pilfered ducks under preparation at that very moment for his dinner. Haley saw no difference between the two incidents of theft, but conceded that "Colonel Merrill is a lawyer, and he doubtless can discriminate."[155] In another regiment, Colonel Lysander Cutler determined to find out who stole some pigs from a local civilian, but dropped the investigation when he learned his own cook had stolen the pork for the colonel's dinner.[156] John Smith, who denigrated the soldiers' propensity to take anything that struck their fancy, had no problem confessing to his mother in a letter that in January 1864 he "went to a fine looking house to see what I could steal."[157]

The Union army did try to halt pillaging before it could occur by issuing orders forbidding their soldiers to despoil civilian property, but the scope of the problem made any effort seem futile and meaningless. With the massive armies moving around a countryside that offered so many opportunities to plunder, officers could not be everywhere, and stopping pillaging became more a matter of chance than design. When encountering soldiers in the act of pillaging, officers often required more than their rank insignia to halt the violation. Faced with armed soldiers, officers often had to use the threat of gunplay themselves. William Sherman, outraged at meeting soldiers riding in a pilfered carriage, forced the soldiers out at gunpoint, unhitched the horses, and "made them draw the carriage back to the owner more than two miles."[158] Coming to the aid of several women, Colonel Wesley Brainerd arrested two cavalryman caught in the act of vandalizing a house. When one turned and fled, Brainerd fired three shots at him but missed.[159] Lieutenant Colonel Strother managed to save a plantation when an officer planned to burn it in retaliation after a bullet fired from the house whizzed past his head. Strother found out that a soldier, stalking a sheep, had fired and missed, and it was his bullet and not a Confederate sniper's, "so the house was not burnt."[160] When three soldier of the Fifth Kentucky committed egregious pillaging, the army responded with the ultimate penalty. Privates William Baldwin, Franklin Bratcher, and James Robinson not only engaged in pillaging; they abandoned their sentry posts to do it, itself a capital offense. To make matters worse, the soldiers not only pillaged a house, they robbed its occupants at gunpoint, and therefore removing any claim of property acquisition to aid the war effort. In response, the army sentenced all three soldiers to death by firing squad, but the three soldiers were a drop in a proverbial bucket and the pillaging continued.[161] The army could not contain its soldiers, but it could make an example out of officers who engaged in the practice. Lieutenant Colonel Frederick Gast of the One Hundred Twenty-third Pennsylvania faced a court-martial that charged him with marauding and encouraging marauding after Gast took "without payment, a horse from the premises of a citizen . . . and did appropriate it to his . . . own use." Found guilty, the court-martial cashiered Gast.[162] Unable to monitor all soldiers everywhere, General Edward Ord permitted civilians in Louisiana to form local militias to protect themselves against "marauders and thieves, white or black."[163]

Besides the use of force, officers could also apply ex post facto punishment, although this created problems of its own. Without an eyewitness, proving a soldier or group of soldiers engaged in pillaging was difficult. Often the only evidence came from a civilian whose loyalty to the Union cause was less than absolute, leading soldiers to complain that officers favored Confederate civilians over their own men. When General William Rosecrans tried to garnish the pay of two Kansas regiments until they "paid the sum of $1053.55, the value of sugar and tobacco destroyed by them in Trenton, Tenn.," the regiments refused to pay and threatened to mutiny if not absolved of the charge.[164] When Charles Haydon made a soldier pay $4 for the pig he stole, "I obtained quite a notoriety among the privates . . . They swear it is the hardest thing they ever heard of . . . & swear awfully abt [about] me when I am gone."[165] If an officer did apply punishment, it was usually of the limited penalty permitted by a regimental court-martial, so often the punishment did not equal the seriousness of the crime. A soldier might destroy a home worth thousands of dollars, but receive only a trifling penalty in comparison. In the One Hundred Fifty-fourth New York, men caught pillaging suffered the indignity of standing guard for long hours wearing a knapsack full of rocks, but that hardly equated to the loss of a home or a year's crop.[166] Other penalties were equally ineffective. David Mowen spent a few day in the guardhouse for stealing apples from an old woman's trees, but he noticed that "Most of the foraging parties were not so unfortunate" as he was to get caught.[167] For stealing hay, the men of a Michigan regiment had to pay a $1 fine, while a soldier who burned down a cotton gin had only to suffer the public indignity of walking about the camp wearing a sign proclaiming his offense.[168] During the Vicksburg campaign, Ulysses Grant billed the officers of the Twentieth Illinois for the depredations of their men, and ordered that each regiment's officers read the orders banning pillaging aloud at roll call for all soldiers to hear in the hopes it might deter some felonious behavior or at least remove the defense of ignorance. But to soldiers determined to steal, "such orders soon got to be a joke with the men."[169]

Pillaging proved most difficult to halt, however, because many officers found it easier to permit the offense instead of stopping it. This attitude led officers to become complicit in the foraging of their men, guilty by tolerance if not by act. Colonel Francis Randall of the Thirteenth Vermont, for instance, stopped a man entering camp with a pilfered pig under his arm, inquiring if the soldier knew about the standing orders regarding foraging. The soldier informed the colonel that the pig was, in fact, a "rabbit," and the colonel permitted him to go on his way. The same colonel denied that his men had anything to do with excessive foraging around his camp, informing angry locals that his regiment was "composed entirely of theology students."[170] The colonel of the Seventh-seventh Illinois protected his men when an irate Kentucky farmer complained of the loss of his sheep. The colonel sent the man away, telling him he "was not in the sheep business just then."[171] The colonel commanding the Fourteenth Wisconsin had a similar attitude. Near Corinth, Mississippi, in August 1862, the officer called out his to "break ranks and go to cooking." When asked what the men were to cook, the colonel responded, "don't you see the pigs & sheep and chickens running around here?"[172] Some officers even developed a sense of pride in their men's ability to forage. Captain Theodore Dodge proudly wrote his family, "You should have seen the boys posting after the sheep and oxen yesterday. It was real fun and they enjoyed it."[173] Even chaplains were not immune from the foraging impulse. During the siege of Petersburg, Chaplain Armstrong admitted, "For dinner to day we are to have two confiscated chickens . . . the good book says "Ask no questions for conscience sake." I suppose I shall have to eat whatever is set before me."[174]

Recognizing that soldiers needed to eat, wanted to punish the enemy, or let off some steam, most officers seemed content to simply look the other way instead of crack down. "Discipline is horrible," General Patrick surveyed in the Army of the Potomac. "There is no responsibility any where & Commanders of every rank cover up the rascality of their Troops. There is a vast deal of stealing."[175] Plenty of evidence existed to show that General Patrick was not exaggerating. Observing men of the Eighth New York Cavalry breaking into a store to obtain tobacco, their colonel opted not to stop them. When queried why, the officer replied he received orders to search for enemy weapons and supplies and his men were merely carrying out the order. The same officer observed that, after arresting more than a hundred men for pillaging a plantation, an officer let the men go after each offered "a rigamarole apology, one breaking in after another until the whole band were in full blast like an orchestra."[176] In an attempt to play upon the masculine instincts of his men, Colonel Edward Bacon of the Sixth Michigan Heavy Artillery tried to regulate the foraging instead of allowing it to go unchecked. After confronting soldiers who left camp at night to forage for vegetables, Bacon chastised his men: "If you want any potatoes and peaches . . . go out like men in open day and ask for them. If denied, why take them in broad daylight, and not like thieves in the darkness."[177] Forced by public outrage to account for a raid by the Seventh Kansas Cavalry into Missouri that led to the burning of a number of farms and the looting of their contents, Brigadier General James W. Denver replied with merely a token written reprimand that reminded the regiment's officers of their obligation to report and inventory everything seized from the enemy.[178] The same General Sherman who forced soldiers to return a carriage at gunpoint in 1862 winked at pillaging by 1864. When confronted by Sherman with the products of his pillaging, a soldier reminded the general of his own orders to "forage liberally on the country," and Sherman let him go.[179]

The pursuit of plunder even caused units to pillage from each other, or at least try to shift the blame for destruction onto another unit. When an officer stopped a soldier from the Ninth New York outside of his column and asked which regiment to which he belonged, the soldier claimed he was from the Sixteenth Maine "forgetting that he had a figure 9 a foot long in red paint on his Knapsack."[180] George Otis remembered fondly a trick his Second Wisconsin played on soldiers of the Twenty-fourth Michigan. Waiting until the Michigan troops had slaughtered and dressed the sheep they had confiscated, a Wisconsin officer angrily ordered them to return what they had stolen, at which point the Wisconsin troops quickly stole the product of their labor. "The Second boys had a fine breakfast," Otis remembered, ". . . and the Twenty-fourth boys were hopping mad."[181] Charles Wills liked his unit's duty to sweep the area around his camp to discourage pillaging because "whenever they catch a man with poultry or meat of any kind they relive him thereof, take him under guard to his regimental commander, and Company G [his unit] eats up" whatever they took from the plunderers.[182] Weary of walking during the Peninsular Campaign, Private Charles Veil came across a cavalryman taking a nap alongside the road, and, "taking saddle and all," mounted his horse and rode away.[183]

Pillaging persisted throughout the war regardless of Confederate displeasure with the practice. The loss of property, in some cases the product of years of hard labor, enraged both the victims and the Confederate government. One Southerner told a Vermont soldier that his losses had firmly turned him against the Union. "I never had any niggers, don't want them," the farmer ranted, "but if soldiers should come into your country and steal your goods, wouldn't you fight?"[184] Instead of suffering but one assault, another Southerner who "had in my charge a small building filled with articles," suffered numerous pillagings when "they [Union soldiers] repeatedly broke into [the building], carrying off what they chose."[185] Accustomed to stories of torched towns, the citizens of Orangeburg, South Carolina, "made them selves busey [*sic*] . . . doing up what little clothing and beding they had," presuming that Union troops would burn the town. "Some weman [*sic*] were crying bitterly," John Ferguson observed. "Other seemed sullen and independent" as the town went up in flames.[186] Other Confederate civilians risked their lives to save their property. Confronted by a woman with a pistol who threatened to shoot anyone who tried to take her horse, Union soldiers opted to leave the animal behind. "I suppose they admired her grit," a soldier explained.[187] A farmer named John Koontz in the Shenandoah Valley saved his farm from destruction in 1864 by playing upon the Union army's sympathy. Instead of confronting the Union soldiers sent to burn his barn, Koontz invited them to a hearty meal, and in gratitude the soldiers mounted up and rode away, leaving his farm unmolested.[188] Occasionally, civilians complained about their losses and officers had to act. Even Colonel Randall, commanding his "theology students," could not always look the other way. When an old man came to complain about the loss of his chickens, Randall let him look through the camp until the man identified the culprits by spotting chicken feathers outside of their tent. Randall had the offenders strapped to a tree, and lectured the assembled troops on obeying orders regarding foraging. The lesson was not necessarily to not forage chickens, but to avoid leaving incriminating evidence upon which Randall would have to act.[189]

Foraging and pillaging had its risks, however. While safe in the company of a large numbers of Union troops, single soldiers or small groups separated from the rest of the army were vulnerable to Confederate retaliation. Marching through enemy country and committing acts that outraged their Southern enemies, Union soldier caught in the act of thievery could expect little mercy. Union soldiers captured while pillaging were usually summarily executed, either being shot or having their throats slit, and their bodies often left alongside the road to deter other pillagers. During Sherman's March through Georgia in 1864, for instance, at least sixty-four Union soldiers died at the hands of Confederate troops and militia while engaging in property destruction, both authorized and unauthorized, and more than a hundred during his Carolinas campaign in 1865.[190] In retaliation, Sherman threatened to execute a Confederate prisoner for every one of his soldiers killed. "It is officially reported to me," Sherman wrote to Confederate General Wade Hampton, "that our foraging parties are murdered after capture, and labeled

'Death to all Foragers,'" and informed Hampton, "I have ordered a similar number of prisoners in our hands to be disposed of in like manner."[191]

DISPOSED TO COMMIT WANTON property crimes, soldiers also proved willing to commit violent crimes as well. As war-related violence propagated, soldiers became more and more prone to personal violence, often on the thinnest of provocations. Describing the offenders held for court-martial in Missouri in 1861, Sergeant Charles Wills noted that the first offender "murdered a comrade . . . Smote him on the head with a club," while those awaiting trail "this morning they had a man stabbed, a day before yesterday they confined one of their men for trying to kill two others."[192] Daniel Chisholm recalled watching a case of mistaken identity that led to attempted murder. Chisholm saw a man brandishing "a big cheese knife" knock down and stab a man "seven times in the breast." The attacker had quarreled with another soldier, and mistook his victim for his previous antagonizer. "I could hear the knife cut the bones where I stood, at least twenty paces away," Chisholm marveled, but "heard afterward that the wounded man recovered."[193] Money was a common motivation for murder or attempted murder. "One of our men was brought in with his throat partially cut," Lieutenant Edmund Halsey wrote to his cousin, ". . . some men attacked him from behind, attempted to murder him and took some $300 he had with him. The wound is not considered mortal but the affair is not a pleasant one." The victim thought they were civilians, but Halsey postulated that it was soldiers of the victim's own company as "The new men [include] some hard men among [the] substitutes and recruits."[194] Sometimes, however, the attacker did not get away. Private Miguel Oliver tried to rob Private Giacomo Antonali as he slept in their tent. Awakening to find Oliver trying to cut through his clothes to steal his money, Antonali retrieved a knife by his bed and stabbed Oliver to death.[195] As with many violent acts, alcohol also played a part in many rash acts of violence. In the New Mexico Territory, a drunken sergeant, resisting arrest by his lieutenant, fired five times at close range and only managed to graze the officer. In response, "Other officers near by [sic] emptied their revolvers" at the sergeant who ended up, unwounded, in the guardhouse to await trial.[196]

The most frequent violent offense was assault upon another person. Assault was a different offense than soldiers simply fighting amongst themselves. Fights occurred over spontaneous triggers and usually involved minor injuries that did not warrant legal proceedings. Assault, on the other hand, implied premeditation of the circumstances of when and how the assault would occur, as well as clear intent to inflict substantial, if not deadly, physical harm. The commission of an assault offense also implied a knowing decision to violate Article 33 of the Articles of War, which forbade "violence . . . against the person or property of any citizen of any of the United States."[197] The definition of assault is particularly relevant as the offense encompassed cases of attempted murder. The Articles did not include a specific charge of attempted murder. Instead, soldiers faced a charge of assault with extenuating circumstances, such as assault with a deadly weapon or assault with the intent to kill. This complicated the proceedings as subsequent courts-martial had to prove intent as well as fact, and the court also had to devise a suitable punishment somewhere between simple assault and murder.

Nearly any confrontation might cause a violent response. In the Thirty-eighth New York, an altercation between a sergeant and a private ended when the private retrieved an iron bar and struck the sergeant with it, breaking his arm and earning the private thirty days hard labor while wearing a ball and chain.[198] Private Carroll Dobbins beat Private James Ingram with a pistol in an argument over the ownership of a blanket, sending Dobbins to prison for six months.[199] Private Henry McGill beat another soldier so badly that the court hearing his case decided the only suitable punishment was an equally brutal sentence of five years at hard labor.[200] Private Levi Hansleman of the First Ohio did not just assault a fellow soldier; he "did strike . . . a soldier from the hospital, with a sling shot," injuring him severely.[201] Assault also became a blatant form of insubordination. Angry at his sergeant, Private Austin Horan followed him into his quarters and "did commit upon him of a violent and outrageous character, by striking him several times with his clenched hands," earning him a sentence of imprisonment at hard labor for the remainder of his term of enlistment.[202] In Charles Haydon's company, soldiers assaulted a corporal who they believed was acting a bit too self-important. Cornering the corporal in a tent, soldiers bearing a "red hot poker & the other a red hot shovel" forced the NCO to dance about for their amusement, "hold up is right hand & swear eternal fidelity to his squad," and to stand on his head. "The last feat being performed," Haydon wrote, "he was allowed to retire to his bunk."[203] In the Sixty-first New York, soldiers and officers, fed up with the poor quality of his services, committed a "gross outrage" by physically seizing their chaplain and tying him "to a Battery Waggon."[204]

If soldiers committed particularly vicious assaults or if military authorities believed the assailant intended to inflict more injury than just a severe beating, then military courts could consider additional outside considerations that amounted to a charge of attempted murder. By considering charges that a soldier committed a physical attack with an additional condition, such as "assault with a deadly weapon" or "assault with the intent to kill," army commanders could impose harsher sentences than for simple assault. Private Patrick McGill received a sentence of six years in the Washington,

DC, penitentiary when he "did take a loaded musket and discharge it at . . . Private Otto Glime . . . with the intent to kill him."[205] When Private Isam Meadows used "a deadly weapon" against Private Daniel Guinn, the action led to Meadows serving a year in prison after an altercation that nearly ended in murder. Meadows fired his weapon at Guinn, "the ball grazing the left cheek and ear, and passing through the rim" of Guinn's hat.[206] When Corporal Edward Carter of the One Hundred Thirteenth New York violated the 9th Article of War by attempting to shoot Captain J.M. Murphy, he exacerbated the act by doing so "with the intent to kill." Even though Carter was not successful in wounding Murphy, the additional condition ensured that Carter received a death sentence.[207]

Although assault and attempted murder were somber offenses, murder charges took military justice to a new level of serious attention. When murder occurred within the army, the army had the legal right to adjudicate the offense within its own jurisdiction. The army tried violent offenses such as murder much in the same way as civilian courts, with some unique elements to the actual procedure (see next chapter). The prosecution of murder and attempted murder was rather straightforward, with the court-examining eyewitnesses, considering motive, and allowing extenuating circumstances. Self-defense was one such circumstance. "Two drunken soldiers got into a fight and one drew his pistol and shot the other in the leg," Lieutenant Pollock wrote his mother, "I arrested them and the wounded fellow was sent to the hospital and the other proved that he did it in self-defense so he got clear."[208] Unlike some other offenders, however, murderers received no sympathy or consideration from their comrades. The accounts of murder and attempted murder recorded in soldiers' letters and diaries did not contain much of a spectrum of opinion, unlike other elements and events of the soldiers' life. Instead, violent offenders commonly received unemotional descriptions of the sad events, reflecting the writer's disdain for such unsavory behavior. This, in turn, permitted the army to conduct a vigorous prosecution of violent offenders because the enlisted men approved of their actions instead of perceiving the subsequent trials as unfair control or persecution.

When civilians became involved in violent crimes against the Union army, however, legal proceedings became complicated. The intrusion of military law into civilian legal matters became even more contested when the army charged civilians with the murder of Union military personnel. Nothing in the Constitution, the Articles of War, or the Lieber Code clarified which legal system, civilian or military, held precedence in cases when enemy civilians murdered army officers. In the antebellum period, when civilians committed crimes against soldiers in peacetime, the army tended to allow civilian courts to render judgment. During the Civil War, however, there often were no civilian courts to take the case, and there was also no clear policy on the legitimacy of civilian courts if they did exist. If the Confederate states were the enemies of the Union army, then civilian courts were, by extension, also enemies and had no jurisdiction in military crimes. On the other hand, if the Confederacy, as the Lincoln administration contended, was still part of the United States but simply a region in rebellion, then civilian courts could press for jurisdiction in clashes between military and civilian law.[209] In most cases, the army opted to view what few local courts existed as enemy institutions, and imposed military law upon those civilians who committed violent crimes upon Union soldiers.

In occupied areas of the Confederacy, the army represented the only law and order in regions where civilian legal authority had ceased to exist. Forced to become ad hoc police, Union soldiers arrested, prosecuted, and punished those who committed crimes, particularly violent ones. In May 1863, for instance, Brigadier General George Wagner ordered a court-martial to try three Confederate citizens for the brutal murder of a Unionist family near Murfreesboro, Tennessee, leading to the execution of the convicted criminals a month later.[210] The army tried Reuben Laster, a Missouri civilian, by military court for the murder of another civilian, Buck Pearkins, because no other court existed in the area. The court accused Laster of killing Pearkins "by shooting him to death with a pistol loaded with gunpowder and leaden bullets" but lacked the evidence to convict and acquitted Laster.[211] David Wright, a physician from Norfolk, Virginia, faced a military tribunal for the death of Lieutenant Alanson Sanborn. Incensed at the presence of USCT units in Norfolk that forced white citizens to walk in the street, Dr. Wright impulsively voiced his disapproval to a passing column of soldiers. When Lieutenant Sanborn tried to arrest him for his comments, Wright mortally wounded Sanborn. After a nine-day trial, accompanied by an examination of his sanity when Dr. Wright exhibited some strange behavior, the court-martial rendered a verdict of guilty, and the army executed Wright by hanging in October 1863.[212] Unlike Dr. Wright's impulsive act, other murders by civilians were intentional acts of violence. Theodore Dodge recorded the arrest of "a man who has cut the throat of five of our stragglers. He confesses as much, and says he don't care if they do hang him."[213] A similar fate befell two Union deserters in Texas, "found dead . . . on the Chihuahua road yesterday morning," killed by either by highwaymen or vengeful Confederates. Civilians were often the source and target of attempted murder. When partisans ambushed and killed four Union soldiers in Missouri, their comrades suspected a local resident had lured them into the trap. "The boys all think him guilty," Charles Wills commented, "and have tried to get him away from the guard to kill him, but unsuccessfully so far."[214] Union soldiers in St. Louis also desired to get their hands on a "Mrs. Willow and a free colored woman named Hannah Courtena," who authorities "arrested yesterday for selling poisoned pies to the soldiers."[215] The first poisoning cases showed up in September, when a soldier informed his parents that "secessionists are thick here . . . they poison fruit & pies for the soldiers[,] 12 or so has been killed in this way."[216] The arrest of Mrs. Willow did not stop the poisonings in St. Louis, however, as seven months later Private David Helmick wrote to his family that "two of the 16th Iowa Regt. was poisoned to death by a woman by eating pies she sold them." He could not discern which woman sold the poisoned goods because "The barracks is full of women selling apples and eggs, pies, [and] cakes." Eager for revenge, Helmick promised, "If they find out who poisoned the boys she will have to suffer worse than death a dozen times."[217]

To prevent soldiers from engaging in retaliatory killings, the army took special pains to prosecute and punish soldiers convicted of maliciously killing civilians, with the death penalty a common instrument of punishment. When one of William Sherman's men robbed and murdered a civilian for his money, a court-martial quickly sentenced him to death as a sign of the army's resolve to protect civilian lives and property.[218] Private Peter Boileau of the First Delaware killed a boy named William Zoelnner of Baltimore. Despite an insanity plea, a court-martial sentenced Boileau to death only three weeks after the crime occurred.[219] In cases where murders took place in areas of the North where civilian trials were in operation, the army occasionally opted to turn soldiers over for civilian trial when civilians were the victims. Such was the case against Private Thomas Boyle. Accused of murdering a civilian in the New Mexico Territory, Boyle found himself in front of a civilian judge after his court-martial decided, "this case is turned over for trial by the civil authorities."[220]

The army reacted quickly when civilians forced the army to act, but when Union officers killed their fellow officers the army rarely pursued the matter. In two notable instances during the Civil War, high-ranking officers murdered other officers but received no significant punishment. On September 29, 1862, Union Brigadier General Jefferson C. Davis shot and killed Brigadier General William Nelson in Louisville, Kentucky. Although not his superior officer, Nelson, who had a reputation as a bully, treated Davis impolitely and ordered him out of Louisville lest Nelson place him under arrest. Davis, a native Indianan, appealed for assistance from Indiana Governor Oliver Morton, who accompanied Davis back to Louisville to confront Nelson regarding his rude behavior. When the two men met at the Galt Hotel, the two men argued and Nelson struck Davis and insulted Governor Morton before returning to his rooms on the second floor. Davis borrowed a pistol from a bystander, followed Nelson upstairs, and shot Nelson in the chest.[221] The other incident occurred in April 1863, when

Colonel Michael Corcoran, riding to inform the separated regiments of his brigade to prepare to move out, encountered Lieutenant Colonel Edgar Kimball on the road. When Corcoran insisted on passing through Kimball's guard without giving a password and Kimball barred his progress, Corcoran shot Kimball dead. The facts of the incident are confusing. Corcoran claimed that Kimball was drunk and drew his sword first, while Kimball's supporters claimed that Corcoran fired without provocation.[222] In both cases, the army declined to prosecute and punish either officer. The army subjected Corcoran to a nonjudicial board of inquiry, but did not file criminal charges. Shielded by the influential Governor Morton, Davis faced no inquiry or punishment at all. Why the army failed to press for prosecution in these cases is open to conjecture. In both instances, the murders took place in the heat of the moment, the impulsive act was obviously not premeditated, and a charge of murder without premeditation was hard to prove. Another possibility is that both of these incidents involved defense of honor, and as this was a personal matter between gentlemen, the army was disinclined to interfere. Regardless of the reasoning, both officers continued their careers without as much as a fine or formal reprimand. There was also an absence of prosecution when officers summarily killed soldiers. Rather than quarrels to protect their reputations, officers killed soldiers as a demonstration of discipline, and the army generally supported such actions. To common privates there was little distinction between summary justice and the outright murder of a soldier by an overbearing officer who possessed the power to determine their very life or death. After Lieutenant Virginius Van Geison summarily killed Sergeant Andrew Ekens for drunkenly defying his authority, an army inquiry determined that Van Geison acted properly, determining, "It was necessary to kill this Sergeant" and that all "Good soldiers will rejoice that the officer did his duty firmly." Ekens' friends did not agree, and some of them "attempted to take the life of the Lieutenant; no less than seven of them entering his boarding-house at one time for that purpose recently," but without success.[223]

When soldiers killed each other, it was usually the result of too much whiskey, too much free time, and too free access to weaponry. Teamster Daniel E. Bruce observed two drunken soldiers quarreling, resulting in a death when one of them struck the other over the head with a club, killing him instantly.[224] Whiskey turned otherwise good friends against each other. "A man in Co. B by the name of Burk that was stabed [sic] with a knife so that he died the other day by a man in the same mess," Henry Bear wrote his wife. "They was allways good friends before. The murderer was drunk. . . . It will go hard with him for it was murder in the first degree."[225] A quarrel in Colonel Elijah Cavins' regiment led to a knife fight between two men, ending with the death of one man and the arrest of the other, "a shocking affair [that] marred the beauty and quiet of this sabbath day."[226] The killing of a soldier by another soldier did not elicit much excitement amongst the officers. When soldiers killed officers, however, the retaliation for this blatant challenge to army authority was quick and severe. When a recruit murdered Captain Thomas McKay, his regiment quickly gathered $2000 as a reward for the apprehension of the offender, who eventually faced a court-martial and a death sentence after his capture.[227] Private Robert Kerr murdered Lieutenant Samuel Allyne on December 20, 1863, and the army prosecuted and executed him in Franklin, Texas, four months later.[228] Private Larkin Ray shot a surgeon in a tavern in Baton Rouge, Louisiana, mistaking the doctor for an officer that Ray had a physical altercation with earlier in the evening. Ray could not mount much of a defense, and died by hanging a few weeks later.[229] Private George Stetter tried to murder Major William Bell when he, as described in his court-martial, "coolly and deliberately did attempt to take the life of Major Bell by taking deliberate aim and firing." Stetter missed and received a five-year prison sentence.[230]

The institutional collision between the army and civilians also affected the army's prosecution of rape as a violent offense. As an intolerable offense in both the peacetime army and in civil society, the army granted no tolerance to soldiers accused of rape. The offense tainted both the reputation of the Union army and sullied the honor of being a soldier, and army leadership quickly moved to assure such denigrations did not occur. Unlike murder cases, where courts-martial followed the same legal practice to prosecute murder as in civil courts, military courts had more latitude in prosecuting rape cases. Civil courts required corroborating evidence, an eyewitness, or the direct testimony of the victim (whose character and reputation the defense might question) to obtain a conviction.[231] Army courts-martial, however, permitted a much looser prosecution. Victims could submit affidavits instead of testifying in person, substantiated evidence was not necessary, and although the reputation of the victim was open to question, the reputation and standing of the defendant amongst his regiment was of more importance to the court. That is not to say that the community standing of a rape victim did not come into account. A court-martial sentenced Private William Cole to ten years hard labor for raping a Maryland woman in 1864. Cole attempted to have his case reviewed, charging that he had consensual sex with a prostitute, as the alleged victim and her daughter "are lewd women" and "they keep a bawdy house."[232]

Sexual assault was a relatively rare occurrence, at least as far as its presence in disciplinary records seemed to indicate. About two hundred Union soldiers faced charges of rape and sexual assault during the war, a considerable number but still only a small fraction of the more than 100,000 total courts-martial. The number of cases may be slightly higher than perceived, however. Because sexual assault and rape made a civilian a victim, the army often proved willing to turn the offender over for prosecution in civilian courts. Therefore, while still rare compared to other violent offenses, the number of rapes committed by the Union army is likely higher than records indicate. Also difficult to ascertain is the precise definition of rape and/or sexual assault. Instances when authorities were not certain whether a sexual assault took place or not demonstrate the difficulties in establishing clear definitions. Private Robert Strong noted the insulting behavior of some Georgia women, whom the soldiers punished by spanking their "bare flesh," a sexual assault by modern standards but not one that attracted attention at the time.[233] On the other hand, when Thomas Clark, a teamster, "did, willfully, maliciously and feloniously lay violent hands upon the person of Sophia Morrison," the army court-martialed him for committing upon her "a grossly indecent outrage of exposing her person and drenching her with water." The court-martial sentenced Clark to four months at hard labor, but Major General Samuel Curtis thought the punishment too lenient, saying "The Army . . . has too proud a position to allow an act of indecency toward a female . . . to pass without the utmost condemnation" and believed that Clark should "be, at least, shot."[234] The army prosecuted still others soldiers for assaulting women by adding the additional charge of "assault with intent to rape," but in many of these cases the charge proved difficult to prove as a matter of intent and courts-martial proved unwilling to convict on such an amorphous charge.

Another issue relating to the extent of sexual assault is the modern interpretation of the intent to commit sexual assault and how that affected the perception of Union soldiers by Confederate civilians. Modern definitions of sexual assault include the threat, stated or implied, of rape as a form of sexual assault, and this broader definition certainly applied to the behavior of Union soldiers. Southern women developed a strong fear of violation as a product of Confederate propaganda, which played upon the predatory fears of isolated women to motivate their war effort.[235] Fearful that Union troops might find her in her remote home, Grace Elmore "thought long and intently upon the righteousness of suicide should that worst of all horrors happen."[236] Enough instances of implied or threatened use of sexual assault occurred to keep such fears active. Confederate authorities accused Major Thomas Jordan of the Ninth Pennsylvania Cavalry of forcing the women of Sparta, Tennessee, to prepare meals for his men or "upon failure he said he would turn his men loose upon them and he would not be responsible for anything they might do." Understandably, "The ladies understood this as a threat of rape."[237] In South Carolina, Louise Cornwell recounted how, when searching her home, Union soldiers "compelled her to unfasten her dress and they examined her person until they were satisfied" she was not concealing any valuables.[238] When in the process of robbing two civilian women, Private Geacomo Antonali crossed the line into sexual assault when, not believing their claims of not having any money, forcibly searched them without their consent.[239]

The army took the threat of sexual assault on lone women seriously. Although he did not sexually assault her, the army court-martialed 2nd Lieutenant Joseph Stoops after he "without authority and without the consent or permission of the occupant, enter the private room of a lady" and "insist[ed] upon remaining; this without her consent or permission, in an insulting and ungentlemanly manner, and against the expressed wishes of the lady." The court found Stoops guilty and dismissed him from the army.[240] When another soldier armed with a knife entered the home of a lone woman and refused to leave, Lieutenant Whitman Smith confronted the soldier and, armed with a knife provided by the lady of the house, removed and arrested the intruder.[241] Private John Mower faced a court-martial after he "without authority, enter[ed] the residence of Susan H. Dale, a person of African descent" and refused to leave. When Dale pushed him out, Mower struck her with "rock, stone, or portion of brick-bat," resulting in "a painful injury." When arrested and questioned by an officer about the incident, Mower became indignant that the army seemed more concerned about an African American civilian than him, stating "whatever a damned nigger said was all right, but what a white man said was nothing." His racist outrage aside, a court-martial sentenced him thirty days at hard labor.[242]

Swift retribution was the solution to the instances of sexual assault that the army did record. In case soldiers were unaware that rape was a capital offense, Major General Irvin McDowell ordered the printing and circulation around the army of General Order number 12, reminding soldiers that "The punishment for rape will be death; and any violence offered a female, white or colored, with the evident intent or purpose to commit a rape, will be considered as one, and punished accordingly." The order also ordered division commanders to "order immediate execution, by hanging" of all arrested rapists, "or by shooting, if the former should not be convenient."[243] Arrests of suspected rapists occurred quickly, even if in an inconvenient place or situation. Deep in South Carolina, a soldier reported the arrest of a member of his regiment. "Ben Allen Co K sent to Provost Marshalls [*sic*]," James Chapin noted in his diary, "for attempt to commit Rape & deserting [his] Post while acting as flanker."[244] If a court-martial found a soldier guilty of sexual assault, the usual method of death was hanging instead of a firing squad. Hanging was an ignominious death, the method of dispatching common criminals. By hanging sexual offenders, the army imposed an additional shame while also disassociating themselves from the condemned man, who was no longer an honorable soldier. General Patrick moved quickly when "a Mrs. Stiles here, who identified a man named Gordon, of the 72 New York, as the man who committed the outrage upon her person last Saturday." Patrick arrested Private Ransom Gordon immediately, and only two days later Patrick reported, "The Court Martial has finished the trial of the Rapers this evening" and sentenced Gordon and his accomplice to death by hanging.[245] When a Union soldier raped an elderly woman, the army conducted a public execution for the convicted offender, causing one observer to note that "hanging was too good for him."[246] Hanging was not always the final punishment. Private William Jones died by firing squad instead of hanging after convicted of rape in Kansas in 1864. Private Lewis Hardin and Corporal Daniel Tierce escaped a date with the hangman following their conviction for rape, instead receiving prison sentences at hard labor, ten years for Hardin and twelve years for Tierce.[247] Like other offenses, the army granted some, but not much, latitude for those accused of attempted rape and sexual assault. When Private John Keahl of the Sixteenth Illinois Cavalry "did assault . . . a girl thirteen years old . . . with the intent to commit rape," a court-martial found him guilty, sentenced him to a year at hard labor, and imposed a dishonorable discharge by drumming him out of camp so that his fellow soldiers might vent their disgust upon him as he left.[248] When Private John Locker committed assault and battery with the intent to commit rape, he received a relatively light three months at hard labor and a $40 fine.[249]

While the army moved to quell sexual assault among the white civilians of the Confederacy, it paid less regard to rape of female slaves. For various reasons, the army did not consider the sexual assault of black slaves as great an offense (or rarely, even an offense at all) as assaulting white women. Theories on this behavior included the stereotypical belief in the hypersexuality of slaves, the violation of slave women as the property of the Confederate enemy, and the separation of emancipation and military victory as the objectives of Union soldiers.[250] While rape was overall a rare offense, female slaves became the most common victims of the crime. Because army records and soldier correspondence provided little account of the extent of the offense, the records of the victims are the only measure of the crime. Esther Hill Hawks, a Northern relief worker in South Carolina, spoke of the frustration and outrage of the victims when she stated, "no colored woman or girl was safe from the brutal lusts of the soldiers—and by soldiers I mean both officers and men." Hawks detailed the assault of several women and the wounding of others who resisted an improper advance. Colonel Richard White, the commander of the Fifty-fifth Pennsylvania, Hawks charged, "kept colored women for his especial needs" and did nothing to stop the depredations of his men.[251] Southern newspapers included accounts of slaveowners who witnessed sexual assaults upon their slaves. Although one could presume that at least some of the accounts were fictional or exaggerated to inflame Southern opinion against their Northern enemy, enough reports existed to confirm that slave women were a common target of sexual assault. In 1863, the *Richmond Whig* reported that four Union soldiers raped two black women in front of their own family members.[252] A year later, in another sexual assault, "he [a Union soldier] caught her and forced her to a Brutal act," a slaveowner told the *Daily Richmond Inquirer* in reporting an assault, "in full view of my dwelling and Wife."[253] When the army did prosecute soldiers for assaulting African American women, a frequent lack of evidence led to either an acquittal or a minimal punishment. When two soldiers raped a slave woman in Cedar Creek, Virginia, for instance, the punishment was only a minor fine.[254]

THE INSTANCES OF THEFT, pillage, and violence perpetrated by the Union army reflected the new reality of the war. Instead of the youthful exuberance of new recruits, the Union army, by the second year of the war, became an army of grim survivalists. Confronted by a war that defied any military attempt to achieve victory and surrounded by defiant civilians that openly supported the enemy, Union soldiers gave in to some of the baser behaviors. Actions that, as law-abiding civilians only a short time earlier, the common Union soldier would have eschewed became common and expected behavior. The distinction between the property of the enemy and the property of the civilian blurred to the point of erasure, leading to personal violations that a perpetrator would have done his best to hide in his prewar existence. Instead, Union soldiers engaged in pillaging in large numbers, defiled the dead for souvenirs, and perpetrated violence upon each other in ways unthinkable to their families at home. Violent crimes, while not the most commom offense, still demonstrated that soldiers who killed on the battlefield were quite willing to kill in camp as well. While officers could not stop the activity at the point of occurrence, the army had to maintain order. As will be seen, the army was fully prepared to use its powers to try offenders by trial and inflict suitable punishments upon those convicted of serious offenses. Trying offenders, however, came with problems of its own, and Civil War military justice found out that a trial did not always amount to justice.

"NO PUNISHMENT CAN BE TOO SEVERE"

The Process of Courts-martial

Military justice has always existed in an odd relationship with the civilian courts most familiar to Americans. The Constitution recognized the unique nature of military law, and codified a separate court system for the army and navy of the United States, but their uniqueness is what made military courts seem so alien, unyielding, and harsh. Military courts have the popular representation of rigid and severe proceedings, but the perception existed largely because of the different procedures permitted to military courts than anyone familiar with civilian courts found restrictive and repressive. An easy association became if the Constitution ensured such liberal legal rights to every American, then any system that did not emulate those rights must be something inferior, and military courts were certainly something different. The structure, personnel, evidence rules, and offenses associated with military trials seemed like a foreign and, therefore, un-American and un-Constitutional way to prosecute offenders. In its own way, however, the Civil War courts-martial, while very different than civilian legal practice, proved very flexible and lenient when circumstances permitted. The judges seated to hear courts-martial undoubtedly had procedures and regulations to follow, but there was room for legal interpretation, clemency, and a system of review and appeal that ensured that courts-martial were anything but rigid and unmerciful.

Courts-martial were but the end of the military justice system, compared to the Provost Marshals, the law-enforcement section of the army. The Provost Marshals of the Union army were the face of military justice to the individual soldiers, the "authorities" who tried to block their access to whiskey, shut down the brothels, and keep them from sneaking out of camp. Provost Marshals, like any law enforcement branch, were often unpopular with the soldiers, as the marshals were the ones who denied soldiers their freedom and their ability to monitor themselves. Besides serving as the instrument that controlled the soldiers' freedom to engage in illicit activity, the marshal represented another form of army oversight. To citizen-soldiers and masculine warriors, the marshals represented the army's efforts at control. Citizen-solders resented the implication that their efforts needed monitoring, as a free citizen fighting for his country did so out of self-motivation and not because the army made him. Marshals also represented a challenge to masculine behavior, denying soldiers the ability to demonstrate their masculinity by drinking, whoring, stealing, or fighting when they saw fit. Instead, marshals were the instruments of army restraint, and the free masculinity of the Union soldier resented such restraint. While there were certainly plenty of Union soldiers who welcomed the presence of a marshal who made the more lawless elements of the army toe the line, for most Union soldiers the idea that the army needed a police force seemed excessive. Unfortunately, their own actions proved that an effective court system and law enforcement body was exactly what the army needed.

THE IDEA OF A MILITARY POLICE force did not occur until the Civil War. In the antebellum period, army units policed themselves, arrested their own offenders, and conducted their own courts-marital. As long as regimental officers obeyed the rules in the Army Regulations regarding the conduct of trials, courts-martial attracted little attention. The military realities of the Civil War changed the nature of military justice, however, and the army soon found a need for a police force of its own. The army received its first inkling of the discipline level of volunteer troops when the first regiments reached Washington in the summer of 1861. These citizen-soldiers, away from home in the nation's capital, had yet to witness their first battle, and their enthusiasm remained undampened. Pandemonium reigned in Washington as thousands of soldiers, ignoring their elected volunteer officers, ran rampant in the taverns and brothels of the city. The army could only maintain order by detaching elements of the Regular Army to police the streets.[1] The army commander, Irvin McDowell, authorized each regiment to appoint a single officer as regimental Provost Marshal, backed by ten enlisted men to serve as a police force. In a standard regiment of more than a thousand men, this represented merely a handful of personnel dedicated to ensuring the discipline of the other 99 percent of the regiment.[2] The system was unable to curb disciplinary infractions, and this bad situation became even worse following the Union army's defeat at the First Battle of Bull Run in July. As the defeated army streamed back into Washington, discipline broke down entirely. Ignoring their officers, demoralized soldiers defied attempts by their officers to reorganize them for the defense of the city, and thousands of soldiers remained beyond the control of the army, causing a total collapse of law enforcement and army discipline.[3]

When Abraham Lincoln appointed Major General George B. McClellan to command the Union armies around Washington, McClellan began the task of reasserting discipline. He appointed Colonel Andrew Porter to the new post of Provost Marshal for the city of Washington and authorized him to return soldiers to their units. Porter began his efforts by "closing up the liquor saloons in the capital, around which much drunkenness and riotous conduct has existed for some days."[4] An effective method of keeping officers with their units was to search the city's theaters in the evenings, and "the provost guard took several officers from the audience during the performance as they could not show their passes, having overstayed their limit. . . . The theaters are visited every night about 9 p.m."[5] To enforce his orders, Porter had at his disposal a force of one thousand infantry, a battery of artillery and a squadron of cavalry. In addition, Porter authorized each army division to appoint a divisional Provost Marshal, who could in turn organize as large a provost guard as was necessary to maintain order in their division.[6] Porter served effectively at his post, but poor health led McClellan to replace him with Brigadier General Marsena Patrick in October 1862. Soon after he assumed his post, Patrick revised the divisional system when General Ambrose Burnside assumed command of the Army of the Potomac. As part of his reorganization of the army, Burnside emphasized the importance of the Provost Marshals in maintaining discipline, and reflected this importance by reorganizing the Provost Marshals along corps instead of divisional lines, giving them more prominence and authority over larger groups of soldiers.[7] When Ulysses Grant received command of all Union forces, he further elevated the importance of the Provost Marshals to an advisory post in every army headquarters and senior command organization, where Grant considered them "necessary for the efficient working of the department."[8]

Other generals began to create similar positions in their commands early in the war, but they were ad hoc arrangements with relatively little central direction. None of the new Provost Marshals knew exactly what their duties were, but McClellan's directives to Porter and Patrick show the broad scope of issues faced by the armies. In his *Report on the Organization and Campaigns of the Army of the Potomac*, McClellan described the duties of the Provost Marshals as suppressing of marauding and depredations, controlling houses of vice, regulating stragglers on the march, executing arrests and supervising punishments, regulating public forms of amusement, handling deserters and POWs from the enemy, and responding to all complaints from citizens regarding the army's behavior.[9] This wide range of duties ensured that marshals became involved in all aspects of the war and became the primary instruments of military law enforcement. Later in the war, the addition of other duties led to a more formalized Provost Marshal structure. By 1862, the proliferation of desertion required additional marshals and the authority to work with local law enforcement to arrest deserters. In 1863, when Congress passed the Enrollment Act and the Union began to conscript soldiers, Provost Marshals gained the responsibility for enforcing the draft, registering potential draftees, and escorting recruits to the front lines. To facilitate these new duties, Secretary of War Edwin Stanton created the position of Provost Marshal General on September 24, 1862, a post to supervise the activities of the collective Provost Marshals (the Provost Marshal Corps or PMC) attached to the armies. In addition, the Provost Marshal General assumed all duties related to the conduct of the draft, the apprehension of deserters, and the maintenance of peace and order in occupied areas of the Confederacy.[10] Simon Draper served temporarily as the first Provost Marshal General, until replaced in March 1863 by Colonel James B. Fry. Under his leadership, Fry soon created a large organization divided into specialist branches. The Enrollment Branch conducted the draft, the Medical Branch conducted all physical examinations of potential recruits and draftees, the Volunteer Recruiting Branch distributed federal bounty money and other volunteer enticements, the Disbursing Branch handled all bookkeeping and finance issues, and the Deserters Branch oversaw the pursuit of deserters. In addition, the Veterans Reserve Corps reported to Fry, who used its members to hunt deserters and escort recruits to the front.[11] Although Fry was officially in charge of all Provost Marshals, his duties largely involved conducting the draft (especially as the draft became increasingly unpopular), which left the day-to-day regulation of military discipline to the army Provost Generals.

True to the description established by McClellan, Provost Marshals undertook a wide range of tasks, and every violation of the Articles of War fell under their authority to act. The duties varied depending upon where the marshal served. In army camps near the front line, their job was to maintain camp discipline. "There has been a new feature introduced into our camp duties," Charles Haydon wrote, "to wit a Provost Guard of 80 men & the necessary officer. . . . Their duty is to arrest soldiers who are more than ¼ mile from the camps without a pass. To prevent stealing from peddlers. To seize all liquor & beer . . . [and] To keep prostitutes off the ground . . . They have no posts but roam about in squads wherever there is a probability of their service being needed."[12] In cities close to the front line, the marshals had the responsibility for maintaining order and stopping desertion from the army. On provost guard in Washington, DC, Alfred Bellard described his duty as "to preserve order, arrest all soldiers without passes and see that no one, citizen or soldier, was on the streets after 10 o'clock at night without a countersign." To demonstrate their resolve, Bellard noted that their officers instructed them, in plain view of the public, "to load with ball cartridge so that the people could see in passing that we were fully prepared to shoot should the occasion require it."[13] Marshals in occupied areas of the Confederacy had the responsibility to "attend to all prisoners, deal with citizens (administer oaths, take paroles, etc.), give all passes for citizens and soldiers leaving, have charge of all soldiers straggling from their regiments, issue permits to sutlers, and overlook the cotton trade."[14] A marshal on draft duty in the North had the burden of "Enrolling all qualified men, conducting the draft, enlisting recruits, tracking down deserters, dealing with enrollment evaders and draft resistors, and contracting for supplies, sustenance, and transportation."[15] Once a battle commenced, provost troops were "everywhere . . . escorting and guarding the Generals . . . rallying the lines at broken places . . . filling up gaps in the lines until larger bodies [of troops] could come up . . . acting as Aides-de-camp . . . [or] carrying dispatches."[16] Soldiers from the Fifth USCT assigned to the provost guard had the thorny problem of dealing with civilians in the absence of civilian law and order, untangling local disputes, protecting former slaves, and policing freedmen.[17]

Provost Marshals themselves were as close as the Union army came to creating a formal military police force, but they were but a relative handful of officers in a very large army. To provide force to the marshals' actions, the armies assigned units to provost duty. These soldiers, in turn, became extemporized law enforcement, making the arrests, stopping the deserters, and administering the punishments that military discipline demanded. As problems mounted, the army had to devote more and more soldiers to the task of keeping their fellow soldiers from breaking the rules. By 1864, for instance, Marsena Patrick required a full brigade and several unassigned companies of infantry, along with additional cavalry and artillery units, to maintain order. The provost guard numbered 6100 officers and men, out of a total strength of 185,400 soldiers in the Army of the Potomac. This represented 3 percent of the total army strength, a far cry from the fraction of a percent that Irvin McDowell thought sufficient.[18]

As a rule, soldiers enjoyed their tenure on the provost guard, as the benefits outweighed the disadvantages. Soldiers serving as provost guards usually did not have to stand on picket duty, did not have to drill, enjoyed more comfortable lodgings and better provisions, and, as an extension of their duties, got to stand around and do nothing for long periods of time. Soldiers certainly enjoyed the perks that provost duty garnered them. Private Charles Wills was glad to go on the provost guard as "It relieves us from picket duty, fatigue, etc.," and the soldiers got to enjoy "quarters in a house (there are a sofa, two rocking chairs, soft-bottomed chairs, a library," and other amenities that other soldiers certainly did not enjoy. Wills felt absolutely no guilt about his lodgings, believing "I've soldiered long enough to never refuse these little good things Providence throws in my way."[19] Samuel Bliss, in a letter to his wife from Beaufort, South Carolina, related his great pleasure at serving as a provost guard as he could go anywhere he wanted, had a real roof over his head, and had someone else to cook his meals for him.[20]

There were other unofficial perks to serving on provost duty. Alfred Bellard enjoyed being on the provost guard, especially when the local merchants provided them with free freshly baked bread and cigars.[21] William Clayton preferred provost duty at Fort Gaines, Alabama, despite the tasks that meant "We do not get much rest" because "Balls and dances have been the order of the day (or rather night) for some time past. Ladies are quite numerous here."[22] With such social mixing, relationships became an inevitable result. "Weddings, white and colored, are just now the subject of gossip," Zenas Haines wrote while on the provost guard in New Bern, North Carolina, "One of our own corporals has been and gone and done it, and one of the pretty natives of Newburn [sic] is now Mrs. Lawrence."[23] It is not surprising that when soldiers came off provost duty they were not particularly happy about the change. "We were relieved from provost duty here yesterday," William Bentley wrote from North Carolina. ". . . [S]ome of the boys are not in a very good humor about the arrangement."[24] The Fourteenth Wisconsin lost its comfortable provost duty because the colonel of the Seventy-second Illinois managed to finagle his regiment into the desirable duty.[25]

In exchange for the benefits of provost duty, the army expected soldiers serving as marshals to undertake the essential, mundane, and sometimes dangerous tasks necessary to keep the army together. Provost guards were the main enforcers of regulations regarding alcohol, the suppressors of plundering, and the deterrent against desertion. None of these duties were pleasant, some of them were dangerous, and all of them caused resentment by the soldiers under the eye of the provost guard. "The duty is not very hard," James Newton wrote his parents. ". . . I have to station a guard at the Gang-plank of every board as soon as it lands and examine all passes and search all baggage belonging to citizens before allowing them on board" in Natchez, Mississippi.[26] As part of this responsibility to search everything, provost guards drove off whiskey dealers, prevented soldiers from leaving camp, and shut down brothels. Soldiers on provost duty had the unenviable task of herding reluctant recruits and bounty-jumpers to the front line, using deadly force to get them there if necessary. When battles ended, the soldiers of the provost guard also endured the ghastly task of arranging for the burial of the dead.[27] As a mid-war expediency, the PMC also became an intelligence service. Displeased with the quality of intelligence information generated Allan Pinkerton, his predecessor's" chief intelligence officer, General Joseph Hooker organized a Bureau of Military Information though his Provost Marshals in the Army of the Potomac. Colonel George H. Sharpe headed the new intelligence service, which began operations in March 1863 and performed superior service throughout the war.[28]

As the face of law and order, soldiers had no particular fondness for Provost Marshals, and their actions proved it. Finding a Provost Marshal's office with no one around, soldiers in New Orleans pillaged the place and carried off what they wanted.[29] Angry with Provost Marshals who arrested some of their comrades, soldiers from the Twenty-seventh USCT nearly rioted, and one of the soldiers fired at one marshal before the mob dispersed.[30] The Seventy-ninth New York so disliked the marshal attached to their unit that they lured him into a cave in Tennessee and rolled a large rock across the entrance to entrap him inside. Other soldiers rescued the marshal a short time later, but the event leaves an observer to wonder if it was a prank or a real attempt to finish off the marshal.[31] Alcohol invariably caused problems. When a "Corporal Fraser . . . detailed as a detective by the Provost Marshal" shut down a number of liquor dealers near their camp, angry soldiers waited until he visited the latrine "into which he was rudely thrust and forced under until he was nearly choked by what he was forced to swallow, and before he was allowed to scramble out and escape."[32] Alcohol also generated violence toward marshals. A drunken officer fired at provost officer Second Lieutenant William Tyrell as he tried to arrest him in Washington, DC. The officer wounded Tyrell in the neck, but Tyrell fired three shots in return and killed his assailant.[33]

Soldiers may not have liked the restraints the marshals placed upon them, but many communities did. At the mercy of large numbers of ill-disciplined soldiers, many communities had only the protection of the Provost Marshals in maintaining law and order. Recognizing that the marshals kept the peace, some communities demonstrated their thanks. "The Provost Guards are an imperative necessity," the Indianapolis *Daily Journal* reported in 1864. "They protect us and we should sustain them."[34] After the occupation of Fredericksburg, Virginia, Provost Marshals instituted a tight curfew, cracked down on rowdy taverns, and purged almost the entire city of prostitution. Crime and disorder declined, although the occasional miscreant disrupted the peace, such as Private Thomas Stewart, whom the marshals described as "dressed in female dress and very disorderly."[35] Policing cities also meant preventing soldiers from engaging in theft or plundering. John Ferguson was unhappy about the limited pickings around his regimental camp because "2 regiments are on provo [*sic*] duty and aresting [*sic*] every soldier they find doing anything wrong."[36] The Forty-eighth Pennsylvania did such a good job of protecting civilian property in Newport News, Virginia, that the local citizenry circulated a petition to keep them on the job when they received order to report for field duty.[37]

Provost Marshals also supervised soldiers whom courts-martial sentenced to periods of incarceration or hard labor. Each division in the army had a sub-depot for housing short-term prisoners, while those serving long-term sentences spent their time in state penitentiaries. These sub-depots housed prisoners for only a short time while courts-martial or other procedures decided the prisoners' final disposition. Under ideal circumstances, these sub-depots segregated their prisoners into ordinary military offenders of the Union army, prisoners of war from the Confederate army, and "prisoners of the state," civilians arrested for violations against the Union army and government. Under most circumstances, however, such clear separation proved impossible due to small facilities and the transient nature of the prisoners held in them.[38] In the chaotic days after Bull Run, the Provost Marshals in Washington, DC, arrested a large number of state prisoners. Often arrested on the slightest of evidence in a climate that saw Confederate treachery everywhere, prisons operated by the Provost Marshals bulged with numerous prisoners, even if most of the accused were soon released.[39] The bulk of the prisoners handled by the Provost Marshals, however, were ordinary military offenders sentenced to short-term prison sentences. "There has not been a day since we were paid that there has not been some of our boys drunk," Daniel Sawtelle wrote. "One of them is in the provost [jail] at Hilton Head sentanced [*sic*] there for six months."[40]

In the course of their duties, Provost Marshals dealt with issues involving civilians who were ostensibly beyond the control of military law, yet committed offenses or undertook actions that affected military operations around them. When such situations occurred, marshals did their best to muddle through the ill-defined border between civilian rights (especially those of a rebellious people) in wartime. Usually, these cases involved situations where Provost Marshals had to act as ersatz local police in occupied areas. Under normal circumstances, the use of soldiers as police was not the perfect solution. Soldiers were not trained in the nuances of negotiation and restraint necessary for police work, but in the absence of local law enforcement no other alternative existed. "The soldier is still a citizen," Colonel Henry Scott wrote in his *Military Dictionary*, "lying under the same obligation, and invested with the same authority to preserve the peace." At the same time, however, soldiers were not above the law when acting as police forces, and "all occasions when the troops are employed in restoring or maintaining public order . . . [for] the loss of life or limb . . . a military man may be called to stand at the bar of a criminal court."[41] Attached to the Tenth New York, Provost Captain Charles Stocking arrested a "noted Secessionist in the vicinity" of the regimental camp in possession of "a considerable quantity of commissary stores" stolen from the army. "Captain Stocking and his guard," an observer noted approvingly, "are wide awake, and will not be slow to bring justice to all offenders against military law and order."[42] At Murfreesboro, Tennessee, occupying Union soldiers conducted the execution of a local civilian, "a murderer" who "cut a man's tongue out and ears off and killed him because he would not tell where his money was."[43] Stationed in Texas, the army expected the Twenty-ninth USCT to perform many tasks, including "to act as a magistrate in all cases of dispute."[44] Relations between occupied Confederates and army soldiers/police was always tense, but even more so when USCT troops performed the duty. When a local resident confessed that he wished to see a passing USCT captured and subjected to Confederate reprisal, the "assistant Provost Marshal, after scaring him pretty well, made him go before the negro company and (upon bended knees) ask their forgiveness."[45] If locals made life difficult for the Union army, the Provost Marshals could supplant local government and place a town under martial law. Finding a disruptive community as the Army of the Potomac pursued the Confederates after Gettysburg, Marsena Patrick entered Warrenton, Virginia, "put the town under Martial Law & went to work."[46]

THE PMC'S CLOSEST ALLY in military justice was the JAG Corps. The army reinstated the position of judge advocate in the aftermath of the Mexican War, a conflict that saw the army embroiled in some murky legal situations. Major John F. Lee, appointed to the reestablished post in 1849, still held the position when the Civil War broke out. Lee soon found himself overwhelmed by the work generated by the new conflict, incapable of rendering timely decisions regarding difficult matters, and under suspicion because of his Virginia ancestry. As the sole legal representative of the army, Lee participated in every general court-martial case that arose during 1861 and early 1862, a task that proved impossible for one man to accomplish. He further questioned many of the wartime policies and practices of the Union army, especially those that seemed to impinge upon civilian rights and property. This placed Lee, a mere major, in the difficult position of judging and occasionally overturning the dictates of not only higher-ranking offices but also the President and the Secretary of War. He especially lost the confidence of the War Department when he halted the execution of Ebenezer Magoffin, brother of the Governor of Kentucky, on charges of murder and engaging in guerilla activity on the grounds that military commissions could not supplant civilian courts and "military commanders have no power to inflict death except by sentence of courts-martial."[47] Lee's ruling proved unpopular, as it seemed to deny the army the ability to enforce national law and restore order in areas controlled by disloyal elements and lacking loyal civilian leadership. Not surprisingly, when the War Department moved to expand the Judge Advocate General office, Lee was not part of the army's plan. He subsequently resigned his commission and retired, later serving in the Maryland state senate.[48]

Uncertain leadership was not the only problem facing the army's legal arm. Like the Mexican War, the Civil War generated complex questions regarding civilian rights and property issues. The Civil War, however, was even more complex because the enemy was ostensibly protected by the same Constitution that the Union army claimed to honor and defend. As soldiers seized property, took slaves from their owners, occupied Confederate soil, and arrested those deemed disloyal to the Union cause, each occurrence generated a potential legal quandary that required an agent to explain the army's reasons and justifications for its actions. A single JAG could not represent the army in all instances, especially one whose loyalties were in question and who lacked formal legal training. Pressed by its legal burdens, in July 1862, Congress authorized the creation of ten field judge advocates who served in the field armies and department commands, and reported to a senior JAG. The JAG himself coordinated the actions of the field judge advocates, served as a central registry of court cases, and consulted with the War Department and other government agencies regarding legal issues related to military matters. The new position carried the equivalent rank of colonel, giving the position more leverage than Lee's rank of major.[49] The man selected to fill the new position was Joseph Holt. A prominent lawyer in his early career, Holt was also a respected political figure. He had served as Postmaster General and, after the resignation of John Floyd, Secretary of War in the final months of James Buchanan's administration. Despite his association with the Buchanan's Democratic administration, Holt threw his support behind the Lincoln administration and used his influence to ensure that his native Kentucky remained loyal to the Union. Holt remained in his post for the rest of the war, overseeing several major legal debates and major cases, including the court-martial of Major General FitzJohn Porter, the prosecution of Congressman Clement Vallandigham, the Northwest Conspiracy and the subsequent case of *Ex Parte Milligan*, and the conviction and execution of the Lincoln conspirators.[50]

Tasked with confirming the sentences of field judge advocates, Holt had the obligation to ensure the legal propriety of all convictions. Although acting in relatively unclear legal waters in the early years of the war, the War Department gave Holt much clearer instructions on how to proceed following the publication of *General Order 100: Instruction for the Government of Armies of the United States in the Field*, also known as the Lieber Code, in April 1863. A broad clarification of the rights, obligations, and limitations imposed upon soldiers under the accepted practices of war, the Lieber Code provided clear definitions of what soldiers could do and what they could not do in relation to the enemy. This was a clear distinction from the limitations and obligations of the Articles of War. The Articles were regulations that defined the soldiers' place within the army structure and delineated the powers the government and army had over the average soldier's existence. The Lieber Code, however, defined the boundaries of behavior in relation to a soldier's contact with enemy forces, occupied civilians, the appropriation of property, and other questions of civilian and rebel rights generated by the war up to that point. Created by a panel headed by legal expert Francis Lieber and a number of military advisors, the Code became the first codification of the laws of war, a model adopted by later efforts such as the Hague Conventions. In addition to Francis Lieber, the Code was the product of Generals George Cadwalader, George L. Hartsuff, Ethan A. Hitchcock, and John H. Martindale. All were senior officers, graduates of West Point, and, with the exception of Hartsuff, considered too elderly to hold major field commands. Not surprisingly, the subsequent code reflected their preference for Regular Army levels of discipline and determination to rein in the looser discipline of the masses of citizen-soldiers.

Despite the influence of these senior officers, the Code most reflected the legal, political, and military opinions of Francis Lieber, a man whose background and ideology made him particularly suited to create the Union army's policy for subduing the South. Born in Prussia in 1798, Lieber grew up in the turbulent years of the Napoleonic Wars. He became an ultranationalist and supported the idea of a unified Germany, but one led by a democratic style of government, not the rule of a Prussian Hohenzollern. Lieber became a follower of the political teachings of Friedrich Jahn, an ultranationalist organizer whose followers created a number of Burschenschaften, student-led patriotic fraternities, throughout Germany. Prussian authorities cracked down on the movement when one of its members assassinated August von Kotzebue, and Jahn and Lieber found themselves in prison. Although jailed only four months, the incident tainted Lieber's reputation, and he found it difficult to complete his university education. Growing disenchanted with political developments in Prussia, Lieber went to Greece to support the Greeks in their bid for independence from the Ottoman Empire in 1821.[51] After fighting for three years, Lieber returned to Germany to find he was still considered a political outcast. He lived in England for a year before immigrating to America in 1827. Lieber engaged in a number of academic pursuits in Boston, including the founding of the *Encyclopedia Americana*, a task that put him in contact with many notable political and scholarly figures. In 1837, he accepted a position to teach history and economics at South Carolina College (now the University of South Carolina) in Columbia. Lieber remained at the institution until 1856, when the growing sectional rivalry prompted him to accept a teaching post at Columbia University. Lieber had become an ultranationalist for his adopted country, and his defense of the Constitution and antagonism toward the (as he viewed it) undemocratic control of the South by the planter class made his tenure in Columbia impossible. Not every member of the Lieber family agreed, however. Lieber's eldest son, Oscar, stayed behind in Charleston, later joined the Confederate army, and died at the 1862 Battle of Williamsburg.[52] When the Civil War broke out, Lieber's intellectual and legal reputation attracted the attention of General Henry W. Halleck, who served as Abraham Lincoln's military advisor. Halleck approached Lieber about writing a number of legal opinions and advisory statements in support of actions taken by the Lincoln administration. Between 1861 and 1862, Lieber wrote a number of documents supporting the legality of actions ranging from the blockade of Southern ports to the retention of fugitive slaves to dealing with guerillas. Therefore, Halleck considered Lieber the ideal person to formulate a formal government policy that defined the parameters of military law, the document that became General Order 100.

The Lieber Code provided a great service in its clarity in defining both the laws and usage of war. The laws of war, behaviors generally accepted by all warring nations in the Western military tradition, embraced such general concepts as the distinction between combatants and noncombatants, the protection of prisoners of war, and the moral conduct of soldiers. Most nations, for instance, accepted as the laws of war that prisoners, especially civilians, were not to be massacred, that it was acceptable to fire on advancing enemy soldiers but not at retreating ones, or that armies might appropriate civilian property suitable to sustain an army (contraband) but personal property unsuitable for military operations was to remain inviolate. Before the Civil War, the relatively small armies of professional soldiers, especially in Europe, collectively knew the laws of war and did not need a codified system to remind them. The mass of volunteer regiments made up of citizen-soldiers that comprised the Union army, on the other hand, had no institutional memory when it came to the laws of war. The citizen army, as one postwar observer opined, was "composed in great part, of men taken from civil pursuits; most of whom were unfamiliar with military affairs, and so utterly unacquainted with the usages of war" that "great harm not infrequently resulted before the decisions could be reversed by competent [read: professional] authority."[53] In support of the laws of war, General Order 100 codified many generally accepted limitations on military force. Article 76, for instance, demanded that "Prisoners of war shall be fed upon plain and wholesome food, whenever practicable, and treated with humanity," while Article 38 ensured that "Private property, unless forfeited by crimes or by offenses of the owner, can be seized only by way of military necessity, for the support or other benefit of the Army or of the United States." Article 29 best summed up the entire purpose for the laws of war: "Peace is their normal condition; war is the exception. The ultimate object of all modern war is a renewed state of peace."[54]

If the Lieber Code was innovative because it codified the laws of war for the first time, it was also regressive because it merely codified elements of the war that already existed, and therefore legalized what was already happening instead of creating boundaries out to which armies could expand their activities. These cases of retroactive codification reflect the usage of war, the particular circumstances outside of the laws of war that are particular to an individual conflict, which emerged from the Civil War. The Civil War introduced a number of thorny legal issues involving the confiscation of civilian property at a time when the belligerent status of Confederate civilians was not certain. The Union army began the process of dismantling the institution of slavery, and military commissions established law and order in occupied portions of the South. The army engaged in these activities as a matter of expediency and from the broad viewpoint that any Southern resident, regardless of purported Union sympathies, was a rebel until proven otherwise. Southern property became not only assets for Union military campaigns, but a means to defeat the enemy as economic warfare became a common feature of all military campaigns. The American army had no qualms about seizing enemy property in earlier wars, but the pillaging of personal property reached epidemic proportions and motivated the Confederacy to fight only harder. Instead of acting to squelch this activity, General Order 100 acted to retroactively legalize and justify such behavior.

The justification for legalizing the usages of war is summed up in the final article, number 157, that declares, "Armed or unarmed resistance by citizens of the United States against the lawful movements of their troops is levying war against the United States, and is therefore treason." Under such a declaration, any effort to suppress the rebellion that did not reach the level of outrageous cruelty achieved legitimacy. Articles 27 and 28 legalized retaliation against an enemy outrage, recognizing, "A reckless enemy often leaves to his opponent no other means of securing himself against the repetition of barbarous outrage" than "a means of protective retribution." Article 84 granted soldiers the authority to summarily deal with "Armed prowlers . . . who steal within the lines of the hostile army for the purpose of robbing, killing, or of destroying . . . are not entitled to the privileges of the prisoner of war." Lieber admonished armies to protect "works of art, libraries and scientific collections" but at the same time permitted armies to "tax the people or their property, to levy forced loans, to billet soldiers, or to appropriate property, especially houses, lands, boats or ships, and the churches, for temporary and military uses." Especially crucial, Articles 42 and 43 justified the seizure of slaves from their owners not only as a military necessity, but from the moral principle that "as the law of nature is concerned, all men are equal." Any slave freed by the army or who fled to the army for protection was "immediately entitled to the rights and privileges of a freeman," adding additional legal weight to the recently enacted Emancipation Proclamation.[55] In the end, General Order 100 did not modify the army's behavior in the field. Quite the opposite, it promoted previously unacceptable activities, especially property crimes, as acceptable military practice.

GROUCHO MARX ONCE QUIPPED that "Military justice is to justice what military music is to music." The implication that military trials denied fundamental liberties to its defendants is an easy, if not inaccurate, leap to make. Armies required discipline, and discipline required the threat of force to establish its legitimacy. Invariably, soldiers fell afoul of the rules and faced the consequences by finding themselves in front of a military tribunal. Denied the right to do as they pleased, convicted soldiers found it easy to complain about a legal system that treated them unfairly, even if the procedure followed clearly established rules to the letter. Disgruntled soldiers in the Civil War were no different, and criticisms of the military justice system appeared almost as soon as the war started. "However plausible the principles," a critic of military law promulgated, ". . . in actual practice they dwindle to little else than the will of the officer who details the court." Instead of the measured and controlled climate of a civilian court, "Heaven help . . . [common soldiers] who have their cases put through at lightening speed, before a court under marching orders, and expecting momentarily to move."[56] Neither the accusation of rigid discipline nor trials on the march are correct, however, as the Union army's military justice system worked reasonably well. Despite times when the system almost had too many cases to handle, courts-martial never lost the flexibility to apply the flexible notion of justice to the inflexible letter of the law.

Guided by the Articles of War, Regulations of the Army, and General Order 100, the army established and operated a judicial system patterned on those of previous wars. A two-tier system emerged with general courts-martial reserved for major violations that threatened the security and success of the army, and regimental courts-martial reserved for minor offenses within the unit. The army also recognized garrison courts-martial, which were the equivalent of regimental courts-martial but distinguished between units in fixed locations and regimental courts-martial for units in the field. In 1862, when the number of courts-martial cases began to escalate, Congress changed the regimental courts-martial, which required a panel of officers from the same regiment, to Field Officer Courts, which could use officers from any regiment on the judgment panel. Despite the change, diaries and letters for the remainder of the war still called the lesser courts "regimental courts-martial."[57] Clear jurisdictional boundaries separated the two tiers of the courts-martial system. While regimental commanders could try lesser cases within their own units, only a senior officer (a corps or department commander) or the attached JAG could call a general court-martial. Due to its elevated status as the superior court-martial, general courts-martial heard only specific types of cases, offenses placed beyond the jurisdiction of a regimental court-martial. Among the offenses restricted to the jurisdiction of general courts-martial were disobeying orders, desertion, bounty-jumping, mutiny, pillaging of property, sleeping while on duty, revealing passwords to the enemy, or espionage.[58] Regimental courts-martial had jurisdiction in all other cases, handling such offenses as insubordination, drunkenness on duty, straggling, minor theft, or a catchall offense known as "conduct prejudicial to good order and military discipline." This offense, Article 99 of the Articles of War, theoretically made any action performed by a soldier a criminal offense if his superior officer deemed it as detrimental to unit discipline.[59] Unable to control a soldier through traditional means, an Article 99 court-martial was often a last resort. Regimental court-martials, due to their limited jurisdiction, could impose only limited punishments. Lesser courts-martial could demote NCOs convicted of offenses, impose minor fines or suspensions of pay, or imprison a convicted soldier (either at hard labor or not) for no more than one month. Regimental courts-martial often got around the punishment limit by imposing a punishment for each charge in the offense, rather than for the single finding of guilt. Only general courts-martial could impose more serious punishments, such as a dishonorable discharge, cashiering of an officer, lengthy prison terms, or the death penalty. Both courts had the discretion to imprison soldiers either in solitary confinement or on a diet of bread and water, but the duration of the punishment was limited to avoid unnecessary cruelty. The punishment could only last fourteen days, and the same number of days had to elapse before the punishment resumed, and the total number of days could not exceed eighty-four in any one year.[60] Every officer and soldier in the Union army faced the potential of judicial punishment, as did honorary officers, such as chaplains and surgeons, and civilians that had regular support roles within the army, such as teamsters and sutlers.[61] Civilians with military contracts were also liable to face courts-martial for criminal offenses related to their contracts. Army authorities arrested William Cozens of Philadelphia, for instance, for fraud and bribery associated with the issuing of an army contract for tents. Tried by military court in February 1865, the panel fined Cozens nearly $74,000 and ordered his confinement until he paid the fine.[62]

Regardless of the type of court-martial, the proceedings began with an officer filing both charges and specifications against the accused soldier. The charge identified the specific violation of the Articles of War, and the specification included the time, place, and specific details about the violation. Clarity was necessary when an officer began a legal proceeding. Officers could not file a charge without filing specifications, or vice versa, at the same time. Officers could not file charges against unknown persons or an entire group or unit, and if specifications were not clear more often than not the charge would not proceed to trial. Upon receipt of the specifications and charges, the regimental commander (regimental courts-martial) or judge advocate (general court-martial) seated a panel to hear the case. In general courts-martial, the JAG himself might not participate in a trial, but instead seat a panel for a set duration of time to hear any cases that should arise in their jurisdiction over that time period. This permitted the JAG to supervise multiple trial sessions at the same time, and became particularly useful when desertions and other major violations began to escalate. In such instances, a court-martial heard a variety of cases. Seated on one panel in 1864, Lieutenant Edmund Halsey heard cases ranging from desertion to petty theft.[63] Unlike civilian trials, where a defendant faced a single judge and multi-person jury, the panel of officers (under the Articles of War, only commissioned officers could adjudicate a court-martial, which eliminated those who held honorary officer ranks, such as chaplains and surgeons) acted as both judge and jury. In regimental courts-martial, officers of the accused soldier's own regiment served on the panel, although outside officers could sit if not enough officers were available. For general courts-martial, any commissioned officer could sit on the panel except in cases were an officer was the defendant. In those cases, Article 75 of the Articles of War stipulated that officers on the panel had to be of equivalent or higher rank; a junior officer could not judge a superior. While only three officers comprised a panel for a less court-martial, for general courts-martial the panel required at least five but not more than thirteen officers.[64] A Judge Advocate presided over the proceedings, and also took part. In regimental courts-martial, one of the officers served as the Judge Advocate, while in general courts-martial the judge advocate or an officer appointed by him served as the chief court officer. The JAG's role was not to serve exclusively as a judge (although he did get a vote in the judgment phase of the trial), but instead was to act as the ensurer of justice. The Judge Advocate's obligation was to ensure a fair trial, to guarantee to make sure the defendant's rights were upheld, to make sure that the court engaged in legal use of evidence and procedure. The Judge Advocate, therefore, had to perform duties of both prosecutor and defender. The Judge Advocate also appointed a panel member as secretary of the proceedings, charged with maintaining a written account of the trial, the same task performed by a court reporter today.

Once the panel was seated, the defendant entered the court. In the presence of the defendant as required by the Articles of War, both the panel and judge advocate swore an oath to conduct a fair and unbiased trial. The judge advocate then introduced the members of the panel and asked the defendant if he had any reservations about any of the officers seated to hear his case. If the defendant had reservations, he could request the removal of the officer in question. The panel could either remove the officer or make inquires as to why the soldier objected. If the panel ruled the soldier's objections were not valid, the officer stayed. At the court-martial of Private William Hammond, for example, "He objected to Lieutenant Davison because he had expressed an opinion in substance that the Boys then under 'charges would be Shot.' . . . Maj. Lugenbeel, when satisfied Hammond's grounds were tenable, excused Davison," but in the next regimental court-martial when Private Lloyd Sands objected to the presence of a particular officer the officer remained because "being President of the Court [judge advocate] saved him."[65] In the vast majority of cases, however, soldiers simply approved the panel to move the proceedings forward. The judge advocate then read the charges and specifications against the defendant, and asked the accused soldier to plead guilty or not guilty to each of the individual charges. As in a civilian court, the court-martial considered any nonresponse as a not guilty plea.[66] If a soldier pled guilty, then the proceedings went immediately to the sentencing phase, as the court-martial had no interest in why a soldier committed his crimes, only that the proceedings reach a conclusion. Some officers preferred that soldiers show at least some contrition, and when soldiers pled guilty as an act of defiance, some feathers got ruffled. "We have just tried a Corpl. upon the charge of engaging in a sort of mob against a guard," Major Charles Mattocks noted in his diary. "The graceless scamp pleads guilty, and . . .

displays a most unlimited amount of 'cheek,' but a good sentence will bring him to his senses."[67]

After entering the defendant's pleas, the panel began the questioning of witnesses. Both the army (prosecution) and accused (defense) could compel military personnel to testify on their behalf. Courts-martial had no authority, however, to subpoena civilians to testify.[68] As an inducement to participate in military justice, judge advocates could provide civilian witnesses $3 per day to compensate them for travel and other expenses.[69] As in civilian trials, the rules governing testimony evidence were strict. Witnesses had to have firsthand knowledge of either the defendant or the circumstances described in the specifications. Hearsay or implied knowledge was not admissible, nor could the questioning lead the witnesses toward evidence they did not possess. Perjury, as in civilian courts, brought severe repercussions. Both the prosecution and defense had the right to cross-examine the witnesses produced by the other, but in these circumstances a soldier was at a disadvantage. While the Army Regulations permitted a soldier to have an advocate present in court, the advocate served only as an advisor and was not permitted to speak directly to the court or query the witnesses. "A lawyer is not recognized by a court-martial," one court manual opined, "though his presence is tolerated, as a friend of the prisoner, to assist him by advice in preparing questions for witnesses, in taking notes, and shaping the defense."[70] They could advise the defendant on what questions to ask or what witnesses to call, but against a judge advocate with previous legal experience, a soldier was at a great disadvantage.

At the end of the cross-examination, the panel adjourned to render a decision. Unlike civilian trials, the panel did not have to render a unanimous verdict; only a majority decision was necessary. The exception was capital cases, where two-thirds of the panel had to confirm a death sentence. Upon reconvening the court to announce the decision, the panel at that point permitted the defendant or his advocate to issue a statement to the court. If a soldier wanted to present a justification for his accused actions, the court permitted him the courtesy, as such diversions were not permitted during cross-examination. Some statements were quite eloquent. "It seems that no kind of punishment except some kind calculated to degrade a man . . . suits our Captain," penned a soldier accused of disobeying orders, "No man among us objects to performing manual labor . . . but when we are to suffer the degradation of being made beasts of burden we think it should be ordered done by the sentence of a General Court Martial."[71] Other soldiers threw themselves on the mercy of the court. "I am well aware of the position in which I am placed," Private George Johnson pleaded. ". . . If you could consistently allow me to return to duty . . . I will guarantee you will find me a soldier."[72] The court then announced its decision, handing down either a positive ("guilty" or "proven") or negative ("not guilty" or "not proven") finding for each charge and specification. The court then retired to consider the soldier's statement to the court as a mitigating factor or announced the sentence imposed for the offense. If found not guilty, the panel ordered the accused to immediately return to his unit, but if found guilty the convicted soldier entered the custody of the Provost Marshals who oversaw his punishment.

On its face, the military justice system seemed to function with clockwork precision. Reality, however, was very different, as any number of difficulties could derail, disrupt, and prevent the timely application of justice. Some general courts-martial found it difficult to seat the minimum number of suitably ranked officers, although the Army Regulations permitted courts-martial to continue with less than the usual number. On occasion, courts-martial operated a few officers short. General courts-martial were supposed to have at least five officers, but only if "that number can be convened without manifest injury to the service" by depriving too many units of their officers. In a pinch, the War Department ruled that Marine Corps officers could sit on army courts-martial, but not navy officers.[73] In regions where discipline was especially bad, the amount of work demoralized the officers caught on court-martial duty, unable to leave until their dockets were clear. "This court-martial will occupy us for months," John DeForest complained while sitting on a panel in New Orleans. "We commenced with sixty cases and get an average of four new ones a day, while we dispose of perhaps two."[74] Lieutenant Edmund Halsey at one stretch spent four months on court-martial duty, and that was not unusual.[75] Once seated, all members of a court-martial panel had to appear in court before proceedings could begin, and a single missing officer meant an entire day might be wasted. To ensure a full panel, the officers seated to hear one series of cases agreed amongst themselves that if an officer appeared late, he had to buy "cigars for the entire court," including the defendant.[76]

Other courts, however, operated with such ruthless proficiency that justice seemed a secondary concern to clearing cases. Colonel Wesley Brainerd's court-martial panel was so efficient "that I could dispose of half a dozen cases in the morning and attend to drilling the Battalion in the afternoon."[77] Some courts-martial faced the displeasure of senior officers who did not like the panel's decisions. General Alfred Torbert, for instance, ordered the court-martial of Private Peter Clancy because Clancy stole some candy from Torbert's tent. When the court-martial panel gave Clancy only a minor punishment, Torbert angrily adjourned the court-martial and ordered the officers back to their regiments.[78] Yet other officers actually enjoyed the process and easy work of court-martial duty and did not want to resume regular duties. Major Mattocks received with "surprise as well as disgust" orders to temporarily assume command of his regiment because the two senior officers were on leave. Mattocks, in good citizen-soldier fashion, especially enjoyed court-martialing officers. "I take more pleasure in 'hazing' these shoulder-straps than in putting poor privates through," Mattocks wrote his mother. ". . . I have ordered one Lieutenant before a Board of Examination and have court-martialed one Capt. who will probably be dismissed [from] the service."[79] Charles Wills also liked court-martial duty, but as a sergeant serving "as sheriff of a court-martial." Providing courtroom security as a sort of bailiff, Wills enjoyed that he had at his disposal "four men a day to guard the prisoners and two orderlies to send errands for me, so I play big injun strongly."[80]

Like any court, military legal proceedings had its own trappings and protocols that signified its importance. The judges, for instance, seated themselves in the same manner as the Supreme Court, with the judge advocate sitting in the middle of the panel and the other panel members sitting on either side, alternating by seniority.[81] By custom, trials began at eight in the morning and ended by three in the afternoon to allow the officers on the panel to attend to their regular duties. The court demanded a level of decorum, and required all participants to attend in their best uniforms. This meant officers had to attend with their dress swords, although with some latitude. "The decorum and ceremoniousness of our court observances are rather solemnizing," Captain DeForest commented. "We are in full uniform, except that we may lay our swords and sashes on the table before us."[82] The exception was if the accused was an officer. When the army arrested any officers, it was custom to deny them the privilege of carrying a sword, the symbol of their authority, until a court-martial or military commission (a noncriminal investigative process) decided their fate.[83] The court required gentlemanly conduct when performing its business, and did not allow disruptive behavior. The court possessed the authority to "punish at its discretion, all riotous and disorderly proceedings or menacing words, signs, or gestures" that might intimidate a witness or member of the court.[84] For volunteer officers not accustomed to the nuances of military trials, the procedure was sometimes daunting. Fortunately, two manuals on courts-martial and military justice were widely available by the start of the war. Captain William C. DeHart first published his *Observations on Military Law and the Constitution and Practices of Courts-Martial* in 1846, which was later supplemented by Captain Stephen V. Benet's *A Treatise on Military Law and the Practice of Courts-Martial* in 1861. Both proved invaluable in explaining the expectations and practices of military courts to volunteer officers who lacked legal training. When in doubt about procedure, the existing literature proved useful. "Courts Martial are governed by very simple but effective laws," Colonel Wesley Brainerd found when appointed to his first panel.

"The principle [*sic*] authorities which govern Courts Martial are DeHart and Benet."[85] Detailed to court-martial duty by General Henry Slocum, Colonel Seymour Hall demurred because "my knowledge of military law and the practice of courts-martial is quite limited." Instead of replacing Hall with a more prepared officer, Slocum instructed Hall, "You have DeHart, get Benet, [and] read them."[86] In addition to these published manuals, the army also provided basic written instructions to officers on court-martial duty. General Ambrose Burnside, when in command of the Department of Ohio in 1863, issued an eight-page basic primer on the conduct of court-martial to educate volunteer officers.[87]

The nature of military courts made them very different from civilian courts, but they did have several elements in common with nonmilitary legal proceedings. Courts provided for a statute of limitations, as an officer could not charge a soldier with an offense that occurred more than two years previously. Military trials also provided protection against double-jeopardy, as no soldier "shall be tried a second time for the same offense," and if any irregular events resulted in a mistrial the court immediately voided the charges against the accused soldier and returned him to his unit.[88] Article 79 of the Articles of War guaranteed a speedy trial, as "no officer or soldier who shall be put in arrest shall continue in confinement more than eight days, or until such time as a court-martial can be assembled."[89] All persons participating in the trial did so under oath to tell the truth. Even the officers of the panel had to swear an oath to "duly administer justice" under the Articles of War "without partiality, favor or affection" for the defendant.[90] Although pledged to serve with objectivity, some officers lost their perspective as impartial observers. "Have had some more victims today before the Court Martial," one officer bragged. "All of them are skulks, and will get but scanty justice."[91] To ensure a valid defense, the court-martial regulations required the court to provide the defendant with a written copy of the charges and specifications before the trial began, and a soldier found guilty by court-martial had the right to obtain a copy of the trial's written record kept by the appointed secretary.[92] In cases where witnesses could not attend the schedule court date, defendants had the right to submit any deposition "taken before some justice of the peace." The sole exception was capital cases. If a defendant's life was at risk, the panel insisted upon hearing witness testimony firsthand.[93] Another comparison to modern courts was the occasional defense of temporary insanity. Captain James D. Thompson used the defense when he stood court-martialed for vociferously protesting the brigade commander's order to hold inspection on Sunday. When his trial finally began, one of the panel members commented that "It is certainly a curious kind of insanity, which will leave a poor man so suddenly, and yet stand him in good play on occasion."[94] Other courts, however, did recognize mental instability in a defendant. Private Rodgers Coleman attacked and stabbed Private John Bridenbaugh in Washington, DC. His court-martial found him guilty, but added the codicil that Coleman committed the act "while laboring under a temporary fit of insanity." The court sentenced Coleman "To be confined in a Military Lunatic Asylum . . . for such time as a board of examining surgeons may deem proper." Upon his release, Coleman "was to serve out the balance of his term of enlistment in the field," with no other punishment attached.[95]

The army even provided a form of appeals process. Soldiers could not appeal their sentences to civilian courts, but that did not mean that the actions of a court-martial were not reviewed. As a senior officer ordered the creation of a court-martial, its findings were, by extension, also his responsibility, and the senior officer who seated a court-martial had the right to review all findings and provide recommendations regarding findings and sentences. If a senior officer offered suggestions to a court-martial panel, the panel had the prerogative to accept the recommendations or leave their findings as originally stated; they were not obligated to consider the senior officer's suggestions as an order. Reviewing officers could also vacate or reduce the sentence imposed by a court-martial, but could not increase the severity of the punishment. If the court-martial panel committed evidential or procedural errors, or if the senior officer did not like the outcome, the senior officer could simply reject the findings outright and return the soldier to his unit. In capital cases, the review process had an additional level of review, as all death sentences required the approval of either the Secretary of War or the President. After Congress established the Judge Advocate General's Office in 1862, the JAG could also approve death sentences, although Joseph Holt usually still referred all cases to Lincoln and the War Department.[96]

Enough harsh court-martial findings occurred to maintain the image of brutal military justice. One regimental court-martial cracked down on a sixteen-year-old drummer boy for failing in his duty, and a regimental court-martial in a Michigan unit sentenced a soldier to twenty days hard labor and fined him a month's pay for merely "swearing at a Corpl."[97] But courts-martial also were within their bounds to grant leniency, as the codification of military justice did not extend to sentencing. The Regulations and Article of War set maximum punishment for some offenses, but did not set minimal limits. Trying a soldier for desertion, a court-martial refused to levy a punishment as the soldier, fighting alongside his father in the same regiment, saw his father killed before his own eyes at Fredericksburg.[98] Edward Jenkins escaped a capital sentence because his mother wrote a plea to the panel, as Jenkins "is the only support I have."[99] If the army had already imprisoned accused soldiers for a lengthy amount of time, courts-martial were inclined to let them off with time served. "I have had two tiresome days on Court Martial," Lieutenant Haydon wrote wearily. ". . . The men have already been 40 days in the guard house & we concluded to let them all off with a fine of $8.00 each."[100] Courts granted leniency, on the other hand, in cases that hinged more on cronyism than facts. Writing of two officers court-martialed in his brigade whose friends sat on the panel, Colonel Patrick Guiney had "no doubt that if punished at all the sentence will be very light if not a total acquittal. Thus it is in the Army—the greater the scamp the more favor and friends."[101]

While the army tried to be lenient and conscientious in its legal proceedings against common soldiers, officers sometimes found the legal system used against them. The occasional officer even found himself convicted by a court-martial of which he was unaware. A court-martial, for instance, cashiered Colonel Louis Butler for conduct unbecoming an officer, despite Butler confessing he was "entirely unacquainted with the circumstances of the case," while Colonel Everard Bierer received the same punishment for purportedly stealing civilian property.[102] Both officers claimed they were the victims of professional rivals who sought to discredit them. Their defense is not without merit, as court-martial became a convenient way to dispose of unwanted or unpopular officers, whether legitimate charges existed or not. On the losing side of an internal squabble in the Fifth New Hampshire, two junior officers accused Lieutenant Colonel Richard Cross of public drunkenness, an accusation that got Cross cashiered.[103] Displeased with Colonel Albert Hall's "unfortunate failing of getting intoxicated," one of his subordinate officers "informed the gentlemen that should I hear of the occurrence again, a court-martial would investigate the same."[104] A court-martial did not remove Captain John Boyle of the Twenty-seventh Indiana, but it compelled him to resign his commission. Arrested on a charge of cowardice, Boyle went under arrest in May 1862, was not court-martialed until July, and at the time he resigned his commission in September was still under arrest as the court still had not rendered a decision.[105] Not all such abuses of the court-martial system were successful, however. Colonel John Reynolds, a West Pointer, disapproved of the performance of volunteer Captain Thomas Spires as he "showed ignorance of his duties and great indifference upon the subject." Reynolds tried to remove Spires by court-martialing him for incompetence, but the panel did not agree with Reynolds' assessment and allowed Spires to keep his commission.[106]

One last type of court-martial occurred during the Civil War, but the conduct of these courts were irregular, infrequent, and illegal. Drumhead courts, proceedings that tried and punished defendants in short order without the benefit of a formal trial, occurred on occasion during the war, but without the mandate of the government or the army. Drumhead courts, named for the imagery of an ad hoc court occurring with an officer using a drum as a makeshift desk, were an unofficial tradition held over from British military justice. In British practice, drumhead trials were a necessity of element of governance in remote areas of the empire, where access to formal courts and senior authority was not practical. In the absence of regular courts, the British condoned drumhead courts-martial as "one of those cases in which a court-martial . . . may be held at any hour," recognizing that circumstances create a situation where "it may be necessary to try the crime, and on proof, punish the offender at once."[107] In American practice, drumhead courts officially did not exist anywhere within the Articles of War or the Constitution, but rare circumstances did arise where officers felt the need to take the law into their own hands. As in British practice, these instances occurred in remote locations, where access to higher guidance and approval was impossible under the immediate circumstances. The most infamous such case in American history was the 1842 *Somers* Incident, where, fearful that one of his junior officers was plotting a mutiny, Captain Alexander Slidell Mackenzie arrested, tried, and executed three alleged mutineers. Navy regulations required the President to confirm all capital sentences before their execution, but Mackenzie, in the middle of the Atlantic Ocean en route to St. Thomas, countered that he was beyond the immediate reach of his superiors and had to act with dispatch. The subsequent court-martial agreed with Slidell and exonerated him of all wrong-doing.[108] During the Mexican War, General Winfield Scott used the same justification when he ordered the execution of men condemned to death by court-martial, including the deserters of the San Patricio Battalion.[109]

During the Civil War, however, improvements to transport and communications meant that units rarely ventured beyond the control of the army hierarchy, and the telegraph and the JAG removed any reason for officers to act independent of army judicial policy. There were instances of drumhead trials, however, but they are notable less for their legality and more for their unusualness. In some cases, the implications of the trials were relatively minor. In May 1864, Sergeant Austin Stearns recorded that "a drumhead Court-martial was ordered" to punish two corporals who straggled during a march. Their only punishment was demotion to the ranks, but demotion still required the formality of a regimental court-martial and they did not get one.[110] Sergeant George Hand found himself arrested for neglect of duty, convicted by a drumhead trial, sentenced, and pardoned all in the same day.[111] Other drumhead trials, however, resulted in capital sentences, with the subsequent executions clearly in violation of the Articles of War and any sense of justice. When recaptured by his own regiment after deserting to the enemy, William Ormsby faced a firing squad barely forty-eight hours after his arrest, the consequence of a drumhead court-martial.[112] Captain Thomas Galwey recalled in his memoirs that a soldier of the Nineteenth Massachusetts who deserted from his regiment on May 18, 1864, was arrested a day later, and the day after that he received a drumhead at six o'clock in the morning and by "eight he was dead. Poor fellow!"[113] In Florida, when officers arrested three soldiers who tried to desert by stowing away on a supply ship, "the military court met immediately and . . . in a period of two hours they were found guilty, sentenced to death, and shot."[114] Besides denying the condemned men the opportunity for a legitimate trial, their quick executions also failed to permit any sort of review by a senior officer, robbing the soldiers of their limited ability to appeal their sentence.

WHILE THE COURT-MARTIAL procedure enjoyed the benefit of manuals, tradition, and clear directions for conduct, the actual cases and their outcomes were much more problematic. The courts recognized neat and well-defined offenses, but for every clear case there was at least another whose facts and outcomes were entirely open to debate. For every prosecution witness that testified that a soldier was absolutely guilty, a soldier could produce a character witness of his own that swore the soldier was innocent. Even if soldiers admitted their guilt, excuses and justifications made rendering a verdict a difficult task. When faced with finding the truth and rendering an appropriate punishment, how well did courts-martial administer justice? A representative sample of courts-martial cases[115] provide a cross-section of the military justice experience, and demonstrates the courts' level of consistency and effectiveness.

During the Civil War, the Union army conducted approximately 80,000 general courts-martial and an inestimable number of regimental courts-martial, making military justice an obvious element of army life during the Civil War. Every rank, every service, and every area of the war saw the presence of military justice. The army court-martialed more privates than any other rank (66 percent of the total sample), but considering the proportion of privates in the total army this was not surprising. About 5 percent[116] of cases involved NCOs, 8 percent involved officers, and the remainder included various positions that fell under army authority (medical personnel, chaplains, sutlers, teamsters, and civilians associated with the armies or the War Department). Senior officers also faced court-martial, like Colonel William Halstead of the First New Jersey Cavalry, who faced a trial for embezzlement in 1862.[117] As the largest service branch, infantry faced the most courts-martial (61 percent of the total sample), followed by cavalry (13 percent), artillery (11 percent), and a scattering of courts-martial among

Quartermasters, Signal Corps, medical personnel, engineers, chaplains, and other groups. Six percent of courts-martial took place in the Western states and territories, 13 percent took place in Northern states, 19 percent in the Trans-Mississippi Theater, 26 percent in the Western Theater, and 40 percent in the Eastern Theater.[118] Courts-martial took place at all times of year, be it winter, spring, or summer.[119] Most courts-martial took place in winter (42 percent, compared to only 29 percent the spring and summer seasons), when the armies were inactive, soldiers had time on their hands, and desertion and French leave were common occurrences. More trials occurred in winter, but the season had no effect on the outcome, with soldiers either acquitted or convicted at the same rate.[120]

The crimes committed by Union soldiers fall into five offense categories: desertion, violent crimes, disciplinary offenses, antiauthority offenses, and theft.[121] There is a clear pattern of when the army prosecuted different offense categories. Desertion went from about 25 percent of the cases in the first two years of the war to more than 40 percent for the last three years. In the same time frames, theft went from 8 percent to 12 percent, as Union armies pressed into Confederate territory and had more opportunities to forage and pillage. The same time frames, however, also saw a significant drop in one category, as disciplinary offenses declined from about 40 percent of early-war cases to about 20 percent in the latter years of the war. A possible explanation is that as soldiers learned their duties the number of disciplinary offenses were bound to fall. The prosecution of violent crimes and antiauthority crimes remained steady throughout the war.[122] The three main branches of the army also demonstrate group patterns of criminal behavior. The infantry tended to have more disciplinary offenses (33 percent of offenses committed by their service branch) and antiauthority offenses (18 percent) than the other branches, but deserted less. Artillerymen deserted at a higher rate than the other branches (49 percent), but had the lowest rate of violent crime (4 percent). Cavalry not only committed a higher ratio of violent crimes (10 percent) than the other service; they also committed more thefts (11 percent) because of their higher mobility compared to the slower infantry and artillery.[123] Their respective offenses also earned each branch a higher proportion of certain punishments than the others. Because of their higher desertion rate, artillerymen found themselves sentenced to hard labor (55 percent) than the other services. For their antiauthority offenses, more infantrymen received a dishonorable discharge (14 percent) and served a prison sentence (9 percent) than the other services. Because of their propensity to steal, courts-martial punished cavalrymen with fines (26 percent) more than the other branches.[124]

One of the most important questions the representative sample answers is the issue of the fairness of military trials. Unlike the image of military justice where panels invariably find defendants guilty regardless of the evidence or circumstances, a significant number of soldiers found the court finding in their favor. Over the course of the war, panels found 83 percent of defendants guilty (76 percent guilty outright and 7 percent guilty of a lesser charge), the great majority of the latter cases where courts-martial charged soldiers with desertion but found them guilt of AWOL. Courts found the other 17 percent not guilty. Over the course of the war, the pattern does not significantly change. During 1861 and 1864, the percentage of defendants found guilty stayed in the 80–81 percent range, defying some claims that courts-martial became harsher as the war progressed.[125] The only major change came in 1865, when courts found only 77 percent of soldiers guilty, perhaps because the war was winding down and the army opted to release soldiers instead of retaining them only to punish them.[126] The number of courts-martial did increase as the war progressed, with 17 percent of the total cases heard in 1861, up to 19 percent in 1863, before peaking at 32 percent in 1864. Only 17 percent of the total courts-martial cases came up in 1865, but the sample ends in July 1865; extrapolated to the end of the year, 1865 would have been as busy as 1864. Despite the increasing numbers of cases, however, the percentage of defendants found guilty remained consistent. The rank of those court-martialed also played a part in the issue of fairness. Courts-martial found different rank groups guilty at a higher rate than others. Panels found privates (78 percent) and junior officers, that is lieutenants and captains (76 percent), guilty at the overall average or higher. Trials found senior officers, i.e., majors, colonels, and generals (64 percent) and NCOs (66 percent) guilty less often than the overall sample.[127]

The claim that courts-martial became increasingly harsh is also disproved when examining the punishments issued by courts over time. Over the course of the war, the most common primary punishment[128] was a term at hard labor (42 percent of cases), but monetary fines were the next most frequent (20 percent) and dishonorable discharge from the service was next (11 percent), followed by incarceration (9 percent) and capital punishment (6 percent). Extrapolated over the years of the war, the relative percentages of the most frequent punishments remain more or less the same. There was a sharp decline in the number of soldiers punished by dishonorable discharge (from 11 percent of 1862 sentences to 7 percent in 1864) because soldiers who wanted to go home would gladly accept a dishonorable discharge and the punishment lost much of its deterrence. There was also a significant increase in the application of the death penalty (from 3 percent in 1862 to 8 percent of punishments by 1864), but that corresponded to a growing number of violations eligible for a capital sentence, particularly when desertion numbers escalated, and does not necessarily reflect a consensus attitude to impose harsher punishments.[129] Nor did other punishments greatly increase in severity. In 1861, a majority (57 percent) of soldiers sentenced to hard labor received a sentence of three months or less, remaining the same through 1863 (55 percent). In 1864, only 27 percent received a sentence of three months or less, but 47 percent received six months or less at hard labor, numbers that remained steady in 1865.[130] The same trend appeared for soldiers sentenced to long-term incarceration. Nearly half (47 percent) received a prison sentence of one year or less in 1861, remaining the same in 1863. Only 25 percent of soldiers sentenced to prison received a sentence of a year or less in 1865, but 30 percent wound up serving out the terms of their enlistment in prison. Most of these cases involved soldiers who enlisted late in the war, and then deserted when the war ended.[131] When fined by the court-martial that found them guilty, soldiers generally did not pay very much. In 1861, 42 percent of soldiers fined by their courts-martial paid only a month's wages, and 73 percent paid three months' worth or less. By 1863, those paying three months' or less fell to only 41 percent, but it rose to 63 percent in 1864 and 59 percent in 1865.[132] Officers also received a large dose of leniency. Article 83 of the Articles of War mandated that "any commissioned officer, convicted before a general court-martial, of conduct unbecoming an officer and a gentleman, shall be dismissed from the service." In courts-martial where panels found officers guilty of such offenses, courts-martial decided not to dismiss the officers 30 percent of the time, choosing instead to issue a reprimand (16 percent), a fine (10 percent), or temporarily suspend the officers from their rank (4 percent).

The leniency of courts-martial is also reflected in the relative paucity of death sentences. The Articles of War contained plenty of offenses that warranted a capital sentence if the court-martial opted to impose it, ranging from mutiny to desertion to sleeping on guard duty. However, for cases in the sample where a death sentence was a possible outcome, the court-martial rendered some other punishment 91 percent of the time. In only 9 percent of the cases did a soldier facing the death penalty actually receive it, with deserters (57 percent) and murderers (17 percent) comprising the majority of those sentenced to death.[133] The army committed a lot of effort to stopping desertion, including, as seen in the next chapter, punishing deserters with death. But only a small number of deserters faced a firing squad because of the offense. The army condemned only 6 percent of the deserters in their courts, reserving the death penalty more for perpetrators of violent crimes (14 percent) and antiauthority crimes (7 percent).[134] The army did apply the death penalty in greater numbers as the war progressed, with 3 percent of cases resulting in a capital sentence in 1861, rising to 5 percent in 1863 before cresting at 7 percent in 1864, but the overall low percentage of cases ending by execution defies the image of the army executing soldiers with reckless abandon.[135] Instead of executions, most deserters received a stretch at hard labor (38 percent) or a fine (25 percent) as their primary punishment instead of death.

The trend toward leniency was also apparent in the significant number of cases that warranted a severe sentence, but received only punishments on the low end of the scale. A significant number of soldiers received relatively light sentences for relatively serious offenses. More than a quarter of all courts-martial (28 percent) ended with the defendants receiving no more punishment than a fine, a demotion, a reprimand, or a dishonorable discharge. Almost half (43 percent) of those who received such minor punishments were soldiers convicted of desertion. The lenient attitude was not just a feature of the early war years, as each year of the war saw roughly the same number of cases resulting in lenient outcomes.[136] The most lenient cases were instances where panels found soldiers guilty, but imposed no penalty at all by declaring that "no criminality was attached" to the soldiers actions. In other words, the soldier did commit an offense, but the offense had no negative consequence, so the panel opted not to punish anyone. Two officers in the Trans-Mississippi Theater, for instance, found themselves court-martialed and convicted of disobeying orders, but the panel declined to punish them because of their good previous behavior and character.[137] Both Private Edward Roedel and Captain C.W. Tillotson found themselves convicted of AWOL, but also returned to their units with no criminality attached.[138] Other soldiers, such as Private John Dunn of the Second Illinois Artillery or Private William Harris of the First Michigan Colored Infantry, even deserted, but enjoyed a reprieve when their courts-martial chose to attach no criminality.[139] Private Jefferson Littleton of the Fifty-ninth USCT shot at a civilian who caught him foraging melons from his garden, but received no punishment.[140]

These relatively minor punishments should not give the impression that courts-martial were always lenient. Rather, they could extend leniency when circumstances permitted such clemency. When offenses merited harsh punishment, courts-martial proved more than willing to impose hardship and retribution. The death penalty was one such method of dealing with a soldier who deserved the highest punishment the courts could inflict, but there were other harsh measures at the panels' disposal. Placing a soldier at hard labor for a lengthy period of time certainly sent a stern warning about violating the rules, and courts-martial proved willing to use the sentence. Among soldiers sentenced to hard labor, nearly a quarter (23 percent) received sentences of two years or more, with nearly one out of every seven (13 percent) at hard labor for five years or more. The recipient of the longest sentence in the sample, a bounty-jumper named Charles Wilson, got a sentence of twenty-one years at hard labor.[141] Not all incarceration involved hard labor, but long prison sentences were nothing to laugh at. Fifteen percent of soldiers incarcerated in state penitentiaries for major offenses (mostly desertion, theft, or violent crimes) received sentences ranging from four to ten years, while another 9 percent were sentenced to spend the rest of their terms of enlistment behind bars, and panels sentenced yet another 14 percent to be indefinitely confined until the end of the war, whenever that might occur.

The court could also impose financial hardship in the form of fines. In many cases the level of financial hardships is unclear, as panels forced soldiers to remit all pay and allowances due to them (10 percent of cases with fines as the primary punishment) without any indication of exactly how much pay and allowances the army owed a soldier. As pay was often months in arrears, this could be a considerable sum, or it could be only a month or two. But in cases where the court established an exact fine amount, the penalties reached serious levels. In one case, a court-martial sentenced a bounty-jumper named Absalom Smoke to serve his three-year military obligation at hard labor and fined him every penny of his army wages for the full three years.[142] Courts could also inflict additional hardships to standard sentences. On top of prison sentences, hard labor, or other primary punishments, courts-martial inflicted other penalties such as a lesser fine (56 percent of cases), dishonorably discharging a soldier at the end of this punishment (22 percent), forcing a soldier at hard labor to wear a ball and chain (11 percent), demoting the offender (2 percent), or placing him in solitary confinement (2 percent).

The most interesting group of soldiers who faced military justice was those who committed offenses that did not fit into any particular charge category. The army employed Article 99 of the Articles of War to suppress all activity that was "to the prejudice of good order and military discipline," effectively creating a mechanism to punish any activity they chose to deem disruptive. The charge of conduct prejudicial accounted for 9 percent of all general courts-martial, and the group represented a wide range of inappropriate behavior. Privates accounted for 69 percent of offenders in this category, NCOs were 11 percent, and officers accounted for the other 19 percent, indicating the charge was not just a means to control the enlisted men. As the bulk of the army, infantrymen suffered the highest proportion of cases (75 percent). The yearly distribution of the charge, however, was unbalanced. More than half of the cases (55 percent) occurred in the first two years of the war, and the ratio declined for the remaining three years of the war. Either the army found new ways to control its enlisted men, or the military justice system opted to not employ such an inexact charge. The charge showed up most often in the Eastern Theater (43 percent of the cases, compared to only 27 percent in the Western Theater). Because an officer could level a charge of conduct prejudicial upon a specific soldier for a specific behavior, the rate at which courts-marital found soldiers guilty of the charge was much higher. While courts found 83 percent of defendants in the general sample guilty, those charged with conduct prejudicial suffered an 89 percent conviction rate. The most common punishment was a term at hard labor (37 percent), somewhat higher than in the general sample (34 percent).

Because conduct prejudicial was such an amorphous offense, it tended to encompass a variety of infractions that did not fit under any other category. Sergeant Alexander Johnson found himself accused of the charge for gambling with one of his guardhouse prisoners, while 2nd Lieutenant Frederick Klentz stood trial for drinking with a prisoner.[143] Private Frank Butt faced trial for carelessly using his firearm, as did Private William Ellis.[144] Privates Quintin Crawford and Corydon Baybrook found themselves accused of the charge for ransacking a civilian home.[145] Private August Ott stole a keg of beer, Private George Parker forged a check, Sergeant John Tingle circulated a petition complaining about his hospital care, and Lieutenant Marshall Saunders consorted with his enlisted men by having a drink with them.[146] Major J.D. Moriarty committed an act prejudicial to good order when, publicly drunk in Washington, DC, he "precipitated in an undignified and unseemly manner upon the ground."[147] Colonel John Hottenstein faced the charge for a variety of unseemly activities, not the least of which was the allegation that he "brought into the camp of his regiment and introduced to his officers as his wife a woman who was not his wife."[148]

Alcohol played a huge role in the large number of criminal offenses that wound up in front of courts-martial. Considering the great, and often illegal, efforts by soldiers to obtain alcohol, not to mention the disruptive behavior caused by whiskey, it is not surprising that many a drunken soldier wound up facing military justice. "We tried fifty men, found forty-five of them guilty, gave two dozen ball and chain, and docked the pay of everybody," Captain DeForest wrote in describing a day's work on a court-martial panel. "It is worth noting that every solitary case of misbehavior originated in whiskey."[149] While many alcohol-related offenses found resolution at the company and regimental level, enough found their way to general courts-martial to warrant attention. Twelve percent of all courts-martial were alcohol-related, either because the defendant or his victim was drunk, the defendant tried to steal alcohol, or alcohol played some significant part in triggering the offense. When soldiers became drunk, the majority of their offenses fell into obvious categories. Charges of drunkenness on duty, drunkenness on guard, and the broad "conduct prejudicial" charge together combined to comprise more than half (57 percent) of the alcohol-related offenses. Soldiers also used alcohol as an excuse in the defense of their actions. Desertion and AWOL combined to account for 9 percent of alcohol-related offenses, as soldiers claimed that they did not intentionally desert, but instead wandered off while intoxicated. Using alcohol as a defense, however, not only failed to gain a defendant pity from the court, but rather made the panel more likely to convict. While panels found 83 percent of defendants guilty in the general sample, courts-martial in alcohol-related offenses found the accused guilty at a rate of 89 percent. That was the highest conviction rate of any circumstance or offense. Courts-martial did not even convict soldiers of desertion at that high of a rate, ruling against accused deserters in 75 percent of the proceedings.[150]

Alcohol played a significant part in the outcome of courts-martial, but generally race did not, as courts-martial applied discipline proportionately across the army. Statistically, African Americans were underrepresented in courts-martial statistics, as African Americans comprised about 12 percent of the Union army but were subjected to only 6 percent of the courts-martial.[151] African Americans pled guilty at a lower rate (27 percent of cases) than white soldiers (37 percent)[152] but were found guilty by courts-martial at the same rate (both 76 percent).[153] There is some statistical dispersion in the relationship between charge groups and race. Using race as a factor, African American and white troops were court-martialed at about the same rate for desertion, violent crimes, and theft. White soldiers, however, committed a higher percentage of antiauthority crimes than African Americans (19 percent for whites versus 7 percent for blacks), but USCT units committed more disciplinary offenses (35 percent to 28 percent).[154] In punishments levied by courts-martial, there was some statistical significance when considering the race of the defendants. While white defendants received a higher percentage of prison sentences, fines, dishonorable discharges, and demotions, courts-marital involving African American soldiers issued hard labor and the death penalty at a higher percentage than white soldiers. In the case of the death penalty, courts handed it down at twice the percentage of white soldiers (13 percent of African American defendants to only 7 percent of white defendants).[155] Alcohol was also a significant factor, with booze influencing 13 percent of white cases compared to only 2 percent of African American cases.[156] In other punishments, however, race played no significant part in the courts' decisions. When it came to extra punishments, such as fines,[157] labor at ball and chain,[158] demotion,[159] sustenance on bread and water,[160] or solitary confinement,[161] black and white soldiers received the extra penalties at the same proportion.

The Lieber Code, issued in April 1863, clarified military practices by approving or disapproving specific actions facing the Union army during the Civil War. It is possible, but impossible to prove, that the Lieber Code dissuaded soldiers from committing banned offenses, but it certainly had little effect on the outcome of courts-martial. The Code, for example, did not affect the finding of courts-martial, and the conviction rate remained the same for pre- and post-Code trials.[162] There were significant changes in the percentages of the charge groups, but these had less to do with the Code and more with evolving circumstances. Violent, disciplinary, and antiauthority crimes showed up at the same percentage after the enacting of the Code as before it. There were more desertion prosecutions, but that simply reflected the growing number of desertions, offenses that occurred without consideration of the Code. There was a major jump in the number of theft offenses (8 percent before the Code; 11 percent after) that might reflect the antipillaging language in the Code or it might simply reflect how the advancement of the army presented more opportunities for pillaging.[163] In a similar manner, the ratio of soldiers who pled not guilty at courts-martial also increased, from 57 percent before the Code to 69 percent after. There is no way to determine if soldiers felt safer taking their chances in a post-Code court-martial, or if soldiers pled guilty in larger numbers because they felt justified in their actions.[164]

The Code also had a significant, but explainable, impact upon sentences handed down by panels. While the percentage of cases that ended in hard labor or a fine remained consistent, some punishment categories showed major shifts. The number of cases that received a dishonorable discharge declined sharply, as the army refused to give soldiers the release from the army that they sought, and the percentage of capital sentences after the implementation of the Code tripled from the percentage before the Code. The Code provided a number of circumstances when the army could put a prisoner, spy, or deserter to death, but few of these circumstances applied to the common soldier or already existed under the Articles of War. Instead of the Code generating more death sentences, the increased number of death sentences reflected the Union army's attempts to stem desertion.[165] For punishments less than death, the Code had no measurable effect. The percentage of cases that wound up in fines, hard labor, incarceration, solitary confinement, ball and chain, or bread and water reflect an insignificant difference in the pre- and post-Code courts-martial.[166]

The only appeal available to soldiers in typical courts-martial cases was the final review of the sentence by the senior officer who seated the court-martial. In most cases, this was the army, department, or district commander, who had the authority to alter the sentence (but not the verdict), return it for reconsideration by the panel, or void the entire trial if the panel committed an evidential or procedural error. In 79 percent of the cases in the sample, the reviewing officer approved the sentence as issued. There was a significant amount of dissent, however, as in 4 percent of the cases the reviewing officer approved the sentence but only after voicing some personal criticism of the sentence or behavior of the court. In the other 17 percent of cases, the reviewing commander altered the sentence by diminishing what he considered a too harsh punishment, kept some portion of the punishment but remitted other elements, or simply voided the trial and returned the soldier to his unit. In cases where the senior officer criticized but approved the sentence, the criticism fell into broad complaints about the failure of the courts to implement a proper sentence. In most cases, the commanding officer believed the court-martial was too lenient. When a court-martial fined 2nd Lieutenant George Stoddard only a month's pay for abandoning his post, the reviewing officer, Brigadier General John Cook, was "somewhat surprised at the very mild sentence for so grave an offense" and believed that "Lieut. Stoddard may congratulate himself on so light a punishment."[167] When Private George Chaffee got only a two-month sentence at hard labor for going AWOL, Major General John Wool was amazed "that the Court should have inflicted so light a punishment. Instead of suppressing crime, it would seem that the only object was to encourage it."[168] Private Francis Burns of the Thirteenth New Hampshire deserted and found himself sentenced to a year at hard labor, but Major General Benjamin Butler found the punishment "entirely disproportionate to the offense . . . he should have been shot to death."[169] Conversely, when a court-martial sentenced three soldiers of the Fifth Kentucky to death for robbery and abandoning their post to pillage, Major General George Thomas applauded the panel's resolve to impose the penalty because "Severe measures must be resorted to, to prevent such outrages."[170] Privates were not the only ones that reviewing officers thought got off too easy. When Lieutenant John Kearney refused to join his company during the Battle of Malvern Hill, his subsequent court-martial cashiered him on the charge of disobeying direct orders. In his approval of the sentence, McClellan wondered why he was not charged with a more serious offense, and commented, "If the Court had affixed the death penalty to the offense the General Commanding is of the opinion that there should be not have been any interposition of executive clemency."[171]

In other cases, the reviewing officer questioned the outcome of a trial based upon the severity of the charge, but allowed a relatively minor sentence based upon a specific recommendation of the court. Most of these cases involved circumstances where the court ruled as the Articles of War required them, but requested mercy from the reviewing officer, who had the luxury of latitude not granted to the panel. A panel found Private John Murphy guilty of desertion in 1862, but imposed only a dishonorable discharge because "The Court is of [the] opinion that the accused, by reason of mental imbecility, is unfit to perform the duties of a soldier." McClellan concurred, stating "This punishment would be incongruous but for the fact stated by the Court," and approved the sentence.[172] Brigadier General Ralph Buckland also accepted a panel's request for mercy in the case of Private Taylor Murrin, whom they punished for sleeping at his post, a capital offense, by only fining him a month's pay "In consideration of the extreme youth of the prisoner, who is apparently not more than 13 to 15 years of age."[173] When necessary, commanding officers approved sentences but chastised panels for insufficiently tending to their duties. In his review after a court-martial found Captain Henry Bartlett not guilty of disobeying orders and AWOL, Brigadier General Daniel Sickles chastised Lieutenant Colonel Sonis Francine for preferring charges against Bartlett that he knew to be false. Francine, Sickles stated, committed "a gross abuse of the right to prefer charges—a prerogative conferred upon officers as an auxiliary to discipline, and not as a weapon of oppression, or for the gratification of spite. . . .[T]his record illustrates the conspicuous incapacity of Lieutenant Colonel Francine."[174] Brigadier General John Hawkins approved the sentences of several USCT soldiers court-martialed at Vicksburg, Mississippi, in the summer of 1864, but criticized the court for failing to maintain the required number of panel members. "The records show many cases of absence of Officers from Court, and no reasons given," Hawkins wrote in his critique. He also warned that "The practice of Officers standing as counsel for an accused person" was appropriate because "Soldiers often need counsel and should have it," but he also warned that "Only those should assume the position [of counsel] who are animated by a desire to see justice done, and not for a desire to display wonderful legal or literary abilities."[175]

In the remaining 17 percent of cases, the reviewing officer disapproved the sentence, and either reduced the sentence or voided it altogether. Officers had plenty of reasons to totally void a sentence. While some officers only rebuked panels that did not adhere to the rules regarding the conduct of courts-martial, some panels committed violations so egregious that justice demanded a discharge of the sentence, even the death sentences of serious offenders. Nearly one-tenth of the cases disapproved by a reviewing officer failed to pass muster because of evidence errors on the part of the panel, and specifically the judge advocate running the trial. After an early-war court-martial sentenced several soldiers to death or long stretches at hard labor for various offenses, McClellan disapproved and released several soldiers because of inappropriate presentation of evidence. McClellan ruled that the evidence used to convict Private Charles Stodenher, sentenced to death for desertion, "indicates rather the offense of desertion without leave than that of desertion," and the evidence applied against Private Charles Howell "do not sustain a sentence of punishment" and both men "will be released from confinement and returned to duty."[176] Convinced in the desertion case against Private John Griffith that in the "charge and specification the evidence is insufficient," Major General Nathaniel Banks ordered "the sentence is suspended until the pleasure of the President can be known."[177] Major General George Thomas had the harshest words for the court-martial that sentenced Private Samuel Tead to death. Rejecting the sentence because the finding was "not supported by such direct and positive proof as would justify . . . the extreme penalty of the law," Thomas scolded the panel because "Soldiers are sentenced to *Death* for trifling offenses, or upon the most doubtful and inadequate evidence. . . . The position of a member of a General Court Martial is no sinecure, but imposes upon him who holds it the most sacred obligations."[178]

In the interests of protecting the rights of soldiers facing courts-martial, reviewing officers also voided sentences because of procedural errors. Such faults might include seating an ineligible panel member, failing to record the proceedings, improperly following the mandated formula for conducting a court-martial, or any other deviation from established methods. This occurred twice as often as cases with evidence errors, comprising 21 percent of the cases disapproved by higher authority and 4 percent of all of the cases in the sample. Brigadier General Eugene Carr disregarded a court-martial's sentence of five months at hard labor for Private William Powley because he abandoned his post. "The evidence . . . shows that the accused was unsound of mind at the time the offense was committed," Carr opined, and instead ordered Powley transferred to the Soldier's Asylum outside Washington, DC, for evaluation.[179] Brigadier General Robert Mitchell dismissed the punishments imposed upon Hospital Steward Lewis Ewald, Corporal William Forsyth, and Private James William by a court-martial in Omaha, Nebraska Territory, because "a Surgeon is incompetent to act as a member of a General Court Martial. Surgeon [George C.] Underhill of the 11th Ohio Vol. Cavalry was detailed and acted as a member of the Court."[180] Captains Ross Deegan and Horace Brown had their sentences dismissed because the judge advocate made the mistake of allowing "These officers . . . [to be] tried by courts some of the members of which were of an inferior rank to the accused."[181] Major M.S. Hasie, facing a charge of conduct unbecoming an officer because he altered and forged a soldier's pass, escaped punishment when sentenced to lose his pay for twenty days because Major General Henry Halleck reminded the court that the mandatory sentence for a conduct unbecoming conviction was "dismissal from the service of the United States. The Court cannot change the penalty."[182] Although convicted of striking his superior officer with a club and threatening to kill him, Hugh Shaw, a wagoner in the Fifty-eighth Indiana, escaped his death penalty when William Rosecrans voided the conviction because "the record of the Court is fatally defective in not showing that the Judge Advocate was duty sworn in the presence of the prisoner," an act required at the start of every courts-martial. "There is no palliation for such gross errors," Rosecrans aimed at Lieutenant Colonel William Young, the judge advocate for the trial, "and if a sense of duty is not a sufficient prompter to . . . discharge the duties of Judge Advocate" then Rosecrans promised "prompt and speedy punishment to all delinquents in the future."[183]

Along similar lines, Brigadier General John McNeil dismissed Private Henry Laubey's conviction for desertion because he was not granted the chance to challenge the presence of any member of the panel, as was his right.[184] Private Thomas McElmore of the Fifteenth USCT escaped a death penalty for threatening his superior officer because his panel did not establish a two-thirds consensus, and "the examination of the witnesses seems to have been conducted in a loose and irregular manner," according to Major General Lovell Rousseau.[185] Private Peter Dugan of the Seventh Missouri also escaped a death sentence for mutinous conduct when Major General James McPherson noted, "the proceedings in this case are fatally defective, as the record does not show the finding of the Court upon the 1st Charge." In other words, the court did not formally state its finding in the official record, thereby committing a sufficient procedural error to void the court-martial.[186] Not all procedural cases involved capital cases, and failure on the part of a judge advocate meant that even minor offenders enjoyed protection against procedural irregularities. Lieutenant John Ellis avoided a dismissal from the service because of his conviction on the charges of "Gross neglect of duty" and being "Disgracefully defective in point of military discipline" because, as Major General John Schofield pointed out, "No such charges as those made against him are known to the rules and articles of war."[187] Although a panel sentenced Private Thomas Gordon to five years in prison for robbing civilians of their personal property, General Rousseau believed "strong suspicion is thrown upon the character of the evidence in the case by a comparison . . . of all those engaged in the commission of the same offenses."[188]

In addition to overriding the sentences of courts-martial for procedural mistakes, officers might also consider pleas of mercy from the court in cases where the panel followed procedure and evidence correctly, but believed that special circumstances should mitigate the mandated punishments. Private Lewis McClusky of the Veterans Reserve Corps disobeyed the orders of his superior officer, but instead of serving his original sentence of five days confinement in the guardhouse, the panel recommended clemency because of the "extreme debility of the prisoner," and Brigadier General John Martindale agreed to return McClusky to his unit.[189] Private John Norbert of the Eighty-fourth USCT deserted, receiving an initial sentence of three years at hard labor. Norbert claimed he left because he was permanently lame, and the court urged Brigadier General Daniel Ullman to consider his claims. Instead of hard labor, Ullman ordered that Norbert be "surveyed by the Surgeon, and if found permanently disabled he will be discharged from the service."[190] In addition to physical hardship, panels also asked reviewing officers to consider prior good service. Captain C.H. Nichols of the Sixth Connecticut found himself convicted of improperly arresting the regimental surgeon and then acting impertinently to a superior officer who ordered him to release the prisoner. He faced the prospect of being cashiered, except that Brigadier General John Brannan agreed with the court's assessment that Nichols exhibited "excellent character hitherto" his conviction and opted to keep him in the army.[191] If the army cashiered an officer, the sentence forever prohibited him from serving in the army, a fate that Captain Barnabas Hayden of the Seventh Kentucky Cavalry managed to avoid. Cashiered for filing false muster rolls, the court recommended clemency because of Hayden's otherwise effective leadership, and General Thomas altered the sentence from cashiering Hayden to merely dishonorably discharging him, allowing him the opportunity to join some other regiment.[192]

In the interest of mercy, commanders also decreased sentences they considered too harsh by reducing the length of a prison term, the amount of a fine, or the extent of a punishment. This occurred in about 20 percent of the cases not approved by higher authorities. The most startling reductions involved capital cases. Private Morris Haley received the death penalty for drawing a pistol on a superior officer, but Secretary of War Edwin Stanton, "upon the recommendation of . . . executive clemency," instead reduced the sentence to hard labor for the duration of the war in the Dry Tortugas.[193] He soon had company. Commanding officers reviewed the death sentences of Privates John Sebert, John Burt, Jean Girien, Maurice Andrews, and Hugh Shannon in separate courts-martial, and placed them in the Dry Tortugas instead of in front of a firing squad. John Burt was a Confederate prisoner who stood trial for the murder of another Confederate prisoner at the POW camp at Rock Island, IL. Despite his heinous act, Burt somehow received mercy due to his "general good conduct and good character."[194] Major General Oliver O. Howard eased the death sentence imposed upon Private William Galbreth for desertion to hard labor for the duration of the war "in the Penitentiary at Nashville, Tenn."[195] Commanders also reduced sentences in the effort to discipline soldiers who broke the rules without imposing too much suffering. Numerous reviews of sentences resulted in lower fines or reductions in the number of months sentenced to hard labor in the hopes that the soldier would learn his lesson without imposing financial hardship upon his family or ruining his reputation.

Along with the reduction of sentences, commanders also remitted, or voided, portions of the sentence they deemed unfair or excessive. These cases (21 percent of the unapproved sentences) usually involved the additional burdens placed upon soldiers in addition to fines or hard labor. Remitting sentences was a common occurrence in court-martial reviews. Senior officers wound up remitting all or part of 14 percent of all cases ending with the defendant serving hard labor, 14 percent of all punishments by fines, 17 percent of all incarceration sentences, 20 percent that ended in dishonorable discharge, and an astounding 58 percent of capital cases.[196] Privates Don Carlos Alvarez, Robert Brown, Michael Collins, and James Faulkner all received their sentences at the same court-martial session in New Orleans in 1864, sentenced to varying time periods of hard labor while wearing a ball and chain. Major General Joseph J. Reynolds lessened their sentences "so much of them as requires that prisoners wear a ball and chain during their confinement, is remitted."[197] For cowardice in battle, Private Benjamin Harbaugh suffered a sentence of three years hard labor in the Dry Tortugas "wearing a ball weighing twenty pounds attached to his leg by a chain not less than four nor more than six feet in length," but luckily for him General Meade remitted the ball and chain.[198] Because a sentence in the Dry Tortugas was such a hardship, not sending soldiers there became a welcome remittance. Major General John C. Fremont approved the sentence of hard labor for the duration of the war for Conrad Kuhl, a civilian who, along with two other civilians, murdered a Union soldier. But while his two accomplices suffered the death penalty by hanging, Fremont remitted Kuhl's incarceration in the Dry Tortugas, instead committing him to serve his sentence at Camp Chase, Ohio.[199] Instead of sending two deserters to the Dry Tortugas, General Thomas remitted that portion of their sentence, instead holding them at the military prison in Nashville at hard labor "for the terms specified in their sentences," two years for one and the duration of the war for the other.[200] In the interests of fairness and mercy, officers also remitted prison sentences altogether if judged too punitive for the proven accusation.

Generals also alleviated the additional suffering of a diet of bread and water. Instead of an $18 fine and a week on bread and water, Private Edward Anglin only had to pay the fine thanks to Brigadier General Lewis G. Arnold.[201] A court-martial threw the book at Private Frank Riley of the One Hundred-first Pennsylvania for disobeying orders. The panel imposed a $60 fine and hard labor for 60 days while wearing a ball and chain on a diet of bread and water, but Major General John J. Peck remitted the bread and water punishment.[202] Generals also had to rein in overzealous panels that imposed clearly illegal punishments. Immediately after the disastrous failure at Fredericksburg, when discipline in the Army of the Potomac was at low ebb, a court-martial in the III Corps sentenced Private Michael Burns of the Eleventh Massachusetts, who assaulted and disobeyed a corporal, to serve the remainder of his term of service in the army at hard labor on the Rip Raps "during which time to wear an iron neck-yoke round his neck weighing seven pounds, with three prongs placed at equal distance on the outside, six inches long each." General Sickles, however remitted the yoke portion of the sentence, and rebuked the penalty as "being too barbarous a character to be executed during the present age."[203]

Reviewing officers also voided sentences altogether, freeing the soldiers from any punishment and returning them to the units, for a totally different reason than mercy and compassion. In 5 percent of the cases with disapproved sentences, the reviewing officer vacated the sentence because the sentence, instead of too harsh, was too lenient. One purpose of courts-martial was to decide the guilt of an accused offender and render a sufficient punishment. The other was to deter future offenses by demonstrating the army's resolve to enforce the rules, convict the guilty, and punish within the bounds of authority. If courts arrived at a sentence that did not sufficiently punish an offender, commanding generals feared that soldiers might not appreciate the seriousness of a court-martial and the risk of violating the rules. This, in turn, might generate additional violations, and undermine the goal of tight discipline. Rather than allow that to happen, reviewing officers preferred to void the sentence as a personal rebuke to the officers on the panel to ensure that, if tasked with court-martial duty in the future, they would address future charges with an appropriate level of justice. The formal disapproval of the sentence usually involved a personal censure of the panel members, reflecting the generals' displeasure at their unwillingness to support the larger duty of military justice. When Private Oscar Tucker deserted and remained away from his regiment for more than three months, his court-martial sentence merely fined him three months pay and issued a formal reprimand. General John Pope found the sentence entirely unsatisfactory. "It is hardly worth while to take officers away from the discharge of their duties," Pope harangued, "and incur a heavy expenditure of money and more valuable time, to obtain such results as these. It is simply . . . trifling with justice and discipline." In setting aside the sentence, Pope stated that "A reprimand can be keenly felt only by those who are imbued with the spirit of soldierly honor," and Tucker, "cannot, reasonably, be supposed susceptible to any shame that could be awakened by a reprimand."[204] Having determined that "The sentence is a farce," General Banks rejected the sentence imposed upon Sergeant Elijah Fish for destroying government property when he cut down the flagpole in his camp. To compensate the government, the panel fined Fish five cents, perhaps the lowest penalty in the history of military justice.[205]

As in civilian courts, offenders of the most serious nature could expect little sympathy or mercy, and when offenses warranted a capital sentence, reviewing officers expected courts-martial to demonstrate the resolve to inflict death. When a panel convicted Private Alexander McBride of murdering a fellow soldier, General Howard quickly confirmed the sentence, agreeing, "For crimes of this aggravated nature, no punishment can be too severe."[206] But not every potential capital case resulted in an execution. Courts-martial could inflict the death penalty, but they did not have to. The Articles of War defined the parameters of capital punishment as "death, or such other punishments as, by sentence of a court-martial, shall be inflicted." If a panel decided that a minor punishment fit a major crime, it was within their powers to render such a decision. In doing so, however, court-martial panels faced the reproach of senior officers who expected discipline and wondered why panels did not provide it. Private Charles Gleason, for instance, twice struck a superior officer, but instead of sentencing him to a potential death penalty, the panel who heard his case imposed only a $5 fine. "Such offenders are punishable *capitally*," George McClellan wrote in dismissing the sentence, "The paltry penalty exacted of the prisoners now under consideration is a burlesque upon military justice," and McClellan opted to "dispense with the farce of executing the sentences awarded."[207] Private John Feaney received a double dose of charity. Instead of desertion, his court-martial convicted him of AWOL and sentenced him to a reprimand, a sentence that General Sickles considered "an absurd punishment for an enlisted man, convicted of absence without leave."[208] General Rousseau censured a panel in his district when they convicted Private John Locker of conduct prejudicial for his attempted rape of a civilian. "The findings . . . are not approved," Rousseau replied, "An indecency of such a flagrant and disgusting character should have been made the occasion for exemplary punishment," but the panel declined to issue a death warrant.[209]

FOR ALL THE STEREOTYPES of inflexible military law, the reality of Civil War military justice is one of flexibility, leniency, and individuality. Far from the rigid and stern administrators of harsh justice, the Union officers who sat on Civil War courts-martial took circumstances into account, listened to both sides of the issue, and operated a system that administered proper justice in the vast majority of cases. While the courts operated by a procedure very different than civil courts, the differences did not amount to an abuse of liberty or the rights of citizens. Military law had its own means of ensuring a fair trial, with objective judges, fair representation, and a limited appeals mechanism. Plenty of Union soldiers faced the possibility of a death sentence, but panels restrained the wider impulse to put soldiers to death or imprison them for long periods of time, and many capital cases ended with a much more lenient sentence. Considering the lack of legal experience held by the masses of volunteer officers appointed to court-martial duty, their performance was a credible example of maintaining a disciplined army. "Disciplined," that is, by the primary definition of the word, being an army with the will to stand, fight, and defeat the enemy. Considering the large number and wide range of cases that showed up in front of courts-martial, it is clear that the Union army was often not a disciplined army by the secondary definition, that is, an army that knew, respected, and obeyed the rules. The massive number of offenders threatened to overwhelm the army's legal system and, if sentenced to the harsher degree, to force the army to spend massive amounts of time and effort to administering punishments instead of fighting the enemy. It was a good thing for the Union army that it possessed such a flexible legal system Had the army shot every soldier found guilty of a capital offense or punished to the ultimate degree every defendant who stole a chicken or got drunk, the army itself might well have revolted. Confronted with men trying to demonstrate their masculinity and citizen-soldiers unaccustomed to such a foreign trial procedure, the army wisely opted to place practical justice over perfect justice. Soldiers who perhaps deserved severe punishment instead got off lightly, or failed to receive a punishment at all. This may not be the ideal example of pure justice, but if military law existed to maintain order and create an effective fighting force, then the Union army's legal system worked well enough. A sentence was not the end of the army's troubles when it came to disciplining citizen-soldiers with a strong idea of individual rights and liberty. Courts-martial, sitting in legal isolation, might have the luxury of judging and issuing a suitable sentence, but it did not have the burden of imposing its punishment. The army had a much more troubling time actually imposing its punishment.

"WE HAVE NO RIGHT TO SHOOT THEM"

The Application of Punishment

Punishing guilty offenders was the end process of the military justice system, an act that brought closure to the series of events that led to the penalty: offense, intervention by an office, judgment, and sentence. The infliction of a penalty, as far as the army was concerned, ended the matter. The army did not institutionally monitor the behavior of soldiers post-punishment, and, unless an officer provided evidence that a soldier was a chronic disciplinary problem, did not hold past offenses against an offender. Closing the book on a particular crime for the army, however, meant something entirely different to soldiers who had to endure the consequences. Military offenses required military punishments, but if soldiers objected to officers controlling their lives and determining their fates, then discipline was even worse. The very idea of subjecting oneself to military discipline divided the opinions of Union soldiers. To the average Civil War soldier, steeped in the citizen-soldier ethos that defense of the nation meant dedication of cause, a flawed soldier who broke the rules deserved his fate. Furthermore, the demonstration of masculinity obliged soldiers to bear their obligations manfully, even if that meant accepting punishment for violating the rules. To other soldiers, however, military punishment was the purest form of despotism, the epitome of the clash between soldiers, determined to maintain their rights and individuality, and officers equally determined to enforce order and discipline. In an effort to justify their position as the arbiter of an offender's fate, the army framed its punishment in the context of the soldier as a failed individual who, if only temporarily, did not live up to his obligations and required corrective action. Any true soldier, in the army's view, could not disagree with this approach as it preserved the honorable name of the army and the soldiers who filled its ranks. While some soldiers accepted this opinion and approved of the punishment of flawed offenders, other soldiers refused to buy the argument. With the realization that life was fragile, death was near, and war was not glamorous, many men viewed army discipline as another example of petty officers exercising petty duties and a faceless army bureaucracy stepping on the rights of citizen-soldiers. Instead of seeing flaws in a punished offender, soldiers expressed sympathy for another victim of army injustice.

Punishment itself, as the final step of the disciplinary process, was no small event. The army inflicted penalties for rule violations to demonstrate that commanders would not accept such behavior in the future. Punishment, therefore, served the function of deterrence as well as retribution, with soldiers chastised for past behavior and hopefully predisposed to avoiding such infractions in the future. Inflicting a painful punishment was certainly an effective means of achieving these goals, but not always appropriate to the crime. Instead, humiliation and disgrace became the common features of discipline regardless of crime, both minor and major, or mechanism of punishment, from demotion to execution. Almost every punishment included a feature intended to humble a soldier, belittle his masculinity, and impress upon him the power and authority of the officers above him. Humiliation, however, only had true effect if others observed the denigrated soldiers in the midst of his punishment, so army penalties by definition became public ones. Whether standing on a barrel or standing in front of a firing squad, military discipline was a public event shared by many. This model of discipline was not by accident. Solely punishing a soldier accomplished the objective of disciplining and deterring the offender, but if others saw the consequences of misbehavior, they might also turn away from inappropriate conduct. To maximize the impact of a shameful penalty, punishments took on ritualistic forms. Instead of ad hoc punishments that concentrated only upon the offender, many disciplinary processes had specific steps and nuances intended to emphasize and maximize the humiliation of the offender and demonstrate the army's authority to any and all witnesses. The level of ritualistic punishment corresponded to the severity of the offense, with minor offenses punished by relatively simple rituals (such as a public demotion) and major offenses warranting a complex ritual (such as the elaborate process of a public execution).

AS PREVIOUSLY DISCUSSED, general courts-martial possessed the sole authority to hear certain cases and inflict certain punishments. For many offenses under their jurisdiction, the army was quick to impose a fine, either as the sole punishment or as an additional penalty. The imposition of a financial penalty certainly got a soldier's attention, especially one who suffered a form of permanent penalty. Demotion was a unique penalty for NCOs who violated the rules. Privates were already on the lowest rung of the rank ladder, and the Articles of War dictated that officers who committed major offenses were to be cashiered, not demoted to the ranks. This left only NCOs to suffer the loss of financial compensation and public face after their demotion for failing to do their duty. At the same time, however, the newly promoted NCOs had to maintain the respect of their fellow enlisted men without appearing condescending or pompous. Many NCOs found the transition difficult, as they did not hold the full authority of officers (who still ordered them about as subordinates) and were still considered as authority figures by the privates (who regarded them as unwelcome symbols of control). Being an NCO, according to Corporal George Cadman, was "being everyone's dog and nobody's boss."[1] Consequently, the turnover of NCOs reached epidemic proportions in some units. Over the duration of the war, for example, Colonel Cyrus Colgrove of the Twenty-seventh Indiana demoted almost forty NCOs for various offenses.[2]

In compensation for their extra duties, NCOs earned additional pay. Compared to the $13 per month paid to privates, corporals earned $20 and sergeants $34, so the loss of rank had a direct financial impact.[3] After a regimental court-martial demoted an orderly sergeant down to private, an officer noted it was "quite a change from 34 to 13 dols. per month."[4] The army had high expectations of its NCOs, so consequently there were plenty of reasons to demote them for failures of their duty. "A Corporal of Co. G was reduced [to the ranks] the other day . . . for neglect of duty," Charles Mattocks noted, while Corporal Michael Kelly lost his stripes for gambling with his men, and Sergeant Edward Hanrahan became a private again after getting drunk on duty.[5] Sergeant Thomas Blincoe lost his position after "making himself a public spectacle" by drinking too much and falling off his horse on a city street for all to see.[6] Corporal Albert W. Bolen "was reduced to the ranks for non-attention on Dress parade."[7] A similar fate befell "Corpls. Ball & Coleman," who "could not desist from talking & laughing in the ranks." When informed of the loss of rank, "They went back to their tents & commenced ripping off their stripes & chevrons while the big tears were rolling down their cheeks. . . . They came out the next morning in the list of privates & in private's uniform."[8] Given the difficulties of staying an NCO, Sergeant Peter Welsh proudly informed his wife, "i [*sic*] never got into any trouble nor got into any disgrace nor received a single reprimand . . . since i joined the regiment."[9]

The loss of rank, status, and pay was a severe punishment, but at least the offenders maintained their personal freedom, unlike those subjected to imprisonment. When encamped for any length of time, regimental or brigade commanders constructed a guardhouse, a jail that represented the minimal level of incarceration for military offenses. Guardhouses served as holding pens for soldiers found guilty of minor offenses, either of regimental rules or at a regimental court-martial. Housing those convicted at courts-martial in the guardhouse prevented the burden of shipping the soldiers to an outside location for their punishment and instead kept them close to their regiments so they could quickly return to duty when their sentences ended. It did not take some soldiers long to find their way into the guardhouse. William Lamson recalled the arrival of some new recruits who got to fighting and wound up spending their first day in the army in the guardhouse.[10] The massive number of offenses committed by soldiers, however, meant that building, maintaining, and guarding the guardhouses was itself a major effort. Describing his duty as an engineer, Private Charles Barber listed his most frequent duties as "build and repair road and bridges[,] build guard houses[,] and bury the dead."[11] Most regiments, however, either constructed their own guardhouses or converted an existing building to that purpose. Most were little more than squalid huts, and soldiers dreaded the prospect of spending any time there. "Our guard-house is a miserable affair, being seldom used," Wilber Fisk commented, "It is seldom fit to use."[12] Robert Sneden described one regimental guardhouse as a simple "log guard house for delinquents. . . the only light is admitted to the inside by a narrow slit in the flat roof."[13]

A stay in the guardhouse was never easy or pleasurable. Often overcrowded, guardhouses soon became filthy and unhealthy, exacerbating the common practice of turning any available structure into a guardhouse whether it was suitable or not. "I found one of the most wretched and filthy holes imaginable," Surgeon Thomas Ellis stated in describing the guardhouse in his camp. Besides the tearing of floorboards for firewood, Ellis found other major structural failures in the building, along with "a heap of filth, composed of the rejected food and offal of every kind, which sent forth an intolerable and unhealthy stench."[14] Soldiers did not just sit around and do nothing in the guardhouse, as officers made sure to keep them occupied lest they become too comfortable and forget their incarceration was punishment. Observing the guardhouse after church services one Sunday, Marcus Woodcock "saw about 50 men 'marking time' at common, quick, and double-quick time" as a sergeant marched them back and forth, "rending the affair rather amusing."[15]

Because of the foul environment and restrictive conditions, many soldiers tried to escape from the guardhouse, although what they planned to do next was open to conjecture. Presumably, most of the prospective escapees intended to further desert from the service, which perhaps explains the harsh response by guards and officers to attempted escapes. Angry at the imprisonment of their comrades, soldiers sometimes plotted to spring them from jail. "Nothing to do today but out guarding the prisson [sic]," Private Thomas Walton wrote, maintaining extra guard vigilance because "It was [threatened] to be broken open by the company to get out prissoners."[16] Other escapes were successful, however. Private George Martin, held in a guardhouse awaiting court-martial, managed to escape and elude a search for him. Angry at his escape, his guards remained "on the lookout for Martin with orders to kill him on sight. If they see him he is a cooked goose."[17] On occasion, ineptitude permitted soldiers to escape the guardhouse. Lieutenant William Seward, struggling with his new responsibilities as an officer, failed to manage the guard around the guardhouse of the Second Michigan. As a consequence, all of the guards wandered off, along with most of the prisoners.[18] Other escapes came by way of organized violence. Unhappy at their confinement for leaving camp without a pass, imprisoned soldiers of the One Hundred Fifty-fourth New York conducted a mass breakout that ended with the guardhouse burned to the ground.[19]

Bound by duty to maintain the guard while confronted with violence from the prisoners, guards often had little compunction about using violence themselves to arrest and contain prisoners. In one incident, pickets had a difficult time subduing an armed and drunken soldier who wandered into their camp. He bolted out the door of the guardhouse before the provost guard could close it, but "He didn't get far before he was overhauled. . . . The rascal came back with a broken head," and one of the provost guards "came back with a broken gun, and as I understand there was a very intimate connection between the two."[20] The use of force to maintain guardhouse security could also reach irrational levels. Tired of the constant "holering [sic] and swaring" coming from the guardhouse that kept them awake at night, James Greenalch watched as, "the officers, two or three of them, would pitch on one man and knock him down and pound him all up" before leaving him "tied down to the benches groaning and yelling." When that did not work, another officer brandished his pistol, warning the prisoners that if "they did not sit down and be still he would give them the contence [sic]." Instead, the officers gave the guards the authority to shoot if it became necessary to maintain the peace, and consequently "last night two men were shot by the goard [guard]." Greenalch explained that "They were told to stop and did not and they [the guards] fired. . . . One was shot dead, the other was brought in to the hospital this morning, and another was shot the night before."[21]

Officers who faced court-martial did not have to suffer the indignity and discomfort of a stay in the guardhouse. The customs of military law granted officers the preferential treatment of more comfortable accommodations if charged with offenses. Instead of occupying the guardhouse, officers who faced criminal proceedings could remain in their tents in a form of house arrest. The exception was when an officer faced a charge "so severe as to afford a natural temptation to escape from justice," causing the army to impose "a state of confinement as secure as the closest civil imprisonment." If an officer left his tent in violation of his arrest, he violated Article of War 77 by breaching his arrest and faced a mandatory cashiering if found guilty.[22] Lieutenant Colonel Orlando Moore of the Thirteenth Michigan, for instance, refused to turn over his sword to the provost guard and insisted on continuing his duties while awaiting his court-martial for threatening a superior officer. Moore soon found himself stripped of his rank.[23] Lieutenant John O'Brien of the Thirty-sixth USCT lost his commission for drunkenness, compounded when he breached his arrest to plead his case with his commanding officer.[24] The Fifteenth Kentucky lost one of its captains when Richard H. Crupper refused a direct order, compounded the charge by insulting a superior officer, and then breached arrest by leaving his tent to commiserate with fellow officers.[25]

As bad as a stint in the guardhouse could be, most soldiers found it preferable to a lengthy prison stay. A relatively short sentence in the guardhouse was the usual outcome of a regimental court-martial for a minor offense, but a prison sentence meant a soldier committed a major offense that warranted a substantial punishment but did not merit the death penalty. Assaulting an officer, chronic AWOL, and theft of military property were the most common offenses that led to a prison sentence, a penalty with little interest in rehabilitation and every intention of punishing the offender. Finding a place to incarcerate prisoners was the army's first problem. In the small antebellum army, local jails and prisons sufficed for the limited number of major offenders. No formal military prison existed when the Civil War began, and the army did not establish its first dedicated prison until the Congress authorized the construction of the United States Military Prison (later the United States Disciplinary Barracks) at Ft. Leavenworth, Kansas, in 1874.[26] The need to create a system of prisoner of war (POW) camps provided the opportunity to established separate military prisons at the same time. The army did not want to house Confederate prisoners and Union convicts together lest it cause disciplinary problems, although in some cases it was unavoidable. Like the

POW camps, military prisons were quickly constructed and ill-planned affairs. The army initially established prisons on little-used or obsolescent military posts. The army pressed masonry forts, made obsolete by modern rifled naval guns, into service as makeshift prisons. Such forts included Fort Jefferson in the Dry Tortugas or Castle Williams on Governor's Island in New York Harbor. In California, the uninhabited island of Alcatraz in San Francisco Harbor acquired its first prison when the army turned it into a temporary holding area for military offenders.[27] Because of their make-shift conversions, the facilities were inadequate, often overcrowded, and inhospitable.

The worst facility, however, was the military prison at Alton, Illinois, twenty-five miles north of St. Louis. Constructed as a state penitentiary in 1833, the state of Illinois abandoned the prison in 1860 after constructing a new facility in Joliet. In need of a prison, Major General Henry Halleck contacted Illinois Governor John Yates about acquiring the empty facility. After spending a mere $2500 on improvements, the army sent its first prisoners to the new Federal Military Prison in February 1862, although conditions were unsatisfactory. The buildings were in poor repair, the prison sat on unstable swampy ground, there was an inadequate water supply, and overcrowding (at one point two thousand prisoners lived there) meant that a portion of the prison population lived outside in tents exposed to sweltering summers and harsh winters.[28] Due to these factors, about 1300 of the prison's estimated 12,000 occupants died while at the prison, a rate exceeded only by the POW camp at Elmira, New York.[29] To make matters worse, in 1863 the War Department ordered the Tenth Kansas to the prison to act as guards. Their commander, Colonel William Weer, was a chronic alcohol abuser whose inept leadership caused additional hardship until a court-martial finally cashiered him in 1864.[30] Although the majority of its occupants were Confederate POWs and civilians arrested for their pro-Southern activities, the army established a separate ward for Union military prisoners from the Western Theater of the war. August Scherneckau, a private in the First Nebraska, noted in his diary that three men from his regiment were heading to Alton. Privates John Douglas and Thomas Mason received sentences of two and six months, respectively, for allowing prisoners to escape from their custody, while another private received a surprisingly light two-month sentence after "He shot at an officer and wounded him in the head."[31]

Regardless of facility, life in military prisons was never pleasant. Prisoners often had to engage in hard labor, either as a portion of their court-martial sentence (and often while wearing a ball and chain) or simply to maintain the crumbling facility itself.[32] The Rip Raps in particular needed constant labor to prevent erosion, so a constant flow of labor went there. "We passed quite near the Rip Raps," Charles Mattocks wrote, commenting on the prisoners sent there, "where so many worthless soldiers are condemned to serve their time."[33] In contrast, Fort Jefferson needed relatively little maintenance, and the different labor needs sorted out which prisoners went where. Offenders with life sentences usually went to Fort Jefferson, which needed a relatively small amount of long-term labor, while the larger number of short-term offenders went to the labor-intensive Rip Raps.[34] Food was bland and in short supply, and hygiene was often difficult to maintain. Discipline was harsh, with guards prone to shoot first and ask questions later. Although a Confederate prisoner at Alton, the shooting of Hiram Miller demonstrated the harsh realities of prison discipline. Angry at a guard that stymied his escape attempt, Miller "came at him with a bar of iron," but the guard "ran his bayonet into him" while another guard "placed his gun through the grating and shot Miller thro" the heart."[35] In the Dry Tortugas, guards reportedly permitted sharks to attack and kill prisoners attempting to escape.[36] Overcrowding was a chronic problem, especially in the Dry Tortugas. Intended to house about five hundred prisoners, the prison population swelled after February 1864 when Lincoln commuted every existing death sentence for desertion to incarceration at Fort Jefferson. By the end of the war, the fort held nearly nine hundred prisoners, crammed into cramped gun embrasures hastily converted into jail cells.[37]

In addition to the punishments handed down by general-courts martial, regimental courts-martial also added their own unique penalties. The most dramatic and symbolic was the expulsion of an offender from the army. Drumming a soldier out of the army was actually a very old form of punishment. In ancient Macedonia, a general drummed several of his men out of camp for drunken misbehavior.[38] Drumming returned with the emergence of codified military law during the Thirty Years' War, and expanded throughout European armies. The punishment persisted into the British army, to be handed down as part of the American military justice tradition. The penalty appeared during the American Revolution, where it was applied even to women, and was a common sentence in the antebellum army.[39] Like other types of punishment, the army used the opportunity for punishment to not only penalize the guilty, but to also deter the actions of other soldiers. Like many punishments, drumming out had a symbolic significance, the military equivalent of exiling an undesirable element. By drumming a soldier out of his unit, the army was not only punishing a soldier but stigmatizing him as well, condemning him as someone unfit to hold the honored title of soldier. Moreover, drumming was not just an institutional offense. By requiring soldiers to participate in the drumming out, instead of just observing as in other forms of discipline, the soldiers added their condemnation as well.

Drumming, consequently, was a very public event, and the army orchestrated the procedure with as many soldiers watching as possible in the hopes of deterring witnesses from engaging in illegal acts that might earn them the same humiliating punishment. Attendance at a drumming was mandatory, and all soldiers in the offender's company or regiment had to turn out, to not only watch but also participate. After forming two long lines facing toward each other creating a double line or gauntlet, the provost guard presented the offender to his erstwhile comrades. While the offender still wore his uniform, provost guards often inflicted other physical indignities upon the prisoner, such as shaving his head or, if they wanted a more garish look, shaving only half the offender's head. Once out of the army and back in civilian life, the shaved (or half-shaved) head was an immediate indicator that the former soldier had not left the army voluntarily, but was instead a despised criminal. Once in position at the head of the double line, the offender began his march out of the army. To keep him from marching out too soon and not receiving the full effect of the humiliating experience, provost guards walked in front and behind him, with their bayonets positioned close to his chest and back to prevent him from moving too quickly. As the procession made its way down the line, the regimental band played the music of the "Rogue's March," an old British soldiers' song about regret at joining the army. Soldiers were free to say what they wanted to the departing soldier, as "There were no restraints put upon the language of his [the drummed out soldier's] recent associates, and their vocabularies were worked up to their full capacity at reviling him."[40] At the end of the line, an NCO stripped the offender of all his buttons, insignia, or any other item that might identify him as a soldier, and the offender then marched to the edge of camp with orders not to return lest an even harsher punishment await him.[41] The unit then distributed the drummed soldier's name to other units, so that the offender could not rejoin the army. The discharge from the camp symbolized the ousting of the offender from the fraternity of soldiers, a membership the drummed soldier could never again attain as he had lost the respect of his comrades.

Like other punishments, certain offenses tended to earn a drumming out more than other types of violations. Soldiers who could not contain their alcohol use, and therefore were a weak link in their companies, frequently found themselves drummed. A regimental court-martial ordered Private Patrick Bolen, after having "one side of his head shaved," to suffer the humiliation of being "drummed out of the service" for chronic drunkenness.[42] Another soldier had the same punishment inflicted upon him after he drunkenly stumbled into a photographer's studio, insisted upon having his picture taken, and then slugged the corporal sent to arrest him.[43] As an offense that also indicated personal failure and loss of faith with one's comrades, theft also often resulted in a drumming out. "We drummed a nigar [*sic*] soldier out of the service the day before yesterday," Corporal John Point wrote regarding a thief. "We first shaved the wool off his head and made him . . . [march] clear down the line."[44] Soldiers also faced the punishment for stealing from civilians. As a soldier passed through Parkersburg, West Virginia, "one of the men of Co. K stole a coat, a shawl, and some other things." After "He was tried by court martial and sentenced to be drummed out of camp in disgrace," the army made arrangements to turn him "over to civil authorities to be tried by them. They will be apt to put him in the penitentiary."[45] Soldiers certainly understood the humiliation of a public ceremony like a drumming out, and they determined to avoid the same disgrace. Describing how "Everything was quiet until about 3 or 4 o'clock," Private Aurelius Voorhis fell "into line to see a man drummed out of service" for "stealing money from a fellow soldier." Observing the event, Voorhis got the message the army was sending; "Such a discharge," he wrote, "I don't want in mine."[46]

Other offenses that commonly earned a drumming out, however, had the odd effect of giving the offenders exactly what they wanted. For soldiers who did not want to fight, either by cowardice or by desertion, a drumming out might be a humiliating experience, but they got what they desired—a separation from the army. Cowards and deserters, examples of men who lacked masculinity or failed to uphold the obligations of a citizen-soldier, were also, like alcoholics and thieves, considered failed soldiers whom a company or regiment was better off without. Humiliating them by drumming them out of camp highlighted their shortcomings or failures, providing a sufficient punishment in itself. In some cases the army sentenced soldiers to a drumming out, followed by a stint in confinement. In other cases, however, especially early in the war, regiments drummed out deserters and cowards as the sole punishment, leaving the former soldier to return home and the inevitable questioning of his manhood. As the war continued, however, and more and more soldiers began to desert or expose themselves less to danger, a drumming out seemed less like a punishment and more like a means to escape. If a head-shaving and a dishonorable discharge was the worst that happened to a soldier who wanted out of the army, then such a punishment was a winning proposition. Consequently, drumming out became less common as the war progressed, and if courts-martial did impose the punishment it came with an additional prison sentence in some unpleasant place. In the Iron Brigade, seven soldiers received a "drumming-only" punishment for charges of cowardice and desertion in a single day. After enduring the mocking of their comrades and the "humiliating punishment on the poor wretches," the disgraced soldiers reached the edge of camp. Defending his actions, one of the drummed out soldiers, Private Patrick Dunn, declared, "I'd rather be a live ass than a dead lion."[47] At a drumming in the Fourth Minnesota, the drummed soldier "acted as if he enjoyed the fun and seemed glad to get out of the service," Corporal Alonzo Brown marveled. ". . . When out of the camp, he kicked up his heels, put his thumb to his nose, and gracefully waved his hand."[48]

Deserters also endured the shameful process. Describing two deserters drummed out at the same time in his regiment, a soldier observed the two "culprits appeared, hand-cuffed" for their drumming out. After undergoing the usual drumming procedure, where "the finger of scorn pointed at them from every one," the two offenders "was [sic] sent to work on fortification for the period of two years, without pay."[49] Instead of serving a prison sentence after his drumming out, Private John A. Mallory of the Eighteenth Regulars served his six-month term in Nashville first, and the army shipped him to the Army of the Cumberland at Chattanooga to receive his drumming out before releasing him.[50] In September 1862, the Seventy-sixth Ohio drummed out four men, one for insubordination and the other three for desertion, when stationed in Helena, Arkansas. The insubordinate soldier suffered only the drumming out, "a consummation he was devoutly glad for in order to get out of the service," in the opinion of one soldier. Two deserters went to a regional jail to serve six months at hard labor, but the other deserter left under escort to serve the remainder of his term at the military prison at Alton.[51]

Most soldiers despised those drummed out, and many recognized the need to avoid experiencing the punishment themselves. Private John Rippetoe admitted it was "a bad looking spectacle after his [a deserter's] head was shaved" and confessed "how bad I should hate to be in his place" but also recognized the effectiveness of the process, acknowledging that the deserter "can never do any good where he is known" after being "disgraced this way."[52] One Union soldier had an answer for his drummed-out appearance. Convicted at regimental court-martial for "robbing his dead comrades after the battle of Lookout Mountain," the soldier had to suffer a drumming out. To further his humiliation, "a colored barber appeared with a bucket of water and a razor" to shave his head, which he explained away when he got home as a necessity because of a "camp fever."[53] Enlisted men might have some empathy for the subject of a drumming out, but officers felt no such consideration. "They shaved his head and drummed him out of camp," Charles Haydon wrote of a deserter from his regiment, "He had a splendid looking foretop, his hair cut & haggled in some placed tight to his head & in others left abt 1 inch long. The tonsorial operation was performed in the presence of the whole Co."[54]

General courts-martial, with their formalized procedures and rules of evidence, often gain the most attention when studies examine military justice. The authority of general courts-martial to impose the harshest of retribution made them dramatic examples of the application of judicial punishment. More often than not, however, a soldier faced lower forms of discipline than general courts-martial. For minor infractions of the Articles of War, soldiers found themselves punished by lower regimental courts-martial. These less formal proceedings occurred much more frequently as they took place within the regiment and did not need the level of formality and protocol demanded by general courts-martial. In addition, soldiers also faced on-the-spot punishments for violations of regimental rules. Each regimental colonel was at his own discretion in imposing his own personal policies on leave, military duties, and camp life, and violators of these policies were at the immediate mercy of the regimental officers without any other recourse or formal procedure. Consequently, the punishments meted out at the regimental level became the most common form of military discipline, with many soldiers receiving some form of penalty in their military career.

Officers, clinging to the traditional concept that discipline in camp meant discipline on the battlefield, often felt stymied by the general courts-martial system, especially when courts proved more lenient than an officer might have preferred. Officers also believed that, while they requested the court-martial, the panel actually punished the soldier, not them, leaving them with the attitude that soldiers feared judicial punishment more than their actual officers. Based upon this combination of elements, officers stretched their internal powers to impose punishment to the limit. Within their own camps and below the legal threshold of a court-martial, the army granted officers the liberty to establish their own rules and policies, and to punish violators of these camp policies as they saw fit. The imposition of these "camp punishments" were the only way that officers could directly moderate the behavior of their soldiers and demonstrate the direct ability to inflict punishment without resorting to a court-martial. Determined to have the discipline they desired, officers had no qualms about punishing soldiers to the extent of their ability, in the hopes of achieving the desired outcome. Captain John Knight, upon taking command of his company, determined to straighten the unit out. Within a matter of days, Knight had men performing extra drill, laboring in the sun on bread and water, carrying heavy objects as punishment, and throwing soldiers in the guardhouse with no concern other than improving discipline. "I wonder if you will think I am cruel," Knight wrote to his wife in describing his disciplinary barrage. "I think it justice and believe it a duty. I got the worst company [when I arrived] . . . [but] One of the officers remarked to me yesterday he believed I had the best company in the detachment."[55] Major Henry Abbott approved of the hard line his colonel, Francis Palfrey of the Twentieth Massachusetts, took with undisciplined soldiers. "Palfrey has good sense enough to see that such cases demand prompt treatment," Abbott wrote to his parents, "such as tying a man up by his thumbs & keeping him in a cell on bread & water with the mercury below freezing."[56] Soldiers, of course, saw such an adherence to discipline quite differently. Instead of making them better soldiers, such strident adherence to rules was the sign of a tyrannical officer. In at least some cases, the soldiers were correct. John Ferguson, for instance, was outraged when his friend was punished when he refused to go on fatigue duty "because he had no shoes."[57]

Free to make any punishment for regimental offenses that they saw fit within the restrictions set by Congress and the Constitution, regimental officers used their imaginations when imposing penalties on offenders in their units. Camp punishments could not exceed the limits set by the formal military justice system. They obviously could not impose the death sentence or a lengthy prison term, nor could they impose severe punishments on a par with general courts-martial. If a soldier warranted a punishment equal to a general court-martial, military justice dictated the soldier should face a general court-martial. Limited in what physical penalties they could impose, officers instead emphasized humiliation and physical discomfort as a punishment. Offenders endured punishments that publicly shamed them, reduced their social standing to something less than a soldier, or inflicted a painful, but temporary, reminder against breaking the rules. A good example was the practice of placing a minor offender on extra duty about camp while wearing a ball and chain. It was not exactly the hard labor that a general court-martial might inflict, but it drew unwanted attention to the offender, reduced him to the level of a common laborer instead of performing the duties of a soldier, and certainly made him physically exhausted. Forcing a soldier to wear a ball and chain also had some practical value. It did not permanently injure or disfigure a soldier, it did not cause financial hardship as might a fine, and it required less physical investment than a guardhouse. As a relatively simple piece of equipment, a ball and chain was easy to keep around, as some soldiers found out. In preparation for punishments that he presumed were coming from a regimental courts-martial, one officer ordered "the Blacksmith to make six Balls and Chains, so certain is he that the Commanding General will approve the Courts Proceedings."[58] Noting the diverse population at Hilton Head, South Carolina, contained, amongst others, "deserting spies, bounty-jumpers, and the like," John Holahan observed, "the 'ball and chain' is a common ornament" among the worst of the residents.[59]

Not all camp punishments involved both the humiliation and physical discomfort elements that a ball and chain combined so well. Depending upon the infraction or the officer, an offense might earn a soldier a sentence from a spectrum of camp punishments intended to highlight a disgrace or physically deter an action. On the humiliation end of the spectrum were punishments that made a display of the soldier, designed to draw attention and disgrace to the offender. Forcing a soldier to stand atop a barrel in a public place for a set period of time was a common method of achieving humiliation. One soldier, who refused to stand guard duty on the Sabbath due to his religious beliefs, changed his mind "After standing on the barrel for 12 hours."[60] Conversely, in the Thirteenth Illinois an officer made a soldier stand on a barrel "some hours for refusing to attend religious services."[61] After forging a pass to leave camp, one soldier, whose only defense was that he wanted to find some onions as a cold remedy, spent four hours a day for ten days standing on a barrel.[62] Sometimes instead of standing on the barrel, the soldier wore it. "There was a man with a heavy Barrell [sic] with a hole cut through the bottom big enough to put his head through," Private Joseph Rogers observed, "with the Barrell over his head, he was kept marching all the time. That is the effect of not obeying orders."[63] In another regiment, two soldiers arrested for stealing from another soldier also had to wear barrels and march "with a guard at their side, around the camp all day yesterday and till midnight last night, and commenced again this morning."[64] Instead of facing general courts-martial and possible execution for cowardice, "two fellows who ran away from the battle of Fredericksburg," Private William Morse wrote, instead had only a regimental court-martial that sentenced them to "have $10 per month deducted from their pay for four months and stand on a barrel . . . for six days with the word 'Cowardice' on their backs."[65]

Another common form of public humiliation was to force a miscreant to wear a sign or placard identifying his offense. Standing silent, unable to justify their acts, a soldier had to endure the scorn of anyone who looked upon him. Like using a barrel, placards emphasized humiliation without undue physical discomfort, and the army applied the punishment for a variety of offenses. "One of our deserters was caught a few days hence," James Horrocks wrote, ". . . his head was shaved and he is placed upon a gun carriage every day with the word deserter on his back."[66] In front of their entire regiment assembled for dress parade, two soldiers in William Davis' unit "were marched to the front of the Regt" to receive "the word 'Thief' written on card board on their chests and backs."[67] Another thief, William Lamson observed, "has been marching back and forth along the street" with sheets of paper pinned to his breast and back marked in "large Captable [sic] letters 'Thief,'" for the offense of stealing "a canteen half full of molasses."[68] Describing the punishment of a "skulker in the face of the enemy," an observer lost count of the number of times "he was marched through the camp & back again." Another soldier was supposed to share the punishment, but "he was so drunk they were obliged to keep him till

Sunday."[69] Unfairly singled out for their failures at Chancellorsville, soldiers of the XI Corps who straggled or shirked duty wore only "a large piece of board in the shape of a crescent . . . the badge worn by the 11th Corps," signifying to all the soldiers' membership in the disgraced unit.[70]

Slightly up the punishment scale was forcing soldiers to "ride the pole" or "ride the horse." The "pole" was simply a cross beam elevated high enough off the ground so that a soldier sitting on it could not place his feet on the ground. The pole in the Fifth USCT was only four inches wide and eight feet off the ground.[71] The "horse" was like the pole, except that provost guards had garishly decorated the pole to make it look like a wooden horse, emphasizing the humiliation of sitting upon such a ridiculous looking structure. Riding the pole or the horse was a more difficult punishment because it involved some physical discomfort as well as humiliation. Perched upon a narrow rail, a soldier's entire body weight pressed down on his legs or crotch, causing pain and discomfort as he sat there for hours on end. To emphasize the discomfort and to make sure the soldier did not dismount without permission, officers might also bind the offender's ankles together.[72] Undisciplined recruits in the Twenty-seventh Michigan had to sit astride a horse in their camp "full of riders, day and night." With their legs tied together and "unable to sit on the animal, and grasping one another, they turn, heads down and hang like so many chickens at market, until they are righted by the guards."[73] While not an excessively painful punishment, riding the pole was certainly no light penalty. Like the barrel, it had the benefit of simplicity, and many different offenders found themselves perched on the pole. "There has been a good deal of drunkenness," Charles Haydon observed in his company, so ". . . Tomorrow we are going to have some of them astride a pole all day."[74]

Instead of riding a pole, some soldiers had to carry one. A bit more up the harshness scale was the practice of compelling a soldier to carry a heavy object while in a public place. The pole soldiers had to bear was usually a hewn log or fence post weighing as much as seventy pounds. For missing roll call one morning, an officer punished a soldier "by making him march up and down the company quarters with a fence rail or pole on his shoulders," while another soldier, caught sneaking out of camp, was soon "packing a rail in front of the camp guardhouse."[75] Some soldiers caught stealing from civilians had an extra bit of humiliation added to their pole punishment. After toting "a heavy stick of cordwood" around the camp "for an hour or two," the provost guard brought the offenders before General Michael Lawler who "put them through the manual of arms for a while with their cordwood muskets" to remind them that they were still soldiers and he expected them to act like such.[76] Even large groups suffered the punishment. For "making some observations distasteful" to their colonel, Sergeant Hartwell's entire company had "to each carry a rail & walk in a ring until further orders."[77] Because they failed so utterly in their drills, John Holahan's entire company was "set to work 'grinding cider,' the military term for walking around a large circle carrying a log of wood on the shoulder."[78] Because the punishment produced physical exhaustion, soldiers did not particularly care for bearing their logs. When the physical appearance of some members of the Twenty-ninth USCT became slovenly, their officers punished them by ordering them to carry a rail, an action that produced a near-riot.[79] Men of the Twenty-second Iowa marched with logs until finally, fed up with the punishment, "one of the boys declared he would march no longer" and dropped his log, and other soldiers followed suit. Major Edward White, who had the respect of the men, talked them into picking up their logs again lest some general "make additional trouble for him."[80]

Broadly similar to forcing a soldier to carry a log was placing him on "knapsack drill," filling his knapsack with stones and requiring him to march about the camp or go about his regular duties with his extra burden. Unlike carrying a log, which replaced the tools of a soldier with a simplistic substitute, knapsack drill reinforced the burden of being a soldier by using his own equipment against him. Private Enos Vail, writing about a soldier who could not seem to stay out of trouble, described the burden placed on the chronic offender. "He would be compelled to march up and down, accompanied by a guard," Vail wrote. "His punishment was to carry a knapsack filled with stones."[81] Captain Washington Elliott had so many offenders in his company that knapsack drill became a group activity, and he forced a number of men to "walk round a ring almost sixty feet in circumference, each man carrying a knapsack filled with stones."[82] For one soldier, the knapsack drill was particularly appropriate. Some "roguish fellows had made a practice of throwing stones" in the barracks after lights out, but Colonel Joel Baker, "sufficient proof being found to convict" one of the offenders, put him on "Knapsack drill for one hour at double quick" for two days.[83]

The army inflicted other camp punishments for the sole purpose of impressing a lesson upon the soldier through physical pain and discomfort. The intent was not to permanently injure or cripple the offender, but rather to inflict just enough torment to deter future inappropriate behavior. Officers had to be careful, however, to not punish too severely, lest they violate the army's limits on punishments or alienate their soldiers even further. Citizen-soldiers understood the need for discipline while at the same time not entirely embracing it. Offenders needed punishment, but if an officer became, in their estimation, too sadistic and imposed penalties too harsh, then citizen-soldiers also had the right to rein in abusive officers. Insubordination, mutiny, and rioting often resulted from excessive punishments. An excessive level of discipline also risked a masculine backlash. Soldiers expected those punished to accept their punishments like men by bearing the responsibility and discomfort that a punishment imposed. A punishment that exceeded the pain level that any normal man could bear, however, led to crying, pleading, and other forms of unmasculine behavior, and many soldiers retaliated for such an abuse of masculine status.

The minimal level of physical punishment was to bind a soldier, either by simply tying his limbs together or by binding him to a tree or other immovable object. This punishment had a certain degree of humiliation attached to it, as an officer might have a soldier bound in a public place. The main purpose was to inflict sufficient pain to deter future behavior, however, and if the bound soldier appeared in public it was more for the effect of also deterring his fellow soldiers. Any offense might result in an officer ordering a soldier bound, but insubordination and drunkenness were the most common, as Robert Sneden noted when he observed, "Sometimes the drunken soldiers . . . have to be put in irons."[84] Lieutenant Haydon, always quick to impose a punishment, used the penalty to quiet drunken soldiers. "We just tie their hands & feet," Haydon described, "gag them & put them to bed till they get sober."[85] To punish two soldiers who deserted together, Colonel Patrick Guiney decided to punish them together. Among other penalties, the two soldiers had to spend "one day from Reveille to Retreat tied by hands" to each other.[86] Officers bound other offenders, by rope or chains, for a plethora of offenses. When one of his soldiers was under arrest for "trying to steal a pistol," an officer "tied him to a post for punishment," while officers of the Thirty-ninth Ohio tied a multiple deserter to a tree to ensure he stayed long enough for his court-martial.[87] Finding a drunken soldier celebrating New Years, Captain Dodge had him bound to a tree, "which effectually quenched his mirth."[88] Lieutenant Haydon, who had drunks in his company sitting up on poles, also had no qualms about tying soldiers as well, because "In this way you are pretty sure to find them if you have to go away a few minutes." Haydon also "proposed to have a chain put around their necks & fastened to a tree" but limited himself to rope.[89] It was a good decision by Haydon, for as much as soldiers hated being tied by rope, chains were much worse. Because chains invoked imagery of common prison convicts or, even worse, slaves, soldiers were more apt to rebel and resist binding by chains. After one jail period in chains, Private John Murphy, stationed in Omaha, Nebraska Territory, threatened First Sergeant Michael Evans that he would shoot him if he tried to put him in chains again. Living up to his threat, Murphy shot Evans when an officer ordered the sergeant to place Murphy in chains for getting drunk, earning Murphy a prison sentence for the remainder of the war.[90]

Other forms of physical punishment, however, made no pretext about disgracing the offending soldiers and instead relied entirely upon intense, if temporary, pain to teach a lesson. The two most common forms of causing such pain were bucking and gagging or hanging soldiers up by their thumbs. Soldiers dreaded both punishments, not certain which was worse. Bucking and gagging a soldier involved seating the offender on the ground with his legs bent so his knees were resting against his chest, a length of wood placed under the knees, the soldier's arms wrapped around his knees and tied to the stick, and something tied into his mouth to silence him (often a bayonet). Once bound "as secure as a traped [*sic*] rat," the soldier then sat there unable to move for hours on end until his cramped muscles ached for relief.[91] Such a sight elicited sympathy from their fellow soldiers, seeing their comrades "In this helpless position . . . tumbled over on one side, lying the hot sun with flies over their faces, or in the rain and mud."[92] Recalling what it was like to be bucked and gagged, Private Frank Wilkerson described it as "highly disagreeable and painful too . . . calculated to make a man's eyes to stick out of his head as a lobster's eyes do," but a soldier could not express his pain except for "inarticulate sounds indicative of his suffering."[93]

Bucking and gagging was such a horrendous punishment that when Captain William Hamilton of the Thirty-second Ohio gave two men the choice between a few hours of the dreaded punishment or knapsack drill for two hours a day for two weeks "with fifty pounds of broken stones," both soldiers took the knapsack drill.[94] Although inflicted upon soldiers for regular punishments, officers also tended to use the punishment as a way to lash out at miscreants who offended or angered them. "Called up 3 times in the night," by drunken soldiers in the guardhouse, Lieutenant Haydon found "it necessary to have them gagged & tied or there was no sleep."[95] Unable to subdue a drunk in the Twelfth Wisconsin, a lieutenant decided that "the fellow was so crazy drunk that that they could do nothing with him" but buck and gag him.[96] Angry at soldiers who violated his rules about pillaging, officers of the Seventh Minnesota had several soldiers bucked and gagged for "killing some goats belonging to a civilian."[97] Lieutenant Lawrence Immell ordered men in his artillery battery bucked and gagged when they had the temerity to complain about their moldy rations.[98] Because officers imposed the punishment so quickly, soldiers often took offense at the flippant use of the penalty, and opposed its practice. Determined to free a bucked and gagged prisoner while encamped in Jefferson City, Missouri, soldiers with fixed bayonets almost got into a violent clash with Regular soldiers led by an officer determined to maintain the punishment. Despite the rapid escalation of the situation, cooler heads prevailed and the volunteers returned to their camp, leaving one of them to decide that "the punishment of the man was inhumane. . . . After such an ordeal a man is justified in deserting."[99]

Soldiers also reacted negatively to the practice of tying a man up by this thumbs. This involved binding a soldier's thumbs to an overhead crossbar set just high enough that the soldier's toes barely touched the ground. Unable to rest his entire body weight upon his feet, the bound soldier felt most of the pressure in his thumb joints, which became excruciatingly painful in a matter of minutes into a sentence that might last for hours. Describing one man who he tied up, Sergeant Daniel Sawtelle observed that within only a few minutes "his hands were already black," and after only a short period "his hands were so swollen that I have to cut the rope" to bring him down. The soldier forgave Sawtelle, as he was only doing what an officer ordered him to do, but he promised "he would kill that officer if he got a chance. He never got a chance, as the threat earned him a court-martial and sentence in the Dry Tortugas.[100] In his diary, Daniel Chisholm made the observation that Private Charles Yauger was "tied up for [giving] lip to the capt."[101] For stealing an apple, a "baby faced lieutenant" in Wesley Brainerd's brigade tied up a soldier until he was "thumping and scratching the pole in the severest pain" and his face turned "white as chalk."[102] The punishment could also be a group affair. After a civilian came to camp to complain about the group stripping her apple trees bare, Captain Dodge's response was "I have got the whole drum corps tied up this morning . . . I am going to keep them there all day."[103] One hardy soldier, tied up for assaulting another soldier, spent an entire afternoon and an entire morning tied up by the thumbs because he would not confess to his offense.[104] One officer had to use thumb tying as a last-resort punishment. When a soldier in his company refused to report for roll call, the officer had him bucked and gagged. When he refused to show up again the next morning, "I took him and tied him up by the thumbs," a move that finally achieved compliance.[105]

One big difference between bucking and gagging and tying a soldier up by this thumbs is that the latter soldier was usually not gagged. A bucked and gagged soldier might be in dire pain and unable to express his predicament because of the gag in his mouth. A thumb-bound soldier, however, was free to express not only his outrage at the punishment but convey the unbearable pain he was enduring. This often motivated his fellow soldiers to act on his behalf, sometimes with violent results. When an orderly sergeant tied up a soldier in the Second Massachusetts Cavalry for refusing to perform duties beyond his responsibilities, his entire company confronted their company captain and made it clear that if he did not release the man, they would release him themselves. Outnumbered, the captain agreed.[106] Incensed that "a captain [who] was noted as a tyrant" had tied up two men by their thumbs, soldiers in a New Jersey regiment nearly mutinied, but refrained when their colonel agreed to release the bound men. The men of the regiment never forgot the incident, however, characterizing the tyrannical captain as the type of officer who "received a stray ball occasionaly [*sic*] on the field of battle" from his own men.[107] After soldiers gathered to cut down a man whom Colonel Thomas Livermore had tied up for theft, Livermore "realized that this meant mutiny in my own regiment." In a show of force, he raced to the scene of the disturbance with pistol in hand and managed to get the soldiers back into their tents, but also only kept the man tied for "half an hour longer . . . then I released him" to avoid further trouble.[108] Caught between officers and enlisted men, the NCOs responsible for implementing the punishment found themselves alienated from both sides. Sergeant Evan Gery of the Ninety-sixth Pennsylvania followed orders and tied a soldier up by the thumbs, only to see the man released by his comrades. When ordered to tie the man up again, Gery refused despite the threat that his superiors "would court-martial me for not doing it." Instead, Gery suggested that the officer "should do it himself, but nothing happened."[109] Gery took a bold stance and was lucky he did not pay the price for it, as in another regiment in which "one of the sergeants [was] tied up on his tiptoes by the thumbs for four hours to a limb of a tree for disobeying orders."[110]

To volunteer soldiers who retained a sense of their citizen-soldier ethos, hanging by the thumbs came to represent a form of Regular Army discipline, and something that anyone who respected his liberty could not abide. This led to clashes between the volunteers and Regulars over the use of the punishment. Near Charlie Mosher's camp, when "the regulars had a man strung up by the thumbs," the men decided that "It was more than our volunteer blood could stand" and persuaded the regimental surgeons to cut the man down for medical reasons.[111] Incensed when a Regular officer tied up one of their own for a trivial offense, volunteers of the Fourteenth Pennsylvania Cavalry got "A mob raised and cut him down & raised a general row all though camp" before officers could restore order.[112] Tented near the Eighteenth Regulars, soldiers of the Second Minnesota and Ninth Ohio, angered by the "pitiful cries" of thumb-tied men emanating from the Regulars' encampment that "could be heard all over the camp," cut the bound man down without permission. When the Regulars strung him up again, the volunteers cut him down again. The Regulars regained control of their camp only by driving the volunteers out at bayonet point.[113] Tired of the "ugly sight" of seeing men constantly tied in General John W. Geary's camps, volunteer soldiers in Robert Strong's regiment refused to abide by army discipline, and "more than once our boys cut the men down" without permission.[114] General William Nelson received a taste of what volunteers would not accept. When Nelson refused Colonel Isaac Suman's advice that volunteer soldiers would not stand for such a harsh punishment and ordered several soldier tied up, soldiers in the Ninth Indiana crept up to Nelson's tent. Ascertaining that Nelson was lying down, the soldiers fired a volley "at the extreme top part of the tent." Realizing the errors of his ways, Nelson had the soldiers untied and he "cautiously slipped away."[115]

Because regimental offenses came in all forms, regiments might have a variety of camp punishments going on simultaneously, depending upon the severity of the misbehavior. "The punishment in the army are queer institutions," Henry Gangewer wrote while describing the activities of his encampment on Roanoke Island, "Some have their heads put through a barrel, others have to stand on a store box armed and equipped, others are bucked and gagged, others are made to attend Company and Battalion Drill with heavy knapsacks on."[116] Near Washington, soldiers endured periods staked out spread-eagle on the ground or subjected to dunking in cold water.[117] To punish drunks in a Maine regiment, officers made some of them stand knee-deep in an icy stream, but made others wear a barrel with the words "Rum Did It" painted upon it.[118] Over several days in the Ninth Pennsylvania Cavalry, an officer listed various offenses and punishments that included a day in the guardhouse for challenging an officer, the demotion of a corporal who left camp without permission, a month-long jail term for disobeying orders, a man tied up by his thumbs for accidentally shooting his horse, and two soldiers standing on barrels for fighting (only to start fighting again while standing on the barrels).[119]

AS PART OF THE CODIFICATION of military justice under the Articles of War, the army limited the type of physical punishments that a court or officer could impose, and limited the severity of its application, as when the original Articles limited the number of lashes a soldier might receive. The trend between the creation of the Articles and the Civil War continued to be one of restraint and leniency. Examples of this tendency include the denial of the death penalty except during wartime, and Congress' banning of flogging as a punishment in August 1861.[120] That did not stop some officers, however, from flaunting the rules or coming up with inventive punishments of their own, such as the cold bath to dissuade drunkenness. Using the same justification as the *Somers* Incident, some commanders in remote locations imposed illegal or particularly brutal punishments they believed necessary to impose discipline in their isolated outposts. The requirement to have all court-martial proceedings approved by higher authority, however, prevented the imposition of most of the unauthorized punishments. For lesser punishments, the only limit on the punishment was the limits of the officers' imagination, and some officers devised some creative penalties.

Some punishments did not occur very often, and were the product of an inventive officer instead of traditional penalties. Tired of Private John Blanchard's "continued insubordination," Colonel William Lee put him on "bread and water until further orders."[121] A physician at an army hospital, unable to contain soldiers from coming and going as they pleased, finally resorted to taking away his patients' clothing, forcing them to stay in bed.[122] Instead of having his officers shame a coward, the colonel of the Forty-eighth Pennsylvania had a man bucked and gagged, ordered the rest of the men into column, and permitted them to spit in the coward's face as they walked by. While some soldiers charitably "scarcely reached his face with any spittle," others gave him the "full benefit of all that tobacco chewing could bring forth."[123] To sober up a drunken soldier, officers ordered "A drunken fellow thrown into a blanket and tossed up," a chaplain witnessed with considerable amusement, "He cut the most ludicrous figure . . . looking very wild, and much like a monstrous frog, of some remote geological period" as the soldiers "tried to shake the whiskey out of him."[124] The Twenty-third Massachusetts tried to revive the use of stocks, an old punishment whereby offenders sat, their heads and hands encased in a wooden frame, in a public place as an open demonstration of their crimes. "The officers have introduced the stocks as punishment for the men have receive[d] a sentence at the hands of a regimental court-martial," Private Frederick Osborne wrote to his mother, but the men did not like it. Refusing to submit to the punishment, obstinate soldiers refused to leave the guardhouse and go into the stocks, and when a lieutenant tried to force them he was "knocked down and kicked out himself by the prisoners" along with two sergeants. Bringing in reinforcements, the officers got the prisoners into the stocks, but "If an officer came within sight of hearing, he had all his shortcomings laid out before him as loud as they could howl."[125]

Another unusual and barbaric punishment was the use of branding. Marking a soldier with a hot iron was another punishment handed down from British practice, and retained by the army throughout the antebellum period. The army reserved the punishment, however, only for soldiers who defiled their status as soldiers, deserving a punishment that lasted beyond their time in uniform. As in the case of the San Patricios during the Mexican War, branding soldiers imposed a lifetime of shame because the brand ·was permanent and marked the soldier as a criminal worthy of perpetual scorn. Compounding the shame, the army followed every branding with a drumming out, leaving the soldier with a fresh indicator of his failure as a soldier. In the aftermath of Fredericksburg, Private Edwin Weist described a drumming out that culminated when the offender "was then branded with the letter D on the hip and marched up and down the ranks of the whole Brigade to the tune of the rogues march."[126] The brand was usually a letter that corresponded to the offender's crime. In the Seventy-fifth Indiana, a deserter was "branded on the right cheek with a red hot iron in the shape of the letter D."[127] In the Seventeenth Maine, two other deserts received the same punishment, except instead of the face the provost guard applied the brand to the hip, while in the Twentieth Indiana a deserter had the brand placed "on his right thigh."[128] Private John Doxy, a deserter, received a "D" on both legs, apparently to make sure the mark was visible.[129] For stealing $15 from a tent mate, Private James Arrison was "marked indelibly with the letter 'T,'" for theft at Fort Monroe, Virginia, in April 1862, the same penalty inflicted upon Private Patrick Callaghan, convicted of robbery in the New Mexico Territory in November 1861.[130] In central Virginia in 1863, a court-martial sentenced Private Henry Degraw to receive "the letter D branded one inch broad on his right hip, and be drummed out of the service of the United States."[131] In the same year, another court-martial sentenced Private George Durrill to pay a fine, perform labor "on Government works" for the duration of his term, and "then to have the letter D branded on his left hip."[132] Private Charles Vanhee of the Third Regulars received perhaps the worst branding, however. Convicted of the specifications of desertion and "utter worthlessness as a soldier," Vanhee received a "D" brand on his left hip and a "W" on his right.[133]

Branding was similar to drumming out in that it was an early-war punishment. Although court-martial records indicate the imposition of brandings as late as 1863, most of the instances occurred in the last half of 1861 and first half of 1862. To avoid criticism for branding a soldier, court-martial euphemized the penalty by ordering an offender to be "indelibly marked" instead of overtly branded. In the remote Department of the Pacific, headquartered in San Francisco, a court-martial ordered that three soldiers guilty of desertion be "indelibly marked with the letter 'D' two and a half inches long on the left hip," along with other punishments.[134] At isolated Fort Pickens, near Pensacola, Florida, a court-marital also penalized Private Jonathan Brightbill with a 'D' on his left hip for desertion.[135] These examples were both of remote locations and of sentences imposed early in the war. In addition, a disproportionate number of Regulars (nearly three-quarters of the identified cases in the court-martial sample) became the victims of branding and marking, identifying the penalty as an antebellum army practice for which volunteer soldiers cared little.

The use of marking persisted despite soldier opposition. Besides its association as a Regular Army form of punishment, most soldiers viewed branding as the most barbaric and degrading punishment possible. As citizen-soldiers, they recognized that their obligation to the army was only temporary, and, even if someone was a failure as a soldier, a criminal in military court had the right to return to civilian life just as anyone else did. They may have to subject themselves to a punishment, such as fine or a prison sentence, but those punishments had a firm ending. A brand, on the other hand, lasted forever, marking the man as a failed soldier even decades after military obligation ended. Soldiers also disapproved of the practice as it was means of marking common property, either cattle or, in the South, slaves. Unwilling to associate themselves as the mere property of the army, soldiers sympathized with the branded offender instead of condemning him. John Haley, who witnessed the branding of the aforementioned coward, considered "Branding a human being like a pork barrel is a relic of barbarism," and he and several members of his regiment disregarded strict orders to remain silent at the proceedings. "Any commander who thinks we would honor such a display is ignorant of the American character," Haley remonstrated, "We haven't lost quite all our sense of decency, nor our courage to rebuke such uncivilized spectacles."[136] Lieutenant Robert S. Robertson of the Ninety-third New York also opposed the practice. After witnessing the branding of two deserters, "one on the shoulder and the other on the *ham*," Robertson stated that "branding is a relic of barbarism that should be abolished and would prefer to see them shot to witnessing such an operation again."[137] As an alternative to branding, the army sometimes called for an offender to receive a permanent tattoo. The use of tattooing provided the enduring stigma the army sought without the negative association of marking property. PMC surgeons, for instance, on occasion marked suspected bounty jumpers with nitrate of silver to prevent them from enlisting at another recruiting station.[138] In New York City in 1864, a court-martial ordered Privates Loren Chase and Alexander Chisholm "to be branded with the letter 'D,' two and one half inches long, in Indian ink, upon the left hip" in lieu of branding with a hot iron.[139] Private William Anderson also received a tattoo "in indelible ink" for deserting from the Sixty-second New York.[140]

Although some courts-martial officers could not restrain themselves from branding guilty soldiers, thankfully at least some senior officers refused to permit the penalty from occurring. In about half of the cases where a panel imposed a branding, the reviewing authority overruled the court-martial and remitted the branding. Brigadier (later Major) General Edwin Sumner, for instance, remitted a number of brandings as commander of the Department of the Pacific. In June 1861, for instance, Sumner remitted the branding imposed upon Private Emanuel Oppenheimer, and later remitted the marking and drumming out of five soldiers court-martialed in July 1861.[141] Unfortunately for the soldiers under his command, the army promoted Sumner in October 1861, and the Department of the Pacific fell under the command of Brigadier General George Wright, who had no compunction about approving branding sentences. In the Department of New Mexico, Colonel (later Major General) Edward E. Canby also remitted multiple branding punishments, including those of Privates John Daily, John Flanigan, and John Gilden after they deserted.[142] But not every general remitted the penalty, and brandings continued until at least the mid-point of the war. The last recorded branding occurred in November 1863, when a soldier of the Seventeenth New York "dezerted [sic]," and received a brand "wich [sic] was done in the presence of the whole Division."[143] On the same day and in another regiment, two other soldiers received their brands during division parade. After using "an artillery forge" to heat the iron, officers applied "the letter D on the right hand" of both offenders.[144]

NO PUNISHMENT, HOWEVER, was as harsh as the death penalty. The Articles of War and General Order number 100 provided for numerous instances whereby the army could excise the decision to penalize a soldier by ending his life. Aside from the offenses that paralleled civilian crimes (i.e., murder or rape), several uniquely military offenses had the potential to end with a capital sentence (i.e., assaulting a superior officer, pillaging, sleeping on duty). Because of this difference, the soldiers of the Union army had a wide range of opinions when it came to the death penalty. Some soldiers sympathized with the condemned man, as they sympathized for the victims of a branding, reflecting their citizen-soldier scorn for disproportionate military punishment. To them, executions were simply examples of the army's excessive brutality, elitist scorn for the common soldier, or abusive policies toward their nonprofessional troops. Other observers, from the same citizen-soldier viewpoint, applauded the use of executions to purge the army of men who could not meet the standard of soldiery demanded by true patriots, or who had failed in the test of masculinity that army life represented. In the former group, soldiers who committed offenses that shamed the uniform and army were prime examples of those deserving death, while in the latter case, soldiers who cried or begged for mercy at the moment of their execution certainly fit into this category. Most officers supported the opinion that executions culled flawed individuals from the army, and went even further by hoping that executions might teach a lesson to the unlucky individuals who had to witness one. Like many other disciplinary attitudes, the army sought to deter future misbehavior by making a public spectacle out of the punished soldier. The more serious the offense, the more serious the punishment, and, the army hoped, the deeper the impression that such a serious and violent punishment might make on the minds of enlisted men. To accomplish this, the army conducted executions in dramatic fashion by ending the soldier's life at the end of an elaborate ritual, following a well-regulated script to achieve the maximum deterrent factor. Instead of a private procedure, condemned soldiers exited the world in front of hundreds, sometimes thousands, of witnesses upon whom the army hoped to strike great reverence for army discipline and fear of violating army rules. To emphasize the importance of the event, officers forced soldiers to treat the execution as a significant occurrence. "This morning we received order to 'fix up'—that is, clean our guns, brush clothes, black shoes, etc.," Captain George Squier wrote his wife, "And what was this fuss for? Only to see one of the 55th O.V.I. [Ohio Volunteer Infantry] boys shot for desertion."[145] Despite the army efforts, not all soldiers recognized the intent or impact of the tragedy played out before them, leaving the army with an inconsistent outcome from its death penalty practices.

The process of executing a soldier involved a very public ritual, spelled out in clear guidelines in the Army Regulations. Soldiers ordered to witness an execution stood in attention in ranks around the pre-dug grave. The Provost Marshal led the formal procession into the execution area, followed by a band, "drums muffled, playing the dead [man's] march." Behind the band came the firing squad, a detail carrying the condemned man's coffin, and, finally, the unfortunate soldier, accompanied by a clergyman and his guards. As in a drumming out, the army stripped the convicted offender of all trappings of soldiery, so the doomed man usually wore only the simplest clothing instead of a uniform. On at least one occasion, however, a condemned man wore a shirt with a "red peice of cloth sewed on his shirt bosom & a little to the left" to serve as an aiming point.[146] The Provost Marshal then read the charges against the soldier, the sentence of guilty, and the death warrant sanctioning the execution. The marshal then stepped aside, directed the firing squad to a distance of only six paces from the doomed soldier, and gave the order to fire. The Provost Marshal then had the gruesome duty of administering a coup de grace if the firing squad failed to hit their target. To give soldiers a good look at the dead soldier and hopefully make them refrain from committing similar offenses, the Provost Marshal closed the execution by ordering the witnesses to "break into columns by the right and move past the corpse in slow time."[147]

In some executions where the condemned soldier committed a particularly despicable act, Provost Marshals not only ended their lives but also erased their existence. Knowing that soldiers feared leaving behind an unmarked grave, some marshals placed the corpse facedown in the coffin and leveled off the dirt, leaving no sign of the burial site. Those buried facedown, instead of witnessing the dawn of Judgment Day, could only observe the hell that awaited them, resting, as one soldier put it, in the "sleep that knows no waking."[148] Following the execution of Private Henry Beardsley at Fairfax Station, Virginia, in October

1863, marshals took great pains in "leveling off the ground so that no passerby would detect the presence of a burial."[149] Two months earlier, marshals inflicted a similar demonstration upon the corpse of an execution victim: "The body was placed face downward in the box and lowered into the grave. The grave was then filled and the earth leveled. No mound or headboard marked the spot where the deserter was lying. Such was the ignominious end."[150]

The army hoped this elaborate ritual not only convinced soldiers that some offenses were not worth committing, but also that the army acted appropriately in applying the sentence. The execution of a deserter, after all, only provided deterrence if the soldiers watching it saw it as a fitting and deserved punishment. Some offenders sentenced to death met their end with little opposition from the men of the Union army. These doomed individuals included offenders of moral law, enemy soldiers who violated the rules of war, and Union soldiers whose offenses threatened the security of other Union troops—in short, the type of flawed individuals that citizen-soldiers believed misrepresented their cause, denigrated the name of the Union army, or manifested the worst elements of their Confederate foes. Guerillas, for instance, faced summary execution for violating the tenets of soldiery. Because Union forces had to contend with irregular forces as soon as they occupied any region of the Confederacy, the army defined the threat posed by unconventional enemy forces and dealt with them accordingly. The Lieber Code established clear distinctions between guerillas, undisciplined and informal insurgency groups, and partisans, semi-formal regional militias still bound by the laws of war because they answered to the enemy's central command, unlike guerillas who acted only of their own accord.[151] John S. Moseby's activities in Virginia were a prime example of legitimate partisan activity. Guerillas received no consideration or formal process of military justice, but partisans enjoyed the protection of the Articles of War and the Lieber Code.

When confronted by guerillas, the Union army was quick to exercise its codified policy of quick executions. The practice of quickly dealing with guerillas soon became the norm. "Four men were taken out of prison today to be executed," Private Voorhis noted in his diary, because "they are guerillas." Two months later, Voorhis expected to see three more men die, "charged with guerillaing," but two of them received a reprieve "on account of their youth and unfitness for death."[152] Charles Musser wrote his father that no great excitement occurred around his camp "except and occasional Brush with the Bushwhackers, which don't amount to much neither way—only the Hanging of a rascal when caught."[153] Other guerillas died in the process of capture, events that amounted to little more than summary execution. Capturing a suspected deserter in his bed, Union soldiers wound up shooting him "through the stomach" to subdue him. After removing the body to outside of the home and discovering he was still alive, "they gave him two more balls through his head" and burned the house before leaving.[154] After catching a "half dozend [*sic*] bushwhakers . . . murdering a Union familie," while on Sherman's March march through Georgia, Union troops exacted revenge by leaving the guerillas "strung up on telegraph poles and left hanging, a warning for others."[155] Some executions were questionable, however, as soldiers either leapt to conclusions or simply did not want to take the time to establish facts. Soldiers of the Thirty-sixth Ohio, for instance, summarily shot a man they caught making bullets, a skill that most rural hunters possessed, on the conclusion the man intended them for the Confederate army.[156]

Partisans had the protection of military law, but spies did not, and Confederate spies that fell into Union hands soon found themselves dangling from the end of a noose. In central Tennessee in 1863, Jacob Bartmess recorded, "There were a couple of spies hung . . . they were going around with forged pass from Gen. [William] Rosecrans and in officers [*sic*] uniforms, but they were caught in their deception and strung up." Bartmess also noted that "There are to be . . . two women hung next friday [*sic*] at Murfreesboro. The women are spies."[157] Sergeant Hartwell not only had a "fine view of the crossing" along the Potomac River, but also "of a Spy that was taken in our lines & hunt on a tree on a high point of land in view of the enemy. He is to hang [for] 48 hours."[158] Blatant brutality often accompanied the search and punishment of suspected spies. "An old camp peddler was seized by our men and hung to a tree," Private Sneden observed, after soldiers found "plans and estimates of the forces" on his person. The angry soldiers produced a confession from him by hanging him briefly until "he confessed he was a Rebel spy. The last time he went up he stayed there."[159] Outraged when a suspected spy resisted arrest, leading to the death of one Union soldier and the wounding of four others, men of the Thirty-second Iowa "run three bayonetts [*sic*] through him and shot him once and then hung him on a lim[b] and then dug a hole and rolled him like a hog and covered him about eighteen inches deep, then some of the bad boys drove sticks through him."[160] The rare spy received the privilege of a court proceeding. Captured in Little Rock, Arkansas, in December 1863 with encoded descriptions of the Union defenses of the city, David O. Dodd, a seventeen-year-old resident, faced a court-martial. Although ably advised by two local attorneys, the evidence found in Dodd's possession sealed his fate. His subsequent hanging turned Dodd into a victim of the cause, the "Boy Martyr of the Confederacy," although the trial plainly proved his guilt.[161] The most well-documented execution of a spy occurred in Frederick, Maryland, where a man named William Henderson, "found with various maps of the country around Gettysburg," was "strung up without trial or due warning." To ensure that plenty of soldiers and civilians alike saw the consequences of espionage,

General John Buford ordered the corpse to hang "three days before being taken down."[162] The Army of the Potomac passed through Frederick in its pursuit of the Confederates after Gettysburg, so a large number of men saw the execution and its aftermath. "While at Frederick we saw a man dangling by the neck from a tree," John Haley wrote, a peddler of "writing papers and envelopes" who a few days before had observed Union camps and had followed the army south until his arrest and execution.[163] Private White, passing by the dangling corpse, remembered "how out of place this hanging body seemed in the midst of this beautiful landscape, made doubly beautiful by the rays of the setting sun."[164]

Rapists also received no sympathy from the crowds assembled to watch them die. Comments on their demise reflect either satisfaction with the execution or only direct commentary with no hint of empathy. Describing the execution of two soldiers convicted of rape, General Patrick described their deaths by hanging: "The feet were tied, the eyes bandaged, the ropes adjusted, the tap upon the drum & the drop fell! Scarcely a convulsion, both being killed instantly."[165] James Newton applauded the execution of "three men who committed an outrage upon the person of a defenseless female.[166] When another convicted rapist flaunted his pending execution by dramatically stating, "You may break my neck, but you cannot break my manly spirit," witnesses were not impressed and watched impassively as "he was launched into eternity."[167] The closest to sympathy that any convicted rapist received came in North Carolina, where Sergeant Francis McAdams managed to avoid observing the execution of a rapist. Having witnessed a number of executions, McAdams decided, "I do not desire to witness another scene like this."[168] The army imposed a disgraceful hanging on convicted rapists as a means of separating itself from the offender. Soldiers who committed offenses died by firing squad, a soldier's death, but common criminals died by hanging. Using the latter means of execution served to indicate that the army did not associate itself with the condemned man. Convicted rapists certainly fit into this category, and to demonstrate the full rejection of the offender, the Union army occasionally hanged rapists in plain view of the enemy to demonstrate that their behavior did not represent the morals and values of the Union army. Instead of merely executing Private William Johnson of the Twenty-third USCT during the siege of Petersburg, the army arranged a cease-fire and hanged Johnson in the no-man's-land between the two armies. The army possibly meant the execution to be a demonstration that freed slaves could not expect free rein to pillage and abuse their former owners, but the Confederates used the event for their own propaganda by showing local slaves the body and telling them this was their fate if they fled to the Union for protection.[169] General Patrick, responsible for conducting the execution, went about it in businesslike fashion. The day before the hanging, Patrick noted in his diary that he "Slept well and [arose] up early. Made my Sunday toilet & then gave the necessary orders for hanging Johnson, the negro, for Rape, tomorrow morning at 9 [a.m.]." Arriving at the execution site the next day, Patrick noticed the Confederates were shelling "the very place where the Gallows were erected so that I had to form the troops below the crest & leave as few exposed as possible." Apparently, Patrick did not move the observers back far enough, as a shell struck "George Polley, Sergeant Major of the 10th Massachusetts, who died in a few minutes.[170] Marshals placed Johnson on the scaffold "& the drop fell, He never knew any thing after."[171] In another example, Major General Regis de Trobriand arrived in camp and observed "two wagoners of the Seventy-second New York had been hanged." The pair had sexually assaulted a woman living nearby, and after a brief trial, the army hanged them "in full view of the enemy's lines, to show the rebels how justice was done amongst us."[172]

Certain deserters also met their end without a tear shed by their former comrades. Soldiers particularly hated those convicted of bounty-jumping, and resoundingly approved of their execution. On December 18, 1863, Winslow Allen died at the hands of a firing squad for bounty jumping. After deserting the Seventy-sixth New York in 1862, he had jumped another bounty the following year, "tempted by the bounty of three hundred dollars," only to have the titanic bad luck of having the army assign him to his old regiment. Spotted by his former comrades, Allen faced court-martial and then a firing squad, leaving him "lifeless upon his coffin."[173] Surgeon Charles Clark of the Thirty-ninth Illinois complimented the firing squad for their accurate shooting in dispatching a bounty jumper, whom Clark described as "a most reckless piece of humanity," with "two shots through the heart; six within a circumference of four inches of it."[174] Other firing squads were not as lenient. In the Second Pennsylvania Heavy Artillery, a bounty jumper lived for several minutes after he was shot "everywhere but in a vital spot," leaving an observer to wonder if the firing squad did so on purpose to inflict agony upon the jumper, stating, "It was, evidently, intended on the part of the executioners."[175] A bounty jumper in the Fourth Maryland, who confessed to jumping sixteen times and collecting more than $20,000, also did not die right away after the firing squad did its work, requiring the soldiers "to put another volley in him."[176] Another soldier described the execution of a man who not only bounty-jumped, he deserted in the midst of battle while serving as a color guard. Caught when "tempted by the large bounties," he reenlisted in the Regular Army. Trying to curry sympathy with his captors, the soldier said "all he cared for were his wife and children, when, in fact he had none."[177]

Soldiers who deserted to the enemy likewise received no empathy. Many Union soldiers deserted to the enemy on the presumption the Confederates intended to issue them paroles permitting them to go home. Some, however wound up serving in the Southern cause, and the soldiers unfortunate enough to actively support the Confederacy only to fall again into Union hands received no compassion from their erstwhile comrades, who considered them active traitors. Wilbur Fisk witnessed the execution of a former Union soldier who not only deserted, but also "added the double disgrace of deserting to the enemy and then turning spy against us," an offense where he "paid the penalty of his crimes on the gallows."[178] Soldiers of the Fourth Indiana spotted one of their deserters, Private David Blazer "wearing a dirty rebel gray Cavallery [sic] suit," among some recently captured prisoners. He was immediately executed in "an impressive Ceremony," Captain Otto described, that "no doubt saved many from a like fate" by dissuading them from deserting.[179] Similar to the unfortunate William Allen, Private Frank McElhenny deserted from the Twenty-fourth Massachusetts in 1862. Two years later, some Confederate deserters entered the Twenty-fourth's lines to surrender, among them Private McElhenny. He, like Allen, also soon died in front of a firing squad.[180] Privates were not the only ones to feel the army's wrath. Lieutenant John Cox served in the Confederate army after deserting the Fourth New Jersey in the summer of 1864. Union forces captured him at Petersburg, Virginia, six months later and executed him less than a month after that.[181] Their deaths, and the deaths of any Union soldier who switched sides, generated no compassion. When the army executed three additional deserters who entered Confederate service in 1864, many soldiers "saw the prisoners meet their fate. No loyal heart gave them any sympathy."[182] In describing the hanging of two soldiers who had "deserted our Army and went to the rebles [sic] and took up arms against us," Private Sylvester McElheney found the proceedings "a pretty hard site [sic]" but believed the two traitors brought their deaths upon themselves.[183]

WHEN IT CAME TO EXECUTIONS for other offenses, however, soldier support was not universal. In other capital offenses, such as cowardice, sleeping on guard, and, especially, desertion, Union soldiers did not agree on the propriety of a capital sentence. The soldiers who opposed the death penalty for these crimes did not excuse the commission of the offense; soldiers understood that there had to be consequences for one's actions. But like soldiers who experienced or witnessed the desertion, cowardice, and shortcomings of their comrades, there was a spectrum of opinion ranging from retribution to indifference to pity. A soldier who disparaged the manhood of a deserter probably had no qualms about seeing a deserter in front of a firing squad, but at the same time a soldier who recognized that desertion was sometimes justified could be expected to believe that a firing squad was not the best remedy to the problem. A soldier's position on the death penalty also depended upon the number of times he had to witness one. Soldiers who supported the most extreme of punishments left the event with either their opinion reinforced or fundamentally changed by what they saw. Some witnesses, affected by the solemn ceremony orchestrated by the Provost Marshals, accepted the propriety of shooting or hanging offenders, while others left the scene with their views altered by the horror and repugnance of the scene.

A number of reasons existed why soldiers opposed the use of the death penalty. Some soldiers objected to the application of the death penalty from the viewpoint of a citizen-soldier. In civilian life, courts reserved the death penalty for specific and heinous crimes. In the army, however, where a soldier might face discipline for offenses that had no civilian equivalent, the application of the death penalty for some offenses violated their sense of civilian equality and justice. Executions for such purely military capital offenses as sleeping on guard duty, assaulting an officer, or leaving camp became examples of disciplinary excess. In civilian life, soldiers reasoned, there was no penalty (especially death) for sleeping at your job, punching someone who deserved it, or coming and going as one pleased, so they further reasoned that the army's use of the death penalty in these cases was simply irrational. Others were opposed to the impersonal mechanism of the execution. Each execution was little different than the last, and occurred with such frequency that soldiers began to perceive that perhaps the army leadership simply enjoyed putting men to death because they could. Some soldiers noted the almost-routine nature of executions, which typically took place on Fridays at noon. Instead of a deeply personal event, the establishment of an execution routine made the death of a soldier of no more consequence than scheduling drill or time to do the laundry. Outside of Petersburg in January 1865, for instance, Private James Holmes recounted the execution of a New Jersey soldier who deserted to the enemy, adding, "There is some sixteen more to he hung, every Friday untill [*sic*] the whole are gone through with."[184] Private James Burrell wrote to his sister that, despite the double execution he had just witnessed, "we have near 30 deserters under us now" awaiting execution.[185] Coupled to the idea of the frequency of executions was the loss of shock value. Soldiers who castigated convicted offenders and welcomed their deaths at their first execution lost that outrage the more executions they witnessed. While not a majority, many soldiers observed two or more executions, and the frequency of the event tended to lessen the impact of the lesson. "To day [*sic*] our division was ordered out to see a man of the 5th New Hampshire Regt. shot," Daniel

Chisholm wrote matter of factly. "He was shot at 12 O'Clock, the time they always shoot or hang them."[186]

An important element that affected how soldiers perceived an execution was the demeanor of the condemned man. A soldier who showed weakness or conducted himself in an unmanly way earned no sympathy and contributed to the perception of the offender as a failure as a man and as a soldier. Crying, pleading for mercy, or physically shrinking from the obligation to die well were only some of the ways that witnesses determined that convicted soldiers deserved their deaths. Other negative determinants included statements to the crowd full of bravado but empty of contrition, relying too heavily on the comfort of a clergyman as a sign that the offender was not certain about the state of his soul, or simply remaining quiet and meekly accepting the looming penalty. The soldier who wanted to hurry his early-morning execution along because he wanted to "get to Hell for dinner" probably did not gain a lot of sympathy, nor did the USCT soldier who futilely "broke down & clasping his hands entreated to be spared," nor the condemned man who "threw his bandage from his eyes twenty times" to delay the proceedings.[187] On the other hand, condemned men could gain the sympathy of witnesses and some measure of redemption through their actions on the execution ground. Men who accepted the consequences of their actions (a key masculine trait), confessed to their offenses, showed contrition, and asked for forgiveness from their comrades earned some redemption. Likewise, soldiers who urged others to avoid their mistakes and not disgrace the uniform, flag, or cause also regained some standing as a citizen-soldier. When given the opportunity to speak before a firing squad ended his life, Private Robert Gay confessed his crimes, asked the assembled body for forgiveness, and absolved the firing squad of any guilt they might have for shooting him, a performance that gained Gay a great deal of redemption.[188] Likewise, at the aforementioned execution of William Ormsby, the condemned man made an impassioned speech where he apologized for his offenses and begged the witnesses to "take warning from my example, and whatever comes do not desert the old flag for which I am proud to die."[189] Approving the behavior of a condemned man who was "perfectly cool and took it as an everyday occurrence," Private Paul Hilliard noted his comrades' appreciation of the man's farewell to the members of his regiment present to watch his death and refusal to wear a blindfold, claiming he "was never afraid to face death and preferred doing so then."[190] Bravery in the face of death also promoted a masculine image, although such bravery was in the eye of the beholder. A statement by a condemned man that he did not fear death might fall under the category of contrived bravado or sincere manliness. A witness might characterize an offender standing silently with a firm jaw and steady walk as bravely accepting his fate or cowardly unable to speak at a time when he should.

Most officers fully sanctioned the use of executions. As the monitors, arbiters, and inflictors of army discipline, officers, with rare exceptions, approved of executing men who deserved their fate and received the benefit of the full court-martial process. Lieutenant Axel Reed of the Second Minnesota embraced the deterrent value of executions, believing that executions "certainly would have a great tendency towards deterring others from committing a similar crime."[191] Chaplain John R. Adams of the Nineteenth Massachusetts thought witnessing the execution of Private John Starbird improved the discipline in that unit, describing "men who had straggled and kept out of battle now were in the ranks."[192] Although he considered executions "a sad sight," Lieutenant John Irwin believed it the only way to stem the problem of desertion and bounty jumping, acknowledging, "There is not much mercy shown in such cases."[193] Other officers had no such minimal concerns, and fully embraced the idea of execution as deterrent. "Desertion has increased at a most alarming extent." Charles Haydon wrote in 1863, "It must at once be punished with Death speedy & certain or the army is ruined."[194] Colonel Patrick Guiney agreed. When the increasing desertion rate triggered an increased execution rate, Guiney observed that "This shooting men for desertion is something new in this Brigade—but it is better late than never. It should have been done long ago."[195]

Proof of the Union army's commitment to capital deterrence was evident in the number and frequency of executions. Despite the leniency of the court-martial process, enough offenders received the death penalty to make the solemn execution procedure a common occurrence. When desertion and other forms of indiscipline reached uncontrollable levels by 1863, the number of executions increased proportionately. Colonel Cavins noticed the increase in executions, writing his wife, "There had been quite a number of deserters shot in this army lately. There were two shot in our division, who belonged to the 14th Connecticut."[196] In September 1863, Major General John W. Geary wrote to his wife, "Yesterday, two soldiers of this Division were executed for crime of desertion . . . There was also one man shot for same crime in the first Division of this Corps. and 16 within the entire army [of the Potomac]. Thus you see the crime of desertion will no longer go unpunished, when so may expiate their crimes upon the same day."[197] Starting in Fall 1864, the tempo of executions increased, with more than fifty executions in the Army of the Potomac alone in the subsequent six months.[198]

Most Union officers wished for frequent executions, but Abraham Lincoln did not. As Commander in Chief, Lincoln's orders caused the death of thousands of men, but when it came to commuting death sentences, the lawyer-President did his utmost to find a legal justification to grant clemency, commute sentences, and vacate death penalties when he could. John Hay, Lincoln's private secretary, often noted that the President eagerly leapt upon any factor that allowed him to issue a reprieve.[199] Excusing himself away from an acquaintance, Lincoln explained that "I must go through these papers and see if I cannot find some excuse to let these poor fellows off."[200] Lincoln held great optimism that soldiers granted a second chance would not waste it, and he was usually correct. In 1864, Lincoln pardoned Private Roswell McIntyre, sentenced to die for deserting his unit, provided that McIntyre "returns to his Regiment and faithfully serves out his term." McIntyre lived up to his promise, dying in combat near Five Forks, Virginia, in the last days of the war.[201] Ultimately, Lincoln commuted all death sentences for desertion by Executive Order on February 26, 1864, removing the need to come up with creative legal maneuvering to spare soldiers' lives.[202] Soldiers certainly appreciated Lincoln's efforts, but it drove army commanders to distraction. Instead of receiving free rein to impose military justice as they saw fit, officers complained that Lincoln undermined their authority by denigrating the power of the court-martial process. They also believed that Lincoln's benevolence eroded the deterrence factor of executions by leading soldiers to presume that their appeals might find a sympathetic ear. Captain Henry Abbott, pleased that "Deserters are shot every Friday, 5 or ten at a time," considered that "the evil will soon be cured" by using such harsh measures. Because he believed that individual soldiers were ultimately responsible for their own conduct, he bitterly criticized the President: "I think Lincoln is responsible to God for the deaths of many poor men, since . . . he persistently spared every case of death for desertion until [soldiers thought] the crime trivial."[203] Colonel Theodore Lyman, a member of General Meade's staff, believed that the majority of offenses in the Army of the Potomac came directly from the undeterred behavior of soldiers who relied upon the "uncertainty of the death penalty through the false merciful policy of the President."[204] Writing to Judge Advocate General Holt in 1864, General William Sherman stated his belief that "punishment should be prompt . . . or lose it efficacy. . . . Forty or fifty executions now would in the next twelve months save a thousand lives."[205]

Not every officer agreed with the execution process and, as citizen-soldiers themselves, found the process disagreeable and pointless. Forced to watch when "a private belonging to the 19th Mass. was hanged in the presence of the whole division," Lieutenant Colonel Selden Connor of the Seventh Maine found the entire proceedings "a horrible sight" and believed it did not change the behavior of a single witness.[206] Captain Elijah Rhodes noted in his diary in regards to the execution of a deserter. The execution procedure went off without a hitch, but Rhodes found no satisfaction in the outcome, believing "The man rightly deserved his fate, but I prefer not to see such justice meted out even to rascals."[207] Captain Marcus Woodcock attended an execution in his brigade, but at the order to fire "I involuntarily turned my eyes away from the scene and waited several seconds . . . and a glance toward the prisoner told me that he was no more."[208] Lieutenant Edmund Halsey sat on many courts-martial that handed down death penalties, but when he actually witnessed one, he became so ill that "I came back with a terrible headache."[209]

Because an undercurrent of sympathy existed to counter-balance the orchestrated drama of a formal execution, a spectrum of attitudes emerged amongst soldiers when it came to executions for desertion, cowardice, and other offenses where blame and guilt were more quantifiable. There were plenty of soldiers who embraced the deterrent effect of executions or agreed that harsh discipline was an unfortunate necessity to have the tight discipline necessary to win the war. Wilbur Fisk noted with approval the execution of two deserters, "Privates John Tague and George Blewers were shot dead in the presence of whole division," topped by the "Five men of the 118th PA [who] were executed this afternoon, witnessed by the whole corps."[210] The sentiments of many soldiers echoed the anger they felt at deserters who left their units in time of need. "I assure you none of us regretted their deaths," John L. Smith wrote his mother, "as we are very bitter against deserters."[211] Robert Robertson looked forward to executions in his regiment because, as an independently assigned regiment, "we are not in a Corps and will have to do our own shooting" instead of the Provost Marshals.[212] "The only trouble [with executions]," John Vautier expounded, "is that there has not been half enough executions for bounty jumpers, deserters, and other desperadoes that infest every Regiment in the Service. Discipline should be enforced& the lawless spirits sent where they could do our cause no harm."[213] Private Abel C. Thomas of the Ninety-fifth Pennsylvania was in total agreement. "If any man deserves an ignominious death, he deserved it," Thomas wrote to his brother of an executed soldier, "not simply because he was a deserter . . . but because he aimed at the destruction or capture of his companions. . . . [T]reachery is the worst form of sin . . . [and] we turn away in abhorrence of the foul deed."[214]

Few soldiers were as enthusiastic about executions, and most recorded a sense of resignation regarding their necessity. Some soldiers had a particular resentment about a particular offense. "I abhore [*sic*] executions," Wyman White wrote after witnessing the shooting of a deserter to the enemy, "but in his one I felt very little pity for the victim."[215] Corporal James Woodworth represented those who resignedly accepted that executions were a necessary evil. "There was another execution for desertion in our Division today," he wrote his family. ". . . It is horrible to look upon, but there is no alternative."[216]

Daniel Mower also did not like the procedure, but realized "Strenuous measures had to be taken to prevent desertion and bounty jumping," an opinion similar to Private David Nichol's assessment that "It was a painful sight [to see three deserters shot], but it will set an example for others."[217] Private William Clark represented those soldiers who balanced the unsavory act of executing a comrade with some sense of legal necessity. "All of the Division were [sic] out in line to see the execution," Clark told his brother, "It is pretty hard to see a fellow soldier shot in such a manner, but I think it just."[218] Other soldiers approved of executions as a means of judging their own masculinity and dedication to their citizen-soldiers' cause. Impressed by the dire nature of their duty, some witnesses came away from executions with a renewed determination to protect their reputations, shoulder their obligations, and avoid such a public humiliation. "I would sooner be brought home in my coffin," John Pardington wrote to his wife and child after seeing a deserter die, than "bring such disgrace on you and my little darling."[219] Despite an execution where the condemned man was hit by "eleven musket balls, almost shot to pieces," Franklin Boyts decided "this is the right way to fix them. They need not run away from the Army. Let them stay and be shot by the Rebels, and do at least a little good for the country."[220]

Although certain offenders received no consideration from their comrades, other condemned men did. Soldiers who committed common violations, such as desertion, that generated different responses among their units also received varied reactions to their executions as well. Witnesses to executions were, in effect, the third party in the event. The Provost Marshal and the firing squad represented discipline and military order, while the offender represented someone who failed in his obligations as a soldier. Although the army's carefully staged execution procedure intended to impress soldiers with the solemnity of violating military law and isolate the doomed man from his colleagues, some soldiers chose to view the execution in their own way. Just as soldiers found means to justify or minimize the severity of various offenses, they also made self-determinations on the propriety of capital sentences. Unhappy with the excessive control that officers exercised over their existence, soldiers rebelled at the idea that they should by definition agree with the army's right to execute major offenders. Instead, soldiers sometimes sided with the executed man. They could not stop the execution, but they could defy the army's intent from the execution ritual and devise their own outlook on how a condemned soldier was remembered.

Although he detested one condemned man because "he had deserted six times, thee of these he had received large bounties," Private Jacob Bechtel sympathized with the soldier's family. "What will his wife think when she hears of this," Bechtel pondered, "or his children think of their father years here after."[221] Angry at what he considered an abuse of military authority, Private Ferdinand Davis believed "To me it was a dreadful thing to see a human being sat on a box, blindfold[ed] & his life taken in such a savage barbarous manner."[222] Disgusted at seeing his first execution (which used an amazing "24 men to shoot at him"), Private Francis Carron decided "I never saw nor never want again to see one of our men shot for desirting [sic]. It was a hard thing I tell you to look at."[223] Private William Jones was even more explicit in his opposition to the "most heartrendering sights a mortal man could behold, two men shot for desertion." Dismissing the fact that one of the men was a bounty jumper, Jones objected to the process because "I have seen men shot in battle, that was nothing compared to this. . . . I could hardly control my feelings. I never felt so bad in my life."[224] This remembrance was very similar to that of Private Albert Reid, who had "seen men killed and wounded, mangled so that they could hardly be recognized . . . and scarcely made notice of it. But this occasion was so solemn that I can never forget it."[225] Instead of internalizing their negative reaction to executions, others externalized their feelings in pity for the condemned. Claiming "they did not deserve what they got," David Lilley characterized two doomed men as dying "like heroes. They never flinched but stood up erect and were shot down like dogs. I pittied [sic] them."[226] All soldiers exhibited strong reactions to executions, not just inexperienced recruits. "Men who had faced death many a time without quailing or faltering," Private William Switz described, "now turned their hands & silent tears run down bronzed cheeks, for sympathy for a fellow being."[227] Mutilation of the body, a side effect of the firing squad's lack of aim, also alienated witnesses. Soldiers commented negatively on the mangling of one condemned man's body and face, with "one hole in his forehead . . . one in the mouth, and four in the breast."[228] Condemned men even faced mutilation after death. In a "scene [with] a touch of the supernatural," soldiers assembled to witness the execution of a soldier from the Third New Hampshire observed a seagull trying to devour the freshly dead body, and "It was only by repeated efforts that the guard was able to keep the voracious bird away."[229]

Out of their sympathy, soldiers tried to find alternative blame for the failure of the condemned soldier. As a soldier like themselves, they reasoned, an external factor was to blame for the offenders's lack of masculine behavior. An officer in the Tenth Connecticut, put off by the necessity "to repair to "Execution Hill" to witness the shooting of two young men," did not blame the offenders for their actions. Instead, the officer claimed, "they are the victims of depraved, vicious, unpatriotic, cowardly, and demoralized public opinion at home," ignoring similar and openly expressed opinions amongst the soldiers themselves.[230] Sergeant Sawtelle excused the man he saw executed, claiming, "the Copperheads of the North had secured another victim to their already long list . . . I firmly believe that a larger percent of the desertions were caused by those brawling stay-at-homes, too cowardly to go out and fight . . . and too mean to keep their mouths shut."[231] Wyman White blamed the officers for executions, claiming that if they knew their jobs such punishments would not be necessary. "It seemed to me," White wrote of a comrade's execution, "that this man might have been made a brave and good soldier if his officers had taken the right course with him."[232] Even worse, from the soldiers' perspective, was the realization that executions did nothing to stop men from deserting if they determined to try. "The penalty attaching to desertion is death by shooting, and this was no uncommon sight in the army," John Billings wrote, "but it did not seem to stay the tide of desertion in the least."[233] Because the odds of arresting a deserter remained relatively low, a dedicated deserter stood a fair chance of eluding efforts to bring him back. An officer of the Tenth Connecticut observed the lack of fear amongst deserters. "A few [deserters] will be picked up," he wrote, but "not over one-fifth are caught usually. Once into the swamps, and they are completely safe."[234] Witnessing executions failed to deter deserters even in the short term. Mere hours after witnessing a firing squad at work, Major Edward Woodward wrote incredulously, "a man who had witnessed the execution was shot and captured by our pickets while attempting to desert to the enemy."[235] Knowing better than the officers what soldiers endured during the war, soldiers were more apt to propose practical solutions to the problem of desertion than execution. "If a man is a coward and can't control himself, he should be removed from the ranks and detailed for some duty he is fitted for," Private Haley proposed, "Such men have a right to desert and we have no right to shoot them."[236]

Nothing generated more sympathy for executed men than a botched execution. The administration of justice was one thing, but soldiers always objected, regardless of the punishment, to the infliction of needless pain and agony upon an offender. Soldiers opposed bucking and gagging and tying up by thumbs because it caused excessive pain and humiliation, and protested and rioted against its use as a disproportionate application of authority over citizen-soldiers. A mishandled execution was the ultimate example of such an unnecessary penalty. Soldiers rationalized that an offender who committed a particularly heinous act deserved his punishment, but exacerbating the penalty by imposing undue pain by prolonging his death was simply torture. Unfortunately, any number of things could complicate an execution, ranging from inadequate weapons to unnerved firing squads to poorly designed scaffolds. At one execution, five deserters faced death, each by a twelve-man firing squad, requiring sixty men in the firing squads.

After the order to fire, a witness reported "to our astonishment each man yet remained standing, showing conclusively that the [firing squad] detail had fired high." Because of the minimal chances to conduct target practice, firing squads frequently missed their targets. But in this case, it was far more likely that the sixty men, either singly or together, decided not to fire a fatal shot. Outraged by the failure of the firing squads, a Provost Marshal ordered the replacement squads to take their position and fire.[237] That was not the only firing squad that refused to shoot a fellow soldier, but during one execution such compassion had tragic consequences. Unwilling to kill a comrade, a sympathetic firing squad fired high, but "onlookers across the plaza, not realizing the danger, were sprayed with musket balls and some were killed."[238] Military observers who witnessed the execution of two soldiers from the Fourteenth Connecticut described the proceedings as "a very bungling affair . . . not more than one cartridge out of five did any service," requiring the employment of replacement shooters who fired at such close range that the blast "blew half his face off, and . . . his clothes took fire from the powder flame."[239] Poor aim on the part of another firing caused another bungled execution when "the men who were selected to do the shooting made a botch of it and hit the man everywhere except in a vital part. He rolled on the ground, writhing in agony until the reserve [firing squad] . . . [blew] his brains out . . . This man was simply butchered by blunderers."[240] A "scene of butchery that all eyes were turned away from it and all hearts shocked by it" was how a soldier described another botched execution that required three different firing squads to finish off a condemned man after the first firing squad only wounded him.[241]

Soldiers also objected to the unfortunate duty that Provost Marshals occasionally had to perform at executions. If the firing squad failed to kill an offender in the first volley, the Provost Marshal could order a reserve squad to fire either another volley or he could use his pistol to finish off the wounded man himself. Soldiers understood the necessity of the former, but objected to the latter. To many soldiers, already resentful of the personal power that officers had over their lives, this seemed the ultimate power of all—the power of life or death. Instead of soldiers shooting a soldier, an act of justice within their own social group, a coup de grace administered by a Provost Marshal represented an intrusion into the community of soldiers and reminded enlisted men of just how little control they had over their own lives. To other privates, a killshot administered in mercy seemed more like a murder than an execution. This was not death on the battlefield, where the mass of enemy made death an anonymous event. Instead this was face to face, and someone pulled a trigger with the sole intent of killing the person in front of him. A Provost Marshal had to complete the execution of Private

William Hill of the Fifteenth Massachusetts, firing a shot that "caused the brain to ooze out on the grass," although "it was two full minutes before life was extinct."[242] At another execution, a Provost Marshal erred by loading the firing squad's muskets himself the night before the shooting. Moisture seeped into the gunpowder, and the rifles failed to fire when the marshal ordered. Angry at the firing squad's failure, the marshal produced his revolver, "placed the muzzle against the man's head, and discharged all the barrels of it."[243] Private Thomas Dawson faced death by hanging in 1864, but events did not unfold as planned, leaving a marshal to kill him in a particularly gruesome fashion. The Provost Marshal miscalculated the length of rope needed to hang the prisoner, and Dawson landed on his feet instead of dangling in midair. The marshal, to rectify his error, "seized the end of the rope and jerked the prisoner upward until death slowly came" by strangulation.[244]

THE STUDY OF PUNISHMENTS in the Union army is a study in contrasts. The army had to maintain order and impose discipline, but had to do so without costing itself the confidence and support of its soldiers. Imprisonment, drumming out, and executions demonstrated the army's resolve to enforce the Articles of War, but also took valuable soldiers out of their units and demoralized those that remained. Punishments intended to diminish the status of the miscreant instead generated pity and resentment. To the citizen-soldiers of the Union army, discipline was not the mechanism to create an effective fighting force. Instead, discipline was the antithesis of the ideals they fought for, with officers as the violators of individual rights. Instead of denigrating the manhood of a failed soldier subjected to punishment, soldiers found masculine traits in those who bore up to heavy punishments. Soldiers, thinking and acting in the independent manner that characterized their entire attitude toward military discipline, established their own definitions about what constituted fair and reasonable punishment. They supported their officers when penalties corrected behavior and opposed commanders who used discipline as retaliation. They supported humiliating punishments for soldiers who earned their disgrace, but rejected the approach when applied to soldiers who committed crimes subject to the soldiers' flexible morality. For a process intended to bring closure to the disciplinary process, punishment instead created the opposite effect.

EPILOGUE

When the war ended in the summer of 1865, the soldiers of the Union army looked forward to not only peace, but a change in status. Thousands of citizen-soldiers anticipated the day when they became merely citizens, and could put their army careers behind them. After years of fighting, soldiers who pessimistically assessed their chances of survival discovered they were going home after all, and elation replaced pessimism. Although the assassination of Abraham Lincoln dampened their joy, the realization that they were about to resume their interrupted lives made for an ebullient army. Some significant obligations, however, slowed the soldiers' path to their front doors. The Army of the Potomac was ready to go home immediately after Lee's surrender at Appomattox, but there were still other Confederate army units in the field and hostile Confederate citizens that posed possible security threats. Despite the end of the war, soldiers still had to be careful. Sergeant Robert Larimer, whose Sixty-second Ohio was encamped near Richmond, reported that "Capt. [Henry K.] Hitchcock was set upon by 3 men near the city and badly beaten, they taking all the contents of his pockets, shoes, and Hat."[1] There were also peacetime duties. The army had to occupy the South to compel compliance with Reconstruction legislation, and until the Regular Army could assume that duty, at least some volunteers had to stay in place. Soldiers who wanted to go home found themselves compelled to remain in the army, for several months in some cases. Recently enlisted or drafted soldiers faced the possibility of remaining in the army for longer periods, despite their insistence that the war was over and so was their obligation to the army. The clash between army needs and soldier expectations created a tense disciplinary situation throughout the summer of 1865, providing one last clash between the army and its citizen-soldiers.

DESPITE THE LOGISTICAL PROBLEMS of processing, paying, and transporting thousands of men eager for civilian life, the army worked an administrative miracle and the army rapidly shrank as its regiments disbanded and its soldiers went home. To avoid confusion by allowing regiments to demobilize themselves, the army essentially had regiments retrace their steps. The army designated assembly points in each army department where regiments initially encamped as part of the discharge process. At the assembly points, units filled out their final muster rolls and other paperwork before progressing to the next stage of the process. Regiments then returned, when given permission to ensure an orderly process, to the state encampments where their regiments first organized. This step allowed the army to escort units in an intact fashion back to their home states under army regulation instead of allowing thousands of unsupervised soldiers to make their way home on their own. At their original encampments, soldiers turned in their weapons for storage at a state arsenal (unless soldiers chose to purchase their rifles for $6), received their back pay, and accepted their honorable discharges.[2] With few exceptions, the system worked remarkably well. The Union army could muster just over one million men in May 1865, but controlled only 460,000 by August, and 215,000 by October. A year after the war ended, in May 1866, the Union army consisted of only 80,000 men. In July, Congress passed the Army Reorganization Act, which fixed the long-term size of the Regular Army at 54,000 soldiers and eliminated all volunteer regiments.[3] Throughout the process, however, soldiers still in the army were still soldiers, and even without an enemy to fight the army expected its men to submit to army discipline. In April 1865, Sherman issued a general order to his men reminding them, "All details of military discipline must still be maintained," and he hoped his army's reputation "is not stained by any violence, vulgarity, rowdyism or petty crime."[4]

Soldiers, however, saw the situation differently. With the war over, they were soldiers in name only, and camp discipline, always tenuous at the best of times, began to erode. The army as an institution wanted to maintain discipline, but the army as a living force began to act like civilians whether the institution wanted them to or not. As citizen-soldiers who answered their nation's call to defend its cause, soldiers now expected their nation to release them from their obligation. "When I went into the service I made up my mind to "see the thing thro[ugh]," John Brobst grumbled, "& now that it is wound up they cant [sic] discharge me a minute too soon."[5] Charles Musser was more direct. "We offered our services to the country to help put down the rebellion," he complained, "that object has been accomplished, and our time is out, and we are no longer needed."[6] In the nature of a true citizen-soldier, one man believed, "We shall all be glad when we are able to throw the yoke of military rule off and return to civil life." Weary of waiting to go home, the same man demanded action: "We have had four years of it; and the War is over, we do not want to learn any more of military discipline, . . . we have been fighting for freedom and independence . . . we want our freedom. Give us our discharge, and we will be independent enough."[7] Reflecting their newly rediscovered civilian outlook, soldiers began to rebel against the personal inconveniences they had been inclined to accept in the name of being good soldiers, but now rejected because they were about to become free men. Standing guard duty and performing manual labor became an insult instead of an obligation. The Nineteenth Iowa, for instance, refused to share the lower deck of their transport with a number of mules, a condition they might have accepted during the war but not in July 1865. The Iowans drove the mules off the steamer, only to have officers drive them back on board and threaten to shoot anyone who interfered. With a clash looming, Colonel John Bruce, commanding the Iowans, himself led the regiment off the transport and announced they would rather wait for another ship than suffer the indignity offered them.[8]

As weeks went by and their regiments remained mustered in Federal service, soldiers became bored and restless. This, in turn, bred conditions where discipline began to break down. Captain George Bowen experienced the full brunt of soldier dissatisfaction. "It is difficult, almost impossible, to enforce discipline," he wrote exasperatedly, "as every man feels he is no longer a soldier."[9] Lacking anything else to pass the time, soldiers of a Wisconsin regiment conducted mock trials amongst themselves, "suing one another, having regular lawsuits, sworn witnesses, we have our lawyers, judges, juries, and all in good style."[10] Others opted to leave camp in search of recreation. "It was so much work to get a pass from the General," Sergeant Sawtelle wrote while on occupation duty near Richmond, "that we decided just to . . . risk getting picked up by the Provo Guard" and go into town anyway.[11] If unable to leave, soldiers were content to stay in camp provided they had entertainment of their own. With the conclusion of the war, soldiers saw no reason why the army's restrictions on drinking remained. "More liquor was smuggled into camp and of course there was another row," Chaplain Armstrong lamented. "One man drew a loaded and cocked revolver on Colonel Telford." Armstrong claimed the whiskey got into camp because "women were allowed to come into camp to peddle fruit cakes, etc. and they were caught with a score of bottles of whiskey dangling under their skirts" and from sutlers selling cider "so drugged that two glasses would make a man crazy."[12] Because of the prevalence of drink, regular army routine also broke down. "Some of company H who had been absent over night came back to camp in a hilarious condition," William Wiley noted, "and had a little bedlam of their own and were put under guard."[13] As during the war, the failure of officers to maintain their own personal discipline provided a ready justification for soldiers to engage in questionable behavior. A chaplain wrote in despair that by early May 1865 discipline in his regiment near Washington, DC, was so bad that "whiskey, beer, and strumpets" saturated the encampment, and even the officers "were drunk last night, and those in shoulder straps were gallanting strumpets about the camp, and taking them into their tents," while the enlisted men engaged in "Fights, with bloody heads and noses . . . [and] Profanity is shockingly prevalent."[14] The army also continued to undermine its alcohol policies, especially on holidays. "A committee has been appointed to go to New Orleans," Rufus Kinsey wrote of the upcoming Fourth of July holiday, "to get lager beer, whiskey, and wines, fireworks and guests. I think we shall have a regular Dutch drunk."[15]

Drinking helped to pass the time, but it did not settle the issue of when soldiers were getting out of the army. Private Henry Heisler, who reenlisted along with other veterans in 1864, believed he was not leaving the army any time soon. Writing to his sister, Heisler opined, "I don't expect to get out of this service till my time expires, which is three years unless sooner shot."[16] Pondering on the meaning of the Fourth of July, Captain Rufus Kinsley wrote in his diary, "I . . . thank God for the return of this anniversary. How much hollow hypocrisy has characterized our rejoicing on this anniversary in the years that are past." Nevertheless, Kinsley was "ready to beat my sword into a plowshare . . . I can afford to retire from the field of Mars. I cannot afford to spend any more time here." Eight days later, Kinsley resigned his commission and went home.[17] Albert Allen and his comrades in the Tenth Rhode Island had their own idea on how to get out of the army. Convinced that their colonel was delaying their discharge, the men of the regiment threatened to "arrest Colonel [Charles H.] Tompkins and . . . sue him for damages and try to get out of the service on the plea of being enlisted under false pretenses."[18]

For soldiers who could not wait any longer to get out of the army, the simplest answer was to desert. Soldiers who enlisted late in the war feared the army would compel them to serve out their terms of service. Private Thomas Walton, for instance, enlisted for a year's service in the One Hundred Ninety-fifth Pennsylvania barely a month before Lee's surrender at Appomattox. He witnessed the dissolution of his company as men, unwilling to stay in an army with no one to fight, deserted away. Between June and November 1865 (the unit did not muster out of army service until January 1866), Walton's company suffered thirty-two desertions, nearly half its strength.[19] A similar circumstance decimated the Seventh Kansas Cavalry. Declaring that they had enlisted for three years or until the end of the war, the Kansans wanted their immediate discharge. Instead, in July 1865 the army ordered them to remote Fort Kearny in the Nebraska Territory to fight the Indians, causing more than one hundred men to desert almost immediately and forcing the officers themselves to stand armed guard over the regiment's horses to keep the men from using them to escape. The unit did not muster out until November of that year.[20] The worst postwar discipline occurred in Texas. Immediately after Lee's surrender, Grant detached Major General Philip Sheridan to assume control of Union forces west of the Mississippi River. Reinforced by the IV and XXV Corps, Sheridan was there to "rattle the saber" at France's occupation of Mexico in violation of the Monroe Doctrine.[21] Sheridan's force remained only though the summer months, but, fearing a much longer stay, his men proved almost unmanageable. "The Whole regt. has lost all confidence in Col. [Thomas H.] Benton." Charles Musser wrote from Clarkesville, Texas, in July 1865, "They all blame him for our comeing [*sic*] to Texas, and they curse him for his imbecility and slowness." Musser described, "dissatisfaction prevails among the boys here. It sometimes almost breaks out in open mutiny" and the "officers have no controll [*sic*] of the men . . . the only way to avoid some of these difficulties is to muster the troops out as quick as possible." The men were particularly incensed when they found out they had to serve longer than they anticipated. Expecting to muster out in August 1865, three years from their date of enlistment, they found out they had to serve until November, the third anniversary of their unit's formal organization.[22] At least the army had men in Texas to complain about their position. A number of men deserted from Twenty-ninth USCT when, as part of the XXV Corps, they received word to prepare for the trip to Texas. Once there, discipline went into a sharp decline, with official inspections full of criticisms of the officers' lack of leadership.[23]

There was an absolute limit, however, to what punishment the army could inflict for desertion and mutinous conduct. An end to the war also brought an end to the death penalty. Army Regulations only permitted capital punishment during wartime, so the army could no longer impose the penalty at postwar courts-martial. Soldiers court-martialed and sentenced to die before the end of the war still faced their punishments, and a small number of executions continued during the summer of 1865. Denied the ability to execute for major offenses, such as desertion, the army reverted to drumming out instead. Soldiers of the One Hundred Ninety-second New York witnessed the drumming out of two deserters in June 1865, viewing the soldiers being "paraded through all the camps in the division" in lieu of facing a firing squad.[24]

The army could not permit discipline to erode to the point of collapse but responded with force only when no other option existed. To stem a growing wave of insubordination, Colonel Joseph Fisher issued a regimental general order that addressed "a species of insubordination growing up in this command." Recognizing "it is desirable that we should all get to our homes and families," Fisher reminded his men, "it is the part of a good Soldier to serve the government as long as his services are required" and that while he sympathized with their complaints, "acts of insubordination cannot, must not, and will not be allowed."[25] While stern and emphatic about making his point, Fisher's tone was entirely different from orders issued during the war, with an element of sympathy and accommodation that wartime general orders usually lacked. To tighten discipline and remind their men they were still soldiers, officers tried to stem the flow of personnel leaving their camps without permission. "We are not allowed to go into town without a pass from the captains and signed by the colonel and our Brigade Commander," Henry Heisler complained in May 1865, "Two men out of every fifty can go out once every morning."[26] The army held officers and NCOs to the same standard. In Daniel Chisholm's regiment, Captain John Weltner found himself under arrest for "being absent without leave" on June 4, 1865. Weltner was still under arrest, according to Chisholm, on June 13, awaiting the seating of a court-martial.[27] Brigadier General William F. Bartlett, commanding a division of the IX Corps, found his troops "restless and dissatisfied about getting mustered out" to the point "it is almost impossible to get men and officers to do their duty." Consequently, Bartlett wrote, "I have roughed more officers and reduced more noncoms to the ranks, these last two or three weeks, than in any other year of service."[28] To help maintain order and to improve relations with Southern civilians, the army ordered all foraging and pillaging to end under the threat of severe punishment. John Ferguson, who enjoyed pillaging as much as any soldier in the Union army, noted the new attitude. "The orderly of each company is ordered to call the company roll every time the command halts to provent [sic] any one from leaving the road to pillage," he noted, "and all such pillagers when caught will in instantly and sovearly [sic] dealt with." Instead of taking what they wanted to eat, "Quarter masters [sic] only will have the right to precure forage and they must be prepaired to pay cash for it."[29]

Alcohol remained the army's main problem. Most disciplinary problems were the product of too much whiskey and too much free time, creating situations that taxed an officer's charity to its limits. When a number of men in the Seventy-seventh Illinois "got on a drunk and became mutinous and cursed and threatened their officers" in May 1865, Captain James Secord "was very patient with the poor drunk fools and got the other men to go and talk to them and try to quiet them." When they refused to quiet down, however, "Secord had to order out a guard and have the worst of them tied up." Because of the row, "Some of them were tried by courtmartial [*sic*] and sent to the dry tortugas when they might have been on their way home." An observer could only shake his head at "the poor foolish creatures [who] after serving their country faithfully for three long years and just on the eve of being honorably discharged . . . [were] condemned to hard labor in the dry tortugas for six months."[30] In a similar event in August 1865, when ten inebriated soldiers from a Pennsylvania regiment incited a mutiny by refusing to go on guard duty, the army court-martialed them and sent them to the Dry Tortugas for a six-month stretch.[31]

Keeping soldiers in camp lessened the alcohol problem, but did not stop it entirely. To stem the drinking problem, the army ended one of the most prevalent sources of alcohol when it shut down its own liquor supply. In a general order dated June 29, 1865, the Adjutant General's Office announced, "The whiskey ration will no longer be supplied to troops of the United States by the Subsistence Department." Instead of one last binge, the army ordered, "the whiskey now on hand will be sold under the order of the Commissary General of Subsistence," and soldiers found it harder to obtain a drink.[32] Other officers shut down saloons near their posts, kept soldiers encamped as far away from towns as possible, and periodically searched the soldiers' personal possessions for hidden whiskey. Officers had to be careful, however, as restraining the soldiers' newly rediscovered sense of freedom came with consequences. To reinforce his ban on soldiers from leaving camp to get drunk in New Orleans, General William Benton increased the number of perimeter guards and restricted the soldiers' liberty to leave camp. In response, "some of the more reckless boys" placed some loose gunpowder and a fuse in "an old canteen" to make a loud, but nonlethal, firework. After the device went off with a bang in his tent, the "General concluded that a camp guard had ceased to be a success and didn't order anymore [*sic*]."[33] Alcohol's symbol of civilian freedoms when civilian life seemed tantalizingly close ensured that soldiers pursued alcohol with perhaps more vigor than ever before. As a sign they were free men and able to drink when they chose, soldiers of the One Hundred Fourth Illinois conducted a "grand raid" upon a saloon outside of their camp on the day they received their discharges, in full view of their erstwhile officers who could do nothing to stop them.[34]

THE REMAINING DECADES of the nineteenth century saw the army slip back into its antebellum roles. Soldiers occupied the South as part of the Reconstruction effort, manned a relative handful of coastal fortifications near major ports, and defended the frontier through a series of small isolated posts. The army faced a number of post-war issues that affected recruiting. Most of the army lived in rustic conditions in isolated posts on the frontier, where nearly constant conflict with Native Americans meant that death in this "peacetime" army was a real possibility. The officer corps suffered as promotions crawled to a virtual halt, leading many officers to leave the army and causing discipline to suffer.[35] Army pay, the most consistent source of complaint among enlisted men, stagnated and even shrank during the post-war years. When the Civil War ended, privates made $16 per month. In 1871, Congress reduced this amount to only $13 per month, and a third of the army's enlisted men deserted within a matter of months. Congress kept the monthly wage at $13, but added longevity pay to reward soldiers in the latter months of their enlistment, a compromise that did little to settle soldiers' complaints.[36]

Consequently, as during the war, desertion became a common problem. In any given year between 1866 and 1890, about 15 percent of the army's enlisted men deserted.[37] To an army limited to a firm personnel limit by Congress and facing severe recruitment problems, high desertion rates were the last thing they needed. To combat the desertion problem, the army enacted new policies in 1890. To keep soldiers from leaving, the army withheld $4 from their wages every month, returning it (with interest) when the soldier received an honorable discharge at the end of his term of service. The army retained its five-year enlistment term, but gave soldiers the option of leaving without penalty after three years. After one year of service, soldiers could also purchase their discharge for a set fee. These changes encouraged soldiers to endure their terms of service and leave the army under legal rather than illegal means. Soldiers responded to the changes; the desertion rate plummeted in the years after the new policies went into effect.[38] Although many Civil War-era penalties persisted (ball and chain, guardhouse, fines) into the post-war era, the army did make some efforts to reform its disciplinary system less toward punishment and more toward reward. The army further codified its disciplinary code to avoid excessive or disproportionate punishment for similar offenses in a new penal code in 1891. The army began to house long-term offenders at the new prison at Fort Leavenworth, although the relatively small number of inmates led the army to turn the facility over to the Justice Department in 1894. After the growth of the standing army in the early twentieth century, however, the army reclaimed the Leavenworth military prison in 1906.[39]

Officers also experimented in ways to preempt behavior offenses and indiscipline instead of merely punishing soldiers after the fact, although with mixed results. Boredom on remote posts inevitably caused excessive drinking, and the army finally took a long-overdue look at the problems alcohol inflicted upon the service. Bans and punishment did not work during the war, so the army had to find another answer. The long-term solution to the drinking problem was to have the army permit, but directly supervise, the alcohol consumed by soldiers. In 1880, the army established its first post canteen, an on-base facility where soldiers could purchase and consume alcohol under controlled conditions. Only licensed vendors could serve alcohol at canteens, and, as they were on-base, they were always under observation by the post commander. The new system worked as intended. Drunkenness declined because the army permitted soldiers to drink, but not to excess. AWOL diminished because soldiers did not have to sneak out of camp to get a drink, and the number of minor offenses declined because drunken soldiers were not wandering about causing mischief. Near his camp, Colonel Richard Dodge reported, "three saloons . . . had closed" because of a lack of soldier business.[40] Prostitution proved a more difficult matter. Officers tried athletic competitions and other wholesome diversions to persuade soldiers from indulging in the prostitutes in nearby towns, but seldom succeeded. One soldier summed up the enlisted man's position on the prostitution issue by mockingly complaining that soldiers were only "thinking where he can get a drink of beer, or a girl," and, unfortunately, at his post "you couldn't get any beer."[41] Local communities jealously guarded their authority to maintain law and order, and resisted army efforts to eradicate prostitution in nearby towns. Admitting failure, the army continued to consider prostitution a civilian crime and did little to control the behavior of their soldiers when it came to sex.[42]

At an institutional level, military justice also experienced reform. Recognizing the need for a lasting military legal presence, Congress permitted the army to retain the position of Judge Advocate General on a permanent basis. Joseph Holt remained in the post, overseeing the trial of the Lincoln conspirators and providing legal insight on proposed army reforms, until his retirement in 1875.[43] His last major service was a clarification of the Articles of War in 1874 that addressed several procedural and punishment issues raised by the war. Holt's replacement was Brevet Brigadier General William M. Dunn, who had served as Holt's assistant JAG during the war. Appointing Dunn to the position was a wise move, as it retained someone in the army's top legal post who had experienced the evolution of military justice during the Civil War, retaining the institutional memory of the JAG. The Civil War and its association with the JAG came full circle in 1895, when Brigadier General Guido N. Lieber, Francis Lieber's son, assumed the position.[44] The army retained its JAG, but lost its Provost Marshal General. James Fry had operated the Provost Marshal Corps with efficiency, but in a manner that often stepped on political toes. Fry's aggressive pursuit of deserters and draft dodgers in New York City made him an enemy of Roscoe Conkling, the powerful New York Congressman, who determined to undermine Fry by not permitting an extension of the federal legislation that created his position, which was due to expire in 1866. Accusing Fry of unfounded charges of inefficiency, brutality, and corruption, Conkling eliminated the PMC and the post of Provost Marshal General as part of the aforementioned Army Reorganization Act. Fry remained in the service until 1881, retiring as a major general in the Regular Army. He produced a number of books on his wartime experiences, including *New York and Conscription* (1885), summarizing his conscription activities in New York and *The Conkling and Blaine-Fry Controversy* (1893) that defended his reputation in the face of Conkling's accusations.[45] Without a PMC, the service reverted to ad hoc internal police forces, and the Office of the Provost Marshal General and a professional Corps of Military Police did not return until the eve of America's entry into World War II.[46]

THE ATTEMPTS AT REFORM indicated that the army did indeed learn something about administering discipline during the war, and afterward army discipline continued to evolve along paths established by wartime experience. Although wartime pressures prevented the army from making institutional reforms during the war, the institutional reforms put in place in the postwar period showed that the army was a flexible institution more in touch with the popular mood of the country and, more importantly, its soldiers than it was in the antebellum period. Although the army reverted to a Regular Army model, it was not the same army as before the Civil War. Gone was the Regular Army mentality, where soldiers themselves created a mode of behavior and level of professionalism to which volunteers had to measure up. Instead, the attitudes of the volunteer became the attitude of the Regular enlisted man. In the post-Civil War army, the ethos of the citizen-soldier, something new in the Civil War, became the new behavioral model for the army. Soldiers, aware of the combative streak that identified the enlisted men of the Union army, continued to challenge the authority of their officers, defy the rules when they could, and yearn for the day when they could be civilians again. The self-regulatory conduct of the prewar Regulars was gone forever, replaced by the almost-expected disgruntlement of the common soldier in future wars, whether it be the World War I doughboy, the World War II G.I., or the Vietnam grunt. Disciplinary regulations remained somewhat flexible, more so at the unit level than the institutional level, and the best officers realized they could no longer rule by decree. The harshest punishments disappeared, replaced by a system more in line with civilian courts and penalties. The army adopted a more rational approach to alcohol, although problems relating to other soldier vices remained unresolved. Officers retained the final voice of authority, but soldiers influenced the level and purpose of discipline through their collective voice and knowledge of wartime precedents. Aware of the new attitude among enlisted men, Major General John Schofield, addressing the Corps of Cadets at West Point in 1879, urged the future leaders of the army to remember, "discipline which makes the soldiers of a free country reliable in battle is not to be gained by harsh or tyrannical treatment," but rather "He who feels the respect which is due to others cannot fail to inspire in them regard for himself."[47]

All of these changes occurred because soldiers of the Union army forced these changes. The social demands of masculinity and the tradition of the citizen-soldier combined to challenge the ironclad disciplinary code of the U.S. Army. The result was a populist reformation of how the army viewed its powers over its soldiers, and how soldiers viewed their responsibility to the army. Distrust of authority caused a level of distrust between enlisted men and officers that seldom improved during the war. The continual need to demonstrate masculinity and preserve the concept of citizen-soldiery led to an almost constant struggle between soldiers and officers despite the formalized Articles of War meant to contain the independent impulses of erstwhile civilians. As a consequence of the social clash, soldiers engaged in a variety of offenses that challenged both the collective expectations of soldier behavior and the written army regulations. The massive number of volunteers in the new industrial army generated so many disciplinary offenses that the army could only cope by changing its disciplinary system lest it face a collapse of discipline altogether. Finding a new middle ground in the midst of war was never easy, especially as the soldiers themselves often could not agree on what was proper soldier behavior, and offered differing views, interpretations, and reactions to army discipline. At every level—from offense, to arrest, to prosecution, to punishment—army and soldiers struggled over the proper relationship between men doing their duty while maintaining their sense of identity and an army upholding its regulations while trying to win a war. The by-product was a mixed experience when it came to the two definitions of discipline, both battlefield conduct and judicial behavior. The Union army certainly had "discipline" enough to win a long, tough war, but few officers who had to lead, administer, arrest, try, or punish their subordinates would agree that the Union army practiced "discipline."

NOTES

Introduction

1. Alexis de Tocqueville, *Democracy in America* (New York: Colonial Press, 1899), 284–285.

2. Carl E. Skeen, *Citizen Soldiers in the War of 1812* (Lexington: University Press of Kentucky, 1999), 18.

3. Ernest F. Fisher, *Guardians of the Republic: A History of the Non-Commissioned Officer Corps of the United States Army* (Mechanicsburg, PA: Stackpole Books, 2001), 109–111.

4. Elizabeth D. Samet, *Willing Obedience: Citizens, Soldiers, and the Progress of Consent in America, 1776–1898* (Palo Alto, CA: Stanford University Press, 2004), 3.

5. David Crockett, *Life of Col. David Crockett* (Philadelphia: G.G. Evans, 1860), 224. Robert J. Higgs. *God in the Stadium: Sports and Religion in America* (Lexington: University of Kentucky Press, 1995), 95.

6. Michael Kimmel, *Manhood in America: A Cultural History* (New York: Free Press, 1996), 22–36.

7. Julie M. Fenster, *The Case of Abraham Lincoln: A Story of Adultery, Murder, and the Making of a Great President* (New York: Palgrave MacMillan, 2007), 20–26.

8. Carl S. Anthony, *First Ladies: The Saga of the Presidents' Wives and their Power, 1789–1961* (New York: HarperCollins, 1992), 162.

9. Peter Gay, *Pleasure Wars: The Bourgeois Experience, Victoria to Freud* (New York: Norton, 1998), 18. Michael E. McGerr, *A Fierce Discontent: The Rise and Fall of the Progressive Movement in America, 1870–1920* (New York: Simon and Schuster, 2003), 60–61.

10. Charles M. Hubbard, *Lincoln and his Contemporaries* (Macon, GA: Mercer University Press, 1999), 47.

1—"Ancient un-American articles"

1. Samuel T. Ansell, "Some Reforms in Our System of Military Justice," *Yale Law Journal*, vol. 32, no. 2 (December 1922): 147. Serving in the Judge Advocate General's office, Ansell participated in the 1920 revision of the Articles of War, the first major change since 1806.

2. Edward M. Byrne, *Military Law*, 3rd ed. (Annapolis, MD: Naval Institute Press, 1981), 5–6.

3. Henry L. Scott, *Military Dictionary* (New York: Greenwood Press, 1968 reprint), 56.

4. Sylvia R. Frey, *The British Soldier in America: A Social History of Military Life in the Revolutionary Period* (Austin: University of Texas Press, 1981), 81–85.

5. J.D. Droddy, "King Richard to *Solorio*: The Historical and Constitutional Bases for Court-Martial Jurisdiction in Criminal Cases," *Harvard Law Review*, vol. 103, no. 8 (June 1990): 93.

6. Scott, 60. The English troops mutinied over the perceived preference of King William III for his native Dutch troops to his new English military forces.

7. Droddy, 89–91.

8. Stuart L. Bernath, "George Washington and the Genesis of American Military

Discipline," *Mid-America: An Historical Review*, vol. 49, no. 2 (April 1967): 95.

9. William Winthrop, *Military Law and Precedents* (Whitefish, MT: Kessinger, 2005; reprint), 949.

10. Bernath, 95.

11. Winthrop, 955.

12. Winthrop, 957.

13. Winthrop, 950–951.

14. John C. Fitzpatrick, ed., *Writings of George Washington from the Original Manuscript Sources* (39 volumes) (Washington, DC: Government Printing Office, 1931–1944), vol. 6; 91 and 114.

15. The other members of the 1775 Articles of War committee were Philip Schuyler, Silas Deane, Thomas Cushing, and Joseph Hewes. Washington, with heavy responsibilities for running the Continental Army, attended only one meeting of the committee. Ironically, Philip Schuyler, serving as a general in the Continental Army in 1777, was court-martialed under the system he himself helped to create, after abandoning Fort Ticonderoga to the British.

16. Jonathan Lurie, *Arming Military Justice*, vol. 1: *The Origins of the United States Court of Military Appeals, 1775–1950* (Princeton, NJ: Princeton University Press, 1992), 5.

17. Page Smith, *John Adams* (Westport, CT: Greenwood Press, 1969), 289.

18. Charles F. Adams, *The Works of John Adams, Second President of the United States*, vol. III (Boston: Little, Brown, 1865), 68.

19. The other members of the 1776 Articles of war committee were John Rutledge, James Wilson, and R.R. Livingstone.

20. Worthington C. Ford, *Journals of the Continental Congress, 1774–1779* (Washington, DC: Government Printing Office, 1905), 374.

21. *The Army Lawyer: A History of the Judge Advocate General's Corps: 1775–1975* (Washington, DC: Government Printing Office, 1975), 11.

22. James McMichael, "Diary of Lieutenant James McMichael of the Pennsylvania Line, 1776–1778," *Pennsylvania Magazine of History and Biography*, Vol. 16 (1892), 139.

23. Harry M. Ward, *George Washington's Enforcers: Policing the Continental Army* (Carbondale: Southern Illinois University Press, 2006), 22–23.

24. Harry M. Ward, *The American Revolution: Nationhood Achieved, 1763–1788* (New York: St. Martin's, 1995), 220.

25. Bonnie S. Stadelman, "The Amusements of the American Soldiers during the Revolution" (Ph.D. dissertation, Tulane University, 1969), 81–110.

26. Louis Beebe, "Journal of Dr. Louis Beebe." *Pennsylvania Magazine of History and Biography*, LIX (1935), 352.

27. Fitzpatrick, VIII, 28–29.

28. Ward, *American Revolution*, 237.

29. S. Sydney Bradford, "Discipline the Morristown Winter Encampments," *Proceedings of the New Jersey Historical Society*, LXXX, no. 1 (1962): 19–20.

30. Bradford, 16–19.

31. Arthur J. Alexander, "Desertion and Its Punishment in Revolutionary Virginia," *William and Mary Quarterly*, III (1946): 386.

32. Ward, *American Revolution*, 239.

33. James C. Neagles, *Summer Soldiers: A Survey & Index of Revolutionary War Courts-Martial* (Salt Lake City, UT: Ancestry Incorporated, 1986), 40 and 277 [emphasis in the original].

34. Allen Bowman, *The Morale of the American Revolutionary Army* (Port Washington, NY: Kennikat Press, 1964), 89.

35. Ward, *American Revolution*, 239–240.

36. Alexander, 397.

37. Bowman, 90–91.

38. Joseph B. Turner, *The Journal and Order Book of Captain Robert Kirkwood of the Delaware Regiment of the Continental Line* (Port Washington, NY: Kennikat Press, 1970), 17.

39. William Denny, "Soldier of the Republic: The Life of Major Ebenezer Denny" (Ph.D. dissertation, Miami University, 1978), 27.

40. Harry M. Ward, *George Washington's Enforcers*, 195.

41. Turner, 218–219.

42. Fitzpatrick, VIII, 8, 17, 161.

43. Fitzpatrick, XXI, 175–176 and 294.

44. Ward, *American Revolution*, 248.

45. Turner, 15.

46. Louis C. Hatch, *The Administration of the American Revolutionary Army* (New York: Longmans, Green, 1904), 138–140.

47. Turner, 52.

48. Maurer Maurer, "Military Justice under General Washington," *Military Affairs*, vol. 28, no. 1 (Spring 1964): 12. Bernath, 97.

49. Washington perhaps recognized what Napoleon Bonaparte enunciated later. In 1804, when an old revolutionary criticized Napoleon's creation of the Legion of Honor as a mere "bauble," Napoleon replied that "It is with baubles that men are led,"50. Bernath, 92–94.

51. Bradford, 15–19.

52. Silvia R. Frey, 72.

53. Lyman H. Butterfield, "Psychological Warfare in 1776: The Jefferson-Franklin Plan to Cause Hessian Desertions," *Proceedings of the American Philosophical Society*, 94, no. 3 (June 1950): 233–241.

54. Frey, 73.

55. Arthur N. Gilbert, "The Changing Face of British Military Justice, 1757–1783," *Military Affairs*, vol. 49, no. 2 (April 1985): 80–84, and Frey, 80–82.

56. Ward, *Washington's Enforcers*, 158–160.

57. C.E. Carver, "The Significance of the Military Office in America, 1763–1765," *American Historical Review*, vol. 28, no. 3 (April 1923): 475–488.

58. Frederick B. Wiener, *Civilians under Military Justice: The British Practice since 1689, Especially in North America* (Chicago: University of Chicago Press, 1967), 105–106.

59. Frederick B. Wiener, "The Military Occupation of Philadelphia in 1777–1778," *Proceedings of the American Philosophical Society*, vol. 111, no. 5 (Oct., 1967): 310–313. Edwald G. Schaukirk, "Occupation of New York City by the British," *Pennsylvania Magazine of History and Biography*, vol. 10, no. 1 (1886): 418–445.

60. Wiener, *Civilians under Military Justice*, 87–92 and 141–153.

61. Frey, 74–78.

62. Oscar T. Barck, *New York City during the War for Independence: With Special Reference to the Period of British Occupation* (Port Washington, NY: Friedman, Inc., 1966; reprint of 1931 edition), 120–127. For a full discussion of the impact of the legislation, see Henry Wagner, "The Prohibitory Act: A Cause of the American Revolution," M.A. thesis, Syracuse University, 1960.

63. John Andre, *Major Andre's Journal: Operations of the British Army under Lieutenant Generals Sir William Howe and Sir Henry Clinton* (Whitefish, MT: Kessinger, 2007; reprint of 1930 edition), 481 and 504.

64. Wiener, *Civilians under Military Justice*, 91.

65. Cornwallis Orderly Book, General Orders numbers 36 and 39, Orderly Book Collection, Clements Library, University of Michigan, Ann Arbor Michigan. Author's database of Wiener research. Author's database of Wiener research.

66. Wiener, *Civilians under Military Justice*, 74–91.

67. Barck, 141–143, and Wiener, *Civilians under Military Justice*, 147.

68. Wiener, *Civilians under Military Justice*, 277–300.

69. Richard J. Koke, "Washington and Captain Joshua Huddy," *New York Historical Society Quarterly*, vol. 41, no. 3 (1957): 330–335. Sheila L. Skemp. *William Franklin: Son of a Patriot, Servant of a King* (New York: Oxford, 1990), 260–264.

70. Frey, 78–79.

71. John P. Kaminski, et al., *The Documentary History of the Ratification of the Constitution* (21 volumes) (Madison: State Historical Society of Wisconsin, 1976–2007), vol. 15, 244.

72. Richard H. Kohn, "The Constitution and National Security: The Intent of the Framers" in Richard H. Kohn, *The United States Military under the Constitution of the United States, 1789–1989* (New York: NYU Press, 1991), 64–67.

73. Kaminski, vol. 15, 492.

74. Lawrence D. Cress, "Republican Liberty and National Security: American Military Policy as an Ideological Problem, 1783 to 1789," *William and Mary Quarterly*, 3rd Ser., vol. 38, no. 1 (January 1981): 73–96.

75. U.S. Constitution, Article I, Section 8.

76. U.S. Constitution, Article II, Section 2, and Article I, Section 9.

77. Lurie, 7–9.

78. Walter T. Cox III, "The Army, the Courts, and the Constitution: The Evolution of Military Justice," *Military Law Review*, vol. 118, no. 1 (1987): 9.

79. Frederick B. Wiener, "Courts-Martial and the Constitution: The Original Understanding, *Harvard Law Review* 72 (1957): 268.

80. John F. Callan, *The Military Laws of the United States Relating to the Army, Marine Corps, Volunteers, Militia, and to Bounty Lands and Pensions, From the Foundation of the Government to the Year 1858* (Baltimore, MD: John Murphy, 1858), 300.

81. *Army Lawyer*, 34.

82. *Dynes v. Hoover*, 61 U.S. (20 How.) 65 (1857). Lurie, 29–30. Droddy, 101–102.

83. *United States v. Hudson*, 7 Cranch 32 (1812).

84. *Walker v. Morris*, 3 Am. Jurist 281 (Mass. 1830). *American Jurist*, April 1830, 17.

85. *Martin v. Mott*, 25 U.S. 19 (1827).

86. Allan R. Millett, "The Constitution and the Citizen-Soldier," in Kohn, 102–105.

87. Mary Ellen Rowe, *Bulwark of the Republic: The American Militia in the Antebellum West* (Westport, CT: Praeger, 2003), 75–79, 117–118, and 205–206.

88. Stanley S. Graham, "Life of the Enlisted Soldier on the Western Frontier," M.A. thesis, North Texas State University, 1972, 201–202.

89. Mark A. Vargas, "The Military Justice System and the Use of Illegal Punishments as Causes of Desertion in the U.S. Army, 1821–1835," *Journal of Military History*, vol. 55, no. 1 (January 1991): 1–19.

90. Lurie, 7.

91. Edward M. Coffman, *The Old Army: A Portrait of the American Army in Peacetime, 1784–1898* (New York: Oxford University Press, 1986), 197.

92. Mark A. Vargas, "The Progressive Agent of Mischief: The Whiskey Ration and Temperance in the United States Army," *Historian*, vol. 67, no. 2 (Summer 2005): 204.

93. Vargas, "Progressive Agent of Mischief," 205.

94. Dale R. Steinhauer, "'Sogers': Enlisted Men in the U.S. Army, 1815–1860," Ph.D. dissertation, University of North Carolina, 1992, 153–154.

95. Vargas, "Progressive Agent of Mischief," 214.

96. *Army Lawyer*, 8–23.

97. Henry Flanders, *The Lives and Times of the Chief Justices of the Supreme Court of the United States* (Philadelphia: Lippincott, 1874), 298.

98. *U.S. Statutes at Large*, 270.

99. *Army Lawyer*, 26–29.

100. *Army Lawyer*, 34–42.

101. Richard B. Winders, *Mr. Polk's Army: The American Military Experience in the Mexican War* (College Station: Texas A & M University Press, 1997), 60.

102. To the prewar army of only 6500 officers and men, the Regular Army enlisted an additional 35,000 men. K. Jack Bauer. *The Mexican War, 1846–1848* (Lincoln: University of Nebraska Press, 1992; reprint of 1974 edition), 397. Paul Foos, *A Short, Offhand, Killing Affair: Soldiers and Social Conflict during the Mexican-American War* (Chapel Hill: University of North Carolina Press, 2002), 61–62.

103. Winders, 60.

104. Approximately 70,000 volunteer soldiers and 3,000 officers. Justin H. Smith, *The War with Mexico* (New York: MacMillan, 1919), 537.

105. Foos, 87.

106. Bauer, 270.

107. Allan Peskin, *Volunteers: The Mexican War Journals of Private Richard Coulter and Sergeant Thomas Barclay, Company E, Second Pennsylvania Infantry* (Kent, OH: Kent State University Press, 1991), 226.

108. Winders, 80–85.

109. Luther Giddings, *Sketches of the Campaign in Northern Mexico, in Eighteen-Hundred Forty Six and Seven* (New York: G.B. Putnam, 1953), 280.

110. Joseph Wheelan, *Invading Mexico: America's Continental Dream and the Mexican War, 1846–1848* (New York: Caroll & Graf, 2007), 176–177 and 181. For a full account of the dilemma posed by the Rangers, see Ian B. Lyles, "Mixed Blessing: The Role of the Texas Rangers in the Mexican War, 1846– 1848," M.A. thesis, Army Command and General Staff College, 2003.

111. Daniel Henry Hill diary, entry for October 17, 1846. Southern Historical Collection, Wilson Library (Manuscripts Department), University of North Carolina, Chapel Hill, North Carolina.

112. Foos, 124.

113. Claude M. Fuess, *The Life of Caleb Cushing* (2 volumes) (New York: Harcourt, Brace, 1923), vol. 2, 54 and 58.

114. Foos, 104. Peter F. Stevens, *The Rogue's March: John Riley and the St. Patrick's Battalion* (Washington, DC: Brassey's, 1999), 48–49.

115. Foos, 96. Stevens, 53 and 56.

116. Abbe Domenech, *Missionary Adventures in Texas and Mexico* (London: Longmans, Brown, & Green, 1857), 69–72. Winders, 115.

117. Giddings, 276.

118. Henry W. Webb, "The Story of Jefferson Barracks," *New Mexico Historical Review* 21 (1946): 197–198.

119. Winders, 83.

120. Winders, 63. A lieutenant colonel, a major, two captains, and five lieutenants were killed at Molino del Rey, and forty-seven other officers were wounded.

121. *Niles National Register*, October 9, 1847.

122. Stevens, 170. Foos, 102. Smith, 318–319.

123. Stevens, 81–87.

124. Foos, 105–106.

125. William S. Henry, *Campaign Sketches of the War with Mexico* (New York: Arno Press, 1973; reprint of 1847 edition), 240.

126. Robert R. Miller, *Shamrock and Sword: The Saint Patrick's Battalion in the U.S.-Mexican War* (Norman: University of Okalahoma Press, 1989), 32 and 187–192.

127. Miller, 103.

128. Edward S. Wallace, "Deserters in the Mexican War," *The Hispanic American Historical Review*, vol. 55, no. 3 (August 1935): 374–383.

129. Dana O. Jensen, "The Memoirs of Daniel M. Frost," *Missouri Historical Society Bulletin*, vol. 26, no. 3 (1970): 222.

130. Winders, 135–138.

131. John S. Eisenhower, *Agent of Destiny: the Life and Times of General Winfield Scott* (New York: Free Press, 1997), 287.

132. Foos, 127.

133. General Order 20, reprinted in Scott, 383.

134. Harold L. Kaplan, "Constitutional Limitations on Trials by Military Commissions," *University of Pennsylvania Law Review and American Law Register*, vol. 92, no. 2 (December 1943): 119–149. Scott R. Morris, "The Laws of War: Rules by Warriors for Warriors," *Army Lawyer*, December 1997, DA-PAM 27–50–301, 9. Foos, 117.

135. Dennis E. Berge, "A Mexican Dilemma: The Mexico City Ayuntamiento and the Question of Loyalty, 1846–1848," *The Hispanic American Historical Review*, vol. 50, no. 2 (May 1970): 229–256.

136. Foos, 121–122.

137. James K. Holland, "Diary of a Texan Volunteer in the Mexican War," *Southwestern Historical Quarterly*, vol. 30, no. 1, 1–33.

138. Foos, 136.

139. *American Military History: Army Historical Series* (Washington, DC: Center for Military History, 1989), 181. In 1855, Congress authorized the Army to create four additional regiments, creating the Regular Army that existed at the outbreak of the Civil War.

140. *Army Lawyer*, 42–46.

2—"Damn Fool!"

1. James Ames, letter to mother dated December 15, 1860, James W. Ames Papers, United States Army Military History Institute, Carlisle, Pennsylvania.

2. Joseph A. Frank, *With Ballot and Bayonet: The Political Socialization of American Civil War Soldiers* (Athens: University of Georgia Press, 1998), 22 and 62.

3. Peter Welsh, undated letter to brother, Peter Welsh Papers, New York Historical Society, New York, New York.

4. Frank, 25.

5. Gerald F. Linderman, *Embattled Courage: The Experience of Combat in the American Civil War* (New York: Free Press, 1987), 7–16.

6. David Lilley, undated letter to sister, David Lilley Papers, University of Delaware Library, Newark, Delaware.

7. John Lynch, letter to cousin dated February 17, 1863, John J. Lynch Papers, Chicago Historical Society, Chicago, Illinois.

8. Darryl Lyman, *Civil War Quotations* (Conshohocken, PA: Combined Books, 1995), 75.

9. James Dunn, letter to wife dated May 29, 1861. James Dunn Papers. Joseph Baer, letter to wife dated October 13, 1862, Joseph Baer letters, both Alderman Memorial Library, University of Virginia; Charlottesville, Virginia.

10. Frank, 23–24.

11. Marcia Reid-Green, *Letters Home: Henry Matrau of the Iron Brigade* (Lincoln: University of Nebraska Press, 1993), 12.

12. James Wiggins, letter to parents dated January 19, 1864, James B. Wiggins Papers, Virginia Historical Society; Richmond, Virginia.

13. A.T. Votwiler, "Letters from a Civil War Officer," *The Mississippi Valley Historical Review*, vol. 14, no. 4 (March 1928): 510.

14. Letter to wife dated May 29, 1861. Samuel Selden Partridge letters. Website "War Letters: Rochester Writes Home," http://www.wxxi.org/warletters/civil.html.

15. Barbara A. Smith, *The Civil War Letters of Col. Elijah H.C. Cavins, 14th Indiana* (Owensboro, KY: Cook-McDowell Publications, 1981), 1.

16. Diary entry for July 8, 1864. Claudius B. Grant papers, Bentley Historical Library, University of Michigan. Ann Arbor, Michigan. Grant was later Chief Justice of the Michigan Supreme Court.

17. Lance J. Herdegen, *The Men Stood Like Iron: How the Iron Brigade Won Its Name* (Bloomington: Indiana University Press, 1997), 78.

18. Richard S. Skidmore, *The Civil War Journal of Billy Davis: From Hopewell, Indiana to Port Republic, Virginia* (Greencastle, IN: Nugget, 1989), 2–3.

19. James Woodworth, letter to wife dated April 14, 1863, Clements Library, University of Michigan; Ann Arbor, Michigan.

20. James Carman, letter to father dated July 18, 1862. Website "The Valley of the Shadow: Two Communities in the American Civil War," http://etext.lib.virginia.edu/etcbin/civwarlett-browse?id=F0689.

21. George Beidelman, letter to father dated August 5, 1862. George Washington Beidelman Papers. Musselman Library, Gettysburg College. Gettysburg, Pennsylvania.

22. William B. Philips, letter to wife dated September 13, 1864. William H. Philips Papers. Ohio Historical Society. Columbus, Ohio.

23. George Cadman, letter to wife dated March 6, 1864 and George Gear, letter to Esther Cadman dated January 19, 1865, George H. Cadman Papers, Southern Historical Collection, University of North Carolina; Chapel Hill, North Carolina.

24. Barbara B. Smith and Nina B. Baker, *Burning Rails as We Pleased: The Civil War Letters of William Garrigues Bentley, 104th Ohio Volunteer Infantry* (Jefferson, NC: McFarland, 2004), 61.

25. Herdegen, 48.

26. George S. Avery, letter to wife dated July 2, 1861, George Smith Avery Papers, Chicago Historical Society, Chicago, Illinois.

27. William Barnitz, letter to the Pennsylvania *Telegraph* dated March 27, 1863. "The Valley of the Shadow," http://etext.lib.virginia.edu/etcbin/civwarlett-browse?id=FN0000.

28. Julie Holcomb, *Southern Sons, Northern Soldiers: The Civil War Letters of the Remley Brothers, 22nd Iowa Infantry* (DeKalb: Northern Illinois University Press, 2004), 84.

29. George Avery, letter to wife dated September 11, 1864, Avery Papers.

30. Donald E. Carmony, "Jacob W. Bartmess Civil War Letters," *Indiana Magazine of History*, vol. 52, no. 1 (March 1956): 63.

31. Wayne Mahood, *Charlie Mosher's Civil War: From Fair Oaks to Andersonville with the Plymouth Pilgrims (85th N.Y. Infantry)* (Hightstown, NJ: Longstreet House, 1994), 276. Margaret Brobst Roth, *Well Mary: Civil War Letters of a Wisconsin Volunteer* (Madison: University of Wisconsin Press, 1960), 65.

32. James Abraham, letter to brother dated August 7, 1862, Civil War Letters of James, Isaac, and William Abraham and James Sturgis, Historical Society of Pennsylvania, Philadelphia, Pennsylvania.

33. David W. Blight, *When This Cruel War is Over: The Civil War Letters of Charles Harvey Brewster* (Amherst: University of Massachusetts Press, 1992), 169.

34. Robert Mitchell, letter to wife dated February 22, 1863. Robert Mitchell Papers, Chicago Historical Society, Chicago, Illinois.

35. Mashies L. Lord, diary entry for August 19, 1862. "War Letters: Rochester Writes Home," http://www.wxxi.org/warletters/civil.html.

36. William E. Hughes, *The Civil War Papers of Lt. Colonel Newton T. Colby, New York Infantry* (Jefferson, NC: McFarland, 2003), 48.

37. Holcomb, 161–162.

38. Welsh Papers, letter to wife dated January 4, 1863.

39. Ella J. Bruen and Brian M. Fitzgibbons, *Though Ordinary Eyes: The Civil War Correspondence of Rufus Robbins, Private, 7th Regiment, Massachusetts Volunteers* (Westport, CT: Praeger, 2000), 73–74.

40. Peter H. Buckingham, *All's for the Best: The Civil War Reminiscences and Letters of Daniel W. Sawtelle, Eighth Maine Volunteer Infantry* (Knoxville: University of Tennessee Press, 2001), 252.

41. Herdegen, 37.

42. Alfred F. Duncan, letter to family of William Abraham dated August 16, 1864, Abraham Papers.

43. Alvin Voris, letter to wife, July 3, 1863. Alvin Voris Papers, Virginia Historical Society, Richmond, VA.

44. Henry C. Forbes, letter to officers of the Seventh Illinois Cavalry, Henry C. Forbes Papers, Chicago Historical Society, Chicago, Illinois.

45. Kenneth W. Noe, *A Southern Boy in Blue: The Memoir of Marcus Woodcock, 9th Kentucky Infantry (U.S.A.)* (Knoxville: University of Tennessee Press, 1996), 115–116.

46. Ashley Halsey, *A Yankee Private's Civil War* (Chicago: Henry Regnery, 1961), 82.

47. Alan D. Gaff, *On Many a Bloody Field: Four Years in the Iron Brigade* (Bloomington: Indiana University Press, 1996), 44.

48. Abraham Papers, "Incidents," 65.

49. Robert G. Scott, *Fallen Leaves: The Civil War Letters of Major Henry Livermore Abbott* (Kent, OH: Kent State University Press, 1991), 73–74.

50. Stuart Murray, *A Time of War: A Northern Chronicle of the Civil War* (Lee, MA: Berkshire House, 2001), 68.

51. Richard E. Matthews. *The 149th Pennsylvania Volunteer Infantry Unit in the Civil War* (Jefferson, NC: McFarland, 1994), 122.

52. Joseph S. Johnston, diary entry for August 16, 1862, Joseph Sturge Johnston Papers, Chicago Historical Society, Chicago, Illinois.

53. Voris Papers, letter to wife dated March 3, 1862.

54. Ruth L. Silliker, *The Rebel yell & the Yankee Hurrah: the Civil War Journal of a Maine Volunteer* (Camden, Maine: Down East Books, 1985), 179.

55. Versalle F. Washington, *Eagles on Their Buttons: A Black Infantry Regiment in the Civil War* (Columbia: University of Missouri Press, 1999), 46.

56. Joseph C. Fitzharris, "Field Officer Courts and U.S. Civil War Military Justice," *The Journal of Military History*, vol. 68, no. 1 (2004): 60.

57. Gaff, 25.

58. *The War of the Rebellion: A Compilation of the Official Records of the Union and Confederate Armies*, 130 volumes (hereafter as ORA) (Washington, DC: Government Printing Office, 1880–1901), vol. 7, 79.

59. James H. Croushore, *A Volunteer's Adventures: A Union Captain's Record of the Civil War* (Hamden, CT: Archon Books, 1970), 79. A noted author before the war, John W. DeForest wrote a number of novels after the war, most notable *Miss Ravenel's Conversion from Secession to Loyalty* (New York: Harper & Brothers, 1867).

60. James Hughlett, letter Abraham Lincoln dated November 1, 1864, James W. Hughlett Papers, Abraham Lincoln Presidential Library, Springfield, Illinois.

61. Jason H. Silverman, "The Excitement had Begun!: The Civil War Diary of Lemuel Jeffries, 1862–1863," *Manuscripts*, vol. 30, no. 4 (Fall 1978): 268.

62. Hughes, 183.

63. Brian H. Reid and John White, "A Mob of Stragglers and Cowards: Desertion from the Union and Confederate Armies, 1861–1865," *Journal of Strategic Studies*, vol. 8, no. 1 (March 1985): 69.

64. Alexander M. Stewart, *Camp, March, and Battlefield: Or Three Years and a Half with the Army of the Potomac* (Philadelphia: Rodgers, 1865), 280.

65. Fred A. Shannon, *The Civil War Letters of Sergeant Onley Andrus* (Urbana: University of Illinois Press, 1947), 53.

66. Clifton Fadiman and Andre Bernard, *Bartlett's Book of Anecdotes* (Boston: Little, Brown, 2000), 274.

67. Mark H. Dunkelman, *Brothers One and All: Esprit de Corps in a Civil War Regiment* (Baton Rouge: Louisiana State University, 2004), 109.

68. Wilbur Fisk, diary entries for April 23 and May 16, 1863. Wilbur Fisk Papers, Library of Congress (Manuscript Division), Washington, DC.

69. Voris Papers, letter to wife dated February 23, 1865.

70. Edward F. Keuchel and James P. Jones, "Charley Schreel's Book: Diary of a Union Soldier on Garrison Duty in Tennessee," *Tennessee Historical Quarterly*, vol. 36, no. 2 (Summer 1977): 199–200.

71. Thomas G. Bennett, letter to his sister dated January 20, 1863, Thomas G. Bennett Papers, United States Army Military History Institute, Carlisle, PA.

72. Samuel Eells, letter to friends dated June 25, 1862, Samuel H. Eells Papers, Library of Congress (Manuscript Division), Washington, DC.

73. George Wagner, letter to Samuel Rikker dated March 25, 1862, George E. Wagner Papers, Alderman Memorial Library, University of Virginia, Charlottesville, Virginia.

74. Silliker, 230.

75. Buckingham, 256.

76. Kathleen Kroll and Charles Moran, "The White Papers," *Massachusetts Review*, vol. 18, no. 2 (Summer 1976): 261–262.

77. Peter G. Boag, "Dear Friends: The Civil War Letters of Francis Marion Elliot, A Pennsylvania Country Boy," *Pittsburgh History*, vol. 72, no. 4 (December 1989): 195.

78. John L. Smith, letter to his mother dated December 15, 1862, John L. Smith Letterbook, Historical Society of Pennsylvania, Philadelphia, Pennsylvania.

79. Samuel S. Partridge letter to family dated July 24, 1861. "War Letters: Rochester Writes Home," http://www. wxxi.org/warletters/civil.html.

80. Daniel Pulis letter to wife dated September 21, 1862. "War Letters: Rochester Writes Home."

81. Alden Murch, letter to his wife dated April 12, 1863, Alden Faunce Murch Papers, Fredericksburg and Spotsylvania National Military Park, National Park Service, Fredericksburg, Virginia.

82. Marshall Miller, letter to wife dated October 30, 1864, Marshal Mortimer Miller Papers, Library of Congress (Manuscript Division), Washington, DC.

83. Mary S. Dix, "And Three Rousing Cheers for the Privates: A Diary of the 1862 Roanoke Island Expedition," *North Carolina Historical Review*, vol. 71, no. 1 (January 1994): 75.

84. James Abraham, "Incidents," 65, Abraham Papers.

85. Dunkelman, 228.

86. Charles Bowen, letter to wife dated June 1, 1863. Charles Bowen Papers, National Park Service (Gettysburg National Battlefield), Gettysburg, Pennsylvania.

87. John Follmer, diary entry for November 8, 1863, John P. Follmer Papers, Historical Society of Pennsylvania, Philadelphia, Pennsylvania.

88. Marsena Patrick, diary entry for October 8, 1863. Marsena Patrick Papers, Library of Congress (Manuscript Division), Washington, DC.

89. Smith, *Civil War Letters of Elijah Cavins*, 111.

90. Norman C. Delaney, "Letters of a Maine Soldier Boy," *Civil War History*, vol. 5 (March 1959), 58.

91. Franklin Boyts, letter to parents dated May 21, 1863, Franklin Boyts Papers, Historical Society of Pennsylvania, Philadelphia, Pennsylvania.

92. Catherine H. Vanderslice, *The Civil War Letters of George Washington Beidelman* (New York: Vantage Press, 1978), 178. Beidelman did not, in fact, die at Gettysburg. He survived the war, dying in 1893 at the age of 64.

93. Charles Haydon, diary entries for July 24, 1861, August 4, 1861, and June 20, 1863. Charles B. Haydon Papers, Bentley Historical Library, University of Michigan, Ann Arbor, Michigan.

94. Follmer Papers, diary entry for December 31, 1863.

95. Thomas L. Livermore, *Days and Events, 1860–1866* (New York: Houghton Mifflin, 1920), 182.

96. Frank Dickerson, letter to father dated February 17, 1863, Frank W. Dickerson Papers, United States Army Military History Institute, Carlisle, Pennsylvania.

97. George Robbins, "Some Recollections of a Private in the War of the Rebellion," page 5, George Robbins Papers, Connecticut Historical Society, Hartford, Connecticut.

98. Haydon Papers, May 12, 1861.

99. Julius Murray, letter to brother dated September 24, 1861. Julius A. Murray Papers, Wisconsin Historical Society, Madison, Wisconsin.

100. Silas Stevens, letter to brother dated August 31, 1903. Silas C. Stevens Papers, Chicago Historical Society, Chicago, Illinois.

101. Skeen, 41 and 182.

102. *U.S. Statutes at Large,* volume, 12, 270.

103. Fred A. Shannon, *The Organization and Administration of the Union Army, 1861–186,* vol. 1 (Gloucester, MA: Peter Smith, 1965), 169.

104. John Campbell, diary entry for December 21, 1861, John Quincy Adams Papers, Western Reserve Historical Society, Cleveland, Ohio.

105. Mahood, 31.

106. George Meade, letter to wife dated November 24, 1861, George G. Meade Papers, Library of Congress (Manuscript Division), Washington, DC.

107. Dunkelman, 219–220.

108. Josiah Hill, diary entry for April 16, 1864. Josiah Hill Papers, Troy Historical Society, Troy, Ohio.

109. Virgil Andruss, letter to mother dated May 14, 1864, Virgil Andruss Papers, Chicago Historical Society, Chicago, Illinois.

110. Campbell Papers, diary entry for June 24, 1863.

111. Aurelius Voorhis, diary entry for January 31, 1865. Aurelius L. Voorhis Papers, Indiana Historical Society, Indianapolis, Indiana.

112. Gunther Barth, *All Quiet on the Yamhill: The Civil War in Oregon, The Journal of Corporal Royal A. Bensell, Company D, Fourth California Infantry* (Eugene: University of Oregon Books, 1959), xi.

113. Silliker, 24.

114. James Abraham, letter to sister dated May 27, 1864, Abraham Papers.

115. William Ferry, letter to wife dated May 14, 1862. Ferry Family Papers, Bentley Historical Library, University of Michigan, Ann Arbor, Michigan.

116. Eugene F. Ware, *The Lyon Campaign in Missouri: Being a History of the First Iowa Infantry* (Topeka, KS: Crane, 1907), 151.

117. Shannon, *Andrus Letters*, 71.

118. Bruce Catton, *America Goes to War* (Garden City, NJ: Doubleday, 1953), 53.

119. Noe, 59.

120. Gaff, 44–45.

121. James H. Otto, 'War Memories' volume 2, page 13, James Henry Otto Papers, Wisconsin Historical Society, Madison, Wisconsin.

122. Mary E. Kellogg, *Army Life of an Illinois Soldier: Including a Day-by-Day Record of Sherman's March to the Sea* (Carbondale: Southern Illinois University Press, 1996), 37.

123. Fitzharris, 50.

124. Howard Coffin, *Nine Months to Gettysburg: Stannard's Vermonters and the Repulse of Picket's Charge* (Woodstock, Vermont: Countryman Press, 1997), 88.

125. Washington, 35.

126. ORA, series III, vol. 10, 227–228.

127. Otto Papers, vol. 3, 4.

128. Charles E. Davis, Jr., *Three Years in the Army: The Story of the Thirteenth Massachusetts Volunteers* (Boston: Estes & Lauriat, 1894), 261.

129. Shannon, *Andrus Letters*, 53.

130. Coffin, 152–153.

131. Haydon Papers, diary entry for May 25, 1861. Wilbur D. Jones. *Giants in the Cornfield: The 27th Indiana Infantry* (Shippensburg, PA: White Mane, 1997), 47.

132. Jones, 18.

133. Simpson S. Hamrick, letter to his father dated April 10, 1862, Simpson Solomon Hamrick Papers, Roy O. West Library, DePauw University, Greencastle, Indiana.

134. Winschel. 26.

135. Anita Palladino, *Diary of a Yankee Engineer: The Civil War Story of John H. Westervelt, Engineer, 1st New York Volunteer Engineer Corps* (New York: Fordham University Press, 1997), 72.

136. Samito, 5.

137. Voris Papers, letters to wife dated July 1 and July 5, 1863. Edward Braddock was killed on July 13, 1755, while commanding an expedition against the French near modern-day Pittsburgh during the French and Indian War. The militia Colonel whose advice Braddock derided was George Washington.

138. Royal Bensell, diary entry for January 18, 1863, Royal August Bensell Papers, University of Oregon Libraries, Eugene, Oregon. Samito, 5.

139. Bensell Papers, diary entry for January 18, 1864.

140. Mark C. Wilson, *Patriots in Blue: Civil War Letters of the Mark E. Rogers Family of Fairfax, Virginia* (West Lafayette, IN: self-published, 1987), 26.

141. Haydon Papers, diary entry for June 23, 1861.

142. Smith Letterbook, letter to mother dated April 24, 1863.

143. Jason H. Silverman, "The Excitement Had Begun: The Civil War Diary of Lemuel Jeffries, 1862–1863," *Manuscripts*, vol. 30, no. 4, 269.

144. Patrick Papers, diary entries for July 27, 1863 and March 8, 1865.

145. Neil B. Carmony. *The Civil War in Apacheland: Sergeant George Hand's Diary: California, Arizona, West Texas, New Mexico, 1861–1864* (Silver City, NV: High-Lonesome Books, 1996), 157.

146. Thomas P. Lowry, *Tarnished Eagles: The Courts-Martial of Fifty Union Colonels and Lieutenant Colonels* (Mechanicsburg, PA: Stackpole Books, 1997), 150–153.

147. Letter to wife dated July 29, 1861. Samuel Selden Partridge letters, *War Letters: Rochester Writes Home*.

148. Dunn Papers, letter to wife dated August 11, 1862.

149. Scott, *Abbott Diary*, 156–158.

150. Elmore Day, letter to parents dated October 25, 1862. Elmore Day Papers, Chicago Historical Society, Chicago, Illinois.

151. William B. Styple, *Writing and Fighting the Civil War: Soldiers Correspondence to the New York Sunday Mercury* (Kearny, NJ: Belle Grover, 2000), 191.

152. William B. Jordan, Jr., *Red Diamond Regiment: The 17th Maine Infantry, 1862–1865* (Shippensburg, PA: White Mane, 1996), 83.

153. Bruce Chadwick, *Brother against Brother: The Lost Civil War Diary of Lt. Edmund Halsey* (New York: Carol, 1997), 206.

154. George K. Leet, letter to William Rowley, William R. Rowley Papers, Abraham Lincoln Presidential Library, Springfield, Illinois.

155. A.S. Lewis, *My Dear Parents: The Civil War Seen by an English Union Soldier* (New York: Harcourt, Brace, Jovanovich, 1982), 106. Jordan, *Red Diamond Regiment*, 46. Allan Nevins, *A Diary of Battle: The Personal Journals of Colonel Charles S. Wainwright, 1861–1865* (New York: Harcourt, Brace & World, 1963), 109.

156. John Holahan, diary entry for January 2, 1863, John Frederick Holahan Papers, Fredericksburg and Spotsylvania National Military Park, National Park Service, Fredericksburg, Virginia.

157. William Moore, letter to wife dated November 17, 1864, William Reed Moore Papers, Historical Society of Pennsylvania, Philadelphia, Pennsylvania.

158. Edward Longacre, "Chaos Still Reigns in this Camp: Letters of Lieutenant George N. Bliss, 1st New England Cavalry, March–September 1862," *Rhode Island History*, vol. 36, no. 1, 18 and 21.

159. Terrence J. Winschel, *The Civil War Diary of a Common Soldier: William Wiley of the 77th Illinois Infantry* (Baton Rouge: Louisiana State University Press, 2001), 65. William H. Bentley, *History of the 77th Illinois Infantry, September 2, 1862–July 10, 1865* (Peoria, IL: Hine, 1883), 161.

160. Follmer Papers, diary entry for February 19, 1864.

161. William Martin, letter to wife dated June 7, 1863, William H. Martin Papers, U.S. Military History Institute, Carlisle, Pennsylvania. Henry C. Lind, *The Long Road for Home: The Civil War Experiences of Four Farmboy Soldiers of the Twenty-seventh Massachusetts Regiment* (Rutherford, NJ: Fairleigh Dickinson University Press, 1992), 84.

162. "Letters from the Californians in the Army of the Potomac," *Daily Alta Californian*, March 22, 1864.

163. David McCordick, *The Harmony Boys are All Well: The Civil War Letters (1862–1865) of Private Henry Kauffman* (Queenstown, Ontario: Edwin Mellen Press, 1991), 67.

164. John C. Williams, *Life in Camp: A History of the Nine Months' Service of the Fourteenth Vermont Regiment* (Claremont, VT: Claremont Manufacturing, 1864), 66.

165. Jack K. Overmyer, *A Stupendous Effort: The 87th Indiana in the War of the Rebellion* (Bloomington: Indiana University Press, 1997), 53. Herdegen, 304.

166. Edward Wightman, letter to brother dated January 3, 1863, Edward King Wightman Papers, Manuscript, Archives, and Rare Book Library, Emory University, Atlanta, Georgia.

167. Aaron C. Kepler, diary entry for March 1, 1862. Aaron Kepler Papers, Richmond National Battlefield Park, National Park Service, Richmond, Virginia.

168. Voris Papers, letter to wife dated November 17, 1862. Emory Sweetland, letter to wife dates April 9, 1863. Michael Winey Collection, United State Military History Institute, Carlisle, Pennsylvania.

169. Smith, 131. Temple,154.

170. Welsh Papers, letter to wife dated November 25, 1863.

171. Bensell Papers, diary entry for March 20, 1862.

172. Michael Schellhammer, *The 83rd Pennsylvania Volunteers in the Civil War* (Jefferson, NC: McFarland, 2003), 152.

173. Wightman Papers, letter to brother dated September 12, 1862.

174. Joseph Heffelfinger, diary entry for May 10, 1864, Joseph Heffelfinger Papers, United States Army Military History Institute, Carlisle, Pennsylvania.

175. William H. Abel, letter to William Ballard dated August 26, 1863, Charles A. Heckman Papers, Historical Society of Pennsylvania, Philadelphia, Pennsylvania.

176. Delaney, 51.

177. Wightman Papers, letter to brother dated September 12, 1862.

178. Donald C. Elder. *A Damned Iowa Greyhound: The Civil War Letters of William Henry Harrison Clayton* (Iowa City: University of Iowa Press, 1998), 31–32.

179. Marilyn T. Williams, *Washing "the Great Unwashed": Public Baths in Urban America, 1840–1920* (Columbus: Ohio State University Press, 1991), 10–14.

180. Cadman Papers, letter to wife dated April 24, 1864.

181. Mary E. Kellogg, *Army Life of an Illinois Soldier* (Toronto: Globe, 1906), 21.

182. Lorien Foote, "Rich Man's War, Rich Man's Fight: Class, Ideology, and Discipline in the Union Army," *Civil War History*, vol. 51, no. 3 (September 2005), 275.

183. Croushore, 29.

184. James Newton, letter to parents dated June 18, 1862, Newton Family Papers, Wisconsin Historical Society, Madison, Wisconsin.

185. Michael Bacarella, *Lincoln's Foreign Legion: The 39th New York Infantry, The Garibaldi Guard* (Shippensburg, PA: White Mane, 1996), 153.

186. Halsey, 80. This was not mere pettiness on the officer's part. Black powder left a considerable amount of residue behind, creating the hazard of a misfire in combat if a soldier did not keep his weapon scrupulously clean.

187. John Holahan, diary entry for February 28, 1863, Holahan Papers.

188. Mike Pride and Mark Travis, *My Brave Boys: To War with Colonel Cross and the Fighting Fifth* (Hanover, NH: University Press of New England, 2001), 201.

189. Sears, 267. Fatigue duties were assignments necessary for the maintenance of camp life, such as digging latrines, collecting trash, or gathering firewood. In later wars, fatigue duty was replaced by "KP" or kitchen police duty.

190. George Hugunin, memoirs entry for March 13, 1864, George Hugunin Papers, Fredericksburg and Spotsylvania National Military Park, National Park Service, Fredericksburg, Virginia.

191. Dunkelman, 79.

192. Warren Wilkinson, *Mother, May You Never See the Sighs I Have Seen: The Fifty-Seventh Massachusetts Veteran Volunteers in the Army of the Potomac, 1864–1865* (New York: Harper & Row, 1990), 10.

193. Haydon Papers, diary entry for May 22, 1861.

194. Cadman Papers, letter to wife dated February 3, 1863.

195. Thomas Bennett, letter to sister dated April 27, 1863, Thomas G. Bennett Papers, United States Army Military History Institute, Carlisle, Pennsylvania.

196. Noe, 16.

197. Gaff, 126. Jordan, *Red Diamond Regiment*, 16.

198. William C. Harris, *In the Country of the Enemy: The Civil War Reports of a Massachusetts Corporal* (Gainesville: University Press of Florida, 1999), 53. Eric J. Wittenberg, *One of Custer's Wolverines: The Civil War Letters of Brevet Brigadier General James H. Kidd, 6th Michigan Cavalry* (Kent, OH: Kent State University Press, 2000), 120.

199. Ann Gebhard, "Doubly Paid for any Sacrifice," *Michigan History*, vol. 74, no. 2 (March/April 1990): 12–13.

200. Wayne C. Temple, "The Civil War Letters of Henry C. Bear: A Soldier in the 116th Illinois Volunteer Infantry," *Lincoln Herald*, vol. 62 (Winter 1960): 146.

201. Henry F. Charles, "Civil War Record, 1862–1865," www.dm.net/~neitz/charles/obit.html.

202. Donald F. Carmony, "Jacob W. Bartmess Civil War Letters," *Indiana Magazine of History*, vol. 52, no. 1 (March 1956): 53.

203. John Ferguson, diary entry for January 2, 1864, John H. Ferguson Papers, Library of Congress (Manuscript Division), Washington, DC.

204. Fisk Papers, diary entry for April 18, 1863.

205. Smith Letterbook, letter to mother dated December 26, 1862.

206. William C. Niesen, "The Consequence of Grandeur: A Union Soldier Writes of the Atlanta Campaign," *Atlanta History*, vol. 33 (Fall 1989): 9 and 16.

207. Fisk Papers, diary entries for April 22 and April 23, 1863.

208. Fisk Papers, letter to wife dated September 24, 1863.

209. Ann Hartwell Britton and Thomas J. Reed, *To My Beloved Wife and Boy at Home: The Letters and Diaries of Orderly Sergeant John F.L. Hartwell* (Rutherford, NJ: Fairleigh Dickinson University Press, 1997), 174.

210. William Morse, diary entry for December 25, 1862, William H. Morse Papers, Androscoggin Historical Society, Auburn, Massachusetts.

211. Niesen, 6.

212. Holahan Papers, diary entry for October 16, 183.

213. Smith Letterbook, letter dated March 25, 1863.

214. William Jones, letter to brother dated October 21, 1861, William T. Jones Papers, Historical Society of Pennsylvania, Philadelphia, Pennsylvania.

215. Thomas E. Pope, *The Weary Boys: Colonel J. Warren Keifer and the 110th Ohio Volunteer Infantry* (Kent, OH: Kent State University Press, 2002), 19. Ed Malles, *Bridge Building in Wartime: Colonel Wesley Brainerd's Memoir of the 50th New York Volunteer Engineers* (Knoxville: University of Tennessee Press, 1997), 242.

216. Silliker, 54.

217. William Papers, diary entry for January 4, 1863.

218. Brobst Papers, letters to wife dated December 17 and December 18, 1864. McCordick, 55 and 73. Silliker, 205.

219. Smith Papers, letter to mother dated March 18, 1865.

220. Charles Heckman, letter to J.J. DeForest dated June 8, 1863, Correspondence Book, Charles Heckman Papers, Historical Society of Pennsylvania, Philadelphia, Pennsylvania.

221. David Coe, *Mine Eyes Have Seen the Glory: Combat Diaries of Union Sergeant Hamlin Alexander Coe* (Madison, NJ: Farleigh Dickinson University Press, 1975), 75.

222. Dunn Papers, letter to wife dated September 11, 1863.

223. Forbes Papers, correspondence between Forbes and Captain John Maxwell and Colonel Edward Prince dated April 2, 3, 4, and 7, 1864.

224. Bensell Papers, diary entry for January 2, 1863.

225. Pride and Travis, 74–75.

226. Mahood, 232, 268, and 271.

3—"Fields of Satan"

1. Mark E. Lender and James K. Martin, *Drinking in America: A History* (New York: Free Press, 1987), 59–61.

2. G. J. Barker-Benfield, *The Horrors of the Half-Known Life: Male Attitudes toward Women and Sexuality in Nineteenth-Century America* (New York: Harper & Row, 1976), 277.

3. Kimmel, 48–50.

4. See Donald T. Courtwright, *Violent Land: Single Men and Social Disorder from the Frontier to the Inner City* (Cambridge, MA: Harvard University Press, 1996).

5. Haydon Papers, diary entry for December 25, 1861.

6. Follmer Papers, diary entry for July 7, 1863.

7. Mildred Throne, *The Civil War Diary of Charles F. Boyd, Fifteenth Iowa Infantry, 1861–1863* (Baton Rouge: Louisiana State University Press, 1998), 42.

8. James I. Robertson, Jr., *Soldiers Blue and Gray* (Columbia: University of South Carolina Press, 1988), 116.

9. Shannon, *Organization of the Union Army*, 175.

10. Emory Sweetland, letter to wife dated January 20, 1865. Michael Winey Collection, United States Army Military History Institute, Carlisle, Pennsylvania.

11. Barry Popchock, *Soldier Boy: The Civil War Letters of Charles O. Musser, 29th Iowa* (Iowa City: University of Iowa Press, 1995), 149 and 158.

12. Lyman D. Ames, diary entry for March 3, 182. Lyman D. Ames Papers, Ohio Historical Society, Columbus, Ohio.

13. W. Springer Menge and J. August Shimrak, *The Civil War Notebook of Daniel Chisholm: A Chronicle of Daily Life in the Union Army, 1864–1865* (New York: Orion Books, 1989), 5.

14. Hallock F. Raup, *Letters from a Pennsylvania Chaplain at the Siege of Petersburg, 1865* (Kent, OH: Kent State University Press, 1961), 12.

15. Campbell Papers, diary entry for November 12, 1863.

16. Welsh Papers, letter to wife dated February 22, 1863.

17. Terrence J. Winschel, *The Civil War Diary of a Common Soldier: William Wiley of the 77th Illinois Infantry* (Baton Rouge: Louisiana State University Press, 2001), 9.

18. Webster W. Moses, letters to Nancy Mowry dated March 19 and April 24, 1864. Webster W. Moses Papers, Kansas State Historical Society, Topeka, Kansas.

19. Barth, 9.

20. Buckingham, 184.

21. Dunkelman, 176.

22. Richard E. Matthews, *The 149th Pennsylvania Volunteer Infantry Unit in the Civil War* (Jefferson, NC: McFarland, 1994), 33.

23. Richard E. Beaudry. *War Journal of Louis N. Beaudry, Fifth New York Cavalry: The Diary of a Union Chaplain, Commencing February 16, 1863* (Jefferson, NC: McFarland, 1996), 14.

24. Dunkelman, 177.

25. Philip J. Reyburn and Terry L. Wilson, *Jottings from Dixie: The Civil War Dispatches of Sergeant Major Stephen F. Fleharty, U.S.A.* (Baton Rouge: Louisiana State University Press, 1999), 15.

26. Follmer Papers, diary entry for April 24, 1864.

27. David T. Hedrick and Gordon B. Davis, Jr., *I'm Surrounded by Methodists . . .: Diary of John H.W. Stuckenberg, Chaplain of the 145th Pennsylvania Volunteer Infantry* (Gettysburg, PA: Thomas Publications, 1995), 69 and 103.

28. Silas Wesson, diary entries for September 27 and November 27, 1862, Silas D. Wesson Papers, Civil War Times Illustrated Collection, United States Army Military History Institute, Carlisle, Pennsylvania.

29. Follmer Papers, diary entry for April 24, 1864.

30. Jerry Voorhis, Sr., *The Life and times of Aurelius Lyman Voorhis* (New York: Vantage Press, 1976), 238.

31. Delaney, 54.

32. Hedrick and Davis, 103.

33. Joseph Johnston, diary entry for November 4, 1861, Joseph Sturge Johnston Papers, Chicago Historical Society, Chicago, Illinois.

34. Eliot Norton, "Tales at First Hand," *Blackwood's*, vol. 233 (January 1933), 37–39.

35. Raup, 8 and 37.

36. David Myers, letter to brother dated March 8, 1863, David Myers Papers, Chicago Historical Society, Chicago, Illinois. Henry Thompson, letter to wife dated July 5, 1861, Henry J.H. Thompson Papers, Perkins Library (Manuscript Collections), Duke University, Durham, North Carolina.

37. Croushore, 43.

38. Wightman Papers, letter to brother dated September 15, 1862.

39. William Moore, letter to wife dated November 17, 1864, William Reed Moore Papers, Historical Society of Pennsylvania, Philadelphia, Pennsylvania.

40. Joseph Blackburn, letter to wife dated January 31, 1862, Joseph Blackburn Papers, United States Army Military History Institute, Carlisle, Pennsylvania.

41. Edwin Emery, letter to sister dated January 5, 1864, Perkins Library (Manuscript Collections), Duke University,, Durham, North Carolina.

42. Smith, *Civil War Letters of Elijah Cavins*, 101.

43. Malles, 39–40.

44. Pride and Travis, 203.

45. Thomas Orwig, letter to friend dated March 14, 1863, Thomas G. Orwig Papers, Civil War Times Illustrated Collection, United States Army Military History Institute, Carlisle, Pennsylvania.

46. Lafayette Church, letter to daughter dated January 29, 1864, Lafayette Church Papers, Clarke Historical Library, Central Michigan University, Mount Pleasant, Michigan.

47. Hedrick and Davis, 30.

48. Steven Vincent Benet, *A Treatise on Military Law and the Practice of Courts-Martial* (New York: D. Van Nostrand, 1862), 336.

49. Joseph Gibbs, *Three Years in the "Bloody Eleventh": The Campaigns of a Pennsylvania Reserves Regiment* (University Park: Pennsylvania State University Press, 2002), 44–45.

50. Malles, 40.

51. Jennifer C. Bohrnstedt, *Soldiering With Sherman: Civil War Letters of George F. Cram* (DeKalb: Northern Illinois University Press, 2000), 24.

52. Raup, 44–45.

53. Thomas E. Parson, *Bear Flag and Bay State in the Civil War: The Californians of the Second Massachusetts Cavalry* (Jefferson, NC: McFarland, 2001), 87–88.

54. George Squier to wife, letter dated December 15, 1862. George W. Squier Papers, Lincoln Museum, Fort Wayne, Indiana.

55. Ann Hartwell Britton and Thomas J. Reed, *To My Beloved Wife and Boy at Home: The Letters and Diaries of Orderly Sergeant John F.L. Hartwell* (Madison, NJ: Fairleigh Dickinson University Press, 1997), 336–337.

56. Beaudry, 25.

57. Hedrick and Davis, 106.

58. Virgil Andruss, letter to mother dated July 21, 1864, Virgil Andruss Papers, Chicago Historical Society, Chicago, Illinois.

59. John Smith, letter to mother dated November 13, 1863, John L. Smith Letterbook, Historical Society of Pennsylvania, Philadelphia, Pennsylvania.

60. Karla J. Husby and Eric J. Wittenberg, *Under Custer's Command: The Civil War Journal of James Henry Avery* (Washington, DC: Brassey's, 2000), 125.

61. Morton H. Bassett, *From Bull Ran to Bristow Station* (St. Paul, MN: North Central, 1962), 8.

62. Steven E. Woodworth, *While God is Marching On: The Religious World of Civil War Soldiers* (Lawrence: University Press of Kansas, 2001), 185.

63. Throne, *Charles F. Boyd Diary*, 24–25.

64. Croushore, 80.

65. Pride and Travis, 203.

66. Bacarella, 141 and 187.

67. George Hand, diary entry for September 17, 1862, George O. Hand Papers, Library of Congress (Manuscript Division), Washington, DC.

68. Patrick Papers, entry for October 8, 1863.

69. Thomas Bell, diary entry for March 11, 1864, Thomas Bell Papers, Civil War Miscellaneous Collection, United States Army Military History Institute, Carlisle, Pennsylvania.

70. Robert F. Crawford, "The Civil War Letters of S. Rodman and Linton Smith," *Delaware History*, vol. 21 (Fall 1984): 96. [Emphasis in original].

71. Hedrick and Davis, 106.

72. James Abraham, letter to brother dated August 7, 1862, Civil War Letters of James, Isaac, and William Abraham and James Sturgis, Historical Society of Pennsylvania, Philadelphia, Pennsylvania.

73. W. S. Nye, *The Valiant Hours: Narrative of "Captain Brevet," an Irish-American in the Army of the Potomac* (Harrisburg, PA: Stackpole, 1961), 93.

74. Haydon Papers, diary entry for July 30, 1861.

75. Barth, 57; Buckingham, 143.

76. Harris, 7.

77. Orlando Poe, letter to sister dated April 3, 1865. Orlando M. Poe Papers, Library of Congress, Manuscript Division, Washington, DC.

78. Raup, 13.

79. Johnston Papers, diary entry for April 7, 1863.

80. C.V. Tevis, *History of the Fighting Fourteenth* (Brooklyn: Brooklyn Eagle Press, 1911), 194.

81. Buckingham, 154.

82. Johnston Papers, diary entry for October 14, 1861.

83. Charles Mattocks, diary entry for April 18, 1863, Charles P. Mattocks Collection, Maine Historical Society, Portland, Maine.

84. William Benedict, letter to wife dated November 27, 1863, Benedict Family Papers, Bailey/Howe Library, University of Vermont, Burlington, Vermont.

85. Lilley Papers, letter to sister dated January 17, 1862.

86. Wilbur Fisk, letter to family dated March 23, 1864, Wilbur Fisk Papers, Library of Congress, Manuscript Division, Washington, DC. Emil Rosenblatt, *Anti-Rebel: The Civil War Letters of Wilbur Fisk* (New York: Croton-on-Hudson, 1983), 204–205.

87. Mildred Throne, "Reminiscences of Jacob C. Switzer of the 22nd Iowa (Part I)," *Iowa Journal of History*, vol. 55, no. 3 (October 1957): 324.

88. Alan Siegel, "Battle in the Snow: Union Troops Take Sides, "*Civil War Times Illustrated*, vol. 23 (December 1984), 22–23 and 50.

89. Haywood Emmill, diary entry for April 22, 1863. Haywood Emmill Papers, Fredericksburg and Spotsylvania National Military Park, National Park Service, Fredericksburg, Virginia.

90. James Decker, letter to sister dated April 27, 1863. James Decker Papers, Fredericksburg and Spotsylvania National Military Park, National Park Service, Fredericksburg, Virginia.

91. Barth, 78 and 87.

92. Gaff, 293.

93. Smith Letterbook, letter to mother dated March 18, 1865.

94. Jeffrey L. Patrick, *Three Years with Wallace's Zouaves: The Civil War Memoirs of Thomas Wise Durham* (Macon, GA: Mercer University Press, 2003), 158–159.

95. Malles, 133. This is probably the accident also reported by Colonel Patrick Guiney. Guiney listed the deceased man as Quartermaster Thomas Mooney and the injured man as an unnamed surgeon from the Thirty-second Massachusetts. Christian G. Samito, *Commanding Boston's Irish Ninth: The Civil War Letters of Colonel Patrick R. Guiney, Ninth Massachusetts Volunteer Infantry* (New York: Fordham University Press, 1998), 170.

96. James C. Mohr and Richard E. Winslow, *The Cormany Diaries: A Northern Family in the Civil War* (Pittsburgh: University of Pittsburgh Press, 1982), 302.

97. Henry Fitzgerald Charles, "Civil War Record," www.dm.net/~neitz/charles/hfcharles.pdf.

98. David H. Donald, *Gone for a Soldier: The Civil War Memoirs of Private Alfred Bellard* (Boston: Little, Brown, 1975), 33.

99. Barth, 113.

100. Donald E. Carmony, "Jacob W. Bartmess Civil War Letters," *Indiana Magazine of History*, vol. 52, no. 1 (March 1956): 62.

101. Lewis Luckenbill, diary entry for April 12, 1863, Lewis Luckenbill Papers, Fredericksburg and Spotsylvania National Military Park, National Park Service, Fredericksburg, Virginia.

102. Mahood, 270.

103. Edwin Weist, diary entry for November 26, 1863, Edwin B. Weist Papers, Fredericksburg National Battlefield, National Park Service, Fredericksburg, Virginia.

104. Parson, 31–32 and 90–92.

105. Kellogg and Simon, 27, 193, and 218.

106. Haydon Papers, diary entry for January 25, 1862.

107. Follmer Papers, diary entry for August 1, 1863.

108. Kathleen Kroll and Charles Moran, "The White Papers," *Massachusetts Review*, vol. 18 (Summer 1976), 258.

109. Kellogg and Simon, 213.

110. James Ames, letter to mother dated May 7, 1863, James A. Ames Papers, Civil War Miscellaneous Collection, United States Army Military History Institute, Carlisle, Pennsylvania.

111. Jedediah Mannis and Galen R. Wilson, *Bound to be a Soldier: The Letters of Private James T. Miller, 111th Pennsylvania Infantry, 1861–1864* (Knoxville: University of Tennessee Press, 2001), 112–113.

112. David Nichol, letter to sister dated June 20, 1863, David Nichol Papers, Civil War Miscellaneous Collection, United States Army Military History Institute, Carlisle, Pennsylvania.

113. Parson, 57.

114. Husby and Wittenberg, 10.

115. Samito, 169–170.

116. Roderick M. Engert, *Maine to the Wilderness: The Civil War Letters of Pvt. William Lamson, 20th Maine Infantry* (Orange, VA: Publisher's Press, 1993), 13.

117. Stephen W. Sears, *On Campaign with the Army of the Potomac: The Civil War Journal of Theodore Ayrault Dodge* (New York: Cooper Square, 2001), 101. Alvin Voris, letter to wife dated October 13, 1863. Alvin Voris Papers, Virginia Historical Society, Richmond, Virginia.

118. Hedrick and Davis, 14.

119. Henry Heisler, letter to sister dated March 6, 1863, Henry C. Heisler Papers, Library of Congress (Manuscript Division), Washington, DC.

120. Silliker, 29 and 166.

121. Anita Palladino, *Diary of a Yankee Engineer: The Civil War Story of John H. Westervelt, Engineer, 1st New York Volunteer Engineer Corps* (New York: Fordham University Press, 1997), 204–205.

122. William L. Burto, *Melting Pot Soldiers: The Union's Ethnic Regiments* (Ames: Iowa State University Press, 1988), 187.

123. William Dunn, letter to sister dated April 2, 1863. William E. Dunn Papers, United States Army Military History Institute, Carlisle, Pennsylvania [Emphasis in original].

124. During the Civil War, the Union made several attempts to bolster enlistments. One way was to offer enlistment lengths shorter than the standard three year term of service. Some units, like the Pennsylvanians, served a nine-month term, but other troops served only ninety days.

125. Gaff, 282.

126. Raymond G. Barber and Gary E. Swinson, *The Civil War Letters of Charles Barber, Private, 104th New York Volunteer Infantry* (Torrance, CA: Swinson, 1991), 139.

127. Norwich [CT] *Morning Bulletin*, January 12, 1865.

128. Brobst Papers, letter to friend dated February 7, 1864.

129. Fisk Papers, diary entry for April 26, 1863.

130. Richard F. Miller, *Harvard's Civil War: A History of the Twentieth Massachusetts Volunteer Infantry* (Hanover, NH: University Press of New England, 2005), 286.

131. Wightman Papers, January 3, 1863.

132. John White, diary entry for January 8, 1865, John Chester White Papers, Library of Congress (Manuscript Division), Washington, DC.

133. Barth, 122. Ironically, Veteran Regiments also received a $402 bounty from the federal government. Thus, veteran soldiers became 'bounty men' themselves, the very thing they claimed to despise.

134. George Merryweather, letter to parents dated January 27, 1864, George Merryweather Papers, Chicago Historical Society, Chicago, Illinois.

135. Cadman Papers, letter to wife dated April 9, 1864.

136. Robert U. Johnson and Clarence C. Buel, *Battles and Leaders of the Civil War* (volume 4) (New York: Century, 1888), 671.

137. John Gibbon, *Personal Recollections of the Civil War* (New York: G.B. Putnam's, 1928), 12–14.

138. John Brobst, letter to friend dated February 7, 1864. John F. Brobst Papers, Wisconsin Historical Society, Madison, Wisconsin.

139. Abraham Papers, William Abraham to brother dated June 7, 1864.

140. Mushkat, 142 and 247.

141. Halsey, 89.

142. Joseph T. Glatthaar, *The March to the Sea and Beyond: Sherman's Troops in the Savannah and Carolinas Campaigns* (Baton Rouge: Louisiana State University Press, 1985), 31 and 33.

143. Halsey, 84.

144. Simpson Hamrick, letter to brother dated March 14, 1863. Simpson S. Hamrick Papers, Roy O. West Library, DePauw University, Greencastle, Indiana.

145. Patrick, 155–156.

146. Mildred Throne, "Reminiscences of Jacob B. Switzer of the 22nd Iowa" (Part 2), *Iowa Journal of History*, vol. 56, no. 1 (January 1958): 52.

147. Menge and Shimrak, 91.

148. Silliker, 278.

149. Throne, "Jacob Switzer Reminiscences," 321.

150. Robert Baird, letter to wife dated April 7, 1864, Baird Family Papers, Ohio Historical Society, Columbus, Ohio.

151. Gerald J. Prokopowicz, *All for the Regiment: The Army of the Ohio, 1861–1862* (Chapel Hill, NC: University of North Carolina Press, 2001), 50.

152. William Fogg, letter to sister dated December 18, 1862, William Fogg Papers, United States Army Military History Institute, Carlisle, Pennsylvania.

153. Edward A. Miller, *The Black Civil War Soldiers of Illinois: The Story of the Twenty-ninth U.S. Colored Infantry* (Columbia: University of South Carolina Press, 1998), 43.

154. Campbell Papers, diary entry for November 7, 1863.

155. Bacarella, 126.

156. Popchock, 215.

157. Matthews, 48.

158. William Wilson, letter to Governor John Andrew dated June 27, 1861, John A. Andrew Papers, Massachusetts Historical Society, Boston, Massachusetts.

159. Sears, 67.

160. Alan S. Brown, *A Soldier's Life: The Civil War Experiences of Ben C. Johnson* (Kalamazoo, MI: Western Michigan University Press, 1962), 41.

161. Thomas P. Lowry, *Tarnished Eagles: The Courts-Martial of Fifty Union Colonels and Lieutenant Colonels* (Mechanicsburg, PA: Stackpole Books, 1997), 208–209.

162. Gibbs, 47.

163. New York *Sunday Mercury*, May 7, 1865.

164. Samuel Rikker, letter to wife dated December 9, 1861, George E. Wagner Papers, Special Collections, University of Virginia, Charlottesville, Virginia.

165. Wightman Papers, letter to brother dated September 19, 1862.

166. Gibbs, 46.

167. Campbell Papers, diary entry for February 22, 1862.

168. James Newton, letter to parents dated August 19, 1862, Newton Family Papers, Wisconsin Historical Society, Madison, Wisconsin.

169. Buckingham, 150.

170. Parson, 88.

171. Robert A. Taylor, *A Pennsylvanian in Blue: The Civil War Diary of Thomas Beck Walton* (Shippensburg, PA: Burd Street Press, 1995), 11.

172. Elisha Peterson, letter to parents dated June 1, 1863, Elisha A. Peterson Papers, Perkins Library, Duke University, Durham, North Carolina.

173. David Mace, letter to parents dated September 12, 1862, John Bricker Papers, Civil War Miscellaneous Collection, United States Army Military History Institute, Carlisle, Pennsylvania.

174. Wallace F. Workmaster, "The Frank H. Shiras Letters, 1862–1865," *Western Pennsylvania Historical Magazine*, vol. 40 (Fall 1957): 181.

175. Harlan Bailey, letter to sister dated February 26, 1864, Harlan P. Bailey Papers, Fredericksburg National Battlefield, National Park Service, Fredericksburg, Virginia.

176. Ferguson Papers, diary entry for February 26, 1864.

177. Skidmore, 56.

178. Engert, 22–23 and 87.

179. Wayne C. Temple, "The Civil War Letters of Henry C. Bear: A Soldier in the 116th Illinois Volunteer Infantry," *Lincoln Herald*, vol. 62 (Fall 1960): 127.

180. Jones, 85.

181. Haydon Papers, diary entry for September 18, 1861.

182. Skidmore, 40.

183. Campbell Papers, diary entry for September 20, 1861.

184. ORA, series I, vol. 48, 73.

185. Heisler Papers, letter to sister dated March 24, 1862.

186. James M. Volo and Dorothy D. Volo, *The Antebellum Period* (New York: Greenwood, 2004), 17–18. Marilynn W. Hill, *Their Sisters' Keepers: Prostitution in New York City, 1830–1870* (Berkeley: University of California Press, 1993), 29. William B. Sanger, *The History of Prostitution: Its Extent, Causes, and Effects Throughout the Ages* (New York: Harper & Bros., 1876), 450–627.

187. Theodore J. Karamanski, *Rally 'round the Flag: Chicago and the Civil War* (New York: Rowman & Littlefield, 2006), 229. In 1860, Chicago had a population of 109,260 people and 298,977 in 1870. The average of the two populations is 204,119. The percentage of prostitutes in the general population is based upon the city average for the Civil War era.

188. Barbra Meil Hobson, *Uneasy Virtue: The Politics of Prostitution and the American Reform Tradition* (Chicago: University of Chicago Press, 1990), 11–12.

189. Michael Meranze, *Laboratories of Virtue: Punishment, Revolution, and Authority in Philadelphia, 1769–1835* (Chapel Hill: University of North Carolina Press, 1996), 278. Anne M. Boylan, *The Origins of Women's Activism: New York and Boston, 1797–1840* (Chapel Hill: University of North Carolina Press, 2002), 49. John D'Emilio and Estelle B. Freedman, *Intimate Matters: A History of Sexuality in America* (Chicago: University of Chicago Press, 1998), 143–144.

190. Edward M. Coffman, *The Old Army: A Portrait of the American Army in Peacetime, 1784–1898* (New York: Oxford, 1986), 107–108.

191. Larry H. Whiteaker and W. Calvin Dickinson, *Civil War Letters of the Tenure Family, Rockland County, N.Y., 1862–1865* (New York: Historical Society of Rockland County, 1990), 57–58.

192. Woodworth, 186.

193. James Boyd, Jr., "A Tale of Two Cities: The Hidden Battle against Venereal Disease in Civil War Nashville and Memphis," *Civil War History*, vol. 31, no. 3 (September 1985): 270–276.

194. Carmony, *Civil War in Apacheland*, 116.

195. Mohr and Winslow, 360.

196. New York *Sunday Mercury*, March 23, 1863.

197. Silliker, 32.

198. Haydon Papers, diary entry for August 22, 1861.

199. Britton and Reed, 203–204 [Emphasis in original].

200. Patrick Papers, diary entry for July 10, 1864.

201. Voorhis, Sr, 238–239.

202. John Vautier, diary entry for April 2, 1863, John D. Vautier Papers, United States Army Military History Institute, Carlisle, Pennsylvania.

203. William E. Hughes, *The Civil War Papers of Lt. Colonel Newton T. Colby, New York Infantry* (Jefferson, NC: McFarland, 2003), 253.

204. National Archives and Records Administration (hereafter as NARA): Record Group 153: Records of the Judge Advocate General (hereafter as RG153), File number NN2933.

205. Richard Harwell, *Colorado Volunteers in New Mexico, 1862* (Chicago: Lakeside Press, 1962), 209–210.

206. John Holahan, diary entry for June 14, 1861, John F. Holahan Papers, Fredericksburg National Battlefield, National Park Service, Fredericksburg, Virginia.

207. Ferguson Papers, diary entry for February 20, 1864.

208. Jordan, *Red Diamond Regiment*, 111. Dunn Papers, letter to wife dated April 21, 1863.

209. Donald, 256.

210. Longacre, "Bliss Letters," 18.

211. Marshall Miller, undated letter to wife (sometime in October 1863), Marshall M. Miller Papers, Library of Congress (Manuscript Division), Washington, DC.

212. Smith, 187.

213. Gregory J.W. Urwin, "The Lord has not Forsake Me and I Won't Forsake Him: Religion in Frederick Steele's Union Army, 1863–1864," *Arkansas Historical Quarterly*, vol. 52, no. 3 (1993): 325.

214. Throne, *Boyd Diary*, 57.

215. Jordan, *Red Diamond Regiment*, 194.

216. W. Mark McKnight. *Blue Bonnets O'er the Border: The 79th New York Cameron Highlanders* (Shippensburg, PA: White Mane Books, 1998), 92.

217. Smith, 182.

218. George Bates, letter to father dated April 27, 1863, George Henry Bates Papers, Schoff Collection, Clements Library, University of Michigan, Ann Arbor, Michigan.

219. Jenny O'Leary and Harvey H. Jackson, "The Civil War Letters of Captain Daniel O'Leary, U.S.A.," *Register of the Kentucky Historical Society*, vol. 77 (Summer 1979), 170.

220. Haydon Papers, diary entry for January 8, 1862.

221. John F. Marszalek. *Sherman's Other War: The General and the Civil War Press* (Kent, OH: Kent State University Press, 1999), 117–118.

222. Lowry, *Tarnished Eagles*, 111–115 and 199–203.

223. Smith, 41.

224. Jordan, *Red Diamond Regiment*, 46.

225. Knox Mellon, Jr., "Letters of James Greenalch," *Michigan History*, vol. 44, no. 2 (June 1960): 230.

226. O'Leary and Jackson, 168.

227. George Avery, letter to wife dated June 22, 1863, George S. Avery Papers, Chicago Historical Society, Chicago, Illinois.

228. Mohr and Winslow, 246.

229. Husby and Wittenberg, 11–12.

230. Herdegen, 39–40.

231. Selden Connor, letters to father dated January 9, 1863 and April 27, 1864, Selden Connor Papers, Brown University Library, Providence, Rhode Island.

232. Rufus Kinsley, diary entry for May 14, 1864, Rufus Kinsley Papers, Vermont Historical Society Library, Barre, Vermont. Edwin C. Bearss, *Historic Resource Study Ship Island Harrison County, Mississippi Gulf Islands National Seashore Florida/ Mississippi* (Denver: National Park Service, 1984), 220–230.

233. United States Surgeon General's Office. *The Medical and Surgical History of the War of the Rebellion*, vol. 1 (Washington, DC: Government Printing Office, 1888), 891.

234. Coffman, 191.

235. ORA, series I, vol. 46, 1097.

236. Gerald M. Capers, "Confederates and Yankees in Occupied New Orleans, 1862–1865," *Journal of Southern History*, vol. 30, no. 4 (November 1964): 415.

237. Darla Brock, "Memphis's *Nymphs Du Pave*: The Most Abandoned Women in the World," *West Tennessee Historical Society Quarterly*, vol. 50, no. 1 (1996): 58. David Kaser, "Nashville's Women of Pleasure in 1860," *Tennessee Historical Quarterly*, vol. 23, no. 4 (1964): 379–382.

238. Lee Kennett. *Sherman: A Soldier's Life* (New York: Perennial, 2001), 173–174. Marszalek, 121–122.

239. Cadman, Papers, letter to wife dated May 18, 1863.

240. Memphis *Bulletin*, August 8, 1862.

241. *Medical and Surgical History of the War of the Rebellion*, vol. 1, 895.

242. Brock, 63–66.

243. Nashville *Daily Press*, July 14, 1863.

244. James B. Jones, Jr., "A Tale of Two Cities," *North and South*, vol. 10, no. 5 (2008): 66.

245. Thomas P. Lowry, "The Army's Licensed Prostitutes," *Civil War Times Illustrated*, vol. 41, no. 4 (August 2002): 31–35.

246. Thomas P. Lowry, *The Story the Soldiers Wouldn't Tell: Sex in the Civil War* (Mechanicsville, PA: Stackpole Books, 1994), 55–59. Paul R. Abramson and Steven D. Pinkerton, *With Pleasure: Thoughts on the Nature of Human Sexuality* (New York: Oxford, 2002), 180.

247. Patrick Papers, diary entries for June 8 and 10, 1863.

248. Beaudry, 75–76.

249. Popchock, 159.

250. Lowry, *Tarnished Eagles*, 202. The accusations against the orderly, William McFarland, surfaced in the court-martial of Colonel Ebenezer Peirce. The witness testifying against Peirce is possibly talking about the same book. He may have mistaken *Frances Hall* for *Fanny Hill*, a novel written by British author John Cleland (1709–1789), which he subtitled *Memoirs of a Woman of Pleasure*. Oxford University Press still publishes *Fanny Hill* as part of its Oxford World's Classics series.

251. Orr and Mary Kelly. *Dream's End: Two Iowa Brothers in the Civil War* (New York: Kodansha America, 1998), 57.

252. Joseph W. Slade, *Pornography and Sexual Representation: A Reference Guide* (New York: Greenwood Press, 2000), 44. Donald A. Downs, *The New Politics of Pornography* (Chicago: University of Chicago Press, 1989), 12.

4—"Brawls, riots, and midnight orgies"

1. Frederick Marryat, *Diary in America: With Remarks on Its Institutions*, vol. I (London: Longman, Orme, Brown, Greene & Longmans, 1839), 124–125.

2. Longacre, "Bliss Letters," 20.

3. Stuart Murray, *A Time of War: A Northern Chronicle of the Civil War* (Lee, MA: Berkshire House, 2001), 117.

4. Sears, 136.

5. Ida B. Adams, "The Civil War Letters of James Rush Holmes," *Western Pennsylvania Historical Magazine*, vol. 44, no. 2 (June 1961): 114.

6. John W. Rowell, *Yankee Artillerymen: Through the Civil War with Eli Lilly's Indiana Battery* (Knoxville: University of Tennessee Press, 1973), 34–35.

7. Rufus R. Dawes, *Service with the Sixth Wisconsin Volunteers* (Marietta, OH: E.R. Alderman & Sons, 1890), 34–35.

8. James Gillette, letter to parents dated July 2, 1863, James Gillette Papers, Civil War Times Illustrated Collection, United States Army Military History Institute, Carlisle, Pennsylvania.

9. Donald Yacovone, *A Voice of Thunder: The Civil War Letters of George E. Stephens* (Urbana: University of Illinois Press, 1997), 156.

10. Dawes, 194.

11. Neil B. Carmony, *The Civil War in Apacheland*, 82.

12. Amy S. Greenberg, *Manifest Manhood and the Antebellum American Empire* (Cambridge: Cambridge University Press, 2005), 10. Elaine Frantz Parsons, *Manhood Lost: Fallen Drunkards and Redeeming Women in the Nineteenth-century United States* (Baltimore: Johns Hopkins University Press, 2003), 54.

13. John Phelps, letter to sister dated February 2, 1859, John W. Phelps Papers, New York Public Library, New York, New York.

14. Mark A. Vargas, "The Progressive Agent of Mischief: The Whiskey Ration and Temperance in the United States Army." *Historian* 67, no. 2 (Summer 2005): 199, 204, and 213–214.

15. Josiah Bunting III, *Ulysses S. Grant* (New York: Henry Holt, 2004), 29–32.

16. Vargas, 205.

17. Lewis, 29.

18. Barth, xiii.

19. James I. Robertson, *Soldiers Blue and Gray* (Columbia: University of South Carolina Press, 1988), 99. Gaff, 104. Silliker, 88.

20. Wightman Papers, letter to brother dated January 15, 1863.

21. Cornelius Cartwright, diary entry for February 21, 1865, Cornelius Courtright Papers, Chicago Historical Society, Chicago, Illinois.

22. Donald E. Reynolds and Max H. Kele, "A Yank in the Carolinas Campaign: The Diary of James W. Chapin, Eighth Indiana Cavalry," *North Carolina Historical Review*, vol. 46, no.1 (January 1969): 52–53.

23. Longacre, "Bliss Letters," 17.

24. Bensell Papers, diary entry for April 24, 1862.

25. Haydon Papers, diary entry for June 13, 1861.

26. Lewis, 71.

27. Helen Hudson, *Civil War Hawks* (Hagerstown, IN: Historic Hagerstown, 1974), 11.

28. Mark E Lender and James K. Martin, *Drinking in America: A History* (New York: Free Press, 1987), 58–60.

29. William L. Burton, *Melting Pot Soldiers: The Union's Ethnic Regiments* (Ames: Iowa State University Press, 1988), 83.

30. Husby and Wittenberg, 126.

31. Wightman Papers, April 13, 1863.

32. Milwaukee *Sentinel*, November 20, 1861.

33. Coe, 74.

34. Croushore, 41.

35. Carmomy, *Apacheland*, 82.

36. Welsh Papers, letter to wife dated January 27, 1863.

37. Edmund Halsey, diary entry for November 7, 1862, Edmund Halsey Papers, United States Army Military History Institute, Carlisle, Pennsylvania.

38. William C. Harris, *In the Country of the Enemy: The Civil War Reports of a Massachusetts Corporal* (Gainesville: University of Florida Press, 1999), 170.

39. Dix, 71.

40. Morse Papers, diary entry for January 1, 1863.

41. Franklin Boyts, diary entry for January 20, 1863, Franklin Boys Papers, Historical Society of Pennsylvania, Philadelphia, Pennsylvania.

42. Buckingham, 19.

43. Raymond Herek, *These Men Have Seen Hard Service: The First Michigan Sharpshooters in the Civil War* (Detroit: Wayne State University Press, 1998), 74–75.

44. Frederick Trautmann, *"We Were the Ninth:" A History of the Ninth Regiment, Ohio Volunteer Infantry"* (Kent, OH: Kent State University Press, 1987), 268.

45. Beaudry, 39.

46. Yacovone, 148.

47. Malles, 51.

48. Joseph Gibbs, *Three Years in the Bloody Eleventh: The Campaigns of a Pennsylvania Reserves Regiment* (University Park: Pennsylvania State University Press, 2002), 46.

49. Yacovone, 156.

50. Follmer Papers, diary entry for January 1, 1865.

51. Marshall J. Pixley, *The Adams Express Company*, http://www.floridareenactorsonline.com/adamsexpress.htm.

52. Daniel H. Mowen Papers, "Reminiscences of the Civil War by a Veteran of the Union Army," Fredericksburg and Spotsylvania National Military Park, National Park Service, Fredericksburg, VA, 7.

53. Donald, 253.

54. Margaret Leech, *Reveille in Washington, 1860–1865* (New York: Harper & Brothers, 1941), 217.

55. Holahan Papers, diary entry for March 24, 1863.

56. Brown, *Soldier's Life*, 73.

57. Philip J. Reyburn and Terry L. Wilson, *Jottings from Dixie: The Civil War Dispatches of Sergeant Major Stephen F. Fleharty, U.S.A.* (Baton Rouge: Louisiana State University Press, 1999), 148–149.

58. Mahood, 35.

59. Charles Scribner, letter to friend dated June 22, 1862, Charles Scribner Papers, Fredericksburg and Spotsylvania National Military Park, National Park Service, Fredericksburg, Virginia.

60. Donald, 33.

61. Stephen V. Benet, *A Treatise on Military Law and the Practice of Courts-Martial* (New York: D. Van Nostrand, 1862), 39.

62. Welsh Papers, letter to wife dated October 7, 1863. A standard issue Union canteen held three pints.

63. United States Army, Adjutant-General's Office. *General Orders Affecting the Volunteer Force* (Washington, DC: Government Printing Office, 1862), 13.

64. ORA, volume 11, series III, 93–94.

65. Carl A. Morrell, *Seymour Dexter, Union Army: Journal and Letters of Civil War Service In Company K, 23rd New York volunteer Regiment of Elmira, with Illustrations* (Jefferson, NC: McFarland, 1996), 131.

66. Indianapolis *Daily State Sentinel*, August 19, 1861.

67. Shannon, *Organization of the Union Army*, 221.

68. New York *Times*, November 3, 1861.

69. Haydon Papers, diary entry for August 19, 1861.

70. Campbell Papers, diary entry for December 11, 1861.

71. Daniel Mowen, "Reminiscences of the Civil War by a Veteran in the Union Army," Part I, 2. Fredericksburg and Spotsylvania National Military Park, National Park Service, Fredericksburg, Virginia.

72. Winschel, 8.

73. Yacovone, 157.

74. Darius Starr, letter to brother dated June 3, 1863, Darius Starr Papers, Fredericksburg and Spotsylvania National Military Park, National Park Service, Fredericksburg, Virginia.

75. Edward Bassett, letter to family dated December 31, 1861, Edward H. and George S. Bassett Papers, Minnesota Historical Society, St. Paul, Minnesota.

76. Rufus Kinsley, diary entry for July 19, 1864, Rufus Kinsley Papers, Vermont Historical Society, Barre, Vermont.

77. NARA, Washington, DC. Record Group 94 (hereafter as RG94): Records of the Adjutant General, Eighty-third Pennsylvania, Regimental Orders Book, Report of Lt. John Wilson, December 1, 1861.

78. Adams, 114.

79. Henry Heisler, letter to sister dated January 7, 1862, Henry Clary Heisler Papers, Library of Congress (Manuscript Division), Washington, DC.

80. ORA, vol. 29, series II, 78–79.

81. Donald, 195. Sears, 13.

82. Croushore, 94.

83. Brown, *Soldier's Life*, 110.

84. Richard F. Miller and Robert E. Mooney, *The Civil War: The Nantucket Experience* (Nantucket, MA: Wesco, 1994), 27.

85. Sears, 140.

86. Albert Allen, letters to sister dated December 20, 1863 and January 16, 1864, Albert and Charles Allen Papers, Special Collections Library, University of Virginia, Charlottesville, Virginia.

87. Jones Papers, letter to brother dated October 21, 1861.

88. Wyman White, diary entry for January 1, 1865. Wyman S. White Papers, Fredericksburg and Spotsylvania National Military Park, National Park Service, Fredericksburg, Virginia.

89. Lender and Martin, 12–16.

90. U.S. War Department, *Revised Regulation for the Army of the United States, 1861* (Philadelphia: J.B. Lippincott, 1861), 244.

91. John D. Billings, *Hardtack and Coffee: Or the Unwritten Story of Army Life* (Boston: George M. Smith, 1887), 140.

92. Bell I. Wiley, *The Life of Billy Yank* (Baton Rouge: Louisiana State University Press, 1979), 230–231.

93. Charles Bryan and Nelson Lankford, *Eye of the Storm: A Civil War Odyssey* (New York: Free Press, 2000), 9.

94. NARA (Washington, DC). Record Group 107: Records of the Office of the Secretary of War. General Orders number 21, Fourth Division, dated July 9, 1864.

95. Ella Jane Bruen and Brian M. Fitzgibbins, *Through Ordinary Eyes: The Civil War Correspondence of Rufus Robbins, Private, 7th Regiment, Massachusetts Volunteers* (Westport, CT: Praeger, 2000), 150.

96. Ferguson Papers, diary entry for January 20 1864. At full strength (which they almost never were), a company contained one hundred men.

97. Frank H. Hamilton, *A Treatise on Military Surgery and Hygiene* (New York: Bailliere Brothers, 1865), 71–72.

98. Haydon Papers, diary entry for September 16, 1861.

99. Sears, 174.

100. Fisk Papers, diary entry for February 13, 1864.

101. Mushkat, 82.

102. William Jackson, diary entry for November 20, 1863, William N. Jackson Papers, Indiana Historical Society, Indianapolis, Indiana.

103. Robert Sneden, diary entry for July 6, 1862, Robert Knox Sneden Papers, Virginia Historical Society, Richmond, Virginia.

104. Dunkelman, 214.

105. Holcomb, 42.

106. John Bates, diary entry for February 20, 1865 John W. Bates Papers, Civil War Miscellaneous Collection, United States Army Military History Institute, Carlisle, Pennsylvania.

107. Sneden Papers, diary entries for July 20 and July 23, 1862.

108. James L. Swanson and Daniel R. Weinberg, *Lincoln's Assassins: Their Trial and Execution* (Santa Fe, NM: Arena Editions, 2001), 2.

109. Samito, 170.

110. John Mottram, diary entry for February 22, 1865, John Mottrom Papers, University of Virginia (Special Collections Library), Charlottesville, Virginia.

111. Shannon, *Andrus Letters*, 72.

112. Jones Papers, letter to father dated December 25, 1863.

113. Dodge Papers, diary entry for December 31, 1862.

114. Sylvester Hadley, diary entry for January 3, 1963, Sylvester Hadley Papers, Fredericksburg and Spotsylvania National Military Park, National Archives, Fredericksburg, Virginia.

115. John Smith, letter to parents dated January 9, 1865, John L. Smith Papers, Historical Society of Pennsylvania, Philadelphia, Pennsylvania.

116. John White, letter to wife dated December 25, 1863, John Chester White Papers, Library of Congress (Manuscript Division), Washington, DC.

117. Welsh Papers, letter to wife dated December 25, 1862.

118. Henry Fitzgerald Charles Civil War Records, www.dm.net/~neitz/charles/index.html, 21.

119. Josiah Williams, letter to parents dated May 18, 1862, Josiah Clinton Williams Papers, Vigo County Public Library, Terre Haute, Indiana.

120. Arthur A. Kent, *Three Years with Company K: Sergt. Austin C. Stearns, Company K 13th Mass. Infantry (Deceased)* (Rutherford, NJ: Fairleigh Dickinson University Press, 1976), 29.

121. Rowell, 35.

122. NARA, Record Group 15: Records of the Veterans Administration, Patrick Brennan Pension file.

123. Herman J. Viola, *The Memoirs of Charles Henry Veil: A Soldiers' Recollections of the Civil War and the Arizona Territory* (Thorndike, ME: Thorndike Press, 1994), 162.

124. Thomas L. Livermore, *Days and Events, 1860–1866* (New York: Houghton Mifflin, 1920), 56.

125. New York *Sunday Mercury*, January 5, 1863.

126. David Gould and James B. Kennedy, *Memoirs of a Dutch Mudsill: The 'War Memories' of John Henry Otto, Captain, Company D, 21st Regiment Wisconsin Volunteer Infantry* (Kent, OH: Kent State University Press, 2004), 37.

127. Gibbs, 45.

128. Hughes, 251.

129. Amos Farling, *Life in the Army: Containing Historical and Biographical Sketches, Incidents, Adventures and Narratives of the Late War* (Buchanan, MI: self-published, 1874), 9.

130. Ferguson Papers, diary entries for February 21 and 27, 1864.

131. Dunkelman, 182–183.

132. William Jackson, diary entry for September 14, 1862, William N. Jackson Papers, Indiana Historical Society, Indianapolis, Indiana.

133. Carmony, *Apacheland*, 139.

134. Coffin, 150.

135. George Hugunin, diary entry for March 17, 1863, George Hugunin Papers, Fredericksburg and Spotsylvania National Military Park, National Park Service, Fredericksburg, Virginia.

136. Joseph K. Newell, *"Ours": Annals of the 10th Regiment, Massachusetts Volunteers* (Springfield, MA: C.A. Nichols, 1875), 52.

137. Silas Wesson, diary entry for June 23, 1864, Silas D. Wesson Papers, Civil War Times Illustrated Collection, United States Army Military History Institute, Carlisle, Pennsylvania.

138. Ferguson Papers, diary entry for January 16, 1864.

139. Winschel, 153.

140. Husby and Wittenberg, 137.

141. Croushore, 41.

142. Coffin, 152.

143. George H. Allen, *Forty-Six Months with the Fourth R.I. Volunteers in the War of 1861 to 1865* (Providence, RI: J.A. and R.A. Reid, 1887), 126.

144. Kent, 255.

145. Frederick Pell, diary entries for December 25 and 26, 1863, Frederick Pell Papers, Civil War Times Illustrated Collection, United States Army Military History Institute, Carlisle, Pennsylvania.

146. Temple, "Henry C. Bear Letters," Winter 1960.

147. Shannon, *Andrus Letters*, 72.

148. Bensell Papers, diary entry for October 9, 1862.

149. Noe, 146.

150. Dodge Papers, journal entry for March 10, 1863.

151. Donald, 33.

152. Ferguson Papers, April 3, 1864.

153. Kroll and Moran, 257–258.

154. Haydon Papers, September 6, 1861.

155. Carmony, *Apacheland*, 81.

156. Fredericksburg (VA) *Christian Banner*, June 18, 1862.

157. Silliker, 181.

158. Napoleon Bartlett, letter to brother dated June 6, 1864, Napoleon Bartlett Papers, Chicago Historical Society, Chicago, Illinois.

159. Mannis and Wilson, 112.

160. Carmony, *Apacheland*, 113.

161. Mark W. Johnson, *That Body of Brave Men: The U.S. Regular Infantry and the Civil War in the West* (New York: DaCapo Press, 2003), 141.

162. Patrick Papers, diary entry for July 12, 1864.

163. NARA, Record Group 110 (hereafter as RG 110): Provost Marshal Records, Entry 3853, Descriptive Book of Arrested Deserters: District of Columbia, 7.

164. Bacarella, 162.

165. Campbell Papers, diary entry for December 12, 1861.

166. Miller Papers, letter to his wife dated March 25, 1862.

167. NARA, RG 110: Provost Marshal Records, Entry 3853, Descriptive Book of Arrested Deserters: District of Columbia, 6.

168. Hughes, 249.

169. Croushore, 41.

170. Parson, 25.

171. Silliker, 29.

172. Carmony, *Apacheland*, 82.

173. Palladino, 28.

174. Lewis, 71.

175. Carmony, *Apacheland*, 82–83.

176. Noe, 100 and 267.

177. Haydon Papers, diary entry for September 25, 1861.

178. Hudson Hyatt, "Captain Hyatt: Being the Letters Written during the War Years 1863–1864 to His Wife Mary," *Ohio State Archaeological and Historical Quarterly*, vol. 53 (1944): 169.

179. Winschel, 85.

180. Lender and Martin, 37–38.

181. *Medical and Surgical History of the War of Rebellion*, vol. 1, Part 3, 143.

182. Robertson, 99.

183. Silliker, 216.

184. Buckingham, 195.

185. Donald, 15 and 23.

186. Richard E. Matthews, *The 149th Pennsylvania Volunteer Infantry Unit in the Civil War* (Jefferson, NC: McFarland, 1994), 34.

187. Sears, 100.

188. Dunkelman, 215–216.

189. Husby and Wittenberg, 11.

190. Croushore, 46.

191. Haydon Papers, diary entry for November, 19, 1861.

192. Daniel B. Weber, *The Diary of Ira Gillaspie of the Eleventh Michigan Infantry* (Mount Pleasant: Central Michigan University Press, 1965), 22.

193. Mary S. Dix, "And Three Rousing Cheers for the Privates: A Diary of the 1862 Roanoke Island Expedition," *North Carolina Historical Review*, vol. 71, no. 1 (January 1994): 66.

194. George Sinclair, letter to wife dated January 6, 1863, George B. Sinclair Papers, Civil War Miscellaneous Collection, United States Army Military History Institute, Carlisle, Pennsylvania.

195. Ovando J. Hollister, *Colorado Volunteers in New Mexico, 1862* (Chicago: Lakeside Press, 1962), 159.

196. Britton and Reed, 319.

197. Thomas Watkins, diary entries for August 21, 1861 and March 18, 1862, Thomas C. Watkins Papers, Civil War Times Illustrated Collection, United States Army Military History Institute, Carlisle, Pennsylvania.

198. Palladino, 53.

199. East Saginaw *Courier*, January 27 1864.

200. Lewis, 26.

201. Silliker, 225.

202. Holahan Papers, diary entry for April 24, 1861.

203. Blackburn Papers, letter to wife dated January 21, 1862.

204. New York *Weekly Anglo-African*, January 18, 1862.

205. D. Alexander Brown, *The Galvanized Yankees* (Urbana: University of Illinois Press, 1963), 140.

206. Geoffrey Perret, *Lincoln's War: The Untold Story of America's Greatest President as Commander in Chief* (New York: Random House, 2004), 262.

207. Gaff, 103.

208. Boston *Herald*, September 13, 1862.

209. Charles A. Willison, *Reminiscences of a Boy's Service with the 76th Ohio* (Huntington, WV: Blue Acorn Press, 1995), 152–155.

210. Cleveland *Daily Herald*, April 9, 1864.

211. NARA, RG 94: Records of the Adjutant General's Office, Records of the Department of the Gulf, General Order number 7, March 28, 1862.

212. Charles Heckman, General Orders Book, General Order number 8, July 22, 1863, Charles Heckman Papers, Historical Society of Pennsylvania, Philadelphia, Pennsylvania.

213. Hughes, 250 and 254–255.

214. New York *Times*, September 8, 1861.

215. ORA, vol. 42, series II, 837.

216. Patrick Papers, diary entry for January 6, 1865.

217. William D.F. Landon, "Fourteenth Indiana Regiment: Letters to Vincennes *Western Sun*," *Indiana Magazine of History*, vol. 35, no. 1 (March 1938): 71–98.

218. Ronald G. Walters, *American Reformers: 1815–1860* (New York: Hill & Wang, 1978), 123–144.

219. Blackburn Papers, letter to wife dated January 1, 1862.

220. McClellan's comment on abstinence being worth 50,000 men to the army has appeared in a number of secondary sources, but the earliest citation appears in General Order number 40 issued by the Army of the Potomac, where McClellan approves the sentences of several court-martialed soldiers. NARA, RG153: Records of the Judge Advocate General, file number II650.

221. Norman C. Delaney, "Letters of a Maine Soldier Boy," *Civil War History*, vol. 5 (March 1959), 53.

222. Beaudry, 90.

223. Buckingham, 195.

224. Henry Forbes, letter to Major John Rewalt dated May 24, 1862, Henry C. Forbes Papers, Chicago Historical Society, Chicago, Illinois.

225. Eugene H. Berwanger, "Absent so Long from Those I Love: The Civil War Letters of Joshua Jones," *Indiana Magazine of History*, vol. 88, no. 3 (September 1992): 223.

226. Jennifer C. Bohrnstedt, *Soldiering With Sherman: Civil War Letters of George F. Cram* (DeKalb: Northern Illinois University Press, 2000), 109–110.

227. George Merryweather, letter to friend dated April 22, 1864, George Merryweather Papers, Chicago Historical Society, Chicago, Illinois.

228. Palladino, 141.

229. Croushore, 40.

230. Campbell Papers, diary entry for February 26, 1864.

231. John Pardington, letters to wife dated November 27 and December 29, 1862, John H. Pardington Papers, Fredericksburg and Spotsylvania National Military Park, Fredericksburg, Virginia.

232. Britton and Reed, 176.

233. Welsh Papers, letter to his brother dated April 29, 1864.

234. Winschel, 8.

235. Beaudry, 93 and 109.

236. Engert, 20.

237. Arthur H. DeRosier, *Through the South with a Union Soldier* (Johnson City: East Tennessee State University, 1969), 45.

238. Hedrick and Davis, 109.

239. Otto F. Bond, *Under the Flag of the Nation: Diaries and Letters of Owen Johnston Hopkins, a Yankee Volunteer in the Civil War* (Columbus: Ohio State University Press, 1998), 143.

240. Carl A. Morrell, *Seymour Dexter, Union Army: Journal and Letters of Civil War Service in Company K, 23rd New York Volunteer Regiment of Elmira, with Illustrations* (Jefferson, NC: McFarland, 1996), 63.

241. New York *Herald*, October 25, 1862.

242. NARA, RG 94: Records of the Adjutant General's Office, Army of the Potomac, General Order number 53.

243. Benet, 217–220.

244. Follmer Papers, diary entry for September 3, 1863.

245. Delaney, 53.

246. Palladino, 22.

247. Fisk Papers, diary entry for April 6, 1863.

248. Campbell Papers, diary entry for March 22, 1864.

249. Milwaukee *Sunday Telegraph*, March 11, 1883.

250. Haydon Papers, diary entry for August 10, 1861.

251. Dodge Papers, diary entry for February 24, 1863.

252. Cecil D. Eby, Jr., *A Virginia Yankee in the Civil War: The Diaries of David Hunter Strother* (Chapel Hill: University of North Carolina Press, 1961), 13.

253. Kinsley Papers, diary entry for December 26, 1863.

254. Thomas Orwig, letter to friend dated March 14, 1863, Thomas G. Orwig Letters, Civil War Times Illustrated Collection, United States Army Military History Institute, Carlisle, Pennsylvania.

255. Robert F. Harris and John Niflot, *Dear Sister: The Civil War Letters of the Brothers Gould* (Westport, CT: Praeger, 1998), 131.

256. New York *Sunday Mercury*, December 22, 1861.

257. Leech, 140.

258. Beaudry, 80.

259. Ferguson Papers, diary entry for January 7, 1865.

260. Britton and Reed, 175.

261. Winschel, 17.

262. Garber A. Davidson, *The Civil War Letters of the Late 1st Lieut. James J. Hartley, 122nd Ohio Infantry Regiment* (Jefferson, NC: McFarland, 1998), 36.

263. Francis Walter, diary entry for September 18, 1864, Francis A. Walter Papers, Civil War Miscellaneous Collection, United State Army Military History Institute, Carlisle, Pennsylvania.

264. War Department, Department of the Missouri, General Order 153, June 6, 1864.

265. Pride and Travis, 50.

266. Giles Shurtleff, letter to friend dated September 17, 1863, Giles W. Shurtleff Papers, Oberlin College, Oberlin, Ohio.

267. C.P. Weaver, *Thank God My Regiment an African One: The Civil War Diary of Colonel Nathan W. Daniels* (Baton Rouge: Louisiana State University Press, 1998), 121.

268. Thomas P. Lowry, *Tarnished Eagles: The Courts-Martial of Fifty Union Colonels and Lieutenant Colonels* (Mechanicsburg, PA: Stackpole Books, 1997), 53.

269. Silliker, 128.

270. Winschel, 97.

271. ORA, series I, vol. 42, 463–465.

272. ORA, series I, vol. 12, 320–322.

273. David Neely, diary entry for August 4, 1864, David R.P. Neely Papers, Pennsylvania Historical and Museum Commission, Harrisburg, Pennsylvania.

274. Walter H. Hebert, *Fighting Joe Hooker* (Lincoln: University of Nebraska Press, 1999), 225.

275. George Barnard, letter to father dated march 28, 1863, George M. Barnard Papers, Massachusetts Historical Society, Boston, Massachusetts.

276. Bob Taggart, letter to Captain John Taggard dated August 28, 1863, Valley of the Shadow Project.

277. Ferguson Papers, diary entries for February 22 and September 20, 1863.

278. Lowry, *Tarnished Eagles*, 36.

279. Haydon Papers, diary entry for September 25, 1861.

280. NARA, RG153: Records of the Judge Advocate General (Army), Court-martial of Benjamin Hancock, File NN29.

281. Throne, *Boyd Diary*, 93.

282. James Harman, letter to father dated July 18, 1862, Valley of the Shadow Project. [Emphasis in original].

283. James McIvor, letter to Captain Robert Gray dated December 9, 1863, James T. McIvor Papers, New York Historical Society, New York, New York.

284. John Anderson, *History of the 57th Regiment of Massachusetts Volunteers* (Boston: E.B. Stilling, 1896), 267.

285. Weaver, 151.

286. Bensell Papers, diary entry for November 10, 1862.

287. NARA, RG 94: Records of the Adjutant General's Office, Seventh Kansas Regimental Letter and Order Book, letter dated July 13, 1862.

288. Frederic S. Klein, "On Trial," *Civil War Times Illustrated*, vol. 7 (January 1969), 41.

289. Lowry, *Tarnished Eagles*, 40–43.

290. Brobst Papers, letter to wife dated December 27, 1864.

291. Lorna L. Sylvester, "The Civil War Letters of Charles Harding Cox," *Indiana Magazine of History*, vol. 68 (March 1972): 66.

292. Sneden Papers, Diary entry for February 25, 1862.

293. Philip N. Racine, *Unspoiled Heart: The Journal of Charles Mattocks of the 17th Maine* (Knoxville: University of Tennessee Press, 1994), 120–129.

294. Klein, 43.

5—"There were threats to shoot the officers"

1. Byrne, 1–2.

2. Boston *Herald*, December 29, 1862.

3. Croushore, 92–93.

4. George H. Otis, *The Second Wisconsin Infantry* (Dayton, OH: Press of Morningside Bookshop, 1984), 54.

5. Dodge Papers, diary entry for June 30, 1862.

6. Robert L. Bee, *The Boys from Rockville: Civil War Narratives of Sgt. Benjamin Hirst, Company D, 14th Connecticut Volunteers* (Knoxville: University of Tennessee Press, 1998), 137–138.

7. W.S. Nye, *The Valiant Hours: Narrative of "Captain Brevet," an Irish-American in the Army of the Potomac* (Harrisburg, PA: Stackpole, 1961), 76–77.

8. Leech, 198.

9. John J. Hennessy, *Fighting with the Eighteenth Massachusetts: The Civil War Memoir of Thomas H. Mann* (Baton Rouge: Louisiana State University, 2000), 99.

10. Winschel, 63.

11. Donald, 172–173.

12. Fisk Papers, letter to parents dated May 27, 1864.

13. Lowry, *Tarnished Eagles*, 148–149.

14. Lorien Foote, "Rich Man's War, Rich Man's Fight: Class, Ideology, and Discipline in the Union Army," *Civil War History*, vol. 51, no. 3 (September 2005): 283.

15. Timothy Bateman, diary entry for September 14, 1864, Timothy Bateman Papers, Civil War Miscellaneous Collection, United States Army Military History Institute, Carlisle, Pennsylvania.

16. Edwin Weist, diary entry for February 14, 1863, Edwin B. Weist Papers, Fredericksburg and Spotsylvania National Military Park, National Park Service, Fredericksburg, Virginia.

17. Smith Letterbook, letters to mother dated January 5 and April 24, 1863.

18. Haydon Papers, diary entry for September 5, 1861.

19. Nye, 80.

20. Nye, 80.

21. Wightman Papers, letter to brother dated January 3, 1863.

22. Haydon Papers, diary entry for June 20, 1861.

23. Dunkelman, 85.

24. James Newton, letter to parents dated January 24, 1863, Abel D. Newton Collection, Wisconsin Historical Society, Madison, Wisconsin.

25. Leander Stillwell, *The Story of a Common Soldier of Army Life in the Civil War* (Erie, KS: Franklin-Hudson, 1920), 119–120.

26. Welsh Papers, letter to wife dated January 4, 1863.

27. ORA, series I, vol. 40, 140.

28. Bell I. Wiley, *Life of Billy Yank: The Common Soldier of the Union* (Baton Rouge: Louisiana State University Press, 1994), 91.

29. Smith Letterbook, letter to parents dated December 13, 1863.

30. Eugene C. Murdock, "Pity the Poor Surgeon," *Civil War History*, vol. 16, no. 1 (March 1970): 29.

31. Albert Castel, "Malingering: Many . . . Diseases Are . . . Feigned," *Civil War Times Illustrated*, vol. 21, no. 5 (August 1977): 29.

32. Harold A. Small, *The Road to Richmond: the Civil War Memoirs of Maj. Abner R. Small of the 16th Maine Vols.* (Berkeley: University of California Press, 1959), 38–39.

33. Joseph Hotz, letters to wife dated January 22 and 29, 1863, Indiana State Archives, Indiana Civil War Commission, Indianapolis, Indiana.

34. Silliker, 86.

35. Welsh Papers, letter to wife dated September 19, 1863.

36. Kroll and Moran, 254.

37. Jeffrey L. Patrick. *Three Years with Wallace's Zouaves: The Civil War Memoirs of Thomas Wise Durham* (Macon, GA: Mercer University Press, 2003), 108.

38. Haydon Papers, diary entry for October 25, 1861.

39. Charles, "Civil War Record," 4.

40. David Ashley, letter to parents dated June 23, 1862, David C. Ashley Papers, Civil War Miscellaneous Collection, United States Army Military History Institute, Carlisle, Pennsylvania.

41. NARA, RG 110: Records of the Provost Marshal General, Descriptive Book of Arrested Deserters: Vermont, entry number 4.

42. Amos Downing, letter to brother dated August 12, 1861, Amos Downing Papers, Civil War Miscellaneous Collection, United States Army Military History Institute, Carlisle, Pennsylvania.

43. James Wiggins, letter to parents dated December 17, 1861, James B. Wiggins Papers, Virginia Historical Society, Richmond, Virginia.

44. Miller, 43.

45. David W. Blight, *When This Cruel War is Over: The Civil War Letters of Charles Harvey Brewster* (Amherst: University of Massachusetts Press, 1992), 168.

46. Bushrod W. James, *Echoes of Battle* (Philadelphia: Henry T. Coates, 1895), 68–70.

47. Hedrick and Davis, 112.

48. Linderman, 11–12.

49. Tully McCrea, letter to fiancé dated December 18, 1862, Tully McCrea Papers, Fredericksburg and Spotsylvania National Military Park, National Park Service, Fredericksburg, Virginia.

50. Daniel Mowen, "Reminiscences of the Civil War by a Veteran in the Union Army," 4, Daniel Mowen Papers, Fredericksburg and Spotsylvania National Military Park, National Park Service, Fredericksburg, Virginia.

51. Joseph Allan Frank, Rudy A. Pozzatti, and George A. Reaves, *Seeing the Elephant: Raw Recruits at the Battle of Shiloh* (Urbana: University of Illinois Press, 2003), 113.

52. Holahan Papers, diary entry for July 13, 1863.

53. NARA, Washington, DC. RG 94: Records of the Adjutant General, First Michigan Sharpshooters, Letter and Order Book, October 24, 1864.

54. Lande, 152–153.

55. Hagerty, 201.

56. Murdock, 32.

57. Castel, 29.

58. Thomas W.W. Atwood, "From the Diaries and Letters of Pvt. Tobie: Life in a U.S. Army Hospital, 1862," *Army*, vol. 38, no. 1 (January 1988): 54.

59. New York *Sunday Mercury*, May 17, 1863.

60. William Stewart, letter to wife dated August 30, 1862, William S. Stewart Papers, Fredericksburg and Spotsylvania National Military Park, National Park Service, Fredericksburg, Virginia.

61. William Winthrop, *Military Law and Precedents* (Washington, DC: Government Printing Office, 1920), 730.

62. Silliker, 121.

63. Lande, 155–156.

64. Avery Papers, letter to wife dated June 3, 1864.

65. Lewis, 66–67 [emphasis in original].

66. NARA, RG 94: Records of the Adjutant General's Office (Compiled Service Records), Charles Williams.

67. Kent, 86–87. "Minie" refers to the Minié ball, the standard ammunition of Civil War muskets. Invented by Captain Claude-Étienne Minié of the French Army, the Minié ball was actually conically shaped, and was made of soft lead to grip the grooves in the new rifled muskets of the era.

68. Welsh Papers, letter to wife dated October 23, 1862.

69. George Squier, letter to wife dated February 3, 1863, George W. Squier Papers, The Lincoln Museum, Fort Wayne, Indiana.

70. Abraham Papers, "Incidents," 4.

71. McPherson, *For Cause and Comrades*, 35.

72. Buckingham, 75.

73. Patrick, 54–55.

74. Patrick Papers, diary entry for July 6, 1863.

75. Squier Papers, letter to wife dated January 4, 1863.

76. See Gerald Linderman's *Embattled Courage: The Experience of Combat in the Civil War*.

77. Lilley Papers, letter to sister dated November 18, 1863.

78. Kroll and Moran, 253.

79. John Cuzner, letter to fiancé dated September 21, 1862, John B. Cuzner Papers, Connecticut Historical Society, Hartford, Connecticut.

80. Thomas Douglass, letter to parents dated December 1, 1862, Thomas B. Douglass Papers, Civil War Miscellaneous Collection, United States Army Military History Institute, Carlisle, Pennsylvania.

81. Charles Brewster, letter to sister dated July 13, 1862, Brewster Family Papers, Sophia Smith Collection, Five Colleges Archives and Manuscript Collection, Smith College, Northampton, Massachusetts.

82. Dunkelman, 82.

83. Abraham Papers, "Incidents," 4.

84. Charles, "Civil War Record," 4.

85. Patrick Papers, diary entry for August 28, 1862.

86. Silliker, 151. Michael Fellman, et al., *This Terrible War: The Civil War and its Aftermath* (New York: Longman, 2003), 268.

87. George Bowen, diary entry for June 18, 1864, George Bowen Papers, Fredericksburg and Spotsylvania National Military Park, National Park Service, Fredericksburg, Virginia.

88. Wilkinson, 142.

89. Bruce Catton, *A Stillness at Appomattox* (Garden City, NJ: Doubleday, 1954), 82.

90. James M. Paradis, *Strike the Blow for Freedom: The 6th United States Colored Infantry in the Civil War* (Shippensburg, PA: White Mane Books, 1998), 53.

91. Gould and Kennedy, 192–193.

92. Newton Papers, letter to parents dated August 10, 1864.

93. George Fairfield, diary entry for July 23, 1861, George Fairfield Papers, Wisconsin Historical Society, Madison, Wisconsin.

94. Squier Papers, letter to wife dated February 3, 1863 [emphasis in original].

95. Versalle F. Washington. *Eagles on Their Buttons: A Black Infantry Regiment in the Civil War* (Columbia: University of Missouri Press, 1999), 24.

96. Newton Papers, letter to parents dated May 6, 1862.

97. Winschel, 26.

98. Haydon Papers, diary entry for December 27, 1861.

99. Richard Moe, *The Last Full Measure: The Life and Death of the First Minnesota Volunteers* (New York: Henry Holt, 1993), 67–68.

100. Follmer Papers, diary entry for May 2, 1863.

101. ORA, series I, vol. 16, 1062.

102. Silliker, 80.

103. Wightman Papers, letter to brother dated May 31, 1864.

104. Patrick, 132–133.

105. Delaney, 54.

106. Silliker, 129.

107. Gaff, 82. Lowry, *Tarnished Eagles*, 186–187.

108. Linderman. 44–48 and 166–168.

109. Patrick Papers, diary entry for June 24, 1864.

110. Raymond J. Herek, *These Men Have Seen Hard Service: The First Michigan Sharpshooters in the Civil War* (Detroit: Wayne State University Press, 1998), 196–197.

111. John Burrill, letter to parents dated August 8, 1862, John H. Burrill Papers, Civil War Miscellaneous Collection, United States Army Military History Institute, Carlisle, Pennsylvania.

112. Thomas E. Pope, *The Weary Boys: Colonel J. Warren Keifer and the 110th Ohio Volunteer Infantry* (Kent, OH: Kent State University Press, 2002), 21.

113. Robert G. Carter, *Four Brothers in Blue: Or Sunshine and Shadows of the War of the Rebellion, a Story of the Great Civil War from Bull Run to Appomattox* (Norman: University of Oklahoma Press, 1999), 9.

114. Andrew Davis, letter to father dated April 21, 1862, Andrew F. Davis Papers, State Historical Society of Missouri, Columbia, Missouri.

115. George A. Thompson, *Rustics in Rebellion* (Chapel Hill: University of North Carolina Press, 1950), 135 and 140.

116. Byron Andrews, *A Biography of General John A. Logan: With an Account of His Public Service in Peace and War* (New York: H.S. Goodspeed, 1884), 452–453.

117. Donald, 213–214.

118. Jones, 133.

119. Donald, 135.

120. Benet, 205–208.

121. Stephen Z. Starr, *Jennison's Jayhawkers: A Civil War Cavalry Regiment and Its Commander* (Baton Rouge: Louisiana State University Press, 1973), 296–297.

122. Silliker, 52.

123. Bacarella, 46–47.

124. Starr, 189–190.

125. Stuart Murray, *A Time of War: A Northern Chronicle of the Civil War* (Lee, MA: Berkshire House, 2001), 164–165.

126. Wightman Papers, letter to friend dated January 27, 1863.

127. Donald, 116–117.

128. Caleb Woolhizer, letter to wife dated January 25, 1863, C.T. Woolhizer Papers, Fredericksburg and Spotsylvania National Military Park, National Park Service, Fredericksburg, Virginia.

129. Engert, 64–65.

130. Dennis K. Boman, "Conduct and Revolt in the Twenty-fifth Ohio Battery: An Insider's Account," *Ohio History*, vol. 104 (Summer/Autumn 1995): 175.

131. Ann Gebhard, "Doubly Paid for any Sacrifice," *Michigan History*, vol. 47 (March/April 1990), 13.

132. New York *Tribune*, September 16, 1861. Shannon, *Organization of the Union Army*, 180–181.

133. William Sherman, *The Memoirs of General W. T. Sherman*, vol. I (New York: D. Appleton, 1875), 188–189.

134. ORA, series I, vol. 33, 637.

135. Marcia Reid-Green, *Letters Home: Henry Matrau of the Iron Brigade* (Lincoln: University of Nebraska Press, 1993), 12.

136. Rufus R. Dawes, *Service with the Sixth Wisconsin Volunteers* (Marietta: E.R. Alderman and Sons, 1890), 135.

137. Edward Henry, letter to sister dated May 24, 1863, Edward Henry Papers, Fredericksburg and Spotsylvania National Military Park, National Park Service, Fredericksburg, Virginia.

138. Samuel Sneden, letter to parents dated June 14, 1861, *Rochester Writes Home.*

139. Parson, 26.

140. NARA, RG 94: Records of the Adjutant General, Seventh Kansas Cavalry, Regimental Order Book, December 28, 1861.

141. James C. Mohr and Richard E. Winslow, *The Cormany Diaries: A Northern Family in the Civil War* (Pittsburgh: University of Pittsburgh Press, 1982), 246.

142. Bensell Papers, diary entries for November 18 and 20, 1862.

143. Philadelphia *Inquirer*, September 4, 1862.

144. Longacre, *Bliss Letters*, 23.

145. Mushkat, 22–23.

146. Donald, 187–188.

147. Johnson, 133–141.

148. Silliker, 52.

149. Johnson, 62–63.

150. Mahood, 35.

151. Haydon Papers, diary entries for August 14 and 15, 1861. Fort Jefferson was a large masonry fort located in the Dry Tortugas, a cluster of islands in the Gulf of Mexico located seventy miles west of Key West. Construction of the fort began in 1854, but it was incomplete when the Civil War began. The Union retained control of the fort throughout the war, using it as a penal facility due to its remote location.

152. Parson, 31. Boston *Saturday Evening Express*, June 28, 1863. Edward W. Emerson, *The Life and Letters of Charles Russell Lowell* (Boston: Houghton & Mifflin, 1907), 31. Lowell was later killed in 1864 at the Battle of Cedar Creek. His brother-in-law was Robert Gould Shaw, the colonel of the Fifty-fourth Massachusetts, the African American regiment portrayed in the motion picture *Glory*.

153. Edwin Gordon, diary entry for April 8, 1865, Edwin A. Gordon Papers, Wyandot Country Historical Society, Sandusky, Ohio.

154. Edward A. Miller, *The Black Civil War Soldiers of Illinois: The Story of the Twenty-ninth U.S. Colored Infantry* (Columbia: University of South Carolina Press, 1998), 154.

155. Carmony, *Apacheland*, 22–23.

156. Fitzgerald, *Civil War Record*, 2–3.

157. Gould and Kennedy, 35–37.

158. Crawford, 96.

159. Bensell Papers, diary entries for April 16 and May 19, 1862.

160. Dodge Papers, diary entry for June 2, 1863.

161. Leech, 111.

162. Jones, 127.

163. Pride and Travis, 56.

164. Halsey, 86.

165. Lowry, *Tarnished Eagles*, 131.

166. Haydon Papers, diary entry for February 4, 1963.

167. Susan T. Puck, *Sacrifice at Vicksburg: Letters from the Front* (Shippensburg, PA: Burd Street Press, 1997), 50.

168. Gould and Kennedy, 33.

169. Herdegen, 66.

170. Malles, 51.

171. Lowry, *Tarnished Eagles*, 201.

172. Popchock, 103 [Emphasis in the original].

173. Wightman Papers, letter to brother dated January 3, 1863.

174. Delaney, 53.

175. Silliker, 43.

176. Donald, 169. In 1858, while a member of the House of Representatives, Sickles killed Philip Barton Key, the son of Francis Scott Key, for sleeping with his wife. Sickles mounted one of the first temporary insanity defenses in American legal history, and the jury acquitted him of all charges. His attorney was Edwin Stanton, who served as Abraham Lincoln's second Secretary of War. See Thomas Keneally, *American Scoundrel: The Life of the Notorious Civil War General Dan Sickles* (New York: Doubleday, 2002).

177. Gaff, 125. Gibbon was born in Philadelphia, but his family moved to North Carolina when Gibbon was ten years old.

178. Winschel, 85. Wiley is modifying the phrase 'to heave Jonah' referring to

vomiting, in reference to the Old Testament prophet swallowed by a whale.

179. W. Mark McKnight, *Blue Bonnets O'er the Border: The 79th New York Cameron Highlanders* (Shippensburg, PA: White Mane Books, 1998), 26–27.

180. Silliker, 65 and 83.

181. Orr Kelly and Mary Davies Kelly, *Dream's End: Tow Iowa Brothers in the Civil War* (New York: Kodansha America, 1998), 119.

182. Edwin Haradon, diary entry for May 10, 1865, Edwin Albert Haradon Papers, Fredericksburg and Spotsylvania National Military Park, National Park Service, Fredericksburg, Virginia. White Papers, letter to parents dated January 2, 1865.

183. Salvatore G. Cilella, "The 121st New York State Infantry Regiment," M.A. thesis, State University of New York–Oneonta, 1972, 189–190.

184. Albert Sprague, letter to wife dated January 25, 1863, Albert G. Sprague Papers, Chicago Historical Society, Chicago, Illinois.

185. Smith Letterbook, letters to mother dated December 26, 1862 and January 25, 1863.

186. Mary E. Kellogg, *Army Life of an Illinois Soldier* (Carbondale: Southern Illinois University Press, 1996), 192.

187. Malles, 132.

188. Popchock, 148.

189. Johnson, 192.

190. Mowen Papers, diary entry for July 15, 1862.

191. Patrick, 108.

192. Bensell Papers, diary entry for April 26, 1862.

193. Haydon Papers, diary entry for January 1, 1862.

194. George K. Collins, *Memories of the 149th Regiment, New York Volunteer Infantry* (Hamilton, NY: Edmonston Pub., 1891), 38.

195. Silliker, 88.

196. Halsey, 83–84 and 87–88.

197. Skidmore, 44 and 86.

198. Frank A. O'Reilly, *The Fredericksburg Campaign: "Stonewall" Jackson at Fredericksburg: The Battle of Prospect Hill, December 13, 1862* (Lynchburg, VA: H.E. Howard, 1993), 94.

199. Klein, 41.

200. Charles Perkins, diary entry for August 1, 1863, Charles C. Perkins Papers, Civil War Times Illustrated Collection, United States Army Military History Institute, Carlisle, Pennsylvania.

201. Haydon Papers, diary entry for November 7, 1861.

202. Lewistown [PA] *Democrat and Sentinel*, September 4, 1861.

203. NARA, RG 94: Records of the Adjutant General's Office, Independent Cavalry Brigade Records, Michael Keefe court-martial, Washington, DC.

204. NARA, RG153: Records of the Provost Marshal General's Office, Files KK418 and KK643.

205. James B. Shaw, *History of the Tenth Regiment Indiana Volunteer Infantry: Three Months and Three Years Organizations* (Lafayette, IN: Burt-Haywood, 1912), 171–172.

206. Patrick Papers, diary entry for January 4, 1863.

207. Harwell, 218.

208. Welsh Papers, letter to wife dated May 13, 1863.

209. Weaver. 160.

210. Gaff, 201.

211. Gould and Kennedy, 203–205.

212. Dodge Papers, diary entry for June 10, 1863.

213. Klein, 40–41.

214. James S. Olsen, *Historical Dictionary of the 1970s* (New York: Greenwood Press, 1999, 161.

215. Newton Papers, letter to parents dated May 26, 1862.

216. Sneden Papers, diary entry for September 29, 1861.

217. Billings, 152.

218. Gould and Kennedy, 256–257.

219. New York *Sunday Mercury*, April 5, 1863.

220. Lucille Griffith. *Yours till Death: The Civil War Letters of John W. Cotton* (Tuscaloosa: University of Alabama Press, 1951), 58.

221. Haley, 85.

222. Haydon Papers, diary entry for July 27, 1861.

223. Samuel H.M. Byers, *With Fire and Sword* (New York: Neale, 1911), 14 and 26–27.

224. Jacob Van Zwaluwenburg, diary entry for April 11, 1862, Jacob Van Zwaluwenburg Papers, Schoff Civil War Collection, Clements Library, University of Michigan, Ann Arbor, Michigan.

225. Silliker, 129.

226. Britton and Reed, 136.

6—"The Pernicious Practice of Treasonable Persons"

1. James Connolly, letter to wife dated September 22, 1863, James A. Connolly Papers, Illinois State Historical Library, Springfield, Illinois.

2. ORA, series III, vol. 4, 706.

3. *House Executive Document*, 39th Congress, First Session, vol. 4, 232–235.

4. Shannon, *Union Army Organization*, 178–179. This number differs slightly from the postwar report of Colonel James B. Fry, the Provost Marshal General, who tallied 268,530 deserters in his final report to Congress dated March 17, 1866.

5. Coffman, 193.

6. "Report of the Provost-Marshal-General, Appendix to the Report of the Secretary of War," 39th Congress, 1st Session, 1866.

7. Arthur C. Cole, *The Centennial History of Illinois*, vol. III: *The Era of the Civil War, 1848–1870* (Springfield: Illinois Centennial Commission, 1919), 306. Harris, 29.

8. James McLean, *California Sabers: The 2nd Massachusetts Cavalry in the Civil War* (Bloomington: Indiana University Press, 2000), 18.

9. ORA, series I, vol. 38, 329.

10. Washington, 47.

11. Gaff, 223.

12. Reid and White, 64.

13. Haydon Papers, diary entry for June 19, 1861.

14. Wilkinson, 142.

15. Palladino, 167.

16. John Pardington, letter to father dated March 24, 1963, John H. Pardington Papers, Fredericksburg and Spotsylvania National Military Park, National Park Service, Fredericksburg, Virginia. Sweetland papers, letter to wife dated January 8, 1863.

17. Dunkelman, 89.

18. Dunkelman, 90.

19. Harwell, 128–129.

20. Anson Shuey, letter to wife dated November 2, 1863, Anson B. Shuey Papers, Civil War Miscellaneous Collection, United States Army Military History Institute, Carlisle, Pennsylvania.

21. Wilkinson, 319. Hughes, 186.

22. Jones, 131.

23. Silas Wesson, diary entry for October 10, 1862, Silas D. Wesson Papers, Civil War Times Illustrated Collection, United States Army Center for Military History, Carlisle, Pennsylvania.

24. Benjamin A. Gould, *Investigation in the Military and Anthropological Statistics of American Soldiers* (New York: Hurd and Houghton, 1869), 29.

25. Robert G. Scott, *Fallen Leaves: The Civil War Letters of Major Henry Livermore Abbott* (Kent, OH: Kent State University Press, 1991), 205 [Emphasis in original].

26. Augustus Hall, letter to cousin dated February 17, 1863, "Rochester Writes Home."

27. Bohrnstedt, 116.

28. Trautmann, 118–19.

29. Haydon Papers, diary entry for January 26, 1863 [Emphasis in original].

30. Benson Bobrick. *Testament: A Soldier's Story of the Civil War* (New York: Simon & Schuster, 2003), 227.

31. The conclusions in this discussion derive from Judith Lee Hallock's "The Role of the Community in Civil War Desertion," *Long Island Historical Journal*, vol. 6, no.2 (Spring 1994): 254–265 and Dora L. Costa and Matthew E. Kahn's "Cowards and Heroes: Group Loyalty in the American Civil War," *Quarterly Journal of Economics*, vol. 118, no. 2 (May 2003): 519–548.

32. New York *Times*, January 16, 1863.

33. Reid and White, 67.

34. War Department, *Revised Regulations for the Army of the United States, 1861* (Philadelphia: J. G. L. Brown, 1861), 30–31.

35. Washington, 74–75.

36. War Department, *Index of General Orders: Adjutant General's Office, 1862* (Washington, DC: Government Printing Office, 1863), General Order number 92, July 31, 1862.

37. Carl A. Morrell, *Seymour Dexter, Union Army: Journal and Letters of Civil War Service in Company K, 23rd New York Volunteer Regiment of Elmira, with Illustrations* (Jefferson, NC: McFarland, 1996), 16.

38. Hughes, 219.

39. Wilkinson, 17. Wightman Papers, letter to family dated February 10, 1863.

40. Wightman Papers, letter to brother dated June 6, 1863.

41. Charles A. Ramsey, "Story of a Headquarters Clerk and Sergeant Major" in Joseph W. Muffly, *The Story of Our Regiment: A History of the 148th Pennsylvania Vols.* (Des Moines, IA: Kenyon, 1904), 336.

42. Alan S. Brown, *A Soldier's Life: The Civil War Experiences of Ben C. Johnson* (Kalamazoo: Western Michigan University Press, 1962), 50–51.

43. Mohr and Winslow, 260.

44. Buckingham, 28.

45. Mahood, 34–35.

46. Ferguson Papers, diary entry for May 27, 1865.

47. Engert, 16.

48. Ferguson Papers, diary entry for January 5, 1865.

49. Winschel, 43.

50. Samito, 171–172.

51. Newton Papers, letter to parents dated January 15, 1862.

52. John Cook, diary entry for August 9, 1865, John H. Cook Papers, Wisconsin Historical Society, Madison, Wisconsin.

53. Husby and Wittenberg, 24 and 87.

54. Bassett, 23.

55. Brobst Papers, letter to friend dated March 27, 1864.

56. William C. Harris, *In the Country of the Enemy: The Civil War Reports of a Massachusetts Corporal* (Gainesville: University of Florida Press, 1999), 52.

57. Buckingham, 17–18.

58. James Simpson, letter to friend dated October 29, 1863, James R. Simpson Papers, Civil War Miscellaneous Collection, United States Army Military History Institute, Carlisle, Pennsylvania.

59. Naomi B. Baker, *Letters Home: Joel B. Baker, A Collection of "Letters Home" from the Civil War* (Delevan, NY: N.B. Baker, 1996), 49.

60. Mannis and Wilson, 8.

61. Lilley Papers, letter to sister dated July 11, 1861.

62. Hughes, 111.

63. Croushore, 79.

64. Haydon Papers, diary entry for November 7, 1861.

65. Knox Mellon, "Letters of James Greenalch," *Michigan History*, vol. 44 (June 1960): 193.

66. Baker, 49.

67. Mowen Papers, diary entry for May 23, 1863.

68. Malles, 40–41.

69. See Ella Lonn, *Desertion during the Civil War* (Gloucester, MA: Peter Smith, 1966), 127–144.

70. Dunkelman, 88.

71. ORA, series I, vol. 25, 78.

72. Harwell, 50.

73. Noe, 47.

74. Washington, 47.

75. Dorothy S. Cannell, "Facing Court-Martial," *Michigan History*, vol. 82, no. 4 (July/August 1998): 86.

76. Solomon Hamrick, letter to father dated February 12, 1862, Solomon S. Hamrick Papers, Indiana Historical Society, Indianapolis, Indiana.

77. NARA, RG 110: Records of the Provost Marshal General's Office, Entry 2253: Descriptive Book of Deserters (New York 28th and 29th Districts), 34.

78. NARA, RG 110: Records of the Provost Marshal General's Office, Entry 3853: Arrested Deserters (District of Columbia), 7.

79. Simeon Royse, letter to father dated February 14, 1863, Royse Family Papers, Perkins Library, Duke University,, Durham, North Carolina.

80. George Sinclair, letter to wife dated January6, 1863, George B. Sinclair Papers, Civil War Miscellaneous Collection, United States Army Military History Institute, Carlisle, Pennsylvania.

81. James Decker, letter to sister dated February 15, 1863, James E. Decker Papers, Fredericksburg and Spotsylvania National Military Park, National Park Service, Fredericksburg, Virginia.

82. Lewis, 71.

83. Patrick Papers, diary entry for January 11 and 16, 1863.

84. Albert Sprague, letter to wife dated January 25, 1863, Albert G. Sprague Papers, Chicago Historical Society, Chicago, Illinois.

85. Lewis, 69.

86. Lesley J. Gordon, *I Never Was a Coward: Questions of Bravery in a Civil War Regiment* (Milwaukee: Marquette University Press, 2005), 19.

87. Philadelphia *Christian Recorder*, February 18, 1864.

88. NARA, RG 110: Records of the Provost Marshal General's Office, Entry 770: Descriptive Book of Deserters (Vermont).

89. NARA, RG 110: Records of the Provost Marshal General's Office, Entry 770: Descriptive Book of Deserters (Vermont).

90. United States Army, 6th New York Artillery, Company D Deserter Roll, Virginia Historical Society, Richmond, Virginia.

91. Welsh Papers, letter to wife dated October 23, 1862.

92. Squier Papers, letter to wife dated January 20, 1863.

93. Thomas E. Pope, *The Weary Boys: Colonel J. Warren Keifer and the 110th Ohio Volunteer Infantry* (Kent, OH: Kent State University Press, 2002), 28.

94. Lewis, 66.

95. Kent, 81.

96. NARA. RG 110: Records of the Provost Marshal General's Office, Entry 2253:

Descriptive Book of Arrested Deserters (New York 28th and 29th Districts), 1. Entry 1100: Descriptive Book of Deserters (Connecticut), 54.

97. Voorhis, 75.

98. Hedrick and Davis, 106.

99. Fisk Papers, diary entry for April 15, 1864.

100. Dodge Papers, diary entry for June 7, 1862.

101. Lande, 18.

102. John Bates, diary entry for June 18, 1865, John W. Bates Papers, Civil War Miscellaneous Collection, United States Army Military History Institute, Carlisle, Pennsylvania.

103. John Dunbar, letter to sister dated February 1, 1863, John M. Dunbar Papers, Fredericksburg and Spotsylvania National Military Park, National Park Service, Fredericksburg, Virginia.

104. Henry F. W. Little, *The Seventh Regiment New Hampshire Volunteers in the War of the Rebellion* (Concord, NH: Ira Evans, 1896), 191.

105. George Hand, diary entry for September 7, 1862, George O. Hand Papers, Library of Congress (Manuscript Division), Washington, DC.

106. Charles F. Morse, *Letters Written during the Civil War, 1861–1865* (privately printed, 1898), 122.

107. New York *Herald*, September 11, 1861.

108. Johnson, 513–514.

109. Reid and White, 69.

110. Wilkinson, 35.

111. Parson, 50.

112. Herek, 75.

113. D. Alexander Brown, *The Galvanized Yankees* (Urbana: University of Illinois Press, 1963), 123.

114. James M. Greiner, *Subdued by the Sword: A Line Officer in the 121st New York Volunteers* (Albany, NY: SUNY Press, 2003), 17.

115. Miller, 165.

116. Donald, 198.

117. Sullivan Green, diary entry for February 1, 1863, Sullivan D. Green Papers, Wisconsin Historical Society, Madison, Wisconsin.

118. Jordan, *Red Diamond Regiment*, 38.

119. Wyman White, "The Civil War Diary of Wyman S. White," 66, Fredericksburg and Spotsylvania National Military Park, National Park Service, Fredericksburg, Virginia.

120. The exact number paroled by Grant at Vicksburg was 28,892 officers and men. Another 709 men who refused to sign a parole became prisoners of war in Northern camps. Henry C. Adams, *Indiana at Vicksburg* (Indianapolis, IN: State Printing and Binding, 1910), 195.

121. William B. Hesseltine, *Civil War Prisons* (Columbus: Ohio State University Press, 1930), 74.

122. McCordick, 34 and 57.

123. Catton, *Glory Road*, 99.

124. Lewis, 109.

125. Robert I. Alotta, *Stop the Evil: A Civil War History of Desertion and Murder* (San Rafael, CA: Presidio Press, 1978), 81.

126. Michael E. Stevens, *As if It Were Glory: Robert Beecham's Civil War from the Iron Brigade to the Black Regiments* (Madison, WI: Madison House, 1998), 174.

127. NARA. RG 110: Records of the Provost Marshal General's Office, Entry 1100: Descriptive Book of Deserters (Connecticut), 59–61 and 98–99.

128. Bacarella, 78.

129. Wightman Papers, letter to brother dated June 6, 1863.

130. Henry Charles, "Civil War Record," 5.

131. Sneden Papers, diary entry for January 1, 1862.

132. George Jones, letter to friends dated December 27, 1862, George M. Jones Papers, Fredericksburg and Spotsylvania National Military Park, National Park Service, Fredericksburg, Virginia.

133. Menge and Shirak, 4.

134. Robertson, 135.

135. Arnold M. Shankman, *The Pennsylvania Antiwar Movement, 1861–1865* (Rutherford, NJ: Fairleigh Dickinson University Press, 1980), 142.

136. ORA, series I, vol. 34, 233.

137. ORA, series I, vol. 25, 73.

138. Billings, 161.

139. Husby and Wittenberg, 155.

140. Louisville *Daily Democrat*, January 14, 1863.

141. NARA, RG 110: Records of the Provost Marshal General's Office, Entry 3853: Arrested Deserters (Washington DC), 6.

142. Francis Hall, diary entry for January 22, 1863, Frances B. Hall Papers, Fredericksburg and Spotsylvania National Military Park, National Park Service, Fredericksburg, Virginia.

143. Sarah Sleeper, letter to mother dated July 20, 1863, Sarah Sleeper Papers, Abraham Lincoln Presidential Library, Springfield, Illinois.

144. United States Congress. *United States Statues at Large, 1862–1863* (Washington, DC: Government Printing Office, 1863), chapter 75, section 24.

145. Trevor K. Plante, "The Shady Side of the Family Tree: Civil War Union Court-Martial Case Files," *Prologue*, vol. 30, no. 4 (Winter 1998): 24.

146. Patrick Papers, diary entry for January, 1865.

147. Pride and Travis, 219–220.

148. Gaff, 410.

149. Hughes, 216.

150. ORA, series III, vol. 2, 146.

151. New York *Sunday Mercury*, February 10, 1864.

152. Palladino, 203.

153. Smith and Baker, 117.

154. Barber and Swinson, 69.

155. Dunkelman, 56.

156. ORA, series I, vol. 25, 10–12.

157. Brewster Papers, letter to wife dated February 21, 1863.

158. David M. Jordan, *Happiness Is Not My Companion: The Life of General G.K. Warren* (Bloomington: Indiana University Press, 2001), 66.

159. *Elmira* (New York) *Advertiser*, March 7, 1863.

160. Dodge Papers, diary entry for February 25, 1863.

161. Dunbar Papers, letter to sister dated December 28, 1863.

162. ORA, series I, vol. 19, 111.

163. Johnson, 514.

164. Herek, 266–267.

165. Jones, 127.

166. James Durkin and Jennifer M. Whitcomb, *This War Is an Awful Thing: Civil War Letters of the National Guards: The 19th and 90th Pennsylvania Volunteers* (Glenside, PA: Santarelli, 1994), 87–89.

167. Brian H. Reid and John White, "A Mob of Stragglers and Cowards: Desertion from the Union and Confederate Armies, 1861–1865," *Journal of Strategic Studies*, vol. 8 (March 1985): 68.

168. Welsh Papers, letter to wife dated September 19, 1863.

169. Matthews, 30–32.

170. Kelly and Kelly, 58.

171. Roger Tusken, "In the Bastile of the Rebels," *Journal of the Illinois State Historical Society*, vol. 56 (Summer 1963): 320–321.

172. Steven E. Woodworth, *The Musick of the Mocking Birds, the Roar of the Cannon: The Civil War Diary and Letters of William Winters* (Lincoln: University of Nebraska Press, 1998), 25.

173. Parson, 102–104.

174. Jonathan T. Dorris, *Pardon and Amnesty under Lincoln and Johnson* (Chapel Hill: University of North Carolina Press, 1953), 63–64. ORA, series I, vol. 42, 555–556.

175. Jennifer C. Bohrnstedt, *Soldiering with Sherman: Civil War Letters of George F. Cram* (DeKalb: Northern Illinois University Press, 2000), 40.

176. Lonn, 161.

177. Pride and Travis, 254.

178. Gould and Kennedy, 50–51.

179. Palladino, 122.

180. Sylvanus Cadwallader, *Three Years with Grant, As Recalled By War Correspondent Sylvanus Cadwallader* (New York: Knopf, 1955), 246.

181. Smith and Baker, 135.

182. Frederick Trautmann, *"We Were the Ninth": A History of the Ninth Regiment, Ohio Volunteer Infantry, April 17, 1861 to June 7, 1864* (Kent, OH: Kent State University Press, 1987), 118.

183. Henry F. Charles, "Civil War Record," 5.

184. Carmony, "Bartmess Letters," 60–61.

185. Robert A. Taylor, *A Pennsylvanian in Blue: The Civil War Diary of Thomas Beck Walton* (Shippensburg, PA: Burd Street Press, 1995), 23. Eric J. Wittenberg, *We Have It Damn Hard Out Here: The Civil War Letters of Sergeant Thomas W. Smith, 6th Pennsylvania Cavalry* (Kent, OH: Kent State University Press, 1999), 75.

186. Edward J. Hagerty, *Collis' Zouaves: The 114th Pennsylvania Volunteers in the Civil War* (Baton Rouge: Louisiana State University Press, 1997), 131.

187. Salvatore G. Cilella, "The 121st New York State Infantry Regiment, 1862–1865," (M.A. thesis, State University of New York College at Oneonta, 1972), 180.

188. NARA, RG153: Records of the Provost Marshal General's Office, File OO132.

189. Rowell, *Yankee Artillerymen*, 24.

190. Miller Papers, letter to wife dated October 9, 1862.

191. Joseph Baer, letter to wife dated December 31, 1863, Joseph Baer Papers, Special Collections Library, University of Virginia, Charlottesville, Virginia. The Rip Raps was a small man-made island at the entrance to Hampton Roads, Virginia, covered by Fort Calhoun (renamed Fort Wool after the Civil War). The fort provided security for the harbor, but the massive tidal flow in and out of the harbor constantly eroded the island, requiring continuous maintenance.

192. Lonn, 160.

193. Herek, 60.

194. Lonn, 167.

195. Ruth Currie-McDaniel, *Carpetbagger of Conscience: A Biography of John Emory Bryant* (New York: Fordham University Press, 1999), 40.

196. Cilella, 10.

197. Matthews, 34. Alotta, 81.

198. Wightman Papers, letter to brother dated November 28, 1864. Lonn, 163.

199. Hagerty, 100.

200. Herek, 60.

201. Starr, 127.

202. Patrick Papers, diary entries for January 31 and September 26, 1863.

203. Lonn, 176.

204. Charles Cox, letter to his sister dated December 5, 1862, Charles H. Cox Papers,

Manuscripts, Archives and Rare Book Library, Emory University, Atlanta, Georgia.

205. Kent, 253.

206. Harold A. Small, *The Road to Richmond: The Civil War Memoirs of Maj. Abner R. Small of the 16th Maine Vols., With His Diary as a Prisoner of War* (Berkeley: University of California Press, 1959), 113.

207. NARA, RG 110: Records of the Provost Marshal General's Office, Entry 6567: Special Order Issued (District of Nebraska), 2.

208. NARA, RG153: Records of the Judge Advocate General, file number II647.

209. NARA, RG 110: Records of the Provost Marshal General's Office, Entry 1100: Descriptive Book of Deserters (Connecticut), 11 and 37.

210. Rufus Kinsley, diary entry for December 20, 1862, Rufus Kinsley Papers, Vermont Historical Society, Leahy Library, Barre, Vermont.

211. NARA, RG 110: Records of the Provost Marshal General's Office, Entry 5590: Descriptive Book of Arrested Deserters (Illinois), entries 583 and 691.

212. NARA, RG 110: Records of the Provost Marshal General's Office, Entry 771: Descriptive Book of Deserters (Vermont), entries number 20 and number 52. Entry 5590: Descriptive Book of Arrested Deserters (Illinois).

213. ORA, series I, vol. 48, 73.

214. Voris Papers, letter to wife dated March 23, 1863.

215. Fred Pelka, *The Civil War Letters of Colonel Charles F. Johnson, Invalid Corps* (Amherst: University of Massachusetts Press, 2004), 11–13. Geoffrey Perret, *Lincoln's War: The Untold Story of America's Greatest President as Commander in Chief* (New York: Random House 2004), 289. Physically fit veterans who had completed their terms of service in the army could also enlist in the Veteran Reserve Corps.

216. ORA, series III, vol. 5, 543–567.

217. Lonn, 177.

218. Paula A. Cimbala and Randall M. Miller, *Union Soldiers and the Northern Home Front: Wartime Experiences, Postwar Adjustments* (New York: Fordham University Press, 2002), 197.

219. William F. Zornow, "Lincoln and Private Lennan," *Indiana Magazine of History*, vol. 44, no. 3 (September 1953): 267.

220. William W. Hummel, "The Military Occupation of Columbia County," *Pennsylvania Magazine of History*, vol. 80, no. 3 (July 1956): 329.

221. Lande, 51.

222. Donald, 240.

223. Hagerty, 103.

224. Lonn, 176.

225. ORA, series III, vol. 2, 286–287.

226. ORA, series III, vol. 2, 286–287.

227. NARA. RG 110: Records of the Provost Marshal General's Office. Entry 3853: Descriptive Book of Arrested Deserters (District of Columbia), 21. Entry 1870: Descriptive List of Arrested Deserters (New York 13th District), 3–4.

228. ORA, series I, vol. 42, 1086.

229. NARA. RG 110: Records of the Provost Marshal General's Office. Entry 675: Descriptive Book of Deserters and Other Persons Arrested (New Hampshire).

230. Lonn, 220–221.

231. NARA, Record Group 393: Records of the United States Army Continental Commands, William Truesdail, letter to William Rosecrans dated February 16, 1863.

232. NARA, RG 110: Records of the Provost Marshal's Office, Entry 6073: Descriptive Book of Deserters (Michigan). Ella Lonn's study of deserters cites a number of "15,000 or 16,000 in Canada, Mexico, and abroad," but does not discern between deserters from the ranks and refugees from the draft. Lonn, 203.

233. Herek, 87.

234. Dunkelman, 87.

235. ORA, series III, vol. 2, 321–322 and 329.

236. Herek, 21.

237. NARA, RG 110: Records of the Provost Marshal General's Office, Entry 6073: Descriptive Book of Deserters (Michigan).

238. NARA, RG 110: Records of the Provost Marshal General's Office, Henry Bans, letter to Edwin Stanton dated July 10, 1863. Murdock, 53.

239. *Statutes of the United States, 1862–1863* (Washington, DC: Government Printing Office, 1863), Chapter 75, Section 21, 26.

240. Samito, 223.

241. In his book *Civil War Justice*, Robert Alotta demonstrates that the official number of 267 executions in the Union Army is undoubtedly incorrect, and he identifies a number of executions missing from the official list. My research, in turn, has discovered executions that Alotta overlooked. Because of the loose nature of Civil War records keeping, the true numbers of executions will most likely never be known.

242. Rowell, 18–19.

243. Johnson, 316–317.

244. Dunkelman, 224–225.

245. Holcomb, 48.

246. Paradis, 51–52.

247. Haydon Papers, diary entry for August 14, 1861.

248. William McCutcheon, letter to James Cole dated March 9, 1862, James M. Cole Papers, Illinois State Historical Library, Springfield, IL.

249. Mary A. Livermore, *My Story of the War: The Civil War Memoirs of the Famous Nurse, Relief Organizer, and Suffragette* (New York: DaCapo, 1995), 559.

250. Gaff, 222, 319, and 409.

251. Britton and Reed, 382.

252. Gibbs, 212.

253. Parson, 147.

254. Patrick Papers, diary entry for March 9, 1865.

255. Nancy N. Baxter, *Gallant Fourteenth: The Story of an Indiana Civil War Regiment* (Cincinnati, OH: Emmis Books, 1999), 41.

256. ORA, series III, vol. 2, 527.

257. ORA, series I, vol. 25, 149, and series III, vol. III, 60–61.

258. James H. Stine, *History of the Army of the Potomac* (Washington, DC: Gibbons Brothers, 1893), 312. Wayne C. Temple, "The Civil War Letters of Henry C. Bear: A Soldier in the 116th Illinois Volunteer Infantry, Part III," *Lincoln Herald*, vol. 63 (Spring 1961): 8.

259. Matthews, 49.

260. Trautmann, 125.

261. Britton and Reed, 176.

262. Fisk Papers, diary entry for February 25, 1863.

263. Gaff, 227.

264. Parson, 35.

265. McCordick, 26.

266. Gibbs, 237.

267. Gould and Kennedy, 155–156.

268. NARA, RG153: Records of the Judge Advocate General's Office, File NN1887.

269. Herek, 20.

270. Haydon Papers, diary entry for May 6, 1861.

271. Throne, 326.

272. Lonn, 175.

273. Stevens, 173.

274. Holahan Papers, diary entry for February 27, 1863.

275. Michael T. Smith, "The Most Desperate Scoundrels Unhung: Bounty Jumpers and

Recruitment Fraud in the Civil War North," *American Nineteenth Century History*, vol. 6, no. 2 (June 2005): 159–165.

276. Edward K. Spann, *Gotham at War: New York City, 1860–1865* (Wilmington, DE: Scholarly Resources, 2002), 183. ORA, series III, vol. 4, 1231.

277. Reid and White, 75.

278. Murdock, 85.

279. Hartford *Daily Courant*, February 25, 1865.

280. New York *Tribune*, January 2, 1865.

281. Matthews, 214.

282. Lewis, 23.

283. Robertson, 39.

284. Zornow, 268–269.

285. Jones, 131–132.

286. NARA, RG 110: Records of the Provost Marshal General's Office, Entry 3853: List of Arrested Deserters (Washington, DC), 12.

287. Small, 38.

288. Eugene C. Murdock, *Patriotism Limited: The Civil War Draft and the Bounty System* (Kent, OH: Kent State University Press, 1967), 91.

289. Robert H. Rhodes, *All for the Union: The Civil War Diary and Letters of Elisha Hunt Rhodes* (New York: Vintage Books, 1985), 198.

290. Frederick M. Osborne, *Private Osborn, Massachusetts 23rd Volunteers: Burnside Expedition, Roanoke Island, Second Front Against Richmond* (Jefferson, NC: McFarland, 1999), 169.

291. Beaudry, 119.

292. Elmira, NY, *Daily Advertiser*, February 13, 1865.

293. Smith Letterbook, letter to mother dated August 14, 1863.

294. Herek, 62.

295. Jordan, *Red Diamond Regiment*, 89.

296. Baker, 103.

297. Murdock, 87–88.

298. Durkin, 131.

299. Frank Wilkeson, *Recollections of a Private Soldier in the Army of the Potomac* (New York: G.P. Putnum's Sons, 1887), 13.

300. Holahan Papers, diary entry for February 29, 1864.

7—"Descend to the level of the barbarians"

1. J. Brit McCarly, "Feeding Billy Yank: Union Rations between 1861 and 1865," *Quartermaster Professional Bulletin* (December 1988), http://www.qmfound.com/feeding_billy_yank.htm.

2. James Abraham, "Civil War Letters," 3, Abraham Papers, Historical Society of Pennsylvania, Philadelphia, Pennsylvania.

3. Cornelius Courtright, diary entry for October 21, 1864, Cornelius Courtright Papers. James Sinclair, diary entry for May 3, 1865, James C. Sinclair Papers, Chicago Historical Society, Chicago, Illinois.

4. Frederick Pell, diary entry for February 28, 1865, Frederick Pell Papers, Chicago Historical Society, Chicago, Illinois.

5. Jordan, *Red Diamond Regiment*, 111.

6. Winschel, 74.

7. Ida B. Adams, "The Civil War Letters of James Rush Holmes," *Western Pennsylvania Historical Magazine*, vol. 44, no. 2 (June 1961): 110.

8. Charles W. Bardeen, *A Little Fifer's War Diary* (Syracuse, NY: self-published, 1910), 47.

9. Lewis Luckenbill, diary entry for May 20, 1863, Lewis Luckenbill Papers, Fredericksburg and Spotsylvania National Military Park, National Park Service, Fredericksburg, Virginia.

10. White, 22–23.

11. John Bates, diary entry for June 21, 1865, John W. Bates Papers, Civil War Miscellaneous Collection, United States Arm Military History Institute, Carlisle, Pennsylvania.

12. Franklin Horner, diary entry for August 29, 1863, Franklin Horner Papers, United States Army Military History Institute, Carlisle, Pennsylvania.

13. Boyts Papers, diary entry for February 21, 1863.

14. George Hitchcock, diary entry for January 23, 1865, George A. Hitchcock Papers, Fredericksburg and Spotsylvania National Military Park, National Park Service, Fredericksburg, Virginia.

15. Palladino, 202.

16. Charles Curtiss, diary entry for August 3, 1864, Charles C. Curtiss Papers, Chicago Historical Society, Chicago, Illinois.

17. Evan Gery, diary entries for January 7, March 3, March 27, April 2, and May 20, 1863, Fredericksburg and Spotsylvania National Military Park, National Park Service, Fredericksburg, Virginia.

18. Mottram Papers, diary entry for January 4, 1865.

19. White Papers, diary entry for January 8, 1865.

20. Smith Letterbook, letter dared December 9, 1862.

21. Patrick Papers, diary entry for September 18, 1864.

22. Overmyer, 50–51.

23. McKnight, 86.

24. Kellogg, 120–121.

25. Haydon Papers, diary entry for June 13, 1861.

26. Smith, 92.

27. Hughes, 182.

28. Dix, 76.

29. Smith Papers, letter to mother dated November 25, 1863. Adams, 113. Amos Abbott, diary entry for July 5, 1862, Amos S. Abbott Papers, Civil War Miscellaneous Collection, United States Army Military History Institute, Carlisle, Pennsylvania. McCordick, 104.

30. Smith and Baker, 144–145. By the end of the war, inflation had rendered Confederate currency worthless, even to the Confederates.

31. Buckingham, 140.

32. Charles E. Benton, *As Seen in the Ranks: A Boy in the Civil War* (New York: Putnam & Sons, 1902), 167.

33. Charles Woolhizer, letter to brother dated November 20, 1862, Fredericksburg and Spotsylvania National Military Park, National Park Service, Fredericksburg, Virginia.

34. Willison, 166.

35. Wightman Papers, letter to brother dated September 27, 1862.

36. Smith Letterbook, letters to mother dated August 6, 1863 and August 21, 1864.

37. Smith Papers, letter to mother dated June 18, 1864.

38. William Landon, "Last Letters to the *Vincennes Sun*," *Indiana Magazine of History*, vol. 35, no. 1 (March 1935): 76–94.

39. NARA, RG 110: Records of the Provost Marshal General, Entry 3853: Descriptive Book of Arrested Deserters, District of Columbia, July 1863–July 1865, 14.

40. Fisk Papers, diary entry for August 18, 1863.

41. White, "The Civil War Diary of Wyman S. White," 140, Fredericksburg and Spotsylvania National Military Park, National Park Service, Fredericksburg, Virginia.

42. Holahan Papers, diary entry for May 16, 1861.

43. Jonathan Stowe, diary entry for December 15, 1861, Jonathan P. Stowe Papers, Civil War Times Illustrated Collection, United States Army Military History Institute, Carlisle, Pennsylvania.

44. Mottram Papers, front cover of diary.

45. Kevin C. Murphy, *The Civil War Letters of Joseph K. Taylor of the Thirty-seventh Massachusetts Volunteer Infantry* (Lewiston, ON: Edwin Mellen Press, 1998), 186.

46. Engert, 54.

47. John Withrow, letter to sister dated March 27, 1863, John D. Withrow Papers, Fredericksburg and Spotsylvania National Military Park, National Park Service, Fredericksburg, Virginia.

48. Elmore Day, letter to parents dated January 27, 1862, Elmore Day Papers, Chicago Historical Society, Chicago, Illinois.

49. James Ames, letter to father dated January 4, 1863, James A. Ames Papers, Civil War Miscellaneous Collection, United States Army Military History Institute, Carlisle, Pennsylvania.

50. Welsh Papers, letter to wife dated January 29, 1864.

51. Patrick Papers, diary entry for July 5, 1863.

52. Bond, 19.

53. Noe, 138.

54. Kathleen Kroll and Charles Moran, "The White Papers," *Massachusetts Review*, vol. 18 (Summer 1976): 260.

55. Bassett, 32–33.

56. Smith Papers, letter to mother dated July 26, 1863.

57. Ames Papers, letter to mother dated January 12, 1863.

58. New York *Tribune*, March 24, 1862.

59. David Ashley, letter to parents dated May 17, 1862, David C. Ashley Papers, Civil War Miscellaneous Collection, United States Army Military History Institute, Carlisle, Pennsylvania.

60. Dunn Papers, letter wife dated August 15, 1862.

61. Bacarella, 160–161.

62. Kellogg, 123.

63. Hedrick and Davis, 18.

64. Dodge Papers, diary entry for April 23, 1863. Winschel, 92.

65. Gould and Kennedy, 203.

66. Murray, 165.

67. NARA, RG153: Records of the Judge Advocate General, file number KK646.

68. Avery Papers, letter to wife dated May 30, 1863.

69. NARA, RG153: Records of the Judge Advocate General, file number OO724.

70. Samuel J. Martin. *Kill-Cavalry: The Life of Union General Hugh Judson Kilpatrick* (Mechanicsburg, PA Stackpole Books, 2000), 57.

71. Jones, 52.

72. Lon Carter Barton, "The Reign of Terror in Graves County," *Register of the Kentucky Historical Society*, vol. 46 (April 1948): 491–492.

73. Lowell H. Harrison, *Lincoln of Kentucky* (Lexington: University of Kentucky Press, 2000), 206–207.

74. War Department, *General Orders of the War Department, Embracing the Years 1861, 1862, and 1863* (New York: Derby & Miller, 1864), 185–190.

75. Bacarella, 131.

76. Scott, 306–309.

77. Stephen D. Engle, *Don Carlos Buell: Most Promising of All* (Chapel Hill: University of North Carolina Press, 1999), 79.

78. Grimsley, 21–22. Grimsley's *The Hard Hand of War* also offers an excellent discussion of the definition of "total war," which Grimsley convincingly argues does not apply to the Civil War.

79. Gibbs, 59.

80. Ethan S. Rafuse, *McClellan's War: The Failure of Moderation in the Struggle for the Union* (Bloomington: Indiana University Press, 2005), 371–372.

81. Grimsley, 158–160.

82. ORA, series I, vol. 12, 50.

83. Mannis and Wilson, 28.

84. Kent, 60.

85. Smith, 82.

86. Silliker, 259.

87. Wightman Papers, letter to brother dated February 2, 1863.

88. Smith Letterbook, letter to mother dated December 26, 1862.

89. Gerald J. Prokopowicz, *All for the Regiment: The Army of the Ohio, 1861–1862* (Chapel Hill: University of North Carolina Press, 2001), 122.

90. Starr, 350.

91. Ambrose, 31.

92. Fisk Papers, diary entry for April 19, 1863.

93. Williston, 102–103.

94. Smith and Baker, 145.

95. Julius Murray, letter to family dated March 17, 1862, Julius Murray Papers, Wisconsin Historical Society, Madison, Wisconsin.

96. Susan T. Puck, *Sacrifice at Vicksburg: Letters from the Front* (Shippensburg, PA: Burd Street Press, 1997), 44.

97. Trautmann, 82.

98. Coffin, 150–151.

99. Ferguson Papers, diary entry for February 4, 1865.

100. Smith and Baker, 142.

101. Rochester, Indiana *Chronicle*, February 26, 1863.

102. Smith Letterbook, letter to mother dated September 4, 1864.

103. Holcomb, 49–50.

104. Clara Dunlap, letter to sister dated July 24, 1864, Fred J. Herring Collection, Arkansas History Commission & State Archives, Little Rock, Arkansas.

105. D. F. Fleharty, *Our Regiment: A History of the 102nd Illinois Infantry Volunteers* (Chicago: Brewster & Hanscom, 1865), 122.

106. Bruce Catton, *Grant Moves South* (Edison, NJ: Castle Books, 2000), 335–336.

107. Wightman Papers, letter to brother dated September 29, 1862.

108. Brobst Papers, letter to friend dated February 7, 1864.

109. Gaff, 252.

110. Brown, *Soldier's Life*, 58–59.

111. Brobst Papers, letter to friend dated April 28, 1864.

112. Brown, *Soldier's Life*, 58.

113. Ferguson Papers, diary entry for January 15, 1865.

114. Holcomb, 86.

115. Dodge Papers, diary entry for May 4, 1863.

116. Kelly and Kelly, 143.

117. Sneden Papers, diary entry for December 3, 1861.

118. Britton and Reed, 136.

119. Thomas H. O'Connor, "Lincoln and the Cotton Trade," *Civil War History* volume 7, no. 1 (1961): 20–29.

120. Richard H. Abbott, *Cotton & Capital: Boston Business Men and Anti-Slavery Reform, 1854–1868* (Amherst: University of Massachusetts Press, 1991), 72–93.

121. United States Congress, "Report of the Joint Committee on the Conduct of the War at the Second Session, Thirty-eighth Congress, Red River Expedition" (Washington, DC: Government Printing Office, 1865), 81.

122. Winschel, 96.

123. William O. Rogers, "Cotton and Clover Hill, " *Civil War Times Illustrated*, vol. 14 (August 1975): 20–23.

124. Voorhis, 109.

125. Catton, *Glory Road*, 65.

126. Oliver W. Norton, *Army Letters, 1861–1865* (Chicago: O.L. Deming, 1903), 130.

127. Smith Letterbook, letter to mother dated December 28, 1862.

128. Curtis Pollack, letter to mother dated December 18, 1862, Curtis C. Pollock Papers, Civil War Miscellaneous Collection, United States Army Military History Institute, Carlisle, Pennsylvania.

129. Hedrick and Davis, 38.

130. Nye, 58.

131. Dennis K. Boman, "Conduct and Revolt in the Twenty-fifth Ohio Battery: An Insider's Account," *Ohio History*, vol. 104 (Summer/Autumn 1995): 174.

132. Winschel, 26.

133. Ferguson Papers, diary entry for May 18, 1864.

134. Raup, 23. William T. Lusk, *War Letters of William Thompson Lusk* (New York: privately printed, 1911), 52.

135. Britton and Reed, 113.

136. Dodge Papers, diary entry for June 22, 1863.

137. Carmony, *Apacheland*, 82. Viola, 152.

138. Alan T. Nolan, *A Full Blown Yankee in the Iron Brigade: Service with the Sixth Wisconsin Volunteers* (Lincoln: University of Nebraska Press, 1999), 107.

139. Winschel, 81.

140. William B. Westervelt, *Lights and Shadows of Army Life: As Seen by a Private Soldier* (Marlboro, NY: C.B. Cochrane, 1886), 2.

141. Husby and Wittenberg, 87.

142. Wightman Papers, letter to brother dated September 29, 1862.

143. Dunkelman, 184–185.

144. Noe, 89.

145. Eby, 168.

146. Danbury [Connecticut] *Times*, April 17, 1862.

147. Smith, 86.

148. Henry Sherman, diary entry for May 6, 1863. Henry S. Sherman Papers, Princeton University,, Princeton, New Jersey.

149. Bond, 15.

150. Thomas Bennett, letter to sister dated March 28, 1863, Thomas G. Bennett Papers, Civil War Miscellaneous Collection, United States Army Military History Institute, Carlisle, Pennsylvania.

151. Dunn Papers, letter to wife dated July 26, 1862.

152. Laurinan Russell, letter to daughter dated October 4, 1861, Laurinan H. Russell Papers, Perkins Library (Manuscript Collection), Duke University, Durham, North Carolina.

153. John Bates, diary entry for January 14, 1864, John W. Bates Papers, United States Army Military History Institute, Carlisle, Pennsylvania.

154. Follmer Papers, diary entry for April 30, 1863.

155. Silliker, 46 and 161.

156. Gaff, 302–303.

157. Smith Letterbook, letter to mother dated January 24, 1864.

158. James Denver, letter to wife dated November 29, 1862, James W. Denver Papers, Harrisonburg Civil War Roundtable Collection, United States Army Military History Institute, Carlisle, Pennsylvania.

159. Malles, 170.

160. Eby, 9.

161. NARA, RG153: Records of the Judge Advocate General, file number KK808.

162. Ibid., file number KK646.

163. ORA, series I, vol. 26, 763.

164. Starr, 188–189.

165. Haydon Papers, diary entry for December 29, 1861.

166. Dunkelman, 221.

167. Mowen Papers, diary entry for October 13, 1862.

168. Haydon Papers, diary entry for January 10, 1862. James Sinclair, diary entries for November 30 and December 1, 1862, James C. Sinclair Papers, Chicago Historical Society, Chicago, Illinois.

169. Catton, *Grant Moves South*, 336.

170. Coffin, 149.

171. Winschel, 18.

172. Ambrose, 31.

173. Dodge Papers, diary entry for July 3, 1862.

174. Raup, 24.

175. Patrick Papers, diary entry for July 22, 1863.

176. Eby, 48 and 169.

177. Brown, *Soldier's Life*, 112.

178. Starr, 108–109.

179. Adin B. Underwood, *Three Years' Service of the Thirty-third Mass. Infantry Regiment 1862–1865* (Boston: A. Williams, 1881), 244.

180. Kent, 122–123.

181. Otis, 63.

182. Kellogg, 134.

183. Viola, 74–75.

184. Coffin, 151.

185. H.V. Redfield, "Characteristics of the Armies," in *The Annals of War: Written by Leading Participants, North and South* (Philadelphia: Times, 1879), 363.

186. Ferguson Papers, diary entry for February 12, 1865.

187. Husby and Wittenberg, 127.

188. John L. Heatwole, *The Burning: Sheridan in the Shenandoah Valley* (Charlottesville, VA: Rockbridge, 1998), 210–211.

189. Coffin, 149–150.

190. Glatthaar, 128.

191. Frank Moore and Edward Everett, *The Rebellion Record: A Diary of American Events*, vol. 11 (New York: Van Nostrand, 1868), 387.

192. Kellogg, 37–38.

193. Menge and Shimrak, 4.

194. Chadwick, 269.

195. Bacarella, 122–124.

196. Harwell, 85.

197. War Department, *Revised Regulations for the Army of the United States, 1861* (Philadelphia: J.G.L. Brown, 1861), 504–505.

198. Bacarella, 112.

199. NARA, RG153: Records of the Judge Advocate General, file numberOO186.

200. Ibid., file number NN3594.

201. Ibid., file number NN809.

202. Ibid., file number II538.

203. Haydon Papers, diary entry for January 10, 1862.

204. Patrick Papers, diary entry for September 22, 1864.

205. NARA: RG153: Records of the Judge Advocate General, File number II647.

206. Ibid., file number NN2933.

207. NARA, RG 94: Records of the Adjutant's General's Office, Army of the Potomac, General Orders number 38, March 31, 1863.

208. Pollock Papers, letter to mother dated June 8, 1863.

209. For a discussion of the problems of running civilian courts in occupied areas of the Confederacy, see Elisabeth J. Doyle, "New Orleans Courts under Military Occupation, 1861–1865," *Mid-America: A Historical Review*, vol. 42, no. 2 (July 1960): 185–192.

210. Gould and Kennedy, 130–131.

211. NARA, RG153: Records of the Judge Advocate General, file number OO136.

212. For a full account of the events, see E.L. Jordan, "A Painful Case: The Wright-Sanborn Incident in Norfolk, Virginia, July-October 1863." M.A. thesis, Old Dominion University, 1979. For a description of Wright's execution, see Henry F. Gladdings, letter to mother dated October 26, 1863, Virginia Historical Society, Richmond, Virginia.

213. Dodge Papers, diary entry for June 23, 1863.

214. Kellogg, 55.

215. New York *World*, September 12, 1861.

216. Arthur Corwin, letter to parents dated September 20, 1861, Arthur Corwin Papers, Civil War Miscellaneous Collection, United States Army Military History Institute, Carlisle, Pennsylvania.

217. David Helmick, letter to family dated March 25, 1862, David Helmick Papers, Civil War Miscellaneous Collection, United States Army Military History Institute, Carlisle, Pennsylvania.

218. Glatthaar, 73.

219. NARA, RG153: Records of the Judge Advocate General, file number NN3029.

220. Ibid., file number II524.

221. Jack K. Overmyer, *A Stupendous Effort: The 87th Indiana in the War of the Rebellion* (Bloomington: Indiana University Press, 1997), 30–31.

222. Wightman Papers, letter to brother dated April 13, 1863. Eight months after the incident, Corcoran died when his horse stumbled and rolled over him, crushing his skull.

223. New York *Sunday Mercury*, January 5 and April 5, 1863.

224. Daniel Bruce, diary entry for November 29, 1862, Daniel E. Bruce Papers, Indiana State Library, Indianapolis, Indiana.

225. Tempe, 8.

226. Smith, 212.

227. Scott, 223–224.

228. Carmony, *Apacheland*, 152.

229. NARA, RG153: Records of the Judge Advocate General, file number NN3261.

230. Klein, 43.

231. Hal Goldman, "A Most Detestable Crime: Character, Consent, and Corroboration in Vermont's Rape Law, 1850–1920," in Merril D. Smith, *Sex without Consent: Rape and Sexual Coercion in America* (New York: New York University Press, 2001), 179–180.

232. Plante, 317–318.

233. Halsey, 45.

234. NARA, RG153: Records of the Judge Advocate General, file number KK833.

235. Lisa T. Frank, "To Cure Her of Her Pride and Boasting: The Gendered Implications of Sherman's March," Ph.D. dissertation, University of Florida, 2001, 189.

236. Marli F. Weiner, *A Heritage of Woe: The Civil War Diary of Grace Brown Elmore, 1861–1868* (Athens: University of Georgia Press, 1997), 81–82.

237. ORA, series II, vol. 4, 876–877.

238. Katherine M. Jones, *When Sherman Came: Southern Women and the "Great March,"* (Indianapolis: Bobbs-Merrill, 1964), 22.

239. NARA, RG 94: Records of the Adjutant's General's Office, Army of the Potomac, General Orders number 38, March 31, 1863.

240. NARA, RG153: Records of the Judge Advocate General, File number NN1591.

241. Carmony, *Apacheland*, 82.

242. NARA: RG153: Records of the Judge Advocate General, file number OO661.

243. Department of the Rappahanock, General Order 12, in Samuel Breck Papers, Fredericksburg and Spotsylvania National Military Park, National Park Service, Fredericksburg, Virginia.

244. Donald E. Reynolds and Max H. Kele, "A Yank in the Carolinas Campaign: The Diary of James W. Chapin, Eighth Indiana Cavalry," *North Carolina Historical Review*, vol. 46, no. 1 (January 1969): 48.

245. Patrick Papers, diary entries for June 25, June 27, and July 15, 1864.

246. Isaac Hadden, letter to friend dated April 27, 1864, Isaac C. Hadden Papers, New York Historical Society, New York, New York.

247. NARA, RG153: Records of the Judge Advocate General, file number NN3232.

248. Ibid., file number NN106.

249. Ibid., file number OO857.

250. Catherine Clinton and Nina Silber, *Divided Houses: Gender and the Civil War* (New York: Oxford University Press, 1992), 241. Reid Mitchell, *The Vacant Chair: The Northern Soldier Leaves Home* (New York: Oxford University Press, 1993), 107–109.

251. Gerald Schwartz, *A Woman Doctor's Civil War: Esther Hill Hawks' Diary* (Columbia: University of South Carolina Press, 1984), 34.

252. Richmond *Whig*, January 10, 1863.

253. *Daily Richmond Inquirer*. October 29, 1864.

254. Thomas P. Lowry, "Johnny Reb, Billy Yank, and Betty Sue," *North & South*, vol. 9, no. 4 (August 2006): 30.

8—"No punishment can be too severe"

1. Moore, 5.

2. ORA, series I, vol. 2, 744.

3. New York *Times*, July 31, 1861.

4. *Harper's Weekly*, vol. 5 (August 17, 1861): 515.

5. Sneden Papers, diary entry for January 1, 1862.

6. ORA, series I, vol. 2, 744 and volume 3, 295.

7. ORA, series I, vol. 19, 545 and 557.

8. ORA, series I, vol. 33, 804.

9. George B. McClellan, *Report on the Organization and Campaigns of the Army of the Potomac* (New York: Sheldon, 1864), 73–74.

10. ORA, series III, vol. 2, 937.

11. ORA, series III, vol. 5, 612–613.

12. Haydon Papers, diary entry for August 22, 1861.

13. Donald, 20.

14. Wills, 135.

15. Murdock, 43.

16. Regimental History Committee, *History of the Third Pennsylvania Cavalry in the American Civil War* (Philadelphia: Franklin Printing, 1905), 422–423.

17. Washington, 74.

18. David S. Sparks, *Inside Lincoln's Army: The Diary of Marsena Rudolph Patrick, Provost Marshal General, Army of the Potomac* (New York: Yoseloff, 1964), 18. ORA, series I, vol. 21, 925.

19. Kellogg, 133.

20. Samuel Bliss, letter to wife dated December 21, 1862, Samuel Bliss Papers, Civil War Miscellaneous Collection, United States Army Military History Institute, Carlisle, Pennsylvania.

21. Donald, 21.

22. Donald C. Elder, *A Damned Iowa Greyhound: The Civil War Letters of William Henry Harrison Clayton* (Iowa City: University of Iowa Press, 1998), 148–150.

23. Harris, 170.

24. Smith and Baker, 141.

25. Newton Papers, letter to parents dated September 14, 1863.

26. Newton Papers, letter to parents dated September 6, 1863.

27. ORA, series I, vol. 27, 119.

28. ORA, series I, vol. 25, 167. See also Edwin C. Fishel, *The Secret War for the Union:*

The Untold Story of Military Intelligence in the Civil War (Boston: Houghton-Mifflin, 1996).

29. Winschel, 74.

30. Henry Spaulding, letter to Edward G. Smith dated March 25, 1865, Henry Spaulding Papers, Manuscript Collections, University of Virginia Library, Charlottesville, Virginia.

31. McKnight, 104–105.

32. White Papers, diary entry for January 8, 1865.

33. Donald, 264.

34. Indianapolis *Daily Journal*, April 21, 1864.

35. Gaff, 131.

36. Ferguson Papers, diary entry for May 4, 1864. 'Provo' became a common name for any Provost Marshal.

37. Henry Heisler, letter to sister dated May 6, 1863, Henry C. Heisler Papers, Library of Congress (Manuscript Division), Washington, DC.

38. ORA, series I, vol. 11, 93–94.

39. Mark E. Neely, Jr., *The Fate of Liberty: Abraham Lincoln and Civil Liberties* (New York: Oxford University Press, 1991), 4–24.

40. Buckingham, 252.

41. Scott, *Military Dictionary*, 265 and 275.

42. New York *Sunday Mercury*, March 8, 1863.

43. Carmony, "Bartmess Letters," 63.

44. Joseph M. Califf, *Record of the Services of the Seventh Regiment U.S. Colored Troops* (Providence, RI: Freeman, 1878), 74.

45. Coe, 97–98.

46. Patrick Papers, diary entry for July 27, 1863.

47. ORA, series I, vol. 8, 158 and 292–353.

48. *Army Lawyer*, 43.

49. United States Army, *Military Laws of the United States*, Fourth Edition (Washington, DC: Government Printing Office, 1901), 268.

50. Lurton D. Ingersoll, *A History of the War Department of the United States* (Philadelphia: Claxton, Remsen, & Haffelfinger, 1880), 520–522.

51. Many Philhellenes, European liberals who supported widespread political change, fought in Greece. The most famous of them, the poet Lord Byron, died supporting the Greeks.

52. Lewis R. Harley, *Francis Lieber: His Life and Political Philosophy* (New York: Columbia University Press, 1899), 1–80 and 164. Lieber's other two sons fought in the Union Army. Hamilton Lieber lost an arm at Fort Donelson, while Guido served without injury, eventually serving as an instructor at West Point and Judge Advocate General.

53. George B. Davis, *Outlines of International Law* (New York: Harper & Brothers, 1887), 395.

54. War Department, *Subject Index to the General Orders and Circulars of the War Department and the Headquarters of the Army Adjutant General's Office from January 1, 1860 to December 31, 1880* (Washington, DC: Government Printing Office, 1913), 104–116.

55. Ibid.

56. Henry Morford, William H. Armstrong, and Jacob G. Frick, *Red Tape and Pigeon-Hole Generals: As Seen From the Ranks during a Campaign in the Army of the Potomac* (New York: Carleton, 1864), 264.

57. Fitzharris, 47–72.

58. Stephen V. Benet, *A Treatise on Military Law and the Practice of Courts-martial* (New York: Van Nostrand, 1862), 41–42.

59. War Department, *Articles of War* (Washington, DC: Government Printing Office, 1863), 27.

60. Benet, 40 and 44.

61. Article 60 of the *Articles of War*.

62. Cozens' arrest, trial, and conviction stretched over a nine-month period. For a

full account, see William B. Cozens Papers, Historical Society of Pennsylvania, Philadelphia, Pennsylvania.

63. Chadwick, 196–203 and 198–209.
64. Benet, 23.
65. Bensell Papers, diary entry for December 16, 1862.
66. Article 70 of the *Articles of War*.
67. Philip N. Racine, *Unspoiled Heart: The Journal of Charles Mattocks of the 17th Maine* (Knoxville: University of Tennessee Press, 1994), 108.
68. Scott 673.
69. Article 1139 of the *Regulations of the United States Army*.
70. Scott, 635.
71. Barth, 66–67.
72. Brown, *Soldier's Life*, 141–142.
73. Benet, 22–23.
74. Croushore, 45.
75. Chadwick, 190.
76. Malles, 185.
77. Malles, 181.
78. Chadwick, 202–203.
79. Racine, 102 and 109.
80. Kellogg, 37.
81. Article 61 of the *Articles of War*.
82. Croushore, 44.
83. Benet, 47.
84. Article 76 of the *Articles of War*.
85. Malles, 183–185.
86. *War Talks in Kansas: A Series of Papers Read before the Kansas Commandery of the Military Order of the Loyal Legion of the United States* (Kansas City, MO: Franklin Hudson, 1906), 182.
87. NARA, RG94: Records of the Adjutant General's Office, Department of the Ohio, General Order 160, September 25, 1863.
88. Article 87 of the *Articles of War*. Scott, 632.
89. Article 79 of the *Articles of War*.
90. Scott, 629.
91. Racine, 90.
92. Scott, 633.
93. Scott, 633.
94. Racine, 101.
95. NARA, RG153: Records of the Judge Advocate General, File number NN2463.
96. *Army Lawyer*, 51–52.
97. Jones, 128. Haydon Papers, diary entry for October 22, 1861.
98. Richard F. Miller and Robert F. Mooney, *The Civil War: The Nantucket Experience* (Nantucket, MA: Wesco, 1994), 93.
99. Durkin, 188–189.
100. Haydon Papers, diary entry for January 10, 1862.
101. Samito, 180–181.
102. Bond, 257. Gibbs, 234–235.
103. Pride and Travis, 264.
104. Weaver, 121.
105. Jones, 134.
106. Gibbs, 61.
107. William Hough, *The Practice of Courts-Martial and Other Military Courts* (London: Parbury, Allen, 1834), 235.
108. For a full account of the *Somers* Incident, see Harrison Hayford, *The Somers*

Mutiny Affair: A Book of Primary Source Materials (New York: Prentice-Hall, 1959), and Buckner F. Melton, Jr., *A Hanging Offense: The Strange Affair of the Warship Somers* (New York: Free Press, 2003).

109. Miller, 103.

110. Kent, 268–269.

111. Carmony, *Apacheland*, 22.

112. Parson, 103.

113. Nye, 219.

114. James S. Pula, *The Memoirs of Ludwik Zychlinski: Reminiscences of the American Civil War, Siberia, and Poland* (New York: Columbia University Press, 1993), 50.

115. The sample referenced for the remainder of this chapter comprise five thousand court-martial cases randomly selected by the author from the NARA, RG153: Records of the Judge Advocate General.

116. All percentages are rounded to the nearest whole number.

117. NARA, RG153: Records of the Judge Advocate General's Office, File number II609.

118. The Western states and territories comprise the states of California, Oregon, and Kansas, and the Nebraska, Washington, Utah, and New Mexico Territories. The Northern Theater comprises the states that did not secede from the Union, but excludes the Border States of Missouri, Kentucky, West Virginia, and Maryland. The Trans-Mississippi Theater comprises Missouri, Arkansas, Texas, and any jurisdiction in Louisiana other than the Department of the Gulf. The Western Theater comprises all states south of the Ohio River, east of the Mississippi River, west of the Appalachian Mountains, and regions of Louisiana under the jurisdiction of the Department of the Gulf. The Eastern Theater comprises all states south of the Mason-Dixon Line and east of the Appalachian Mountains.

119. For the purposes of this study, the year has only three seasons. Winter is the months between November and February, spring is March through June, and summer is July through October. This roughly corresponds to the active seasons of armies during the Civil War. Armies usually resided inactive in winter camp between November and February; warmer weather in spring presaged the start of the campaigning season, with most fighting taking place during the summer months of July through October.

120. Chi-square significance, .319.

121. Instead of dealing with a multitude of offenses, the study groups offenses into five broad categories, comprising desertion-related crimes (such as desertion, attempted desertion, or abetting desertion), violent crimes (such as murder, attempted murder, rape, or assault), disciplinary crimes (offenses that cause a break down of army discipline, such as drunkenness on duty, conduct prejudicial, or neglect of duty), antiauthority crimes (offenses that challenge the authority of the army, such as mutiny, mutinous conduct, disobey order, or insubordination), and theft in any form (such as robbery, pillaging, burglary, or embezzlement).

122. Chi-square significance, .000.

123. Chi-square significance, .000.

124. Chi-square significance, .004.

125. Robertson, "Military Executions," 34.

126. Chi-square significance, .000.

127. Chi-square significance, .000.

128. Courts-martial frequently imposed more than a single punishment, i.e., a term at hard labor and a fine or a prison sentence and a dishonorable discharge. The term 'primary punishment' refers to the most significant punishment issued by the court to the exclusion of any additional sentences.

129. Chi-square significance, .000.

130. Chi-square significance, .000.

131. Chi-square significance, .000.

132. Chi-square significance, .000.

133. Chi-square significance, .000.

134. Chi-square significance, .000. Antiauthority crimes included all forms of insubordination, disobeying orders, or mutinous conduct.

135. Chi-square significance, .002.

136. Chi-square significance, .442.

137. NARA, RG153: Records of the Judge Advocate General, file number II545.

138. Ibid., file numbers OO1146 and NN1250.

139. Ibid., file numbers OO858 and NN2413.

140. Ibid., file number NN3577.

141. Ibid., file number OO604.

142. Ibid., file number NN3599.

143. Ibid., file numbers NN1554 and KK360.

144. Ibid., file number OO655.

145. Ibid., file number NN1876.

146. Ibid., file numbers II837, NN3031, NN3223, and NN657.

147. Ibid., file number II644.

148. Ibid., file number NN2114.

149. Croushore, 30.

150. Chi-square significance, .000. In desertion cases, courts-martial found 9 percent of defendants not guilty and 16 percent guilty of the lesser charge of AWOL.

151. Gregory J.W. Urwin, "United States Colored Troops," in David S. Heidler and Jeanne T. Heidler, *Encyclopedia of the American Civil War: A Political, Social, and Military History*, vol. 4 (Santa Barbara, CA: ABC-CLIO, 2000), 2002–2003.

152. Chi-square significance, .000.

153. Chi-square significance, .833.

154. Chi-square significance, .004.

155. Chi-square significance, .000.

156. Chi-square significance, .000.

157. Chi-square significance, .675.

158. Chi-square significance, .235.

159. Chi-square significance, .068.

160. Chi-square significance, .894.

161. Chi-square significance, .186.

162. Chi-square significance, .798.

163. Chi-square significance, .000.

164. Chi-square significance, .000.

165. Chi-square significance, .000.

166. Chi-square significance, 671.

167. NARA, RG153: Records of the Judge Advocate General, file number NN3480.

168. Ibid., file number II507.

169. Ibid., file number LL1246.

170. Ibid., file number KK808.

171. Ibid., file number KK092.

172. Ibid., file number II650.

173. Ibid., file number NN3181.

174. Ibid., file. number KK643.

175. Ibid., file number NN2489.

176. Ibid., file number II501.

177. Ibid., file number LL847.

178. Ibid., file number OO115 [emphasis in original].

179. Ibid., file number KK656.

180. Ibid., file number NN2585.

181. Ibid., file number LL849.

182. Ibid., file number KK105.

183. Ibid., file number KK489.

184. Ibid., file number OO661.
185. Ibid., file number OO855.
186. Ibid., file number OO111.
187. Ibid., file number NN1591.
188. Ibid., file number OO857.
189. Ibid., file number OO116.
190. Ibid., file number NN3575.
191. Ibid., file number KK486.
192. Ibid., file number OO724.
193. Ibid., file number NN1374.
194. Ibid., file numbers OO151 and NN 1374.
195. Ibid., file number NN3031.
196. Chi-square significance, .000.
197. NARA, RG153: Records of the Judge Advocate General, File number OO150.
198. Ibid., file number OO151.
199. Ibid., file number II832.
200. Ibid., file number OO722.
201. Ibid., file number KK067.
202. Ibid., file number NN1258.
203. Ibid., file number KK643.
204. Ibid., file number NN2416.
205. Ibid., file number LL849.
206. Ibid., file number NN3031.
207. Ibid., file number II650 [emphasis in original].
208. Ibid., file number KK643.
209. Ibid., file number OO857.

9—"We have no right to shoot them"

1. Quenzel, 130.
2. Jones, 126.
3. Philip Katcher, *The Civil War Source Book* (New York: Facts on File, 1982), 304.
4. Palladino, 47.
5. Racine, 101. Brown, *Galvanized Yankees*, 135. Wilkinson, 355–356.
6. Lande, 88–89.
7. Menge and Shimrak, 64.
8. Haydon Papers, diary entries for January 11 and January 16, 1862.
9. Welsh Papers, letter to wife dated September 19, 1863.
10. Engert, 90.
11. Barber and Swinson, 168.
12. Fisk Papers, diary entry for March 24, 1865.
13. Sneden Papers, diary entry for September 29, 1861.
14. Thomas T. Ellis, *Leaves from the Diary of an Army Surgeon; Or, Incidents of Field, Camp, and Hospital Life* (New York: J. Bradburn, 1863), 24.
15. Noe, 46–47.
16. Taylor, 23.
17. Carmony, *Apacheland*, 118–119.
18. Haydon Papers, diary entry for December 28, 1861.
19. Dunkelman, 221.
20. Fisk Papers, diary entry for March 24, 1865.
21. Mellon, 192.
22. Benet, 46–47.
23. Clifford L. Swanson, *The Sixth United States Infantry Regiment, 1855 to Reconstruction* (Jefferson, NC: McFarland, 2001), 147.

24. Wilbert L. Jenkins, *Climbing Up to Glory: A Short History of African Americans during the Civil War and Reconstruction* (Lanham, MD: Rowman & Littlefield, 2002), 42.

25. Kirk C. Jenkins, *The Battle Rages Higher: The Union's Fifteenth Kentucky Infantry* (Lexington: University of Kentucky Press, 2003), 378.

26. Todd M. Kerstetter, "Leavenworth Penitentiary" in David J. Wishart ,*Encyclopedia of the Great Plains* (Lincoln: University of Nebraska Press, 2004), 455.

27. Michael Esslinger, *Alcatraz: A Definitive History of the Penitentiary Years* (Carmel, CA: Ocean View, 2003), 37.

28. Harriet Stevens, *The Graybeards: The Family of Major Lyman Allen during the American Civil War* (Iowa City, IA: Press of the Camp Pope Bookshop, 1998), 17.

29. Margaret E. Wagner, et. al., *The Library of Congress Civil War Desk Reference* (New York: Simon and Schuster, 2002), 605.

30. Lande, 83–85.

31. James E. Potter and Edith Robbins, *Marching with the First Nebraska: A Civil War Diary* (Norman: University of Oklahoma Press, 2007), 207–208.

32. Elizabeth D. Leonard, *Lincoln's Avengers: Justice, Revenge, and Reunion after the Civil War* (New York: Norton, 2004), 138.

33. Racine, 68.

34. Francis H. Buffum, *A Memorial of the Great Rebellion: Being a History of the Fourteenth Regiment New Hampshire Volunteers* (Boston: Franklin Press, 1882), 120.

35. Alton [Illinois] *Telegraph*, April 8, 1864.

36. Samuel Carter, *The Riddle of Dr. Mudd* (New York: Putnam, 1974), 227 and 233–234.

37. William L. Miller, "Lincoln's Pardons and What They Mean" in Charles M. Hubbard, *Lincoln Reshapes the Presidency* (Macon, GA: Mercer University Press, 2001), 119. At the end of the war, President Andrew Johnson issued a general pardon to all military prisoners at Fort Jefferson and permitted them to go home with dishonorable discharges.

38. Victor D. Hanson and John Keegan, *The Western Way of War: Infantry Battle in Classical Greece*, 2nd ed. (Berkeley: University of California Press, 2000), 128.

39. Harry M. Ward, *The War for Independence and the Transformation of American Society* (New York: Routledge, 1999), 124. James M. McCaffrey, *The Army in Transformation, 1790–1860* (New York: Greenwood Press, 2006), 68.

40. Billings, 155.

41. Robertson, 134. Donald, 206. Benet, 168. Benet specifically mentions that a drumming out must include the "Rogue's March."

42. Lande, 105–106.

43. Bob Zeller, *The Blue and Gray in Black and White: A History of Civil War Photography* (New York: Greenwood, 2005), 154.

44. John Point, letter to his brother dated January 20, 1865, John Point Papers, Historical Society of Delaware, Wilmington, Delaware.

45. Garber A. Davidson, *The Civil War Letters of the Late 1st Lieut. James J. Hartley, 122nd Ohio Infantry Regiment* (Jefferson, NC: McFarland, 1998), 12.

46. Voorhis, 158.

47. Nathanial Rollins, diary entry for February 22, 1863, Nathanial Rollins Papers, Wisconsin Historical Society, Madison, Wisconsin. Dunn is paraphrasing the Bible, Ecclesiastes 2:24, "A live dog is better than a dead lion."

48. Alonzo L. Brown, *History of the Fourth Minnesota Infantry Volunteers during the Great Rebellion, 1861–1865* (St. Paul, MN: Pioneer Press, 1892), 154.

49. Herek, 76.

50. Johnson, 440–441.

51. Willison, 26.

52. John W. Rowell, *Yankee Artillerymen: Through the Civil War with Eli Lilly's Indiana Battery* (Knoxville: University of Tennessee Press, 1975), 19.

53. John R. Boyle, *Soldiers True: The Story of the One Hundred and Eleventh Regiment Pennsylvania Veteran Volunteers and of Its Campaigns in the War for the Union, 1861–1865* (New York: Eaton & Mains, 1903), 193.

54. Haydon Papers, diary entry for May 23, 1861.

55. John Knight, letter to wife dated June 20, 1862, John H. Knight Papers, Wisconsin Historical Society, Madison, Wisconsin.

56. Scott, 95–96.

57. Ferguson Papers, diary entry for April 25, 1864.

58. Bensell Papers, diary entry for December 18, 1862.

59. Holahan Papers, diary entry for January 12, 1864.

60. Raup, 44.

61. *Military History and Reminiscences of the Thirteenth Regiment of Illinois Volunteer Infantry in the Civil War in the United States, 1861–1865* (Chicago: Woman's Temperance, 1892), 18.

62. William C. Davis, *A Taste for War: A Culinary History of the Blue and the Gray* (Mechanicsburg, PA: Stackpole Books, 2003), 78.

63. Joseph Rogers, letter to sister dated September 26, 1862, Joseph S. Rogers Papers, Fredericksburg and Spotsylvania National Military Park, National Park Service, Fredericksburg, Virginia.

64. Carmony, "Bartmess Letters," 51.

65. William Morse, diary entry for January 18, 1863, William H. Morse Papers, Fredericksburg and Spotsylvania National Military Park, National Park Service, Fredericksburg, Virginia.

66. Lewis, 26.

67. Skidmore, 94.

68. Engert, 26.

69. Francis Hall, diary entry for December 29, 1862, Francis B. Hall Papers, Fredericksburg and Spotsylvania National Military Park, National Park Service, Fredericksburg, Virginia.

70. Pittsburgh *Evening Chronicle*, May 26, 1863.

71. Washington, 35.

72. Sheldon B. Thorpe, *The History of the Fifteenth Connecticut Volunteers in the War for the Defense of the Union, 1861–1865* (New Haven, CT: Price, Lee, and Adkins, 1893), 28.

73. Holahan Papers, diary entry for February 27, 1863.

74. Haydon Papers, diary entry for January 22, 1862.

75. Patrick, 108. Viola, 64.

76. Winschel, 74–75.

77. Britton and Reed, 295–296.

78. Holahan Papers, diary entry for June 22, 1861.

79. Miller, 154.

80. Throne, "Switzer Letters," 39–40.

81. Enos B. Vail, *Reminiscences of a Boy in the Civil War* (Brooklyn, NY, privately printed, 1915), 66.

82. George M. Vickers, *Under Both Flags: A Panorama of the Great Civil War* (Philadelphia: Fidelity, 1896), 575.

83. Baker, 48–49.

84. Sneden Papers, diary entry September 29, 1861.

85. Haydon Papers, diary entry for January 22, 1862.

86. Samito, 175.

87. Rowell, *Yankee Cavalrymen*, 112. Robertson, *Blue and Gray*, 38.

88. Dodge Papers, diary entry for January 1, 1863.

89. Haydon Papers, diary entry for December 20, 1861.

90. NARA, RG153: Records of the Judge Advocate General, File number NN3585.

91. Donald, 81–82.

92. Halsey, 85.

93. Frank Wilkerson, *Recollections of a Private Soldier in the Army of the Potomac* (New York: Putnam, 1887), 35.

94. William D. Hamilton, *Recollections of a Cavalryman of the Civil War After Fifty Years, 1861–1865* (Columbus, OH: F.J. Heer, 1915), 50–51.

95. Haydon Papers, diary entry for September 22, 1861.

96. Hosea W. Rood, *Story of the Service of Company E, and the Twelfth Wisconsin Regiment, Veteran Volunteer Infantry, in the War of the Rebellion* (Milwaukee: Swain and Tate, 1893), 86.

97. Theodore G. Carter, "The Tupelo Campaign," *Publications of the Mississippi Historical Society*, vol. 10 (Oxford, MS: Mississippi Historical Society, 1909), 92.

98. Peter Cozzens, *The Darkest Days of the War: The Battles of Iuka and Corinth* (Chapel Hill: University of North Carolina Press, 2006), 87.

99. Ware, 151–152.

100. Buckingham, 185–187.

101. Menge and Shimrak, 10.

102. Palladino, 82.

103. Dodge Papers, diary entry for June 22, 1863.

104. Kent, 228–230.

105. Patrick, 108–109.

106. James McLean, *California Sabers: The 2nd Massachusetts Cavalry in the Civil War* (Bloomington: Indiana University Press, 2000), 22.

107. Donald, 188.

108. Thomas L. Livermore. *Days and Events: 1860–1866* (Boston: Houghton-Mifflin, 1920), 475.

109. Evan Gery, diary entry for January 7,1863, Evan M. Gery Papers, Fredericksburg and Spotsylvania National Military Park, National Park Service, Fredericksburg, Virginia.

110. John Crater, diary entry for November 11, 1862, John P. Crater Papers, Fredericksburg and Spotsylvania National Military Park, National Park Service, Fredericksburg, Virginia.

111. Mahood, 35.

112. Albert Artman, diary entry for March 10, 1864, Albert H. Artman Papers, Fredericksburg and Spotsylvania National Military Park, National Park Service, Fredericksburg, Virginia.

113. Lowry, *Tarnished Eagles*, 131–132.

114. Halsey, 84–85.

115. Washington Davis. *Camp-fire Chats of the Civil War* (Chicago: Lewis, 1888), 221–222.

116. Dix, 77–78.

117. Leech, 112.

118. Silliker, 63.

119. Rowell, *Yankee Cavalrymen*, 38.

120. Benet, 39. This was actually the second time that Congress had banned flogging. In May 1812, Congress banned all forms of corporal punishment, only to reverse itself in 1833 when the army was permitted to flog soldiers convicted of desertion. Callan, 194 and 310.

121. Richard F. Miller. *Harvard's Civil War: A History of the Twentieth Massachusetts Volunteer Infantry* (Boston: University Press of New England, 2005), 37.

122. Atwood, 54.

123. Joseph Gould. *The Story of the Forty-eighth: A Record of the Campaigns of the Forty-eighth Regiment Pennsylvania Veteran Volunteer Infantry* (Philadelphia: Frank A. Taylor, 1908), 177–178.

124. Hedrick and Davis, 112–113.

125. Marcotte, 116–117.

126. Edwin Weist, diary entry for January 18, 1863, Edwin B. Weist Papers, Fredericksburg and Spotsylvania National Military Park, National Park Service, Fredericksburg, Virginia.

127. Rowell, *Yankee Artillerymen*, 19.

128. Jordan, 36. Thomas Stephens, diary entry for January 18, 1863, Thomas W. Stephens Papers, Civil War Miscellaneous Collection, United States Army Military History Institute, Carlisle, Pennsylvania.

129. Malles, 185.

130. NARA, RG153: Records of the Judge Advocate General, File numbers II837 and II525.

131. Ibid., file number KK643.
132. Fisk Papers, diary entry for March 17, 1863.
133. NARA, RG153: Records of the Judge Advocate General, File number II397.
134. Ibid., file number II358.
135. Ibid., file number II636.
136. Silliker, 66–67.
137. Robert Robertson, letter to parents dated November 19, 1863, Robert S. Robertson Papers, Fredericksburg and Spotsylvania National Military Park, National Park Service, Fredericksburg, Virginia.
138. Murdock, 104.
139. NARA, RG153: Records of the Judge Advocate General, File number NN1364. Chisholm's sentence included the reference to "Indian ink," but Chase's sentence only mentioned he should be branded. One could presume, however, that the court-martial panel intended the same punishment for both as the sentence is otherwise identical.
140. Ibid., file number II643.
141. Ibid., file numbers II390 and II398.
142. Ibid., file number II530.
143. Albert Reid, diary entry for November 23, 1863, Albert J. Reid Papers, Fredericksburg and Spotsylvania National Military Park, National Park Service, Fredericksburg, Virginia.
144. Fisk Papers, diary entries for November 17 and November 23, 1863.
145. George Squier, letter to wife dated June 8, 1863, George W. Squier Papers, Lincoln Museum, Fort Wayne, Indiana.
146. Robert F. Harris and John Niflot, *Dear Sister: the Civil War Letters of the Brothers Gould* (New York: Praeger, 1998), 129.
147. The ritual of execution is spelled out in DeHart, 247–248.
148. Hennessy, 203.
149. Jordan, 96.
150. Robertson, *Blue and Gray*, 138.
151. Section IV (Articles 81 through 85) of the Lieber Code delineated the differences between soldiers, guerillas, and partisans, and defined how the Union army was to treat each classification.
152. Voorhis, 248 and 252.
153. Popchock, 161.
154. McCordick, 24–25.
155. Gould and Kennedy, 265.
156. William Dunham, letter to wife dated October 28, 1861, William H. Dunham Papers, Civil War Miscellaneous Collection, United States Army Military History Institute, Carlisle, PA.
157. Carmony, "Bartmess Letters," 63.
158. Britton and Reed, 113.
159. Sneden Papers, diary entry for December 4, 1861.
160. David B. Danbom, "Dear Companion: Civil War Letters of a Story County Farmer," *Annals of Iowa*, vol. 47 (Fall 1984): 540.
161. Kelly and Kelly, 73–80.
162. Boyts Papers, diary entries for July 5 and July 7, 1863.
163. Silliker, 110. Thompson Snyder, diary entry for July 10, 1863, Thompson A. Snyder Papers, Fredericksburg and Spotsylvania National Military Park, National Park Service, Fredericksburg, Virginia.
164. White Papers, diary entry for July 10, 1863.
165. Patrick Papers, diary entries for July 14 and July 15, 1864.
166. Newton Papers, letter to parents dated June 22, 1864.
167. Miller and Mooney, 116–117.
168. Francis M. McAdams, *Every-day Soldier Life: Or A History of the One Hundred Thirteenth Ohio Infantry* (Columbus, OH: Charles M. Cott, 1884), 148.

169. Ervin L. Jordan, Jr., *Black Confederates and Afro-Yankees in Civil War Virginia* (Charlottesville: University Press of Virginia, 1995). See William A. Frassanito, *Grant and Lee: The Virginia Campaigns, 1864–1865* (New York: Scribner's and Sons, 1983), 220–223 for photographs of Johnson's execution.

170. Boston *Evening Transcript*, June 20, 1864.

171. Patrick Papers, diary entries for June 19 and June 20, 1864.

172. Regis de Trobriand, *Four Years with the Army of the Potomac* (Boston: Ticknor, 1889), 604–605.

173. Abram P. Smith, *History of the Seventy-sixth Regiment New York Volunteers* (Syracuse, NY: Truair, Smith, & Miles, 1867), 260–262.

174. Charles M. Clark, *The History of the Thirty-Ninth Regiment Illinois Volunteer Veteran Infantry* (Chicago: self-published, 1889), 248.

175. George W. Ward, *History of the Second Pennsylvania Veteran Heavy Artillery* (Philadelphia: George W. Ward, Printer, 1904), 129–130.

176. Charles P. Bosson, *History of the Forty-second Regiment, Massachusetts Volunteers* (Boston: Mills, Knight, 1886), 451.

177. White Papers, diary entry or December 18, 1863.

178. Fisk Papers, diary entry for July 18, 1864.

179. Gould and Kennedy, 131–133.

180. Alfred S. Roe, *The Twenty-fourth Regiment, Massachusetts Volunteers* (Worcester, MA: Twenty-fourth Veteran Association, 1907), 424–432.

181. Chadwick, 291.

182. Billings, 162–163.

183. Sylvester McElheney, letter to wife dated December 14, 1864. Valley of the Shadow Project.

184. Ida B. Adams, "The Civil War Letters of James Rush Holmes," *Western Pennsylvania Historical Magazine*, vol. 44, no. 2 (June 1961): 125.

185. James Burrell, letter to sister dated September 1, 1863, John D. Withrow Papers, Fredericksburg and Spotsylvania National Military Park, National Park Service, Fredericksburg, Virginia.

186. Menge and Shimrak, 56.

187. Robertson, "Military Executions," 39. Lester L. Swift, "Letter from a Sailor on a Tinclad," *Civil War History*, vol. 7, no. 2 (March 1961): 60–61. Silliker, 230.

188. Albert F. Bridges, "The Execution of Private Robert Gay," *Indiana Magazine of History*, vol. 20, no. 2 (June 1924): 174–186.

189. Parson, 102–104.

190. Paul Hilliard, letter to sister dated November 24, 1864, Paul H. Hilliard Papers, Perkins Library (Manuscript Collections), Duke University, Durham, North Carolina.

191. Axel Reed, letter to family dated April 1, 1865, Axel Reed Papers, Minnesota Historical Society, St. Paul, Minnesota.

192. John R. Adams, *Memorial and Letters of Rev. John R. Adams, D.D.* (Cambridge, MA: Harvard University Press, 1890), 94.

193. John Irwin, letter to father dated October 2, 1863, John F. Irwin Papers, Fredericksburg and Spotsylvania National Military Park, National Park Service, Fredericksburg, Virginia.

194. Haydon Papers, diary entry for January 26, 1863.

195. Samito, 210–212.

196. Smith, 193.

197. John Geary, letter to wife dated September 19, 1863, John W. Geary Papers, Historical Society of Pennsylvania, Philadelphia, Pennsylvania.

198. Robertson, "Military Executions," 36.

199. William R. Thayer, *John Hay: In Two volumes* (New York: Houghton Mifflin, 1915), 218.

200. Don E. Fehrenbacher and Virginia Fehrenbacher, *Recollected Words of Abraham Lincoln* (Palo Alto, CA: Stanford University Press, 1996), 441.

201. Harry E. Fosdick, *The Meaning of Faith* (New York: Association Press, 1918), 259–260.

202. NARA, RG 94: Records of the Adjutant General's Office, War Department, General Orders number 76, February 26, 1864.

203. Scott, 207.

204. Theodore Lyman, *Meade's Headquarters, 1863–1865* (New York: Atlantic Monthly Press, 1922), 117.

205. ORA, series II, vol. 7, 19.

206. Connor Papers, letter to father dated April 27, 1864.

207. Rhodes, 198–199.

208. Noe, 165–167.

209. Chadwick, 160–161.

210. Fisk Papers, diary entry for December 18, 1863. Franklin Horner, diary entry for August 29, 1863, Franklin Horner Papers, Fredericksburg and Spotsylvania National Military Park, National Park Service, Fredericksburg, Virginia.

211. Smith Letterbook, letter to mother dated September 4, 1863.

212. Robertson Papers, letter to parents dated September 1, 1863.

213. John Vautier, diary entry for August 13, 1864, John D. Vautier Papers, Civil War Miscellaneous Collection, United States Army Military History Institute, Carlisle, Pennsylvania.

214. Abel Thomas, letter to friend dated January 1, 1862, Abel C. Thomas Papers, Virginia Historical Society, Richmond, Virginia.

215. White Papers, diary entry for December 23, 1864.

216. James Woodworth, letter to family dated September 18, 1864. David Nichol, letter to sister dated June 20, 1863, David Nichol Papers, Civil War Miscellaneous Collection, United States Army Military History Institute, Carlisle, Pennsylvania.

217. Mowen Papers, diary entry for July 15, 1863.

218. William Clark, letter to brother dated September 19, 1863, William M. Clark Papers, Chickamauga-Chattanooga National Military Park, National Park Service, Chattanooga, Tennessee.

219. Coralou P. Lassen, *Dear Sarah: Letters Home from a Soldier in the Iron Brigade* (Bloomington: Indiana University Press, 1999), 76–77.

220. Boyts Papers, letter to brother dated September 27, 1863.

221. Jacob Bechtel, letter to wife dated August 23, 1863, Jacob Bechtel Papers, Gettysburg National Military Park, National Park Service, Gettysburg, Pennsylvania.

222. Ferdinand Davis, *Memoir of the Civil War*, 63–64, Bentley Historical Library, University of Michigan, Ann Arbor, Michigan.

223. Francis Carron, letter to friend dated August 19, 1863, Francis M. Carron Papers, Fredericksburg and Spotsylvania National Military Park, National Park Service, Fredericksburg, Virginia.

224. Jones Papers, letter to father dated December 25, 1863.

225. Albert Reid, diary entry for December 18, 1863, Albert J. Reid Papers, Fredericksburg and Spotsylvania National Military Park, National Park Service, Fredericksburg, Virginia.

226. Lilley Papers, letter to sister dated August 28, 1863.

227. Vautier, diary entry for October 2, 1863.

228. David A. Ward, "Amidst a Tempest of Shot and Shell: A History of the Ninety-sixth Pennsylvania Volunteers," M.A. thesis, Southern Connecticut State University, 1988, 64.

229. Virginia M. Adams, *On the Altar of Freedom: A Black Soldier's Civil War Letters from the Front* (New York: Warner Books, 1991), 92–93.

230. Norwich [Connecticut] *Morning Bulletin*, January 14, 1865.

231. Buckingham, 151.

232. White Papers, diary entry for December 4, 1864.

233. Billings, 161.

234. Norwich [Connecticut] *Morning Bulletin*, February 7, 1865.

235. E.M. Woodward, *History of the One Hundred and Ninety-Eighth Pennsylvania*

Volunteers (Trenton, NJ: MacCrellish & Quigley, 1884), 17–18.

236. Silliker, 251.

237. Robertson, 139.

238. Carmony, *Apacheland*, 96.

239. Charles D. Page, *History of the Fourteenth Regiment, Connecticut Volunteer Infantry* (Hartford: Horton Printing, 1906), 185. Silverman, 276–277.

240. Silliker, 251.

241. Sears, 171.

242. Boston *Journal*, September 1, 1863.

243. Nye, 145.

244. William Corby, *Memoirs of a Chaplain Life: Three Years Chaplain in the Famous "Irish Brigade,"* Army of the Potomac (New York: Scholastic Press, 1984), 220–228. Alotta, *Civil War Justice*, 107–108.

Epilogue

1. Robert Larimer, diary entry for June 8, 1865, Robert Larimer Papers, University of Virginia, Special Collections Library, Charlottesville, Virginia.

2. William B. Holberton, *Homeward Bound: The Demobilization of the Union & Confederate Armies, 1865–66* (Mechanicsburg, PA: Stackpole Books, 2001), 7–10.

3. Albert A. Nofi, *A Civil War Treasury* (New York: Da Capo Press, 1995), 402. Jerold E. Brown, *Historical Dictionary of the U.S. Army* (Westport, CT: Greenwood, 2001), 39.

4. NARA, RG 94: Records of the Adjutant General's Office, Army of Tennessee, General Orders number 59, April 29, 1865.

5. Brobst Papers, letter to parents dated May 17, 1865.

6. Popchock, 214–215.

7. New York *Sunday Mercury*, June 22, 1865.

8. Winschel, 176.

9. George Bowen, diary entry for June 1, 1865, George A. Bowen Papers, Fredericksburg and Spotsylvania National Military Park, National Park Service, Fredericksburg, Virginia.

10. Brobst Papers, letter parents dated May 11, 1865.

11. Buckingham, 188–189.

12. Raup, 37–38.

13. Winschel, 171.

14. Raup, 33.

15. Kinsley Papers, diary entry for June 26, 1865.

16. Henry Heisler, letter to sister dated May 13, 1865, Henry C. Heisler Papers, Library of Congress (Manuscript Division), Washington, DC.

17. Kinsley Papers, diary entries for July 4 and July 12, 1865.

18. Albert Allen, letter to sister dated July 20, 1865, Albert and Charles Allen Papers, University of Virginia, Special Collections Library, Charlottesville, Virginia.

19. Taylor, 46–47.

20. Starr, 373–374.

21. Philip H. Sheridan, *Personal Memoirs of P.H. Sheridan*, vol. II (New York: Charles L. Webster, 1888), 208–209. ORA, series I, vol. 48, 476.

22. Popchock, 212–213.

23. Miller, 156–161.

24. New York *Sunday Mercury*, June 25, 1865.

25. Taylor, 28–29.

26. Henry Heisler, letter to sister dated May 5, 1865, Henry C. Heisler Papers, Library of Congress (Manuscript Division), Washington, DC.

27. Menge and Shimrak, 94.

28. Francis W. Palfrey, *Memoir of William Francis Bartlett* (Boston: Houghton, Osgood, 1879), 155.

29. Ferguson Papers, diary entry for April 29, 1865.

30. Winschel, 162–163.

31. Taylor, 57–58.

32. NARA, RG 94: Records of the Adjutant General's Office, War Department, General Orders number 120, June 29, 1865.

33. Winschel, 166–167.

34. Courtright Papers, diary entry for June 11, 1865.

35. Charles A. Byler, *Civil-Military Relations on the Frontier and Beyond, 1865–1917* (Westport, CT: Praeger Security International, 2006), 51–54.

36. Coffman, 346.

37. Byler, 43.

38. Coffman, 374.

39. Robert V. Ladow, "United States Prisons and Prisoners" in Charles R. Henderson, et al., *Correction and Prevention* (New York: Charles Publication Committee, 1910), 177–178.

40. Wayne R. Kime, *Colonel Richard Irving Dodge: The Life and Times of a Career Army Officer* (Norman: University of Oklahoma Press, 2006), 497–498.

41. Coffman, 311–312.

42. Anne M. Butler, *Daughters of Joy, Sisters of Misery: Prostitutes in the American West, 1865–1890* (Urbana: University of Illinois Press, 1987), 153–154.

43. Leonard, 291–301.

44. *Army Lawyer*, 71–85.

45. "James B. Fry" in Heidler and Heidler, vol. II, 791–792.

46. NARA, Record Group 389: Records of the Office of the Provost Marshal General, "Administrative History of the Office of the Provost Marshal General," 3–4. The army recreated a temporary Provost Marshal General during World War I, along with an ad hoc military police force, but the army dissolved the position again in 1919.

47. Robert D. Heinl, *Dictionary of Military and Naval Quotations* (Annapolis, MD: Naval Institute Press, 1966), 93.

WORKS CITED

Manuscript Collections

Abraham Lincoln Presidential Library (Springfield, Illinois)

James W. Hughlett Papers
William R. Rowley Papers
Sarah Sleeper Papers

Androscoggin Historical Society (Auburn, Massachusetts)

William H. Morse Papers

Arkansas History Commission & State Archives (Little Rock, Arkansas)

Fred J. Herring Collection

Brown University (Providence, Rhode Island)

Selden Conner Papers

Central Michigan University (Mount Pleasant, Michigan)

Lafayette Church Papers

Chicago Historical Society (Chicago, Illinois)

Virgil Andruss Papers
George Smith Avery Papers
Napoleon Bartlett Papers
Cornelius Courtright Papers
Charles C. Curtiss Papers
Elmore Day Papers
Henry C. Forbes Papers
Joseph Sturge Johnston Papers
John J. Lynch Papers
George Merryweather Papers
Robert Mitchell Papers
David Myers Papers
Frederick Pell Papers
James C. Sinclair Papers
Albert G. Sprague Papers
Silas C. Stevens Papers

Chickamauga and Chattanooga National Military Park (Chattanooga, Tennessee)
William M. Clark Papers

Connecticut Historical Society (Hartford, Connecticut)
John B. Cuzner Papers
George Robbins Papers

DePauw University (Greencastle, Indiana)
Simpson Solomon Hamrick Papers

Duke University (Durham, North Carolina)
Edwin Emery Papers
Paul H. Hilliard Papers
Elisha A. Peterson Papers
Royse Family Papers
Laurinan H. Russell Papers
Henry J. H. Thompson Papers

Emory University (Atlanta, Georgia)
Charles H. Cox Papers
Edward King Wightman Papers

Five Colleges Archives and Manuscript Collection (Northampton, Massachusetts)
Brewster Family Papers, Sophia Smith Collection

Fredericksburg and Spotsylvania National Military Park (Fredericksburg, Virginia)
Albert H. Artman Papers
Harlan P. Bailey Papers
George Bowen Papers
Samuel Breck Papers
Francis M. Carron Papers
John P. Crater Papers
James Decker Papers
John M. Dunbar Papers
Haywood Emmill Papers
Evan M. Gery Papers
Sylvester Hadley Papers
Francis B. Hall Papers
Edwin Albert Haradon Papers
John Frederick Holahan Papers
Edward Henry Papers
George A. Hitchcock Papers
Franklin Horner Papers
George Hugunin Papers
John F. Irwin Papers
George M. Jones Papers
Lewis Luckenbill Papers
Tully McCrea Papers

William H. Morse Papers
Daniel H. Mowen Papers
Alden Faunce Murch Papers
John H. Pardington Papers
Albert J. Reid Papers
Robert S. Robertson Papers
Joseph S. Rogers Papers
Charles Scribner Papers
Thompson A. Snyder Papers
Darius Starr Papers
William S. Stewart Papers
Edwin B. Weist Papers
Wyman S. White Papers
John D. Withrow Papers
Caleb C. T. Woolhizer Papers

Gettysburg College (Gettysburg, Pennsylvania)

George Washington Beidelman Papers

Gettysburg National Battlefield Park (Gettysburg, Pennsylvania)

Jacob Bechtel Papers
Charles Bowen Papers

Historical Society of Delaware (Wilmington, Delaware)

John Point Papers

Historical Society of Pennsylvania (Philadelphia, Pennsylvania)

Civil War Letters of James, Isaac, and William Abraham and James Sturgis
Franklin Boyts Papers
William B. Cozens Papers
John P. Follmer Papers
John W. Geary Papers
Charles A. Heckman Papers
William T. Jones Papers
William Reed Moore Papers
John L. Smith Papers

Illinois Historical Society (Springfield, Illinois)

James A. Connolly Papers

Illinois State Historical Library (Springfield, Illinois)

James M. Cole Papers

Indiana Historical Society (Indianapolis, Indiana)

Solomon S. Hamrick Papers
William N. Jackson Papers
Aurelius L. Voorhis Papers

Indiana State Archives (Indianapolis, Indiana)
Joseph Hotz Papers

Indiana State Library (Indianapolis, Indiana)
Daniel E. Bruce Papers

Kansas State Historical Society (Topeka, Kansas)
Webster W. Moses Papers

Library of Congress (Washington, DC)
Samuel H. Eells Papers
John H. Ferguson Papers
Wilbur Fisk Papers
George O. Hand Papers
Henry C. Heisler Papers
George G. Meade Papers
Marshal Mortimer Miller Papers
Marsena Patrick Papers
Orlando M. Poe Papers
John Chester White Papers

Lincoln Museum (Fort Wayne, Indiana)
George W. Squier Papers

Maine Historical Society (Portland, Maine)
Charles P. Mattocks Papers

Massachusetts Historical Society (Boston, Massachusetts)
John A. Andrew Papers
George M. Barnard Papers

Minnesota Historical Society (St. Paul, Minnesota)
Edward H. and George S. Bassett Papers
Axel Reed Papers

New York Historical Society (New York, New York)
Isaac C. Hadden Papers
James T. McIvor Papers
Peter Welsh Papers

New York Public Library (New York, New York)
John W. Phelps Papers

Oberlin College (Oberlin, Ohio)
Giles W. Shurtleff Papers

Ohio Historical Society (Columbus, Ohio)

Lyman D. Ames Papers
Baird Family Papers
William H. Philips Papers

Pennsylvania Historical and Museum Commission (Harrisburg, Pennsylvania)

David R. P. Neely Papers

Princeton University (Princeton, New Jersey)

Henry S. Sherman Papers

Richmond National Battlefield Park (Richmond, Virginia)

Aaron Kepler Papers

State Historical Society of Missouri (Columbia, Missouri)

Andrew F. Davis Papers

Troy Historical Society (Troy, Ohio)

Josiah Hill Papers

United States Army Military History Institute (Carlisle, Pennsylvania)

Joseph Blackburn Papers
Frank W. Dickerson Papers
William E. Dunn Papers
William Fogg Papers
Edmund Halsey Papers
Joseph Heffelfinger Papers
Franklin Horner Papers
William H. Martin Papers
John D. Vautier Papers
Amos S. Abbott Papers, Civil War Miscellaneous Collection
James A. Ames Papers, Civil War Miscellaneous Collection
David C. Ashley Papers, Civil War Miscellaneous Collection
Timothy Bateman Papers, Civil War Miscellaneous Collection
John W. Bates Papers, Civil War Miscellaneous Collection
Thomas Bell Papers, Civil War Miscellaneous Collection
Thomas G. Bennett Papers, Civil War Miscellaneous Collection
Samuel Bliss Papers, Civil War Miscellaneous Collection
John Bricker Papers, Civil War Miscellaneous Collection
John H. Burrill Papers, Civil War Miscellaneous Collection
Arthur Corwin Papers, Civil War Miscellaneous Collection
Thomas B. Douglass Papers, Civil War Miscellaneous Collection
Amos Downing Papers, Civil War Miscellaneous Collection
William H. Dunham Papers, Civil War Miscellaneous Collection
David Helmick Papers, Civil War Miscellaneous Collection
David Nichol Papers, Civil War Miscellaneous Collection
Curtis C. Pollock Papers, Civil War Miscellaneous Collection
William M. Sayre Papers, Civil War Miscellaneous Collection

Anson B. Shuey Papers, Civil War Miscellaneous Collection
James R. Simpson Papers, Civil War Miscellaneous Collection
George B. Sinclair Papers, Civil War Miscellaneous Collection
Thomas W. Stephens Papers, Civil War Miscellaneous Collection
Francis A. Walter Papers, Civil War Miscellaneous Collection
James Gillette Papers, Civil War Times Illustrated Collection
Thomas G. Orwig Papers, Civil War Times Illustrated Collection
Charles C. Perkins Papers, Civil War Times Illustrated Collection
Jonathan P. Stowe Papers, Civil War Times Illustrated Collection
Thomas C. Watkins Papers, Civil War Times Illustrated Collection
Silas D. Wesson Papers, Civil War Times Illustrated Collection
James W. Denver Papers, Harrisonburg Civil War Roundtable Collection
Emory Sweetland Papers, Michael Winey Collection

University of Delaware Library (Newark, Delaware)

David Lilley Papers

University of Michigan (Ann Arbor, Michigan)

Ferdinand Davis Papers, Bentley Historical Library
Ferry Family Papers, Bentley Historical Library
Charles B. Haydon Papers, Bentley Historical Library
Claudius B. Grant papers, Bentley Historical Library
Cornwallis Orderly Book, Orderly Book Collection, Clements Library
George Henry Bates Papers, Schoff Collection, Clements Library
Jacob Van Zwaluwenburg Papers, Schoff Collection, Clements Library
James R. Woodworth Papers, Schoff Collection, Clements Library

University of North Carolina (Chapel Hill, North Carolina)

George H. Cadman Papers, Southern Historical Collection
Daniel Henry Hill Papers. Southern Historical Collection

University of Oregon (Eugene, Oregon)

Royal August Bensell Papers

University of Vermont (Burlington, Vermont)

Benedict Family Papers

University of Virginia (Charlottesville, Virginia)

Albert and Charles Allen Papers
Joseph Baer Papers
James Dunn Papers
Robert Larimer Papers
John Mottrom Papers
Henry Spaulding Papers
George E. Wagner Papers

Vermont Historical Society (Barre, Vermont)

Rufus Kinsley Papers

Vigo County Public Library (Terre Haute, Indiana)

Josiah Clinton Williams Papers

Virginia Historical Society (Richmond, Virginia)

Henry F. Gladdings Papers
Robert Knox Sneden Papers
Abel C. Thomas Papers
United States Army Collection
Alvin Voris Papers
James B. Wiggins Papers

Western Reserve Historical Society (Cleveland, Ohio)

John Quincy Adams Papers

Wisconsin Historical Society (Madison, Wisconsin)

John F. Brobst Papers
John H. Cook Papers
George Fairfield Papers
Sullivan D. Green Papers
John H. Knight Papers
Julius Murray Papers
Newton Family Papers
James Henry Otto Papers
Nathanial Rollins Papers

Wyandot Country Historical Society (Sandusky, Ohio)

Edwin A. Gordon Papers

Books and Articles

Abbott, Richard H. *Cotton & Capital: Boston Business Men and Anti-Slavery Reform, 1854–1868*. Amherst: University of Massachusetts Press, 1991.

Abramson, Paul R. and Pinkerton, Steven D. *With Pleasure: Thoughts on the Nature of Human Sexuality*. New York: Oxford, 2002.

Adams, Charles F. *The Works of John Adams, Second President of the United States*. Boston: Little, Brown, 1865.

Adams, Henry C. *Indiana at Vicksburg*. Indianapolis, IN: State Printing and Binding, 1910.

Adams, Ida B. "The Civil War Letters of James Rush Holmes." *Western Pennsylvania Historical Magazine*, vol. 44, no. 2 (June 1961).

Adams, John R. *Memorial and Letters of Rev. John R. Adams, D.D.* Cambridge, MA: Harvard University Press, 1890.

Adams, Virginia M. *On the Altar of Freedom: A Black Soldier's Civil War Letters from the Front*. New York: Warner Books, 1991.

Alexander, Arthur J. "Desertion and Its Punishment in Revolutionary Virginia." *William and Mary Quarterly*, vol. 3 (1946).

Allen, George H. *Forty-Six Months with the Fourth R.I. Volunteers in the War of 1861 to 1865.* Providence, RI: J.A. and R.A. Reid, 1887.

Alotta, Robert I. *Stop the Evil: A Civil War History of Desertion and Murder*. San Rafael, CA: Presidio Press, 1978.

American Military History: Army Historical Series. Washington, DC: Center for Military History, 1989.

Anderson, John. *History of the 57th Regiment of Massachusetts Volunteers*. Boston: E.B. Stilling, 1896.

Andre, John. *Major Andre's Journal: Operations of the British Army under Lieutenant Generals Sir William Howe and Sir Henry Clinton*. Whitefish, MT: Kessinger, 2007. Reprint of 1930 edition, 481 and 504.

Andrews, Byron. *A Biography of General John A. Logan: With an Account of His Public Service in Peace and War*. New York: H.S. Goodspeed, 1884.

The Annals of War Written by Leading Participants, North and South. Philadelphia: Times, 1879.

Ansell, Samuel T. "Some Reforms in Our System of Military Justice." *Yale Law Journal*, vol. 32, no. 2 (December 1922).

Anthony, Carl S. *First Ladies: The Saga of the Presidents' Wives and their Power, 1789–1961*. New York: Harper, Collins, 1992.

Armstrong, Warren B. *For Courageous Fighting and Confident Dying: Union Chaplains in the Civil War*. Lawrence: University Press of Kansas, 1998.

The Army Lawyer: A History of the Judge Advocate General's Corps: 1775–1975. Washington, DC: Government Printing Office, 1975.

Atwood, Thomas W.W. "From the Diaries and Letters of Pvt. Tobie: Life in a U.S. Army Hospital, 1862." *Army*, vol. 38, no. 1 (January 1988).

Bacarella, Michael. *Lincoln's Foreign Legion: The 39th New York Infantry, The Garibaldi Guard*. Shippensburg, PA: White Mane, 1996.

Baker, Naomi B. *Letters Home: Joel B. Baker, A Collection of 'Letters Home' from the Civil War*. Delevan, NY: N.B. Baker, 1996.

Barber, Raymond G., and Swinson, Gary E. *The Civil War Letters of Charles Barber, Private, 104th New York Volunteer Infantry*. Torrance, CA: Swinson, 1991.

Barck, Oscar T. *New York City during the War for Independence: With Special Reference to the Period of British Occupation*. Port Washington, NY: Friedman, Inc., 1966. Reprint of 1931 edition.

Bardeen, Charles W. *A Little Fifer's War Diary*. Syracuse, NY: self-published, 1910.

Barker-Benfield, G.J. *The Horrors of the Half-Known Life: Male Attitudes toward Women and Sexuality in Nineteenth-Century America*. New York: Harper & Row, 1976, 277.

Barth, Gunther. *All Quiet on the Yamhill: The Civil War in Oregon, The Journal of Corporal Royal A. Bensell, Company D, Fourth California Infantry*. Eugene: University of Oregon Books, 1959, xi.

Barton, Lon C. "The Reign of Terror in Graves County." *Register of the Kentucky Historical Society*, vol. 46 (April 1948).

Bassett, Morton H. *From Bull Ran to Bristow Station*. St. Paul, MN: North Central, 1962.

Bauer, K. Jack. *The Mexican War, 1846–1848*. Lincoln: University of Nebraska Press, 1992. Reprint of 1974 edition.

Baxter, Nancy N. *Gallant Fourteenth: The Story of an Indiana Civil War Regiment*. Cincinnati, OH: Emmis Books, 1999.

Bearss, Edwin C. *Historic Resource Study Ship Island Harrison County, Mississippi Gulf Islands National Seashore Florida/ Mississippi*. Denver: National Park Service, 1984.

Beaudry, Richard E. *War Journal of Louis N. Beaudry, Fifth New York Cavalry: The Diary of a Union Chaplain, Commencing February 16, 1863*. Jefferson, NC: McFarland & Company, 1996.

Bee, Robert L. *The Boys from Rockville: Civil War Narratives of Sgt. Benjamin Hirst, Company D,*

14th Connecticut Volunteers. Knoxville: University of Tennessee Press, 1998.

Beebe, Louis. "Journal of Dr. Louis Beebe." *Pennsylvania Magazine of History and Biography*, LIX (1935).

Benet, Steven V. *A Treatise on Military Law and the Practice of Courts-Martial*. New York: D. Van Nostrand, 1862.

Bentley, William H. *History of the 77th Illinois Infantry, September 2, 1862–July 10, 1865*. Peoria, IL: Hine, 1883.

Benton, Charles E. *As Seen in the Ranks: A Boy in the Civil War*. New York: Putnam & Sons, 1902.

Berge, Dennis E. "A Mexican Dilemma: The Mexico City Ayuntamiento and the Question of Loyalty, 1846–1848." *The Hispanic American Historical Review*, vol. 50, no. 2 (May 1970).

Bernath, Stuart L. "George Washington and the Genesis of American Military Discipline." *Mid-America: An Historical Review*, vol. 49, no. 2 (April 1967).

Berwanger, Eugene H. "Absent so Long from Those I Love: The Civil War Letters of Joshua Jones." *Indiana Magazine of History*, vol. 88, no. 3 (September 1992).

Billings, John D. *Hardtack and Coffee: Or the Unwritten Story of Army Life*. Boston: George M. Smith & Co., 1887.

Blight, David W. *When This Cruel War is Over: The Civil War Letters of Charles Harvey Brewster*. Amherst: University of Massachusetts Press, 1992.

Boag, Peter G. "Dear Friends: The Civil War Letters of Francis Marion Elliot, A Pennsylvania Country Boy." *Pittsburgh History*, vol. 72, no. 4 (December 1989).

Bobrick, Benson. *Testament: A Soldier's Story of the Civil War*. New York: Simon & Schuster, 2003.

Bohrnstedt, Jennifer C. *Soldiering With Sherman: Civil War Letters of George F. Cram*. DeKalb: Northern Illinois University Press, 2000.

Boman, Dennis K. "Conduct and Revolt in the Twenty-fifth Ohio Battery: An Insider's Account." *Ohio History*, vol. 104 (Summer/Autumn 1995).

Bond, Otto F. *Under the Flag of the Nation: Diaries and Letters of Own Johnston Hopkins, A Yankee volunteer in the Civil War*. Columbus: Ohio State University Press, 1998.

Bosson, Charles P. *History of the Forty-second Regiment, Massachusetts Volunteers*. Boston: Mills, Knight, & Co., 1886.

Bowman, Allen. *The Morale of the American Revolutionary Army*. Port Washington, NY: Kennikat Press, 1964.

Boyd, James. "A Tale of Two Cities: The Hidden Battle against Venereal Disease in Civil War Nashville and Memphis." *Civil War History*, vol. 31, no. 3 (September 1985).

Boylan, Anne M. *The Origins of Women's Activism: New York and Boston, 1797–1840*. Chapel Hill: University of North Carolina Press, 2002.

Boyle, John R. *Soldiers True: The Story of the One Hundred and Eleventh Regiment Pennsylvania Veteran Volunteers and of Its Campaigns in the War for the Union, 1861–1865*. New York: Eaton & Mains, 1903.

Bradford, S. Sydney. "Discipline the Morristown Winter Encampments." *Proceedings of the New Jersey Historical Society*, LXXX, Number 1 (1962).

Bridges, Alfred F. "The Execution of Private Robert Gay." *Indiana Magazine of History*, vol. 20, no. 2 (June 1924).

Britton, Ann Hartwell and Reed, Thomas J. *To My Beloved Wife and Boy at Home: The Letters and Diaries of Orderly Sergeant John F.L. Hartwell*. Rutherford, NJ: Fairleigh Dickinson University Press, 1997.

Brock, Darla. "Memphis's *Nymphs Du Pave*: The Most Abandoned Women in the World." *West Tennessee Historical Society Quarterly*, vol. 50, no. 1 (1996).

Brown, Alan S. *A Soldier's Life: the Civil War Experiences of Ben C. Johnson*. Kalamazoo, MI: Western Michigan University Press, 1962.

Brown, Alonzo L. *History of the Fourth Minnesota Infantry Volunteers during the Great Rebellion, 1861–1865*. St. Paul, MN: Pioneer Press, 1892.

Brown, D. Alexander. *The Galvanized Yankees*. Urbana: University of Illinois Press, 1963.

Brown, Jerold E. *Historical Dictionary of the U.S. Army*. Westport, CT: Greenwood, 2001.

Bruen, Ella J., and Fitzgibbons. Brian M. *Though Ordinary Eyes: The Civil War Correspondence of*

Rufus Robbins, Private, 7th Regiment, Massachusetts Volunteers. Westport, CT: Praeger, 2000.

Bryan, Charles, and Lankford, Nelson. *Eye of the Storm: A Civil War Odyssey.* New York: Free Press, 2000.

Buckingham, Peter H. *All's for the Best: The Civil War Reminiscences and Letters of Daniel W. Sawtelle, Eighth Maine Volunteer Infantry.* Knoxville: University of Tennessee Press, 2001.

Buffum, Francis H. *A Memorial of the Great Rebellion: Being a History of the Fourteenth Regiment New Hampshire Volunteers.* Boston: Franklin Press, 1882.

Bunting, Josiah. *Ulysses S. Grant.* New York: Henry Holt & Co., 2004.

Burton, William L. *Melting Pot Soldiers: The Union's Ethnic Regiments.* Ames: Iowa State University Press, 1988.

Butler, Anne M. *Daughters of Joy, Sisters of Misery: Prostitutes in the American West, 1865–1890.* Champaign: University of Illinois Press, 1987.

Butterfield, Lyman H. "Psychological Warfare in 1776: The Jefferson-Franklin Plan to Cause Hessian Desertions." *Proceedings of the American Philosophical Society,* 94, no. 3 (June 1950).

Byler, Charles A. *Civil-Military Relations on the Frontier and Beyond, 1865–1917.* Westport, CT: Praeger Security International, 2006.

Byrne, Edward M. *Military Law* 3rd Edition. Annapolis, MD: Naval Institute Press, 1981.

Cadwallader, Sylvanus. *Three Years with Grant, As Recalled By War Correspondent Sylvanus Cadwallader.* New York: Knopf, 1955.

Califf, Joseph M. *Record of the Services of the Seventh Regiment U.S. Colored Troops.* Providence, RI: Freeman, 1878.

Callan, John F. *The Military Laws of the United States Relating to the Army, Marine Corps, Volunteers, Militia, and to Bounty Lands and Pensions, From the Foundation of the Government to the Year 1858.* Baltimore, MD: John Murphy & Co., 1858.

Cannell, Dorothy S. "Facing Court-Martial." *Michigan History,* vol. 82, no. 4 (July/August 1998).

Capers, Gerald M. "Confederates and Yankees in Occupied New Orleans, 1862–1865." *Journal of Southern History,* vol. 30, no. 4 (November 1964).

Carmony, Donald E. "Jacob W. Bartmess Civil War Letters." *Indiana Magazine of History,* vol. 52, no. 1 (March 1956).

Carmony, Neil B. *The Civil War in Apacheland: Sergeant George Hand's Diary: California, Arizona, West Texas, New Mexico, 1861–1864.* Silver City, NV: High-Lonesome Books, 1996.

Carter, Robert G. *Four Brothers in Blue: Or Sunshine and Shadows of the War of the Rebellion, A Story of the Great Civil War from Bull Run to Appomattox.* Norman: University of Oklahoma Press, 1999.

Carter, Samuel. *The Riddle of Dr. Mudd.* New York: Putnam, 1974.

Carter, Theodore G. "The Tupelo Campaign." *Publications of the Mississippi Historical Society,* vol. 10 (Oxford, MS: Mississippi Historical Society, 1909).

Carver, C.E. "The Significance of the Military Officer in America, 1763–1765." *American Historical Review,* vol. 28, no. 3 (April 1923).

Castel, Albert. "Malingering: Many . . . Diseases Are . . . Feigned." *Civil War Times Illustrated,* vol. 21, no. 5 (August 1977).

Catton, Bruce. *A Stillness at Appomattox.* Garden City, NJ: Doubleday, 1954.

———. *America Goes to War.* Garden City, NJ: Doubleday, 1953.

Chadwick, Bruce. *Brother Against Brother: The Lost Civil War Diary of Lt. Edmund Halsey.* New York: Carol, 1997.

Cilella, Salvatore G. "The 121st New York State Infantry Regiment," M.A. thesis, State University of New York-Oneonta, 1972.

Cimbala, Paula A., and Miller, Randall M. *Union Soldiers and the Northern Home Front: Wartime Experiences, Postwar Adjustments.* New York: Fordham University Press, 2002.

Clark, Charles M. *The History of the Thirty-Ninth Regiment Illinois Volunteer Veteran Infantry.* Chicago: self-published, 1889.

Clinton, Catherin, and Silber, Nina. *Divided Houses: Gender and the Civil War.* New York: Oxford University Press, 1992.

Coe, David. *Mine Eyes Have Seen the Glory: Combat Diaries of Union Sergeant Hamlin Alexander Coe*. Rutherford, NJ: Fairleigh Dickinson State University Press, 1975, 97–98.

Coffin, Howard. *Nine Months to Gettysburg: Stannard's Vermonters and the Repulse of Picket's Charge*. Woodstock, Vermont: Countryman Press, 1997.

Coffman, Edward M. *The Old Army: A Portrait of the American Army in Peacetime, 1784–1898*. New York: Oxford University Press, 1986.

Cole, Arthur C. *The Centennial History of Illinois*, vol. III: *The Era of the Civil War, 1848–1870*. Springfield: Illinois Centennial Commission, 1919.

Collins, George K. *Memories of the 149th Regiment, New York Volunteer Infantry*. Hamilton, NY: Edmonston Pub., 1891.

Corby, William, *Memoirs of a Chaplain Life: Three Years Chaplain in the Famous "Irish Brigade," Army of the Potomac*. Scholastic Press, 1984.

Costa, Dora L. and Kahn, Matthew E. "Cowards and Heroes: Group Loyalty in the American Civil War." *Quarterly Journal of Economics*, vol. 118, no. 2 (May 2003).

Courtwright, Donald T. *Violent Land: Single Men and Social Disorder from the Frontier to the Inner City*. Cambridge, MA: Harvard University Press, 1996.

Cox, Walter T. "The Army, the Courts, and the Constitution: The Evolution of Military Justice." *Military Law Review*, vol. 118, no. 1 (1987).

Cozzens, Peter. *The Darkest Days of the War: The Battles of Iuka and Corinth*. Chapel Hill, University of North Carolina Press, 2006.

Crawford, Robert F. "The Civil War Letters of S. Rodman and Linton Smith." *Delaware History*, vol. 21 (Fall 1984).

Cress, Lawrence D. "Republican Liberty and National Security: American Military Policy as an Ideological Problem, 1783 to 1789." *William and Mary Quarterly*, 3rd Ser., vol. 38, no. 1 (January, 1981).

Crockett, David. *Life of Col. David Crockett*. Philadelphia: G.G. Evans, 1860.

Croushore, James H. *A Volunteer's Adventures: A Union Captain's Record of the Civil War*. Hamden, CT: Archon Books, 1970.

Currie-McDaniel, Ruth. *Carpetbagger of Conscience: A Biography of John Emory Bryant*. New York: Fordham University Press, 1999.

Danbom, David B. "Dear Companion: Civil War Letters of a Story County Farmer." *Annals of Iowa*, vol. 47 (Fall 1984).

Davidson, Garber A. *The Civil War Letters of the Late 1st Lieut. James J. Hartley, 122nd Ohio Infantry Regiment*. Jefferson, NC: McFarland & Company, 1998.

Davis, Charles E. *Three Years in the Army: The Story of the Thirteenth Massachusetts Volunteers*. Boston: Estes & Lauriat, 1894.

Davis, George B. *Outlines of International Law*. New York: Harper & Brothers, 1887.

Davis, Washington. *Camp-fire Chats of the Civil War*. Chicago: Lewis, 1888.

Davis, William C. *A Taste for War: A Culinary History of the Blue and the Gray*. Mechanicsburg, PA: Stackpole Books, 2003.

Dawes, Rufus R. *Service with the Sixth Wisconsin Volunteers*. Marietta, OH: E.R. Alderman & Sons, 1890.

Delaney, Norman C. "Letters of a Maine Soldier Boy." *Civil War History*, vol. 5 (March 1959)

D'Emilio, John and Freedman, Estelle B. *Intimate Matters: A History of Sexuality in America*. Chicago: University of Chicago Press, 1998..

Denny, William. "Soldier of the Republic: The Life of Major Ebenezer Denny," Ph.D. dissertation, Miami University, 1978.

DeRosier, Arthur H. *Through the South with a Union Soldier*. Johnson City: East Tennessee State University, 1969.

de Tocqueville, Alexis. *Democracy in America*. New York: Colonial Press, 1899.

de Trobriand, Regis. *Four Years with the Army of the Potomac*. Boston: Ticknor & Co., 1889.

Dix, Mary S. "And Three rousing Cheers for the Privates: A Diary of the 1862 Roanoke Island Expedition." *North Carolina Historical Review*, vol. 71, no. 1 (January 1994).

Domenech, Abbe. *Missionary Adventures in Texas and Mexico*. London: Longmans, Brown, & Green, 1857.

Donald, David H. *Gone for a Soldier: The Civil War Memoirs of Private Alfred Bellard*. Boston: Little, Brown, 1975.

Dorris, Jonathan T. *Pardon and Amnesty under Lincoln and Johnson*. Chapel Hill: University of North Carolina Press, 1953.

Downs, Donald A. *The New Politics of Pornography*. Chicago: University of Chicago Press, 1989.

Doyle, Elisabeth J. "New Orleans Courts under Military Occupation, 1861–1865." *Mid-America: A Historical Review*, vol. 42, no. 2 (July 1960).

Droddy, J.D. "King Richard to *Solorio*: The Historical and Constitutional Bases for Court-Martial Jurisdiction in Criminal Cases." *Harvard Law Review*, vol. 103, no. 8 (June, 1990).

Dunkelman, Mark H. *Brothers One and All: Esprit de Corps in a Civil War Regiment*. Baton Rouge: Louisiana State University, 2004.

Durkin, James and Whitcomb, Jennifer M. *This War is an Awful Thing: Civil War Letters of the National Guards: The 19th and 90th Pennsylvania Volunteers*. Glenside, PA: Santarelli, 1994.

Eby, Cecil D. *A Virginia Yankee in the Civil War: The Diaries of David Hunter Strother*. Chapel Hill: University of North Carolina Press, 1961.

Eisenhower, John S. *Agent of Destiny: the Life and Times of General Winfield Scott*. New York: Free Press, 1997.

Elder, Donald C. *A Damned Iowa Greyhound: The Civil War Letters of William Henry Harrison Clayton*. Iowa City: University of Iowa Press, 1998.

Ellis, Thomas T. *Leaves from the Diary of an Army Surgeon; Or, Incidents of Field, Camp, and Hospital Life*. New York: J. Bradburn, 1863.

Emerson, Edward W. *The Life and Letters of Charles Russell Lowell*. Boston: Houghton & Mifflin, 1907.

Engert, Roderick M. *Maine to the Wilderness: The Civil War Letters of Pvt. William Lamson, 20th Maine Infantry*. Orange, VA: Publisher's Press, 1993.

Engle, Stephen D. *Don Carlos Buell: Most Promising of All*. Chapel Hill: University of North Carolina Press, 1999.

Esslinger, Michael. *Alcatraz: A Definitive History of the Penitentiary Years*. Carmel, CA: Ocean View, 2003.

Fadiman, Clifton and Andre Bernard, Andre. *Bartlett's Book of Anecdotes*. Boston: Little, Brown, 2000.

Farling, Amos. *Life in the Army: Containing Historical and Biographical Sketches, Incidents, Adventures and Narratives of the Late War*. Buchanan, MI: self-published, 1874.

Fatout, Paul. *Letters of a Civil War Surgeon*. West Lafayette, IN: Purdue University Press, 1961.

Fehrenbacher, Don E. and Fehrenbacher, Virginia. *Recollected Words of Abraham Lincoln*. Palo Alto, CA: Stanford University Press, 1996.

Fenster, Julie M. *The Case of Abraham Lincoln: A Story of Adultery, Murder, and the Making of a Great President*. New York: Palgrave MacMillan, 2007.

Fishel, Edwin C. *The Secret War for the Union: The Untold Story of Military Intelligence in the Civil War*. Boston: Houghton-Mifflin, 1996.

Fisher, Ernest F. *Guardians of the Republic: A History of the Non-Commissioned Officer Corps of the United States Army*. Mechanicsburg, PA: Stackpole Books, 2001.

Fitzharris, Joseph C. "Field Officer Courts and U.S. Civil War Military Justice." *The Journal of Military History*, vol. 68, no. 1 (2004).

Fitzpatrick, John C. *Writings of George Washington from the Original Manuscript Sources*. 39 vols. Washington, DC: Government Printing Office, 1931–1944.

Flanders, Henry. *The Lives and Times of the Chief Justices of the Supreme Court of the United States*. Philadelphia Lippincott, 1874.

Fleharty, D.F. *Our Regiment: A History of the 102nd Illinois Infantry Volunteers*. Chicago: Brewster & Hanscom, 1865.

Foos, Paul. *A Short, Offhand, Killing Affair: Soldiers and Social Conflict during the Mexican-American War*. Chapel Hill: University of North Carolina Press, 2002.

Foote, Lorien. "Rich Man's War, Rich Man's Fight: Class, Ideology, and Discipline in the Union Army." *Civil War History*, vol. 51, no. 3 (September 2005).

Ford, Worthington C. *Journals of the Continental Congress, 1774–1779.* Washington, DC: Government Printing Office, 1905.

Fosdick, Harry E. *The Meaning of Faith.* New York: Association Press, 1918.

Frank, Joseph A. *With Ballot and Bayonet: The Political Socialization of American Civil War Soldiers.* Athens, University of Georgia Press, 1998.

Frank, Joseph A., Pozzatti, Rudy A., and Reaves, George A. *Seeing the Elephant: Raw Recruits at the Battle of Shiloh.* Champagne: University of Illinois Press, 2003.

Frank, Lisa T. "To Cure Her of Her Pride and Boasting: The Gendered Implications of Sherman's March," Ph.D. dissertation, University of Florida, 2001.

Frassanito, William A. *Grant and Lee: The Virginia Campaigns, 1864–1865.* New York: Scribner's and Sons, 1983.

Frey, Sylvia R. *The British Soldier in America: A Social History of Military Life in the Revolutionary Period.* Austin: University of Texas Press, 1981.

Fuess, Claude M. *The Life of Caleb Cushing.* 2 vols. New York: Harcourt, Brace, 1923.

Gaff, Alan D. *On Many a Bloody Field: Four Years in the Iron Brigade.* Bloomington: Indiana University Press, 1996.

Gay, Peter. *Pleasure Wars: The Bourgeois Experience, Victoria to Freud.* New York: Norton, 1998.

Gebhard, Ann. "Doubly Paid for any Sacrifice." *Michigan History*, vol. 74, no. 2 (March/April 1990).

Gibbon, John. *Personal Recollections of the Civil War.* New York: G.B. Putnam's, 1928.

Gibbs, Joseph. *Three Years in the "Bloody Eleventh": The Campaigns of a Pennsylvania Reserves Regiment.* University Park: Pennsylvania State University Press, 2002.

Giddings, Luther. *Sketches of the Campaign in Northern Mexico, in Eighteen-Hundred Forty Six and Seven.* New York: G.B. Putnam, 1953.

Gilbert, Arthur N. "The Changing Face of British Military Justice, 1757–1783." *Military Affairs*, vol. 49, no. 2 (April 1985).

Glatthaar, Joseph T. *The March to the Sea and Beyond: Sherman's Troops in the Savannah and Carolinas Campaigns.* Baton Rouge: Louisiana State University Press, 1985.

Gordon, Lesley J. *I Never Was a Coward: Questions of Bravery in a Civil War Regiment.* Milwaukee: Marquette University Press, 2005.

Gould, Benjamin A. *Investigation in the Military and Anthropological Statistics of American Soldiers.* New York: Hurd and Houghton, 1869.

Gould, David and Kennedy, James B. *Memoirs of a Dutch Mudsill: The 'War Memories' of John Henry Otto, Captain, Company D, 21st Regiment Wisconsin Volunteer Infantry.* Kent, OH: Kent State University Press, 2004.

Gould, Joseph. *The Story of the Forty-eighth: A Record of the Campaigns of the Forty-eighth Regiment Pennsylvania Veteran Volunteer Infantry.* Philadelphia: Frank A. Taylor, 1908.

Graham, Stanley S. "Life of the Enlisted Soldier on the Western Frontier," M.A. thesis, North Texas State University, 1972.

Greenberg, Amy S. *Manifest Manhood and the Antebellum American Empire.* Cambridge: Cambridge University Press, 2005.

Greiner, James M. *Subdued by the Sword: A Line Officer in the 121st New York Volunteers.* Albany, NY: SUNY Press, 2003.

Griffith, Lucille. *Yours Till Death: The Civil War Letters of John W. Cotton.* Tuscaloosa: University of Alabama Press, 1951.

Hagerty, Edward J. *Collis' Zouaves: The 114th Pennsylvania Volunteers in the Civil War.* Baton Rouge: Louisiana State University Press, 1997.

Hallock, Judith Lee. "The Role of the Community in Civil War Desertion." *Long Island Historical Journal*, vol. 6, no. 2 (Spring 1994).

Halsey, Ashley. *A Yankee Private's Civil War.* Chicago: Henry Regnery Company, 1961.

Hamilton, Frank H. *A Treatise on Military Surgery and Hygiene.* New York: Bailliere Brothers, 1865.

Hamilton, William D. *Recollections of a Cavalryman of the Civil War After Fifty Years, 1861–1865.* Columbus, OH: F.J. Heer, 1915.

Hanson, Victor D., and Keegan, John. *The Western Way of War: Infantry Battle in Classical Greece*, 2nd Edition. Berkeley: University of California Press, 2000.

Harley, Lewis R. *Francis Lieber: His Life and Political Philosophy*. New York: Columbia University Press, 1899.

Harris, Robert F., and Niflot, John. *Dear Sister: The Civil War Letters of the Brothers Gould*. Westport, CT: Praeger, 1998.

Harris, William C. *In the Country of the Enemy: The Civil War Reports of a Massachusetts Corporal*. Gainesville: University Press of Florida, 1999.

Harrison, Lowell H. *Lincoln of Kentucky*. Lexington: University of Kentucky Press, 2000.

Harwell, Richard. *Colorado Volunteers in New Mexico, 1862*. Chicago: Lakeside Press, 1962.

Hatch, Louis C. *The Administration of the American Revolutionary Army*. New York: Longmans, Green, 1904.

Hayford, Harrison. *The Somers Mutiny Affair: A Book of Primary Source Materials*. New York: Prentice-Hall, 1959.

Heatwole, John L. *The Burning: Sheridan in the Shenandoah Valley*. Charlottesville, VA: Rockbridge, 1998.

Hebert, Walter H. *Fighting Joe Hooker*. Lincoln: University of Nebraska Press, 1999.

Hedrick, David T., and Davis, Gordon B. *I'm Surrounded by Methodists...: Diary of John H.W. Stuckenberg, Chaplain of the 145th Pennsylvania Volunteer Infantry*. Gettysburg, PA: Thomas Publications, 1995.

Heidler, David S., and Heidler, Jeanne T. *Encyclopedia of the American Civil War: A Political, Social, and Military History*. Santa Barbara, CA: ABC-CLIO, 2000, 2002–2003.

Heinl, Robert D. *Dictionary of Military and Naval Quotations*. Annapolis, MD: Naval Institute Press, 1966.

Henderson, Charles R. *Correction and Prevention*. New York: Charles Publication Committee, 1910.

Hennessy, John J. *Fighting with the Eighteenth Massachusetts: The Civil War Memoir of Thomas H. Mann*. Baton Rouge: Louisiana State University, 2000.

Henry, William S. *Campaign Sketches of the War with Mexico*. New York: Arno Press, 1973; reprint of 1847 edition.

Herdegen, Lance J. *The Men Stood Like Iron: How the Iron Brigade Won Its Name*. Bloomington: Indiana University Press, 1997.

Herek, Raymond. *These Men Have Seen Hard Service: The First Michigan Sharpshooters in the Civil War*. Detroit: Wayne State University Press, 1998.

Hesseltine, William B. *Civil War Prisons*. Columbus: Ohio State University Press, 1930.

Higgs, Robert J. *God in the Stadium: Sports and Religion in America*. Lexington: University of Kentucky Press, 1995.

Hill, Marilynn W. *Their Sisters' Keepers: Prostitution in New York City, 1830–1870*. Berkeley: University of California Press, 1993.

Hobson, Barbara M. *Uneasy Virtue: The Politics of Prostitution and the American Reform Tradition*. Chicago: University of Chicago Press, 1990.

Holberton, William B. *Homeward Bound: The Demobilization of the Union & Confederate Armies, 1865–66*. Mechanicsburg, PA: Stackpole Books, 2001.

Holcomb, Julie. *Southern Sons, Northern Soldiers: The Civil War Letters of the Remley Brothers, 22nd Iowa Infantry*. DeKalb: Northern Illinois University Press, 2004.

Holland, James K. "Diary of a Texan Volunteer in the Mexican War." *Southwestern Historical Quarterly*, vol. 30 (July 1926).

Hollister, Ovando J. *Colorado Volunteers in New Mexico, 1862*. Chicago: Lakeside Press, 1962.

Hough, William. *The Practice of Courts-Martial and Other Military Courts*. London: Parbury, Allen, & Co., 1834.

Hubbard, Charles M. *Lincoln and his Contemporaries*. Macon, GA: Mercer University Press, 1999.

———. *Lincoln Reshapes the Presidency*. Macon, GA: Mercer University Press, 2001.

Hudson, Helen. *Civil War Hawks*. Hagerstown, IN: Historic Hagerstown, 1974.

Hughes, William E. *The Civil War Papers of Lt. Colonel Newton T. Colby, New York Infantry*. Jefferson, North Carolina: McFarland & Company, 2003.

Hummel, William W. "The Military Occupation of Columbia County." *Pennsylvania*

Magazine of History, vol. 80, no. 3 (July 1956).

Husby, Karla J., and Wittenberg, Eric J. *Under Custer's Command: The Civil War Journal of James Henry Avery*. Washington, DC: Brassey's, 2000.

Hyatt, Hudson. "Captain Hyatt: Being the Letters Written during the War Years 1863–1864 to His Wife Mary." *Ohio State Archaeological and Historical Quarterly*, vol. 53 (1944).

Ingersoll, Lurton D. *A History of the War Department of the United States*. Philadelphia: Claxton, Remsen, & Haffelfinger, 1880.

Jenkins, Kirk C. *The Battle Rages Higher: The Union's Fifteenth Kentucky Infantry*. Lexington: University of Kentucky Press, 2003.

Jenkins, Wilbert L. *Climbing Up to Glory: A Short History of African Americans during the Civil War and Reconstruction*. Lanham, MD: Rowman & Littlefield, 2002.

Jensen, Dana O. "The Memoirs of Daniel M. Frost." *Missouri Historical Society Bulletin*, vol. 26, no. 3 (1970).

Johnson, Mark W. *That Body of Brave Men: The U.S. Regular Infantry and the Civil War in the West*. New York: DaCapo Press, 2003.

Johnson, Robert U., and Buel, Clarence C. *Battles and Leaders of the Civil War*. New York: The Century Company, 1888.

Jones, James B. "A Tale of Two Cities." *North and South*, vol. 10, no. 5 (2008).

Jones, Katherine M. *When Sherman Came: Southern Women and the "Great March,"*. Indianapolis: Bobbs-Merrill, 1964.

Jones, Wilbur D. *Giants in the Cornfield: The 27th Indiana Infantry*. Shippensburg, PA: White Mane, 1997.

Jordan, David M. *Happiness Is Not My Companion: The Life of General G.K. Warren*. Bloomington: Indiana University Press, 2001.

Jordan, E.L. "A Painful Case: The Wright-Sanborn Incident in Norfolk, Virginia, July–October 1863," M.A. thesis, Old Dominion University, 1979.

Jordan, Ervin L. *Black Confederates and Afro-Yankees in Civil War Virginia*. Charlottesville: University Press of Virginia, 1995.

Jordan, William B. *Red Diamond Regiment: The 17th Maine Infantry, 1862–1865*. Shippensburg, PA: White Mane, 1996.

Kaminski, John P. *The Documentary History of the Ratification of the Constitution*. Madison: State Historical Society of Wisconsin, 1976–2007.

Kaplan, Harold L. "Constitutional Limitations on Trials by Military Commissions." *University of Pennsylvania Law Review and American Law Register*, vol. 92, no. 2 (December 1943).

Karamanski, Theodore J. *Rally 'round the Flag: Chicago And the Civil War*. New York: Rowman & Littlefield, 2006.

Kaser, David. "Nashville's Women of Pleasure in 1860." *Tennessee Historical Quarterly*, vol. 23, no. 4 (1964).

Katcher, Philip. *The Civil War Source Book*. New York: Facts on File, 1982.

Kellogg, Mary E. *Army Life of an Illinois Soldier*. Carbondale: Southern Illinois University Press, 1996.

Kelly, Orr, and Kelly, Mary D. *Dream's End: Two Iowa Brothers in the Civil War*. New York: Kodansha America, 1998.

Kennett, Lee. *Sherman: A Soldier's Life*. New York: Perennial, 2001.

Kent, Arthur A. *Three Years with Company K: Sergt. Austin C. Stearns, Company K 13th Mass. Infantry. Deceased*. Rutherford, NJ: Fairleigh Dickinson University Press, 1976.

Keuchel, Edward F. and Jones, James P. "Charley Schreel's Book: Diary of a Union Soldier on Garrison Duty in Tennessee." *Tennessee Historical Quarterly*, vol. 36, no. 2 (Summer 1977).

Kime, Wayne R. *Colonel Richard Irving Dodge: The Life and Times of a Career Army Officer*. Norman: University of Oklahoma Press, 2006.

Kimmel, Michael. *Manhood in America: A Cultural History*. New York: Free Press, 1996.

Kohn, Richard H. *The United States Military under the Constitution of the United States, 1789–1989*. New York: New York University Press, 1991.

Koke, Richard J. "Washington and Captain Joshua Huddy." *New York Historical Society Quarterly*, vol. 41, no. 3 (1957).

Kroll, Kathleen, and Moran, Charles. "The White Papers." *Massachusetts Review*, vol. 18, no. 2 (Summer 1976).

Landon, William D.F. "Fourteenth Indiana Regiment: Letters to Vincennes *Western Sun.*" *Indiana Magazine of History*, vol. 35, no. 1 (March 1938).

Lassen, Coralou P. *Dear Sarah: Letters Home from a Soldier in the Iron Brigade*. Bloomington: Indiana University Press, 1999.

Leech, Margaret. *Reveille in Washington, 1860–1865*. New York: Harper & Brothers, 1941.

Lender, Mark E, and Martin, James K. *Drinking in America: A History*. New York: Free Press, 1987.

Leonard, Elizabeth D. *Lincoln's Avengers: Justice, Revenge, and Reunion after the Civil War*. New York: Norton, 2004.

Lewis, A.S. *My Dear Parents: The Civil War Seen by an English Union Soldier*. New York: Harcourt, Brace, Jovanovich, 1982.

Lind, Henry C. *The Long Road for Home: The Civil War Experiences of Four Farmboy Soldiers of the Twenty-seventh Massachusetts Regiment*. Rutherford, NJ: Fairleigh Dickinson University Press, 1992.

Linderman, Gerald F. *Embattled Courage: The Experience of Combat in the American Civil War*. New York: Free Press, 1987.

Little, Henry F.W. *The Seventh Regiment New Hampshire Volunteers in the War of the Rebellion*. Concord, NH: Ira Evans, 1896.

Livermore, Mary A. *My Story of the War: The Civil War Memoirs of the Famous Nurse, Relief Organizer, and Suffragette*. New York: DaCapo, 1995.

Livermore, Thomas L. *Days and Events, 1860–1866*. New York: Houghton Mifflin, 1920.

Longacre, Edward. "Chaos Still Reigns in this Camp: Letters of Lieutenant George N. Bliss, 1st New England Cavalry, March-September 1862." *Rhode Island History*, vol. 36, no. 1 (1911).

Lowry, Thomas P. "The Army's Licensed Prostitutes." *Civil War Times Illustrated*, vol. 41, no. 4 (August 2002).

———. "Johnny Reb, Billy Yank, and Betty Sue." *North & South*, vol. 9, no. 4 (August 2006).

———. *The Story the Soldiers Wouldn't Tell: Sex in the Civil War*. Mechanicsville, PA: Stackpole Books, 1994.

———. *Tarnished Eagles: The Courts-Martial of Fifty Union Colonels and Lieutenant Colonels*. Mechanicsburg, PA: Stackpole Books, 1997.

Lurie, Jonathan. *Arming Military Justice, vol. 1: The Origins of the United States Court of Military Appeals, 1775–1950*. Princeton, NJ: Princeton University Press, 1992.

Lusk, William T. *War Letters of William Thompson Lusk*. New York: privately printed, 1911.

Lyles, Ian B. "Mixed Blessing: The Role of the Texas Rangers in the Mexican War, 1846–1848," M.A. thesis, Army Command and General Staff College, 2003.

Lyman, Darryl. *Civil War Quotations*. Conshohocken, PA: Combined Books, 1995.

Lyman, Theodore. *Meade's Headquarters, 1863–1865*. New York: Atlantic Monthly Press, 1922.

Mahood, Wayne. *Charlie Mosher's Civil War: From Fair Oaks to Andersonville with the Plymouth Pilgrims. 85th N.Y. Infantry*. Hightstown, NJ: Longstreet House, 1994.

Malles, Ed. *Bridge Building in Wartime: Colonel Wesley Brainerd's Memoir of the 50th New York Volunteer Engineers*. Knoxville: University of Tennessee Press, 1997.

Mannis, Jedediah, and Wilson, Galen R. *Bound to be a Soldier: The Letters of Private James T. Miller, 111th Pennsylvania Infantry, 1861–1864*. Knoxville: University of Tennessee Press, 2001.

Marryat, Frederick. *Diary in America: With Remarks on Its Institutions*, vol. I. London: Longman, Orme, Brown, Greene & Longmans, 1839.

Marszalek, John F. *Sherman's Other War: The General and the Civil War Press*. Kent, OH: Kent State University Press, 1999.

Martin, Samuel J. *Kill-Cavalry: The Life of Union General Hugh Judson Kilpatrick*. Mechanicsburg, PA: Stackpole Books, 2000.

Matthews, Richard E. *The 149th Pennsylvania Volunteer Infantry Unit in the Civil War.* Jefferson, NC: McFarland & Company, 1994.

Maurer, Maurer. "Military Justice under General Washington." *Military Affairs,* vol. 28, no. 1 (Spring 1964).

McAdams, Francis M. *Every-day Soldier Life: Or A History of the One Hundred Thirteenth Ohio Infantry.* Columbus, OH: Charles M. Cott, 1884.

McCaffrey, James M. *The Army in Transformation, 1790–1860.* New York: Greenwood Press, 2006.

McClellan, George B. *Report on the Organization and Campaigns of the Army of the Potomac.* New York: Sheldon & Co., 1864.

McCordick, David. *The Harmony Boys are All Well: The Civil War Letters. 1862–1865 of Private Henry Kauffman.* Queenstown, Ontario: Edwin Mellen Press, 1991.

McGerr, Michael E. *A Fierce Discontent: The Rise and Fall of the Progressive Movement in America, 1870–1920.* New York: Simon and Schuster, 2003.

McKnight, W. Mark. *Blue Bonnets O'er the Border: The 79th New York Cameron Highlanders.* Shippensburg, PA: White Mane Books, 1998.

McLean, James. *California Sabers: The 2nd Massachusetts Cavalry in the Civil War.* Bloomington: Indiana University Press, 2000.

McMichael, James. "Diary of Lieutenant James McMichael of the Pennsylvania Line, 1776–1778." *Pennsylvania Magazine of History and Biography,* vol. 16 (1892).

Mellon, Knox. "Letters of James Greenalch." *Michigan History,* vol. 44, no. 2 (June 1960).

Melton, Buckner F. *A Hanging Offense: The Strange Affair of the Warship Somers.* New York: Free Press, 2003.

Menge, W. Springer, and J. Shimrak, August. *The Civil War Notebook of Daniel Chisholm: A Chronicle of Daily Life in the Union Army, 1864–1865.* New York: Orion Books, 1989.

Meranze, Michael. *Laboratories of Virtue: Punishment, Revolution, and Authority in Philadelphia, 1769–1835.* Chapel Hill: University of North Carolina Press, 1996.

Military History and Reminiscences of the Thirteenth Regiment of Illinois Volunteer Infantry in the Civil War in the United States, 1861–1865. Chicago: Woman's Temperance Publishing Association, 1892.

Miller, Edward A. *The Black Civil War Soldiers of Illinois: The Story of the Twenty-ninth U.S. Colored Infantry.* Columbia: University of South Carolina Press, 1998.

Miller, Richard F. *Harvard's Civil War: A History of the Twentieth Massachusetts Volunteer Infantry.* Hanover, NH: University Press of New England, 2005.

Miller, Richard F., and Mooney, Robert F. *The Civil War: The Nantucket Experience.* Nantucket, MA: Wesco, 1994.

Miller, Robert R. *Shamrock and Sword: The Saint Patrick's Battalion in the U.S.-Mexican War.* Norman: University of Oklahoma Press, 1989.

Mitchell, Reid. *The Vacant Chair: The Northern Soldier Leaves Home.* New York: Oxford University Press, 1993.

Moe, Richard. *The Last Full Measure: The Life and Death of the First Minnesota Volunteers.* New York: Henry Holt & Company, 1993.

Mohr, James C., and Winslow, Richard E. *The Cormany Diaries: A Northern Family in the Civil War.* Pittsburgh: University of Pittsburgh Press, 1982.

Moore, Frank, and Everett, Edward. *The Rebellion Record: A Diary of American Events.* New York: Van Nostrand, 1868.

Morford, Henry, Armstrong, William H., and Frick, Jacob G. *Red Tape and Pigeon-Hole Generals: As Seen From the Ranks during a Campaign in the Army of the Potomac.* New York: Carleton, 1864.

Morrell, Carl A. *Seymour Dexter, Union Army: Journal and Letters of Civil War Service In Company K, 23rd New York volunteer Regiment of Elmira, with Illustrations.* Jefferson, NC: McFarland & Company, 1996.

Morris, Scott R. "The Laws of War: Rules by Warriors for Warriors." *The Army Lawyer,* December 1997, DA-PAM 27–50–301.

Morse, Charles F. *Letters Written during the Civil War, 1861–1865*. Privately printed, 1898.

Muffly, Joseh W. *The Story of Our Regiment: A History of the 148th Pennsylvania Vols.*. Des Moines, IA: Kenyon, 1904.

Murdock, Eugene C. *Patriotism Limited: The Civil War Draft and the Bounty System*. Kent, OH: Kent State University Press, 1967.

———. "Pity the Poor Surgeon." *Civil War History*, vol. 16, no. 1 (March 1970).

Murphy, Kevin C. *The Civil War Letters of Joseph K. Taylor of the Thirty-seventh Massachusetts Volunteer Infantry*. Lewiston, ON: Edwin Mellen Press, 1998.

Murray, Stuart. *A Time of War: A Northern Chronicle of the Civil War*. Lee, MA: Berkshire House, 2001.

Neagles, James C. *Summer Soldiers: A Survey & Index of Revolutionary War Courts-Martial*. Salt Lake City, UT: Ancestry Incorporated, 1986.

Neely, Mark E. *The Fate of Liberty: Abraham Lincoln and Civil Liberties*. New York: Oxford University Press, 1991.

Nevins, Allan. *A Diary of Battle: The Personal Journals of Colonel Charles S. Wainwright, 1861–1865*. New York: Harcourt, Brace & World, 1963.

Newell, Joseph K. *'Ours': Annals of the 10th Regiment, Massachusetts Volunteers*. Springfield, MA: C.A. Nichols & Co., 1875.

Niesen, William C. "The Consequence of Grandeur: A Union Soldier Writes of the Atlanta Campaign." *Atlanta History*, vol. 33 (Fall 1989).

Noe, Kenneth W. *A Southern Boy in Blue: The Memoir of Marcus Woodcock, 9th Kentucky Infantry. U.S.A.*. Knoxville: University of Tennessee Press, 1996.

Nofi, Albert A. *A Civil War Treasury*. New York: Da Capo Press, 1995.

Nolan, Alan T. *A Full Blown Yankee in the Iron Brigade: Service with the Sixth Wisconsin Volunteers*. Lincoln: University of Nebraska Press, 1999.

Norton, Eliot. "Tales at First Hand." *Blackwood's*, vol. 233 (January 1933).

Norton, Oliver W. *Army Letters, 1861–1865*. Chicago: O.L. Deming, 1903.

Nye, W.S. *The Valiant Hours: Narrative of "Captain Brevet," an Irish-American in the Army of the Potomac*. Harrisburg, PA: The Stackpole Company, 1961.

O'Connor, Thomas H. "Lincoln and the Cotton Trade." *Civil War History*, vol. 7, no. 1 (1961).

O'Leary, Jenny, and Jackson, Harvey H. "The Civil War Letters of Captain Daniel O'Leary, U.S.A." *Register of the Kentucky Historical Society*, vol. 77 (Summer 1979).

Olsen, James S. *Historical Dictionary of the 1970s*. New York: Greenwood Press, 1999.

O'Reilly, Frank A. *The Fredericksburg Campaign: "Stonewall" Jackson at Fredericksburg: The Battle of Prospect Hill, December 13, 1862*. Lynchburg, VA: H.E. Howard, 1993.

Osborne, Frederick M. *Private Osborn, Massachusetts 23rd Volunteers: Burnside Expedition, Roanoke Island, Second Front Against Richmond*. Jefferson, NC: McFarland & Co., 1999.

Otis, George H. *The Second Wisconsin Infantry*. Dayton, OH: Press of Morningside Bookshop, 1984.

Overmyer, Jack K. *A Stupendous Effort: The 87th Indiana in the War of the Rebellion*. Bloomington: Indiana University Press, 1997.

Page, Charles D. *History of the Fourteenth Regiment, Connecticut Volunteer Infantry*. Hartford: Horton Printing, 1906.

Palfrey, Francis W. *Memoir of William Francis Bartlett*. Boston: Houghton, Osgood, 1879.

Palladino, Anita. *Diary of a Yankee Engineer: The Civil War Story of John H. Westervelt, Engineer, 1st New York Volunteer Engineer Corps*. New York: Fordham University Press, 1997.

Paradis, James M. *Strike the Blow for Freedom: The 6th United States Colored Infantry in the Civil War*. Shippensburg, PA: White Mane Books, 1998.

Parson, Thomas E. *Bear Flag and Bay State in the Civil War: The Californians of the Second Massachusetts Cavalry*. Jefferson, NC: McFarland & Company, 2001.

Parsons, Elaine Frantz. *Manhood Lost: Fallen Drunkards and Redeeming Women in the Nineteenth-century United States*. Baltimore: Johns Hopkins University Press, 2003.

Patrick, Jeffrey L. *Three Years with Wallace's Zouaves: The Civil War Memoirs of Thomas Wise Durham*. Macon, GA: Mercer University Press, 2003.

Pelka, Fred. *The Civil War Letters of Colonel Charles F. Johnson, Invalid Corps.* Amherst: University of Massachusetts Press, 2004.

Perret, Geoffrey. *Lincoln's War: The Untold Story of America's Greatest President as Commander in Chief.* New York: Random House, 2004.

Peskin, Allan. *Volunteers: The Mexican War Journals of Private Richard Coulter and Sergeant Thomas Barclay, Company E, Second Pennsylvania Infantry.* Kent, OH: Kent State University Press, 1991.

Plante, Trevor K. "The Shady Side of the Family Tree: Civil War Union Court-Martial Case Files." *Prologue*, vol. 30, no. 4 (Winter 1998).

Popchock, Barry. *Soldier Boy: The Civil War Letters of Charles O. Musser, 29th Iowa.* Iowa City: University of Iowa Press, 1995.

Pope, Thomas E. *The Weary Boys: Colonel J. Warren Keifer and the 110th Ohio Volunteer Infantry.* Kent, OH: Kent State University Press, 2002.

Potter, James E. and Robbins, Edith. *Marching with the First Nebraska: A Civil War Diary.* Norman: University of Oklahoma Press, 2007.

Pride, Mark, and Travis, Mark. *My Brave Boys: To War with Colonel Cross and the Fighting Fifth.* Hanover, NH: University Press of New England, 2001.

Prokopowicz, Gerald J. *All for the Regiment: The Army of the Ohio, 1861–1862.* Chapel Hill, NC: University of North Carolina Press, 2001.

Puck, Susan T. *Sacrifice at Vicksburg: Letters from the Front.* Shippensburg, PA: Burd Street Press, 1997.

Pula, James S. *The Memoirs of Ludwik Zychlinski: Reminiscences of the American Civil War, Siberia, and Poland.* New York: Columbia University Press, 1993.

Racine, Philip N. *Unspoiled Heart: The Journal of Charles Mattocks of the 17th Maine.* Knoxville: University of Tennessee Press, 1994.

Rafuse, Ethan S. *McClellan's War: The Failure of Moderation in the Struggle for the Union.* Bloomington: Indiana University Press, 2005.

Raup, Hallock F. *Letters from a Pennsylvania Chaplain at the Siege of Petersburg, 1865.* Kent, OH: Kent State University Press, 1961.

Regimental History Committee. *History of the Third Pennsylvania Cavalry in the American Civil War.* Philadelphia: Franklin Printing, 1905.

Reid, Brian H., and White, John. "A Mob of Stragglers and Cowards: Desertion from the Union and Confederate Armies, 1861–1865." *Journal of Strategic Studies*, vol. 8, no. 1 (March 1985).

Reid-Green, Marcia. *Letters Home: Henry Matrau of the Iron Brigade.* Lincoln: University of Nebraska Press, 1993.

Reyburn, Philip J., and Wilson, Terry L. *Jottings from Dixie: The Civil War Dispatches of Sergeant Major Stephen F. Fleharty, U.S.A.* Baton Rouge: Louisiana State University Press, 1999.

Reynolds Donald E., and Kele, Max H. "A Yank in the Carolinas Campaign: The Diary of James W. Chapin, Eighth Indiana Cavalry." *North Carolina Historical Review*, vol. 46, no. 1 (January 1969).

Rhodes, Robert H. *All for the Union: The Civil War Diary and Letters of Elisha Hunt Rhodes.* New York: Vintage Books, 1985.

Robertson, James I. *Soldiers Blue and Gray.* Columbia: University of South Carolina Press, 1988.

Roe, Alfred S. *The Twenty-fourth Regiment, Massachusetts Volunteers.* Worcester, MA: Twenty-fourth Veteran Association, 1907.

Rogers, William O. "Cotton and Clover Hill." *Civil War Times Illustrated*, vol. 14 (August 1975).

Rood, Hosea W. *Story of the Service of Company E, and the Twelfth Wisconsin Regiment, Veteran Volunteer Infantry, in the War of the Rebellion.* Milwaukee: Swain and Tate, 1893.

Rosenblatt, Emil. *Anti-Rebel: The Civil War Letters of Wilbur Fisk.* New York: Croton-on-Hudson, 1983.

Roth, Margaret B. *Well Mary: Civil War Letters of a Wisconsin Volunteer.* Madison: University of Wisconsin Press, 1960.

Rowe, Mary Ellen. *Bulwark of the Republic: The American Militia in the Antebellum West.* Westport, CT: Praeger, 2003.

Rowell, John W. *Yankee Artillerymen: Through the Civil War with Eli Lilly's Indiana Battery.* Knoxville: University of Tennessee Press, 1973.

———. *Yankee Cavalrymen: Through the Civil War with the Ninth Pennsylvania Cavalry.* Knoxville: University of Tennessee Press, 1971.

Samet, Elizabeth D. *Willing Obedience: Citizens, Soldiers, and the Progress of Consent in America, 1776–1898.* Palo Alto, CA: Stanford University Press, 2004.

Samito, Christian G. *Commanding Boston's Irish Ninth: The Civil War Letters of Colonel Patrick R. Guiney, Ninth Massachusetts Volunteer Infantry.* New York: Fordham University Press, 1998.

Sanger, William B. *The History of Prostitution: Its Extent, Causes, and Effects Throughout the Ages.* New York: Harper & Bros., 1876.

Schellhammer, Michael. *The 83rd Pennsylvania Volunteers in the Civil War.* Jefferson, NC: McFarland & Company, 2003.

Schwartz, Gerald. *A Woman Doctor's Civil War: Esther Hill Hawks' Diary.* Columbia: University of South Carolina Press, 1984.

Scott, Henry L. *Military Dictionary: Comprising Technical Definitions; Information on Raising and Keeping Troops; Actual Service, Including Makeshift and Improver Material; and Law, Government, Regulation, and Administration Relating to Land Forces.* New York: D. Van Nostrand, 1864.

Scott, Robert G. *Fallen Leaves: The Civil War Letters of Major Henry Livermore Abbott.* Kent, OH: Kent State University Press, 1991.

Sears, Stephen W. *On Campaign with the Army of the Potomac: The Civil War Journal of Theodore Ayrault Dodge.* New York: Cooper Square, 2001.

Shankman, Arnold M. *The Pennsylvania Antiwar Movement, 1861–1865.* Rutherford, NJ: Fairleigh Dickinson University Press, 1980.

Shannon, Fred A. *The Civil War Letters of Sergeant Onley Andrus.* Urbana: University of Illinois Press, 1947.

———. *The Organization and Administration of the Union Army, 1861–1865,* vol. 1. Gloucester, MA: Peter Smith, 1965.

Schaukirk, Edwald G. "Occupation of New York City by the British." *Pennsylvania Magazine of History and Biography,* vol. 10, no. 1 (1886).

Shaw, James B. *History of the Tenth Regiment Indiana Volunteer Infantry: Three Months and Three Years Organizations.* Lafayette, IN: Burt-Haywood, 1912.

Sheridan, Philip H. *Personal Memoirs of P.H. Sheridan,* vol. II. New York: Charles L. Webster & Co., 1888, 208–209.

Sherman, William T. *The Memoirs of General W. T. Sherman,* vol. I. New York: D. Appleton, 1875.

Siegel, Alan. "Battle in the Snow: Union Troops Take Sides." *Civil War Times Illustrated,* vol. 23 (December 1984).

Silliker, Ruth L. *The Rebel Yell & the Yankee Hurrah: the Civil War Journal of a Maine Volunteer.* Camden, Maine: Down East Books, 1985.

Silverman, Jason H. "The Excitement had Begun!: The Civil War Diary of Lemuel Jeffries, 1862–1863." *Manuscripts,* vol. 30, no. 4 (Fall 1978).

Skeen, Carl E. *Citizen Soldiers in the War of 1812.* Lexington: University Press of Kentucky, 1999.

Skemp, Sheila L. *William Franklin: Son of a Patriot, Servant of a King.* New York: Oxford, 1990.

Skidmore, Richard S. *The Civil War Journal of Billy Davis: From Hopewell, Indiana to Port Republic, Virginia.* Greencastle, IN: Nugget, 1989.

Slade, Joseph W. *Pornography and Sexual Representation: A Reference Guide.* New York: Greenwood Press, 2000.

Small, Harold A. *The Road to Richmond: the Civil War Memoirs of Maj. Abner R. Small of the 16th Maine Vols.* Berkeley: University of California Press, 1959.

Smith, Abram. *History of the Seventy-sixth Regiment New York Volunteers.* Syracuse, NY: Truair, Smith, & Miles, 1867.

Smith, Barbara A. *The Civil War Letters of Col. Elijah H.C. Cavins, 14th Indiana.* Owensboro, KY: Cook-McDowell Publications, 1981.

Smith, Barbara B., and Baker, Nina B. *Burning Rails as We Pleased: The Civil War Letters of William Garrigues Bentley, 104th Ohio Volunteer Infantry.* Jefferson, NC: McFarland & Company, 2004.

Smith, Justin H. *The War with Mexico.* New York: MacMillan & Company, 1919.

Smith, Merril D. *Sex Without Consent: Rape and Sexual Coercion in America.* New York: New York University Press, 2001.

Smith, Michael T. "The Most Desperate Scoundrels Unhung: Bounty Jumpers and Recruitment Fraud in the Civil War North." *American Nineteenth Century History*, vol. 6, no. 2 (June 2005).

Smith, Page. *John Adams.* Westport, CT: Greenwood Press, 1969.

Spann, Edward K. *Gotham at War: New York City, 1860–1865.* Wilmington, DE: Scholarly Resources, 2002.

Sparks, David S. *Inside Lincoln's Army: The Diary of Marsena Rudolph Patrick, Provost Marshal General, Army of the Potomac.* New York: Yoseloff, 1964.

Stadelman, Bonnie S. "The Amusements of the American Soldiers during the Revolution," Ph.D. dissertation, Tulane University, 1969.

Starr, Stephen Z. *Jennison's Jayhawkers: A Civil War Cavalry Regiment and Its Commander.* Baton Rouge: Louisiana State University Press, 1973.

Steinhauer, Dale R. "'Sogers': Enlisted Men in the U.S. Army, 1815–1860." Ph.D. dissertation, University of North Carolina, 1992.

Stevens, Harriet. *The Graybeards: The Family of Major Lyman Allen during the American Civil War.* Iowa City, IA: Press of the Camp Pope Bookshop, 1998.

Stevens, Michael E. *As if It Were Glory: Robert Beecham's Civil War from the Iron Brigade to the Black Regiments.* Madison, WI: Madison House, 1998.

Stevens, Peter F. *The Rogue's March: John Riley and the St. Patrick's Battalion.* Washington, DC: Brassey's, 1999.

Stewart, Alexander M. *Camp, March, and Battlefield: or Three Years and a Half with the Army of the Potomac.* Philadelphia: Rodgers, 1865.

Stillwell, Leander. *The Story of a Common Soldier of Army Life in the Civil War.* Erie, KS: Franklin-Hudson, 1920.

Stine, James H. *History of the Army of the Potomac.* Washington, DC: Gibbons Brothers, 1893.

Styple, William B. *Writing and Fighting the Civil War: Soldiers Correspondence to the New York Sunday Mercury.* Kearny, NJ: Belle Grover, 2000.

Swanson, Clifford L. *The Sixth United States Infantry Regiment, 1855 to Reconstruction.* Jefferson, NC: McFarland, 2001.

Swanson, James L. and Weinberg, Daniel R. *Lincoln's Assassins: Their Trial and Execution.* Santa Fe, NM: Arena Editions, 2001.

Swift, Lester L. "Letter from a Sailor on a Tinclad." *Civil War History*, vol. 7, no. 2 (March 1961).

Sylvester, Lorna L. "The Civil War Letters of Charles Harding Cox." *Indiana Magazine of History*, vol. 68 (March 1972).

Taylor, Robert A. *A Pennsylvanian in Blue: The Civil War Diary of Thomas Beck Walton.* Shippensburg, PA: Burd Street Press, 1995.

Temple, Wayne C. "The Civil War Letters of Henry C. Bear: A Soldier in the 116th Illinois Volunteer Infantry, Part II." *Lincoln Herald*, vol. 62 (Winter 1960).

———. "The Civil War Letters of Henry C. Bear: A Soldier in the 116th Illinois Volunteer Infantry, Part III." *Lincoln Herald*, vol. 63 (Spring 1961).

Tevis, C.V. *History of the Fighting Fourteenth.* Brooklyn: Brooklyn Eagle Press, 1911.

Thayer, William R. *John Hay: In Two Volumes.* New York: Houghton Mifflin, 1915.

Thompson, George A. *Rustics in Rebellion.* Chapel Hill: University of North Carolina Press, 1950.

Thorpe, Sheldon B. *The History of the Fifteenth Connecticut Volunteers in the War for the Defense of the Union, 1861–1865.* New Haven, CT: Price, Lee, and Adkins, 1893.

Throne, Mildred. *The Civil War Diary of Charles F. Boyd, Fifteenth Iowa Infantry, 1861–1863.* Baton Rouge: Louisiana State University Press, 1998.

———. "Reminiscences of Jacob C. Switzer of the 22nd Iowa (Part 1)." *Iowa Journal of History*, vol. 55, no. 3 (October 1957).

———. "Reminiscences of Jacob B. Switzer of the 22n Iowa (Part 2)." *Iowa Journal of History*, vol. 56, no. 1 (January 1958).

Trautmann, Frederick. *"We Were the Ninth": A History of the Ninth Regiment, Ohio Volunteer Infantry.* Kent, OH: Kent State University Press, 1987.

Turner, Joseph B. *The Journal and Order Book of Captain Robert Kirkwood of the Delaware Regiment of the Continental Line.* Port Washington, NY: Kennikat Press, 1970.

Tusken, Roger. "In the Bastile of the Rebels." *Journal of the Illinois State Historical Society*, vol. 56 (Summer 1963).

Underwood, Adin B. *Three Years' Service of the Thirty-third Mass. Infantry Regiment 1862–1865.* Boston: A. Williams & Co., 1881.

Urwin, Gregory J.W. "The Lord has not Forsake Me and I Won't Forsake Him: Religion in Frederick Steele's Union Army, 1863–1864." *Arkansas Historical Quarterly*, vol. 52, no. 3 (1993).

Vail, Enos B. *Reminiscences of a Boy in the Civil War.* Brooklyn, NY. Privately printed, 1915.

Vanderslice, Catherine H. *The Civil War Letters of George Washington Beidelman.* New York: Vantage Press, 1978.

Vargas, Mark A. "The Military Justice System and the Use of Illegal Punishments as Causes of Desertion in the U.S. Army, 1821–1835." *Journal of Military History*, vol. 55, no. 1 (January 1991).

———. "The Progressive Agent of Mischief: The Whiskey Ration and Temperance in the United States Army." *Historian*, vol. 67, no. 2 (Summer 2005).

Vickers, George M. *Under Both Flags: A Panorama of the Great Civil War.* Philadelphia: Fidelity, 1896.

Viola, Herman J. *The Memoirs of Charles Henry Veil: A Soldiers' Recollections of the Civil War and the Arizona Territory.* Thorndike, ME: Thorndike Press, 1994.

Volo, James M., and Volo, Dorothy D. *The Antebellum Period.* New York: Greenwood, 2004.

Voorhis, Jerry. *The Life and Times of Aurelius Lyman Voorhis.* New York: Vantage Press, 1976, 238.

Votwiler, A.T. "Letters from a Civil War Officer." *The Mississippi Valley Historical Review*, vol. 14, no. 4 (March 1928).

Wagner, Henry. "The Prohibitory Act: A Cause of the American Revolution," M.A. thesis, Syracuse University, 1960.

Wagner, Margaret E. *The Library of Congress Civil War Desk Reference.* New York: Simon and Schuster, 2002, 605.

Wallace, Edward S. "Deserters in the Mexican War." *The Hispanic American Historical Review*, vol. 55, no. 3 (August 1935).

Walters, Ronald G. *American Reformers: 1815–1860.* New York: Hill & Wang, 1978.

War Talks in Kansas: A Series of Papers Read before the Kansas Commandery of the Military Order of the Loyal Legion of the United States. Kansas City, MO: Franklin Hudson, 1906.

Ward, David A. "Amidst a Tempest of Shot and Shell: A History of the Ninety-sixth Pennsylvania Volunteers," M.A. thesis, Southern Connecticut State University, 1988.

Ward, George W. *History of the Second Pennsylvania Veteran Heavy Artillery.* Philadelphia: George W. Ward, Printer, 1904.

Ward, Harry M. *George Washington's Enforcers: Policing the Continental Army.* Carbondale: Southern Illinois University Press, 2006.

———. *The American Revolution: Nationhood Achieved, 1763–1788.* New York: St. Martin's, 1995.

———. *The War for Independence and the Transformation of American Society.* New York: Routledge, 1999.

Ware, Eugene F. *The Lyon Campaign in Missouri: Being a History of the First Iowa Infantry.* Topeka, KS: Crane, 1907.

Washington, Versalle F. *Eagles on Their Buttons: A Black Infantry Regiment in the Civil War.* Columbia: University of Missouri Press, 1999.

Weaver, C.P. *Thank God My Regiment an African One: The Civil War Diary of Colonel Nathan W. Daniels.* Baton Rouge: Louisiana State University Press, 1998.

Webb, Henry W. "The Story of Jefferson Barracks," *New Mexico Historical Review* 21 (1946).

Weber, Daniel B. *The Diary of Ira Gillaspie of the Eleventh Michigan Infantry*. Mount Pleasant: Central Michigan University Press, 1965.

Weiner, Marli F. *A Heritage of Woe: The Civil War Diary of Grace Brown Elmore, 1861–1868*. Athens: University of Georgia Press, 1997.

Westervelt, William B. *Lights and Shadows of Army Life: As Seen by a Private Soldier*. Marlboro, NY: C.B. Cochrane, 1886.

Whiteaker, Larry H., and Dickinson, W. Calvin. *Civil War Letters of the Tenure Family, Rockland County, N.Y., 1862–1865*. New York: Historical Society of Rockland County, 1990.

Wiener, Frederick B. *Civilians Under Military Justice: The British Practice since 1689, Especially in North America*. Chicago: University of Chicago Press, 1967.

———. "Courts-Martial and the Constitution: The Original Understanding," *Harvard Law Review* 72 (1957).

———. "The Military Occupation of Philadelphia in 1777–1778." *Proceedings of the American Philosophical Society*, vol. 111, no. 5 (Oct., 1967).

Wiley, Bell I. *The Life of Billy Yank*. Baton Rouge: Louisiana State University Press, 1979.

Wilkinson, Warren. *Mother, May You Never See the Sighs I Have Seen: The Fifty-Seventh Massachusetts Veteran Volunteers in the Army of the Potomac, 1864–1865*. New York: Harper & Row, 1990.

Williams, John C. *Life in Camp: A History of the Nine Months' Service of the Fourteenth Vermont Regiment*. Claremont, VT: Claremont Manufacturing Co., 1864.

Williams, Marilyn T. *Washing "the Great Unwashed": Public Baths in Urban America, 1840–1920*. Columbus: Ohio State University Press, 1991.

Willison, Charles A. *Reminiscences of a Boy's Service with the 76th Ohio*. Huntington, WV: Blue Acorn Press, 1995.

Wilson, Mark C. *Patriots in Blue: Civil War Letters of the Mark E. Rogers Family of Fairfax, Virginia*. West Lafayette, IN: self-published, 1987.

Winders. Richard B. *Mr. Polk's Army: The American Military Experience in the Mexican War*. College Station: Texas A & M University Press, 1997.

Winschel, Terrence J. *The Civil War Diary of a Common Soldier: William Wiley of the 77th Illinois Infantry*. Baton Rouge: Louisiana State University Press, 2001.

Winthrop, William. *Military Law and Precedents*. Washington, DC: Government Printing Office, 1920.

Wishart, David J. *Encyclopedia of the Great Plains*. Lincoln: University of Nebraska Press, 2004.

Wittenberg, Eric J. *One of Custer's Wolverines: The Civil War Letters of Brevet Brigadier General James H. Kidd, 6th Michigan Cavalry*. Kent, OH: Kent State University Press, 2000.

———. *We Have It Damn Hard Out Here: The Civil War Letters of Sergeant Thomas W. Smith, 6th Pennsylvania Cavalry*. Kent, OH: Kent State University Press, 1999.

Wheelan, Joseph. *Invading Mexico: America's Continental Dream and the Mexican War, 1846–1848*. New York: Caroll & Graf, 2007.

Woodward, E.M. *History of the One Hundred and Ninety-Eighth Pennsylvania Volunteers*. Trenton, NJ: MacCrellish & Quigley, 1884.

Woodworth, Steven E. *The Musick of the Mocking Birds, the Roar of the Cannon: The Civil War Diary and Letters of William Winters*. Lincoln: University of Nebraska Press, 1998.

———. *While God is Marching On: The Religious World of Civil War Soldiers*. Lawrence: University Press of Kansas, 2001.

Workmaster, Wallace F. "The Frank H. Shiras Letters, 1862–1865." *Western Pennsylvania Historical Magazine*, vol. 40 (Fall 1957).

Yacovone, Donald. *A Voice of Thunder: The Civil War Letters of George E. Stephens*. Urbana: University of Illinois Press, 1997.

Zeller, Bob. *The Blue and Gray in Black and White: A History of Civil War Photography*. New York: Greenwood, 2005.

Zornow, William F. "Lincoln and Private Lennan." *Indiana Magazine of History*, vol. 44, no. 3 (September 1953).

Government Records and Publications

House Executive Document, 39th Congress, First Session.

National Archives and Records Administration, Record Group 15: Records of the Veterans Administration.

———. Record Group 94: Records of the Adjutant General's Office.

———. Record Group 107: Records of the Office of the Secretary of War.

———. Record Group 110: Records of the Provost Marshal General's Bureau.

———. Record Group 153: Records of the Office of the Judge Advocate General (Army).

———. Record Group 389: Records of the Office of the Provost Marshal General.

———. Record Group 393: Records of the United States Army Continental Commands.

"Report of the Provost-Marshal-General, Appendix to the Report of the Secretary of War," 39th Congress, 1st Session, 1866.

Statutes of the United States, 1862–1863 (Washington, DC: Government Printing Office, 1863), Chapter 75, Section 21, 26.

U.S. Statutes at Large.

United States Army. *Military Laws of the United States*, Fourth Edition (Washington, DC: Government Printing Office, 1901), 268.

United States Congress, "Report of the Joint Committee on the Conduct of the War at theSecond Session, Thirty-eighth Congress, Red River Expedition" (Washington, DC: Government Printing Office, 1865), 81.

United States Congress. *United States Statues at Large, 1862–1863* (Washington, DC: Government Printing Office, 1863), Chapter 75, Section 24.

United States Surgeon General's Office. *The Medical and Surgical History of the War of the Rebellion*, vol. 1 (Washington, DC: Government Printing Office, 1888), 891.

War Department, Department of the Missouri, General Order 153, June 6, 1864.

War Department. *General Orders of the War Department, Embracing the Years 1861, 1862, and 1863* (New York: Derby & Miller, 1864), 185–190.

———. *Index of General Orders: Adjutant General's Office, 1862* (Washington, DC: Government Printing Office, 1863), General Orders #92, July 31, 1862.

———. *Revised Regulation for the Army of the United States, 1861* (Philadelphia: J.B. Lippincott, 1861), 244.

———. *Revised Regulations for the Army of the United States, 1861* (Philadelphia: J.G.L. Brown, 1861), 30–31.

———. *Subject Index to the General Orders and Circulars of the War Department and the Headquarters of the Army Adjutant General's Office from January1, 1860 to December 31, 1880* (Washington, DC: Government Printing Office, 1913), 104–116.

———, Adjutant-General's Office. *General Orders Affecting the Volunteer Force* (Washington, DC: Government Printing Office, 1862), 13.

The War of the Rebellion: A Compilation of the Official Records of the Union andConfederate Armies, 130 vols. (Washington, DC: Government Printing Office, 1880–1901), vol. 7, 79.

Court Cases

Dynes v. Hoover, 61 U.S. (20 How.) 65 (1857)

Martin v. Mott, 25 U.S. 19 (1827)

Walker v. Morris, 3 Am. Jurist 281 (Mass. 1830)

United States v. Hudson, 7 Cranch 32 (1812)

Newspapers

Daily Alta Californian
Alton (IL) *Telegraph*
Boston *Evening Transcript*
Boston *Journal*
Boston *Herald*
Boston *Saturday Evening Express*
Cleveland *Daily Herald*
Danbury (CT) *Times*
East Saginaw (MI) *Courier*
Elmira (NY) *Advertiser*
Fredericksburg (VA) *Christian Banner*
Harper's Weekly
Hartford *Daily Courant*
Indianapolis *Daily Journal*
Indianapolis *Daily State Sentinel*
Lewistown (PA) *Democrat and Sentinel*
Louisville (KY) *Daily Democrat*
Memphis *Bulletin*
Milwaukee *Sentinel*
Milwaukee *Sunday Telegraph*
Nashville *Daily Press*
New York *Herald*
New York *Sunday Mercury*
New York *Times*
New York *Tribune*
New York *Weekly Anglo-African*
New York *World*
Niles National Register
Norwich (CT) *Morning Bulletin*
Philadelphia *Christian Recorder*
Philadelphia *Inquirer*
Pittsburgh *Evening Chronicle*
Daily Richmond Inquirer
Richmond *Whig*
Rochester (IN) *Chronicle.*

Online Resources

Henry F. Charles
  "Civil War Record, 1862–1865"
  www.dm.net/~neitz/charles/obit.html.

J. Brit McCarly
  "Feeding Billy Yank: Union Rations between 1861 and 1865"
  QuartermasterProfessional Bulletin (December 1988
  http://www.qmfound.com/feeding_billy_yank.htm.

Marshall J. Pixley
  "The Adams Express Company"
  http://www.floridareenactorsonline.com /adamsexpress.htm.

"The Valley of the Shadow: Two Communities in the Civil War."
http://etext.lib.virginia.edu/etcbin/civwarlettbrowse? id=FN0000.
William Barnitz, letter to the Pennsylvania *Telegraph* dated March 27, 1863.
James Carman, letter to father dated July 18, 1862.
Sylvester McElheney, letter to wife dated December 14, 1864.
Bob Taggart, letter to Captain John Taggart dated August 28, 1863

"War Letters: Rochester Writes Home."
http://www.wxxi.org/ warletters/civil.html.
Augustus Hall, letter to cousin dated February 17, 1863
Samuel Partridge, letter to wife dated May 29, 1861.
Daniel Pulis letter to wife dated September 21, 1862.

INDEX

absent without leave, 28, 32, 236–41, 245, 247, 259, 267, 275, 340, 342, 344, 347, 348, 354, 361, 402, 405, 463; after ten days became desertion, 237; as right of citizen-soldier, 237; attempts to control, 238, 239; legitimate reasons for absence, 237; risk of death, 240

Adams, John, 26, 41, 410, 479, 493

Adams Express Company, 250, 497

African American soldiers, 64, 74, 118, 119, 121, 187, 200, 206, 207, 219, 233, 237, 243, 244, 247, 266, 306, 318, 320, 322, 342, 345, 348, 350, 361, 370, 371, 384, 388, 401

alcohol, 27, 28, 29, 44, 45, 80, 103, 126, 135, 136, 137, 138, 151, 153–68, 170, 172–80, 182, 183, 185–87, 189–91, 286, 303, 319, 344, 345, 362, 364, 400, 403–6; alcoholism, 93, 174, 175, 186; attempts to control, 158, 160, 171, 173, 177; concealed in other packaging, 157; deaths caused by, 175; dispensed as a reward, 163; dispensed as compensation, 162; dispensed on special occasions, 164; drinking by immigrant soldiers, 154; drinking by officers, 166, 182, 183, 188; drinking in groups, 137; drunken officers in battle, 187; drunken soldiers fighting officers, 170; drunkenness, 26, 27, 28, 69, 78, 97, 136, 155, 171, 176, 180, 184, 187, 189, 190, 218, 223, 316, 328, 336, 344, 361, 364, 370, 372, 376, 462; foraging for, 165; hangovers and vomiting, 173; liquor dealers, 157; masculinity and, 135, 136; names for alcoholic drinks, 153; national use of, 136; obtained for medical purposes, 161; officers and, 138; opposition to, 179; paydays bring drunkenness, 155; perference for whiskey, 153; price of whiskey, 155; purchased from taverns, 155; reason for failed officers, 80; smuggled by soldiers, 156; smuggled by sutlers, 158; smuggled into camp, 399; smuggled through the mail, 160; stolen from civilians, 166, 167; stolen from the army, 167; symbolism of drinking, 135; temperance efforts, 45, 93, 136, 161, 175, 179–81; use in the postwar army, 402; whiskey ration, 88, 110, 138, 162–64, 179; wine and beer, 88, 124, 153–56, 160, 161, 165, 167, 168, 229, 280, 318, 344, 400, 405; American Revolution, 16, 24, 29, 30, 32, 34, 35, 37, 38, 56, 138, 210, 363, 410, 411, 490, 494

amnesty, 30, 31, 255, 264, 268, 269

antebellum U.S. Army, 15, 16, 20, 44, 138, 361, 363, 378; desertion in, 138, 232; alcohol use in, 44, 45, 138; no need for military police force in, 315

Articles of War (Great Britain), 22–24, 34; adopted by colonies, 24, 25; greater range of punishments, 33

Articles of War (U.S.), 16, 17, 22, 25, 26, 28, 29, 30, 31, 33, 38, 40–42, 45, 46, 51, 53, 86, 90, 92, 94, 99, 100, 118, 123, 133, 134, 171, 183, 192, 209, 211, 220, 229, 231, 240, 266, 304, 305, 317, 324, 328, 330, 334, 337, 341, 343, 346, 347, 354, 358, 367, 376, 380, 382, 396, 405, 407, 409, 410, 460, 461; 1775 version, 25, 26, 30, 99, 410; 1776 version, 26, 27, 29, 30, 31, 32, 33, 41, 45, 410; 1786 version, 40; 1806 version, 41, 44, 46; proposed changes to, 31

Atlanta, GA, 59, 246, 419, 421, 450, 474, 490

boredom, 27, 28, 53, 66, 93, 103–5, 239, 256

bounty-jumping, 270–74, 342, 343; arrests of bounty-jumpers, 273; by men with medical disabilities, 272; despised by soldiers, 270; practiced by professional criminals, 271